LAW, POLICY AND THE INTERNET

This comprehensive textbook by the editor of *Law and the Internet* seeks to provide students, practitioners and businesses with an up-to-date and accessible account of the key issues in internet law and policy from a European and UK perspective. The internet has advanced in the last 30 years from an esoteric interest to a vital and unavoidable part of modern work, rest and play. As such, an account of how the internet and its users are regulated is vital for everyone concerned with the modern information society. This book also addresses the fact that internet regulation is not just a matter of law but increasingly intermixed with technology, economics and politics. Policy developments are closely analysed as an intrinsic part of modern governance. Law, Policy and the Internet focuses on two key areas: e-commerce, including the role and responsibilities of online intermediaries such as Google, Facebook and Uber; and privacy, data protection and online crime. In particular there is detailed up-to-date coverage of the crucially important General Data Protection Regulation which came into force in May 2018.

Law, Policy and the Internet

Edited by
Lilian Edwards

•HART•
OXFORD · LONDON · NEW YORK · NEW DELHI · SYDNEY

HART PUBLISHING

Bloomsbury Publishing Plc

Kemp House, Chawley Park, Cumnor Hill, Oxford, OX2 9PH, UK

HART PUBLISHING, the Hart/Stag logo, BLOOMSBURY and the Diana logo are
trademarks of Bloomsbury Publishing Plc

First published in Great Britain 2019

A catalogue record for this book is available from the British Library.

Library of Congress Cataloging-in-Publication Data

Names: Edwards, Lilian, editor.

Title: Law, policy and the Internet / edited by Lilian Edwards.

Description: Oxford, UK ; Portland, Oregon : Hart Publishing, 2019. | Includes index.

Identifiers: LCCN 2018034244 (print) | LCCN 2018035207 (ebook) |
ISBN 9781509900930 (Epub) | ISBN 9781849467032 (pbk. : alk. paper)

Subjects: LCSH: Internet—Law and legislation. | Data protection—Law and legislation. |
Privacy, Right of. | Internet—Censorship. | Computer security. |
Internet—Law and legislation—Europe. | Internet—Government policy—Europe.

Classification: LCC K564.C6 (ebook) | LCC K564.C6 L39 2019 (print) | DDC 343.09/944—dc23

LC record available at https://lccn.loc.gov/2018034244

ISBN: PB: 978-1-84946-703-2
        ePDF: 978-1-50990-092-3
        ePub: 978-1-50990-093-0

Typeset by Compuscript Ltd, Shannon
Printed and bound in Great Britain by CPI Group (UK) Ltd, Croydon CR0 4YY

To find out more about our authors and books visit www.hartpublishing.co.uk.
Here you will find extracts, author information, details of forthcoming events
and the option to sign up for our newsletters.

Contents

PART III
ONLINE INTERMEDIARIES, E-COMMERCE AND CYBERCRIME

Table of Cases

Table of Legal Instruments

Council of Europe

NATO

OECD

United Kingdom, Secondary Legislation

List of Contributors

Francis Davey

Francis Davey is a practising barrister and senior associate at Anderson Law LLP. After qualifying as a computer scientist from Cambridge University, he carried out research and worked in the field of computing, before qualifying as a lawyer in 2003. He has a particular interest in the interaction between law and computer science. He is particularly well known for his work in the field of open data and sat on a sector transparency panel in the 2010–2015 Parliament. In addition to this, he has had long had an interest in the nature of money in the electronic age and online payment systems. He taught an e-commerce course for three years at the University of Strathclyde on which the book chapters he authored is based.

Lilian Edwards

Lilian Edwards is a Scottish UK-based academic and frequent speaker on issues of Internet law, intellectual property and artificial intelligence. She is on the Advisory Board of the Open Rights Group and the Foundation for Internet Privacy Research and is the Professor of Law, Innovation and Society at Newcastle Law School at Newcastle University.

Andres Guadamuz

Dr Andres Guadamuz is a Senior Lecturer in Intellectual Property Law at the University of Sussex and the Editor in Chief of the Journal of World Intellectual Property. His main research areas are on digital copyright, open licensing, software protection, cryptocurrencies, blockchains, and complexity. Andres has published two books, the most recent of which is *Networks, Complexity and Internet Regulation*, and he regularly blogs at Technollama.co.uk. He has acted as an international consultant for the World Intellectual Property Organization, and since 2005, he has been involved with Creative Commons Scotland (while lecturer at University of Edinburgh and Associate Director of the SCRIPT Centre), Costa Rica and now the UK.

Eleni Kosta

Professor Dr Eleni Kosta is full Professor of Technology Law and Human Rights at the Tilburg Institute for Law, Technology and Society (TILT, Tilburg University, the Netherlands). Eleni is conducting research on privacy and data protection, specialising in electronic communications and new technologies. She has been involved in numerous EU research projects and is teaching 'Capita Selecta Privacy and Data Protection' at the LLM Law & Technology of the Tilburg Law School. In 2014 Eleni was awarded a personal research grant for research on privacy and surveillance by the Dutch Research Organisation (VENI/NWO). Eleni also collaborates as associate with timelex (www.timelex.eu).

Chris Marsden

Chris Marsden is Professor of Internet Law at the University of Sussex and a renowned international expert on Internet and new media law, having researched and taught in the field since its foundation over twenty years ago (1996 was arguably Year Zero). Chris researches regulation by code – whether legal, software or social code. He is author of seven books and over 130 research publications on Internet law and regulation, including 'Net Neutrality: From Policy to Law to Regulation' (2017), 'Regulating Code' (2013 with Professor Ian Brown), 'Internet Co-regulation' (2011). Chris was formerly Professor of Law at Essex (2007–13), having previously researched at RAND (2005–7), Oxford (2004–5), and Warwick (1997–2000). He held Visiting Fellowships at Harvard, Melbourne, Cambridge, Oxford, USC-Annenberg, Keio, GLOCOM Tokyo, and FGV Rio de Janeiro. He has founded and led teams to successful completion of over 20 externally funded international collaborative projects, worth in total over £6m, including Openlaws.eu [2014–16] and FP7 European Internet Science (EINS) [2011–15].

TJ McIntyre

Dr TJ McIntyre is Lecturer in Law, University College Dublin where his research focuses on issues involving information technology law and fundamental rights. He qualified as a barrister in the Honorable Society of King's Inns, Dublin, where he achieved the Antonia O'Callaghan Prize for Advocacy, and was later admitted as a solicitor by the Law Society of Ireland. He is also a member of the New York Bar. He chairs the civil liberties group Digital Rights Ireland and regularly contributes to national and international policy debate on issues of law and technology.

Nóra Ni Loideain

Dr Nóra Ni Loideain is Director and Lecturer in Law of the Information Law and Policy Centre, Institute of Advanced Legal Studies, University of London. Her research interests and publications concern governance, human rights law, and State surveillance. She was awarded a PhD in law from the University of Cambridge which is the focus of her forthcoming monograph concerning the mass retention of communications metadata for law enforcement purposes and European human rights law: Data Privacy, Serious Crime, and EU Policy-Making (Oxford University Press). Nóra is also co-author of the forthcoming textbook: Lynskey and Ni Loideain, *Data Protection Law and Policy* (Oxford University Press). She is a Visiting Lecturer in Law at King's College London in information privacy and data protection law and was previously an Affiliated Lecturer in Law of same at the University of Cambridge. In 2017, she was appointed to the editorial board of the journal for *International Data Privacy Law* (Oxford University Press). Prior to her academic career, she was a Legal and Policy Officer for the Office of the Director of Public Prosecutions of Ireland and clerked for the Irish Supreme Court.

Lachlan Urquhart

Dr Lachlan D Urquhart is a Lecturer in Technology Law at the University of Edinburgh. Prior to this, he was a Research Fellow at the Horizon Digital Economy

Research Institute, School of Computer Science, University of Nottingham. He is a multidisciplinary researcher, primarily working at the boundaries of human-computer interaction (HCI), IT law, and computer ethics. He researches the technical, legal, social, and ethical implications of living with interactive computing (eg, internet of things (IoT) – including smart homes, smart cities and industrial IoT; adaptive architecture; affective computing; robotics etc.) He has law (LL.B – University of Edinburgh; LL.M in IT & Telecommunications Law – University of Strathclyde) and computer science (Ph.D – University of Nottingham) degrees. His doctoral research within the Mixed Reality Lab and Horizon Centre for Doctoral Training, both at Nottingham, examined the role of design(ers) in regulation, particularly how to implement privacy by design for the domestic Internet of Things. Lachlan has worked as a research assistant at the Centre for Internet Law & Policy at Strathclyde twice, and was a visiting researcher at the Centre for Business Information Ethics, Meiji University, Tokyo. For up to date information see his website, www.lachlansresearch.com.

Introduction

Even by the standards of recent years, the topic of Internet law and policy has rarely been more prominent, prolific and contested than it is as I write this introduction. In the UK, a major House of Lords Select Committee enquiry is currently ongoing into how the Internet should be regulated in the widest sense.[1] Another committee has just suggested that drastic measures are necessary to rein in fake news online.[2] A third has declared that the UK can and should lead the way on 'ethical' AI.[3] Facebook, Google, Amazon, AI, driverless cars, the gig economy, sex robots and online trolling (to name but a few random topics) regularly lead the news.

Headlines have been dominated for months in 2018 in particular by the story that political advertising, micro-targeted using data gathered by Cambridge Analytica, and delivered using Facebook's platform, may have turned the fortunes both of the unexpected US Trump election victory and the UK's narrow vote for Brexit.[4] A panoply of actors including everyone from Trump's closest aides to Putin to the leaders of Vote Leave in the UK have been possibly implicated. At the end of July 2018, after months of exposés, Facebook faces an exodus of 3 million of its EU users, another precipitate (though no doubt soon to be reversed) fall in share prices,[5] a growing lake of inquiries, Congressional hearings and damning reports[6] and a half million pound fine from the Information Commissioners Office (ICO)[7] (luckily squeezing under the wire before the General Data Protection Regulation's (GDPR) more stringent penalties cut in. The international love-in with Silicon Valley and its chocolate factories seems finally to be at an end, something even Snowden did not quite achieve[8] and social media is firmly on the naughty step. Welcome to the future, where digital surveillance may just have destroyed democracy as we know it.

---

[1] 'The Internet: to regulate or not to regulate? Inquiry', House of Lords, at https://www.parliament.uk/business/committees/committees-a-z/lords-select/communications-committee/inquiries/parliament-2017/the-internet-to-regulate-or-not-to-regulate/, still ongoing as of July 27 2018 and expected to last till late 2018. See also ch 9.

[2] See DCMS Committee Fake News enquiry; https://www.parliament.uk/business/committees/committees-a-z/commons-select/digital-culture-media-and-sport-committee/inquiries/parliament-2017/fake-news-17-19/publications/.

[3] See 'UK can lead the way on ethical AI, says Lords Committee', 16 April 2018 at https://www.parliament.uk/business/committees/committees-a-z/lords-select/ai-committee/news-parliament-2017/ai-report-published/.

[4] See discussion in Chapter 3.

[5] See https://www.theguardian.com/technology/2018/jul/26/facebook-market-cap-falls-109bn-dollars-after-growth-shock.

[6] See eg Electoral Commission *Report of an investigation in respect of- Vote Leave et al – Concerning campaign funding and spending for the 2016 referendum on the UK's membership of the EU*.17 July 2018; ICO *Democracy disrupted? Personal information and political influence*, 11 July 2018 at https://ico.org.uk/media/action-weve-taken/2259369/democracy-disrupted-110718.pdf.

[7] See https://www.bbc.co.uk/news/technology-44785151.

[8] The fallout from Snowden in terms of scrutiny of state powers of surveillance and data retention are addressed in chs 6 and 7.

1 INTRODUCTION

The Cambridge Analytica story enticingly combines several of the major societal themes around law and the Internet of the last decade: the rise of AI and machine learning algorithms; the dominance of privately owned US based digital and social media platforms over conventional state governance; the lack of transparency around user manipulation, tracking and surveillance;[9] and the loss of faith generally in both industry self-regulation and the protection of personal privacy. Much of this volume is dominated, rightly, by these themes.

This new edited collection is not the direct heir to the *Law and Internet* series which was co-edited by myself and Charlotte Waelde between 1997 and 2009, but it does bear some fraternal resemblances. Charlotte has moved on in her research from a primary focus on the Internet to concentrating on intellectual property 'beyond text' and in particular, the world of dance, and I can only thank her for all her hard work in the past and wish her good luck in her new endeavours. Meanwhile, left to my own devices, the idea was born of a new sole-edited volume, which would not seek to be a comprehensive account of all the aspects of Internet law and digital IP law (now an impossible task to achieve in one volume, though Graham Smith and his team at Bird and Bird may still be attempting it) but would focus on emblematic areas of Internet regulation such as regulation and net neutrality,[10] privacy and data protection;[11] state surveillance;[12] intermediary liability;[13] filtering and censorship;[14] cybercrime and security;[15] and the new wonders of Bitcoin and smart contracts.[16] A decision to exclude digital IP in the main was taken; it has its own textbooks, its own gurus and its own practitioner bibles now, and the need for one volume to cover both areas seems less pressing (and much less possible) than it did in 2009. By contrast, privacy and associated areas now take up over a third of the book; a reflection of the editor's own obsessions perhaps, but also I think a reflection of societal and industry concerns, the volume of new legislation (and litigation) and the dominance of free-to-user data-driven business models, as well as the rise of the Internet of Things.

Above all, the new volume would still be focused on Internet *regulation* (and importantly, on being a practical resource with which to teach Honours and Masters students, as well as hopefully of use both to practitioners and the wider world fascinated with technology in society) but it would also have an overarching interest in how *policy* is evolved, debated and resolved in this arena. To some extent this focus has derived from my own increasing participation in the merry-go-round of parliamentary inquiries, policy consultations, research funder away days, civil society campaigns and industry consultancy – all of which drive home how the post-recession world, especially in Europe, is currently torn between the US-centric neoliberal ideas of 'light touch regulation' to foster and promote innovation, and the more European fears that

---

[9] On these last three points see primarily chs 4 and 5, but also ch 8.
[10] Chs 1 and 2.
[11] Chs 3–5, 8.
[12] Chs 6 and 7.
[13] Ch 9.
[14] Ch 10.
[15] Ch 13.
[16] Chs 11 and 12.

unregulated technology will lose the trust of its users, jeopardising social confidence, cohesion, democracy and fundamental values, exacerbating globalisation resentments and possibly leading to the kind of backlashes that have restrained uptake of the likes of GM crops and human genetic experimentation.

Do we regulate by law, do we refuse to regulate till a clear path can be seen, or do we turn to soft law, self-regulation, 'co-regulation', codes of conduct, technical standards, trustmarks, ethical charters, user democracy, who knows? This is a question much of this author's previous work has raised, but it never gets old. The rise of 'ethics washing', where legislation is staved off by self-regulatory and largely unsupervised ethics charters, looks well set to be the next big trend in Internet governance. Centres which are not-quite regulators – quang-regs, perhaps – are also trending: in AI in the UK, for example, we have seen the arrival of the Office for AI, the AI Council, and shortly, the Centre for Data Ethics and Innovation, all of which interact perhaps a tad messily with the existing Information Commissioner.

Obviously, this is an edited collection and as editor, I owe the most enormous debt of gratitude to the contributors, who have put up, without complaint, with the delays and frustrations of not only (or at least not solely) their editor but also of working in one of the fastest changing areas of law on the planet. I also owe uncountable thanks to several wonderful research assistants who have worked tirelessly on this project, all now forging their own very distinct reputations in the field: Lachlan Urquhart, once my Masters student and now newly appointed Lecturer at Edinburgh University; Edina Harbinja, also an old lag of the Strathclyde LLM in IT and Telecoms Law, and now Senior Lecturer at University of Aston; and finally Laurence Diver, doctoral candidate at the University of Edinburgh. Mark Leiser, now Lecturer at the University of Leiden, also provided helpful research assistance to chapters 11 and 12. At the risk of sounding like an Oscars ceremony, this book also owes a great deal to the incredible creativity and collective brainpower of my motley 'crew' of lawyers, techies, digital rights people, journalists and policy wonks, many of them giving up great expanses of time to worry over unbelievably vital issues on Twitter with me (far more vital than, say, marking exams or preparing classes), answer late night queries about footnotes and occasionally share in threads of bad jokes about the GDPR, Oprah Winfrey and LOLcats; too many to list, but particular gratitude to Michael Veale, Derek Macaulay, Ian Brown, Burkhard Schafer, Daithi MacSithigh, Andres Guadamuz, Chris Marsden, Judith Rauhofer, Tristan Henderson, Nóra NiLoidean and the ongoing cast and crew of Gikii. You are all lovely, you have made me laugh a great deal, and Internet law is the best field to be in, ever.

Lilian Edwards
London, July 2018, on the hottest day of the year

Part I

Regulation and Infrastructure

1

Internet Regulation

ANDRES GUADAMUZ*

How can we regulate the Internet? This seemingly innocent question has been the subject of countless books and articles for just over the past 20 years. Part of the reason why it continues to be a vibrant and relevant topic is the difference of opinions on what is going on. On the one hand, we have those who believe that the Internet is a free and open space that requires no regulation, and/or is incapable of being regulated. On the other hand, we have those who think that regulation is not only desirable, but that the Internet as it exists now is completely regulated because of the prevalence of state surveillance, and that all semblance of freedom is a mere illusion.

I. The Internet

The Internet has become an integral part of our lives, but if you were to ask the average user about how it works, they would not be able to provide any details other than the fact that it is a medium to transmit information. This is as it should be; as technologies become widespread it is not necessary to understand how they operate – it is possible to drive a car without understanding the intricacies of the internal combustion engine.

However, when it comes to regulating the Internet, it is useful to at least have an idea of what lies under the hood, since it is difficult to try to exert some control over something that one does not understand.

From a regulatory perspective, the first element that should be remarked upon is that the Internet is a 'network of networks'[1] that operate using common protocols

---

* Some of the ideas presented in this chapter can be found in my book on complexity and Internet regulation: *Networks, Complexity and Internet Regulation: Scale-Free Law* (Cheltenham, Edward Elgar, 2011). This chapter is both an update and a reworking of some features of the book.

[1] Jianxi Gao Daqing Li Shlomo Havlin, 'From a Single Network to a Network of Networks' (2014) 1:3 *National Science Review* 346.

designed to ensure resilience, distribution, decentralisation and modularity. It is now part of the history of the Internet that started as a military programme intended to create a communication infrastructure that could survive a nuclear strike. To achieve this objective, a communication network needs to be decentralised, with no central point or governing node. Similarly, communications must be able to be broken down and sent through various links in the network, only to be put together automatically by the recipient. The network will also be made of heterogeneous pieces of hardware that should be able to talk to each other using standard communication tools, and everything should have simplicity and modularity in mind.[2]

The best way to understand the Internet is to separate its architectural features in layers of functionality. By doing this, it is possible to identify the various elements with regards to the function that they serve. The Internet has four layers:

1. **Link layer.** The link layer consists of protocols that allow connection of a host with gateways and routers within a network, usually a large area network (LAN) (eg Ethernet protocols).
2. **Transport layer.** This provides end-to-end protocols for communication between hosts in the system, such as the Transmission Control Protocol (TCP) and the User Datagram Protocol (UDP).
3. **Internet layer.** Because the Internet is a network of networks, every computer connected to it must be able to find its components. The Internet Protocol (IP) fulfils this function, and is differentiated from the application and transport layers by the fact that it does not consist of instructions to reach a destination, or is used to make the actual communications, but it allows data packets to reach their destinations by allowing identification of participating computers based on their IP address.
4. **Application layer.** This is the top communication level made up of protocols for user applications such as sending mail (Send Mail Transfer Protocol, or SMTP), sending files (Hyper Text Transfer Protocol, or HTTP); it also includes protocols used for system support, such as that which identifies servers in the system by name instead of IP address (Domain Name System, or DNS).

The idea behind the above classification for regulatory purposes is that some elements are so fundamental to the functioning of the Internet that they cannot be regulated. The first three layers are specifically about communication between networks and computers, and they are made up of protocols that have been established by the various standards-setting bodies such as the Internet Engineering Task Force (IETF), the World Wide Web Consortium (W3C), the Internet Engineering Steering Group (IESG), the Internet Architecture Board (IAB) and the Internet Society (ISOC). The role of the first layers is to distribute information across the networks.

The application layer is different. Most user activity takes place here, and this is where most communication subject to regulation will take place. The standards used to get communications from one computer to the other tend to be irrelevant

---

[2] B Carpenter, 'Architectural Principles of the Internet' (Internet Architecture Board Paper, 1996), available at www.ietf.org/rfc/rfc1958.txt (last accessed 19 June 2018).

for regulators, other than perhaps being of interest from a governance perspective. However, it is the actual communications that matter, and these will take place through applications.

Having said that, the communication layers may be relevant for the type of regulation that is proposed. For example, a country that wants to control the flow of data coming in and out of its jurisdiction would place technical controls at the Internet layer level in order to filter or block content before it reaches its destination.

II. A Tale of Two Internets

Perhaps the best way to explain the two opposing views of Internet regulation is by contrasting two very distinct case studies that exemplify the difference in experience and perception that lead us to see the Internet in such a different light.

A. The Dark Web

As it was explained above, the Internet is made up of common protocols that allow users to communicate and exchange information with one another. The 'visible' Internet makes use of the four layers, and it consists of shared applications such as the World Wide Web, email, social media apps, games, file transfers, etc. Users connect to the network using the communication layers, and they can connect to one another using the application layer.

Beneath the visible Internet exists a network that not many know how to access, known as the Dark Web (or Dark Net). It uses the Internet's own transport layers, but it consists of applications that are shared by a few technically-minded users. This facilitates a space that is rarely visited, highly encrypted and seldom regulated.

James Bartlett describes the Dark Web as follows:

> For some, the dark net is the encrypted world of Tor Hidden Services, where users cannot be traced and cannot be identified. […] It has also become a catch-all term for the myriad of shocking, disturbing and controversial corners of the Net – the realm of imagined criminals and predators of all shapes and sizes.[3]

One of the most visible Internet applications is the World Wide Web, and we commonly surf through it with web browsers that can read web pages created using the Hypertext Markup Language (HTML). However, because the Internet is decentralised and modular, it is possible for anyone to come up with new applications and protocols that use the communication layers. I could program a new browser that uses my own application protocol, and as long as there is someone else using it, then that would still be part of the Internet, but it would be invisible for most users.

---

[3] J Bartlett, *The Dark Net: Inside the Digital Underworld* (London, William Heinemann, 2014).

One such application is the Tor Browser, which uses the TOR Hidden Service Protocol to connect computers that are also connected to the Internet.[4] This is a communications protocol created by a group of encryption enthusiasts designed to anonymise data transferred through the Internet by using voluntary relays and routers that mask a user's identity to prevent traffic snooping and surveillance. By installing the Tor Browser on their computers, users can view websites that are not accessible through a mainstream browser like Firefox or Chrome.

The anonymous nature of the Dark Web makes it possible to post any type of content, and using anonymous and decentralised payment methods like Bitcoin, users can purchase almost anything they desire.[5] At the time of writing, it was possible to access pages on the Dark Web advertising various drugs, UK passports, US identification documents, hacking services, stolen credit cards and hacked social media accounts.

All of this has led the Dark Web to gain a difficult reputation, coupled by the publicity gained in the trial of Ross Ulbricht, the operator of the Silk Road website, a deep web marketplace for any sort of illegal material.[6]

The presence of such vast and unregulated space tends to lend credence to the idea that the Internet cannot be regulated.

B. Snowden's Internet

Thanks to the series of revelations made by former National Security Agency (NSA) contractor Edward Snowden,[7] we have a troubling picture of extreme control due to mass surveillance conducted by the NSA in the US, and the Government Communications Headquarters (GCHQ) in the UK.

Although the Internet is supposed to be a decentralised, distributed and open telecommunications network, the surveillance revelations have unearthed a much more controlled and centralised system than previously thought possible. Snowden left his life as a contractor and travelled to Hong Kong where he contacted journalist Glenn Greenwald and filmmaker Laura Poitras to whom he gave access to a series of files that laid bare the extent of state surveillance.

The revelations showed a troubling amount of surveillance at all levels, and it is not this chapter's remit to cover these in detail. Following the above classification of the Internet's architecture into layers, it is possible to highlight just some of the issues uncovered:

1. **Link layer**. The Tailored Access Operations (TAO) is the NSA's powerful hacking unit, which specialises in breaking into a target's every communication

---

[4] D Dingledine et al, 'Tor: The Second-Generation Onion Router' (2004), available at https://svn.torproject.org/svn/projects/design-paper/tor-design.pdf (last accessed 19 June 2018).

[5] For more about Bitcoin, see A Guadamuz and C Marsden, 'Blockchains and Bitcoin: Regulatory Responses to Cryptocurrencies' (2015) 20(11) *First Monday*, http://dx.doi.org/10.5210/fm.v20i12 (last accessed 21 June 2018).

[6] J Mullin, 'Ulbricht Guilty in Silk Road Online Drug-Trafficking Trial' (*Ars Technica*, 4 February 2015), available at https://arstechnica.com/tech-policy/2015/02/ulbricht-guilty-in-silk-road-online-drug-trafficking-trial/ (last accessed 19 June 2018).

[7] L Harding, *The Snowden Files* (London, Guardian Faber, 2014).

by tinkering with their access points to the network.[8] The unit uses built-in back-doors in hardware such as routers to tap into people's connection at the point of origin.

2. **Transport layer.** The NSA has managed to tap some of the most important underwater cable systems, which make up the very backbone of the Internet.[9] The tapping is possible because the communications in the transport layer are not encrypted by default.

3. **Internet layer.** This is related to the above paragraph. It has been revealed that the NSA may have had a hand in the lack of default encryption in the Internet layer protocols (TCP/IP), as Vint Cerf, one of the fathers of the Internet, has claimed that he was stopped by the NSA from including an encrypted protocol into the transport layer.[10]

4. **Application layer.** One of the most troubling revelations has been that the NSA has managed to obtain collaboration from technology firms to conduct surveillance within applications, including allegedly secure and encrypted communications like Skype.[11] The project Sigint, which stands for signals intelligence, creates partnerships with developers and companies to build exploits into telecommunication tools.

All of the above speaks of a much more controlled Internet, filled with taps, exploits and collusion on the part of industry, culminating in an unprecedented level of surveillance.

C. Will the Real Internet Please Stand Up?

If one reads each of the above two sections separately, then one would conclude very different things about the nature of the Internet, and the need for regulation.

If one were to read only stories about the Dark Web, one would be likely to conclude that the Internet is a lawless anarchic space filled with pornography, drugs and illegal weapons, where paedophiles and terrorists have a free pass.

If one reads about the Snowden revelations, then one could conclude that we live in a dictatorial dystopia of Orwellian proportions, where shadowy agencies monitor our every thought.

As is often the case, the truth lies somewhere in the middle.

The Internet presents a space that is difficult to regulate despite the existence of the surveillance apparatus described above. While it is relatively easy for most people to

---

[8] J Applebaum et al, 'Inside TAO: Documents Reveal Top NSA Hacking Unit' (*Der Spiegel*, 29 December 2013), available at www.spiegel.de/international/world/the-nsa-uses-powerful-toolbox-in-effort-to-spy-on-global-networks-a-940969.html (last accessed 19 June 2018).

[9] *Ibid.*

[10] P Roberts, 'CERF: Classified NSA Work Mucked Up Security For Early TCP/IP' (*Veracode*, 3 April 2014), available at www.veracode.com/blog/2014/04/cerf-classified-nsa-work-mucked-up-security-for-early-tcpip (last accessed 19 June 2018).

[11] J Ball et al, 'Revealed: How US and UK Spy Agencies Defeat Internet Privacy and Security' *The Guardian* (6 September 2013), available at www.theguardian.com/world/2013/sep/05/nsa-gchq-encryption-codes-security (last accessed 19 June 2018).

be identified when they do something online, there is still some level of anonymity in the network, and there is growing evidence that any attempt at exercising enforcement online will result in increased levels of purposeful and directed anonymisation. For example, a study in Sweden found that when regulators tried to enforce new legislation to curb filesharing, the number of users of anonymous services such as proxies and virtual private networks rose.[12] Similarly, jurisdiction continues to be an issue, evidenced by the fact that criminal operations move online because enforcement tends to be ineffective,[13] and the costs attributed to cybercrime continue to rise.[14]

On the other hand, despite the large surveillance apparatus laid bare by Snowden, this has not yet been translated into more control of everyday Internet transactions. Users continue to share files infringing copyright, and in general people manage to use the network in ways that would be expected even without surveillance. But what is emerging is a more centralised experience for large numbers of users, both at the private and public level.

First, state control is possible – the Chinese Internet, with its built-in filtering and censorship mechanisms, demonstrates a more controlled experience for the largest Internet demographic in the world. Closer to home, court injunctions[15] have successfully blocked access to hundreds of infringing sites, such as The Pirate Bay and Isohunt, and while such blocking is easily circumvented by experienced users, for the large majority the filtering and blocking successfully restricts access to illegal material.[16]

Second, the everyday experience of millions of users is predicated on what private enterprises show them. As more and more people browse through mobile applications, their online experience is defined by the app developer. The level of control that these private enterprises hold can be evidenced by the fact that for a growing number of users, the Internet doesn't even exist; for example, in several countries in Asia the number of self-identified Facebook users is larger than the number of Internet users, which leads researchers to believe that in many territories people mistake Facebook for the Internet.[17]

Thus a more nuanced picture of the Internet begins to emerge. A minority of technically-oriented users operate in heavily encrypted spaces with near-impunity from regulation, while a large number of people suffer constant regulation through

---

[12] S Larsson and M Svensson, 'Compliance or Obscurity? Online Anonymity as a Consequence of Fighting Unauthorised File-sharing' (2010) 2(4) *Policy & Internet* 77.

[13] J Naughton, 'These Days Crime Doesn't Pay … Unless it's Done Online' *The Guardian* (29 March 2015), available at www.theguardian.com/commentisfree/2015/mar/29/cybercrime-online-government-cuts-crime-statistics (last accessed 19 June 2018).

[14] R Anderson et al, 'Measuring the Cost of Cybercrime' *Workshop on the Economics of Information Security* (Stockholm, Sweden, 2012), available at www.econinfosec.org/archive/weis2012/papers/Anderson_WEIS2012.pdf (last accessed 19 June 2018).

[15] A series of blocking orders that start with *Twentieth Century Fox Film Corporation & Anor v Newzbin Ltd* [2010] EWHC 608.

[16] eg, this study suggests dropping torrent usage due to the increase in legal streaming use: Sandvine, *Global Internet Phenomena Report* (2013), available at www.sandvine.com/downloads/general/global-internet-phenomena/2013/2h-2013-global-internet-phenomena-report.pdf (last accessed 19 June 2018).

[17] L Mirani, 'Millions of Facebook Users Have No Idea They're Using the Internet' (*Quartz*, 9 February 2015), available at https://qz.com/333313/milliions-of-facebook-users-have-no-idea-theyre-using-the-internet/ (last accessed 19 June 2018).

censorship, blocking and filtering of content. A person's experience of the Internet will therefore be heavily dependent on education, resources and geographical location.

In other words, the Internet resembles more and more the inequality of 'real' life, but where the one per cent has been replaced with a techno elite minority.

III. Regulation Theories

A. Plus ça change?

It is a common display of modern hubris to believe that the Internet is new in a fundamental way. We see the world around us and notice the impact in almost everything that we do, from planning a trip to driving to work. The advent of the Internet was met with some grandiose statements about how it would herald a new golden era of prosperity and global understanding, an age of 'computer-aided peace'.[18] In 1997, Nicolas Negroponte predicted that in 20 years' time children 'are not going to know what nationalism is'.[19] However, 20 years on, such statements look laughable.

The problem is not only a certain lack of imagination on the part of technology enthusiasts, but also a lack of historical awareness. Undoubtedly there are many important developments both in regulation and communication that have been experienced before, and it is pertinent to remember that many of the debates that we tend to think of as inherently digital were experienced before during the adoption of different technologies.

One of the best examples of this is encapsulated in Standage's seminal book *The Victorian Internet*,[20] which draws many parallels between the rise of telegraphy as a means of communication in the nineteenth century, and the rise of the Internet. These parallels include the misuse of the technology for fraudulent purposes, the creation of a highly-skilled technical class of users and operators and the social changes that it brought.

Our current obsession with technology is often similar to earlier debates about the role of communication and media in society. In a now famous *Newsweek* cover in 1970, the magazine asked whether privacy was dead, with a cartoon depicting an anxious couple harassed by computers, telephones, cameras and microphones.[21] One could easily update that cover with modern concerns such as smartphones, CCTV and drones.

As early as 1983, Ithiel de Sola Pool was already discussing some of the social changes and the societal implications of electronic communication before the digital

---

[18] M Dertouzos, *What Will Be: How the World of Information Will Change* (New York, Harper Collins, 1997).

[19] 'Negroponte: Internet is Way to World Peace' (*CNN*, 25 November 1997), available at http://edition.cnn.com/TECH/9711/25/internet.peace.reut/ (last accessed 19 June 2018).

[20] T Standage, *The Victorian Internet: The Remarkable Story of the Telegraph and the Nineteenth Century's on-Line Pioneers* (San Francisco, Berkley Books, 1999).

[21] The cover can be found at www.thedailybeast.com/is-privacy-dead (last accessed 21 June 2018).

era, identifying key elements about media ownership, distance, centralisation, and privacy. In his book *Technologies of Freedom*, he wrote:

> The exercise of regulation and control over communication is a central concern in any treatise of freedom. How much control are policy makers allowed to exercise? What are the limitations on them [...]? May they censor? May the license those who seek to communicate? What norms control the things that communicators may say to each other? What is libel, what is slander, what violates privacy or security? Who is chose to enforce these rules and how?[22]

These questions are just as relevant today; one could easily ask them of the phenomenon of social media. It is logical that we should consider similar questions concerning the regulation of technology, because the very act of regulation hinges on the issues of power and control, and these do not tend to change with different technologies. What changes are the players, and to a large extent the subject of regulation.

Braman makes an excellent point when talking about the changing regulatory landscape as seen by those who are subject to regulation.[23] She comments that in the pre-digital era, media regulation used to be directed almost exclusively at professional entities and organisations. With the Internet, we are witnessing a democratisation of the application of media policy and regulation in fields such as defamation and copyright. Therefore, Internet regulation has shifted from concerns about direct regulation and has moved towards discussion about intermediary liability.[24]

So, while many of the themes of Internet regulation may remain the same over the years, we can begin to identify unique features that make the Internet subject to different rules, raising the question of whether it is possible to regulate it at all.

B. The Return of Cyber-Libertarianism

The idea of the Internet as a separate space subject to different laws and regulations is as old as the term Cyberspace. In some of the most influential science fiction depictions of virtual realities in novels like *Neuromancer*,[25] *Snow Crash*,[26] and *Ready Player One*[27], the Internet tends to be depicted as an almost different physical reality that is subject to its own rules.

The early Web did feel a bit like an unregulated frontier, particularly because regulators were slow to respond and were very much taken aback by the potential of the new technology and the appearance of a global communications network that seemed to be immune from regulation. In an often-cited work on the topic, lyricist John Perry Barlow wrote his *Declaration of Independence of Cyberspace*, in which he

[22] I de Sola Pool, *Technologies of Freedom* (Cambridge, Massachusetts, Harvard University Press, 1983) 9.
[23] S Braman, 'Where has Media Policy Gone? Defining the Field in the Twenty-First Century' (2004) 9(2) *Communication Law and Policy* 153.
[24] See, eg, D Mac Sithigh, 'The Fragmentation of Intermediary Liability in the UK' (2013) 8(7) *Journal of Intellectual Property Law & Practice* 521.
[25] W Gibson, *Neuromancer* (London, Harper Collins, 2011).
[26] N Stephenson, *Snow Crash* (London, Penguin, 1994).
[27] E Cline, *Ready Player One* (London, Arrow, 2012).

set out to attack government intervention in Cyberspace, favouring a quasi-libertarian self-regulated approach. He wrote:

> Cyberspace consists of transactions, relationships, and thought itself, arrayed like a standing wave in the web of our communications. Ours is a world that is both everywhere and nowhere, but it is not where bodies live. [...] Our identities have no bodies, so, unlike you, we cannot obtain order by physical coercion. We believe that from ethics, enlightened self-interest, and the commonweal, our governance will emerge.[28]

Barlow believed that Internet communities would be able to exercise self-regulatory control because governments would not be able to intervene.

Other commentators and scholars adopted Barlow's ideas in the late 1990s, believing that it would be difficult to subject the Web to traditional regulatory methods. The understanding at the time was that the Internet could not be controlled in any effective manner, and so several models of self-regulation were proposed that were intended to organise the network in some coherent fashion.[29] Of note amongst these theories is Post and Johnson's Net Federalism.[30] They argued that Cyberspace is a separate entity clearly bordered with the physical world, and consequently it should be treated as an independent regulatory sphere for all legal purposes. Because the Internet would still require some form of regulation, they argued that the Web should be able to assemble its own legal institutions in a manner similar to the creation of federal states brought together under a unifying ideal. These self-regulated federal 'states' would generate their own sets of rules consistent with practice in that part of Cyberspace.[31]

While some of the arguments in favour of cyber-libertarianism might be persuasive, Barlow, Post and Johnson completely underestimated the regulatory push from governments and international organisations that would take place.[32] Even back in the late 1990s, several authors criticised the cyber-libertarian ideas of unregulated spaces. In particular, Boyle[33] seems to have understood that the premise behind the theories of the impossibility of exercising any credible governance over Cyberspace was not only wrong-headed, but rested on completely untested hypotheses. In his view, cyber-libertarianism was blind to the many avenues of control available to public regulators.

Nonetheless, cyber-libertarianism continues to endure even to this day. Part of its baffling resilience might arise from the sense of regulatory despair that is often awakened when new technological changes take place. It is interesting how the

---

[28] JP Barlow, *A Declaration of the Independence of Cyberspace* (Electronic Frontier Foundation, 1996), available at www.eff.org/cyberspace-independence (last accessed 19 June 2018).

[29] A comprehensive review of most of these ideas can be found in G Greenleaf, 'An Endnote on Regulating Cyberspace: Architecture vs Law?' (1998) 21(2) *University of New South Wales Law Journal* 593, available at www.austlii.edu.au/au/journals/UNSWLJ/1998/52.html (last accessed 19 June 2018).

[30] DR Johnson and DG Post, 'Law and Borders: The Rise of Law in Cyberspace' (1996) 48 *Stanford Law Review* 1367.

[31] Other works of note are J Reidenberg, '*Lex Informatica*: The Formulation of Information Policy Rules through Technology' (1998) 76 *Texas Law Review* 553; and J Boyle, *Shamans, Software, and Spleens: Law and the Construction of the Information Society* (Cambridge, Massachusetts, Harvard University Press, 1996).

[32] eg, the World Intellectual Property Organisation (WIPO) Copyright Treaties. See J Sheinblatt, 'The WIPO Copyright Treaty' (1998) 13 *Berkeley Technology Law Journal* 535.

[33] J Boyle, 'Foucault in Cyberspace: Surveillance, Sovereignty, and Hard-Wired Censors' (1997) 66 *University of Cincinnati Law Review* 177.

'Internet cannot be regulated' mantra is resurrected every few years when we are presented with a new advance online. This was true of virtual worlds, peer-to-peer (P2P) filesharing, 3D printing, social networks, cryptocurrencies and wearable technology, to name just a few examples.[34] When presented with challenges, many tend to revert to a cyber-libertarian default, declaring the new technology as impossible to regulate. This enduring feature of cyber-libertarianism may be fuelled by nothing more than unfamiliarity with either the new technologies or the history of the Web. As the Internet matures, it seems like every new generation believes that its online experience is unique to the one that came before it.

But the real reason for the return of cyber-libertarianism may be more normative than descriptive. With Snowden's revelations, we are being presented with a dystopian surveillance apparatus that does not resemble the free and open Internet ideal that was originally envisaged. On this view, it is not so much that the Internet *cannot* be regulated, but that it *should not* be regulated. Snowden has given us the perfect excuse, if any was needed, to further distrust regulatory structures. During the closing statements at the 2014 Internet Governance Forum (IGF) in Istanbul, Milton Mueller proposed that Barlow was worth a second look, and postulated the idea of an Internet Nation:

> Barlow's idea that the internet was immune from control by existing governments has been discredited. But remember, Barlow drafted a declaration of independence. Such a declaration does not necessarily mean that existing nations have no power; it means that the residents of cyberspace want a distinct nation of their own. [...] There is nothing terribly crazy or controversial about the concept of an Internet community. Clearly, the Internet provides the basis for a community with its own interests, an incipient identity, its own norms and modes of living together. And it is only a small step from community to nation. A nation is just a community that wants its own state.[35]

This is perhaps a proposition that requires a second look. Many of those who laughed at the idea of cyber-libertarianism did so from the perspective that it clashed with practice, and that governments seemed quite adept at regulating certain aspects of the online experience. But perhaps we were asking the wrong question, and we should now be asking whether such regulation is desired.

C. Regulating the Gateways

While cyber-libertarianism may be experiencing a comeback, it still needs to confront the cold reality of power struggles. The rise of Napster in 1999 and the later emergence of P2P filesharing networks,[36] served as clear reminders of the difficulties of enforcing the law in the digital domain. The near-limitless availability of illicit materials online coupled with the widespread availability of infringing content gave the impression that the Internet was a medium where no regulation was possible. Nonetheless, despite the

---

[34] See, eg, A Guadamuz, 'Back to the Future: Regulation of Virtual Worlds' (2007) 4(3) *SCRIPTed* 242.
[35] M Mueller, 'Internet Nation?' (Internet Governance Project, 5 September 2014), available at www.internetgovernance.org/2014/09/05/internet-nation/ (last accessed 19 June 2018).
[36] See S Smith, 'From Napster to Kazaa: The Battle over Peer-to-Peer Filesharing Goes International' (2003) *Duke Law & Technology Review* 8.

glaring failure in shutting down filesharing networks, the early years of the twenty-first century witnessed the deployment of relatively successful regulatory approaches by many national governments.

The landscape of Internet regulation up until around 2000 was a mixture of cyber-libertarianism and half-hearted legislative solutions. The Internet was a global, distributed and borderless network because it had been designed as such. It also demonstrated resilience because of its origins as a military network whereby its design meant that communications could easily route around damage to any one node in the network. Castells describes this as 'architecture of openness'.[37] Vint Cerf, one of the fathers of the modern Web, went as far as stating that the Internet traffic was 'totally unbound with respect to geography'.[38]

However, as Goldsmith and Wu rightly point out, this initial architecture was not entirely set in stone, and unsurprisingly, it soon became clear that national governments were attempting to draw borders in Cyberspace.[39] The most successful attempt to do so was the segregation of the Internet into national intranets. While the Internet was supposed to be globally distributed, several countries started redesigning the entry points into their national networks in order to impose screening mechanisms that would allow them to filter out undesired content.

This state of affairs is a logical result of the manner in which the Internet grew. While the global architecture of the Internet as a distributed network still holds true because of the existence of routers and distributed protocols, the actual physical Internet is often centralised. In the early days of the Internet, a lot of information was spread through the telephone network, which ensured a high, albeit expensive, distribution ratio.[40] Later, a high-speed backbone had to be built to accommodate larger amounts of information being spread throughout the system, first copper cables and satellites, and later optical cables.[41] The end result was a more centralised Internet than was originally envisaged, as the router distribution worked within connected nodes. This can be explained using the UK as an example: the country has many roads, but not being connected to continental Europe, it relies on ports and airports as communication hubs. The modern Internet looks something like that, with physical connections akin to ports where most of the information comes through, and then it is distributed using routers and hosts in the manner in which it was intended. Many countries have reduced the number of physical entry points to their internal networks, effectively creating Internet chokepoints. If a government controls these gateways, then it will be easier to exercise control over the Internet in that particular country as a whole.

---

[37] M Castells, *The Internet Galaxy: Reflections on Internet, Business, and Society* (Oxford, Oxford University Press, 2001) 26.

[38] As cited by L Guernsey, 'Welcome to the Web. Passport, Please?' *New York Times* (15 March 2001), available at www.nytimes.com/2001/03/15/technology/welcome-to-the-web-passport-please.html (last accessed 19 June 2018).

[39] JL Goldsmith and T Wu, *Who Controls the Internet? Illusions of a Borderless World* (Oxford, Oxford University Press, 2006) 58.

[40] Some early networks, such as Fidonet, even sent all of their packets during cheap-rate calling times, see J Naughton, *A Brief History of the Future: The Origins of the Internet* (London, Phoenix, 2000) 190.

[41] B Leiner et al, *A Brief History of the Internet* (Internet Society Paper, 2000), available at www.cs.ucsb.edu/~almeroth/classes/F10.176A/papers/internet-history-09.pdf (last accessed 19 June 2018).

Unfortunately, there are a growing number of examples of just how effective such chokepoint regulation may be. By far the best example of this is the so-called Great Firewall of China, known there as the Golden Shield Project. The Great Firewall is a multi-layered technological solution that takes advantage of the fact that the Chinese Government controls the few Internet gateways into the larger Chinese Internet. This allows the Government to impose effective filtering restrictions to incoming Internet traffic by various means. The most crucial is the filtering of IP addresses originating from blacklisted services, which range from Blogger to Sex.com.[42] While this is in no way a perfect system, it does allow the Chinese Government a level of influence that was thought impossible with the distributed architecture. The Great Firewall works by deploying hardware routers at each of the entry points into the country. These routers are given lists of banned IP addresses, so when an Internet host within China makes a request to access a banned site, the router does not forward the request to the target host, so the site appears not to exist, and a network error message is returned to the client.[43]

Another well-documented phenomenon was the disconnection of the Egyptian Internet during the Arab Spring. On 27 January 2011 at around 10.30 GMT, the entire Egyptian Internet was disconnected from the rest of the world by Egyptian authorities to respond to widespread protests that were made using social media to communicate and organise.[44] This was possible because Egypt, like many other countries in the Middle East, has a national firewall consisting of an extra layer of Internet servers that mediate all traffic in and out of the country through servers running the appropriately named Border Gateway Protocol (BGP). Egyptian authorities managed simultaneously to shut down 3,500 BGP routes into the country, which meant that more than 90 per cent of all traffic in and out of the country could not get through.[45]

Therefore, it has become clear then that the most effective regulatory solution to online content is to exercise control at the access points. This regulation model has been replicated in many other countries,[46] proving that the Internet is decreasingly distributed, and looks increasingly like a network of self-enclosed city states with connecting ports.

Moreover, private enterprises have been co-opted as regulators of their own environments, in what Laidlaw describes as gatekeepers.[47] She identifies two types of gatekeepers – those who broadly control the flow of information, and what she calls Internet information gatekeepers, who 'as a result of the control impact participation and deliberation in the democratic culture'.[48] Under this framework, large parts of

---

[42] Goldsmith and Wu (n 39) 92.

[43] Goldsmith and Wu (n 39) 92–94.

[44] C Williams, 'How Egypt Shut Down the Internet' *The Telegraph* (28 January 2011), available at www.telegraph.co.uk/news/worldnews/africaandindianocean/egypt/8288163/How-Egypt-shut-down-the-internet.html (last accessed 19 June 2018).

[45] L Greenemeier, 'How Was Egypt's Internet Access Shut Off?' *Scientific American* (28 January 2011), available at www.scientificamerican.com/article/egypt-internet-mubarak/ (last accessed 19 June 2018).

[46] For a comprehensive survey, see J Zittrain et al, *Access Denied: The Practice and Policy of Global Internet Filtering* (Cambridge, Massachusetts, MIT Press, 2007).

[47] E Laidlaw, 'A framework for identifying Internet information gatekeepers' (2010) 24(3) *International Review of Law, Computers & Technology* 263.

[48] *Ibid* 266.

the online environment become regulated by private entities through end-user licence agreements and terms of use, where the gatekeeper can unilaterally remove content with little recourse to the creator. The role of intermediaries as gatekeepers becomes an integral part of the regulatory arsenal, and makes it difficult to sustain the contention that the Internet is an environment devoid of any control.

It must be pointed out that the regulation at the gateway level has interesting side effects for regulatory purposes. The first interesting characteristic is a less decentralised and highly balkanised system where countries exercise internal control. The second is that private enterprises exercise an increasingly powerful level of control over their users, either at the prompting of government, or on behalf of other private actors. The result is a much more centralised environment that does not conform to cyber-libertarian ideals.

D. Code

Since its publication in 1999, Lessig's *Code and Other Laws of Cyberspace*[49] has become one of the more influential books on Internet regulation. In it he postulates that there are four main modes of regulation, namely markets, norms, law and architecture.[50] Most theories of regulation up until then accounted for the first three. Lessig's breakthrough came in the way in which he identified the prevalence of architectural regulation in technological settings. Lessig argued that the Internet itself is highly dependent on the technological architecture that sustains it, the 'code' in which it is written, the connectivity layers between domains, the protocols used in order to distribute information from one computer to another, the functional layers of said protocols, the domain name server system that tells one computer's location in the system, and so on.[51] Whether the Internet can be subject to regulatory control will depend entirely on its underlying architecture. For example, some of the constituent code of the Internet is open, that is, it can be inspected, copied and modified by all sorts of people. This code cannot easily be subject to government regulation. However, the protocols and communication tools that make up the online world are more critical than the underlying code because they are needed for connectivity to take place. Whoever controls the underlying 'plumbing', and the protocols, thus controls the Internet.

But who writes the code? Lessig's architectural regulation suggests the existence of some form of self-ordering mechanism. He identifies the 'invisible hand' of cyberspace that exerts an ordering force into the architecture of the Internet:

Control. Not necessarily control by government, and not necessarily control to some evil, fascist end. But the argument of this book is that the invisible hand of cyberspace is building an architecture that is quite the opposite of its architecture at its birth. This invisible hand,

---

[49] L Lessig, *Code: And Other Laws of Cyberspace* (New York, Basic Books, 1999).
[50] *Ibid* 88.
[51] *Ibid* 100–102.

pushed by government and by commerce, is constructing an architecture that will perfect control and make highly efficient regulation possible.[52]

Nonetheless, Lessig's version of the invisible hand of cyberspace is limited in that he believes that it is shaped by code. So, programmers, regulators and policymakers can make conscious decisions that shape what the underlying architecture will look like, hence exercising real control over the shape of the Web.[53] This version of self-organisation is, as a result, limited by conscious decisions, and while Cyberspace may reach its own efficient regulation, it can be subject to change.

While the original text has been updated,[54] and some of the examples feel dated, the work is still as relevant today as it was back then. As the years pass, and more technology developments arise and evolve, it becomes more evident that architectural decisions made at the outset of the development of a technology have huge implications about how it is going to be regulated.

A great example of an architectural decision that has had huge implications is one of the building blocks of the Internet, the TCP/IP protocol suite. The suite is designed to allow packets of information to reach the intended recipient, but it has a well-documented flaw,[55] namely a lack of authentication. This allows a range of common attacks, such as so-called 'IP spoofing', whereby a malicious user pretends to be sending data from an IP address other than its own. Because there is little authentication, the network assumes that it is coming from that address.[56] This security fault has also made mass surveillance easier, prompting accusations that such an oversight was a purposeful decision in order to make such control possible. Vint Cerf has even admitted that there were proposals to create a network encryption layer, but that it would require the use of encryption technology which at the time was restricted.[57]

The TCP/IP authentication vulnerability is a great example of the strengths and weaknesses of the code regulation model. At its heart, the code model relies on the informed decision of coders and policymakers, and we are expected to believe that they will make the best decisions. But this is not always the case. It is possible for regulators to build bad code into the system, and developers are humans and make mistakes as well. We may also code into place solutions that do not work, or are misguided. Brown and Marsden make this point in their book *Regulating Code*. They write:

> Regulation by code can increase the efficacy of regulation but should not be seen as a panacea. Copyright holders' hopes that 'the answer to the machine is in the machine' led them to waste almost twenty years attempting to enforce scarcity-based business models rather than innovate toward the 'celestial jukebox' that is finally emerging in products such as

---

[52] *Ibid* 7.

[53] *Ibid* 106–108.

[54] L Lessig, *Code Version 2.0*, 2nd edn (London, Basic Books, 2006).

[55] Identified as early as the 1980s, see SM Bellovin, 'Security Problems in the TCP/IP Protocol Suite' (1989) 19(2) *Computer Communication Review* 32.

[56] C Chambers, J Dolske and J Iyer, *TCP/IP Security* (Linux Security Document, 2001), available at www.linuxsecurity.com/resource_files/documentation/tcpip-security.html (last accessed 19 June 2018).

[57] J Leyden, 'Vint Cerf Wanted to Make Internet Secure from the Start, but Secrecy Prevented it" (*The Register*, 7 April 2014), available at www.theregister.co.uk/2014/04/07/internet_inception_security_vint_cerf_google_hangout/ (last accessed 19 June 2018).

Spotify. Code is fundamentally a non-state-designed response that can lead to more effective solutions but will tend to undervalue the public interest and lack democratic legitimacy.[58]

Thus, code can be an empowering regulatory tool, but it can also often be misused, wittingly or otherwise. There is no such thing as an invisible hand of Cyberspace, but we are presented with a model in which programmers, regulators and policymakers make conscious decisions that shape the underlying architecture of the Internet. These decisions are in turn limited by existing technology, but also by other constraints such as the basic online structures.

It would be possible to think of code more as a regulation hierarchy, akin to the Kelsen's pyramid with constitutional norms at the top.[59] At the top of the Internet code pyramid are the foundational protocols, such as the TCP/IP suite, which gives us a clear case of a conscious architectural decision. All other Internet protocols tend to rest on the foundational ones, and therefore must respond to the existing characteristics of the network. Developers can make decisions, but those have to respond to the existing constraints.

IV. Complexity and Self-Organisation

All of the above theories explain different parts of the problem of online regulation. The resistance of various corners of the Internet to regulation can explain the baffling endurance of cyber-libertarianism. It is also evident that the regulation of gateways and chokepoints has had an effect in exercising some form of control over the network. Code can help to explain how some behaviour is built into the system's architecture.

It has been the contention of the author in several works that the Internet is a complex network that displays self-organising characteristics.[60] Assuming that the Internet is a complex adaptive system subject to self-organisation,[61] one might postulate that any attempt to regulate specific elements within the network will have to take into account this important emergent attribute of the global communication system. Moreover, it may not be possible to regulate adequately online environments that display self-organising characteristics without some knowledge of the empirical and theoretical features of such environments.

The network is made up of nodes and links that grow according to power laws.[62] Older links in the network accumulate more links, and those successful nodes in turn tend to accumulate more links themselves, creating a 'the rich get richer' situation.

---

[58] I Brown and C Marsden, *Regulating Code: Good Governance and Better Regulation in the Information Age* (Cambridge, Massachusetts, MIT Press, 2013) 170.

[59] H Kelsen, *Pure Theory of Law*, 2nd edn (Clark, New Jersey, The Lawbook Exchange, 2005).

[60] See A Guadamuz, *Networks, Complexity and Internet Regulation* (n *).

[61] Understood as a system that is capable of organising itself, see SA Kauffman, *At Home in the Universe: The Search for Laws of Self-Organization and Complexity* (Oxford, Oxford University Press, 1995).

[62] A power law is a mathematical expression that happens 'when the probability of measuring a particular value of some quantity varies inversely as a power of that value'. See MEJ Newman, 'Power Laws, Pareto Distributions and Zipf's Law' (2005) 46(5) *Contemporary Physics* 323, 323.

The resulting hubs serve as important connectors within the network, which in turn explains the seemingly ordered nature of the system. The nodes themselves often cluster into small world networks where the intervening pathways between nodes tend to be short. The network is fractal in nature, meaning it has the same architectural features be it on a large or short scale, hence the suggestion that it is scale-free.

The scale-free nature of the network makes the Internet resilient to random attacks. However, this also means that other undesired networks which exist within cyberspace are also robust, such as P2P filesharing networks, ransomware or cybercrime rings. Similarly, because of architectural decisions made early on, the network displays high levels of centrality at the national scale.

All of these features, amongst others, offer strong evidence that self-organising forces operate online. Any regulatory effort that ignores this fact is faced with severe difficulties, as the same self-organising forces that shape the Internet's architecture are also working to undermine and even defeat regulatory action.

The father of self-organisation studies in social systems is Niklas Luhmann, particularly his influential theory of autopoiesis.[63] In its broadest sense, Luhmann's theory of autopoiesis matches what we have witnessed online, as he defines it as social systems that respond to internal stimuli instead of relying on external elements; these elements come together to generate stability in the system. It is a common misunderstanding that self-organisation causes chaos,[64] when in reality most chaotic systems tend towards stability in the long run, much in line with what are known as 'fitness landscapes'.[65] If we think of the Internet as an autopoietic system, then we should conclude that it becomes organised because the interaction of its parts favours clustering and stability in order to manage complexity.

When presented with autopoietic systems, regulation theories have two possible strategies. One could accept that the network responds to its own self-organising elements, and therefore cannot be governed. If this is the case, then regulation is not possible. The postulated theory of self-organisation of the Internet adopts the opposite view, that self-regulation need not mean that governance of the system is impossible. While this may be optimistic, it is the only viable avenue to take if one wishes to undertake regulatory efforts. To fail to do this would be to fall prey to an anarchic and/or cyber-libertarian view of governance, where everything is left to the self-organising powers of the system. Even in the face of contradictory evidence, I adopt an optimistic view of regulation, and will assume that some form of order outside of the regulatory effort is possible.

Within the optimistic regulatory philosophy, we could try to build the system to fit the regulatory goals. Following the idea presented in Lessig's *Code*,[66] regulation strategies can be built into the system, assuming that this will seed the elements around

---

[63] Literally meaning self-creation. See N Luhmann, *Social Systems* (Stanford, Stanford University Press, 1995) 22.

[64] Chaos in the strict mathematical sense, meaning that rendering long-term prediction is impossible in general. See KT Alligood, *Chaos: An Introduction to Dynamical Systems* (New York, Springer-Verlag, 1997).

[65] SA Kauffman and EW Weinberger, 'The NK Model of Rugged Fitness Landscapes and its Application to Maturation of the Immune Response" (1989) 141(2) *Journal of Theoretical Biology* 211.

[66] Lessig (n 54).

which self-organisation will occur. As stated, complex systems will usually order them-selves at fitness peaks of higher order. If we know how self-organisation works within the network, then we can try to code situations that will constitute fitness peaks in the overall landscape.

There are two examples that serve to illustrate opportunities for engineered self-organisation. First, in the fight against P2P file-sharing, it seems evident that the networks are robust self-organising entities. But what would happen if one built a network architecture that specifically targets such networks? While there have been some attempts to attack the networks in this manner, perhaps more strict legislation that tackles not the infringers, but the architecture, would have more chance of success. Second, some forms of cybercrime rely heavily on the current open and centralised Internet architecture. A more tightly regulated network, with more gateways and inter-mediaries, may sacrifice the Web's dynamic nature, but may also seriously hinder some forms of cybercrime, particularly denial of service attacks, spam and phishing.

The optimistic view of regulation also presents opportunities for smarter regula-tory efforts by informing decision-makers and stakeholders about the way in which the target system operates. Any attempt to legislate in the areas covered by Internet regula-tion, such as privacy, copyright and cybercrime, must consider the emergent traits of Cyberspace. At some point policymakers will realise that their regulatory efforts are having no effect, and hopefully they will look at some of the research highlighted in this work in search of evidence.

To recap, the self-organisation theory of Internet regulation is as follows: the Internet is a complex system that displays self-organisation. In order to efficiently and successfully regulate the digital environment, it is imperative that one understands how it is organised, what characteristics are present, what elements act as fitness peaks and how architectural decisions affect its emergent features.

V. Epilogue: The Centrality Menace

On 2 March 2013, an unprecedented (and under-reported) event in the history of the Internet took place. A small technical fault arising from a software update took out 785,000 websites that use the popular content delivery network CloudFlare for over an hour.[67] While some downtime is to be expected, what is remarkable about this incident is that it should never have happened. The Internet is planned with a very clear idea in mind, and that is resilience. It was designed in part to respond to an all-out nuclear strike on the communications infrastructure of the US, and therefore it had a clear design goal that has decentralisation at its core. The idea is that all traffic is distrib-uted through other nodes in the network, so if any individual node is knocked down,

---

[67] R Dillet, 'CloudFlare Was Down Due To Edge Routers Crashing, Taking Down 785,000 Websites Including 4chan, Wikileaks, Metallica.com' (*TechCrunch*, 3 March 2013), available at https://techcrunch.com/2013/03/03/cloudflare-is-down-due-to-dns-outage-taking-down-785000-websites-including-4chan-wikileaks-metallica-com/ (last accessed 19 June 2018).

then traffic should be able to be re-directed through another pathway. The CloudFlare outage was possible because the modern Internet is starting to ignore and bypass this very basic rule for convenience purposes. We are increasingly seeing more centralisation as part of the network, and this spells trouble not just from a technical standpoint, but also with respect to how we are sleepwalking into a more centralised, more regulated, and less open global network.

Anyone who is aware of the decentralised nature of the Internet will undoubtedly be worried that the ideal of decentralisation is fast becoming a thing of the past. The Snowden revelations have uncovered an Internet that is highly centralised; a few countries and a handful of private companies have a disproportionate amount of power with regards to its architecture. The Cambridge Analytica[68] debacle gave us a glimpse into the level of centralisation that private entities have accumulated.

The study of Internet regulation in the next few years will have to tackle the growing levels of centrality. Many people, including this author, still believe that the distributed and open Internet is a worthy cause to support. Besides the common fear of government presence in online communities, exemplified by the ideology of cyber-libertarianism, we need to take a hard look at the way in which the Internet has become a sizeable business, and how a few companies command a disproportionate amount of power. These companies no longer respond to self-imposed promises not to be evil; their reason for existing is to make a profit.[69] The Snowden revelations have uncovered a public-private conglomerate of gigantic proportions, with the US Government and many US-based companies at the centre. Each new revelation has uncovered layers of collaboration that many suspected, but the reality seems to surpass even the worst conspiracy theories.

Internet regulation theories must tackle these issues head on.[70]

---

[68] C Cadwalladr, 'I Made Steve Bannon's Psychological Warfare Tool': Meet the Data War Whistleblower' *The Guardian* (18 March 2018), www.theguardian.com/news/2018/mar/17/data-war-whistleblower-christopher-wylie-faceook-nix-bannon-trump (last accessed 21 June 2018).

[69] See also the discussion of the Cambridge Analytica/ Facebook scandal of 2017–2018 in Lilian Edwards' contribution to this volume in Chapter 3.

[70] In Chapter 9 of this book, the editor, Lilian Edwards, picks up this notion of the increasing importance of platforms and intermediaries as nodes of central power on the Internet and the trend towards enrolling them by the threat of regulation as chokepoints, censors or filters for content and online activities.

2

Net Neutrality Law and Regulation

CHRIS MARSDEN[1]

I. Introduction

Without Internet access, there is no content, application, or service to enjoy: it is the *sine qua non* of Internet use. For that reason, internet access providers (IAPs) have a Faustian bargain with government: in exchange for the privilege to provide such a unique public service and the attendant rights to dig up the streets and conduct other works (for instance, enforcing a public Right of Way), IAPs accept that their service is subject to special rules. If this was not previously clear to the general public and politicians, the Snowden revelations of 2013 made it crystal clear. IAPs provide you with access to the Internet and thus can track your every click of a mouse and every bit that is transferred. Their cooperation with law enforcement is vital to mass or individual surveillance, and their long term cooperation with law enforcement is part of that special Faustian bargain with the state.

Net neutrality is the principle that IAPs do not censor, or otherwise commercially manage data which individual users are attempting to access. Telecommunications providers ('telcos') should not block or throttle Voice over Internet Protocol (VoIP, for example Skype or WhatsApp), or video (for example YouTube, BBC iPlayer or NetFlix), except under temporary and narrowly defined technical conditions.[2] Net neutrality regulation is critical to the future of Internet access for businesses and micro-enterprises, as well as students, citizens and all domestic users, and it is therefore

[1] This research was in part funded by the European Commission EU FP7 EINS grant agreement No 288021 and internal funding from the University of Sussex. No IAP or content provider has provided funding to the project since 2008, though several of each funded earlier stages. I am grateful to have been appointed Research Fellow at Melbourne University School of Law in 2012, and FGV Centre for Technology and Society in 2015, in periods of research leave that contributed to this research.
[2] See further C Marsden, *Network Neutrality: From Policy to Law to Regulation* (Manchester, Manchester University Press, 2017), especially Chapter 4.

critical to the future mass adoption of the Internet of Things (IoT), blockchain, cloud computing and Big Data.

Net neutrality directly regulates the relationship between IAPs and content providers, providing rules about how IAPs may contract with and treat the traffic of those content providers, especially that they may not discriminate against certain providers (either blocking their content or favouring commercial rivals such as IAP affiliates). It does not regulate those content providers directly. Net neutrality is therefore a policy of Internet[3] non-discrimination based on innovation, free speech and privacy, achieved through regulation of telco local access networks.[4] Books have been written about net neutrality, competition law[5] and human rights.[6]

The laws and regulations are formally 'Open Internet', rather than 'network neutrality'. Though laws were passed in many countries in 2015,[7] these were not implemented with rigour by regulatory agencies, nor enforced in the courts.[8] It is too early for advocates to claim success: legal prohibition on discrimination by IAPs has not yet resulted in effective net neutrality regulation.[9] In 2014–16, over seven million citizens replied to various net neutrality consultations, including over two million in India, nearly half a million in Europe, and four million in the US.[10] In 2017, the US 'Open Internet' consultation produced 18 million responses, though much anti-neutrality may have resulted from bot-generated accounts rather than real people, which in 2018 led to an investigation by the Government Accountability Office.[11]

---

[3] The 'Internet' is a network of autonomous systems, of which about 50,000 are of a scale that is relevant. See H Haddadi et al, 'Analysis of the Internet's Structural Evolution', Technical Report Number 756 (2009) Computer Laboratory UCAM-CL-TR-756 ISSN 1476-2986.

[4] C Marsden, 'The Net Neutrality Zombie and Net Neutrality "Lite"' (2009) 19(6) *Computers & Law*, available at www.scl.org/articles/1408-the-net-neutrality-zombie-and-net-neutrality-lite (last accessed 19 June 2018), stating: 'No matter how many economists plant a stake in its heart, or come to bury it not praise it, net neutrality will not die'.

[5] K Maniadaki, *EU Competition Law and the Internet: The Case of Net Neutrality* (Kluwer Law, International Competition Law Series, 2015).

[6] CD Nunziato, *Virtual Freedom: Net Neutrality and Free Speech in the Internet Age* (Stanford, Stanford Law Books, 2009). For the opposing view, see B Zelnick, *The Illusion of Net Neutrality: Political Alarmism, Regulatory Creep, and the Real Threat to Internet Freedom* (Standford: CA, Hoover Institution Press, 2013).

[7] See Regulation (EU) 2015/2120 of 25 November 2015 laying down measures concerning open internet access and amending Directive 2002/22/EC on universal service and users' rights relating to electronic communications networks and services and Regulation (EU) No 531/2012 on roaming on public mobile communications networks within the Union ('Open Internet Regulation') [2015] OJ L310/1–18.

[8] N van Eijk, 'About Network Neutrality 1.0, 2.0, 3.0 and 4.0' (2001) 6 *Computers & Law Magazine* 2011–16; Amsterdam Law School Research Paper No 2012-57; Institute for Information Law Research Paper No 2012-15, available at http://papers.ssrn.com/sol3/papers.cfm?abstract_id=2038802 (last accessed 19 June 2018).

[9] C Marsden, 'Chapter 15: Internet Service Providers' in I Walden (ed), *Telecommunications Law and Regulation*, 5th edn (Oxford, Oxford University Press, 2018).

[10] B Obama, 'President Obama's Statement on Keeping the Internet Open and Free' (10 November 2014), available at www.youtube.com/watch?v=uKcjQPVwfDk (last accessed 19 June 2018). See also B Obama, 'Net Neutrality: President Obama's Plan for a Free and Open Internet' (2015), available at https://obamawhitehouse.archives.gov/node/323681 (last accessed 19 June 2018).

[11] A Breland, 'Government Watchdog Agrees to Probe Fake Net Neutrality Comments (*The Hill*, 24 January 2018), available at http://thehill.com/policy/technology/370521-government-watchdog-agrees-to-probe-fake-net-neutrality-comments# (last accessed 19 June 2018). See also H Neidig, 'FCC Extends

The chapter examines the definition of net neutrality, its 'lite' and 'heavy' aspects, and its legal adoption via regulatory action in the United States and Europe, the latter including special emphasis on European law: Regulation 2015/2120.

II. Net Neutrality Definition and Policy

'Net neutrality' is a difficult term to define accurately, as it is a principle and not a regulatory process. Hahn and Wallsten explained that net neutrality:

> usually means that broadband service providers charge consumers only once for Internet access, don't favor one content provider over another, and don't charge content providers for sending information over broadband lines to end users.[12]

Note that all major consumer IAPs are vertically integrated to some extent, with proprietary video, voice, portal and other services. Conventional economic arguments have been broadly negative about the concept of net neutrality, preferring the introduction of tariff-based congestion pricing.[13]

While issues about potential discrimination by ISPs have been current since at least 1999,[14] the term 'network (net) neutrality' was coined by Tim Wu in 2003.[15] Theorists lined up on either side of the debate in the United States and in Europe.[16]

Deadline for Net Neutrality Comments' (*The Hill*, 11 August 2017), available at http://thehill.com/policy/technology/346232-fcc-extends-deadline-for-net-neutrality-comments (last accessed 19 June 2018).

[12] R Hahn and S Wallsten, 'The Economics of Net Neutrality' (AEI Brookings Joint Center for Regulatory Studies, Washington, DC, 2006).

[13] See P David, 'The Evolving Accidental Information Super-Highway' (2001) 17(2) *Oxford Review of Economic Policy* 159.

[14] See M Lemley and L Lessig, 'Ex Parte Declaration of Professor Mark A. Lemley and Professor Lawrence Lessig in the Matter of: Application for Consent to the Transfer of Control of Licenses of MediaOne Group, Inc. to AT&T Corp' (1999), available at https://cyber.harvard.edu/works/lessig/cable/fcc/fcc.html (last accessed 20 June 2018). See further Chapter 1 of C Marsden, *Network Neutrality* (London, Bloomsbury, 2010); and C Marsden, 'Pluralism in the Multi-Channel Market. Suggestions for Regulatory Scrutiny' (1999) 4 *International Journal of Communications Law and Policy* 2000.

[15] T Wu, 'Network Neutrality, Broadband Discrimination' (2003) 2 *Journal on Telecommunications and High-Tech Law* 141.

[16] For those against regulation, see, eg, J Speta, 'FCC Authority to Regulate the Internet: Creating It and Limiting It' (2004) 35 *Loyola University Chicago Law Journal* 15–39; C Yoo, 'Network Neutrality and the Economics of Congestion' (2006) 94 *Georgetown Law Journal* 1847–1908. For those in favour of regulation, see, eg, T Wu, 'Wireless Carterfone' (2007) 1 *International Journal of Communication* 389–426; R Frieden, 'What Do Pizza Delivery and Information Services Have in Common? Lessons From Recent Judicial and Regulatory Struggles with Convergence' (2006) 32 *Rutgers Computer and Technology Law Journal* 247–96; N Economides and J Tåg, 'Network Neutrality on the Internet: A Two-Sided Market Analysis' (2012) 24 *Information Economics and Policy* 91–104; P Weiser, 'The Future of Internet Regulation' (2009) 43 *UC Davis Law Review* 529–90; B Frischmann and B van Schewick, 'Yoo's Frame and What It Ignores: Network Neutrality and the Economics of an Information Superhighway' (2007) 47 *Jurimetrics Journal* 383–428. Since that point, the debate has turned from theory to evidence and implementation details, on which this chapter focuses.

In the period since, the debate was dismissed as 'an American problem due to abandonment of network unbundling' and common carriage (competition is 'inter-modal' between cable and telecoms networks, not 'intra-modal' between different telecoms companies using the incumbents' exchanges to access the 'last mile').[17] The giant regional monopolies, the Regional Bell Operating Companies (RBOCs), re-emerged in 2006 as two super-sized local long-distance internet-wireless combines, now called AT&T and Verizon.[18] Competition economics somewhat misses the point: competition law will not entirely meet the challenge, as this is a consumer law issue.[19]

The lack of trust and security on the Internet, combined with a lack of innovation in the Quality of Service (QoS) offered in the core network, means that development has been focused almost entirely on the application layer. Peer-to-Peer (P2P) programmes such as low-grade VoIP and filesharing as well as the World Wide Web were designed during this period.[20] 'Carrier-grade' VoIP, data and video transmission was restricted to commercial Virtual Private Networks (VPNs) that could guarantee security, with premium content attempting to replicate the same using Content Delivery Networks such as Akamai, or IAPs' own offerings deployed within their networks.

Network congestion and lack of bandwidth at peak times is a feature of the Internet which has always existed. This is why streaming video over the Internet was, until the late 1990s, simply unfeasible. It is also why VoIP often has patchy quality, and why engineers have been trying to create better QoS. Prior to commercialisation in 1995, the Internet had never been subject to regulation beyond that needed for interoperability and competition, building on the Computer I and II inquiries by Federal Communications Commission (FCC) in the United States, and the design principle of 'end-to-end' (E2E). That principle itself was bypassed by the need for greater trust and reliability in the emerging broadband network by the late 1990s, particularly as spam email led to viruses, botnets and other risks. The E2E principle governing internet architecture is a two-edged sword, with advantages of openness and a dumb network, and disadvantages of congestion, jitter, and ultimately a slowing rate of progress for high-end applications such as streaming High Definition Television (HDTV).[21]

---

[17] Communications Act of 1934 as amended by Communications (Deregulatory) Act of 1996, 47 USC §§153(20) (definition of 'information service'), 153(10) (definition of 'common carrier'), 153(43) (definition of 'telecommunications'), and 153(46) (definition of 'telecommunications service').

[18] Federal Communications Commission, 'FCC Approves SBC/AT&T and VERIZON/MCI mergers' (31 October 2005), available at http://hraunfoss.fcc.gov/edocs_public/attachmatch/DOC-261936A1.pdf (accessed 29 September 2017).

[19] L Belli and P De Filippi (eds), *Net Neutrality Compendium: Human Rights, Free Competition and the Future of the Internet* (New York, Springer International, 2016).

[20] I Brown and C Marsden, *Regulating Code* (Cambridge, Massachusetts, MIT Press, 2013) 36–39; R Cannon, 'The Legacy of the FCC's Computer Inquiries' (2003) 55 *Federal Communications Law Journal* 167–205, and references therein.

[21] JH Saltzer, DP Reed and DD Clark, 'E2E Arguments in System Design' (1984) 2 *ACM Transactions on Computer Systems* 288.

It is worth noting the comment of the European regulator group BEREC (Body of European Regulators of Electronic Communications):

> Over the Internet, a guaranteed end-to-end QoS offer is … neither commercially nor technically realistic. Differentiated services (DiffServ), which fall just short of guaranteed end-to-end QoS, exist but continue to be exceptional … where end-to-end QoS arrangements are currently in use, they almost always consist of specialised services (e.g. IPTV), provided not over the Internet but within a closed network within the Internet Access Provider [IAP]'s own network.[22]

A. Net Neutrality 'Lite' and 'Heavy'

Dividing net neutrality into its forward-looking positive and backward-degrading negative elements is the first step in unpacking the term, in comprehending that there are two types of problem: charging more for more, and charging the same for less. IAPs can discriminate against all content or against the particular content that they compete with when they are vertically integrated.

Backward-looking 'net neutrality lite' claims that Internet users should not be disadvantaged due to opaque and invidious practices by their current IAP. That means no throttling, blocking of rival content (for example Skype, BitTorrent, NetFlix or WhatsApp), as well as upholding the 'four freedoms' of Internet users: their own choice of content, applications, services and devices to connect to the Internet. In the US, regulators have a long history of fighting such discrimination.

Forward-looking 'heavy' net neutrality is the new focus of the problem: network owners with vertical integration into content or alliances have enhanced incentives to require content owners (who may also be consumers) to pay a toll to use the higher-speed networks that they offer to end-users. These 'fast lanes' are typically upgraded fibre to the customer's neighbourhood (or road or even house) rather than traditional copper networks. This 'heavy' net neutrality is argued to place a burden on investors in upgrading to faster IAP lines, though the costs have fallen dramatically and most European and US Internet users can in 2018 access a fast broadband line.

Net neutrality 'lite' is becoming regulated, and is less controversial than previously. Governments and regulators that fought net neutrality law fiercely have finally conceded that it may not be as disastrous as they had claimed. They are conceding net neutrality 'lite' because they have secured approval for their IAPs to discriminate on their fast lane services, which are now called 'specialised services'. For example, the European mobile IAPs finally agreed in 2014 to stop fighting for the right to throttle their users' Internet use when it became inevitable that a new European law would be passed in some shape.

The net neutrality problem is complex and far-reaching: European attempts to dismiss it as a problem that can be overcome by local loop (last mile) telecoms competition fail to acknowledge persistent problems of market failure.[23] The physical delivery

---

[22] BEREC (2012) BoR (12) 120.
[23] C Marsden, *Network Neutrality: Towards a Co-Regulatory Solution* (London, Bloomsbury Academic, 2010).

of the Internet to consumers is subject to a wide range of bottlenecks, not simply in the 'last mile' connecting to the end-user. There is little 'middle mile' (backhaul) competition in fixed IAP markets, even in Europe. Even if platforms did compete in, for instance, heavily cabled countries, there would remain market problems in that there is no necessary direct (even non-contractual) relationship between innovative application providers and IAPs, for instance a Korean games developer and a UK IAP. Platforms may set rules to 'tax' data packets that ultimately impoverish the open innovation value chain, thus ultimately causing consumer harm. Thus the archetypal garage start-ups such as Facebook (founded 2003) and YouTube (founded 2005) would have had less opportunity to spread 'virally' across the Internet, as their services would be subject to these extra costs.

B. History of Common Carriage, the Forerunner to Net Neutrality

Net neutrality has been variously defined, most prominently with regard to its forerunner: common carriage. In common-law countries such as the UK and USA, carriers are liable for damage or loss of the goods that are in their possession as carriers, unless they prove that the damage or loss is attributable to certain excepted causes (for example 'acts of God').[24] Common carriage is defined by the duties imposed on public networks in exchange for their right to use public property as a right of way, as well as other privileges. Common carriers are under a duty to carry goods lawfully delivered to them for carriage. The duty does not prevent carriers from restricting the commodities that they will carry. Carriers may refuse to carry dangerous goods, improperly packed goods, or those that they are unable to carry, for example on account of size, legal prohibition, or a lack of facilities.

In the US, it was established in 1901 that a public telegraph company (and more especially the largest) had a duty of non-discrimination towards the public.[25] Telecoms networks were established to be common carriers as they achieved maturity, following telegraphs, railways, canals and other networks. The Internet was held out by early legal and technical analysts to be special, due to its decentred construction, separating it from earlier 'technologies of freedom' including radio and the telegraph. Noam explains: 'it is not the failure of common carriage but rather its very success that undermines the institution. By making communications ubiquitous and essential, it spawned new types of carriers and delivery systems'.[26] He forewarned that net neutrality would have to be the argument employed by those arguing for non-discriminatory access.

---

[24] E Noam, 'Beyond Liberalization II: The Impending Doom of Common Carriage' (1994) 18(6) *Telecommunications Policy* 435–52.

[25] See *Western Union Telegraph Co v Call Publishing Co* 181 US 92, 98 (1901).

[26] Noam (n 25) 435, explaining that: 'When historically they [infrastructure services] were provided in the past by private firms, English common law courts often imposed some quasi-public obligations, one of which one was common carriage. It mandated the provision of service to willing customers, bringing common carriage close to a service obligation to all once it was offered to some.'

Common carriers that claim on the one hand the benefits of rights of way and other privileges, yet on the other claim traffic management for profit rather than network integrity, are trying to both 'have their cake and eat it'.[27] Twenty-first century IAPs that choose to engage in traffic management measures (TMM) in a discriminatory fashion could not be considered common carriers. If they cease being common carriers, they then open themselves to liability for the 'cargo' they inspect before they agree to carry it on a discriminatory basis. This raises a huge number of liability issues considered elsewhere in the book.

C. Deep Packet Inspection and Traffic Management

In order to manage traffic, new technology lets any of the IAP routers (if so equipped) to look inside an unencrypted data packet to 'see' its content, via deep packet inspection (DPI) and other techniques. Previous routers were not powerful enough to conduct more than a shallow inspection that simply established the header information – the equivalent of the postal address for the packet. An IAP can use DPI to determine whether a data packet values high-speed transport – as a television stream does in requiring a dedicated broadcast channel – and thus it can offer higher-speed dedicated capacity to time-dependent content such as high definition video or VoIP. That could make a good business for IAPs that wish to offer higher capability for 'managed services' via DPI.[28] Not all IAPs will do so, and it is quite possible to manage traffic less obtrusively, for instance by using the DiffServ protocol to prioritise traffic streams.[29]

DPI and other techniques that let IAPs prioritise certain types of content also allow them to slow it down, or speed it up for those that pay (and, for example, emergency communications and other 'good' packets). This potentially threatens competitors with that content: Skype offers VoIP using normal Internet speeds; uTorrent and BBC's iPlayer have offered video using P2P protocols. Encryption is common in these applications and partially successful in overcoming these IAP controls. This is because it makes identifying the nature of the content more difficult, but even if all users and applications used strong encryption this would not succeed in overcoming decisions by IAPs simply to route known premium traffic to a 'faster lane', consigning all other traffic, including that encrypted traffic, into a slower non-priority lane (a policy explanation simplifying a complex engineering decision). P2P is designed to make the

---

[27] See R Frieden, 'Invoking and Avoiding the First Amendment: How Internet Service Providers Leverage Their Status as Both Content Creators and Neutral Conduits' (2010) 12 *University of Pennsylvania Journal of Constitutional Law* 1279; K Werbach, 'Off the Hook' (2010) 95 *Cornell Law Review* 535; B Cherry, 'Misusing Network Neutrality to Eliminate Common Carriage Threatens Free Speech and the Postal System' (2006) 33 *Northern Kentucky Law Review* 483–511.

[28] R Frieden, 'Internet Packet Sniffing and Its Impact on the Network Neutrality Debate and the Balance of Power Between Intellectual Property Creators and Consumers' (2008) 18(3) *Fordham Intellectual Property, Media & Entertainment Law Journal* 633–75.

[29] Brown and Marsden (n 20) 144.

most efficient use of congested networks, and its proponents claim that with sufficient deployment, P2P could largely overcome congestion problems.

In 2007, congestion on the Internet was said to be caused by P2P file-sharing, and consumer advocates feared that DPI would lead to pervasive Internet monitoring by IAPs and advertisers. In 2007, no-one had heard of Spotify, Twitter, WhatsApp, SnapChat, Instagram or NetFlix. One could not use a 3G network to download apps from the iTunes Store, because the iPhone was only launched in mid-2007 and data was so slow and expensive that it was assumed downloads all took place on WiFi. The iPad and all other tablet computers did not exist. No-one had heard of Julian Assange or Wikileaks, let alone Edward Snowden. P2P is no longer seen as a significant cause of congestion but merely an artefact of the midband decade in which consumers struggled with 256kbps-4Mbps connections.

On fast broadband networks, it is ultra-high definition television (UHDTV) streaming and downloading which is the concern. Video streaming arose as a policy concern with the blocking of both Norwegian and UK state broadcaster video streaming in the mid-2000s. In the period since 2010, it has been redefined as a commercial concern arising in the US with NetFlix and in varying manifestations in other nations. In addition, audio streaming on mobile has been a concern with various IAPs providing 'free' (i.e. positively discriminated) offers for music services such as Spotify, the 'legitimate' successor to Napster, the P2P service that accompanied much of the early net neutrality controversy. Net neutrality may therefore be returning to its roots in the 1990s – turning the Internet into an on-demand cable TV service where Internet traffic becomes a second-class service to first-class proprietary video (and audio) offerings.

Edward Snowden proved beyond all reasonable doubt that major IAPs had collaborated for years with security agencies in the US, UK and many other countries, to provide monitoring in real time and via retained historic browsing data of all Internet users, both within those territories and whose traffic passed through them. This made the concerns around DPI and advertising both proven and trivial: yes, IAPs clearly had the ability to track all users, but more importantly they had been using this capacity for years and it was funded by both advertisers and in advanced surveillance projects by the security agencies.[30] Snowden's revelations revealed how acutely the privacy concerns of advocates were shown to have been under- rather than over-blown.[31] Net neutrality defined as freedom to use the Internet without interference may be considered a pre-Snowden anachronism, given the knowledge he revealed. Bear in mind that while Snowden's revelations are now historical, dating back to the spring of 2013, surveillance will have advanced considerably in the intervening period.[32]

---

[30] A D'Ignazioa and E Giovannetti, 'Predicting Internet Commercial Connectivity Wars: The Impact of Trust and Operators' Asymmetry' (2015) 31(4) *International Journal of Forecasting* 1127–37.

[31] NM Richards, *Intellectual Privacy: Rethinking Civil Liberties in the Digital Age* (Oxford, Oxford University Press, 2015), available at SSRN: http://ssrn.com/abstract=2554196 (last accessed 20 June 2018).

[32] A Candeub, "Is there Anything New to Say about Network Neutrality?' (2015) *Michigan State Law Review* 455 references my arguments at fn 55.

III. State of the Law on Net Neutrality

Net neutrality has advanced from thwarted regulatory proposal to actual regulatory action in several advanced and developing nations. Notable examples of laws with the date of regulation/legislation are: Chile (2010–11);[33] Brazil (2014–15);[34] Israel (2011);[35] and Costa Rica (2010).[36] Other nations have introduced forms of self-regulation for net neutrality with varying degrees of regulatory commitment, including Norway (2009),[37] the United Kingdom,[38] South Korea (2013),[39] Japan (2009),[40] and Singapore (2011).[41] 'Open Internet' legislation has been passed in the European Economic Area (EEA) via Regulation 2015/2120, and is regulated in the US via the Open Internet Orders of 2010 (transparency provisions) and 2015 (anti-discrimination).[42] Canada has used existing law to regulate.[43] European nations with pre-existing laws included Netherlands (2012),[44] Slovenia (2012),[45] and Finland (2014).[46]

---

[33] Chile, 'Law 20.453 Which Enshrines the Principle of Net neutrality for Consumers and Internet Users' (26 August 2010), available at www.leychile.cl/Navegar?idNorma=1016570&buscar=NEUTRALIDAD+D E+RED (last accessed 20 June 2018).

[34] Brazil Presidency of the Republic, Civil House Legal Affairs Subsection, Law No 12.965 (23 April 2014).

[35] Amending Article 51C(b) Telecommunications Law 1982, summarised by the Ministry of Communications (2015) at http://berec.europa.eu/files/doc/2.%20Israel%20adi%20presentation%20 emerg%2023.6.15%20Israel.pdf (last accessed 20 June 2018).

[36] *Andrés Oviedo Guzmán, Fabio Isaac Masís Fallas Y Juan Manuel Campos Ávila, Contra El Ministerio De Ambiente, Energía Y Telecomunicaciones*, Ministerio De La Presidencia, Sala Constitucional De La Corte Suprema De Justicia, San José (13 July 2010), available at www.tcchnollama.co.uk/wp-content/ uploads/2012/04/Voto2010-12790SalaConstitucionalCR.pdf (last accessed 20 June 2018).

[37] Norway Post and Telecommunications Authority (NPT), 'Network Neutrality – Guidelines for Internet Neutrality' (2009), available at www.legi-internet.ro/fileadmin/editor_folder/pdf/Guidelines_for_network_ neutrality_-_Norway.pdf (last accessed 20 June 2018).

[38] C Marsden, 'Net Neutrality Regulation in the UK: More Transparency and Switching' (2014) *Journal of Law and Economic Regulation* (Seoul, Korea), available on SSRN: http://ssrn.com/abstract=2423284 (last accessed 20 June 2018).

[39] Y Kim, 'Net Neutrality Regulation and Management of Internet Traffic of Korea: Issues and Evaluation' (2014) *Journal of Law and Economic Regulation* (Seoul, Korea) which discusses 'Net Neutrality and Internet Traffic Management Guidelines' (2011); 'Criteria on Reasonable Management and Use of Communications Networks and Transparency in Traffic Management' (October 2013, finalised December 2013).

[40] T Jitsuzumi, 'Recent Development of Net Neutrality Conditions in Japan', presentation at the ITS Europe 2015. Slides available at www.slideshare.net/toshiyajitsuzumi/recent-development-of-net-neutrality-conditions-in-japan (last accessed 20 June 2018).

[41] Info-Communications Development Authority of Singapore, 'IDA's Decision and Explanatory Memorandum for the Public Consultation on Net Neutrality' (2011).

[42] GN Docket No 14-28, 'Protecting and Promoting the Open Internet', Notice of Proposed Rulemaking, 29 FCC Rcd 5561 (2014) (2014 Open Internet NPRM).

[43] Canadian Radio-television and Telecommunications Commission (CRTC), 'Review of the Internet Traffic Management Practices of Internet Service Providers' (2009), available at www.crtc.gc.ca/eng/ archive/2009/2009-657.htm (last accessed 20 June 2018).

[44] Netherlands Telecommunications Act 2012.

[45] Slovenia Law on Electronic Communications, No 003-02-10/2012-32 (20 December 2012), Art 203(4), available at www.uradni-list.si/1/content?id=111442 (last accessed 20 June 2018).

[46] Finland Ministry of Transport and Communications, Information Society Code (917/2014) PART I, s 110, 'Network Neutrality' (2014) at www.finlex.fi/fi/laki/kaannokset/2014/en20140917.pdf (last accessed 20 June 2018). I am grateful to Professor Päivi Korpisaari of Helsinki University.

Table 1 Notable Net Neutrality Laws or Regulations

Country	Legislation/regulation	Published	Date enforced
Norway	Guidelines[47]	24/2/2009[48]	Zero rating NKOM 2014
Chile	Law 20.453[49]	18/8/2010	Decree 368, 15/12/2010[50]
Netherlands	Telecoms Act 2012[51]	7/6/2012	Guidelines 15/5/2015[52]
Slovenia	Law on Electronic Communications 2012[53]	20/12/2012	Zero rating 2015
Finland	Information Society Code (917/2014)[54]	17/9/2014	2014
India	Regulations (No 2 of 2016)	8/2/2016	8 August 2016
Brazil	Law No 12.965 Decree No 8771/2016	11/5/2016	No implementation[55]

In each of the case studies, initial confusion at the lack of clarity in net neutrality laws[56] gave way to significant cases, which have given regulators the opportunity to clarify their legislation or regulation. The majority of such cases relate to mobile (or in US parlance 'wireless') net neutrality, and in particular so-called 'zero rating' practices.

IV. US Network Neutrality

A. Internet Policy Statement – the 'Four Freedoms' 2004–2005

Chair of the FCC, Michael Powell, decided that a statement of consumer-oriented open access policy should persuade ISPs to avoid egregious discrimination. In February 2004 he declared: 'I challenge the broadband network industry to preserve the following Internet Freedoms: Freedom to Access Content; Freedom to Use Applications;

---

[47] Norwegian Communications Authority (NKOM), 'Net Neutrality' (2014), available at http://eng.nkom.no/technical/internet/net-neutrality/net-neutrality (last accessed 20 June 2018).

[48] T Olsen, 'Net Neutrality Activities at BEREC and Nkom, Norwegian Communications Authority' (2015), slide 5, available at http://berec.europa.eu/files/doc/2015-07-13_09_56_36_3.%20Noruega%20Nkom%20net%20neutrality%20-%20Summit%20BEREC-EaPeReg-REGULATEL-EMERG.pdf (accessed 6 July 17).

[49] Chile, 'Law 20.453, which Enshrines the Principle of Net Neutrality for Consumers and Internet Users' (2010), available at www.leychile.cl/Navegar?idNorma=1016570&buscar=NEUTRALIDAD+DE+RED (last accessed 20 June 2018).

[50] See www.subtel.gob.cl/images/stories/articles/subtel/asocfile/10d_0368.pdf (last accessed 20 June 2018).

[51] See www.government.nl/documents/policy-notes/2012/06/07/dutch-telecommunications-act (last accessed 20 June 2018).

[52] Netherlands Department of Economic Affairs, *Net Neutrality Guidelines May 15th, for the Authority for Consumers and Markets (ACM) for the Enforcement by ACM of Article 7.4a of the Netherlands Telecommunications Act 2012* (2015).

[53] 'No 003-02-10/2012-32' available at www.uradni-list.si/1/content?id=11144 (last accessed 20 June 2018).

[54] See www.finlex.fi/fi/laki/kaannokset/2014/en20140917 (last accessed 20 June 2018).

[55] For updates, see 'Ministry of Justice' (2016), available at http://pensando.mj.gov.br/marcocivil/ (last accessed 20 June 2018).

[56] C Marsden, 'Presentation on Net Neutrality' (2013), available at http://chrismarsden.blogspot.co.uk/2013/10/presentation-on-net-neutrality-at.html (last accessed 20 June 2018).

Freedom to Attach Personal Devices; Freedom to Obtain Service Plan Information.'[57] The 'Four Freedoms' were applied in the Internet Policy Statement in which the FCC adopted this policy, though no specific regulation.[58]

B. Regulatory Actions by the FCC 2005–2010

There were three major enforcement actions by the FCC under the policy, namely: *Madison River* (2005), *AT&T/BellSouth* (2007) and *Comcast* (2008). The first regulatory action to prevent blocking of access was against a small ISP that had been blocking a rival VoIP service, Madison River.[59] After *Madison River*, the larger scale regulatory action came in the merger of *AT&T/BellSouth* (2007), when the merged company undertook various commitments not to block other companies' applications directed to their users.[60] AT&T agreed to:

1. follow the FCC's four Internet Freedoms for 30 months;
2. apply network neutrality principles for its broadband ISP between subscribers and the first Internet Exchange point for two years;
3. but it expressly reserved the option not to apply network neutrality principles for its IP Television (IPTV) service, and to any service beyond the first Internet Exchange point.

The FCC then made an Order of 1 August 2008 against Comcast, a major cable broadband ISP.[61] The FCC ordered Comcast, within 30 days, to:

1. disclose to the Commission the precise contours of the network management practices at issue, including equipment utilised, when and under what circumstances it was used, and what protocols were affected;
2. submit a compliance plan to the Commission to transition from discriminatory to non-discriminatory network management practices by the end of 2008; and
3. disclose to the Commission and the public the details of the network management practices that it intends to deploy following the termination of its current practices, including the thresholds that will trigger any limits on customers' access to bandwidth.

The FCC found that 'Comcast has an anti-competitive motive to interfere with customers' use of P2P applications'. This is because P2P offers a rival TV service delivery

---

[57] M Powell, 'Four Freedoms' speech (2004), available at http://hraunfoss.fcc.gov/edocs_public/attachmatch/DOC-243556A1.pdf (accessed 28 August 2017).

[58] FCC 05-151, adopted 5 August 2005.

[59] Madison River Communications, LLC, Order, DA 05-543, 20 FCC Rcd 4295 (2005), available at http://hraunfoss.fcc.gov/edocs_public/attachmatch/DA-05-543A1.pdf (accessed 28 August 2017).

[60] In AT&T Inc and BellSouth Corp (2007) Application for Transfer of Control, 22 FCC Rcd 5562, note the dissent at Appendix F, slip op p 154.

[61] Federal Communications Commission, Formal Complaint of Free Press and Public Knowledge Against Comcast Corp for Secretly Degrading Peer-to-Peer Applications; Broadband Industry Practices; Petition of Free Press et al for Declaratory Ruling that Degrading an Internet Application Violates the FCC's Internet Policy Statement and Does Not Meet an Exception for 'Reasonable Network Management' 2008, Memorandum Opinion and Order, 23 FCC Rcd 13028 ('ComcastOrder').

to cable, which the FCC found 'poses a potential competitive threat to Comcast's video-on-demand (VOD) service'. FCC concluded that Comcast's conduct blocked internet traffic, rejected Comcast's defence that its practice constituted reasonable network management, and also that 'the anticompetitive harms caused by Comcast's conduct have been compounded by the company's unacceptable failure to disclose its practices to consumers'. Then FCC Chairman Martin was not condemning 'metered broadband'. Comcast announced a 250 Gigabyte monthly limit in early September 2008, replacing its previous discretionary Terms of Use reasonable caps.

The FCC justified its regulatory authority to issue the Order, invoking its Title I ancillary jurisdiction under the Communications Act to regulate in the name of 'national Internet policy' as described in seven statutory provisions, all of which speak in general terms about 'promoting deployment', 'promoting accessibility', and 'reducing market entry barriers'. Comcast appealed to the District of Columbia Court of Appeals to overturn the Order on these grounds, winning in 2010 because the FCC failed to tie its assertion of ancillary authority to any 'statutorily mandated responsibility'.[62] This decision occurred as the FCC was then consulting on a draft Notice of Proposed Rule Making (NPRM), with the perhaps inevitable result that the FCC NPRM was immediately appealed in 2010, and finally overturned in 2014 (with the exception of consumer transparency requirements that stayed in force throughout).

C. Open Internet Report and Order 2010

The FCC extended a consultation on net neutrality or 'the open Internet' over 2009–2010, receiving over 27,000 submissions. This process was finishing just as the Court of Appeal judged in April 2010 in *Comcast v FCC* that the FCC's regulatory actions in this area were not justified by its reasoning under the Communications Act 1996. The successful Comcast appeal meant that the FCC had to:

- reclaim Title II common carrier authority for ISPs under the 1996 Telecommunications Act,
- ask Congress to re-legislate to grant it Title I authority, or
- try to assert its own Title I authority subject to legal challenge.

It adopted this last course in its Order of 23 December 2010.[63] The Report and Order was then subjected to an unusual delay in publication in the Federal Register until September 2011,[64] following which it required 60 days before both pro- and anti-net neutrality organisations were able to formally make representations to bring the

---

[62] *Comcast Corp v FCC*, 600 F.3d 642, 2010 United States Court of Appeals for the District of Columbia.
[63] See FCC Report and Order (2010) 'Preserving the Open Internet', 25 FCC Rcd 17905 and FCC Report and Order, 'In the Matter of Preserving the Open Internet and Broadband Industry Practices', GN Docket No 09-191, WC Docket No 07-52, FCC 10-201 §21–30 (2010).
[64] FCC Report and Order (2010), *ibid*.

question of the FCC's authority under the Communications Act to court. A case before the DC Appeals Court led to the FCC being defeated in 2014.[65]

D. Open Internet Order 2015 and NPRM 2017

As a result of its court defeat, the FCC decided in 2014 to implement a new NPRM that reclassified broadband internet access services (BIAS) as Title II common carriers, finalising the rules in February 2015. In *United States Telecom Association v FCC* the telecoms operators appealed that decision, but the FCC ruling was upheld in the DC Court of Appeals in June 2016.[66]

Prior to the 2015 Open Internet Order,[67] the 2010 Order was highly controversial in its exclusion of mobile ('wireless') data, resulting in several data caps being imposed, zero ratings plans being adopted, and the Order itself becoming incapable of effective enforcement following litigation which ended in 2014[68] and resumed in 2015. The Court of Appeals decision on 14 June 2016[69] will possibly be further appealed to the Supreme Court in 2018.[70]

The FCC claimed the 26 February 2015 Open Internet Order offered 'Bright Line Rules':

- No Blocking: broadband providers may not block access to legal content, applications, services, or non-harmful devices.

- No Throttling: broadband providers may not impair or degrade lawful Internet traffic on the basis of content, applications, services, or non-harmful devices.

- No Paid Prioritisation: broadband providers may not favour some lawful Internet traffic over other lawful traffic in exchange for consideration of any kind – in other words, no 'fast lanes'. This rule also bans IAPs from prioritising content and services of their affiliates.[71]

The FCC found itself most able to enforce net neutrality with decisions inserted into merger approvals, as previously in the mergers of AT&T/BellSouth in 2007 and Comcast/NBC Universal in 2011. The 2015 merger of DirecTV into AT&T imposed such conditions on zero rating.[72] Comcast's attempted takeover of Time

---

[65] In Re: Federal Communications Commission, In the Matter of Preserving the Open Internet, Report and Order, FCC 10-201, 76 Fed Reg 59192 (2011), 23 September 2011, Consolidation Order, 1 (Judicial Panel on Multidistrict Litigation, 6 October 2011).

[66] *United States Telecom Association v Federal Communications Commission*, Decided June 14, 2016, DC Cir, No 15-1063.

[67] 2015 Open Internet Order, 30 FCC Rcd at 5706.

[68] *Verizon v Federal Communications Commission*, 740 F.3d 623 (DC Cir 2014); 11–1355, 14 January 2014.

[69] United States DC Court of Appeals No 15-1063 *United States Telecom Association, et al. v Federal Communications Commission* (14 June 2016).

[70] FCC, 'Internet Policy Statement 05–151' (2014), available at https://apps.fcc.gov/edocs_public/attach-match/FCC-05-151A1.pdf (last accessed 20 June 2018). Madison River Communications Order (n 59).

[71] FCC, 'Protecting and Promoting the Open Internet', GN Docket No 14-28, Report and Order on Remand, Declaratory Ruling, and Order, FCC 15-24 (2015), available at https://apps.fcc.gov/edocs_public/attachmatch/FCC-15-24A1.pdf (last accessed 20 June 2018).

[72] Telecom Paper, 'FCC Set to Approve AT&T's DirecTV Takeover with Conditions' (2015), available at www.telecompaper.com/news/fcc-set-to-approve-atandts-directv-takeover-with-conditions/ (last accessed

Warner Cable, abandoned in 2015, would also have been likely to see such conditions imposed alongside interoperability/neutrality in its dealing with third party device authentication – which concerns the freedom to attach devices to the network.[73]

In its AT&T/DirecTV approval of 27 July 2015, the FCC stated at paragraph 395: 'we require the combined entity to refrain from discriminatory usage-based allowance practices for its fixed broadband Internet access service'.[74] Moreover, in response to accusations that AT&T ignored previous commitments in mergers, the FCC at paragraph 398 stated, '[we] require that AT&T retain both an internal company compliance officer and an independent, external compliance officer'.

The FCC announced in July 2015 how to receive case-by-case advice about future plans, for instance zero rating schemes or specialised services, that may risk breaching net neutrality: '[the] new process involves requesting and receiving an advisory opinion on specific, prospective business practices'.[75] At paragraph 30–31 it explained that:

> Although advisory opinions are not binding on any party, a requesting party may rely on an opinion if the request fully and accurately contains all the material facts and representations necessary for the opinion and the situation conforms to the situation described in the request for opinion.[76]

The FCC 'may later rescind an advisory opinion, but any such rescission would apply only to future conduct and would not be retroactive'.[77]

Zero rating is a common practice in the US. For instance, T-Mobile has offered 33 zero-rated music services in its Music Freedom Plan since 2014,[78] avoiding any negative regulatory scrutiny in part due to its offer being non-exclusive, relating to music rather than heavily congesting and expensive video, and also to T-Mobile being the smallest of the national mobile IAPs. As Goldstein argues: 'if a zero-rating plan were exclusive to one company that offers a particular type of service, that likely would draw more scrutiny from the FCC'.[79]

Following the election of President Donald Trump, the new FCC Chair Ajit Pai and his Republican colleague (there were only three Commissioners in the first half of

---

20 June 2018) ('If approved by the commissioners, 12.5 million customer locations will have access to a competitive fibre connection from AT&T. The additional roll-out is around ten times the size of AT&T's current FttP deployment and increases the national residential fibre build by over 40 percent … AT&T will not be permitted to exclude affiliated video services and content from data caps on its fixed broadband connections. It will also be required to submit all competed interconnection agreements with the FCC.')

[73] J Brodkin, 'Comcast to Stop Blocking HBO Go and Showtime on Roku Streaming Devices' (*Ars Technica, Condé Nast Digital*, 2014), available at http://arstechnica.com/business/2014/12/comcast-to-stop-blocking-hbo-go-and-showtime-on-roku-streaming-devices/ (last accessed 20 June 2018).

[74] FCC, *In the Matter of Applications of AT&T Inc and DIRECTV For Consent to Assign or Transfer Control of Licenses and Authorizations MB Docket No 14-90* (2015), available at http://transition.fcc.gov/Daily_Releases/Daily_Business/2015/db0728/FCC-15-94A1.pdf (last accessed 21 June 2018).

[75] FCC, *Open Internet Advisory Opinion Procedures, Protecting and Promoting the Open Internet, GN Docket No 14-28* (Washington DC, 2015).

[76] *Ibid.*

[77] *Ibid.*

[78] L Northrup, 'T-Mobile Now Exempts 33 Streaming Music Services From Data Limits, Adds Apple Music, Consumerist' (2015), available at http://consumerist.com/2015/07/28/t-mobile-now-exempts-33-streaming-music-services-from-data-limits-adds-apple-music/ (last accessed 21 June 2018).

[79] P Goldstein, 'Net Neutrality Rules won't Force Carriers to Get FCC Permission for New Plans' (2015), available at www.fiercewireless.com/story/net-neutrality-rules-wont-force-carriers-get-fcc-permission-new-plans-offic/2015-02-26 (last accessed 21 July 2018).

2017) issued a new NPRM in May 2017 for three months' consultation then adopted in December.[80] As released on 4 January 2018, the Order guts the existing rules of their enforcement power, while staying any investigations into BIAS discrimination in favour of their zero-rated video and audio services (ie not counting to the monthly data cap).[81]

Table 2 below illustrates the decade-long battle to implement net neutrality.

Table 2 United States Regulation and Litigation on Open Internet 2007–15[82]

Phase of Regulation	Phase 1: Policy 2005–10	Phase 2: Open Internet under Title I, 2010–14	Phase 3: Title II Open Internet, 2014–
Challenge to Existing Regulation	Internet Policy Statement 2005 following 'Four Freedoms' speech 2004	Open Internet Order	Response to *Verizon v FCC* (2014)
Commission Proceeding	Comcast investigation 2007–8[83]	Preserving the Open Internet (2009)[84]	Protecting and Promoting Open Internet 2014[85]
Date adopted	2008	21 December 2010[86]	*Open Internet Order* 26 February 2015[87]
Legal effect	No general effect	December 2010	12 June 2015
Date struck down	*Comcast v FCC* Court of Appeals, 6 April 2010	*Verizon v FCC* Court of Appeals, 14 Jan 2014[88]	*Restoring Internet Freedom* Order 2018 – deregulatory

I predict another decade's litigation, legislation and regulation will still not resolve the issue in the US.

---

[80] WC Docket No 17-108 *In the Matter of Restoring Internet Freedom* Adopted: 18 May 2017; Reply Comment Date: 16 August 2017.

[81] FCC (2018) *Restoring Internet Freedom Order*, DA/FCC: FCC-17-166 Released On: 4 Jan 2018; Adopted On: 14 Dec 2017; Issued On: 4 Jan 2018.

[82] An excellent narrative account of the policy and judicial history is H Feld (2015), 'Net Neutrality in Court This Week: The Story of How We Got Here, Public Knowledge' (2 December 2015), available at www.publicknowledge.org/news-blog/blogs/net-neutrality-in-court-this-week-the-story-of-how-we-got-here/ (last accessed 21 June 2018).

[83] Complaint of Free Press & Public Knowledge Against Comcast Corp, File No EB-08-IH-1518 (filed 1 November 2007); Petition of Free Press et al for Declaratory Ruling, WC Docket No 07-52 (filed 1 November 2007).

[84] FCC, *In the Matter of Preserving the Open Internet, Broadband Industry Practices* (Proceeding 09-191) (2009).

[85] FCC, *In the Matter of Protecting and Promoting the Open Internet GN Docket No 14-28* (2014) *NOTICE OF PROPOSED RULEMAKING* Adopted: 15 May 2014; Comment Date: 15 July 2014; Reply Comment Date: 10 September 2014.

[86] GN Docket No 09-191, WC Docket No 07-52, Report and Order, 25 FCC Rcd 17905, 17910, para 13.

[87] Adopted on 26 February 2015, in effect 12 June 2015.

[88] *Verizon v FCC*, 740 F 3d 623 (2014).

V. European Legislation and Regulation of Network Neutrality

In its initial explanation of its reasons to review the law, the Commission noted the US debate but did no more than discuss the theoretical problem.[89] Over 2007–2008, the volume of regulatory reform proposals in the USA,[90] Japan, Canada and Norway had grown along with consumer outrage at ISP malpractice and misleading advertising, notably over notorious fixed and mobile advertisements which presented theoretical laboratory maximum speeds on a dedicated unshared connection and subject to 'reasonable terms of usage' – which meant capacity constraints on a monthly basis, some of these on mobile as low as 100MB download totals.[91]

A. Net Neutrality in the 2009 Directives

Net neutrality became a significant issue, together with a graduated response, in the voting on the First Reading of the 2009 telecoms package in May 2009. The European Parliament voted down the reforms at First Reading prior to imminent parliamentary elections in June. Amendments on consumer transparency and network openness were offered to the Parliament in the Conciliation process, collated in the European Commission's 'Declaration on Net Neutrality',[92] appended to 2009/140/EC:

> The Commission attaches high importance to preserving the open and neutral character of the Internet, taking full account of the will of the co-legislators now to enshrine net neutrality as a policy objective and regulatory principle to be promoted by [NRAs] (Article 8(4)(g) Framework Directive), alongside the strengthening of related transparency requirements (Articles 20(1)(b) and 21(3)(c) and (d) Universal Service Directive) and the creation of safeguard powers for [NRAs] to prevent the degradation of services and the hindering or slowing down of traffic over public networks (Article 22(3) Universal Service Directive).

There, in summary, are the concerns about IAPs discriminating against content they dislike, or in favour of affiliated content.[93] The Directives became effective in Member

---

[89] COM(2006) 334 final Review of the EU Regulatory Framework for electronic communications networks and services, Brussels, 29 June 2006 at s 6.2–6.4.

[90] See J Scott Marcus, 'Network Neutrality: The Roots of the Debate in the United States' (2008) 43 *Intereconomics* 30–37; JP Sluijs, 'Network Neutrality Between False Positives and False Negatives: Introducing a European Approach to American Broadband Markets' (2010) 62 *Federal Comm Law Journal* 77–117; M Cave and P Crocioni, 'Does Europe Need Network Neutrality Rules?' (2007) 1 *International Journal of Communication* 669–79; P Valcke et al, 'Guardian Night or Hands off? The European Response to Network Neutrality: Legal Considerations on the Electronic Communications Reform' (2008) 72 *Communications and Strategies* 89–112.

[91] SEC(2007) 1472 Commission Staff Working Document: Impact Assessment at 90–102 (2007).

[92] European Commission, Declaration on Net Neutrality, appended to Dir 2009/140/EC [2009] OJ L337/37, p 69.

[93] See JP Sluijs, F Schuett, and B Henze, 'Transparency Regulation in Broadband Markets: Lessons from Experimental Research' (2011) 35 *Telecommunications Policy* 592–602 for an experimental analysis of transparency regulation in broadband.

States in May 2011[94] and stated that Member States may take action to ensure particular content is not discriminated against directly (by blocking or slowing it), or indirectly (by speeding up services only for content affiliated with the IAP).

The 2009 Declaration, and the more legally relevant Directive clauses, relied heavily on implementation at national level and on proactive monitoring by the Commission itself, together with national courts, and privacy regulators where content discrimination contains traffic management practices which collate personal subscriber data.[95] Nevertheless, the Directive did lay out the principle of openness and net neutrality. Article 22(3) of the Universal Service Directive stipulated that regulatory authorities should be able to set minimum QoS standards: 'In order to prevent the degradation of service and the hindering or slowing down of traffic over networks, Member States shall ensure that [NRAs] are able to set minimum quality of service requirements'.

As with all telecoms licensing conditions, net neutrality depends on the physical capacity available, and it may be that de facto exclusivity results in some services for a limited time period as capacity upgrades are developed.[96] Regulations passed in licensing can affect network neutrality at a fundamental level. Interoperability requirements can form a basis for action where an IAP blocks an application.

B. Revisions to Dispute Settlement

BEREC noted in 2010 that legal provisions in the Directives permit greater 'symmetric' regulation on all operators, not simply dominant actors, but ask for clarification on these measures: 'Access Directive, Art 5(1) explicitly stated that NRAs are able to impose obligations "on undertakings that control access to end-users to make their services interoperable"'. Furthermore, the new wider scope for solving interoperability disputes could be used from 2011:

> revised Article 20 of the Framework Directive now provides for the resolution of disputes between undertakings providing electronic communications networks or services and also between such undertakings and others that benefit from obligations of access and/or interconnection (with the definition of 'access' also modified in Article 2 Access Directive as previously stated). Dispute resolutions cannot be considered as straightforward tools for developing a regulatory policy, but they do provide the option to address some specific (maybe urgent) situations. The potential outcome of disputes based on the transparency obligations can provide a 'credible threat' for undertakings to behave in line with those obligations, since violation may trigger the imposition of minimum quality requirements on an undertaking, in line with Article 22(3) Universal Service Directive.

---

[94] Directive 2009/136/EC (the 'Citizens Rights Directive') and Directive 2009/140/EC (the 'Better Regulation Directive') both of 25 November 2009, to be implemented within 18 months.

[95] Directive 2006/24/EC of 15 March 2006 on the retention of data generated or processed in connection with the provision of publicly available electronic communications services or of public communications networks and amending Directive 2002/58/EC [2006] OJ L105/54.

[96] See GN Docket No 09-191 Broadband Industry Practices WC Docket No 07-52 'In the Matter of Further Inquiry into Two Under-Developed Issues in the Open Internet Proceeding Preserving the Open Internet'; and Andersen et al, Joint Reply Comments of Various Advocates For The Open Internet, 4 November 2010, Comments on Advancing Open Internet Policy Through Analysis Distinguishing Open Internet from Specialized Network Services.

This repaired a lacuna in the law, in that the 2002 framework did not permit formal complaints to be made by content providers regarding their treatment by ISPs.

C. Interpretation of 2009 Framework by the European Commission, BEREC and Member States

The European Parliament had thus negotiated a very 'lite' net neutrality (rules on blocking/throttling) in 2009 to be implemented via regulatory action and reporting from 2011 under the amended Electronic Communications package.[97] It essentially permitted discrimination (under certain conditions) on speed and price for new network capacity, but insisted that existing networks do not discriminate 'backwards' – that is, they do not reduce the existing levels of service or block content without clear and transparent notice to users, and demonstrable reasonableness of those actions. This had to be adopted by national parliaments in June 2011 – though many delayed. On behalf of the 28 national telecoms regulators, the European Parliament, the European Commission and BEREC all announced investigations into the implementation of net neutrality carried out in the second half of 2010, at the end of which the European Commission presented to Parliament its first annual findings in the area.

The European Commission consultation on network neutrality implementation included BEREC's response in September 2010.[98] BEREC concluded that mobile should be subject to net neutrality provisions, listing breaches of neutrality: 'blocking of VoIP in mobile networks occurred in Austria, Croatia, Germany, Italy, the Netherlands, Portugal, Romania and Switzerland'.[99] BEREC explained:

> mobile network access may need the ability to limit the overall capacity consumption per user in certain circumstances (more than fixed network access with high bandwidth resources) and as this does not involve selective treatment of content it does not, in principle, raise network neutrality concerns.[100]

They explained that though mobile will always need greater traffic management than fixed networks ('traffic management for mobile accesses is more challenging'), symmetrical regulation must be maintained to ensure technological neutrality: 'there are not enough arguments to support having a different approach on network neutrality in the fixed and mobile networks. And especially future-oriented approach for network neutrality should not include differentiation between different types of networks.'

In December 2011, BEREC published its guidelines on transparency and QoS.[101] On transparency, BEREC stated that 'probably no single method will be sufficient'[102]

---

[97] Directive 2009/136/EC and the Declaration appended to Directive 2009/140/EC.
[98] BoR (10) 42 BEREC Response to the European Commission's consultation on the open Internet and net neutrality in Europe.
[99] *Ibid* p 3.
[100] *Ibid* p 11.
[101] Documents BoR (11) 53 'Quality of Service' BEREC: Riga; and BoR (11) 67 'Guidelines on Transparency as a Tool to Achieve Net Neutrality' Berec: Riga.
[102] See BoR (11) 67, *ibid* p 5.

Table 3 BEREC Papers on Net Neutrality 2010–15

Document No	Title
BoR (10) 42	BEREC Response to the European Commission's Consultation on the Open Internet and Net Neutrality in Europe
BoR (11) 44	Draft BEREC Guidelines on Net Neutrality and Transparency
BoR (11) 67	Guidelines on Transparency as a Tool to Achieve Net Neutrality
BoR (12) 33	An Assessment of IP-Interconnection in the Context of Net Neutrality
BoR (12) 32	BEREC Guidelines for Quality of Service in the Scope of Net Neutrality
BoR (12) 30	A View of Traffic Management and other Practices Resulting in Restrictions to the Open Internet in Europe – Findings from BEREC's and the European Commission's Joint Investigation
BoR (12) 31	Differentiation Practices and Related Competition Issues in the Scope of Net Neutrality
BoR (12) 34	BEREC Public Consultations on Net Neutrality Explanatory Paper
BoR (12) 120	Statement with Observations about Net Neutrality for ETNO's Proposal to (ITU) World Conference on International Telecommunications
BoR (13) 117	Ecosystem Dynamics and Demand Side Forces in Net Neutrality: Progress Report and Decision on Next Steps
BoR (14) 117	Monitoring Quality of Internet Access Services in the Context of Net Neutrality
BoR (15) 90	Report on How Consumers Value Net Neutrality

and pointed out the limited role of NRAs. Development of European legal implementation of the network neutrality principles was slow, with the European Commission referring much of the detailed work to BEREC, which undertook an extensive work programme on net neutrality from 2011, leading slowly towards European legislative activity in 2013–2015, and BEREC Guidelines to enforce the 2015 Regulation by August 2016.

Three Member States implemented laws that were much stricter than the 2009 rules. In the Netherlands, questions were asked in Parliament about Skype blocking in 2009.[103] The largest IAP (KPN) was boasting on investor calls about spying on user behaviour so as to block the new messaging app that was leading users to stop texting, namely WhatsApp.[104] When the Netherlands voted on its adoption of the 2009 package, it strengthened the powers of its regulator substantially to outlaw discrimination and the use of the spying technology that KPN had used. The law was later confirmed by the Dutch Senate in April 2012, though the regulations to make detailed rules were not passed until mid-2013. Slovenia adopted even more stringent rules than the

---

[103] Aanhangsel Handelingen II (Appendix Official Report), 2008/09, nr 2765 and 2766.
[104] See www.csmonitor.com/Business/Latest-News-Wires/2011/0623/Skype-Dutch-House-says-mobile-carriers-can-t-limit-its-use (last accessed 21 June 2018).

Netherlands in its telecoms law of December 2012. These laws prompted harmonisation via the new European Regulation passed in 2015.[105]

At national level, other EU Member States were slow to recognise net neutrality problems. The UK Government opposes net neutrality, and Ofcom's role has been both restricted to encouraging self-regulation and, since 2009, to funding research into Traffic Management Practices (TMP),[106] and its effect on consumers. Empirical analysis of UK IAP practices has showed that net neutrality violations have been far more frequent than in the US.[107] The UK regulatory regime focussed on behavioural 'nudge' responses to net neutrality violations, though it has also conducted technical measurement of both broadband speeds and traffic measurement, as well as a study into types of monitoring,[108] so that 'regulators keep a close watch on the operations of the market, using frequent detailed traffic measurement reports'.[109]

VI. European Open Internet Regulation 2015

The European Commission announced the *ConnectedContinent* proposal on 11 September 2013.[110] On 27 October 2015, the Open Internet Regulation was approved by the European Parliament.[111] The Regulation states that the safeguarding of equal and non-discriminatory treatment of Internet traffic became urgent and necessary because 'a significant number of end-users are affected by traffic management practices which block or slow down specific applications or services'. The spread of such discriminatory practices had been clearly demonstrated by a joint investigation of the BEREC and the European Commission in 2012. Reactions to the vote were rather heterogeneous, with the European Commissioners cheering the rules as excellent news, but the Dutch and Slovenian governments pointing out that their domestic laws passed in 2012 were now potentially in conflict with the Regulation.[112]

---

[105] See further C Marsden, *Network Neutrality: From Policy to Law to Regulation* (Manchester, Manchester University Press, 2017), especially Chapter 4.

[106] It was proven by SamKnows in 2008 that British Telecom throttled all P2P traffic aggressively during evening peak: see B Collins, 'Sam Shines a Light on BT's Traffic Shaping' (*Alphr*, 4 August 2008), available at www.alphr.com/news/internet/216252/sam-shines-a-light-on-bts-traffic-shaping (last accessed 21 June 2018).

[107] A Cooper and I Brown, 'Net Neutrality: Discrimination, Competition, and Innovation in the UK and US' (2015) 15 *ACM Transactions on Internet Technology* 1–21.

[108] Ofcom, '12th Annual Communications Market Report' (6 August 2015). See also the Ofcom-commissioned study by Predictable Network Solutions Limited (2015), 'A Study of Traffic Management Detection Methods & Tools', MC 316 (June 2015), available at www.ofcom.org.uk/__data/assets/pdf_file/0024/71682/traffic-management-detection.pdf (last accessed 21 June 2018).

[109] J Crowcroft, 'The UK Doesn't Yet Need net Neutrality Regulations' (*The Conversation*, 4 March 2015), available at http://phys.org/news/2015-03-uk-doesnt-net-neutrality.html (last accessed 21 June 2018).

[110] COM (2013) 627: Proposal for a Regulation of the European Parliament and of the Council laying down measures concerning the European single market for electronic communications and to achieve a Connected Continent, and amending Directives 2002/20/EC, 2002/21/EC and 2002/22/EC and Regulations (EC) No 1211/2009 and (EU) No 531/2012.

[111] Regulation 2015/2120.

[112] IP-15-5927 Press Release, 'Bringing Down Barriers in the Digital Single Market: No Roaming Charges as of June 2017' (2015), available at http://europa.eu/rapid/press-release_IP-15-5927_en.htm (last accessed

Guidelines were issued by BEREC in August 2016 to enforce the rules, and the NRAs' individual and collective actions in enforcing that set of guidelines developed from 2017 onwards.

The Regulation is hideously badly written even by the standards of European law. In particular, it introduces two new definitions which have no objective justification, both signifying 'Electronic Communications Service Provider' (ECPS), the European version of an IAP. Article 2 sets out these definitions based on previous e-communications law,[113] but adds two new types, PECP and IAS:

(1) 'provider of electronic communications to the public' [PECP] means an undertaking providing public communications networks or publicly available electronic communications services;

(2) 'internet access service' [IAS] means a publicly available electronic communications service [PECD] that provides access to the internet, and thereby connectivity to virtually all end points of the internet, irrespective of the network technology and terminal equipment used.

'Virtually all' may have the meaning 'substantially all' or 'most that are technically possible'. It is at least a close approximation of the FCC term 'broadband IAS':

A mass-market retail service by wire or radio that provides the capability to transmit data to and receive data from all or substantially all Internet endpoints ... This term also encompasses any service that the Commission finds to be providing a functional equivalent of the service described in the previous sentence, or that is used to evade the protections set forth in this Part[114]

The assumption is that creating a new definition captures services otherwise excluded by Framework Directive 2002/21/EC, Article 2:

(c) 'electronic communications service' means a service normally provided for remuneration which consists wholly or mainly in the conveyance of signals on electronic communications networks, including telecommunications services and transmission services in networks used for broadcasting, but exclude services providing, or exercising editorial control over, content transmitted using electronic communications networks and services; it does not include information society services, as defined in Article 1 of Directive 98/34/EC, which do not consist wholly or mainly in the conveyance of signals on electronic communications networks.

The Regulation states that the open Internet – not net neutrality, which is not defined or written in the Regulation – is to be preserved in Articles 3–6, which impose duties on IAPs, NRAs and on the Commission itself. Article 3(1) states Powell's 2004

---

21 June 2018), and MEMO-15-5275, 'Roaming Charges and Open Internet: Questions and Answers' (27 October 2015), available at http://europa.eu/rapid/press-release_MEMO-15-5275_en.htm (last accessed 21 June 2018).

[113] Article 2 of Framework Directive 2002/21/EC.

[114] See FCC (2015), 'In the Matter of Protecting and Promoting the Open Internet', GN Docket No 14-28 Report And Order On Remand, Declaratory Ruling, And Order Adopted: 26 February 2015; Released: 12 March 2015 at p 10 para 25. Used in both the 2010 and 2015 Open Internet Orders.

'Four Freedoms', Article 3(2) that contracts/practices cannot limit those rights, and Article 3(3) that traffic must be treated equally:

1.   End-users shall have the right to access and distribute information and content, use and provide applications and services, and use terminal equipment of their choice, irrespective of the end-user's or provider's location or the location, origin or destination of the information, CAS, via their IAS. This paragraph is without prejudice to Union law, or national law that complies with Union law, related to the lawfulness of the CAS.

2.   Agreements between PIAS and end-users on commercial and technical conditions and the characteristics of IAS such as price, data volumes or speed, and any commercial practices conducted by PIAS, shall not limit the exercise of the rights of end-users laid down in paragraph 1.

3.   PIAS shall treat all traffic equally, when providing IAS, without discrimination, restriction or interference, and irrespective of the sender and receiver, the [CAS], or the terminal equipment used.

The general condition is detailed immediately, and three justified exceptions are identified in Art 3:

The first subparagraph shall not prevent providers of IAS from implementing reasonable TMM. In order to be deemed to be reasonable, such measures shall be transparent, non-discriminatory and proportionate, and shall not be based on commercial considerations but on objectively different technical [QoS] requirements of specific categories of traffic. Such measures shall not monitor the specific content and shall not be maintained for longer than necessary.

PIAS in particular shall not block, slow down, alter, restrict, interfere with, degrade or discriminate between specific CAS, or specific categories thereof, except as necessary, and only for as long as necessary, in order to:

(a)   comply with Union legislative acts, or national legislation that complies with Union law, to which the provider of [IAS] is subject, or with measures that comply with Union law giving effect to such Union legislative acts or national legislation, including with orders by courts or public authorities vested with relevant powers;

(b)   preserve the integrity and security of the network, of services provided via that network, and of the terminal equipment of end-users;

(c)   prevent impending network congestion and mitigate the effects of exceptional or temporary network congestion, provided that equivalent categories of traffic are treated equally.

Article 3(4) is a basic privacy reminder.[115] Article 3(5) sets out a Specialised Services ('fast lane') exception:

5. PECP, including PIAS, and providers of CAS shall be free to offer services other than IAS which are optimised for specific CAS, or a combination thereof, where the optimisation is necessary in order to meet requirements of the CAS for a specific level of quality. PECP, including PIAS, may offer or facilitate such services only if the network capacity is sufficient to provide them in addition to any IAS provided. Such services shall not be usable or offered

---

[115] Any TMM may entail processing of personal data only if such processing is necessary and proportionate to achieve the objectives set out in paragraph 3. Such processing shall be carried out in accordance with Directive 95/46/EC and Directive 2002/58/EC.

as a replacement for IAS, and shall not be to the detriment of the availability or general quality of IAS for end-users.

O'Donoghue and Pascoe argue that the Regulation is 'expressed in extremely telegraphic terms ... not exactly a model of clarity and consistency'.[116] Because the exception in Article 3(5) provides a general right and not a derogating exception (as with other elements of Article 3), they argue the 'concept of necessity under Article 3(5) is not only independent of how that concept would be defined in other contexts under EU law, but is even distinct from how necessity is defined in other aspects of the Regulation'. They also argue that judging which qualities are 'necessary' is aided by a recent High Court case accepting reduced latency as a vital element in the Google Maps service.[117] While this remains to be seen, I agree with their conclusion that 'the concept of "reasonable traffic management measures" (TMM) is nebulous and is therefore likely to lead to litigation'.[118] They see the best line of attack as 'to challenge various aspects of the Regulation, or at least certain suggested interpretations of it, on the basis that they would be inconsistent with the concept of non-discrimination as a (higher) general principle under EU law'. They also see litigation grounds on

> compatibly with fundamental rights provided by the EU Charter, including the freedom to conduct a business under Article 16 and the right to property under Article 17 ... restrictions on the provider's right to operate its business in accordance with its own wishes, and those of its customers, should be more limited than the terms of the Regulation might suggest on its face.[119]

Telecoms operators may, if necessary, launch litigation based on these arguments in 2018 and beyond.

Article 4 on transparency may have the most immediate impact on users, as it enforces proper information on use and took effect from 29 November 2015:

1. PIAS shall ensure that any contract which includes IAS specifies at least the following:

(a) information on how TMM applied by that provider could impact on the quality of the IAS, on the privacy of end-users and on the protection of their personal data;

(b) a clear and comprehensible explanation as to how any volume limitation, speed and other quality of service parameters may in practice have an impact on IAS, and in particular on the use of CAS;

(c) a clear and comprehensible explanation of how any services referred to in Article 3(5) to which the end-user subscribes might in practice have an impact on the IAS provided to that end-user.

This mandates minimal consumer protection by IAPs within minimal consumer protection by regulators:

(d) a clear and comprehensible explanation of the minimum, normally available, maximum and advertised download and upload speed of the IAS in the case of fixed networks, or

---

[116] R O'Donoghue and T Pascoe, 'Net Neutrality in the EU: Unresolved Issues under the New Regulation' (2016), available at https://papers.ssrn.com/sol3/Papers.cfm?abstract_id=2741173 (last accessed 21 June 2018).
[117] *Ibid* p 8, fn 10.
[118] *Ibid* p 11.
[119] *Ibid* p 13.

of the estimated maximum and advertised download and upload speed of the IAS in the case of mobile networks, and how significant deviations from the respective advertised download and upload speeds could impact the exercise of the end-users' rights laid down in Article 3(1);

(e)   a clear and comprehensible explanation of the remedies available to the consumer in accordance with national law in the event of any continuous or regularly recurring discrepancy between the actual performance of the IAS regarding speed or other quality of service parameters and the performance indicated in accordance with points (a) to (d).

Providers of Internet Access Services shall publish the information referred to in the first subparagraph.

There is in Article 4 a requirement that users can actually enforce measures, but contract termination is not specified:

2.   PIAS shall put in place transparent, simple and efficient procedures to address complaints of end-users relating to the rights and obligations laid down in Article 3 and paragraph 1 of this Article.

3.   The requirements laid down in paragraphs 1 and 2 are in addition to those provided for in Directive 2002/22/EC and shall not prevent Member States from maintaining or introducing additional monitoring, information and transparency requirements, including those concerning the content, form and manner of the information to be published. Those requirements shall comply with this Regulation and the relevant provisions of Directives 2002/21/EC and 2002/22/EC.

4.   Any significant discrepancy, continuous or regularly recurring, between the actual performance of the [IAS] regarding speed or other [QoS] parameters and the performance indicated by the [PIAS] in accordance with points (a) to (d) of paragraph 1 shall, where the relevant facts are established by a monitoring mechanism certified by the [NRA], be deemed to constitute non-conformity of performance for the purposes of triggering the remedies available to the consumer in accordance with national law. This paragraph shall apply only to contracts concluded or renewed from 29 November 2015.

Minimal harmonisation clauses inside regulations are very rare, and it will be of more general interest to analyse the outcome of this process.

Article 5(1) (Supervision and Enforcement) provides the teeth of the Regulation:

NRAs shall closely monitor and ensure compliance with Articles 3 and 4, and shall promote the continued availability of non-discriminatory [IAS] at levels of quality that reflect advances in technology. For those purposes, NRAs may impose requirements concerning technical characteristics, minimum [QoS] requirements and other appropriate and necessary measures on one or more [PECP], including providers of [IAS]. NRAs shall publish reports on an annual basis regarding their monitoring and findings, and provide those reports to the Commission and to BEREC.

2. At the request of the [NRA], [PECPs], including [PIAS], shall make available to that [NRA] information relevant to the obligations set out in Articles 3 and 4, in particular information concerning the management of their network capacity and traffic, as well as justifications for any [TMM] applied. Those providers shall provide the requested information in accordance with the time-limits and the level of detail required by the [NRA].

Article 5(3) sets out BEREC's duty:

> By 30 August 2016, in order to contribute to the consistent application of this Regulation, BEREC shall, after consulting stakeholders and in close cooperation with the Commission, issue guidelines for the implementation of the obligations of [NRAs] under this Article.

Article 6 deals with penalties:

> Member States shall lay down the rules on penalties applicable to infringements of Articles 3, 4 and 5 and shall take all measures necessary to ensure that they are implemented. The penalties provided for must be effective, proportionate and dissuasive. Member States shall notify the Commission of those rules and measures.

Notification is thus required by the governments on behalf of NRAs. Finally, Article 9 instructs that provisions will be reviewed by 2019:

> By 30 April 2019, and every four years thereafter, the Commission shall review Articles 3, 4, 5 and 6 and shall submit a report to the European Parliament and to the Council thereon, accompanied, if necessary, by appropriate proposals with a view to amending this Regulation.

Given this short timetable, it may be that the 2019 review has nothing to report, or that it recommends codifying the BEREC Guidelines, which are discussed in the next section.

VII. National Legal Implementation

A. BEREC Net Neutrality Guidelines 2016

The European Economic Area implementation of the Open Internet Regulation (EU/2015/2120) has been clarified with BEREC Guidelines issued on 30 August 2016.[120] These provide guidance to national regulators on implementation of the 2015 Regulation, and were primarily drafted by the UK (Ofcom) and Norwegian regulators. BEREC's guidelines at paragraph 45 expressed agnosticism on zero rating: 'It is not the case that every factor affecting end-users' choices should necessarily be considered to limit the exercise of end-users' rights'. At paragraph 46, they warned that the combination of the largest mobile operator with largest social network provider could produce an anti-competitive discriminatory access agreement:

> a practice is more likely to limit the exercise of end-user rights in a situation where, for example, many end-users are concerned and/or there are few alternative offers and/or competing ISPs for the end-users to choose from.

---

[120] BEREC (2016) BoR (16) 127 'Guidelines on the Implementation by National Regulators of European Net Neutrality Rules'.

And at paragraph 48 stated:

> Price differentiation between individual applications within a category has an impact on competition between providers in that class ... and thereby undermine the goals of the Regulation [more] than would price differentiation between classes of application ... the lower the data cap, the stronger such influence is likely to be.

B. National Regulator Responses to Regulation 2015/2120

National regulators' implementation of the 2015 Regulation has resulted in several decisions to prevent telecoms operators from zero rating their affiliated content, following interpretation of paragraphs 45–48 of the BEREC Guidelines 2016, but also the striking down of the provisions in the earlier and broader Netherlands Telecoms law of 2012. In 2017, the Rotterdam administrative court of first instance struck down the Netherlands Telecoms Law 2012, Article 7(4), regarding net neutrality:[121]

> ACM (Dutch regulator) has ordered T-Mobile to discontinue the provision and execution of the Data Free Music service under forfeiture of a penalty payment. At the hearing it appears that Vodafone Ziggo disagrees with the far-reaching suspension by ACM of the burden during a possible preliminary question. The objection lodged at the sitting – as part of the plea note – indicates that the court should have been forwarded within the meaning of Article 7.1a.

> ACM takes the view that zero rating is contrary to Article 3, second and third paragraphs, of the Network Neutrality Regulation and with Article 7.4a, third paragraph, of the Telecoms Law 2012. The court is of the opinion that the neutrality regulation and in particular Article 3 of the Regulation undoubtedly contains no categorical prohibition of price discrimination ('acte clair'). Article 7.4a, third paragraph, is therefore unequivocally contrary to the network neutrality regulation.

> In this connection, the court notes that no other conclusion is possible than the national legislature has acted against by better understanding by Article 7.4a, third paragraph, in spite of the establishment history and the text of Article 3 of the Network Neutrality Regulation.

If similar conclusions are reached in Slovenia, there will be rapid harmonisation on the basis of the Regulation. If the question is referred to the Court of Justice of the European Union, it may be that the UK leaves the European Union prior to the settlement of that law.

The UK Parliament passed a Statutory Instrument in 2016 implementing the EU Regulation, signaling its intention to conform to the European legal framework for the foreseeable future. The Open Internet Access (EU Regulation) Regulations 2016[122] set

---

[121] ROT 17/468, ROT 17/1160 and ROT 17/1932 *T-Mobile v Ziggo BV, Ziggo Services BV, Vodafone Libertel BV* (20 April 2017), available at https://uitspraken.rechtspraak.nl/inziendocument?id=ECLI:NL:RBROT:2017:2940 (last accessed 21 June 2018).

[122] The Open Internet Access (EU Regulation) Regulations 2016 (SI 2016/No 607), available at www.legislation.gov.uk/uksi/2016/607/pdfs/uksi_20160607_en.pdf (last accessed 21 June 2018).

out powers to fine access providers that restrict Internet access to subscribers or fail to cooperate with Ofcom investigations:

> 19.—(1) Where OFCOM determine that there are reasonable grounds for believing that a person is breaching, or has breached an obligation under Articles 3, 4 or 5 of the EU Regulation or under these Regulations they may give that person a notification under this regulation …
>
> 21.—(1) The amount of a penalty notified under regulation 19 … is to be such amount as OFCOM determine to be—
>
> (a) appropriate; and
> (b) proportionate to the breach in respect of which it is imposed,
>> but in the case of a breach of an information requirement not exceeding £2,000,000, and in the case of any other breach of the EU Regulation or these Regulations, not exceeding ten per cent, of the turnover of the notified person's relevant business for the relevant period.

The UK's continued tangible interconnection with the European open Internet suggests that continued harmoniation of regulation in this area will apply, should the UK eventually leave the EU.

VIII. Conclusion

The European legal basis for regulatory intervention is a consumer law framework to prevent competition abuses and prevent discrimination, under which national regulators need the skills and evidence base to investigate unjustified interference with IAPs' traditional 'mere conduit' status and their non-discrimination between data types. Regulators' proactive approach to monitoring and researching non-neutral behaviours will make IAPs much more cognisant of their duties and obligations. While traffic management is proprietary, in reality regulators will only be able to ensure that IAPs 'don't be evil' – that they do not engage in permanent blocking of rival video and voice services, as has occurred in the past. Total neutrality is neither achievable nor desirable, given the congestion issues that a best-efforts Internet will always face.

The pace of change in the relation between architecture and content on the Internet requires continuous improvement in the regulator's research and technological training. Regulators are required to monitor both commercial transactions and traffic shaping by IAPs to detect potentially abusive discrimination. They must also conduct research towards understanding the nature of congestion problems on the Internet and their effect on content and innovation. The issue of uncontrolled Internet flows versus engineered solutions is central to the question of a 'free' versus regulated Internet.[123] Regulations are intended to prevent unregulated non-transparent controls exerted over

---

[123] RE Kahn and VG Cerf, 'What Is The Internet (And What Makes It Work)' (Internet Policy Institute, Washington DC, 1999), available at www.policyscience.net/cerf.pdf (last accessed 21 June 2018).

traffic, whether imposed by IAPs for financial advantage or to use this new technology to filter, censor and enforce copyright and other laws against Internet users.

Ever since the broadband Internet was brought to users in the late 1990s, this has been the messiest issue in both telecoms regulation narrowly and in the Internet generally, and has affected anybody who previously, currently, or in future uses the Internet: which is to say all of us. It is fiendishly difficult to identify abuses of net neutrality, and many corporate economists have claimed it is a solution in search of a problem or abuse: Schrodinger's net neutrality? It is and will continue to be extremely difficult to regulate. Human rights, behavioural science, and innovation economics have been brought to bear on the typically neo-classical economic models used to regulate telco networks through which we connect to the Internet. The telcos and their regulators' corporatist modes of regulation, co- and self-regulation (state-firm bargaining with former state monopolies like British Telecom and foreign investors such as T-Mobile) are now exposed to the clamorous demand of civil society organistions for multistake-holder governance (MSG).[124]

Net neutrality cannot be dismissed as a technical or competition challenge without serious consumer implication and civil society interaction. A fierce net neutrality fight has been waged for over 15 years to secure the future of the Internet: telecoms companies and their lobbyists have claimed it is of no relevance, then fought to oppose it. It was meant to be solved in Europe in 2009, when options for regulation were attached to the 'telecoms package'. It was meant to be solved in the US when the then-President Obama's first FCC Chairman announced that there would be a consultation followed by an 'Open Internet Order' in 2009–10. It was meant to be irrelevant to mobile data or developing countries because net neutrality was a luxury problem, not a question of universal access and human rights. Net neutrality 'lite' law is now 'law on the books' in Europe since 2015, but action in regulating the 'fast lane' (specialised services) and zero rating remains to be carried out.

---

[124] AB Powell, 'Network Exceptionalism: Online Action, Discourse and the Opposition to SOPA and ACTA' (2015) 19(2) *Information, Communication & Society* 249–63.

Part II

Privacy, Data Protection and Surveillance

3

Privacy and Data Protection 1: What is Privacy? Human Right, National Law, Global Problem

LILIAN EDWARDS*

I. Introduction

Privacy is not a simple subject, especially online privacy.[1] Privacy and surveillance now take up half this volume; in its predecessors it was limited to two or three chapters. Before we can even start to look at the substantive law, we need to ask some important preliminary questions. What kind of value *is* privacy? Is it enough that it be recognised as an ethical concept, or a social norm? Or should the law formally protect it as a right? If it is a right, is it a 'fundamental' one, what we sometimes call a basic human right, against which other laws may be judged and found lacking? And if the latter, how should it be balanced against *other* fundamental rights, such as rights to security and freedom of speech, with which it may conflict? Most notably, in an era of terror threats, should the individual's right to privacy cede or be reduced in response to the needs of the state to protect its people from terrorism and crime?[2]

Privacy is a particularly difficult value about which to construct regulation, chiefly because there is little consensus on what it actually is. Privacy has been used to describe everything from anonymity, to secrecy, to solitude, to seclusion (this being the essentially passive right to be 'let alone', in the famous words of Warren and Brandeis[3]),

---

* My grateful thanks to Edina Harbinja, Senior Lecturer in Law, University of Hertfordshire, for research assistance, and to Rowena Rodrigues, now of Trilateral Consulting, for assistance on earlier versions of this chapter.
[1] For a good introduction to the enormous literature examining the value, philosophy and context of privacy in an online context, see H Nissenbaum, *Privacy in Context: Technology, Policy and the Integrity of Social Life* (Stanford University Press, 2010).
[2] See further, Chapter 6 and Chapter 7 of this volume.
[3] S Warren and LD Brandeis, 'The Right to Privacy' (1890) 4 *Harvard Law Review* 193.

to active control of personal data or communications,[4] to diverse ideas of protection of reputation, brand and personality,[5] and it has even been argued that its meaning should embrace control of one's physical body in contexts such as abortion,[6] the right to die,[7] and whether blood tests can be compelled in paternity suits.[8] Many have echoed in more recent decades the words written by one scholar in 1975: '… the most striking thing about the right to privacy is that nobody seems to have any very clear idea what it is',[9] while in 2006 Barendt added ruefully that '[p]rivacy is an elusive concept, so elusive in fact that it has generally proved impossible for English and Australian lawyers to discover its exact whereabouts in the common law'.[10] In this chapter, and this book, we will largely be talking about privacy only in the informational context, although recognising that there may be cases where control of personal data also has important overlaps with physical, or bodily, privacy.[11]

The population themselves seem as uncertain about how they feel about privacy as scholars are confused about what it is. To take a comparison, any democratic society will probably now agree that (for example) deliberate murder, torture and sexual assault are fundamentally wrong and should be uncompromisingly criminalised within conventional legal regimes.[12] Yet empirical evidence shows that feelings about privacy are not so homogeneous. In 1990, in a famous 1990 study, Westin used telephone interviews to classify the US public into three categories: privacy *fundamentalists* or idealists who are distrustful of information sharing and in favour of privacy legislation (c 25 per cent of the population); privacy *pragmatists* who are prepared to balance privacy intrusions against other gains (c 57 per cent); and privacy *'unconcerneds'* (c 17 per cent) who are generally trusting of data collection and are against new privacy regulation. Perhaps surprisingly, even given the enormous technological and societal changes that have occurred since 1990, subsequent studies have roughly agreed that

---

[4] See most notably, AF Westin, *Privacy and Freedom* (Athenaeum Press, 1967). See also S Garfinkel, *Database Nation: The Death of Privacy in the 21st Century* (O'Reilly Media, 2000).

[5] Epstein usefully notes that privacy suffers from what can be called 'conceptual overload', used to mean all things to all men (or women). (RA Epstein, 'Deconstructing Privacy and Putting It Back Together Again' (2000) 17 *Social Philosophy and Policy* 1).

[6] See the Canadian law on abortion, founded from notions of privacy: *R v Morgentaler* [1988] 1 SCR 30.

[7] See, eg, *Pretty v UK*, ECtHR, Application No 2346/02, 29 April 2002.

[8] See in Scotland *Whitehall v Whitehall* 1958 SC 252.

[9] See JJ Thomson, 'The Right to Privacy' (1975) 4 *Philosophy and Public Affairs* 295.

[10] E Barendt, 'Privacy and Freedom of Speech' in A Kenyon and M Richardson (eds), *New Dimensions in Privacy Law* (Cambridge University Press, 2006) 5.

[11] In *Wainwright v United Kingdom*, Application No 12350/04, 26 September 2006, for example, the European Court of Human Rights (ECtHR) held that an unduly intrusive strip search of relatives visiting a prisoner in jail had been a violation of Article 8 of the European Convention on Human Rights (ECHR). Here the right to correspondence and the right to bodily privacy are intertwined. A similar future issue blending the physical and the informational may arise if employers require employees to accept sub dermal transplants of tracking devices, perhaps to enable automated door access or for cash-free environments. For an example of voluntary acceptance of such tech, see 'Barcelona Clubbers get Chipped' *BBC News* (29 September 2004), available at http://news.bbc.co.uk/2/hi/technology/3697940.stm.

[12] There is of course an ongoing debate about whether torture, for example, is exceptionally justifiable in emergency terrorist situations. But few have been so hawkish as to suggest it should be available to police, rather than quasi-extralegal intelligence agencies, and routinely rather than in non-emergency scenarios.

only around a quarter of the population can be described as being seriously worried about privacy at all times.[13]

This leads us to question if privacy can be regulated as an *objective* concept, important in the same way to all persons, or an inherently *subjective* value, in which case it is difficult to know exactly how privacy – thus seen as an individual interest – should be balanced against other interests which are considered 'societal', such as security, innovation and economic growth. When one of the main arguments about many modern intrusive privacy practices (such as targeted advertising) is that they make some – but not all – users feel queasy or 'creeped out'.[14] Is this a good enough basis upon which to involve the law? The alternative is to found privacy laws (and sanctions) in a concrete attempt to objectively assess what *harm* – not only economic, but sometimes emotional or 'dignitary' – is caused by a lack of privacy safeguards. Yet this also suggests the question of what economic loss may flow from privacy protection (for example where it impedes the business models of free-to-the-user data collecting industries, or overwhelms them with regulatory overhead). Quantifying the value of privacy is a difficult foundation for regulation, as 'privacy harms' are notoriously hard to spot, trace and quantify, especially for any one individual, at any one time. (A promising sub science, which tries to assess privacy behaviour in terms of behavioural economics and experimental data rather than normative assertions or philosophical claims has made outstanding contributions here, but still has a long way to go to feed into user and policymaker awareness.[15])

The European tradition has in the main rejected the idea that privacy regulation should be based solely on 'harms', favouring instead a human rights foundation. Human rights, though, can also be a restrictive prism, in that traditional liberal philosophy regards them as an *individual* right and not as a *societal* good. Yet all of us have a stake in the preservation of privacy in our society, even though it may be threatened by the accumulation of numerous individual choices – as seen for example in the rise and modern inescapability of social media culture. Some scholars are therefore now trying to emphasise privacy as a collective social good (like clean air, or unpoisoned water). As Regan puts it, '[m]ost privacy scholars emphasise that the individual is better off if privacy exists. I argue that society is better off when privacy exists'.[16]

A final connected confusion is whether privacy is better seen as a *right* at all, as it is now in the EU under the European Charter of Fundamental Rights as well as

[13] See P Kumaragaru and L Cranor, 'Privacy Indexes: A Survey of Westin's Studies', (Carnegie Mellon Cylab, CMU-ISRI-5-138, December 2005). Of course, at various points awareness of privacy threats rise and attitudes to privacy shift, as shown in surveys conducted after the 'Snowden effect'. Later at p 68 we discuss European attitudes to privacy prior to the GDPR reform process commenced in 2012 and the ePrivacy process commenced in 2017.

[14] See O Tene and J Polonetsky, 'A Theory of Creepy: Technology, Privacy, and Shifting Social Norms' (2013) 16 *Yale Journal of Law and Technology* 59.

[15] On this fascinating area, see *passim* the work of Alessandro Acquisti and his colleagues at Carnegie Mellon University, and F Borgesius, 'Behavioural Sciences and the Regulation of Privacy on the Internet', IvIR Law Research paper No 2014-02.

[16] See P Regan, *Legislating Privacy: Technology, Social Values, and Public Policy* (University of North Carolina Press, 1995). See also C Bennett and C Raab, *The Governance of Privacy*, 2nd edn (MIT Press, 2006).

Article 8 of the European Convention on Human Rights (ECHR), or should instead be seen merely as a *commodity*, that is a piece of property of value which can be freely traded or given away. In the US, which lacks omnibus rights-based regulation of privacy akin to European data protection (DP) law, arguments for 'commodification' of privacy have had some influence. The assertion is that under such arrangements regulation is not needed, since a market will naturally emerge in which personal data is traded at market value and users will be empowered by being paid for giving up their privacy, rather than simply having it taken away for free (or in return for services such as social networking or web search). While such ideas have appeal in a system like the US which fails to fully regulate privacy rights against commercial actors, they are mainly rejected in Europe as undermining the fundamental importance of privacy vis-à-vis other values such as personality, autonomy and expression. In the UK, however, where privacy culture has sometimes been regarded with some distrust by business, the Information Commissioner's Office (ICO) at one point asked consultation respondents to make a 'business case' for privacy,[17] and evidence has come in since the Snowden revelations that a lack of privacy does in fact also have business costs in terms of the loss of trust in the consumer market.[18]

Yet despite these many confusions, historically, at least in post-industrial times and in Europe,[19] privacy has always, I would argue, been seen as a positive, as an important liberal right which defends the individual against the unfettered power of the state, allows space to think and construct one's identity (variously political, social, ethical, sexual, etc) and is an important bulwark for autonomy and a prerequisite for freedom of expression.[20] As such, it was until recently fairly uncontested that privacy was worthy of (some) protection by the law – although what legal regime should be applied, how conflicts with other values such as security and freedom of expression should be resolved, and who should regulate such laws (how can the state regulate privacy when it is itself perhaps the most dangerous invader of privacy?) remained thorny problems.

However, as we will see repeatedly in this and the next several chapters, the value of privacy itself has come under fire to an unprecedented degree in the last decade and a half, partly because of the rise of the Internet and the incredible ease it lends to data collection, processing, sharing and publishing, on a local and global basis, and partly because of a variety of other political, economic and social changes, some associated with digitisation, some not (most obviously the panic around terrorism since 9/11, but

---

[17] ICO, 3 March 2010.

[18] See, eg, projections in August 2013 of losses of $22–35 billion to the US cloud computing industry due to the reluctance of EU users to engage with it following revelations around the National Security Agency (NSA) snooping on US-provided cloud storage services: see www2.itif.org/2013-cloud-computing-costs.pdf. Many companies have responded post-Snowden to a collapse in user trust by emphasising privacy rhetoric and taking measures like adding Ethics Advisory Boards.

[19] It should also be remembered that privacy is a relatively recent invention both in practice and as a positive idea. In the fascinating work, *Privacy and Solitude in the Middle Ages* (Hambledon Continuum, 2007), Diana Webb demonstrates that privacy was almost unknown before modernity for all but the richest and the most religious, and that furthermore seclusion was usually regarded with suspicion rather than as a desirable state (the Roman word *privatus* being the nearest Latin had to a word for privacy but with negative and underhand associations).

[20] See, eg, B Roessler, *The Value of Privacy* (Polity Press, 2004).

also including the rise of managerial society and risk aversion attitudes, the growth of consumerist and atomic (or perhaps, anomic) society, the globalisation of US culture, the incredible rise of social networking, and the sheer drop in the costs of technologies of ubiquitous and mass surveillance). If there was one quote which dominated student essays about privacy and the Internet in the first decade of this century, it was probably the headline-grabbing (and prescient) claim of Scott McNealy, Chief Executive Officer (CEO) of Sun Microsystems, who in 1999 said that '[y]ou have zero privacy anyway. Get over it'.[21] These sentiments were eagerly taken up by other Silicon Valley entrepreneurs in the boom days of the dotcom era, to whom privacy appeared mainly to represent an annoying obstacle on the road to both business profit and consumer gratification. Mark Zuckerberg, founder of Facebook, famously followed in McNealy's path in 2010, declaring that: 'People have really gotten comfortable not only sharing more information and different kinds, but more openly and with more people ... That social norm is just something that has evolved over time.'[22]

Similarly, when he was CEO of Google, Eric Schmidt infamously stated in 2010 that: 'If you have something that you don't want anyone to know,[23] maybe you shouldn't be doing it in the first place.'[24] Yet the pendulum may have swung back the other way, at least a little. What seemed a technologically determined and socially inevitable lurch towards openness and/or pervasive 24/7 surveillance (depending on your views) and away from privacy and individual control over personal data, might have been altered by the actions of one man, Edward Snowden, who in July 2013 revealed the full extent of the covert mass surveillance ongoing by Western intelligence agencies, notably the US's National Security Agency (NSA) and the UK's Government Communications Headquarters (GCHQ), over phone calls, mobile connections, web traffic and almost every aspect of digital life, with the cooperation, forced, voluntary or unknowing (the jury is still out on this one) of many of the world's best-known commercial names such as Google, Facebook, Microsoft, Verizon and Yahoo! et al.[25] At the time of writing the fallout of the Snowden revelations is still being felt: as with previous privacy and breach scandals, such as the loss of the records of 25 million people by HMRC on a CD in October 2007[26] or the revelations of the hacking of Milly Dowler's phone by

---

[21] Quoted in S Manes, 'Private Lives? Not Ours!' (*PC World*, 18 April 2000).

[22] See CNET interview, 'Zuckerberg: I Know that People Don't Want Privacy' (11 January 2010), available at www.cnet.com/au/news/zuckerberg-i-know-that-people-dont-want-privacy/.

[23] This common claim, often encapsulated as 'nothing to fear, nothing to hide' is usefully deconstructed by Daniel Solove in *Nothing to Hide* (Yale University Press, 2011).

[24] Cited by the Electronic Frontier Foundation, CNBC interview, 10 December 2009, available at www.eff.org/deeplinks/2009/12/google-ceo-eric-schmidt-dismisses-privacy. Both have at other times taken a softer line on privacy, or at least, anonymity. Zuckerberg, for example, went back at least partially on Facebook's much-vaunted 'real names' policy in 2014 (see www.networkworld.com/article/2226288/microsoft-subnet/as-facebook-turns-10--zuckerberg-changes-his-mind-about-anonymity.html) while Google also dropped the much disliked real name requirement from their struggling G+ social network in July 2014. On these policies see further L Edwards, 'From the Fantasy to the Reality: Social Media and Real Name Policies' in *Festschrift for Jon Bing* (University of Oslo, 2013).

[25] For a very accessible documentary of how the Snowden leaks were brought to the world, see the excellent *Citizenfour* (Poirtas, 2014 and https://citizenfourfilm.com). For a timeline of the leaks and their consequences, see coverage in *The Guardian*, *passim*, at www.theguardian.com/us-news/edward-snowden, and L Harding, *The Snowden Files* (Guardian Books/Faber and Faber, 2014).

[26] See *BBC News* coverage at http://news.bbc.co.uk/2/hi/uk_politics/7104368.stm.

the *News of the World* in 2011,[27] the initial shock and calls for legal reform may dissipate into a general background of complacency and cynicism in which little changes either in law or in practice. On the other hand, in the short to medium term it seems likely that the Snowden revelations may have propelled a harder line by the EU in how it finalises the comprehensive reform of the DP Directive (see below) as a Regulation. Growing distrust of the US-based cloud computing and social networking industries may encourage European growth in these sectors,[28] while the Court of Justice of the EU (CJEU) has begun to take a harder, and surprisingly radical line, towards the interpretation of existing DP law.[29] Such developments are contributing towards increasing consumer demand for easy and cheap privacy safeguards, such as encryption by default in common user applications such as webmail[30] and messenger services (the success of WhatsApp, even after takeover by Facebook, being a prime example), as well as a welcome growth in Transparency Reports from online service providers.[31]

Just as the fallout from Snowden was perhaps finally turning from shock into ennui, along came another privacy scandal with what may be an even greater potential to derail economic determinism and bolster demands for transparency and control over personal data. Whereas Snowden taught us to distrust our governments, the Cambridge Analytica/Facebook scandal of 2017–18 (ongoing at the time of writing) may teach us to look with equal suspicion on social media and other digital giants of the private sector. Cambridge Analytica (CA) were (they conveniently declared bankruptcy on 2 May 2018) a UK-based data profiling organisation, which offered 'intelligence', in particular on how voters were likely to choose come election time. CA were paid to use its 'psychographic' tools to make targeted online ad purchases for *inter alia* the UK Brexit 'Leave' campaign, the 2016 presidential campaign of Ted Cruz, and the 2016 Trump campaign.[32]

---

[27] See 'News of the World "hacked Milly Dowler phone"' *BBC News* (4 July 2011), available at www.bbc. co.uk/news/uk-14017661. The phone hacking revelations resulted *inter alia* in the closure of the News of the World and an extensive enquiry by Lord Leveson into press ethics and privacy regulation. See further Urquhart in Chapter 8 of this volume.

[28] See speech by Neelie Kroes on 4 July 2013, available at http://europa.eu/rapid/press-release_MEMO-13-654_en.htm, in which she stated: 'If European cloud customers cannot trust the United States government or their assurances, then maybe they won't trust US cloud providers either. That is my guess. And if I am right then there are multi-billion euro consequences for American companies'.

[29] See, eg, the 'right to be forgotten' case of Case C-131/12 *Google Spain v Agencia Española de Protección de Datos (AEPD) and González* (13 May 2014) (see further Chapter 4 of this volume) and the striking down of the Data Retention Directive (Directive 2006/24/EC on the retention of data generated or processed in connection with the provision of publicly available electronic communications services or of public communications networks and amending Directive 2002/58/EC, [2006] OJ L105/54 (March 15 2006)), discussed in Chapter 7.

[30] At the end of December 2017, Google's Transparency Report noted that 90% of emails outgoing from Gmail were encrypted, while 89% of traffic incoming from other providers was so encrypted: www.google. com/transparencyreport/saferemail/. This is a remarkable recent change, driven by providers supplying encryption by default.

[31] Transparency reports typically document what requests have been made by state agencies for restriction of access to content or details of users of online service providers. Sometimes they also report such requests from the private sector, for example IP rightholders. See, eg, Facebook's report at https://transparency.facebook.com/. Google, Verizon, AT&T, Twitter, Apple, Dropbox, Facebook, Yahoo and CloudFlare also currently issue transparency reports. Notably, only Google and Twitter did so before the Snowden revelations.

[32] See, usefully, 'TIMELINE-Cambridge Analytica Lists Events Leading to Facebook Data Row' *Reuters* (22 March 2018), available at www.reuters.com/article/facebook-cambridge-analytica/timeline-cambridge-analytica-lists-events-leading-to-facebook-data-row-idUSL3N1R45J1.

When CA were hired by the Trump campaign, they did not, it seems, feel they had enough data to effectively micro-target US voters, so bought data from GSR, a company run by Alexander Kogan,[33] a Cambridge psychology researcher. Kogan had been allowed by Facebook to gather personal data in 2014 from at least 87 million Facebook users using a personality-quiz app. (Although only about 270,000 people accessed the app, at the time Facebook's rules allowed an app to gather data not just about the user who signed up to the app but also all their Facebook friends). Kogan's app (which was supposed to be used for research purposes only, in his capacity as a Cambridge academic) saved that information into a private database, which was then provided to CA, which in turn used it to make 30 million 'psychographic' profiles about voters. These events came to light in the main when whistleblower, Christopher Wylie, formerly of CA, revealed details in March 2018 to journalist Carole Cadwalladr working for *The Observer* and *New York Times*, along with Channel 4.[34]

In the event, as is well known, both the Brexit vote of 2016 and the 2016 US election produced somewhat unexpected results. The public has since been mesmerised by the implications (though these are very unsubstantiated[35]) that the political 'dark ads' that were sent using CA data, may have been the deciding factor which tipped the recent electoral lurch towards the right, as well as the viral spread of fake news on social media, some of which may also have been financed by Russian agents also seeking to destabilise the US and EU.[36] Legislators in both the US and UK as well as the European Commission have, outraged at this apparent tampering with democracy, demanded that Mark Zuckerberg[37] and the various personnel of CA and GSR give evidence at numerous hearings and select committees, many still ongoing. Most tellingly, Facebook's own stock declined in value by $75 billion in one week (though later to some extent recovered) and a #DeleteFacebook campaign stalked (ironically) social media.

While the 'Russians stole our elections' hype has propelled the CA story onto a thousand virtual front pages, the real fallout in terms of privacy regulation may come from the realisation it has forced on ordinary users of Facebook that they have little or no idea how their personal data is extracted, profiled and used to target them. Consent to share data, much mentioned by Zuckerberg in his various sacrificial hearings, has been seen to be an empty protection, and transparency an illusion. Profiling and

---

[33] Formerly 'Alexander Spectre', he was asked during one UK parliamentary enquiry session if he had changed his name so as not to sound like a Bond villain. He denied this.

[34] See 'Revealed: 50 million Facebook Profiles Harvested for Cambridge Analytica in Major Data Breach' *The Guardian* (17 March 2018), available at www.theguardian.com/news/2018/mar/17/cambridge-analytica-facebook-influence-us-election.

[35] See 'Not Even Cambridge Analytica Believed Its Hype' (*The Atlantic*, 20 March 2018), available at www.theatlantic.com/politics/archive/2018/03/cambridge-analyticas-self-own/556016/.

[36] Who also may have spread fake news to disrupt the Brexit vote. See 'Facebook to Expand Inquiry into Russian Influence of Brexit' *The Guardian* (17 January 2018), available at www.theguardian.com/technology/2018/jan/17/facebook-inquiry-russia-influence-brexit. Note that as much or more fake news may have been spread from East European (or other) sources simply to make money from the ads which were displayed opposite these stories, rather than to achieve any political goals: see 'Inside the Macedonian Fake-News Complex' (*Wired*, 15 February 2017), available at www.wired.com/2017/02/veles-macedonia-fake-news/.

[37] As of May 2018, Zuckerberg had avoided giving evidence in the UK, sending his Chief Technology Officer of Facebook instead. A formal demand served on him to appear before the DCMS (Digital, Culture, Media and Sport) Committee of the House of Commons on 24 May 2018 failed, although he did agree to testify to the European Parliament in the same month.

algorithmic decision making have been shown to be unknown and perhaps uncontrollable phenomena which can destabilise democracies, spread lies and destroy truth as easily as they can share celebrity gossip or cute cat videos. Regulation, whether self-, co-, or top-down of 'fake news' is already in the works and is dealt with in this volume at both Chapters 8 and 9. In the privacy domain, the CA scandal has merged seamlessly into a general panic in the UK around the implementation of the General Data Protection Regulation (GDPR) and created a higher profile for personal data regulation than at any time since Snowden. Meanwhile in the US, a new hunger for privacy regulation seems to have taken root and, quite remarkably, US lawyers and consumers have begun to ask why they too do not have access to the perceived protections of the GDPR.[38]

Against this background of fear, uncertainty and doubt ('FUD'), the main thrust of this chapter will not only be to explain the current rules of DP, primarily as deployed in the GDPR, but to explain why in many senses they are seen as having failed to meet the challenges of the modern networked information society in protecting personal privacy and freedom. To meet this sense of failure, the EU has been arguing since November 2010[39] (and indeed, since much earlier) on how best to reform these rules. Data protection is a very old dog in Internet years, having been conceived of in the aftermath of World War II, spurred on by the rise of surveillance in the Communist post-war era, implemented in some European countries in the 1970s and finally harmonised in 1981 by the Council of Europe and then the EU in 1995. Thus, the rules regulating protection of personal data online were essentially conceived decades before the first iPad, iPhone, FitBit, Facebook profile or Amazon shopping cart was ever built or used. Below (and in the next two chapters) we will examine four topics: first, the historical challenges to privacy rights in response to which DP laws, including, but not limited to, the EU DP Directive (DPD)[40] and then the GDPR, have evolved and spread throughout the globe; second, the key threats to privacy that have arisen since – but were unanticipated by – the DPD, including the growth of the Web, social networking, profiling and online behavioural advertising, Big Data and the Internet of Things; third, the consequent goals of the GDPR reform process; and fourth, the detail of the legal framework as it currently exists.[41] A number of key concerns will be examined in depth, including the notions of personal data, sensitive personal data,

---

[38] Regulation (EU) 2016/679 of the European Parliament and of the Council of 27 April 2016 on the protection of natural persons with regard to the processing of personal data and on the free movement of such data, and repealing Directive 95/46/EC (General Data Protection Regulation) [2016] OJ L119/1. See 'Facebook Data Scandal Opens New Era in Global Privacy Enforcement" (*Politico.eu*, 31 March 2018), available at www.politico.eu/article/facebook-cambridge-analytica-data-protection-privacy-mark-zuckerberg-regulators/.

[39] Communication from EC Commission, *A Comprehensive Approach on Personal Data Protection in the European Union* COM (2010) 609 final, 4 November 2010.

[40] Directive 95/46/EC of the European Parliament and of the Council of 24 October 1995 on the protection of individuals with regard to the processing of personal data and on the free movement of such data [1995] OJ L281/31–0050.

[41] A number of excellent textbooks are devoted fully to the law of data protection, although fewer yet are updated to include the GDPR. For UK law, see R Jay, *Guide to the General Data Protection Regulation: A Companion to Data Protection Law and Practice* (Sweet and Maxwell, 2017); P Carey, *Data Protection: A Practical Guide to UK and EU Law* (Oxford University Press, 2018). For a perspective focusing on human rights and autonomy, see P Bernal, *Internet Privacy Rights: Rights to Protect Autonomy* (Cambridge University Press, 2014). For a general European overview of data protection

anonymisation/pseudonymisation and consent. We also, conscious of the fact that this book may be of use to a non-EU readership, include a brief section on privacy norms and laws outwith the EU.

Special attention will be given as appropriate to the UK and its case law, though as at the time of writing implementation of the GDPR in the UK is yet to be finalised, this coverage will of necessity be incomplete. It is one of life's amusing ironies that EU law requires the GDPR to come into force in Member States by May 2018, which is too early for Brexit to have taken place and therefore too early for the UK to consider its own way forward in DP. In fact, both the ICO and the Government have to date given every impression of expecting to implement the GDPR not only by May 2018 but for the foreseeable future, even after Brexit and the DP Bill passing at the time of writing through Parliament will entrench this. However, our data privacy laws as a whole, including the Investigatory Powers Act, may still not pass muster as 'adequate' under EU law, if and when a departure from the bloc eventually happens. The implications are worrying, as dealt with briefly below.

A final question is whether the GDPR is likely to make a real difference to the protection of privacy in the digital age, and if not, what other ways to protect privacy other than regulation may evolve?

II. Historical and Technological Challenges: The Global Rise of DP Laws

Informational privacy as a concept has its origins in the cumulative fears for individual privacy arising first from Nazi dossier-keeping in World War II and the post-war rise of Stalinism, and later, the emergence of early automated data processing. The pressing fear in Western states, as the world rebuilt in the 1940s and 1950s, was of the total surveillance 'Big Brother' state that had been glimpsed in Germany and the totalitarian Soviet bloc and was immortalised by Orwell.[42]

In the post-war period, new threats to privacy began to emerge with the arrival of the modern digital computer. The rise to prominence of DP law in recent times is generally attributed to the increasing use of computers and electronic communication devices.[43] Digitisation enabled the collection, processing, search and storage of personal data on a scale unprecedented in the analogue era. Huge amounts of digitised data could be stored indefinitely at relatively low cost, searched according to a vast number of criteria in minutes or seconds rather than hours, and be further processed in limitless numbers of useful ways. Crucially, data collected from one source (or one

---

law, see the updated EU Agency for Fundamental Rights' *Handbook on European Data Protection Law* (Publications Office of the European Union, 2018), available at http://fra.europa.eu/en/publication/2018/handbook-european-data-protection-law.

[42] Interestingly, Solove argues that a better metaphor for loss of privacy in the modern information society is that of Kafka's *The Trial* (bureaucracy) rather than Orwell's *1984* (obvious state surveillance). See D Solove, *The Digital Person* (New York University Press, 2004) Ch 3.

[43] *Ibid.*

'database') could be combined with other databases, to generate new data revealing significant connections and comparisons – this is the concept of 'data mining'. 'Profiling', a form of data mining that looks for patterns in data collected or aggregated about a person or group of persons, emerged as a ubiquitous and highly useful technology both for investigatory and commercial purposes.

While all these developments were transformative for businesses, citizens and consumers, they also had extremely worrying possibilities for surveillance, tracking and discriminatory practices.[44] Data might be re-used for functions quite different to the purposes for which it were originally collected: this is the concept of function, or scope, 'creep'. For example, data collected about a person for medical purposes – for example tests showing they are HIV-positive – might theoretically be used later to categorise that person as a risk when they seek to purchase life assurance, or to secure permanent employment. Information on ethnicity, gathered as part of routine demographics, might be later used to target a person of Islamic origin for searches at airports, or to put him or her on a suspect list when random crimes occur. Furthermore, personal data retained or created from new data mining might go out of date or be created or recorded with errors, leading to unfortunate (and harmful) results such as errors in credit histories or conviction or employment records. Users have felt increasingly unable to claim they are in control of both the collection and the uses of their personal data, especially when they began receiving junk mail and unsolicited phone calls from the evolving direct marketing industry.

These concerns manifested themselves first in national DP laws in the latter quarter of the twentieth century – the first being by the state of Hesse in Germany in 1970 – and in a number of important international instruments. The Universal Declaration of Human Rights (UDHR)[45] and the International Covenant on Civil and Political Rights (ICCPR)[46] both enshrine the right to respect for private life,[47] and have both contributed to the emergence of modern DP law. However, the most influential instrument in the creation of modern international privacy law was probably the 1981 Organisation for Economic Co-operation and Development (OECD) Guidelines on the Protection of Privacy and Transborder Flows of Personal Data, revised in 2013.[48] The Council of Europe was then the first organisation to create a binding treaty on DP in Convention 108 of 1981, and it remains the only global instrument specifically protecting privacy online as a human right.[49] Convention 108 was followed by the DPD which required all EU Member States to implement DP laws. Rooted in the right to private life enshrined in Article 8 of the ECHR, DP law was clearly intended

---

[44] We discuss the issues of profiling extensively in the context of online behavioural advertising (OBA) in Chapter 5 of this volume.

[45] General Assembly Resolution (GA Res) 217A (III), UN Doc A/810 at 71 (1948).

[46] GA Res 2200A (XXI), 21 UN GAOR Supp (No 16) at 52, UN Doc A/6316 (1966), 999 UNTS 171, entered into force on 23 March 1976.

[47] See respectively Art 12 of the UDHR, Art 17 of the ICCPR and Art 8 of the ECHR.

[48] Available at www.oecd.org/sti/ieconomy/2013-oecd-privacy-guidelines.pdf.

[49] EC: 108th Convention for the protection of individuals concerning automatic processing of personal data (1981). The Council of Europe Convention has been modernised alongside the GDPR; see now Modernised Convention 108, CM/Inf(2018)15-final at www.coe.int/en/web/data-protection/convention108/modernised.

to protect the privacy of individual citizens against the state, and therefore, with some small exceptions, it protects neither the deceased nor juristic persons (companies and similar unincorporated associations).[50]

The DPD, adopted in October 1995, was, until the arrival of the GDPR, the most comprehensive enactment on informational privacy in the world. The DPD was a minimum harmonisation instrument, and thus Member States were required to enact laws equivalent to its minimum standards but were free to provide greater protection if they wished. The DPD was extended to deal with perceived technological challenges by the 2002 Privacy and Electronic Communications Directive ('PECD'),[51] which was revised in 2009.[52]

More recently, the EU created a new right to the protection of personal data, as distinct from the right to respect for private life, in its 2000 Charter of Fundamental Rights.[53] Although originally only a political document, the Charter became legally binding as EU primary law with the coming into force of the Lisbon Treaty on 1 December 2009.[54]

A. Privacy, DP law, and the UK

This book has, of course, a special interest in the UK legal system, but it makes most sense generally to consider DP law as a European harmonised system with which even a post-Brexit UK will have to engage if it is not to lose the right to trade with, and in the personal data of, European data subjects (see below). The UK implemented the DPD in the DP Act 1998 ('DPA 98'), which wholly replaced the previous 1984 UK Act. The UK also implemented the PECD in the Privacy and Electronic Communications ((EC Directive) Regulations ('PECR')[55] in October 2003. When the PECD was updated in 2009, the UK amended the PECR in 2011.[56] The UK system is policed by the ICO, which has issued extensive legal guidance on the interpretation of the

---

[50] Given the application of DP only to 'natural persons' (DPD, Art 2(a)). A few EU countries have chosen however to extend some DP rights to the deceased (or rather, their representatives), including Bulgaria and Estonia. See discussion of these (at 131) and the arguments for and against post mortem rights of privacy and data protection in L Edwards and E Harbinja, 'Protecting Post-Mortem Privacy: Reconsidering the Privacy Interests of the Deceased in a Digital World' (2013) 32 *Cardozo Arts & Entertainment Law Journal* 101.

[51] 2002/58/EC.

[52] Directive 2009/136/EC of the European Parliament and of the Council of 25 November 2009 amending Directive 2002/22/EC on universal service and users' rights relating to electronic communications networks and services, Directive 2002/58/EC concerning the processing of personal data and the protection of privacy in the electronic communications sector and Regulation (EC) No 2006/2004 on cooperation between national authorities responsible for the enforcement of consumer protection laws [2009] OJ L337/11.

[53] EU (2012), Charter of Fundamental Rights of the European Union [2012] OJ C326/1.

[54] See consolidated versions of European Communities (2012), Treaty on European Union, [2012] OJ C326/1; and of European Communities (2012), TFEU [2012] OJ C326/391. One serious Brexit issue is that although a UK outside the EU will still be very likely to be subject to the ECHR, the Government has indicated its intention not to be governed by the Charter. See further on this Chapter 6 of this volume.

[55] SI 2003 No 2426.

[56] The Privacy and Electronic Communications (EC Directive) (Amendment) Regulations 2011 (SI 2011/ No 1208).

DPA 98,[57] the DP principles and related issues.[58] DP is a UK-wide matter reserved to Westminster, however a Scottish Information Commissioner also exists, with a role in relation to Scottish DP education as well as policing the separate Scottish Freedom of Information (FOI) scheme.

The UK has implemented the GDPR via a new DP Act 2018[59] to replace the 1998 Act; this was passed one day before the GDPR came into operation on 25 May 2018. The structure of the new Act is, to put it mildly, unhelpful. By implication, the GDPR as a Regulation operates in the UK without need for transposition. However the Regulation does give Member States considerable discretion to adapt over 50 designated articles, for eg, in Art 80(2) states have a choice whether to introduce independent rights for civil society organisations to bring litigation relating to the GDPR provisions, or simply to allow data subjects to be represented by such organisations. The UK has chosen the latter option; while other states such as Germany have made the opposite decision. Thus, even after May 2018, DP law will by no means be wholly harmonised in the EU (which is arguably unfortunate given its ambitions to be a comprehensive maximum harmonisation Regulation.)

The structure of the UK DP Act is thus as follows:

- Part 1 sets out an overview of how the Act structure works, and definitions.

- The first major section (Part 2) sets out new rules where the UK has discretion to make choices about how it implements the GDPR. It does *not* however reproduce the GDPR in full. Thus it cannot be read alone as an account of UK DP law. This will be extremely unhelpful for lay readers. This is now to be known as 'the applied GDPR'.

- The second major section (Part 3) transposes the DP Policing Directive.[60] As this is a Directive, the full text of the UK's version of the Directive is presented. This prescribes for the first time the rules about how law enforcement authorities, including the police, must respect some, though not all, DP principles when processing personal data in the course of their duty to prevent, detect, investigate and prosecute crime. It applies to 'competent authorities' as defined in s 30 of the 2018 Act but excludes the intelligence services. Previously in EU law, only transnational sharing of personal data between state law enforcement authorities was regulated by EU DP law, so this is a major change.

- The third major section (Part 4) introduces for the first time a full DP code for UK intelligence services which process personal data. This is not an area subject to EU jurisdiction but the UK has taken the opportunity to harmonise rules across sectors, drawing not only on the GDPR and DP Policing Directive by analogy but

---

[57] See formerly ICO, 'Data Protection Act 1998: Legal Guidance', no longer available on the Web.

[58] See formerly ICO, 'Data Protection Document Library', no longer available on the Web, although some DPA related documents can still be found as of 10 July 2018.

[59] Data Protection Act 2018 c 12.

[60] Directive 2016/680 on the protection of natural persons with regard to the processing of personal data by competent authorities for the purposes of the prevention, investigation, detection or prosecution of criminal offences of the execution of criminal penalties, and on the free movement of such data, and repealing Council Framework Decision 2008/977/JHA [2016] OJ L119/89. See Chapter 4 for more information.

also in parts on the draft reformed Council of Europe Convention No 108.[61] At first sight this would seem, slightly surprisingly, to indicate far greater constraints on intelligence service personal data gathering and use than has historically been the case – eg provision of subject access rights (SARs). However, there is a large caveat in that effectively the pre-existing system, whereby the Secretary of State can designate certain processing as secret for security reasons, is maintained, which excludes many key rights (including SARs). Notwithstanding, this section does go some way towards improving the rule of law in relation to personal data and intelligence services.

- Part 5 makes new rules about the role of the UK supervisory authority, the ICO, in particular introducing a new funding mechanism for the ICO, once fees for notification disappear; in future data controllers will instead pay a kind of tax to the ICO, depending on their level of processing activity.

- A considerable number of exceptions to the GDPR (eg for research) and other types of state discretion left by the GDPR are dealt with in Schedules, including important matters relating to health data, social work and education, as well as many more obscure areas (eg drug testing of athletes).

All in all navigating the new DP Act will not be for the faint hearted!

It should be noted that DP is not the only law relating to privacy in the UK. The law of confidence, which is dealt with in depth by Urquhart elsewhere in this volume,[62] also plays a significant role.[63] The UK has no constitutional protection of privacy as such, but the law of confidence has been transformed in recent years into something very near to a home-grown right of privacy by the incorporation of the ECHR into UK domestic law through the Human Rights Act 1998. Article 8 of the ECHR guarantees the right to respect for private life and, since the 1998 Act, the right to a private life as a fundamental human right can now be pled in any court in the land, with no need to go to Strasbourg to raise the issue.[64] Public bodies (such as social work departments, courts and local authorities) must act in accordance with it and the Government must, in theory at least, certify that legislation passed is compliant with the ECHR. As a remedy of last resort, however, both breaches of the Convention and failures to implement it in domestic law are justiciable before the European Court of Human Rights ('ECtHR').

---

[61] See n 49.

[62] See Chapter 8.

[63] Other areas of law may of course be relevant. Image, reputation and branding, eg, which can all be seen as connected to notions of privacy and personality, can be protected by *inter alia* defamation laws, trademark, passing off and contract (nondisclosure agreements or NDAs). Freedom of information (FOI) law also has a close connection with data protection, since both share a definition of personal data.

[64] It is beyond the scope of this chapter to fully examine ECtHR case law in this area, but it is worth noting that there has been a clear growth in cases emanating from Strasbourg which have significant effects on the law of privacy and data protection. See, eg, the seminal case of *von Hannover v Germany* [2004] ECHR 294; *S and Marper v UK*, Application Nos 30562/04 and 30566/04, 4 December 2008 (on the legality of retaining DNA samples of suspects in a police database); Case 48009/08 *Mosley v UK*, (10 May 2011) (on the right to prior notification of publication of potentially embarrassing material rejected as an aspect of Art 8); *Barbalescu v Romania*, Application No 61496/08, 5 September 2017 (workplace surveillance). It seems that issues of privacy and data protection are now as likely to arise in the Strasbourg Court as in the European Court of Justice (ECJ) in Luxembourg.

The law of confidence prevents a second party from disclosing information which should be kept private between that person and the data subject. It is thus considerably narrower than DP; for example if personal information is seen to have entered the public domain, or to have no character of secrecy, then remedies from the law of confidence will no longer be available.

III. After the DPD: New Challenges and the Need for Reform

Drafted before the mainstream Internet era,[65] the DPD struggled to preserve online privacy almost as soon as it was transposed into Member State law, owing to the effects of cheap and fast networked electronic communications. Since then, it has become engulfed in further challenges, from numerous directions.

A. From Elephants to Mice: Enforcement and Oversight in the Digital Era

DP law was originally designed for a world of mainframe technologies, where relatively few companies processed data; these were the intended targets of DP law. As Swire puts it, such companies were 'elephants':[66] they were few in number, large, slow to change, nationally based with physical headquarters, and as such they were easy targets for national regulators and law enforcement agencies. With corporate reputations to protect, they also had an interest in legal compliance and, generally, the resources available to achieve it. By contrast, the Web's cheap and accessible client-server technology, combined with the decline in the price of both hardware and software, and the subsequent further explosion in smart mobile communications, tablets, 'apps' and social networks, have created a world where data collectors and service providers can operate from anywhere in the world, where data flows instantly between nation states without stopping for police or customs points, where the location of data storage and processing is often completely opaque, and where a move to jurisdictions with a more amenable legal, social and financial climate is as easy as buying a plane ticket. The world of the Web is thus one of 'mice' – very many actors, often small, virtualised, fast moving, hard to control by national agencies, often with no physical headquarters within the EU and no particular interest in legal compliance (for example spammers, scammers, music pirates, et al), scurrying round collecting, processing, storing and selling personal data. This fundamental change has made DP in the twenty-first century extraordinarily hard to enforce, and in some eyes even to justify as a viable regulatory regime.

---

[65] The Internet theoretically begins in 1981 according to most scholars with the expansion of ARPAnet. However, the Web did not arrive until Tim Berners-Lee's invention of the HTTP protocol around 1990, and the commercial Internet took root around 1996 in the UK.

[66] See P Swire, 'Of Elephants, Mice and Privacy: International Choice of Law and the Internet' 32 *International Lawyer* 991.

Indeed, DP was originally conceived of as a bureaucratic, rather detailed and nerdy regime, that would only be the concern of a few large companies. Instead, in the modern Internet era, almost everyone has become potentially subject to DP obligations, including ordinary consumers and non-commercial organisations. As we discuss further in the next chapter, one European Court of Justice (ECJ) case long regarded as something of a counsel of perfection, *Lindqvist*,[67] mandates that every domestic Internet user who posts free-to-air content to the Web on sites like Facebook or Twitter becomes a data controller, with the full set of DP obligations (though not, at least, an exporter of personal data outside the EU). Similarly, another recent ECJ decision has rendered every householder who uses a camera-based security system whose gaze extends beyond their own garden a 'data controller' within the scope of the DPD.[68] Comprehensive enforcement of DP law has thus become impossible in practice, even leaving aside the extraterritorial element. The costs are far too high even for a reactive, complaint-driven approach to be successfully adopted by most DP authorities ('DPAs').[69]

B. Domestic Law Regulating Transnational Data Flows

It follows from the above that DP is now a body of law that is inevitably extraterritorial, with the EU often seeming to struggle to impose its own privacy norms on the wider world – most notably the US – no matter how different the privacy rules and norms in those other jurisdictions. This was foreseen in 1998 at the beginning of the DPD era by Peter Swire, the US creator of Safe Harbor, who noted that:

> Outside of Europe, US and other website operators are [un]likely to comply with the Directive, and many of these operators may remain beyond the jurisdiction of European law. Web sites will also likely be established outside of Europe to process data in ways that are forbidden by the Directive.[70]

The battle to impose EU norms on foreign data controllers thus dominates many of the current DP reform controversies, including the 'right to be forgotten', the requirements for the legality of data exports, and the question of how overseas cloud providers should respond to state demands for access to data in the name of national security.[71]

C. DP vs Businesses and E-Government?

DP has often been seen as being in direct opposition to business interests. In the UK, the commercial sector has seen it historically as irritating and unnecessary red tape,

---

[67] Case C-101/01 *Lindqvist* (ECJ, 6 November 2003).

[68] Case C-212/13 *Rynes* (ECJ, 11 December 2014).

[69] A comparison may be made to the post Internet copyright world, where almost everyone is likely at some point to be a copyright infringer, whereas once it was actually quite difficult to breach copyright without being a major publisher, broadcaster or performer.

[70] P Swire and R Litan, *None of Your Business: World Data Flows, E-Commerce and the European Privacy Directive* (Brookings Institution Press, 1998) 69–70.

[71] See discussions in Chapter 6 and Chapter 7.

impeding its ability to compete with firms in the US and elsewhere. Kuner, writing in 2005 about the whole EU market, noted: 'There have been increasing complaints by companies that European DP law is based on outmoded regulatory models and does not sufficiently take the requirements of electronic commerce into account'.[72]

More recently, and in reaction to the Snowden leaks mentioned above, there has been something of a division in business approaches. Companies that make money selling goods and services are keen to harness the rhetoric of privacy to increase the trust of their customers in an uncertain world. But for companies whose business model it is to provide a service for free – such as web search or digital entertainment – while making money out of advertising on the side, the free use of data – increasingly 'big data'[73] – is vital, and privacy may necessarily come into direct conflict with such business models. Many of the most innovative and successful global brands – Google, Facebook, Amazon, Spotify and many more – fundamentally base their business models (at least initially) on the collection, processing, use and sale of personal data. As the EU Commissioner, Meglena Kuneva, famously said in 2009, personal data has become the 'new oil of the internet and the new currency of the digital world'.[74] Although privacy compliance and engendering public trust will always be important, companies exist in the end to generate profit.

The state also finds sharing and processing personal data useful. In an age of post-recession austerity, struggling public services can save money by digitising services such as voting, tax returns, and health and welfare, these all perhaps being enabled by digital ID cards as has happened in countries like India and Estonia. 'Smart cities' – discussed in Chapter 5 – are the logical end product: connected 'smart' environments where data drives the delivery of every public service, including transport, welfare, sustainability, waste disposal, energy use, crime prevention and policing. But such programmes may also fail to provide adequate privacy safeguards, and risk delivering public data into private, corporate hands. In England, for example, the 'care.data' programme, which intended to foster greater sharing of patient data within and outside the NHS, remains an ongoing red flag between privacy advocates and politicians.[75]

D. DP vs Law Enforcement and Security?

Perhaps the greatest global challenge to DP and privacy laws since 1995 has been the rise of a culture of fear, surveillance and security that was precipitated by the horrendous events of 9/11. The impact on privacy of global demands from law enforcement

---

[72] C Kuner, *European Data Privacy Law and Online Business*, 1st edn (Oxford University Press, 2003) 45–48.

[73] See Chapter 5.

[74] See speech at the Roundtable on Online Data Collection, Targeting and Profiling, Brussels, 31 March 2009, available at http://europa.eu/rapid/press-release_SPEECH-09-156_en.htm. The common conception of 'data as the new oil' is now in fact increasingly contested as a usual metaphor – see, eg, J Thorp, 'Big Data Is Not the New Oil' (Harvard Business Review, 30 November 2012) at https://hbr.org/2012/11/data-humans-and-the-new-oil.

[75] See further www.england.nhs.uk/ourwork/tsd/care-data/; see also R Anderson, 'The Privacy of our Medical Records is being Sold Off" *The Guardian* (28 August 2012), available at www.theguardian.com/commentisfree/2012/aug/28/code-practice-medical-data-vulnerable.

and security agencies for surveillance of homes, workplaces and all kinds of online communications is sketched in more detail in Chapter 6 and Chapter 7.

E. DP vs the Press and Freedom of Expression?

A final constituency which are often vociferously opposed to privacy and DP regulation are the press. A tension has of course always existed between privacy (the right to keep my own data (including images) under my control) and freedom of expression (the right, *inter alia*, to know about and report on, other people),[76] and this conflict is recognised in a partial exemption from the restraints of DP law for journalists.[77] In recent years, however, the UK tabloid press has come under severe criticism for invasions of privacy, which reached its crescendo when the phone hacking activities of the journalists of the *News of the World* were disclosed in 2011, leading to the Leveson Inquiry into press ethics[78] and high profile prosecutions of MGN journalists. Media coverage of certain DP developments which might threaten its interests, such as the 'right to be forgotten', has been notably partisan and negative.[79]

It is important to remember that the 'media' no longer means just newspapers, radio, and TV, but now also includes the mass of citizen journalists, bloggers, tweeters, etc. The English courts have already struggled with whether it is worthwhile to issue injunctions to protect privacy when the intimate details desired to be hidden have already 'gone viral' over the Internet, owing in some cases to the so-called 'Streisand effect'.[80] So far they have decided the game is worth the candle,[81] but the views of many outside the legal sphere might differ.

In summary, then, privacy regulation needs to find a balance between (or, alternatively, not to be overwhelmed by) the interests of:

- *Business*, especially Internet-based industries;
- *Police*, *security agencies* and *law enforcement authorities*;

---

[76] See, helpfully, R Clayton and H Tomlinson, *Privacy and Freedom of Expression* (Oxford University Press, 2010).

[77] See now in the DPA 2018, Sch 2, Part 5.

[78] See 'Leveson Inquiry – Report into the Culture, Practices and Ethics of the Press' (Department for Digital, Culture, Media & Sport, 29 November 2012).

[79] See L Edwards, 'Three Myths that Need Nailed about the Right to be Forgotten (and one Question)' *Pangloss* blog (7 August 2014), available at http://blogscript.blogspot.co.uk/2014/08/three-myths-that-need-nailed-about.html.

[80] 'The Streisand effect is the phenomenon whereby an attempt to hide, remove, or censor a piece of information has the unintended consequence of publicizing the information more widely, usually facilitated by the Internet.' See http://en.wikipedia.org/wiki/Streisand_effect for origin of the term.

[81] See notably the Ryan Giggs case, *CTB v News Group Newspapers* [2011] EWHC 1232 (QB), where an injunction was granted by the English High Court to prevent mention of the affair of a famous footballer with a model, despite the fact the information had circulated widely on Twitter. The injunction did not run to Scotland however, and the details were published by a Scottish newspaper, the *Sunday Herald*, in which it was written: 'Today we identify the footballer whose name has been linked to a court superinjunction by thousands of postings on Twitter. Why? Because we believe it is unsustainable that the law can be used to prevent newspapers from publishing information that readers can access on the internet at the click of a mouse.' (22 May 2011).

- The *press*, and sometimes social media users and citizen journalists; and
- *Government agencies* and *municipal leaders* convinced that data sharing is in the public interest.

F. Public Need/Demand for Privacy Regulation?

Despite these difficulties, surveys have continually shown that the public are unhappy with the state of privacy protection as they perceive it. In 2011 the European Commission found, while drafting the GDPR, that:

- less than one third of EU citizens trusted phone companies, mobile communications companies, and ISPs, and just over one fifth trusted search engines, social networking sites and e-mail providers;
- only a quarter of social network users, and less than a fifth of online shoppers, felt in complete control of their personal data. Specific worries revolved around payment cards (54 per cent concerned), and mobile collection of data (49 per cent concerned);
- 74 per cent felt they should be required to give specific approval before any kind of personal information was collected and processed, in all cases;
- 70 per cent of EU users were concerned their personal data might be used for a purpose other than that for which it was collected; and
- 75 per cent wanted a right to delete all the information about them that had been collected via a website.[82]

The Commission concluded, with some understatement, that 'although the majority of Europeans have accepted the disclosure of personal information as fact of modern life, they appear to be quite concerned about their privacy'. Interestingly, this picture of around three quarters of the population despairing of their control over their personal data is repeated elsewhere around the globe. In 2013, Big Brother Watch surveyed nine countries (the UK, Germany, France, Spain, India, Japan, South Korea, Brazil and Australia), and showed that more than three quarters of consumers globally (79 per cent) were concerned about their privacy online.[83] In a more recent US Pew Internet study of privacy attitudes, carried out following the Snowden revelations, a remarkable 91 per cent of adults in the survey 'agreed' or 'strongly agreed' that consumers have lost control over how personal information is collected and used by companies, and 80 per cent of adults 'agreed' or 'strongly agreed' that Americans should be concerned about the Government's monitoring of phone calls and internet communication.[84]

---

[82] See COM (2010) 609 final (n 39).
[83] See Big Brother Watch, 'Global Attitudes to Privacy Online' (June 2013), available at https://bigbrotherwatch.org.uk/all-work/global-attitudes-to-privacy-online/.
[84] Pew Internet Study, 'Public Perceptions of Privacy and Security in the Post-Snowden Era' (November 2014).

G. Facing Up to the Need for Reform: The Goals of the 2012 Draft General DP Regulation

Bolstered by this evidence, the European Commission finally embarked in 2012 on an ambitious programme of reform for the DP Directive, with the aims both of providing data subjects with more control over their personal data, and promoting the free flow of personal data and so benefiting business and strengthening economic growth.[85] The proposal for a General DP Regulation ('GDPR') had a number of key goals, first articulated in the 2011 Communication *A Comprehensive Approach on Personal Data Protection in the European Union,*[86] and later expanded in the formal proposal of 25 January 2012:[87]

- To address the impact of *new technologies*, with which the PECD (n 51) had evidently failed to cope.
- To improve *harmonisation* of DP within the EU, with a view to enhancing the Single Market.[88] This would be achieved by replacing the existing Directive, which gave Member States considerable freedom as to its domestic transposition, with a Regulation intended to achieve 'maximum harmonisation'. This bold concept proved particularly controversial throughout: the UK saw it as reducing the flexibility of its current 'business friendly' interpretation of the rules; Germany saw it as reducing its robust privacy laws to an unacceptably low common standard; and France interpreted the Regulation's plans to harmonise the rulings of state DPAs as an infringement on the autonomy of its state regulator. The UK was particularly vociferous on this, with the ICO, Parliament, and the Government all characterising the proposal as inflexible, costly, and threatening to the economic growth, and insisting that the Regulation should be 're-cast as a Directive'.[89]
- To improve the *coherence* of DP law by combining in a single instrument rules for law enforcement, which the EU constitution had previously reserved to a different authority, with rules for private and commercial sectors. The advent of the Lisbon Treaty, together with the EU Charter of Fundamental Rights, made this coherence of sectoral rules for the first time both possible, and necessary. In fact, ironically, the original proposal which

---

[85] Full details and all draft texts of the GDPR, as well as supporting studies and empirical data, can be found at http://ec.europa.eu/justice/newsroom/data-protection/news/120125_en.htm.

[86] See COM (2010) 609 final (n 39).

[87] See European Commission, Communication *Safeguarding Privacy in a Connected World: A European DP Framework for the 21st Century* COM (2012) 09 final; and *Proposal for a Regulation of the European Parliament and of the Council on the Protection of Individuals with Regard to the Processing of Personal Data and on the Free Movement of Such Data (General Data Protection Regulation)* COM (2012) 11 final, Brussels, 25 January 2012.

[88] 'The timely adoption of a strong EU General Data Protection framework ... is essential for the completion of the Digital Single Market by 2015.' European Council, *Conclusions,* Brussels, 25 October 2013, EUCO 169/13 at www.consilium.europa.eu/uedocs/cms_data/docs/pressdata/en/ec/139197.pdf.

[89] See, eg, The House of Common Justice Select Committee, *The Committee's Opinion on the European Union Data Protection Framework Proposals – Justice Committee Contents,* October 2012, at www.publications.parliament.uk/pa/cm201213/cmselect/cmjust/572/57202.htm; ICO, *Proposed New EU General Data Protection Regulation: Article-by-Article Analysis Paper,* February 2013; Ministry of Justice, *Government Response to Justice Select Committee's Opinion on the European Union Data Protection Framework Proposals,* January 2013, www.gov.uk/government/uploads/system/uploads/attachment_data/file/217296/response-eu-data-protection-framework-proposals.pdf.

emerged in 2012 did not envisage a unified instrument at all, but rather a Regulation and a draft Directive[90] which would apply similar, but not identical, rules to the law enforcement sector.

Sub-goals, made explicit to a greater or lesser degree, included:

- To strengthen individual rights and enhance individual control over personal data, with the introduction of a new principle of 'minimisation' of data collection, and a number of innovative new rights such as the 'right to be forgotten', rights of data interoperability and new rights against profiling.

- To reduce red tape for businesses, both as a goal in itself and as a *quid pro quo* for acceptance of other, less 'business friendly', provisions. Notably, the intent was to create and trade a new principle of accountability of data controllers for the old and much disliked idea of compulsory notifications by data controllers.

- To introduce stringent new monetary penalties, and rules on mandatory security breach notifications, which would give real teeth to enforcement of DP law against multinational companies.

- To better address the problems of global flows of data, particularly with respect to cloud computing, and by extending existing mechanisms such as Binding Corporate Rules (BCRs).

The progress of this ambitious proposal was halting, to say the least. First envisaged as being settled at the latest by the Spring of 2014, the final finished product emerged only in May 2016.[91] Its gestation outlasted an entire term of European Commissioners, including some of its most fervent advocates. It allegedly had more lobbying money spent on it than any other EU enactment, even, remarkably, those devoted to copyright. Following the initial proposal, an agonisingly complex legislative progress ensued,[92] interspersed with periods of frenzied lobbying and multiple responses from the Article 29 Working Party ('A29 WP'). Battles between lobbyists, states and civil society[93] first came to a head in the 'Albrecht report' produced by the LIBE Committee on 22 November 2013[94] and named after its rapporteur, Jan Albrecht. By this stage, the Snowden revelations had heavily impacted on what were already fraught negotiations, and an amendment – of uncertain, but clearly symbolic, value – was introduced specifically to resist NSA access to the data of EU consumers stored outside of the EU and/or under the control of US service providers.

---

[90] Proposal for a Directive on the protection of individuals with regard to the processing of personal data by competent authorities for the purposes of prevention, investigation, detection or prosecution of criminal offences or the execution of criminal penalties, and the free movement of such data COM/2012/010 final – 2012/0010 (COD). Due to lack of space the DP Policing Directive will not be considered here.

[91] GDPR (n 38).

[92] 4000 amendments were submitted to the LIBE report from various EU committees. 'Lobbyplag', a civil society site at http://lobbyplag.eu/map, gives a fascinating insight into the state of lobbying influence among Members of the European Parliament. It also tracks when the text of amendments was cut and pasted directly from corporate lobbying organisations, such as eBay and Yahoo!.

[93] Privacy advocacy from civil society has been coordinated largely by EDRI – see the comprehensive website http://protectmydata.eu/.

[94] See the Report on the proposal for a regulation of the European Parliament and of the Council on the protection of individuals with regard to the processing of personal data and on the free movement of such data (General Data Protection Regulation) (COM (2012) 0011 – C7-0025/2012 – 2012/0011(COD)).

Following the Albrecht report the dust still failed to settle. Proposals for international data transfers, profiling and the notion of a 'one stop shop' regulator for non-EU businesses operating in multiple EU states (such as Google and Facebook), were key roadblocks.[95] However, compromise was eventually reached out at the 'trilogue' stage, when a joint proposal of the European Parliament, the Council and the Commission emerged blinking into the daylight. Many commentators thought they would never live to see the day. Others noted that the gains, especially on some key points of contention, such as the definition of consent and of personal data, might well not justify the energies expended to get there.

In the next chapter, the key points of the GDPR will be considered. Finally in this chapter however, we will briefly consider the state of privacy and DP laws outside Europe.

IV. DP Laws beyond the EU

Privacy is a cultural concept,[96] interpreted differently in different countries and assuming different connotations.[97] People have different expectations according to their national origin.[98] For example, it is no surprise that post-war Germany with its history of abuse of personal data collection by the Nazis has probably the strongest privacy sensibilities built into its laws of any legal system in the world. A continuing tension in debates over global harmonisation of privacy laws has been the American tendency to prize freedom of speech over privacy, while in Europe the balance is much less clearly staked out. Given these cultural differences, it is unsurprising that privacy laws differ starkly from country to country.

While the GDPR applies only within the EU, it, and the DPD before it, have had enormous influence as a model of *omnibus* privacy protection (that is, protection that applies across all kinds of data collection and processing, in both the private and public sectors) for countries outside Europe. Indeed, Greenleaf argues that some of the newer Asian DP laws, such as those in the Philippines and South Korea, have features which may surpass the protections provided by EU law.[99] Almost all European countries, including some former Soviet bloc states outside the EU, and many Latin American and Asian countries, have now implemented DP-like laws, often drawing on the right to respect for private life as a constitutional norm. However, beyond this general level of similarity, the devil is in the detail and legal systems of the world have

---

[95] See The Council of the EU, *Press Release*, 3298th Council meeting, Justice and Home Affairs, Brussels, 3 and 4 March 2014 at www.consilium.europa.eu/uedocs/cms_Data/docs/pressdata/en/jha/141295.pdf.

[96] D Lyon, *Surveillance Studies: An Overview* (Polity Press, 2007).

[97] RC Post, 'Three Concepts of Privacy' (2001) *Georgetown Law Journal* 89, 2087.

[98] S Nouwt, BR de Vries and R Loermans, 'Analysis of the Country Reports' in S Nouwt, BR de Vries and C Prins (eds), *Reasonable Expectations of Privacy? Eleven Country Reports on Camera Surveillance and Workplace Privacy* (TMC Asser Press, 2005) 352.

[99] See, eg, G Greenleaf, 'Korea's New Act: Asia's Toughest Data Privacy Law' (2012) 117 *Privacy Laws & Business International Report* 1–6.

wildly differing laws relating to informational privacy and can be arranged in a loose taxonomy of privacy-friendliness.

The European DP regime is often touted as the gold standard for privacy regulation worldwide. As we will discuss in more detail in the next chapter, the DP regime contains incentives for other non EU legal systems to implement laws similar in broad ways to DP. Data cannot be exported from the EU to countries which have not been certified as 'adequate' according to EU rules, and the exceptions to this rule (such as 'safe harbour') allowing data exports are under attack. The aim is for the personal data of EU citizens to be protected when it is processed outside the EU with a similar degree of expectation of privacy protection as when this occurs within the EU. On the whole, despite accusations of extraterritorial law making, this data export rule has succeeded in incentivising something of a 'race to the top' in privacy standards, competing with what might have been seen as a likely 'race to the bottom' as states tried to entice businesses with regulation-free 'data havens'.[100]

Very few countries have actually been certified as 'adequate', partly because of the labyrinthine bureaucracy involved and partly because of the alternate routes to enabling data export in the DPD which have been seen as more business-friendly. Those that have been so certified include Canada, Switzerland, Argentina, Israel, Guernsey and the Isle of Man, and Uruguay with recent overtures to Japan not yet finalised. Although no public notification has been made, it is known that a number of countries (such as Australia) have failed to be granted adequacy despite having what might be regarded as sophisticated privacy regulation. By contrast, somewhat to many observers' surprise, Japan has recently been provisionally certified as adequate[101] which may indicate an easing of stringency.

A larger number of countries however have, or are in the process of implementing, rules somewhat akin to DP, despite not having the imprint of 'adequacy'. Often, the intention here is to secure revenue streams as providers of outsourcing and data services to EU companies and consumers. In such states, as noted above, legislation may be driven more by external forces than home grown privacy priorities.

Some countries however are also responding to internalised traditions, eg Commonwealth nations with a strong common law tradition, or where policy elites seek to 'keep up with' the global norm on privacy in the leading nations 'club'.[102] Such countries with a DP-like system might be said to include New Zealand, Hong Kong, Chile, Costa Rica,[103] Uruguay, Mexico and Peru, and most recently, Malaysia[104] and India.[105]

---

[100] Bennett and Raab (n 16) Ch 10.

[101] See http://ec.europa.eu/justice/data-protection/international-transfers/adequacy/index_en.htm and Press Report, 13 September 2017 at http://datamatters.sidley.com/eu-adequacy-ruling-japan-expected/.

[102] See J Rule, 'Conclusion' in J Rule and G Greenleaf, *Global Privacy Protection: The First Generation* (Edward Elgar, 2008).

[103] See www.globallawwatch.com/2011/09/costa-ricas-new-data-protection-statute-may-not-meet-eu-adequacy-lawyers-say/.

[104] See A Rafferty, 'All Eyes on Asia: Emerging Privacy Laws in Asia' (Society for Computers and Law Blog, 24 January 2012), available at www.scl.org/site.aspx?i=ed24603.

[105] See R Ananthapur, 'India's New Data Protection Legislation' (2011) 8:2 *SCRIPTed* 192, available at www.law.ed.ac.uk/ahrc/script-ed/vol8-2/ananthapur.asp. See discussion of India's recent Supreme Court case on privacy at 'Indian Court Rules Privacy a "Fundamental Right" in Battle over National ID Cards' *The Guardian* (24 August 2017) at www.theguardian.com/world/2017/aug/24/indian-court-rules-privacy-a-fundamental-right-in-battle-over-national-id-cards

Guadamuz[106] notes furthermore that in some Latin American countries, even where no formal DP legislation has been drafted, rights over information exist which is known as 'habeas data'. This protection forms part of the constitutional law of most Latin American countries. Some African countries, such as Nigeria and South Africa, also have constitutional guarantees of privacy. In most of these cases though, there are significant weaknesses compared to the EU regime; notably revolving around a lack of enforcement powers or resources; a lack of an independent supervisory body; a lack of effective remedies for data subjects; or simply a general lack of detail beyond a vague constitutional assertion.

These problems are exacerbated in the third group of countries to be considered, the members of the APEC (Asia-Pacific Economic Cooperation) Privacy Framework,[107] which takes in several major data outsourcing countries and 'Asian Tiger' economies and comprises 21 states including, on the one hand, those with strong domestic privacy traditions such as New Zealand and Australia and, on the other, those with very little indigenous privacy tradition or binding law such as Taiwan, Vietnam, China and Thailand. Reaction from Western commentators to the final version of the APEC Principles was not positive. Greenleaf wrote that: 'My initial reaction to the first draft of the APEC proposal was that it was "OECD-Lite". There is nothing in the final framework to change my mind'. Greenleaf goes on to castigate the frame-work as 'at best an approximation of what was regarded as acceptable information privacy principles twenty years ago'.[108] Pounder similarly regards the APEC text as 'unlikely to protect privacy' and a shaky foundation on which to build a global privacy framework.[109] Both identify fatal weaknesses in the APEC rules, including a lack of rules on data retention, data export and automated decision making. Pounder empha-sises the likelihood of inconsistent implementation by APEC Member States resulting in a likely confused hotchpotch of national DP laws and the likelihood of a very weak policing regime. Greenleaf in particular bemoans the fact that the Privacy Principles actually set a lower baseline than already found in many of the APEC countries. In short, the APEC developments seem to have failed to help in the progress towards acceptable global minimum standards for personal DP, in a highly significant group of data importing countries.

This leaves the question of states with no generic privacy regime of any kind. Most of these (eg, much of Africa) are relatively insignificant in terms of global e-commerce policy and data import and export volume (though this may rapidly cease to be the case), but the United States (US) is a different story. As often noted, the US has no omnibus DP regime akin to that of the EU. For historical reasons, the US is often characterised as suspicious of controls on its commercial operators, but fairly ready

---

[106] A Guadamuz, 'Habeas Data: The Latin-American Response to Data Protection' (2000) (2) *The Journal of Information, Law and Technology*, available at www2.warwick.ac.uk/fac/soc/law/elj/jilt/2000_2/guadamuz/.

[107] See   www.apec.org/Groups/Committee-on-Trade-and-Investment/~/media/Files/Groups/ECSG/05_ecsg_privacyframewk.ashx.

[108] G Greenleaf, 'APEC's Privacy Framework' in Rule and Greenleaf (n 102).

[109] C Pounder, 'Why the APEC Framework is Unlikely to Protect Privacy', available at www.out-law.com/page-8550.

to allow US citizens safeguards against its government. Accordingly, the Fourth Amendment gives US citizens strong rights against government or police searches and seizures, while the Privacy Act 1974 gave citizens rights derived from the Fair Information Principles against federal agencies. Regan narrates that at this time it was widely believed the next step would be omnibus privacy legislation for the private sector as well, but instead the commercial lobby successfully diverted efforts to a sector-by-sector approach, with minimal governmental intervention seen as the most appropriate way forward.[110] The result was an incremental and haphazard regulation of pieces of the commercial landscape which seemed to present particular privacy threats at the time, including enactments such as the Cable Communications Policy Act 1984 (reporting requirements of personal data held of subscribers by cable companies) and the Video Privacy Protection Act 1988 (video stores not to disclose what videos customers rented[111]).

More recently, the US has systematically regulated three key areas of personal privacy, with well-respected legislation: relating to health privacy (HIPAA[112]), financial information (the Gramm-Leach-Bliley Act[113]) and children's data (COPPA[114]). Some of these rules may well provide stronger protection in their sector than that supplied by the EU regime. This still leaves considerable gaps in relation to data subjects and the private sector, which are filled (if at all) either by self-regulation or 'soft law' (eg the use of privacy policies and membership of privacy associations or 'seals'); or by adaption of existing general law, such as the Federal Trade Commission's remit to prevent 'deceptive practices' in the consumer world, and the privacy torts as systematised by the US scholar Prosser in 1960.[115]

These torts, as Solove notes,[116] are aimed at redressing specific harms done to individuals – often related to press intrusion or reputation management – but are not well adapted to regulating the everyday flow of personal information into databases or profiles. They comprise: the torts of *intrusion upon seclusion* (protecting against intentional intrusion into 'seclusion' or 'private affairs' where disclosure would be 'highly offensive to the reasonable person'); *public disclosure of private facts* (making public matters relating to private life in a way that would be 'highly offensive' and not of legitimate concern to the public); *false light* (a variation on defamation or libel, giving publicity to matters that place another in false light to the public); and *appropriation* (akin to passing off, appropriating for one's own use the name or likeness of another). These torts fail to control, as DP law at least aspires to, most of the significant crises of the information society relating to data flow, and the system overall fails to provide many of the basic norms of the DP regimes such as user subject access rights, rights to

---

[110] P Regan, 'The United States' in Rule and Greenleaf (n 102) at 58.
[111] Anecdote has it this provision was introduced because a particular Senator Bork had been embarrassed by the Press obtaining a list of the movies he had rented. The Act does not extend to books borrowed, records bought or any other kind of retail or entertainment outlet.
[112] Health Insurance Portability and Accountability Act 1996.
[113] Financial Modernisation Act 1999.
[114] Children's Online Privacy Protection Act 1998.
[115] D Solove, *The Digital Person* (New York University Press, 2014) Ch 4.
[116] *Ibid* at 58. Note that the criticisms made here are of privacy at a federal level. Some US states, most notably California, have state laws adding up to levels of protection comparable to EU DP law.

have data deleted when no longer needed and rights to an independent supervision and enforcement agency. In particular, they fail to deal with disclosures of mundane details which nonetheless add up to privacy threats when compiled into profiles.

All this does not mean that the US (or US states) have no privacy law, merely that it is fractured, sectoral, and in some key cases supported by soft rather than mandatory law, and is thus impossible to square with the EU adequacy requirements. Some research has suggested that in certain sectors US protection may in practice be more effective than European protection[117] and that US commercial practice may have much in common with German practice; and the Federal Trade Commission (FTC) has taken an extremely tough role in recent years[118] in looking towards stronger enforcement of consumer privacy rights against digital giants like Facebook[119] and Google,[120] as well as policing new threats like connected toys for children.[121] But given that the US is the leading e-commerce nation on the planet, and unlikely to agree to implement a European level of omnibus protection any time soon (especially while Trump remains in power[122]), one of the greatest challenges faced by the European system is how to create a meaningful system of privacy protection for EC citizens in a world of trans-border data flows. This problem of 'data exports' is also taken up in the next chapter.

---

[117] See K Bamberger and D Mulligan, *Privacy on the Ground: Driving Corporate Behavior in the US and Europe* (MIT, 2015).

[118] See FTC, *Protecting Consumer Privacy in an Era of Rapid Change* (December 2010), available at www.ftc.gov/os/2010/12/101201privacyreport.pdf.

[119] See FTC consent order relating to Facebook, FILE NO 092 3184, 2011, at http://ftc.gov/os/caselist/092 3184/111129facebookagree.pdf.

[120] See FTC consent order relating to Google, FILE NO102 3136, 2011 at www.ftc.gov/os/caselist/1023136 /110330googlebuzzcmpt.pdf (Google Buzz settlement).

[121] See 'FTC Settles First Children's Privacy Case Involving Connected Toys' (Privacy and International Security Blog, 8 January 2018), available at www.huntonprivacyblog.com/2018/01/08/ ftc-settles-first-childrens-privacy-case-involving-connected-toys/.

[122] There was a brief dawn during the Obama regime that self-regulatory privacy principles might evolve into something more mandatory. These have now been entirely removed from the White House website, although an archived announcement can be found at https://obamawhitehouse.archives.gov/ the-press-office/2012/02/23/fact-sheet-plan-protect-privacy-internet-age-adopting-consumer-privacy-b.

4

Data Protection: Enter the General Data Protection Regulation

LILIAN EDWARDS

In the last chapter, we reviewed the history of privacy as a value, and a human right, and the rise in interest in legal protection of privacy, over the last 30 years of technical and social innovation which led to the creation of the modern networked information society. We also traced how the General Data Protection Regulation (GDPR)[1] came to become the most significant data privacy reform process in history. In this chapter, we will analyse the basic structure and the key building blocks of the GDPR, such as personal data, processing and consent; and analyse how far this unwieldy instrument really makes a difference, both in theory and practice, to the privacy rights of users.

I. Jurisdiction: Material and Territorial Scope

The GDPR applies to 'the processing of personal data wholly or partly by automated means', as well as in limited circumstances to manual filing systems (outwith the scope of this chapter) (GDPR, Art 2(1)). A number of important exemptions from this material scope exist.[2] One is the domestic purposes or 'household exemption' examined in more detail at p 82 below. The other significant exemption for current UK purposes is in relation to criminal justice and policing. This exemption also existed in the Data Protection Directive (DPD), and meant that the treatment of personal data processing

---

[1] Regulation (EU) 2016/679 of the European Parliament and of the Council of 27 April 2016 on the protection of natural persons with regard to the processing of personal data and on the free movement of such data, and repealing Directive 95/46/EC (General Data Protection Regulation or GDPR) [2016] OJ L119/1. All references in this chapter are to the GDPR unless otherwise noted.

[2] GDPR, Art 2(2). Exemptions also include activity which falls outside the scope of Union law and activity related to the common foreign and security policy of the Union.

by law enforcement agencies throughout Europe was essentially unharmonised.[3] As noted in the last chapter, the original GDPR discussions sought to provide a 'comprehensive' solution that is one where the same rules were applied to policing as to other civil, commercial and public matters. This proved impossible, and the result was the separate 'Data Protection Policing Directive' (DP Policing Directive).[4] Partial exemptions allowing national discretion appear in quite a number of places in the GDPR, in relation to employment (Article 88) and in a number of other areas listed primarily in Article 23. It is notable that for an instrument intended to comprehensively harmonise data protection rules across Europe, a remarkable amount of dissensus will still exist if Member States choose to make full use of these options.

In the UK, exemptions are now regulated by the Data Protection Act 2018 (DPA 2018) s 15, which passed one day before the GDPR was due to be brought into operation on 25 May 2018. Here, the most important exceptions continue to include national security, law enforcement and journalism,[5] the latter of which has become heavily contested, invoking as it does the balance between freedom of information and privacy. Interestingly, it is clear that it is not only professional journalists who can claim exemption from EU data protection (DP) law: although the claim of Google to journalistic privileges as a search engine has been dismissed by both the Court of Justice of the European Union (CJEU) and recently, the English High Court.[6]

The *territorial* scope of the GDPR is a fraught issue. Protecting the rights of EU citizens whose data is processed by (say) US-based companies seems both self-evidently necessary and extraordinarily difficult. On the other hand, there is a long international legal tradition which warns against too extensive an extension of extraterritorial jurisdiction for fear of raising hopes of regulation without co-existent enforcement, as well as possibly aggressive-seeming disruption of local legislative sovereignty. This already messy exercise has been complicated further by the enormous growth in cloud-based consumer services, including Gmail, Facebook (FB) and Dropbox, meaning that ordinary users are as likely to have their data stored and processed outside the EU as in it, and even more so now than was true in the days of simple outsourcing. The apparent ease with which the territorial application of EU DP laws can be gamed was demonstrated in April 2018 when FB overnight announced it had switched the data controllership of its non-EU users from Ireland (an EU member) to the US. This decision (which seems not to have involved the physical transfer of data or personnel) has been said at a stroke to have removed the potential data protection rights of 1.5 billion

---

[3] Directive 95/46/EC of the European Parliament and of the Council of 24 October 1995 on the protection of individuals with regard to the processing of personal data and on the free movement of such data [1995] OJ L281/31–0050. Note the Framework Decision on the protection of personal data processed in the framework of police and judicial co-operation (Council Framework Decision 2008/977/JHA), 30 December 2008. However, the main point of this instrument was to enable greater data sharing between national EU police forces. It is replaced by the new DP Policing Directive (see n 4).

[4] Directive 2016/680 on the protection of natural persons with regard to the processing of personal data by competent authorities for the purposes of the prevention, investigation, detection or prosecution of criminal offences or of the execution of criminal penalties, and on the free movement of such data, and repealing Council Framework Decision 2008/977/JHA [2016] OJ L119/89.

[5] See detailed discussion in Chapter 8.

[6] See Case C-131/12 *Google Spain v Agencia Española de Protección de Datos (AEPD) and González*, 13 May 2014 [85] (hereafter '*Google Spain*'); *NT1 & NT2 v Google LLC* [2018] EWHC 799 (QB).

FB users.[7] An alternative framing however is to ask if a corporation has a moral duty to apply EU legal rights of privacy to non-EU data subjects whose data may or may not be processed in the EU and whose local laws may or may not be 'adequate' for EU purposes (see below Pt XI).

In an attempt primarily to protect EU data subjects, the GDPR departs significantly from the DPD in providing three tests of jurisdiction. First, the GDPR applies to processing of personal data in the context of the activities of an *establishment* of a controller or processor in the EU, regardless of whether the processing takes place in the EU or not. Second, if the personal data relating to EU data subjects is processed by controllers who are *not* established in the EU, then they may still be caught if:

(i)   they offer goods or services to data subjects of the EU (and it does not matter if no payment was requested); or
(ii) they monitor the 'behaviour' of data subjects within the EU.[8]

These new and far-reaching 'targeting' provisions, modelled to some extent on similar approaches in the Brussels Regulation on Jurisdiction and Judgments (recast) and elsewhere, are clearly intended to catch large US companies such as Google, FB and Amazon, whether or not they maintain a physical 'establishment' within the EU. In fact, many or most of these companies will operate with offices of some kind in multiple EU Member States, even though the main management activities are usually kept on US soil. If this is the case, do these national outfits qualify as 'establishments'? And, if they do, which DP authority should regulate their activities, and what rights will a data subject in a particular EU state have if the controller claims their *main* establishment is in a different Member State? This is a common situation, since many tech giants have established their EU centre of operations in Ireland, because of its combination of a generous corporation tax regime and (at least so far) an understanding DP authority. Jurisdiction in DP has to some extent become a matter of forum shopping, something the CJEU attacked in *Google Spain*.[9]

In that case, Google's first line of defence was that although it had a marketing office in Spain which sold advertising space, its real EU centre of operations ('main establishment') was in Ireland, and therefore the matter should be referred to the Irish DP authority. To the surprise of many, the CJEU held that (i) Google Spain was

---

[7] See, eg, report at www.irishtimes.com/business/technology/facebook-to-put-1-5bn-users-out-of-reach-of-new-eu-gdpr-privacy-law-1.3466837, 19 April 2018. Prior to 19 April 2018, in respect of US and Canadian FB users, FB asserted FB Inc in the US was the data controller, while for all other FB users' data, including EU and non-EU users, FB Ireland, based in Dublin, was asserted to be the data controller. The claim is slightly disingenuous as it is unlikely that many of these non-EU users before this data had the knowledge or ability to enforce any DPD rights against FB. Other corporations seem to be taking similar measures: eg new terms as of 8 May move non-Europeans to contracts with US-based LinkedIn Corp. However, Twitter has not chosen to move non-US non-EU users to an American data controller.

[8] The Recitals indicate that 'offering goods or services' is more than mere access to a website or email address (see possible confirmation in Case C-191/15 *Amazon* (28 July 2016)), and might be evidenced by use of language or currency generally used in one or more Member States with the possibility of ordering goods/ services there, and/or monitoring customers or users who are in EU. 'Monitoring of behaviour' will occur, for example, where individuals are tracked on the Internet by techniques which apply a profile to enable decisions to be made/predict personal preferences, etc.

[9] *Google Spain* (n 6).

clearly *an* 'establishment' because it engaged in the effective and real exercise of activity through stable arrangements in Spain,[10] and (ii) from this it followed that, even though the Spanish office engaged only in the selling of advertising, processing was nonetheless carried out 'in the context of the *activities* of an *establishment*' (emphasis added).[11] The activities of the search engine, and those of its establishment in Spain, were 'inextricably linked' since Google could not survive profitably without the advertising revenue. The attempt to avoid the jurisdiction of the Spanish courts and regulator was thus firmly rejected.

From the point of view of the multinational company, however, what is most desirable is to have everyday compliance matters regulated by just one DP authority. This so-called 'one-stop-shop' solution was promoted as one of the plus points of the GDPR for large companies, enabling efficient company management, but it will also benefit consumers by improving consistency in how commercial activities are regulated across multiple states. This matter has however been slightly fudged in the GDPR. First, there is an apparently clear provision in Article 56 that the DP authority 'of the *main establishment*[12] ... of the controller or processor shall be competent to act as *lead* supervisory authority for the cross-border processing' of the controller (emphasis added). This is, however, immediately complicated by Article 56(2), which provides that states may derogate from this provision such that their own DP authority 'shall be competent to handle a complaint lodged with it or a possible infringement of this Regulation, if the subject matter relates only to an establishment in its Member State or substantially affects data subjects only in its Member State'. This messy compromise looks likely to lead to a great deal of litigation in the CJEU.[13]

II. Key Terminology

The GDPR uses certain specific and important terminology, most of which is defined in Article 4. Since they are relevant to the material scope we explored above, the definitions of '*personal data*' and '*processing*' are particularly important. Also crucial are an understanding of the difference between a *data controller*, who controls the processing in question, and a *data processor* who, in theory at least, merely carries out processing operations on behalf of the controller.

- 'Personal data'[14] means any information relating to an identified or identifiable natural person (the 'data subject'). An identifiable natural person is one who can be

---

[10] See further, Article 29 Working Party (A29 Working Party), *Update of Opinion 8/2010 on Applicable Law in Light of the CJEU Judgement in Google Spain*, WP 179 update, 16 December 2015.

[11] Following the formulation in Case C-230/14 *Weltimmo* (1 October 2015).

[12] Defined in GDPR, Art 4(16) for a controller with multiple establishments in the EU as its 'place of central administration' or, if it has none, the place where its 'main processing activities' take place.

[13] See adopted guidance from A29 WP, *Guidelines on The Lead Supervisory Authority*, WP244rev.01_en (13 December 2016).

[14] GDPR, Art 4(1). Discussed in greater detail below.

identified, directly or indirectly, in particular by reference to an identifier such as a name, an identification number, location data, an online identifier, or by reference to one or more factors specific to the physical, physiological, genetic, mental, economic, cultural or social identity of that natural person.

- 'Processing'[15] means any operation or set of operations which is performed on personal data or on sets of personal data, whether or not by automated means, such as collection, recording, organisation, structuring, storage, adaptation or alteration, retrieval, consultation, use, disclosure by transmission, dissemination or otherwise making available, alignment or combination, restriction, erasure or destruction.

- A 'data controller'[16] is the natural or legal person, public authority, agency or other body which, alone or jointly with others, determines the purposes and means of the processing of personal data. Where the purposes and means of such processing are determined by Union or Member State law, the controller or the specific criteria for its nomination may be provided for by Union or Member State law. Most duties in the DPD were placed on data controllers. Although this remains true under the GDPR, certain duties have also been extended to data processors. This is primarily because of the uncertain status of cloud service providers (CSPs).[17] Joint data controllers are possible.[18]

- A 'data processor'[19] is any person, natural or juristic, who processes the data on behalf of the data controller, for example a data warehouse, an out-sourcing agency, or a cloud provider of Software, Platform or Infrastructure as a Service (SaaS, PaaS and IaaS, respectively). Data processors were seen as relatively unimportant when the DPD was drafted, as their activities could be (and indeed had to be) fully controlled by an explicit contract with the data controller.[20] Accordingly, their only separate obligation was one of security.[21] However, since the rise of cloud computing it has become increasingly hard to distinguish between data controllers and data processors, which has considerable impact on EU control of data stored and processed in the cloud, often by non-EU cloud service

---

[15] *Ibid*, Art 4(2).

[16] *Ibid*, Art 4(7).

[17] See further, C Millard et al, *Cloud Computing Law* (Oxford University Press, 2013).

[18] See generally Ch IV of the GDPR. Article 25 now deals explicitly with joint controllers. A good recent example of the usefulness of the 'joint controller' concept is Advocate General (AG) Bot's Opinion in Case C-210/16 *Wirtschaftsakademie Schleswig-Holstein* (CJEU, 24 October 2017) where the AG argues that where a FB 'fan page' collected analytics information about visitors via a tool provided by FB ('Facebook Analytics'), FB and the site are joint controllers. Paragraph 62 of the Opinion has an excellent discussion of how in modern Internet commerce, distinct processes occur where often 'numerous parties … themselves have differing degrees of control' at different points in the process. See also ongoing Case C-40/17 *Fashion ID*, (CJEU, 24 March 2017) which concerned a similar scenario involving a website separate from FB which used a social plug-in ('Like' button) to send information about visitors to FB for similar analytics purposes, and from which the AG indicated he would not 'draw an artificial distinction' (at [66]).

[19] GDPR, Art 4(8).

[20] DPD, Art 17(3).

[21] *Ibid*, Art 17(2).

providers.[22] According to the Article 29 Working Party (hereinafter 'A29 WP')[23] in 2010,

> the possibility of pluralistic control caters for the increasing number of situations where different parties act as controllers. The assessment of this joint control should mirror the assessment of 'single' control, by taking a substantive and functional approach and focussing on whether the purposes and the essential elements of the means are determined by more than one party. The participation of parties in the determination of purposes and means of processing in the context of joint control may take different forms and does not need to be equally shared.[24]

- The approach in the GDPR has been to widen the scope of data processors' obligations, including the documenting of processing operations, co-operation with local Data Protection Authorities (DPAs,) and certain obligations relating to security breaches. Yet deciding who is a data controller and who a data processor in complicated areas like modern targeted advertising is maddeningly difficult. FB for example in its post-GDPR revision of terms of service has asserted that advertisers who use its Custom Audiences facilities are data controllers and they are mere data processors. This seems dubious. There is a strong case to be made that every party which processes data should simply apply all data protection obligations as far as is practically possible, and the doomed attempt to construct a binary division be abandoned. Joint controllership may solve some issues but is unlikely to be asserted by a corporation deferring responsibility and will be complex to establish in court.

III. Processing

Processing, as can be seen from the definition quoted above, is defined extremely widely in the GDPR, as was also the case in the DPD. In the CJEU case of *Lindqvist*, a Swedish woman set up a personal web page on which she posted pictures of fellow members of her church, along with some identifying details. It was held that she was indeed 'processing personal data' within the meaning of the DPD, even though the process was only partly automated and involved manual input. Importantly, a defence that her activities were in the course of a purely personal or household activity (or, as DPA 1998 interpreted the phrase, 'domestic purposes'[25]), and so should have fallen

---

[22] Note the A29 Working Party, *Opinion in the SWIFT Case*, Opinion 10/2006 WP 128, 6 December 2006, which determined that SWIFT, a Belgian-based clearing house for international bank transfers made at the instruction of various EU banks, was not a mere data processor but had sufficient independent capacity to be regarded as a data controller, and was thus subject to the full rigour of Belgian DP law. Enormous difficulties are now arising in deciding if cloud computing service providers are processors or controllers. See further Millard (n 17). For general EU work on regulating the Cloud, see the European Cloud Computing Strategy 2012 at http://ec.europa.eu/digital-agenda/en/european-cloud-computing-strategy.

[23] The A29 WP is a group drawn from the Data Protection Authorities (DPAs) of the EU Member States which provide highly persuasive but not mandatory advice on aspects of DP law. Their job is to try to harmonise interpretation of DP law across Europe. In the GDPR, they are replaced by the European DP Board (EDPB) (see p 111 below).

[24] A29 WP *Opinion 1/2010 on the Concept of 'Controller' and 'Processor'* WP 169, 16 February 2010 at 32 and 33.

[25] See DPA 1998, s 36.

outside Art 3(2) of the DPD, was rejected. The Court considered that Mrs Lindqvist's activities could not be seen as having been carried out in private or in the course of her family life, because they involved publication of data on the Internet to 'an indefinite number of people'.[26]

The implications of this case, which is often described as a 'highwater' mark of DP maximalism, have been much criticised. In principle it implies that every user of social networking services (SNSs) whose posts mention any of their friends, and who does not restrict the audience of their posts, is likely technically to be a data controller. Many have argued this is an unnecessary incursion of bureaucracy into the quasi-domestic, and certainly non-profit-making, sphere.[27] The A29 WP has responded by suggesting that users of SNSs should primarily be seen as data subjects, with the main responsibilities of the data controller falling on the social network.[28] The GDPR, despite much debate on the issue, still defines the household exemption as applying only to 'a natural person in the course of a purely personal or household activity'[29] and text which would have limited it to cases 'where it can be reasonably expected that it will be only accessed by a limited number of persons' failed to reach the final text.[30] Indeed, in the more recent case of *Rynes*,[31] the hardline approach to the exemption has been restated, with the Court excluding from the exemption a householder whose CCTV system surveilled the public space beyond his own house, even though the purpose was merely to defend private property. The Court argued that exemptions to a fundamental right must be narrowly construed, especially where video surveillance of public space was concerned. The narrowness of the household exemption is likely to become less problematic in practical terms, however, with the removal of the obligation of notification for data controllers (see p 92 below).

IV. Personal, Anonymous and Pseudonymous Data

'Personal data' is, according to the GDPR, 'any information relating to an identified or identifiable natural person'. An identifiable person is one who can be identified from

---

[26] Case C-101/01 *Lindqvist* (ECJ, 6 November 2003) at [47].

[27] See, eg, R Wong, 'Social Networking: Anybody is a Data Controller!', *BILETA Conference*, 2007, Glasgow Caledonian University; R Wong and J Savaramithu, 'All or Nothing: This is the Question? The Application of Art. 3(2) Data Protection Directive 95/46/EC to the Internet' (2008) 25 *John Marshall Journal of Computer & Information Law*.

[28] Note however in the AG Opinion in *Wirtschaftsakademie Schleswig-Holstein* (n 19), it was asserted that a social network owner of a FB 'fan page' could still be responsible for the collection of analytics data about visitors to that page, even where built-in FB tools were used. Similar results might apply where bloggers run amateur pages on platforms that use built-in Google analytics tools. See further discussion of web analytics cookies in the next chapter.

[29] GDPR, Art 2(c).

[30] See the 'Albrecht report' for the LIBE Committee, ie the Report on the proposal for a regulation of the European Parliament and of the Council on the protection of individuals with regard to the processing of personal data and on the free movement of such data (General Data Protection Regulation) (COM(2012)0011 – C7-0025/2012 – 2012/0011(COD)). Recital 18 of the GDPR does specifically mention social networking as a possible candidate for the household exemption and also emphasises the exclusion of 'professional or commercial activity' from it.

[31] Case C-212/13 *Rynes* (CJEU, 11 December 2014).

that data, directly or indirectly. While the most obvious way of identifying a person is by their name, the Article 4 definition clearly gives examples of non-nymic personal data as including an 'identification number' and 'one or more factors specific to [the data subject's] physical, physiological, genetic, mental, economic, cultural or social identity'. The UK DPA 1998 definition was long notorious for not fully implementing the DPD on this point. It specified, in relation to 'indirectly', that this included the case where the person could not be identified by the information alone, but could be when it was combined with other data 'likely' to be held by the *same* data controller [emphasis added]. This idea of 'mosaic identification' is a common scenario in the age of 'Big Data' (see further next chapter), where users are often profiled and accurately targeted from multiple pieces of personal data held by different data controllers but then merged and mined for insights. The test of likelihood, and the restriction to where two or more pieces of data are held by the same data controller, were not found in the DPD. As we discuss in relation to *Breyer v Germany* below, this transposition would now inarguably be in breach of both the DPD and the GDPR and has vanished from the DPA 2018.[32]

What constitutes personal data is one of the central causes of doubt in the current DP regime, both in the EU generally and in the UK specifically. The definition is crucial, because it is a threshold requirement to the application of any of the DP rules. Yet studies have shown in the past that there is a wide variation across the EU as to how the phrase is interpreted both in law and in practice.[33] The definition of personal data in the UK under the DPA 1998 pre-GDPR, already restricted as noted above, was limited further by judicial activism in the case of *Durant v FSA*[34] in 2003. In that case, the Court held that:

> Mere mention of the data subject in a document held by a data controller does not necessarily amount to his personal data. Whether it does so in any particular instance depends on where it falls in a 'continuum of relevance or proximity' to the data subject as distinct, say, from transactions or matters in which he may have been involved to a greater or lesser degree.

The Court added that if the data was 'biographical in a significant sense, that is, going beyond the recording of the putative data subject's involvement in a matter or event that has no personal connotations', then it was likely to be regarded as personal data.[35]

This restrictive definition had practical consequences, for example in the context of CCTV,[36] and was explicitly criticised by the A29 WP.[37] Under the GDPR after

---

[32] See also DPD, Recital 26.

[33] Case C-582/14 *Breyer v Germany* (19 October 2016). See the excellent pan-EU survey commissioned by the Information Commissioner's Office (ICO), 'What are Personal Data?' (Sheffield University, 2004).

[34] *Durant v FSA* [2003] EWCA Civ 1746. The meaning of personal data in the context of anonymised medical data was also discussed in the Scottish freedom of information case, *Common Services Agency v Scottish Information Commissioner* [2006] CSIH 58. The Scottish judgment was reversed by the House of Lords in [2008] UKHL 47, but their Lordships declined to comment on *Durant* as part of the binding opinion, regarding it as irrelevant to the issue at hand, that of effective anonymisation.

[35] *Durant, ibid* [28].

[36] See discussion of this point in L Edwards, 'Taking the "Personal" Out of Personal Data: *Durant v FSA* and its Impact on the Legal Regulation of CCTV' (2004) 1:2 *SCRIPTed* 341.

[37] A29 WP, *Opinion 4/2007 on the Concept of Personal Data*, WP 136, 20 June 2007.

May 2018, the UK's discretion to minimise the scope of personal data in this way disappeared. Perhaps with this in mind, even pre-GDPR, the courts strove to minimise the effect of *Durant*. In *Edem v Information Commissioner*,[38] the Court of Appeal found that, in most cases, it would simply be obvious if data was personal. In the instant case, the debate was around individuals identified by name, which was, the Court found, obviously about personal data, unless the names were so common 'that without further identification, such as its use in a work context, the person would remain unidentifiable'. Only if the case was 'difficult or uncertain' should recourse be given to the 'notions', such as 'biographical' nature, which Auld J had introduced in *Durant*.

The current battlefield in defining personal data is however mainly not about separating 'biographical' data from other data (though see discussion of *YS and others v Ministry of Immigration*, below),[39] but rather to separate data which when collected and processed has the *potential* to have an impact on the personal privacy of particular users, perhaps including their economic and emotional wellbeing, from data which definitively does *not* have such potential. Increasingly, this distinction does not map neatly to a dichotomy between personal data, which is easily linked to a particular name or identifier, and all other data. Data which originally related to a living person but now claims to be 'anonymised' in some sense – perhaps merely by the substitution of an identifier for a name – can still be both very useful to businesses and very intrusive to personal privacy; thus it is crucial that we think hard about when such data is sufficiently separated from impact on a living data subject so as to fall outside the protections of the GDPR.

Nowadays, much of the most valuable data collected online does not look much like 'traditional' personal data, including the 'cookies' used on most websites,[40] browser fingerprints and, most crucially, Internet Protocol (IP) addresses (and MAC addresses, their equivalent for mobile devices). IP addresses are often used to identify and profile consumers who repeatedly visit a website but have not fully completed some identification or registration process. Such profiling can include activities such as online shopping, web searching,[41] downloading media, etc.

IP addresses do not identify a person. They are simply a string of numbers which uniquely identify a networked device; many people in the household (or office, or university) may use a particular machine without its IP address changing. Often the user's externally-viewable IP address will refer not to their exact device but instead to the networking gateway (router) through which they connect to their Internet Service Provider (ISP), meaning that several devices on an internal home or office network can be identified by one IP address. In addition to this, the assigned address will often be

---

[38] *Edem v Information Commissioner* [2014] EWCA Civ 92.

[39] Joint cases C-141/12 and C- 372/12 *YS and others v Ministry of Immigration* (17 July 2016).

[40] See Chapter 5.

[41] See A29 WP, *Opinion on Data Protection Issues Related to Search Engines*, WP 148, 4 April 2008. The Report clearly asserted that the then-DPD clearly applied to search engines which deposited cookies on the machines of EU resident users, even if the search engine was based economically or physically outside the EU (see DPD, Art 4(1)(a)). See also the earlier *Working document on determining the international application of EU data protection law to personal data processing on the Internet by non-EU based web sites* WP 56, 30 May 2002, as confirmed recently in the *Google Spain* case (n 6).

temporary, since most consumer ISPs dynamically assign and re-assign IP addresses according to demand (dynamic IP addressing).[42] All of this means that identification will often require a combination of the IP address and the ISP's date and usage logs, and even then it will often refer only to a whole household or office rather than a specific device. Despite these issues, the DPD and the GDPR both clearly recognise that non-nymic identifiers *can*, though need not *always be*,[43] personal data. The A29 WP has taken a fairly aggressive line here, arguing that because IP addresses can often be used to identify data subjects (for example when tracking down file- sharers), it is best practice to regard them as personal data.[44]

After endless years of debate, the matter was addressed by the CJEU in *Breyer v Germany*,[45] in which the Court decided helpfully that IP addresses were indeed personal data, at least in certain circumstances. The case is important because it concerns dynamic IP addresses[46] which were collected by public German informa- tion websites for reasons of cybersecurity. The Court held the addresses did constitute personal data, with respect to the operator of the website, but only if:

> the [operator] has the *means which may likely reasonably be used in order to identify the data subject, with the assistance of other persons,* namely the competent authority and the internet service provider, on the basis of the IP addresses stored (at [48] emphasis added).

This approach is expansive in that it clearly rejects the approach found, as we have noted, in the UK DPA 1998, that personal data can only be indirectly identifiable if the pieces of information that add up to identification are held by *one* data controller. On the other hand, it restricts the scope of personal data by requiring that means of iden- tification by a third party must be 'likely' to be reasonably used. (In the *Breyer* case, identification was accepted to be likely because the data controller was the German Government that had statutory powers to require the disclosure of subscriber details from the ISP indicated as the issuer of the IP address). Though somewhat convoluted, this arguably strikes an acceptable balance both between the positions of various EU Member States, and between the stances of large digital corporations, which are often US-based, and EU privacy sensibilities.[47]

Another battlefield around personal data relates to anonymisation. Many businesses claim that much of their activity that might be of concern in privacy terms – for example social networking, targeted advertising and collection of search data – involves the processing only of anonymised data, and hence does not fall within the

---

[42] This problem is further aggravated by the imminent exhaustion of IP addresses under the current version of the protocol (version 4), and the failure to move wholesale to the newer version 6 which provides an essentially unlimited number of unique addresses. Note some providers also refresh identifiers for privacy purposes; Apple devices do this with MAC addresses.

[43] GDPR, Recital 30.

[44] A29 WP, WP 136 (n 37) at 17.

[45] *Breyer* (n 33).

[46] This is why the case is more significant than the brief assessment by the CJEU of static IP addresses in Case C-70/10 *Scarlet v SABAM* (24 November 2011), which was also a special case in being concerned with processing (filtering) by an ISP that could of course easily identify to whom an IP address had been served.

[47] See Bird and Bird, 'CJEU Decision on Dynamic IP Addresses Touches Fundamental DP Law Questions' (21 October 2016), at www.twobirds.com/en/news/articles/2016/global/cjeu-decision-on-dynamic-ip-addresses-touches-fundamental-dp-law-questions, where this is described as the 'subjective/relative' approach.

scope of DP law. In response, privacy advocates argue that since an anonymised profile, even if not connected to a named user, can still be used to target or 'single out'[48] users – for example, to deny access to luxury services or to alter the price at which goods are sold, as well as simply to target ads[49] – then users suffer just as much as if they were being classified or discriminated against by name.

A further key problem is that anonymisation is itself an increasingly unconvincing process. Scholars such as Ohm[50] have pointed out that it is often possible to 're-identify' or 'de-anonymise' individuals, whose identities are hidden in anonymised data, with astonishing ease. This is partly as a result of 'Big Data' (patterns are easier to spot in a large pool of data, and with more variables, people also become more 'unique in the crowd'[51]), partly because of the growth in 'public' data, via social media, governmental 'open' data and data breaches (think about the Equifax breach of 2017 which exposed over 450 million personal records) and partly because of improved re-identification algorithms. Consider, for example, that users often provide the means of their own unmasking by using the same profile image across various social networks or services, some of which (like FB) identify the user by default.[52]

There is no real consensus as to what constitutes an effective anonymisation algorithm, or even what can reasonably be expected of businesses of various sizes handling data of varying degrees of sensitivity for varying purposes; all these issues affect what may be seen as a reasonable desire for a 'risk based' rather than absolute demand for anonymisation. Public interest is also a difficult issue; the more we anonymise in sensitive areas like medical research, the less easily we may be able to feed back results to actually help the subjects in the study, or even conduct the research at all. The UK Information Commissioner's Office (ICO) 'risk based' Code of Practice on anonymisation has been greeted with skepticism by some experts in the field;[53] the A29 WP recommendations on anonymisation are notably tougher with a fundamental requirement that the process not be reversible.[54] Interestingly, debates during the passage of the DP Bill lead to the introduction of a controversial new criminal offence of re-identifying anonymised data, albeit with a defence to reassure security researchers whose work often involves doing exactly that.

---

[48] See GDPR, Recital 29.

[49] See, eg, the work of Latanya Sweeney in the US on racial discrimination by profiling; A Miller, 'What Do We Worry About When We Worry About Price Discrimination? The Law and Ethics of Using Personal Information for Pricing' (2014) 19 *Journal of Technology Law & Policy* 41. See further discussion of price and service discrimination in the next chapter.

[50] P Ohm, 'Broken Promises of Privacy: Responding to the Surprising Failure of Anonymization' (2010) 57 *UCLA Law Review* 1701.

[51] See YA de Montjoye et al, 'Unique in the Crowd: The Privacy Bounds of Human Mobility' (2013) 3 *Scientific Reports* Article number:1376, doi:10.1038/srep01376.

[52] Acquisti, Gross, and Stutzman have proven in a number of experiments that facial images posted to FB can easily be used to re-identify the subject on other social networking sites. See A Acquisti, R Gross and F Stutzman, 'Face Recognition and Privacy in the Age of Augmented Reality' (2014) 6 (2) *Journal of Privacy and Confidentiality*, available at http://repository.cmu.edu/jpc/vol6/iss2/1.

[53] See ICO, *Anonymisation: Managing Data Protection Risk: Code of Practice*, November 2012 and response from R Anderson for the Foundation for Information Policy Research (FIPR) to the draft ICO Code, at www.cl.cam.ac.uk/~rja14/Papers/fipr-ico-anoncop-2012.pdf. The ICO is the DPA or National Regulatory Agency (NRA) of the UK, ie the regulator, independent from the state and from commerce.

[54] See A29 WP, *Opinion 05/2014 on Anonymisation Techniques*, WP 216, 10 April 2014.

The consistent A29 WP response to these issues – now integrated, after much struggle, into the GDPR, albeit only in the Recitals – has been (as adopted in *Breyer*) that if data can be used to identify a person, directly or indirectly, 'by means reasonably likely to be used by the controller or by any other natural or legal person', then it should be regarded as personal.[55] The idea of '*singling out*' as a litmus test for personal identifiability has been borrowed from US practice and incorporated into Recital 29. This rather confusing division of definition between Article 2 and Recitals 26 and 29 reflects the struggle during the passage of the GDPR with US data giants such as Google and FB, which argued that 'the concept of personal data should be defined pragmatically, rather than upon the likelihood of identification'.[56]

In the midst of the GDPR negotiations, a compromise concept emerged of reinventing 'pseudonymous data' as a kind of personal data which can

> no longer be attributed to a specific data subject without the use of additional information, provided that such additional information is kept separately and is subject to technical and organisational measures to ensure that the personal data are not attributed to an identified or identifiable natural person.[57]

Such pseudonymised data is still, explicitly and importantly, personal data, but its processing is seen as presenting less risk to data subjects, and as such it is given certain privileges designed to incentivise its use. For example, pseudonymisation can be seen as evidence that the data controller has fulfilled the Article 5(f) security obligation, and that they have engaged with Article 25's requirement for DP by design.[58] The combination of harm arising from social profiling and sorting and the ease with which anonymised data can be re-identified means that, in this writer's opinion, any serious reduction in the protection of pseudonymised data – which was mooted but rejected part way through the GDPR process – would signal a step down a very dangerous path.

Meanwhile, the definition of personal data just keeps expanding. As Purtova puts it, given that capacity for (re-)identification is increasing each year, 'although perfect identification may still be a myth, one wonders for how long'. As things are going, at least in the EU, it seems that DP law may indeed be the one law to rule them all in the data-driven society, becoming the '*law of everything*'.[59] This seems something that should be fully considered. Is it the correct path to go down for consumer protection in the era of Big Data, or is it unreasonably expansive, given the complexity and severity of the DP regime post GDPR? More interests are concerned here than merely the oft-mentioned advertising and social media industries. Just as the UK courts sought, probably in error of law, to restrict the scope of DP law to cases where they saw some real connection to invasion of privacy in *Durant*, it may be that the CJEU may also conceivably seek means in the future to again narrow the definition of personal data.

---

[55] Recital 26 and see also factors identified in A29 WP, WP 136 (n 37) 15–17.
[56] See, eg, 'Are IP Addresses "Personal Data"?', Peter Fleischer's blog, 5 February 2007. The division of important rules between main text and Recitals is a continual problem in the GDPR.
[57] GDPR, Art 2(5) and Recitals 26–29; Arts. 6, 25, 32, 40 and 89.
[58] See further below p 110.
[59] N Purtova, 'The Law of Everything. Broad Concept of Personal Data and Overstretched Scope of EU Data Protection Law' (9 September 2017). Available at SSRN: https://ssrn.com/abstract=3036355.

Interestingly, one case already points in this direction, namely *YS and others v Ministry of Immigration*.[60] Here, the CJEU excluded the legal analysis made by immigration officers about a particular family's entry rights from the category of 'personal data', thus denying them subject access rights over it. This was, it was said, information about the *law*, not about the data subjects. '[A]lthough it may contain personal data, it does not in itself constitute such data'. Guaranteeing a right of access to such would enable a right to administrative justice 'not in fact serve the directive's purpose of guaranteeing the protection of the ... right to privacy'.[61] This is remarkably and eerily similar to the rationale of the much-despised *Durant* judgment.[62]

A. Special Categories of Data ('Sensitive Personal Data')

Special category data (known in the UK prior to the GDPR as sensitive personal data) is a subset of personal data which is regarded as so intensely private that special safeguards are needed to guard against abusive processing. As defined in the DPD Article 8, special category data meant data relating to race, political opinions, health and sex life, religious and other beliefs, trade union membership and criminal records. These categories betrayed their historical and cultural origins in 1980s Europe; it can be argued that they exclude some important forms of personal information that are valued in the twenty-first century, for example biometric information (such as fingerprints, retinal scans or DNA) and financial data (such as credit card details). Nor is there any consideration of the subject of the data: it might be argued, for example, that *all* data disclosed by a child is 'sensitive'.[63]

The GDPR adopts the DPD definition of personal data, but adds, 'the processing of genetic data [and] biometric data for the purpose of uniquely defining a natural person'.[64] Following the ECJ decision in *Lindqvist*,[65] where a simple photo of a woman with a note that she had had health problems was held to embody sensitive data, there was a perceived danger that almost all personal images might be seen as sensitive because of the information about skin colour and race contained therein.[66] Interestingly, this theory appears to be rebutted by Recital 51 of the GDPR. As we will

---

[60] *YS and others* (n 39).

[61] *YS and others* (n 39) [46].

[62] Further clarification can be found in the case of Case C-434/16 *Nowak v Irish DPC* concerning whether exam scripts, the mark given and the comments made by the markers are 'personal data'; the AG's opinion delivered 20 July 2017 found that comments made by a marker were nonetheless the personal data of the candidate as relating indirectly to the candidate. The opinion was broadly upheld in the final judgment of the CJEU on 20 December 2017.

[63] Compare the US system, which lacks an omnibus regime akin to the EU's data protection law and has no general concept of 'sensitive personal data', but *does* have specific and highly regulated statutory privacy regimes for health, financial and children's data (Health Insurance Portability and Accountability Act of 1996 (HIPAA), Sarbanes-Oxley and Children's Online Privacy Protection Act (COPPA)).

[64] GDPR, Art 9. Biometric and genetic data are themselves defined in Art 2(13)–(14).

[65] *Lindqvist* (n 26).

[66] See, eg, *Murray v Big Pictures (UK) Ltd* [2007] EWHC 1908 (Ch) where the Court noted, *obiter*, with regard to a photo of JK Rowling's (white) baby taken while the infant was wheeled through a public street, that 'if a photograph and the information it contains constitutes personal data, then it is hard to escape from the conclusion that insofar as it indicates the racial or ethnic origin of the data subject it also consists of sensitive personal data' (per Patten J at [80]).

see below, finding lawful grounds to process sensitive data can be challenging for businesses, and in some cases the level of protection may be hard to meet or justify. Wong[67] has suggested that a more contextual, less firmly predetermined attitude to sensitive personal data might be appropriate, but the GDPR rejects such an approach.

A considerable issue which will be discussed in full in the next chapter is that modern machine learning (ML) algorithms have the capacity to process 'ordinary' personal data to produce inferences which may be sensitive. A classic case involved the supermarket Target processing shopping receipts from customers via its loyalty scheme, and generating in one case an inference that a girl was pregnant. Discount vouchers for pregnancy care goods were then sent to her home address. According to urban legend, this caused consternation as her father did not know she was pregnant – but Target's algorithm did. Health data – special category data – had been created out of ordinary receipts.[68] Should the standard of data protection associated with processing such data be the higher standard for special category data? And if so from when should that standard apply? When does the controller know they are dealing with sensitive data? Need they have the intent to produce it and what if it is erroneous (quite possible given the error rate of ML inferencing?). Facebook regularly sells to advertisers insights that a user is 'interested in' gay matters, certain illnesses or particular religions – but deny that this implies they should have got explicit consent to the generation of those *inferences* (as opposed to the collection a priori of sexual, health or religious data). This is a hugely difficult and, ironically, 'sensitive' question in many spheres, eg when data about political views, also special category data, is generated from the analysis of day to day behaviour to send targeted adverts in elections. The European DP Supervisor (EDPS) has recently argued on this point that 'explicit consent would be essential for processing any sensitive information which … *reveals* … political views',[69] which seems to apply the higher standard at the time of *collection* not just at the time of inferencing. Given the increasing power of ML algorithms, this might lead us to the inexorable conclusion that not only is 'everything personal data' as per Purtova, but perhaps even, 'everything is special category data'. This might be a strong argument to reconsider the division entirely. Another pragmatic approach, espoused by the ICO, might be to argue that data is only sensitive when it is processed with intent to exploit its sensitive characteristics.

V. The GDPR Core Principles

Article 5 of the GDPR lays down six fundamental DP principles:

1. *Lawfulness.* Personal data shall be processed fairly, lawfully and in a transparent manner.

---

[67] R Wong, 'Data Protection Online: Alternative Approaches to Sensitive Data?' (2007)(2) *Journal of International Commercial Law and Technology* 9.

[68] See 'How Target Figured Out A Teen Girl Was Pregnant Before Her Father Did' *Forbes* (16 February 2012).

[69] See Opinion 3/2018 EDPS *Opinion on Online Manipulation and Personal Data* 23 March 2018 at 17 (emphasis added). This might be particularly relevant when building such an ML system in terms of the need for a prior DP impact assessment (DPIA).

2.   *Purpose limitation*. Personal data shall be collected for specified, explicit and legit-imate purposes, and shall not be further processed in a manner incompatible with those purposes.

3.   *Data minimisation*. Personal data shall be adequate, relevant and limited to what is necessary in relation to the purpose or purposes for which it is processed.[70]

4.   *Accuracy*. Personal data shall be accurate and, where necessary, kept up to date. If inaccurate it should be erased or updated.

5.   *Storage limitation*. Personal data shall not be kept in a form which permits identi-fication of data subjects for longer than is necessary for the purposes for which it is processed.

6.   *Integrity and confidentiality*. Personal data shall be processed in a manner that ensures appropriate security. Appropriate technical and organisational measures shall be taken against unauthorised or unlawful processing, and against accidental loss, destruction, or damage.

Although not named as such, Article 5(2) also introduces what is effectively a new seventh principle, that of *accountability*. This principle places a burden of proof on businesses to demonstrate their compliance with the GDPR provisions, but it is also supposed to promote substantive compliance not become a mere box-ticking exercise. In order to demonstrate compliance, the data controller is required to employ appro-priate organisational and technological measures, which may be reviewed and updated where necessary.[71] Interestingly, there is an implied element of risk assessment in this: smaller enterprises or those performing more routine processing, perhaps not involv-ing either sensitive data or profiling, may feel required to do less than larger enterprises or those engaging in these forms of processing. The UK strongly advocated a risk-based approach during the GDPR debates, arguing that it reduced the burden of the changes on small and medium sized enterprises (SMEs).[72] The A29 WP on the other hand has argued that a risk-based approach is inappropriate where the protection of a human right is concerned, and that it may well be a stalking horse for a fully-fledged postponement of GDPR obligations from the point of *collection* of data to its mere *use*.[73]

A similarly scaled obligation is placed on all public sector bodies and commer-cial enterprises, which either (i) require regular and systematic monitoring of data subjects on a 'large scale', or (ii) process sensitive data under Article 9 on a 'large scale' and/or personal data relating to criminal convictions and offences, to designate a DP officer (DPO).[74] Enterprises deemed to be carrying out processing with a 'high

---

[70] These three principles are especially important in the context of Big Data and machine learning. See discussion in the next chapter.

[71] GDPR, Art 24. For an interesting examination of this principle, see L Urquhart et al, 'Demonstrably Doing Accountability in the Internet of Things' (22 January 2018), available at https://arxiv.org/abs/1801.07168.

[72] See Ministry of Justice, *Summary of Evidence Submitted in Response to Consultation on the Proposed EU DP Framework*, June 2012.

[73] Which, as we will see in the next chapter, is one of the suggested ways to adjust DP Law to make it more compatible with Big Data. See A29 WP *Statement on the role of a risk-based approach in data protection legal frameworks*, WP 218, 30 May 2014.

[74] GDPR, Art 37. See adopted A29 *Guidelines on Data Protection Officers* ('DPOs'), WP243rev.01_en. The DPO does not need to be an employee and at least one enterprising law firm has launched a scheme to provide 'out-sourced' DPOs.

risk' to the rights and freedoms of users[75] must also carry out DP impact assessments ('DPIAs' – see further below). If such assessment shows a need for measures that can mitigate the risk, the enterprise must seek prior approval from its DPA before engaging in the processing.

The *quid pro quo* for the accountability principle is that it replaces the need for data controllers to notify their local DPA regarding their processing of personal data,[76] a requirement imposed by the DPD which was increasingly seen as needlessly bureaucratic and which also had the potential to criminalise ordinary users of social networks and cloud services which might not benefit from the household exemption (see above p 83) and were unaware of their status as data controllers. There are concerns, however, first that the shift away from notification will cut off the major revenue source of many (already underfunded) DPAs,[77] and second, that accountability, rather than being the panacea it is sometimes portrayed as,[78] may in fact create yet another paper-filling quality assurance industry.

VI. Grounds for Lawful Processing of Data (Art 6)

With respect to the first principle above, the GDPR sets out a number of conditions, only one of which need apply, before personal data may be processed.[79] There is a stricter regime for specified categories of 'special category data' (discussed below), wherein processing is only permitted if one of the Article 6 conditions is met, *and* there is the *explicit* consent of the data subject although in some rare circumstances another exemption may apply.[80]

The best-known ground for rendering processing lawful (though it is given no precedence in the text of the legislation) is that the data subject has given her consent.[81] As we shall see below, however, consent is increasingly failing as an effective threshold condition in a world where users regularly rubberstamp standard term contracts to access online services, effectively giving away their personal data without meaningful consideration, negotiation or safeguards.

[75] GDPR, Arts 35–36.

[76] See formerly DPD, Art 18.

[77] Annual fees charged for notification (£500 pa in 2017 for large controllers, £35 for the rest) were the principal revenue stream of the ICO under the DPA 1998. The Digital Economy Act 2017 ss 108–111 replaced this income with a data controller tax which depends on the size of the data controller and may well be more costly than the previous regime. See AmberHawk Blog 'Large Controller "Registration" Fee Likely to Soar to £7K per Year under the GDPR' (1 April 2017), available at http://amberhawk.typepad.com/amber-hawk/2017/04/large-business-registration-fee-could-increase-to-7k-per-year-as-a-result-of-the-gdpr.html.

[78] See further A29 WP *Opinion on Accountability*, WP 173, 13 July 2010. The A29 WP view is that accountability 'contributes to moving data protection from "theory to practice"'.

[79] GDPR, Art 6. There has been debate as to whether it is legitimate for a controller to suggest that particular data processing is justified by more than one ground. What seems a good rule of thumb is that having a 'fall back' ground might be possible but should not be used to mislead or confuse the user or reduce their rights, eg the Art 17 right to reassure (see below). In particular, if user consent is obtained, the controller should not then 'fall back' on legitimate interests if the consent turns out to be invalid, eg because (see below) it was not 'freely obtained' because it was secured as part of an employment contract.

[80] GDPR, Art 9; see below.

[81] *Ibid*, Art 6(1)(a).

Other important grounds than consent do exist to render processing lawful, *inter alia* that the processing is necessary for the performance of a contract to which the data subject is a party,[82] that it is necessary for compliance with a legal obligation,[83] that it is necessary to protect the data subject's 'vital interests'[84] or that the processing is in the public interest.[85]

One ground which is commercially relevant but sometimes controversial is that in Article 6(1)(f), which says that processing may be carried out if 'necessary' for the purposes of the data processor's 'legitimate interests', *except* where these interests are overridden by the interests or fundamental rights and freedoms of the data subject. (Note that this ground is not available to public authorities, which must depend on a claim of public interest or official, usually statutory, authority.[86]) The terminal sub-clause is essential here, otherwise any business (for example an advertiser) could ride roughshod over the privacy rights of individuals on the grounds that to do so is useful for its lawful business. Traditionally this provision has been seen as setting up a balance between the interests of the business and the rights of the data subjects affected[87]; however, the CJEU case of *Bavarian Lager*[88] suggested instead that where there is any incursion which materially affects the privacy of the individual data subject, the interests of the business must give way.

The most significant recent interpretation of legitimate interests was in the *Google Spain*[89] case (discussed in more depth below) in which Google claimed that its collection and processing of personal data to enable its search engine facility, was lawful on the grounds of Article 6 'legitimate interests'. The Court, which was clearly aware that the 'spidering' of content that enables search engines might invade the privacy of unaware or nonconsenting users, seemed surprisingly relaxed about accepting this argument, claiming that it struck a 'fair balance': 'merely the economic interest' of the operator was not enough on its own, but it was significant that there were also 'legitimate interest[s] of internet users potentially interested in having access to that information'.[90] In other words, the economic interest of Google could well have been trumped by the rights of users who did not wish information about them to be indexed, had it not been for the general *public* interest of all users in being able to access information on the Internet via search engines. This ingenious theory nevertheless does not

---

[82] *Ibid*, Art 6(1)(b).

[83] *Ibid*, Art 6(1)(c).

[84] *Ibid*, Art 6(1)(d).

[85] *Ibid*, Art 6(1)(e). An interesting point is if a private controller can claim they are lawfully processing data in the public interest under (e): there seems no reason why not (even though public authorities in contrast cannot claim the legitimate interests ground under 6(1)(f)) but the processing must be authorised by EU or Member State law (Art 6(3)). Hence, for eg, Google could not claim that the processing of data to build Google Maps was lawful by virtue of Art 6(1)(e), even if it was argued there was public interest in such being built.

[86] *Ibid*, Art 6(1)(e).

[87] See most recently, Case C-13/16 *Rigas* (CJEU, 4 May 2017. Note in this case the CJEU refused to allow a public body to use the legitimate interests ground to process personal data, insisting instead that they use a ground sanctioned by national law; this exclusion from Art 6(1)(f) is now explicit in the GDPR.

[88] Case T-194/04 *Bavarian Lager v Commission of the EC*, Judgment of the Court of First Instance, 8 November 2007.

[89] *Google Spain* (n 6).

[90] *Google Spain* (n 6) [81].

take account of how the processing of *sensitive* (special category) personal data by Google is justified, where 'legitimate interests' are not a lawful ground for processing (see further below).[91] Nor does it really explain how special care is to be taken in the balancing exercise for the interests of children as data subjects as is now required by Article 6(1)(f).

The A29 WP opinion on the legitimate interest of data controllers emphasised that this provision should not be used as '"a last resort" for rare or unexpected situations', and that it should not be 'automatically chosen' or 'unduly extended on the basis of a perception that it is less constraining than the other grounds'.[92] They also provided a useful seven step guide to data controllers on how to carry out the balancing test. While the GDPR does not provide this level of guidance, it is clear in Recital 47 that a great deal will rest on the 'reasonable expectations' of the data subject in the context of the processing. On the other hand, it is also made explicit that both fraud protection[93] and direct marketing may be 'legitimate' reasons for data processing (though as we shall see in the next chapter, separate rules in (currently) the Privacy and Electronic Communications Directive (PECD) (discussed in depth in next chapter) may require prior consent to be obtained from a user to direct marketing, regardless of the chosen ground for lawful processing).

A. Lawful Grounds for Processing Special Category Data

In the case of special category data, the requirement of fair and lawful processing must be satisfied, but in addition to this at least one of a number of further conditions must also be satisfied.[94] These include that

(i)   the data subject has given *explicit consent*;
(ii) processing is necessary to protect the vital interests of the data subject;[95]
(iii) processing relates to data manifestly made public by the data subject;[96]
(iv) processing is necessary for legal reasons (including obligations under employment and social security law), or for the administration of justice;

---

[91] Though see n 96 below. This objection has been spearheaded by David Erdos, see video discussion at www.cam.ac.uk/research/discussion/will-one-be-forgotten-internet-freedom-and-data-protection-after-google-spain http://edu.ava360.com/will-one-be-forgotten-internet-freedom-and-data-protection-after-google-spain_b46dc941f.html.

[92] A29 WP, *Opinion 06/2014 on the notion of legitimate interests of the data controller under Article 7 of Directive 95/46/EC*, WP 217, 9 Apr 2014.

[93] In *Breyer* (n 33), the CJEU accepted that the collection of dynamic IP addresses, which were personal data, could potentially be justified by 'legitimate interests', namely the protection of the security of the data controller's website.

[94] GDPR, Art 9.

[95] *Ibid*, Art 9(2)(c).

[96] *Ibid*, Art 9(2)(e). See further *Murray* (n 66). Interestingly, this would seem to allow processing without *explicit* consent of sensitive data made available on SNSs such as FB – good news both for SNS operators and for third parties such as direct marketers who often collect personal data from SNS pages. It might also provide an explanation for how sensitive personal data could be processed in the *Google Spain* scenario in that only 'public' data is spidered by Google's bots (and even public data can be explicitly excluded from such bots by use of robot.txt files). However, data might have been made public by someone other than the data subject.

(v)   processing is necessary for reasons of 'substantial public interest';[97]

(vi) processing is necessary to establish or defend a legal claim;[98] or

(vii) processing is necessary for the upkeep of public archives or registers, albeit with safeguards for privacy.

It can be seen that in the commercial context the principal requirement for the processing of sensitive data is likely to be 'explicit' consent, which may create difficulties in the increasingly automated and 'smart' world we live in where opportunities for the giving of clear and explicit consent may not always be apparent.[99]

VII. Consent

So what is 'consent', and how does it differ from 'explicit consent'? Consent is one of the key concepts in DP law and yet, oddly, the definition of it from the DPD was never transposed into the DPA 1998 (on the supposition that the nature of consent was well understood in UK law). Under Article 2 of the DPD, consent was defined as 'any freely given specific and informed indication of his wishes by which the data subject signifies his agreement to personal data relating to him being processed'.

The DPD definition of 'ordinary' (non-explicit) consent was seen as less rigorous than the (sometimes equally uncertain) 'explicit consent' required in relation to the processing of *sensitive* personal data.[100] This left a vast chasm of greyness. Could consent be collected via a notice on a website or form with a pre-checked tick box? Did consent mean the same as 'opt in' (a phrase used more associated with the PECD, or did providing a means to 'opt-out' suffice? Could ordinary consent, since it is not required to be explicit, be given by silence or inaction, or was some kind of signifier of affirmation required? Feelings on these matters varied considerably among EU Member States, causing confusion and even the threat of regulatory action.[101]

More important even than these national variations in practice was the growing suspicion that, in the digital consumer world, consent had ceased to be meaningful, or even voluntary, and that users had lost all control over the use of their personal data and, as a result, their trust in online services. This has been described as going beyond the 'privacy paradox' to 'privacy cynicism'. As noted in the last chapter, at the time of the introduction of the draft GDPR, less than one third of EU citizens trusted phone companies, mobile communications companies and ISPs, while just over one fifth trusted search engines, social networking sites and email providers. In countless

---

[97] *Ibid*, Art 9(2)(g). Recital 45 of the GDPR makes it clear that it is up to national law whether private controllers may also benefit from using it – compare the situation with Art 6(1)(f) discussed earlier.

[98] *Ibid*, Art 9(2)(f).

[99] See further in the next chapter.

[100] GDPR, Art 9(2)(a).

[101] An excellent review of the difficulties of consent in the DPD can be found in M Borghi et al, 'Online Data Processing Consent under EU Law: A Theoretical Framework and Empirical Evidence from the UK' (2013) 21 *International Journal of Law and Information Technology* 10.

successive surveys, around 75 per cent of users have reported unease about the uses and re-uses of their personal data, especially in online environments.[102]

When two billion people use FB every day, including children, and people of limited education, or perhaps just limited time, it is beyond credibility that each of them is honestly and meaningfully consenting to the sharing of their personal data in all the ways it is used by FB. (On the other hand we relatively happily accept this illusory standard of consent in relation to most signed documents.) First of all, online consent is primarily obtained by ticking a box, which assumes that the user has read or even scanned the privacy policy on the site. In fact, as boyd[103] and others have extensively shown, privacy policies have become excessively long, are difficult for most non-lawyers to read or understand, change frequently (usually amassing greater complexity and wider sets of permissions), and are almost never read. Indeed, there is arguably no purpose in reading them, since their terms cannot be negotiated. Standard term consumer contracts are nothing new, but competition theory predicts that a market will spawn competitors that offer a variety of choices, including choices in data privacy, to users. However, in the social networking market, and also successively the search engine and cloud services markets, this does not seem to have happened. There are a number of reasons for this, most notably what is known as the 'network effect': the idea that if a large number of people use a data-driven service then it will be difficult to leave, because any new service will not provide equivalent connectivity, and so such markets tend to become monopolistic or at best oligopolistic. This is most vividly demonstrated by social networks: a new social network start-up with no or few users will struggle to attract new ones, even if its features or respect for data privacy surpass the incumbents. People go, or stay, where their f(F)riends are. Thus competition does not operate to create a functioning market, and consent does not operate as a means by which consumers can exert control over their personal data, short of refusing to interact with the digital world at all.[104] And is it reasonable nowadays to say that real consent can be exercised, in conditions of market failure, by refusing to join any social network or use any search engine? I would argue not. Such technoluddism has moved from the inconvenient to the ludicrous: social media these days is where jobs are found, networks forged, identities constructed, goods and services sourced, political dissidence organised. Asking users to protect their privacy by leaving social media is both fruitless and misguided – why should

---

[102] Such surveys of course vary hugely methodologically and in how questions are posed. But see, eg, ICO Annual Track 2016 for UK adults: 'Only 1 in 4 UK adults trust businesses with their personal information. High street banks are the most trusted, internet brands the least' at https://ico.org.uk/about-the-ico/research-and-reports/information-rights-research/; DotEveryone, *People, Power and Technology* (February 2018): 'People are fed up with online products and services which many feel are deliberately designed to obfuscate. 89% of people want clearer terms and conditions; more than half would like to know about the use and security of their data but can't find this out' at http://attitudes.doteveryone.org.uk/files/People%20 Power%20and%20Technology%20Doteveryone%20Digital%20Attitudes%20Report%202018.pdf.

[103] See d boyd, *Its Complicated: The Social Lives of Networked Teens* (Yale University Press, 2014); A McDonald and LF Cranor, 'The Cost of Reading Privacy Policies' (2008–2009) 4 *Journal of Law and Policy for the Information Society* 543.

[104] This complex argument is explained at length in L Edwards, 'Privacy, Law, Code and Social Networking Sites' in II Brown (ed), *Research Handbook On Governance Of The Internet* (Edward Elgar, 2013). It is illustrated however by the long parade of social networks making a feature of better privacy which have failed to make a dent in FB's audiences, eg Ello, Diaspora, Mastodon et al.

they be the ones who suffer for the bad behaviour of the platform? The failure of the #DeleteFacebook movements, even after the Cambridge Analytica scandal of 2018, demonstrates yet again that users cannot be expected to cut off their digital noses to spite their face.[105]

The problem of consent in the context of personal data is most obvious in digital markets, but it is not restricted to them. For example, many employment contracts require employers to consent to employer surveillance of their workplace, their emails and their telephone calls from work. (Universities do this to their students too.) Few employees will actually read and understand such clauses, and even fewer will turn a job down rather than give consent, there being usually no possibility of negotiating the matter. When one considers children, the power differential is obvious between the child and their school demanding fingerprints in order to access the library or canteen.[106] In all these cases it is difficult to argue that consent is 'freely' given.

There is a strong argument that this failure of what in the US is called 'notice and choice' cannot be fixed by altering the definition of consent, but instead requires an entire change of culture and perhaps of business models moving away from a world where personal data is what funds many of the most used sites on the Internet, rather than the direct charging of users. As discussed further in the next chapter, one approach might be to incentivise 'free' sites like FB to offer subscription models which do not involve tracking data as an alternative to, or even instead of, data-driven business models – an approach successfully pioneered by 'freemium' sites like Spotify. Other legal challenges might include consumer protection law, such as the law of unfair contract terms, or competition law, where a site is deemed to have an abusive position in the market.[107] Both approaches have been and are being tried.[108] At the time of writing, some are suggesting that powerful data monopolies like FB and Google might

[105] Early indications as of April 2018, despite intermittent dips in FB's share price, are that the Cambridge Analytica scandal has not significantly reduced FB's audience or revenues: see 'Facebook Profits Soar as it Brushes off Cambridge Analytica Scandal' *Telegraph* (25 April 2018). FB reported a 63% rise in profits over the first quarter of 2018. One reason why leaving FB is fruitless is because FB collects information about people who do not have FB accounts as well as those who do: these 'shadow profiles' have been one of the key features of the Cambridge Analytica revelations.

[106] See English Children's Commissioner's Report, discussed in *The Guardian* (5 January 2017), 'Children in England Sign Over Digital Rights "Regularly and Unknowingly"', available at www.theguardian.com/society/2017/jan/05/children-england-digital-rights-social-media-terms-conditions-anne-longfield?CMP=Share_iOSApp_Other.

[107] See the repeated attempts over the last decade by the European Commission to bring Google to heel on competition grounds.

[108] On unfair terms law, see, eg, the 2015 Belgian Privacy Commission finding that FB's statement of rights and responsibilities did not comply with the Unfair Consumer Contract Terms Directive, reported in *The Guardian* (23 February 2015), available at www.theguardian.com/technology/2015/feb/23/facebooks-privacy-policy-breaches-european-law-report-finds). It is generally thought though that unfair terms challenges will rarely succeed against a free service. More recent action by the Belgian and three other DPAs against FB seems based only on DP law though still referring, *inter alia*, to issues of fairness, which are, of course, part of the first DP principle. See joint statement of 16 May 2017 at https://autoriteitper-soonsgegevens.nl/sites/default/files/atoms/files/common_statement_16_may_2017.pdf; and the decision of the Belgian courts in February 2018 (see 'Facebook Ordered to Stop Collecting User Data by Belgian Court' *The* Guardian (16 February 2018), available at www.theguardian.com/technology/2018/feb/16/facebook-ordered-stop-collecting-user-data-fines-belgian-court.

even be broken up to create competition, as in the US telecoms market of the early 1980s, or even regulated as public utilities: both of these fixes still seem fairly remote. Notwithstanding, in DP law, an undue amount of emphasis continues to fall on 'fixing' the issue of consent.

Because of this the GDPR drafting process saw much to-ing and fro-ing on the definition of consent (at one stage *all* consent was to be explicit; lobbyists quickly forced a revision). The final definition bundles together concepts from various parts of the DPD with A29 WP guidance, all the while attempting to provide greater safeguards for users but actually (despite the furore of re-consenting by direct marketers) making fairly marginal changes from the DPD. Consent in the GDPR is to be a 'freely given, specific, informed and unambiguous indication of the data subject's wishes', and requires 'a clear affirmative action' which 'signifies agreement'.[109] Silence and pre-ticked boxes to indicate consent are specifically banned (Recital 32). Furthermore, the burden of *proving* consent was given is to fall on the data controller.[110] Consent, it is made clear (but was always presumed to be the case by most scholars), can be withdrawn as well as given.[111] A request for consent that forms part of a written declaration (for example a privacy policy) must be 'intelligible' and written using 'clear and plain language',[112] with failure to do so rendering the request non-binding. This is a fine sentiment, but only court cases will show how enforceable it is.

The GDPR does make a few positively new changes. First, it requires that consent to data sharing not be bundled with other matters in a contract. Instead, such requests must be presented 'in a manner clearly distinguishable from other matters'.[113] This still requires that privacy policies be read if there is to be any impact, however. More useful would have been the inclusion firmly in the main text of the provision that consent to data sharing should not be valid if it is tied as a prerequisite to the provision of a service for which the consent was not necessary. At present this remains, ambiguously, in Recital 43. What is left in the main text, however, is merely that such a conditional arrangement is just one factor, albeit of 'utmost' importance, in assessing if consent was indeed given 'freely'.[114]

Second, Recital 43 – but, again, not the main text – now notes that consent should not 'provide a valid legal ground for the processing of personal data in a specific case where there is a clear imbalance [of power?] between the data subject and the

---

[109] GDPR, Art 4(11). See generally the finalised A29 WP *Guidelines on Consent under Regulation 2016/679* (wp259rev.01), 10 April 2018; and the finalised A29 WP *Guidelines on Transparency under Regulation 2016/679*,WP 260, 11 April 2018. In the UK, the ICO has issued in brief its final GDPR consent guidance (https://ico.org.uk/for-organisations/guide-to-the-general-data-protection-regulation-gdpr/lawful-basis-for-processing/consent/.)

[110] GDPR, Art 7(1). This has inspired the idea of 'consent receipts' which should be given to users every time they agree to share data with a service – see blog at www.digitalcatapultcentre.org.uk/consent-receipts-the-future-of-data-sharing/. It is hard to see how this idea can scale to modern social networks, and even harder to see how this kind of transparency tactic can work in a non-competitive marketplace.

[111] *Ibid*, Art 7(4).

[112] *Ibid*, Art 7(2).

[113] *Ibid*, Art 7(2).

[114] *Ibid*, Art 7(4). This issue has become extremely important in the context of online behavioural advertising (OBA) and refusal of tracking, discussed at length in the following chapter.

controller'. This provision, which draws on the history of control of unfair terms in vendor; consumer contracts, has tremendous potential to bring scrutiny of the sort carried out routinely in consumer regulation to the world of DP.[115] Indeed, Recital 42 specifically mentions that consent clauses should not contain unfair terms. The relegation of these provisions from the main text of the Regulation to its Recitals means, however, that their reach is, again, hard to predict.

Consent prior to the GDPR had arguably become a magic wand that could be waived by any popular online service to secure itself a revenue stream of personal data whilst remaining legally compliant. Whether the GDPR will make a major change to this culture remains to be seen. As we will discuss briefly below, academic, though by no means consumer, attention has begun to turn to finding ways of 'giving users back control', not via more fiddling with notice and choice, but via 'code' solutions which allow data subjects to retain possession of and exercise control over their own data, while still being able to interact with the digital world.[116] We discuss these ideas of personal data storage, portability, and better still, interoperability, in the next chapter.

A. Children's Consent

Children, despite their status as 'digital natives', are said to need particular protection in relation to sharing and processing of their personal data because they may be less aware of the risks involved. This is particularly true in relation to marketing, where childrens' data is harvested intensively from video, toy, game and social networking sites, and may result in lasting profiles.

The age of consent for giving permission for data sharing has in the past been a matter of tremendous national variation in the EU and, indeed, even within the UK. On many sites, for example, FB, the age at which children were legally allowed to use the site was set at 13, a choice driven by US law, namely the Children's Online Privacy Protection Act (COPPA). The GDPR, faced with this diversity, gives Member States discretion to pick an age of consent to data processing for children in a band between 13 and 16 (Art 8).

The DPA 2018 harmonises the relevant age for children in England and Wales at 13.[117] In Scotland, however, the idea of a test of 'general capacity for understanding

---

[115] Note especially that the ICO Consultation document on GDPR consent guidance (2 March 2017) asserts that freely given consent will be 'very difficult to obtain in the context of a relationship where there is a clear imbalance between the data subject and controller' in particular for public authorities and employers. Similar guidance from the A29 WP is found at 7–8 (n 109).

[116] See, eg, the Databox project, a personal data container which allows data subjects to store and use their own personal data, which was originated at the University of Nottingham's Horizon Centre (www.databox-project.uk). See further Chapter 5.

[117] DPA 2018, s 9. See also ICO draft *Consultation: Children and the GDPR Guidance* available at https://ico.org.uk/media/about-the-ico/consultations/2172913/children-and-the-gdpr-consultation-guid-ance-20171221.pdf (consultation closed 28 February 2018). Interestingly, Ireland has just chosen to set this age at 16. How this will affect US companies with headquarters and hence a DPA in Ireland, but which provide services throughout the EU, is not yet clear. From first principles, the law governing a child's capacity would normally be the law of that child's domicile or residence.

of what it means to exercise the right or give such consent' is retained from DPA 1998, which might create considerable difficulty for online services.[118] As in the DPA 1998, however, consent is presumed at age 12. Below the age of consent, consent must be supplied by the parent or guardian.[119] Sonia Livingston, the leading researcher in the UK on children in the digital world, has complained that we have 'little knowledge of the best overall age at which children can reasonably consent to commercial providers using their personal data. For the GDPR to have been informed by evidence, new research should have been commissioned. But it was not'.[120] She demonstrates from prior research that understanding is acquired on a sliding scale and is dependent not just on age but education and wealth. Cynics might argue that the age of 13 was picked simply to be compliant with US service provider practices. Perhaps Scotland's idea of gradated consent is not so odd after all. Another issue is how this age is to be verified; here, service providers might borrow from approaches to age verification being pioneered for access to pornography in eg the Digital Economy Act 2017, Pt 3 – or more likely, they may continue as now to be allegedly (ie, not) verified by use of an adult credit card.

VIII. User Rights

A. Continuing Rights

Under the DPD and now under the GDPR, the rights of data subjects include:

(a) *Access.* The right to access their own personal data without excessive delay or expense.[121] This 'subject access right' (or SAR) is subject to a number of exceptions, and is in practice more often used in specialised contexts, such as employment tribunals, or by journalists, than by 'ordinary' users. Data subjects are entitled to a copy of their data in electronic form where they make the request using electronic means, and such data shall be supplied for free and 'in a commonly used electronic form'.

(b) *Rectification.* The right to control the *integrity* of data relating to the data subject, including the right to rectify inaccurate personal data; this may include the right to add material to incomplete data.[122]

(c) *Right to object.* The right to object[123] to the processing of their personal data, but only where it was legitimised under either the 'legitimate interests' ground or the

---

[118] Based on the competency principle established for 'mature minors' in *Gillick v West Norfolk and Wisbeck AHA* [1985] 3 All ER 402.

[119] GDPR, Art 8.

[120] See S Livingstone, 'If children don't know an ad from information, how can they grasp how companies use their personal data?' (LSE, Media Policy Project Blog, 18 July 2017), available at http://blogs.lse.ac.uk/mediapolicyproject/2017/07/18/if-children-dont-know-an-ad-from-information-how-can-they-grasp-how-companies-use-their-personal-data/.

[121] GDPR, Art 15.

[122] *Ibid*, Art 16.

[123] *Ibid*, Art 21.

'public interest' test.[124] Since these grounds did not involve consent, the implication is that a data subject should retain the ability to 'opt out' of the processing. Importantly, this right extends to 'profiling'[125] which was based on personal data obtained via these grounds. The data subject need only demonstrate 'grounds relating to his or her particular situation' in order to exercise his right.[126] This is considerably more expansive than the right previously enshrined in the UK DPA 1998, under which the right to object existed only if the processing was likely to cause damage or distress.[127] However, data subjects have an absolute right to object to the processing of their data for direct marketing purposes.[128]

(d) *Rights restricting automated decision making and profiling.* The right not to be subject to a decision with legal effect, or which 'significantly affects' the data subject, based solely on the automated processing of data.[129] A typical example is a decision to block, withdraw, or refuse to extend financial credit on the basis solely of automated processing. As the ICO put it, data subjects must be able to obtain human intervention (a 'human in the loop'), express their point of view and obtain an explanation of the decision which can be challenged.[130] This right was extended in the GDPR to encompass a more general concept of profiling,[131] something which is a key issue in the worlds of police predictive profiling and of online behavioural targeting of adverts and services.

This right contained in point (d) is becoming highly important in the modern information society. When it was first introduced in the DPD, in the early days of mainframe computing, the general fear was of input error – typos or contextual confusion such as putting down the wrong address – which might then wrongly prejudice a user's credit, taxation, or employment record (for example). Now, however, the fear is a more generic one that important decisions about hiring, student admission, welfare administration, promotion, criminal sentencing, content moderation, etc are increasingly being taken by data-driven algorithmic systems whose operations are an inscrutable 'black box',[132] and not necessarily just to the data subject, but in many cases *also* to the data controller. In such systems, a challenge may be far harder to launch than in the conventional error scenario, given the frequent lack of any facility that can explain the decisions made by modern 'Big Data' algorithms.

---

[124] *Ibid*, Art 6(1)(e) and (f).
[125] Defined in *ibid*, Art 4(4).
[126] *Ibid*, Recital 69.
[127] DPA 1998, s 10.
[128] See GDPR, Art 21(2).
[129] *Ibid*, Art 22. This right is implemented with some augmentation in DPA 2018, ss 14. Profiling, machine learning and algorithms are addressed in more detail in the next chapter. A much more detailed investigation of the right to object to automated processing, as well as the posited 'right to an explanation', can be found in L Edwards and M Veale, 'Slave to the Algorithm? Why a "Right to an Explanation" Is Probably Not the Remedy You Are Looking For' (2017) 16 *Duke Law & Technology Review* 18, 24–27 (hereafter 'Slave'). See also a shorter updated version in L Edwards and M Veale, 'Enslaving the Algorithm: From a "Right to an Explanation" to a "Right to Better Decisions"?' (2018) *IEEE Security & Privacy Magazine* 16(3) 46–54.
[130] ICO *Overview of the GDPR*, 7 July 2016, at 25.
[131] GDPR, Art 4(4).
[132] See F Pasquale, *The Black Box Society: The Secret Algorithms that Control Money and Information* (Harvard University Press, 2015).

Importantly, this right is very limited. First, it applies only when the processing has been carried out *solely* by automated means.[133] Second, the decision must have legal or *'significant'* effects.[134] Third, it does not apply when the data founding the decision was lawfully processed on the basis that it was necessary for entering a contract, that the processing was authorised by law or, most crucially, that it was based on explicit consent.[135] On the other hand, Article 22(4) goes much further than the DPD in making profiling based on *sensitive* personal data illegal *unless* it was based on explicit consent or public interest. Even then, 'suitable measures to safeguard the data subject's rights' must be put in place, which might include *inter alia* the provision of meaningful information about how the profiling is done, DP impact assessments and independent auditing to ensure processing was fair and transparent.[136]

Article 22 is in essence a right to *object* to algorithmic processing, *not* to demand an explanation of how that processing was done ('algorithmic transparency'). However, a right which *might* usefully be employed to procure an explanation of the behaviour of the 'black box' is found not in Article 22 but rather in the information and subject access rights in Article 15, discussed elsewhere in this chapter, which include not just access to the data which a controller holds about the data subject, but also to *'meaningful information about the logic involved'* in cases of automated decision-making and profiling.[137]

Contrary to some over-excited literature, this so-called 'right to an explanation'[138] is not new but has existed in the DPD since 1995.[139] The problems with the right (if we suppose it exists) are twofold: one legal, one practical. First, there has always been an exception to the right in the form of the protection of trade secrets and intellectual property. A request for the logic behind Google's profiling of personal data might well run up against an IP defence. This probably explains the lack of use of this right throughout the EU. Recital 63 of the GDPR does however counsel that this should not justify 'a refusal to provide *all* information to the data subject'.

---

[133] There is considerable argument over whether this excludes cases where human involvement is minor or nominal rubber-stamping. Examples of entirely automated decision-making are few in real life and arguably not 'significant' – eg, targeted advertising. See discussion in A29 WP *Guidelines on Automated Individual Decision-Making and Profiling for the Purposes of Regulation 2016/679* WP 251, 3 October 2017, revised at 9; and commentary on this guidance in M Veale and L Edwards, 'Clarity, Surprises, and Further Questions in the Article 29 Working Party Draft Guidance on Automated Decision-Making and Profiling' (2017) *Computer Law & Security Review: The International Journal of Technology Law and Practice* at 3.1 (hereafter 'Clarity').

[134] See 'Clarity', *ibid*, at 3.2. Interestingly since the Cambridge Analytica scandal, opinion has shifted away from regarding targeted ads as non-significant, at least when they relate to political preferences.

[135] GDPR, Art 9(2). See 'Clarity' (n 133).

[136] See 'Clarity' (n 133) 3.3.

[137] GDPR, Art 13(2)(f), referring itself to Art 22(1) and (4); and Art 15(1)(h).

[138] See B Goodman and S Flaxman, 'EU Regulations on Algorithmic Decision Making and "a Right to an Explanation"' (2016 ICML Workshop on Human Interpretability in Machine Learning (WHI 2016), New York, USA). Recital 71 relating to 'safeguards' under Art 22(3) also refers explicitly to this right but the inconsistency with its exclusion from the main text of Art 22(3) makes it unclear if it is a mandatory right.

[139] DPD, Art 12(a). Opposing the idea that Art 22 contains a right to an explanation, see Sandra Wachter et al, 'Why a Right to Explanation of Automated Decision-Making Does Not Exist in the General Data Protection Regulation' (2017) *International Data Privacy Law* 2, 76–99. In 'Slave' (n 129), this author and M Veale take the view that a limited right to an explanation can possibly be constructed but may be so uncertain and partial that we should look elsewhere for solutions to algorithmic opacity.

Second, and even more problematically, is the difficulty in presenting the raw behaviour of a machine learning algorithm in an intelligible fashion. There may simply be no causal explanation available in what is primarily a statistical correlation and prediction exercise. Algorithms may internally determine factors for decision-making which do not correspond to any human comprehensible theory of how the decision was made, or use so many variables that a human mind could not make sense of them. Edwards and Veale in 'Slave to the Algorithm?' suggest a number of solutions to this problem, including a number of ways in which a data subject can compare their *own* treatment by the algorithm to *other* data subjects ('subject-centric explanations'):

(i)   *Sensitivity-based* subject-centric explanations: what changes in my input data would have made my decision turn out otherwise?
(ii) *Case-based* subject-centric explanations: which data records used to train this model are most similar to mine?
(iii) *Demographic-based* subject-centric explanations: what are the characteristics of individuals who received similar treatment to me?
(iv) *Performance-based* subject-centric explanations: how confident are you of my outcome?[140]

Algorithmic transparency may be an over-rated right. The history of consumer regulation shows that transparency alone is only a first step towards meaningful challenge and power – and if left to fend alone may result in a 'transparency fallacy'. There is a danger that as with consent, we fixate on the tool and neglect to assess if it actually provides real protection to users. Other GDPR rights we will look at below, such as the 'right to be forgotten', the right to data portability, and incentives towards 'privacy by design', may be more actively useful in allowing data subjects to control how they are profiled and in creating fairer algorithms for all of us. Portability, in particular, might open up the possibility of taking one's data to a service provider with a more appealing, more discrimination-aware (or more transparent) algorithm.[141] Certainly this is a major computer (and social) science research area for the foreseeable future.

B. New Rights in the GDPR

i. Rights to Information or 'Fair Processing Information'

These existed in the DPD but have been elaborated considerably in the GDPR.[142] The information required varies according to whether data is obtained directly from the data subject, in which case it should be supplied at the time data is collected, or from a third party.

---

[140] For a fascinating empirical study of using these approaches in an experiment with Oxford students and hypothetical decisions, see R Binns et al, '"It's Reducing a Human Being to a Percentage"; Perceptions of Justice in Algorithmic Decisions' (ACM Conference on Human Factors in Computing Systems (CHI '18), April 21–26, Montreal, Canada) at https://arxiv.org/abs/1801.10408.
[141] See the full version of this argument in 'Slave' (n 129).
[142] GDPR, Arts 12–14.

One of the reasons why 'privacy notices'[143] or privacy policies have become so long[144] is because of the expanding lists of information which must be made available in the interests of (supposed) transparency. As noted above, this author is skeptical about the value of this approach given the overwhelming evidence that such notices are rarely read. In light of this the ICO championed for a time an approach known as 'short privacy notices', which were intended to convey the essence of the full policy to ordinary users in plain language. It is not clear whether consumers benefitted particularly from this. More recently, the ICO has promoted using 'privacy dashboards' and 'just-in-time' pop-ups to inform people of the ways in which their personal information will be used as they move through an application, rather than merely at the first point of entry. Some innovations are emerging even in the commercial world. For example, Google's revised GDPR-ready privacy policy as of May 2018 includes examples with larger fonts and videos. One approach which recurs regularly is to design 'privacy icons' which will convey the key elements of the privacy policy graphically, in the style of laundry washing instructions or food nutrition labels. Despite some inherent appeal, the efficacy of privacy icons has been again and again proven to be poor, partly because universally comprehensible icons about a nuanced conceptual issue like privacy are very hard to create, partly because without effective audit and enforcement they can be deliberately or innocently misleading, and partly because a critical mass of service providers need to use such icons before users find them familiar and helpful. The problem is chicken-and-egg: unless and until providers believe that users will get value out of such icons, they will not invest in implementing them in the absence of a legal mandate requiring them to do so.[145]

ii. Right to Erasure

This right, better (but erroneously) known as the 'right to be forgotten' (RTBF) emerged from the CJEU in the landmark case of *Google Spain*.[146] In that case, Mr González asked Google to remove a link to a newspaper web page which could be

---

[143] Draft guidance on consent and the GDPR from the ICO, 31 March 2017, is available at https://ico.org.uk/about-the-ico/ico-and-stakeholder-consultations/gdpr-consent-guidance/. The ICO has also provided an online privacy notice generator, intended mainly for SMEs.

[144] As one example, in 2010 the *New York Times* noted that the FB privacy policy had gone from 1,004 words in 2005 to nearly 6,000 words in 2010, longer than the US Constitution. See further, Edwards (n 104).

[145] At one point on the progress of the GDPR, privacy icons were to be mandated: in the final version they are merely optional and mentioned ('visualisation') as a possible way to further transparency (Art 12(7) and Recital 58). Privacy icons might also be designed to be machine readable in standardised formats, an approach which was tried but failed in the Platform for Privacy Preferences (P3P) Project experiments of the dot.com period (see www.w3.org/P3P/). A major EU exercise (PrimeLife) produced a large set of privacy icons in 2011 which appear not ever to have been used in the market. Icons were trialled in the UK as of 2016 as part of a joint exercise between the Digital Catapult and the BSI with a view to a standard being produced, but again seem to have had no concrete outcome. See further, L Edwards, *The Use of Privacy Icons and Standard Contract Terms for Generating Consumer Trust and Confidence in Digital Services* (CREATe Working Paper, 2014/15) criticising the general notion of icons and transparency at www.create.ac.uk/blog/2014/10/31/create-working-paper-201415-the-use-of-privacy-icons-and-standard-contract-terms-for-generating-consumer-trust-and-confidence-in-digital-services/.

[146] *Google Spain* (n 6).

found when people searched for his name. The web page contained publicly-mandated information about a social security debt once owed by Mr González but which had long since been paid. The Court held that:[147]

(i)   Google was indeed processing Mr González' personal data under the DPD as a data controller, in that they *inter alia* collected it, retrieved it, recorded it, organ-ised it, indexed it, stored it, disclosed it, and made it available.[148] It did not matter that the data had already been made public. Since Google determined the means and purposes of this processing, namely to provide a search engine, they were clearly a relevant data controller, even though publication was originally done by the newspaper.

(ii) Under Articles 14 and 12(b) of the DPD (see discussion above on the rights to object to processing), data subjects had a right to demand from a data controller that links about them be removed where the data linked was 'inadequate, irrel-evant or no longer relevant, or excessive'.[149] This right was not affected by the fact the data could merely be removed from the newspaper website, or that the data was at one point truthful, or that publication there was not only lawful but indeed was required by law.[150] The Court held that search engines:

> [made it] appreciably easier for any internet user making a search in respect of the person concerned and may play a decisive role in the dissemination of that informa-tion [thus] it is liable to constitute a more significant interference with the data subject's fundamental right to privacy than the publication on the web page.[151]

As such, Mr González' rights to suppress a link to outdated information about him overrode not only the economic interest of the operator of the search engine, but also the interest of the general public in having access to that information pursuant to a search relating to the data subject's name.[152]

Google Spain has been a vastly controversial decision, inaccurately pilloried as taking little or no account of freedom of speech, and its balance with privacy.[153] Wild accusations that the decision was 'one of the most wide-sweeping internet censorship rulings that I've ever seen' (Wikipedia founder Jimmy Wales, speaking to *BBC News*[154]) took little account of the fact that all that was removed (and on valid grounds) was the *link* between a search on a name, and a particular webpage. The information itself

---

[147] The jurisdiction point in *Google Spain* was also important but is dealt with above p 79.
[148] DPD, Art 2. This apparently obvious conclusion was highly controversial, perhaps partly because of the historic position of online intermediaries as 'neutral' and immunised from liability for third party content; see further Chapter 9.
[149] *Google Spain* (n 6) [93].
[150] *Google Spain* (n 6) [62].
[151] *Google Spain* (n 6) [37] and [80].
[152] *Google Spain* (n 6) [97]. See however the distinction drawn in Case C-398/15 *Manni* (CJEU, 9 March 2017), where it was held a RTBF did not apply against public company registers as the need for legal certainty, mandated by law, outweighed the privacy interests of the data subject. However, a right to restrict access might apply after a sufficiently long period and in exceptional circumstances.
[153] For a strong attempt at this line of argument, see S Kulk and F Zuiderveen Borgesius, 'Google Spain v. González: Did the Court Forget About Freedom of Expression?' (2014) *European Journal of Risk Regulation*, also available on SSRN at http://ssrn.com/abstract=2491486.
[154] 14 May 2014. See www.bbc.co.uk/news/technology-27407017.

remained both on the Web, and in Google's index, and was available via the many other possible searches.[155]

Three years on from the *Google Spain* ruling, assertions that a tsunami of applications would engulf both Google and the courts as public figures sought to bury their past misdeeds do not seem to have come to pass. Some countries such as France and Spain have indeed had a fair number of court rulings; in the UK, the first substantive court challenge (*NT1 and NT2 v Google LLC*) has just made it to the High Court.[156]

Google's own report on trends over three years of the RTBF, issued in February 2018,[157] seems to show that the RTBF has overwhelmingly been used by ordinary data subjects rather than public figures seeking to hide their flaws, against both social media (33 per cent) and conventional news outlets (20 per cent), as well as a range of other websites. Of requested URLs, 85 per cent came from private individuals, while minors made up 5 per cent of requesters. Government officials and politicians generated 3.3 per cent of requested URLs and had a lower delisting rate than private individuals; only 11 per cent of such requests were approved. Another 4.1 per cent of requests came from 'non-governmental' public figures, celebrities and their ilk, who had a 35 per cent delisting success rate. This does not seem to show a major assault on access to truth and freedom of the press. On the other hand, Google's figures do show the rise of a new class of reputation managers: 'high volume requesters', often law firms. Of requesters, 0.25 per cent generated 14.6 per cent of requests and 20.8 per cent of delistings. This does perhaps show a trend towards the 'PR society' fears raised after *Google Spain*.

Two matters remain profoundly controversial in relation to the RTBF. First, what the territorial scope of an erasure decision should be (for example, should a French regulator be able to command that a link be removed not just from Google.fr, or even from all EU domains, but also from Google.com?[158]), and second, how the decision to remove a link should be adjudicated, and by whom (Google alone? A local DPA? Some independent free speech-oriented body? And to whom could such decisions be appealed?). Google, itself no lover of the right it has been forced to implement, has responded to critics as well as it can by making public some of its criteria for removal,[159]

---

[155] One hypothesis of this writer is that most commentators have confused a RTBF 'takedown', where no information is actually removed from the Web, with the far more common copyright take down where information *is* in fact removed and supressed; see again, discussion in Chapter 9.

[156] See *NT1 & NT2 v Google* (n 6). A previous UK court application, *ABC v Google Inc* [2018] EWHC 137 (QB), failed on procedural grounds.

[157] See www.google.com/transparencyreport/removals/europeprivacy/?hl=en.

[158] This matter has been litigated in France by its DPA the Commission nationale de l'informatique et des libertés (CNIL),where global delinking was indeed demanded, and is now going to the CJEU for what should be a very interesting decision (Case C-136/17 *GC v CNIL*): see 'Google's Right to be Forgotten Appeal Heading to Europe's Top Court' *TechCrunch* (19 July 2017), available at https://techcrunch.com/2017/07/19/googles-right-to-be-forgotten-appeal-heading-to-europes-top-court/. See also discussion in Brendan Van Alsenoy and Marieke Koekkoek, 'Internet and Jurisdiction after Google Spain: The Extraterritorial Reach of the "Right to be Delisted"' (2015) 5(2) *International Data Privacy Law* 105.

[159] See Advisory Council to Google Report, available at http://docs.dpaq.de/8527-report_of_the_advisory_committee_to_google_on_the_right_to_be_forgotten.pdf. The A29 WP has also issued useful guidance: see *Guidelines on the Implementation of the Court of Justice of the European Union Judgment on 'Google Spain and Inc. v. Agencia Española de Protección de Datos (AEPD) and Mario Costeja González' C-131/12*, WP 225, 26 November 2014, especially the criteria at p 12; see also Google's 'three years on' report at n 160.

as well as convening an ethical board of advisers, and releasing a welcome, but nevertheless limited, amount of information about how many links have been removed over time and connected analysis.[160]

After *Google Spain*, the 'right to be forgotten' also became part of the GDPR, and indeed, one of its most controversial provisions. Originally drafted before *Google Spain*, and mainly intended as a well-meaning attempt to allow children to hide the mistakes of their youth left for all to see on social networks, the final version in Arts 17 and 18 of the GDPR[161] is much wider than *Google Spain*, in that it applies to all data controllers, not just search engines. After a period of lobbying and fierce debates among scholars, technologists and regulators,[162] the 'right to be forgotten' was redubbed with the less contentious term the 'right to erasure'. Arguably, and as Zanfir persuasively narrates,[163] there is still little new in Article 17, given the pre-existing remedies of Articles 12 and 14 of the DPD. However, the right to erasure is now firmly on the map, with 2.4 million requests for removal of URLs made since May 2014[164] (although nearly half of these, 43 per cent, have been rejected).

Article 17 also to an extent clarifies, in a way which the *Google Spain* decision did not, the exceptions to the right. Although still somewhat vague and in need of national transposition, they do firmly include where freedom of expression would be compromised, what constitutes 'public interest' in the area of health, how the right applies to public archives and in the context of scientific, historical and statistical research, and where legal claims must be decided. In general, it is worth noting the words of the *Google Spain* Court that erasure cannot be justified if 'such [is] the role played by the data subject in public life, that the interference with his fundamental rights is justified by the preponderant interest of the general public ...'[165]

These words and the guideline criteria of the A29 WP[166] were tested for the first time in the UK courts in *NT1 & NT2 vs Google LLC*. Two businessmen, both convicted in the past of criminal offences, complained that Google had refused to remove links between their name when searches were made, and news reports of these crimes. Such cases involving the obscuring of past convictions from the public gaze have been one of the key worries around the RTBF. In both cases, the convictions had become 'spent' under rehabilitation of offenders' laws. Both were deemed by the Court to have been 'public figures' because of their business affairs with the public. (Identities were closely

---

[160] See www.google.com/transparencyreport/removals/europeprivacy/?hl=en.

[161] GDPR, Art 18 deals with the lesser remedy of restriction of processing, rather than erasure.

[162] See, eg, P Fleischer, 'The Right to Be Forgotten, or How to Edit Your History', Peter Fleischer's blog, 29 Jan 2012, available at http://peterfleischer.blogspot.co.uk/2012/01/right-to-be-forgotten-or-how-to-edit.html; P Bernal, 'A Right to Delete?' (2011) 2(2) *European Journal of Law and Technology*, available at http://ejlt.org/article/view/75/144; J Koops, 'Forgetting Footprints, Shunning Shadows: A Critical Analysis of the "Right to Be Forgotten" in Big Data Practice' (2011) 8:3 *SCRIPTed* 229, available at https://script-ed.org/?p=43; ML Ambrose and J Ausloos, 'The Right to Be Forgotten Across the Pond' (2013) 3 *Journal of Information Policy* 1, also available on SSRN at http://ssrn.com/abstract=2032325.

[163] G Zanfir, 'Tracing the Right to be Forgotten in the Short History of Data Protection Law: The "New Clothes" of an Old Right' (October 2013), available on SSRN at http://ssrn.com/abstract=2501312.

[164] See the excellent report prepared by Google on the first three years of operation of the RTBF by T Bertram et al at https://drive.google.com/file/d/1H4MKNwf5MgeztG7OnJRnl3ym3gIT3HUK/view.

[165] *Google Spain* (n 6) [98].

[166] See A29 WP, WP 225 (n 159).

kept secret during the case.) However, the Court distinguished between the two cases, ordering Google to remove the links in the case of NT2 but not NT1. Why was this distinction made?

NT2's sentence was shorter, his contact with the public was now limited, his past offending had little relevance to his current business and he had admitted guilt and shown remorse. NT1 by contrast, had never admitted guilt nor shown remorse. Yet as the case narrates, his sentence too had become spent (albeit only because the law had changed since the time of his original sentencing) and he no longer had contact with consumers in his business life. The distinction seems to rest as much on the moral lack of reformation he had shown, as the practical issue of whether the public had a right (or need) to know about his prior convictions. There is a worrying element here as to whether unelected judges should essentially have a discretionary right to overrule even partially the effect of the rehabilitation statutes, even in edge cases like NT1. Future cases will no doubt clarify and expand on interpretative guidance.

iii. Right to Data Portability

This right sits rather oddly in the GDPR, because it might be seen as less a matter of DP and more a right concerned with consumer protection, or competition, law. Alternatively, however, it might be seen as the logical derivative of the subject access rights, discussed above, as applied in the modern information age. Article 20 provides that data subjects have the right to receive their personal data, which they 'provided' to a controller, in a 'structured, commonly used and machine readable format', and that they then have the right to transmit that data to another controller 'without hindrance'.[167]

As noted above in the discussion of the futility of 'notice and choice', one of the problems with markets in data-driven network services is that competition fails to operate properly because users are often locked into 'walled gardens': online services where data is held in proprietary formats and access to it is controlled by the service provider, with little or no way to move that data to another, competing service. Put simply: how does a user move all her posts, photos and contacts from Facebook over to a competing social network? For most of us, this appears to be an impossible task, and it is this problem that the right to data portability is primarily intended to ameliorate. Similar issues arise most prominently in the energy markets: suppliers hold very useful cumulative personal data about the energy consumption of their customers; if users could access that data, the theory is that a new market could evolve that would make it easier to switch providers, thus empowering consumers,[168] fostering innovative new services and also, hopefully, reducing energy consumption.

In fact, the UK was so enamoured with this theory that even prior to the GDPR it had commenced the 'Midata' scheme which encouraged companies, especially in

---

[167] This also included the right to have the data directly transmitted from controller A to controller B, see GDPR, Art 20(2).

[168] See, persuasively, *Personal Data Empowerment: Time for a Fairer Data Deal?* (Citizens Advice Bureau, April 2015) at https://www.citizensadvice.org.uk/about-us/policy/policy-research-topics/consumer-policy-research/consumer-policy-research/personal-data-empowerment-time-for-a-fairer-deal/.

the energy sector, voluntarily to allow portability rights.[169] Midata was a voluntary scheme, but the 2013 Enterprise and Regulatory Reform Act also gave the Government extra potential legislative powers if particular industry sectors reneged on the idea. So far these have not been used.

Neither Article 20 nor Midata provide the next step beyond portability, *interoperability*. A user can now, in theory, ask for all her data held by a provider like FB, and receive it in a machine readable format to take elsewhere.[170] The question arises, however: why would she go elsewhere when all her friends are still on FB and she cannot interact with them online except through that platform? True interoperability would allow users to network with friends on FB using external third-party tools, without providing FB with any personal data as the price of admission. For exactly this reason – that it subverts the business model of free-to-user sites – true interoperability is still a long way down the road, and with it real competition and real consumer empowerment.[171]

Meanwhile, interesting details of the right to portability remain to be clarified. What data exactly does the data subject have the right to export? Just the date explicitly given to a controller by a data subject, or data *observed* by the data controller, for example, the behaviour of a user as the user interacts with a site like FB or Amazon? This 'behavioural' metadata is often as valuable as explicit data in terms of profiling and may also be as privacy-invasive. The A29 WP guidance[172] emphasises that although Art 20 refers to data 'provided by' the data subject, this should also include personal data that are '*observed* from the activities of users such as raw data processed by a smart meter or other types of connected objects, activity logs, history of website usage or search activities'.[173] However, it distinguished, and excluded from portability rights, *inferred* personal data '*created by the data controller* (using the data observed or directly provided as *input*) such as a user profile created by analysis of the raw smart metering data collected' [emphasis added].

This distinction seems strange, particularly when compared to the Art 17 RTBF. Data portability is conceptually a sibling right to Art 17. In theory, a data subject can

---

[169] See www.gocompare.com/money/midata.

[170] This is, famously, what Max Schrems did prior to launching his case against FB. This case will be discussed later in the chapter.

[171] Attempts were made to build interoperability tools as part of the CREATe project of which this author is deputy director (create.ac.uk). The technical team was spearheaded by the Horizon team at Nottingham University. The attempts were stymied by constant changing of the application programming interfaces (APIs) to access and withdraw data from FB – effectively creating an access 'arms race'. A trivial but interesting example of true interoperability can be observed between the niche social network Live Journal and its open source clone, Dreamwidth. Users can post from either site to both sites and receive and answer comments on both sites without needing to log in separately to both sites. Hence the 'friends list' is not lost by moving, as many did, from Live Journal to Dreamwidth. The site Mastodon is currently trying to achieve this for more mainstream social networking.

[172] See A29 WP *Guidelines on the Right to Data Portability,* WP 242 rev.01, revised and adopted on 5 April 2017. The matter has created confusion already in the case of FB which have publicised its Download Your Data tool as allowing users access and control to all the data FB holds on them, ie fulfilling their subject access rights under GDPR, Art 15. However, privacy advocates have found that the data supplied is only that required by Art 20, and does not include inferences about the user, nor data gathered about the user from third party sites; see further, 'What's Not Included in Facebook's "Download Your Data"' *Wired* (23 April 2018).

[173] See A29 WP, WP 242 at 10.

ask for their data to be erased from one site (eg Google) and at the same time ported into their own hands.[174] Yet we seem to have a clear conflict with the already acknowledged right of a data subject to erase an inference from Google's search algorithm under *Google Spain*. Admittedly, that right is derived from the DPD and not as yet any case litigated under the GDPR – but it is hard to see any rolling back of the extent of that right.[175]

Furthermore, Article 20 only applies to data provided by 'consent' (Art 20(1)(a)) – accordingly if data has been collected and profiled under another lawful ground such as the legitimate interests of the data controller, no right to portability exists.[176] Last, it is worth emphasising this right only covers data which was being processed by 'automated means'[177] – though not, as in Art 22, '*solely*' automated means.

IX. Privacy by Design and by Default

As we have seen above, traditional legal safeguards for data privacy, especially consent, are suffering in the modern, data driven world. Policymakers are increasingly considering how 'code'[178] can protect privacy, rather than legislating, as is traditional, to regulate *people* rather than technologies. The European Commission has supported Privacy Enhancing Technologies (PETs)[179] for many years, and the general public too is beginning to understand the value, especially following the Snowden and Cambridge Analytica revelations, of tools such as encryption, Personal Data Containers (PDCs) and, perhaps most significantly, ad-blockers. 'Privacy by Design'[180] is now for the first time incorporated into the general scheme of the GDPR, under the term 'DP by design' ('DPbD'). Article 25 provides that controllers shall apply software design principles as well as organisational measures to 'engineer in' privacy protection throughout the development, as well as the data capture, processes.

Recommended principles to enable 'privacy by design' include pseudonymisation of data (see the discussion above) as well as minimising the collection of data. In particular, Article 25 recommends that, by default, applications or systems collect only the data necessary to fulfil those purposes that have been made known to users.

---

[174] GDPR, Art 20(3). But note the right to erasure covers data 'concerning' a data subject rather than as here, merely 'provided' by the data subject. The latter is considerably more restrictive.

[175] See a fuller discussion of the consequences of this odd dichotomy for machine learning in 'Slave' (n 129) at 5.2.1.1 and 5.2.2.

[176] This bizarre choice can only be explained by thinking of Art 20 as a solution to promote competition by allowing data subjects to make active choices to retrieve their voluntarily posted data from social networks.

[177] GDPR, Art 20(1)(b).

[178] The term 'code as law' originates with L Lessig, *Code Version 2.0* (Basic Books, 2006). See discussion in Guadamuz in Chapter 1.

[179] See *Communication from the Commission to the European Parliament and Council, Promoting Data Protection by PETs* COM (2007) 228 final, 2 May 2007.

[180] Term coined in Canada by A Cavoukian. See *Privacy by Design, Take the Challenge* (Information and Privacy Commissioner of Canada, 2009). See further discussion on PDCs and ad-blockers in the next chapter on profiling.

Data minimisation is of course now a distinct DP principle, but as a business practice, this provision represents a substantial change in norms, especially for US-based companies dependent on data mining and targeted advertising for their revenue streams. Furthermore, there is a strong argument that DPbD is at odds with one of the dominant models of software development, 'agile' programming, where software is built ground-up by iterative processes rather than top-down from a pre-meditated blueprint.[181] In reality, Article 25 is advisory: it acknowledges that efforts to move towards DPbD are restricted by the state of the art, the costs of implementation and the nature of the processing in question. But there is no doubt that it will incentivise the emergent field of privacy engineering and draw attention to the ideas of users' ownership of their personal data, raised above.[182] DP impact assessments ('DPIAs') are required by the GDPR where a system uses new technologies or presents a 'high risk' to the rights of individuals,[183] and will also become an important part of evidencing attempts to comply with Article 25. Automated profiling and machine learning systems, CCTV surveillance schemes, and large scale processing of sensitive personal data are among the activities almost certain to require a DPIA. Again, however, it remains to be seen how far a DPIA will be taken seriously as an opportunity to improve privacy standards, as opposed to merely an exercise in compulsory box ticking.[184]

X. Supervisory Authorities, Enforcement, and Compensation

Enforcement in the UK is part of the role of the ICO, and in other Member States, their national supervisory authority or DPA.[185] DPAs must be independent in the sense that they can act freely without commercial or governmental pressure.[186] They are not, however, able to act without regard for other Member State DPAs, otherwise consistent interpretation of the Regulation would become impossible. Accordingly, the GDPR provides for a harmonisation measure. The newly-established independent European DP Board (EDPB) is to replace the A29 WP and will comprise the

---

[181] See S Gurses and J van Hoboken, 'Privacy After the Agile Turn' in E Selinger et al (eds), *Cambridge Handbook of Consumer Privacy* (Cambridge University Press, 2018).

[182] See, eg, ENISA, *Privacy and Data Protection by Design – from Policy to Engineering* (December 2014).

[183] GDPR, Art 35 and Recital 78, 91–96. See A29 WP adopted guidance *Guidelines on Data Protection Impact Assessment (DPIA) and determining whether processing is 'likely to result in a high risk' for the purposes of Regulation 2016/679*, WP248rev.01, 4 October 2017.

[184] For the idea of a comprehensive Social Impact Assessment (SIA) that would look at issues beyond privacy or data protection to areas such as gender or race discrimination embedded in Big Data machine learning systems, see L Edwards, D McAuley and L Diver, 'From Privacy Impact Assessment to Social Impact Assessment' (2016) *IEEE Security and Privacy Workshops (SPW)* 53.

[185] Each EU state must have at least one DPA, but may have more than one, as in, for example, Germany. See GDPR, Art 51.

[186] *Ibid*, Art 52; see CJEU decisions in Case C-518/07 *Commission v Germany* (9 March 2010) and, more recently, Case C-614/10 *Commission v Austria* (16 October 2012), where the Austrian DPA was found not to be independent.

EDPS and senior representatives of the national DPAs. Its obligations include issuing opinions and guidance, ensuring consistent application of the GDPR and reporting to the Commission. It will also have a key approximation role in the 'one-stop-shop' mechanism already described.

Historically, in the UK at least, the aim of the ICO has often seemed to be sympathetic to business and to encourage compliance from data controllers, rather than to impose penalties as deterrence. Data subjects have been encouraged to complain of breaches to data controllers in the first instance, and data controllers themselves are encouraged to consult with the ICO and to seek advice, with prosecution seen as a last resort if agreement cannot be reached as to compliance. The ICO can currently choose to serve either an information notice (asking the data controller to provide details of their processing activities), a 'special' information notice, or an enforcement notice requiring the data controller to comply with specified DP principles, rather than immediately levying a fine or seeking prosecution. Failure to comply with any of these notices is a criminal offence. The ICO can also serve its own fines (monetary penalty notices), as well as instructing prosecutions. Fines for DP breaches in the UK were in 2010 increased to £500,000,[187] but fines of this scale are extremely rare and in general fines have been used more often against public authorities than private companies. Powers exceptionally to impose jail sentences were enacted but have never been brought into force. Given the lack of resources available to police an ever-more problematic area, the ICO enforcement strategy has due to necessity been primarily educational and reactive, rather than being proactive enough to discourage breaches outside the public and large corporate sectors. Recent investigations involving Cambridge Analytica have shown the deficits in the ICO's powers with respect to powers of entry and withholding or destroying evidence; amendments to bolster these powers are (as of May 2018) likely to be added to the DP Bill before it finally passes into enactment.

This rather 'softly softly' approach stands in sharp contrast to the new enforcement powers given to DPAs under the GDPR. DPAs will be able to impose fines for some infringements of up to the higher of 4 per cent of annual worldwide turnover, or €20 million (for example breach of requirements relating to international transfers or the basic principles for processing, such as conditions for consent). Other less specific infringements will attract a fine of up to the higher of 2 per cent of annual worldwide turnover, or €10 million. Such fines begin to compare with the level of fines levied by the US Federal Trade Commission against tech giants, and are certainly likely to (and are intended to) concentrate the minds of CEOs. There are likely to be lengthy challenges to such fines on grounds of due process and irrationality.[188]

What about data subjects? Alongside their other rights, they have the right to seek compensation for DP breaches (GDPR, Art 82). In the UK there was once doubt that

---

[187] Pursuant to the Data Protection (Monetary Penalties)(Maximum Penalty and Notices) Regulations (2010) SI. No 31, Regulation 2. In practice, the highest penalty to date was £400,000, levied against TalkTalk in October 2016. See https://ico.org.uk/action-weve-taken/enforcement/talktalk-telecom-group-plc-mpn/.

[188] See adopted A20 WP *Guidelines on the Application and Setting of Administrative Fines for the Purpose of the Regulation 2016/679*, WP 253, 3 October 2017.

compensation could be claimed for data breaches involving emotional but not financial loss[189] but this point was clearly settled by *Vidal v Google*.[190]

A. Mandatory Security Breach Disclosure

To the dismay of consumers, large scale security breaches are increasingly common in the corporate world. The last few years have seen the data of millions of users exposed to hackers and scammers in leaks from companies including TalkTalk and Yahoo. It is often suggested that in the corporate sector the negative coverage generated by a disclosed data breach is a far more effective sanction than any meted out by the ICO or the courts.[191] For this reason, the EC introduced mandatory security breach notification, at first only to the telecoms sector, in Article 4 and Recital 20 of the PECD.[192] Data breach disclosure rules have become common in some US states, and in some other systems such as Japan. Their effectiveness remains controversial, however, with some arguing that they are undermined by 'notification fatigue'. Much of the devil is in the detail of the disclosure requirements, for example how serious a security breach must be before it needs to be notified, to whom it should be notified, what details should be notified, who should determine the seriousness of the breach, whether notification should be made to every potential victim of a data breach or just to a regulator or law enforcement agency, and what remedies the public should have in response to such a breach notification.

The instrument that implements the PECD in current UK law, the PECD Regulations or PECR,[193] provides that notification should be made without 'undue delay' to the ICO where the data breach occurs.[194] In addition, where it 'is likely to adversely affect the personal data and privacy of a subscriber or user' the service provider is also obliged to notify the affected individual(s).[195] Where this is not the case, the ICO may nevertheless mandate that the data controller notify the individuals affected (data controllers may voluntarily disclose more widely if they wish). No notification need be made if the data breached is encrypted and thus 'unintelligible' to persons unauthorised to access it.

These proposals received severe criticism from both the A29 WP and the EDPS,[196] mainly because of the limited sector to which they applied. Now Article 33 of the GDPR will apply notification rules for 'personal data breaches' to *all* data controllers. (As a consequence, breach disclosure will be removed entirely from the forthcoming

---

[189] See *Johnson v Medical Defence Union* [2006] EWHC 321 (Ch).

[190] *Vidal v Google* [2015] EWCA Civ 311.

[191] See, eg, 'Damage to brand image following data breach has bigger 'hit' than regulatory fines, admits watchdog' (Outlaw.com, 23 May 2014), available at www.out-law.com/en/articles/2014/may/damage-to-brand-image-following-data-breach-has-bigger-hit-than-regulatory-fines-admits-watchdog/.

[192] 2002/58/EC.

[193] The Privacy and Electronic Communications (EC Directive) (Amendment) Regulations 2011 (SI 2011/No 1208).

[194] Regulation 5A(2).

[195] Regulation 5A(3).

[196] See A29 WP *Opinion 1/2009 on Proposals amending Directive 2002/58/EC*, WP 159, 10 February 2009; Second Opinion of the EDPS on the review of Directive 2002/58/EC concerning the processing of personal data and the protection of privacy in the electronic communications sector, available at www.edps.europa.eu.

e-Privacy Regulation – see next chapter.) The requirement is similar to that contained in the PECD, with the notable change that breaches must be notified to the DPA no later than 72 hours after the breach has occurred. A 'personal data breach' means a breach of security leading to the accidental or unlawful destruction, loss, alteration, unauthorised disclosure of, or access to, personal data transmitted, stored or otherwise processed.[197] The obligation to notify the data subject as well as the DPA arises only where there is a 'high risk to the rights and freedoms of natural persons', the same test used to decide when a DPIA is required. As with the PECD, notification to data subjects is explicitly *not* required if the data in question was encrypted[198] and, more controversially, if it would involve 'disproportionate effort' to do so. In the latter case, controllers are instead required to make a 'public communication'. The question is open as to what constitutes such a communication – a TV broadcast, an advertisement on FB, or perhaps simply a calmly phrased announcement on the company's website?[199]

Overall it seems unlikely that the breach notification provisions, though welcome, will be any kind of panacea for data subjects. The main problem is the current lack of viable civil class action procedures in the UK, and indeed across the EU.[200] The decision in *Vidal v Google* allowing claims for non-economic distress may, however, help in encouraging a compensation culture in the UK. So, too, may GDPR Art 80, which tries to encourage civil society not-for-profit bodies to lodge complaints on behalf of data subjects that might want to seek compensation for DP breaches. Article 80(2) also allows such bodies to bring freestanding actions relating to data protection breaches, but somewhat controversially, the UK Government has chosen not to implement this part in the DPA 2018, although they have undertaken to review this decision in three years' time.

XI. Data Exports: From 'Safe Harbor' to 'Privacy Shield' and Brexit

Article 25 of the DPD introduced for the first time a rule that transfers of personal data to third countries outside the EU[201] could only lawfully take place if the third

---

[197] Art 4(12). There are some exceptions, notably where the breach is 'unlikely to result in a risk to the rights and freedoms of natural persons'. It is interesting to consider if a breach arises through 'unauthorised disclosure' if, eg, the authorisation a user gave to a platform to share her data was invalid for lack of substantive consent; need a 'security' breach indicate solely a technical failure? Surely not given the inclusion in the security principle in Art 5(1)(f) of 'unauthorised processing' and 'organisational measures'.

[198] Art 34(3)(a).

[199] See guidance from the A29 WP *Guidelines on Personal Data Breach Notification under Regulation 2016/679*, WP250rev.01 6 February 2018.

[200] Even in the US, where class action by consumers are common, courts have often failed to allow them in relation to data breaches, thus making effective claims by consumers for damages almost impossible. See A Matwyshwn, 'Behavioural Targeting of Online Advertisements and the Future of Data Protection' (2009) (January) *Journal of Computers and Law*, available at www.scl.org.

[201] Merely making a webpage accessible anywhere in the world does not constitute a transfer of personal data to a third country, since a third party still needs to make the effort to access that data; it must be 'pulled' not just 'pushed'. See *Lindqvist* (n 26).

country in question ensured an 'adequate' level of protection, the question of which had to be assessed in the light of all the circumstances surrounding the data transfer.[202] The aim of this land grab of extraterritorial jurisdiction was simple: to make sure that data exported outside the EU was not then processed in ways completely contrary to the DP laws of Europe, resulting in EU citizens suffering harm. The problem becomes obvious when one considers that personal data about EU data subjects might easily be collected by, for example, a web-based business based in the US, then transferred to data miners in China, or leaked to spammers in Moldova; EU DP law does not operate directly in any of these countries, and there may be little equivalent protection under their local laws.

Relatively few countries have been accredited by the European Commission as providing 'adequate' protection. Those that have include Canada, Israel, Switzerland, Guernsey, Argentina, Uruguay, New Zealand, the Isle of Man and Jersey.[203] The prominent hard case thrown up by the data exports rule was the US, which, as noted in the last chapter, has no omnibus privacy protection of the kind required by EU 'adequacy' rules, preferring instead self-regulation plus piecemeal sectoral-based regulation of parts of the private sector and of government. Furthermore, the US has no independent supervisory authority to which data subjects can apply for redress. Despite this, trade between the EU and US, which inevitably involves the export of personal data, could not suddenly be expected to cease. Accordingly, an ingenious special agreement was negotiated under which *companies* within the US could register to join what was known as 'Safe Harbor' if they agreed to fulfil certain fair information practices, either through their own self-regulatory conduct, or by joining a privacy or trust seal association such as TrustE.

It was fairly clear from quite early on that Safe Harbor was more of a face-saving way out of a dilemma than a genuinely effective attempt at protecting EU citizens' personal data. As early as 2000,[204] Charlesworth argued forcefully that Safe Harbor represented a crucial watering down of the protection afforded to personal data within the EU, in particular in relation to enforcement of Safe Harbor by trust seal bodies. The European Commission expressed considerable dissatisfaction with Safe Harbor in its 2004 and later reviews.

However, matters truly came to a head in the wake of the Snowden revelations, alluded to above. As we all discovered post Snowden, data transfers to the US could be, and were, routinely intercepted as part of blanket surveillance by the National Security Agency of both foreign and US nationals, even when the data was sent to or via private companies such as Google, Facebook and Microsoft. Furthermore, these private companies, even if not actively complicit, could not do much about the surveillance without breaking US federal law, which took precedence over Safe

---

[202] DPD, Art 25(2). See updated guidance for GDPR in A29 WP *Working Document on Adequacy Referential* WP254rev0.1, 28 November 2017.

[203] See European Commission, *Commission decisions on the adequacy of the protection of personal data in third countries* at http://ec.europa.eu/justice/data-protection/document/international-transfers/adequacy/index_en.htm#h2-15.

[204] A Charlesworth, 'Data Privacy in Cyberspace' in L Edwards and C Waelde (eds), *Law and the Internet*, 2nd edn (Hart Publishing, 2000).

Harbor agreements.[205] As such, Safe Harbor was clearly not protecting EU citizens' personal data from illegal scrutiny, and on a vast and blanket mass surveillance basis. The Safe Harbor agreement was finally put out of its misery on these grounds in the famous *Schrems*[206] case heard by the CJEU in 2014.[207] A new agreement, known as 'Privacy Shield',[208] was subsequently created, and was bolstered by some gestures at changes in US law, but it too has faced severe criticism and is already under challenge in the CJEU.[209] So long as US federal law allows, and indeed mandates, covert blanket surveillance of foreign personal data, it is hard to see how Privacy Shield will not fairly soon suffer the same fate as Safe Harbor.

However, alternatives to the adequacy provisions exist, carried over from the DPD to the GDPR, which can legitimise transfers of personal data outwith the EU. The most obvious measure is procuring the explicit consent of the data subject (GDPR, Art 49(1)(a)). However, Recital 111 constrains the utility of such consent considerably, allowing it to be used only where transfer is 'occasional' and 'necessary', and where other grounds are not useable (Recital 113). The A29 WP has strongly set itself against the use of consent in standard terms contracts as a panacea, and its use in future will thus probably be very limited. This leaves the options of standard contractual clauses (SCCs) under Article 46,[210] binding corporate rules (BCRs) under Article 47, and special adequacy decisions, like Privacy Shield, discussed above. All of these measures, with the exception of BCRs, are also, however, under challenge on similar grounds to those presented in *Schrems*[211] and BCRs are of limited application since they only concern transfers within a single multinational company, and are not much liked by many in the commercial sphere. Thus, as Ustaran has stated, '[t]he prospect of

---

[205] See further, 'Communication from the Commission to the European Parliament and the Council "Rebuilding Trust in EU-US Data Flows" COM(2013) 846 final, 27 November 2013, and 'Communication from the Commission to the European Parliament and the Council on the Functioning of the Safe Harbour from the Perspective of EU Citizens and Companies Established in the EU' COM(2013) 847 final, 27 November 2013.

[206] Case C-362/14 *Schrems v DPC for Ireland* (6 October 2015).

[207] See further discussion in Chapters 6 and 7.

[208] Commission Implementing Decision (EU) 2016/1250 of 12 July 2016 asserts that Privacy Shield demonstrates the adequacy of data exports to the US, although this was to be reviewed after a year; see n 209 below. The review agreed that the Shield 'continues to ensure an adequate level of protection for the personal data transferred' but made a number of recommendations for improvement, including that there should be 'regular checks' of whether businesses self-certified under the Privacy Shield are complying with the framework's privacy principles.

[209] See *First Annual Review of the EU-U.S. Privacy Shield*, 18 October 2017; A29 WP *Opinion 01/2016 on the EU-US Privacy Shield Draft Adequacy Decision*, WP 238, 30 May 2016; EDPS Opinion 4/2016 *Opinion on the EU-US Privacy Shield Draft Adequacy Decision*; challenge by Digital Rights Ireland recorded in Politico, 'Privacy Shield Data Agreement Challenged before EU Court' (27 October 2016), available at www.politico.eu/article/privacy-shield-data-agreement-challenged-before-ecj/. See also the strong reaffirmation that mass blanket surveillance cannot be lawful under EU law in CJEU Joined Cases C-203/15 *Tele2 Sverige AB v Postochtelestyrelsen* and C-698/15 *Secretary of State for Home Department v Tom Watson*, (21 December 2016) (discussed in Chapters 6 and 7).

[210] Those model clauses can be found at http://ec.europa.eu/justice/data-protection/international-transfers/transfer/index_en.htm.

[211] The challenge to SCCs by Irish DPA is now heading to the CJEU. See explanatory memo at www.dataprotection.ie/docs/01-02-2017-Update-on-Litigation-involving-Facebook-and-Maximilian-Schrems/1598.htm.

the standard contractual clauses being declared invalid is the Armageddon of lawful global data flows'.[212]

All of this is extremely bad news for a potential post-Brexit UK. While still in the EU the UK has a 'free pass' on adequacy, because it is constrained by, and mandated to, implement EU DP law (even if, as we saw above, its interpretations have sometimes been dubious). Once (or if) it leaves the EU and the European Economic Area (EEA), it will be scrutinised just as the US or China currently are, and it may well fail on the adequacy requirement, which could be catastrophic for trade reliant on personal data.

Such an eventuality, if it comes about, will probably not arise because of the GDPR, since it is almost certain that the UK will implement its provisions prior to the date it exits the EU, and current indications are that such implementation will be retained after that date. The problem lies instead with the recently passed and highly controversial UK Investigatory Powers Act (the 'IP Act', discussed in detail in Chapter 6). It is quite possible that some provisions of the IP Act, especially the bulk collection powers, are fundamentally incompatible with the adequacy test. Such an interpretation can be found in CJEU case law. In *Digital Rights Ireland*,[213] the case which saw the demise of the Data Retention Directive, it was stated clearly that mass untargeted surveillance was unlawful. But the IP Act enables exactly this form of surveillance, and indeed on a wider scale than even its predecessor, the also unsatisfactory Regulation of Investigatory Powers Act (RIPA) 2000. As well as indiscriminate data retention, the IP Act legalises covert state hacking and grants new powers for the bulk acquisition of personal datasets. Subsequent to *Digital Rights Ireland* and as already noted, both *Schrems* and the *Tele2/Davis* case have taken a hard line concerning state interception, access and retention of data.[214] Given that some 70 per cent of UK companies (including SMEs) reportedly store, collect, or process personal data from the EU, this may be (another) one of the great under-considered perils of exiting the EU.

XII. Conclusion

This chapter has given the reader a full outline of the basic structure of European DP law following the passing of the GDPR. In the next chapter we will discuss some of the outstanding challenges and emerging problems for DP and privacy in the civil and commercial world, including online marketing, 'Big Data', behavioural profiling, algorithmic governance and the Internet of Things, before reaching some overall conclusions about the development of privacy and DP law over time.

---

[212] Quoted in IAPP, 'Model Clauses in Jeopardy with Irish DPA Referral to CJEU' (25 May 2016), available at https://iapp.org/news/a/model-clauses-in-jeopardy-with-irish-dpa-referral-to-cjeu/. Another sign of the hard line being adopted by the CJEU post Snowden can be seen in *Opinion 1/15 of the CJEU on the EU/Canada PNR Agreement*, 26 July 2017, which found that the PNR Agreement could not be concluded in its current form because several of its provisions are incompatible with the fundamental rights recognised by the EU.

[213] Joined Cases C-293/12 and 594/12 *Digital Rights Ireland and Seitlinger and others* (8 April 2014).

[214] See Parliamentary briefing note *Brexit and Data Protection*, Number 7838, 10 October 2017, which emphasises the potentially destabilising effect of the UK leaving the EU Charter of Rights after Brexit.

5

Data Protection and e-Privacy: From Spam and Cookies to Big Data, Machine Learning and Profiling

LILIAN EDWARDS[*]

In this chapter, we examine in detail how data subjects are tracked, profiled and targeted by their activities online and, increasingly, in the 'offline' world as well. Tracking is part of both commercial and state surveillance, but in this chapter we concentrate on the former (see Chapters 6 and 7 for detailed consideration of the latter). Driven by the pursuit of money and intelligence, and enabled by the steeply decreasing cost and rising quality of electronic surveillance, tracking technologies have evolved from simple 'cookies', to far more varied and complex means such as browser fingerprinting, location tracking and the sensing of heat and motion, as well as the use of biometric information, for example heart rates or fingerprints. This constantly evolving range of tracking technologies has been described as an 'arms race of commercial surveillance'.[1]

Cookies and less legitimate 'spyware' were the earliest enablers of commercial tracking and were first explicitly regulated in Europe by the Privacy and Electronic Communications Directive ('PECD' or 'e-Privacy Directive')[2] in 2002 (as amended

* My thanks to Lachlan Urquhart who made considerable contributions to this chapter as research assistant; and to Michael Veale for his collaboration on much work cited herein and continuing insights about machine learning. The chapter is based, where applicable, on the version of the e-Privacy Regulation available as of 5 December 2017 (see n 5 below); however it has been possible to take some later events into account in the chapter.

[1] N Nikiforakis and G Acar, 'Browser Fingerprinting and the Online-Tracking Arms Race' (*IEEE Spectrum*, 25 Jul 2014), available at http://spectrum.ieee.org/computing/software/browser-fingerprinting-and-the-onlinetracking-arms-race.

[2] European Parliament and the Council of the European Union, Directive 2002/58/EC of 12 July 2002 concerning the processing of personal data and the protection of privacy in the electronic communications sector (Directive on privacy and electronic communications) [2002] OJ L201/37.

in 2006 and 2009).[3] Technological evolution has however challenged the effectiveness of legal protections, leading to the drafting of a new e-Privacy Regulation (EPR) which may yet be as controversial as its parent instrument, the General Data Protection Regulation (GDPR) (see Chapter 4).[4] It was hoped the EPR would be ready to go at the same time as the GDPR, which came into operation in May 2018, but as of the time of writing, this now seems impossible[5] and given a period of transition, one should probably not expect to see the PECD rules change from their current domestic implementation any time before late 2019. As a result, this chapter still considers in some depth the commercially important rules around cookies and spam as found in the PECD and its implementation in regulations in the UK, while also casting an eye over the likely shape of the upcoming harmonised EPR regime.

The major focus of this chapter is commercial surveillance. In a little over 20 years, we have seen online marketing move from 'broadcast' ads, where millions of people see the same content delivered by email spam or banner ads on websites, to targeted ads based on user behaviour: a phenomenon known as *Online Behavioural Advertising*, or OBA. The theory goes that since these ads are tailored to individual desires, recipients are more likely to read them and to click through to actual websites and perhaps even actually spend money, and so such ads are priced at a premium. The revenues of online giants like Google and Facebook are almost completely dependent on these tailored adverts, and indeed the entire digital advertising spend online is now mainly absorbed by the so-called 'duopoly' of Google and Facebook, with estimates that they take between 65 and 90 per cent of total digital advertising spend – as well as 20 per cent of total advertising spend in all media globally.[6] In the UK, one of the most digital consumer markets, online advertising now takes over half of total ad spend, with roughly 55 per cent of all money spent on advertising online (including mobile).[7]

Because so many business models in the digital era – not just search and social media, but music streaming services, newspapers online, email and messaging services,

---

[3] Unofficial consolidated version is available at https://ec.europa.eu/digital-agenda/sites/digital-agenda/files/24eprivacy_2.pdf. The PECD was initially transposed into UK law by the Privacy and Electronic Communications (EC Directive) Regulations 2003 (SI 2003/No 2426) (hereinafter 'PECR').

[4] Regulation (EU) 2016/679 of the European Parliament and of the Council of 27 April 2016 on the protection of natural persons with regard to the processing of personal data and on the free movement of such data, and repealing Directive 95/46/EC (General Data Protection Regulation or GDPR) [2016] OJ L119/1.

[5] The EPR was introduced in January 2017 as the Proposal for a Regulation of the European Parliament and of the Council concerning the respect for private life and the protection of personal data in electronic communications and repealing Directive 2002/58/EC (Regulation on Privacy and Electronic Communications), Brussels, 10.1.2017 COM(2017) 10 final. The latest version at the time of writing (January 2018), and to which references are made, is the Interinstitutional File of Brussels, 5 December 2017 at http://data.consilium.europa.eu/doc/document/ST-15333-2017-INIT/en/pdf. The text is still likely to be considerably revised by the Council, however. A good guide to understanding the EPR is FJ Zuiderveen Borgesius et al, *An Assessment of the Commission's Proposal on Privacy and Electronic Communications* (Directorate-General for Internal Policies, Policy Department C: Citizen's Rights and Constitutional Affairs, 7 June 2017). Available at SSRN: https://ssrn.com/abstract=2982290 (hereinafter 'LIBE Report').

[6] See, eg, 'How Google and Facebook Have Taken Over the Digital Ad Industry' *Fortune* (4 January 2017), available at http://fortune.com/2017/01/04/google-facebook-ad-industry/; 'Google and Facebook Bring in One-Fifth of Global Ad Revenue' *The Guardian* (2 May 2017), available at www.theguardian.com/media/2017/may/02/google-and-facebook-bring-in-one-fifth-of-global-ad-revenue.

[7] See IAB / PwC Digital Adspend Study (2016), available at www.iabuk.net/research/digital-adspend.

online maps and many more – are based on providing services for free but deriving revenue from advertising or other uses of collected personal data, tracking and profiling have become inextricably mixed up with making money on the Internet. This is what Zuboff has memorably described as 'surveillance capitalism'.[8] Anderson has also predicted, so far not inaccurately, that 'every industry that becomes digital becomes free', in other words, paid for primarily by ads.[9]

Tracking technologies have also become ubiquitous in the true sense of the word. Data is gathered about you not just when sitting at a desktop computer but also in almost every plausible connected environment. Mobile users (smartphones, tablets, smart watches) have driven ad spend in recent years, while data is also collected from our interactions with the 'real world' in the form of the Internet of the Things (see section VI. below). To name only a few examples, data is already likely to be gathered about (i) your viewing preferences from your smart TV and its Netflix app; (ii) your movements from your smart transport card as you use the tube, train or bus; (iii) your tastes in food and other products from your credit card and loyalty card at your local supermarket as you do the weekly shop; and perhaps (iv) even about your personality, using data from your high-end connected car as it assesses from your driving style if you are a careful or risky driver or from the emojis you use to indicate liking or outrage at social media posts (the new discipline of emotional or 'affective' computing[10]). These pieces of information are gathered in enormous volume in the data-intensive information society, leading to the notion of 'Big Data' (see section IV. below) which can be mined for new predictive insights using techniques of *profiling*, especially with the aid of *machine learning* algorithms. Increasingly, therefore, we live in a society where everything we do leads to us being classified in various not wholly transparent ways: as shoppers, as consumers, as viewers, as citizens or as risky members of society or potential terrorists. This is, in the words of Citron and Pasquale, a 'scored society'.[11]

Ubiquitous surveillance means we will also *see* tailored ads everywhere: not just on our laptop and mobile screens but on our smart TVs and games consoles, on 'intelligent billboards' at bus and tram stops, in shops or beamed to our mobiles as we pause and consider a purchase, and perhaps even in our living rooms as we engage with

---

[8] See S Zuboff, 'Big Other: Surveillance Capitalism and the Prospects of an Information Civilization' (2015) 30 *Journal of Information Technology* 75.

[9] See 'Wired Editor-in-Chief Chris Anderson on the Future of Free (*Wired*, 15 June 2009), available at www.wired.com/2009/06/disruptive-by-design-wired-editor-in-chief-chris-anderson-discusses-the-future-of-free/. Non-advertising revenues are of course possible; the newspaper industry is experimenting with paywalls requiring subscriptions, and music streaming services such as Spotify push a model known as 'freemium', where users are first attracted by free, ad-supported services and then weaned onto subscription premium services which benefit from lack of ads, extra features, etc. In more alternative circles such as the arts and cutting edge innovation, crowdfunding or 'patronage' has become a common model via sites such as Kickstarter. However, it is fair to say the predominant business model on the Internet is advertising.

[10] See, eg, A McStay, *Emotional AI: The Rise of Empathic Media* (Sage Publishing, 2018).

[11] D Citron and F Pasquale, 'The Scored Society: Due Process for Automated Predictions' (2014) 89(1) *Washington Law Review* 1. A fantastic fictional rendition of a scored society can be found in the episode 'Nosedive' (series 3, episode 1, 2016) of the Netflix series *Black Mirror*. The scored society however is far from fictional: see the recent Chinese initiative into 'Social Credit': S Brehm and N Loubere, 'China's Dystopian Social Credit System is a Harbinger of the Global Age of the Algorithm' (*The Conversation*, 15 January 2018), available at https://theconversation.com/chinas-dystopian-social-credit-system-is-a-harbinger-of-the-global-age-of-the-algorithm-88348.

virtual reality (VR) for home entertainment. In these scenarios, our location becomes a highly valuable and equally sensitive piece of location and, as we will see, for that reason there have been attempts in Europe specifically to protect location data.

The law struggles to fit these technologies into existing norms and frameworks of privacy and data protection (DP), both legal and extra-legal, for numerous reasons beyond the simple fact that tracking makes money and is therefore resistant to regulation in times of neoliberal and post-austerity capitalism. Legislation is splintered, with privacy, DP, commerce, consumer law, advertising, interception of communications, policing powers and national security law all implicated. A key point which will be revisited later in this volume is that data gathered by private actors for private profit is often now shared with state surveillance authorities for law enforcement or security purposes, whether by choice or under compulsion. These 'public-private assemblages',[12] most vividly exposed by Edward Snowden in 2013, arguably pose the most severe threat to individual and collective privacy yet known, and make both comprehensive and globally-harmonised regulation of surveillance almost impossibly controversial.

Overlapping enforcement turf wars also result. Even at national level, in the UK alone, and even looking only at commercial activity, we might turn to the Information Commissioner's Office (ICO) for privacy oversight, to the Advertising Standards Authority (ASA) for industry self-regulation of advertising, and to OFCOM for regulation of some but not all 'communications', as well as to some specialised regulators such as those for 'tv-like' audiovisual services and premium phone lines. Interestingly, no regulator is clearly in charge of social media services, which often evade traditional broadcasting and press governance.[13] The courts and private litigation may also have an increasing role in enforcement: in the UK, the High Court has recently declared for the first time in *Vidal Hall v Google*[14] that collecting private information via cookies without a user's consent is a tort of misuse of private information in English law, while Art 80 of the GDPR encourages non-governmental organisations (NGOs) and civil liberty groups to represent data subjects in court in relation to privacy breaches, something which may become a first step to US-style 'class actions'.

Spheres like search and social media also impact heavily on the principles of domestic territorial jurisdiction; regulating a multinational giant like Google is difficult, to put it mildly, when their home privacy laws are so different from EU norms and the impact of their withdrawal from any individual EU market (say) could be profound.[15]

---

[12] See Z Bauman and D Lyon, *Liquid Surveillance: A Conversation* (Cambridge, Polity Press, 2012).

[13] Though this too is becoming highly controversial, especially in relation to the rise of 'fake news': see, eg, 'Ofcom Chair Raises Prospect of Regulation for Google and Facebook' *The Guardian* (10 October 2017), available at www.theguardian.com/media/2017/oct/10/ofcom-patricia-hodgson-google-facebook-fake-news. A high profile Carnegie Trust project by Will Perrin and Lorna Woods has recently suggested Ofcom should take over as regulator for social media: see www.carnegieuktrust.org.uk/blog/social-media-regulation/. See further discussion on intermediary liability in Edwards, Chapter 9.

[14] *Vidal Hall v Google* [2014] EWHC 13 (QB).

[15] This is not an idle worry. When faced with regulation of its Google News service in Spain to protect local news sites, which would have harmed its business model, Google simply withdrew its service from that market, causing extreme damage to local Spanish newspapers' websites. See 'Why Google News is Leaving Spain and what it Means for Publishers' (*Digiday*, 12 December 2014), available at https://digiday.com/uk/google-news-spain/. On data protection and territorial jurisdictional rules, see the previous chapter in this volume.

Indeed, it is often said now that the GAFAM (Google, Amazon, Facebook, Apple, Microsoft) giants are more like countries than corporations, regulated as much by their internal cultures, policies and terms of service as by external state regulation. They also control most of the Big Data which is so often regarded as the 'new oil' of future prosperity (see below). How to find privacy solutions in a world of tracking and profiling driven by both commercial and 'soft power' political goals, which can be compatible with both EU fundamental rights, US commercial permissiveness and general Western *laissez faire* capitalism, is easily one of the toughest diplomatic and regulatory challenges of our times.

Just as we saw in the previous chapter with respect to the GDPR, partly because legal harmonisation across borders is so difficult, commentators and politicians often look for solutions to self-regulatory, 'code' or 'privacy by design' solutions. Some of these solutions are led by the marketing industries themselves – others, like ad-blockers, by users and private developers, resulting in another type of ongoing arms war. We will discuss in particular the idea of a technical 'Do Not Track' solution in this chapter, which is to be mandated by law in the forthcoming EPR. Finally, we will discuss whether, given the accumulating challenges from 'Big Data' to the Internet of Things, DP law is genuinely fit for purpose to deter online commercial surveillance, or if we need to look more than rhetorically at different solutions, both legal and technical, to preserve our privacy but also to maximise social benefit in the eras of not just Big, but Smart, Data.

I. Broadcast Marketing – 'Spam'

A. The Technology

Hard as it is to believe, in the earliest days of the Internet, its use for commercial and marketing purposes was, if not legally banned then extremely frowned upon. According to legend, the first 'spam email' – spam being loosely defined as unsolicited commercial communications sent in bulk[16] – was sent in 1994 in the US by two lawyers called Cantor and Siegel, who aimed to capture customers in search of a US Immigration 'green card'. In return they were greeted with one of the first denial of service attacks, which drove them off the Web.[17]

Spam is 'broadcast' marketing – every recipient gets the same offer, however inappropriate (does this female author really need to be offered a larger male organ?), with the only personalisation being the use of email addresses or other tags to direct the message to a particular recipient. Such emails, most often financial and dating scams,

---

[16] For a full discussion of the definitions of spam, see L Edwards and J Hatcher, 'Consumer Privacy Law 2: Data Collection, Profiling and Targeting' in L Edwards and C Waelde (eds), *Law and the Internet*, 3rd edn (Oxford, Hart Publishing, 2009) 492, *et seq.*

[17] 'The Spam that Started It All' (*Wired*, 13 April 1999), available at www.wired.com/1999/04/the-spam-that-started-it-all/. There is an argument that the first true spam email was actually sent on ARPAnet to 400 people in 1978.

ransomware or messages selling illegal goods or services, have, unsurprisingly, very low response rates. Nonetheless the economics of the Internet – the extraordinary ease and cheapness of sending out millions of spam emails, especially now using botnet technology – mean that spam is still financially viable and still a major problem clogging the arteries of the Internet, albeit that it is now in decline from its heyday of the early 2000s.[18] Spam is also a major carrier of malware and viruses and so constitutes a major part of the general insecurity of the Internet. For ordinary users, however, spam has to some extent receded in significance as the email filters run by Internet service providers (ISPs) and webmail suppliers have improved. Spam is therefore arguably now more of a commercial and security problem for service providers, than it is a privacy problem for users. Nevertheless, DP law remains the primary method by which it is dealt with under EU law.

B. The Regulation

The act of spamming is almost always in breach of the general principles of DP law. Most importantly, spammers, by processing the email address of recipients, that is their personal data, invariably fail to meet the most significant DP rule, namely the need for a lawful ground or grounds for processing. The consent of data subjects to the processing of their data will, by definition, not have been obtained, and it is highly unlikely spam would ever be regarded as meeting the balancing test against data subjects' rights demanded by the 'legitimate interests of the data controller' test.[19]

However discrete rules about direct marketing in general, and spam in particular, have also evolved in DP law. The GDPR gives the data subject the specific right under Art 21 to object to the processing of his or her personal data for the purposes of direct marketing by a data controller, and this includes 'profiling' related to direct marketing. This 'opt out' from direct marketing is implemented in the UK by an 'opt out register', the Mailing Preference Service, a voluntary register run by the Direct Marketing Association,[20] which allows consumers to register their preference not to receive direct marketing. Data controllers then come under a duty to search this register and desist from sending junk mail to subscribers, on- or offline.[21] This opt out system, though still requiring activity from primarily inert consumers, worked tolerably well when applied to traditional direct marketers based within UK jurisdiction and subject to enforcement measures. However it had minimal effect on spammers, who are able to operate essentially cost-free from overseas via email and Voice over IP.

---

[18] Spam is now at an all-time low, making up only around 50–60% of global Internet traffic in early 2017, compared with around 70–80% in 2005: see https://securelist.com/spam-and-phishing-in-q1-2017/78221/. This can be attributed more to better filtering and easier ways of making money, for example ransomware scams and identification theft, than to regulation.

[19] GDPR, Art 6(1)(f) – see earlier Chapter 4. Note however GDPR, Recital 47 which does specify that in principle 'The processing of personal data for direct marketing purposes may be regarded as carried out for a legitimate interest'.

[20] See www.mpsonline.org.uk/. Similar voluntary preference services exist for fax and telephone 'cold calling' (the Telephone Preferences Service).

[21] 'Direct marketing' is defined for these purposes in the current Data Protection Act 1998 as 'the communication (by whatever means) of any advertising or marketing material which is directed to particular individuals' (s 11(3)) and so includes spam as well as traditional junk mail.

As a result, after considerable policy debate, Art 13(1) of the PECD was enacted to demand that all EU Member States require prior consent – 'opt in' – to the use of personal data to send unsolicited electronic mail.[22] 'Electronic mail' was widely defined to include 'any text, voice, sound or image message sent over a public communications network which can be stored in the network or in the recipient's terminal equipment until it is collected by the recipient'.[23] The clear intention here was to make the Directive 'technology neutral' and less prone to immediate obsolescence as new forms of communications were invented.

There are, however, significant exceptions to the 'opt in to spam' rule. Prior consent is *not* required if the details of the recipient were previously obtained 'in the context of a sale of a product or service', so long as

a)   the recipient is given a clear, simple and free opportunity to opt out of receiving spam each time a new communication is sent; and

b)   the goods or services were 'similar' to those now being marketed.[24]

One grey area is whether this exception (the 'existing marketing soft opt in', as the ICO calls it) operates only where an *actual* prior sale has occurred, or whether 'in the context of a sale or service' include scenarios where, say, a user had gone so far to place an order but then pulled out, or even merely browsed a site, perhaps to compare prices. The UK PECD Regulations take the latter approach (reg 22). Provided the business has legitimately obtained the contact details (in terms of the requirements of DP law concerning fair collection and processing), details can be used if they have been obtained in the course of the 'sale *or negotiations*' (my emphasis). Guidance from the Information Commissioner suggests that 'negotiations' do not require an actual sale but do require some kind of active expression by the data subject of interest in the company's products.[25]

A right to opt out is of course useless if the address of the sender is disguised. Accordingly, Art 13(4) of the PECD requires that the sending of emails from a disguised address for direct marketing purposes is to be prohibited.[26] Again, however, such a prohibition is largely ineffective in a time when spam emails are nearly always sent from the equipment of innocent users that has been co-opted by malware ('zombie' or 'bot' computers which form part of larger 'botnets'. See the discussion in Chapter 13 below.) Effectively, therefore, the elimination of spam has become part of the general fight against botnets and malware online rather than the task of DP law. To some extent, another software-based solution, the use of 'blacklists' of spamming sites run by organisations like Spamhaus,[27] has also been at least as useful as the law in controlling and reducing the impact of spam.

---

[22] Implemented in the UK PECR, reg 22.

[23] PECD, Art 2(h).

[24] *Ibid*, Art 13(2) and PECR, reg 22(3).

[25] *Privacy and Electronic Communications Directive: Direct Marketing* (ICO, 2018, v2.3 at time of writing), available at https://ico.org.uk/media/for-organisations/documents/1555/direct-marketing-guidance.pdf.

[26] Note also that the Electronic Commerce Directive added 'Labelling': Art 7(1) – unsolicited commercial communications to be 'identifiable clearly and unambiguously as soon as received'.

[27] See www.spamhaus.org/.

Notwithstanding this, Art 16 of the draft EPR retains prohibitions on unsolicited communications in similar form. A new and wider concept of 'direct marketing communications' is introduced to replace the term 'unsolicited communications', and is defined as

> any form of advertising, whether written or oral, sent or presented to one or more identified or identifiable end-users of electronic communications services, including the use of automated calling and communication systems with or without human interaction, electronic messages, SMS, etc' (Art 4(f)).

The real bite will come if and when it is decided that this wider definition includes targeted advertising and OBA (discussed further in section III. below). Article 16 also carries forward the existing exemptions to the requirement of opt in consent, along with the ambiguity around 'in the context of' a sale.

Interestingly, the draft EPR expects to replicate the GDPR in significantly increasing the scope of its financial penalties: Art 23 provides that fines for a breach may be levied at up to 10 million Euros or 2 per cent of the total worldwide turnover of the preceding financial year, whichever is higher. Given the ICO still pursues domestic spammers and cold callers actively, this may concentrate the minds of those who do desire to operate legitimately. For example, political campaigners received something of a wake-up call when Leave.EU, an organisation campaigning for Brexit, was fined £50,000 in May 2016 for failing to take due care to observe the rules on opt in consent in respect of mailing addresses obtained from a third party.[28]

II. Cookies

A. The Technology

Cookies are small text files stored by a website, via the user's web browser, on the local storage of the user's computer or other 'terminal equipment'. They can contain a limited amount of profiling information about that user (up to 4,096 bytes, or characters, of information). Cookies are usually visible to users who know where to look,[29] but the information in the cookie, even if located, will usually be meaningless to the user because it will generally store only a unique identifier which associates the computer where it has been deposited with information held server-side by the business whose website created the cookie.

Most typically, cookies are used on B2C e-commerce sites to track their users from session to session. When a user browses such a site, personal information is collected – for example what pages she views, what search terms she types in, what

---

[28] This is interesting to compare to the US approach in its Federal CAN-Spam Act where political campaign messages are exempted from spam prohibitions. In the UK, see also guidance recently supplied by the ICO: 'Guidance on Political Campaigning" (ICO, 2017, v3.0 at the time of writing), available at https://ico.org.uk/media/about-the-ico/documents/1042560/promotion-of-a-political-party.pdf. The draft EPR still explicitly states in Recital 32 that 'messages sent by political parties' fall under Art 16.

[29] The directories they are stored in depend on the configuration of the system.

images she clicks on, what items she selects – and stored in the website's server-side database. That information is then connected to the user on subsequent repeat visits to that site via the cookie which acts to identify the user. (Sites cannot simply use IP addresses to recognise the user, because most non-corporate users access the Internet via consumer ISPs which typically dynamically assign different IP addresses to users each time they log in.)

'Persistent' cookies[30] of the kind just described are very useful to users: they enable websites to know who you are, in essence, and are sometimes said to give the site a 'memory'; there is no need to log in every time, and data such as delivery addresses and credit card details can usefully be remembered and filled in automatically for the user. Cookies are also very useful to e-commerce businesses, and to online advertisers, since they enable a profile of the user's shopping habits and preferences to be built up. User X, for example, may be revealed by cookies to be repeatedly surfing a particular website for vintage Nike as opposed to Adidas brand trainers. This is valuable information, which can be used by the business itself, sold to competing businesses or to advertisers or used in combination with other information for data mining purposes.[31]

This model has subsequently been expanded through the use of 'third-party cookies'. These are set not by the retailer whose website the user is directly interacting with, but rather by a third-party advertising network: the market leader being the company DoubleClick, which was acquired by Google in 2008. If, for example, a user browses amazon.co.uk, Amazon deposits a cookie in her browser so that it can 'remember' what products she viewed and bought. (This represents how cookies have typically been used: more robust methods of recording user data server-side have since been invented and may be used instead of or as well as cookies.) The business model of DoubleClick is to contract with *numerous* website businesses, which might include Amazon. Once partnered, when our user browses the Amazon website, not only is an Amazon cookie deposited, but so too is a DoubleClick ('third-party') cookie. This way DoubleClick can learn what the user does when she visits not only Amazon, but also other online stores which are DoubleClick partners, for example Waterstones or Blackwells. If the user searches for graphic novels about superheroes, it then becomes fairly easy to work out what adverts (not only for graphic novels, but also (say) the new Marvel movie, or a Netflix science fiction series) may be effective when served to the user when she next visits a DoubleClick-partnered website. This multi-site information provided an early route towards better profiling of the overall activity of a user, and opened up the possibility of serving more relevant or 'targeted' ads which have since come to dominate the online marketing world.

It is important to note that there are different types of cookies. 'Session' effectively glue the pages of a web session together, permitting the 'state' of a website to be retained in the otherwise stateless medium of the Web, for example by retaining the contents of a shopping cart as the user navigates around the website. These cookies

---

[30] 'Persistent' cookies are cookies which are not deleted at the end of a website browsing session but remain on the device's storage more-or-less indefinitely. These should be distinguished from 'session cookies' – see below.

[31] For a history of such uses, see L Edwards and G Howells, 'Anonymity, Consumers and the Internet: Where Everyone Knows You're A Dog' in C Nicoll, JEJ Prins and MJM van Dellen (eds), *Digital Anonymity and the Law* (Asser Press, 2003).

generally have no privacy implications. 'Analytics' cookies allow a website's operator to keep records of who visits it, how often, at what times, using which browsers and which search terms, etc. These are extremely useful to businesses, and if set by the website itself are no different in legal terms from any ordinary cookie. However, an issue is that most websites use analytics tools provided by third parties – most notably Google, with its Analytics product – which means the cookies act effectively as third-party cookies, sharing personal data with the analytics provider. Because 'buying in' free third-party analytics services is so simple and useful, they are often used as a matter of course by web developers with little thought as to their privacy implications, even in sensitive contexts such as NHS health trust sites.[32]

Some other types of cookies that have aroused concern include 'zombie' cookies and 'flash' cookies. These kinds of cookies can evade attempts at user control via browser settings (discussed below), either because they are non-detectable or because they 'respawn' even if deleted.[33]

B. The Regulation

Cookies became an early object of contention during the debates over the EC Electronic Commerce Directive (ECD),[34] when the European Parliament became aware that personal information about consumers browsing the Internet was being collected using third-party cookies, usually without the consumers' explicit consent or knowledge. So horrified were the Parliament that they proposed the total banning of cookies without prior consent ('opt in'), to the utter consternation of European industry.[35] The matter was not resolved within the ECD, and instead, in 2002 the PECD introduced in its Art 5(3) (on 'confidentiality of communications') the relatively lukewarm requirement that cookies might only be set if the consumer was 'supplied with *clear and comprehensive information* … about the purposes of the processing, and is offered the right to *refuse* such processing by the data controller' (my emphasis). The protection extended beyond cookies to all 'devices' stored on 'terminal equipment' of user, including 'spyware, web bugs, hidden identifiers and similar devices'.[36] Importantly, Art 5(3) was not limited to the use of personal data, but covered information generally, since the PECD protects privacy of communications and therefore is not restricted to the protection of personal data, like the GDPR or the DPD before it.

In practice, this 'informed opt out' requirement added very little extra protection. Many websites merely offered a hyperlink to a privacy policy elsewhere on the website (the previous chapter discusses how little read and understood such policies are). Meanwhile, consumer inertia meant that most, informed or not, did not opt out of receiving

---

[32] Over 80% of websites on the Web now use Google Analytics, according to https://w3techs.com/technologies/details/ta-googleanalytics/all/all.

[33] R Singel, 'Privacy Lawsuit Targets "Net Giants over 'Zombie Cookies'"' (*ARS Technica*, 28 July 2010), available at http://arstechnica.com/tech-policy/2010/07/privacy-lawsuit-targets-net-giants-over-zombie-cookies/.

[34] Directive 2000/31/EC on certain legal aspects of information society services, in particular electronic commerce, in the Internal Market (Directive on electronic commerce) [2000] OJ L178/1.

[35] See G Mackay and M Lomas, 'The Cookie Monster' (2002) 12(6) *Computers and Law* 14.

[36] PECD, Recital 24.

such cookies. Furthermore, Recital 25 of the 2002 PECD provided that 'Information and the right to refuse may be offered once … also covering any further use'.

In 2009 the PECD was revised to try and enhance user control over cookies. The reformed law caused enormous controversy. The enhanced opt out was replaced with an enhanced prior *opt in* requirement that the user '*has given … consent, having been provided with clear and comprehensive information*' (Art 5(3)). However, certain exceptions to this requirement in the original PECD (discussed below) were retained, specifically for 'strictly necessary' cookies. The industry was appalled, with fears expressed that users required to give explicit consent every time and everywhere they browsed the Web before actually accessing useful content, would flee the Internet in horror and confusion at the endless pop-up consent windows. The PECD became known (wrongly) solely as the 'Cookie Directive' and one editorial on a normally sober site pleading read 'Please Kill this Cookie Monster to Save EU Websites!'.[37]

In fact, for the majority of websites, the solution found was to reduce the apparently empowering requirement of mandatory prior consent to a banal annoyance which gave consumers no further control at all. In theory, as good practice, before any cookies were set websites should have asked users on arrival at the website to say yes or no to cookies – with clear links to plain language advice. In fact, many or most websites continued to set some cookies automatically once a user arrived, owing in part to the costs involved in re-architecting website software to work otherwise. Worse still, the norm became one of showing a banner saying something like 'by continuing to use this site, you consent to the use of cookies', rather than offering an explicit choice (see Figure 1 below). Was this *really* consent and if it was, was it legal?

Figure 1 Info, no click "By browsing, you agree"

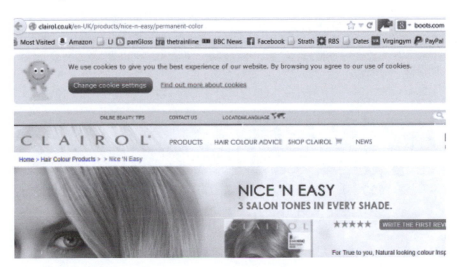

Info, no click: "by browsing, you agree.."

---

[37] The site was the otherwise extremely useful OUT-LAW News, but luckily the article seems to have disappeared from the Internet.

This became a highly conflicted issue, involving the European Commission, the Article 29 Working Party and, in the UK, the ICO, in a seemingly endless battle of consultation documents, guidance and warnings.[38] The PECD recitals were revised by reference in 2009 to add that the 'will to accept cookies', that is, opt in, could be done by 'using the appropriate settings of a browser'.[39] Almost all modern browsers, including Internet Explorer (and Microsoft Edge), Safari, Firefox and Chrome offer users control in the privacy settings over what cookies can be set, as well as the ability to block third-party cookies. The rationale here, then, is that by continuing to allow a browser to set cookies, the user is, by *inaction* (failing to change these settings) *actively* consenting ('opting in') to the continued setting of cookies. This logic is somewhat convoluted. Most browsers' settings allow by default the setting of some if not all cookies (the blocking of some third-party, though not analytics, cookies, as well as potentially malicious cookies, has slowly become the standard). Thus, effectively, websites continued to rely on consumer inertia to continue gathering data about users. The interfaces of more compliant websites (such as the BBC's) which gave users a real choice, were often regarded as merely annoying. It did not help that the functionality of many websites was crippled without cookies enabled. In fact, websites increasingly refused to give access to users who by refusing cookies refused to 'pay their way' in data, a tactic which has become far more common since the arrival of easy to use and browser-integrated ad-blocker tools (we return to this concept of 'tracking walls' below). The issue of zombie cookies, which respawn even when a user has deleted them, also became rather germane.

Figure 2 BBC—true opt in to cookies

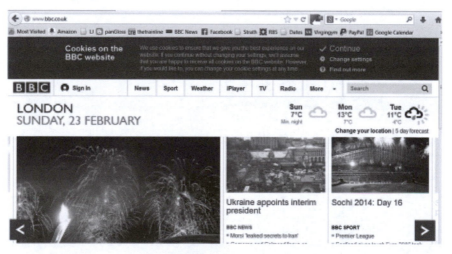

[38] See Article 29 Working Party, *Opinion 15/2011 on the Definition of Consent*, WP 187, 13 July 2011 30, and the refs below, nn 42–44.
[39] PECD as revised 2009, Recital 66.

In the UK, in the face of utter confusion, the Department for Business, Innovation and Skills (BIS) and the ICO agreed to put off enforcement action for a year even after the PECD revisions came into force in May 2011.[40] The ICO issued guidance in 2011 which asserted that 'Consent must involve some form of communication where the individual knowingly indicates their acceptance. This may involve clicking an icon, sending an email or subscribing to a service', and that 'browser settings [were] not sophisticated enough' to 'assume' consent has been given.[41] In 2013, however, the ICO appeared expressly to allow implied consent to cookies where the website owner is 'satisfied their users understand their actions will result in cookies being set'.[42] However, they warned whilst 'implied consent is certainly a valid form of consent … those who seek to rely on it should not see it as an easy way out or use the term as a euphemism for "doing nothing"'.[43] Despite, or perhaps because of, this flurry of advice the 'By using this site …' formulation remains ubiquitous.

C. Exceptions to Cookie Consent

There are of course exceptions to the requirement to obtained 'informed opt in', even after the 2009 amendments. Cookies set for 'technical storage or access for the sole purpose of carrying out the transmission of a communication over an electronic communications network', that is session cookies which usually expire at the end of a browsing session, continue to be allowed without consent. Article 29 Working Party guidance on the 'sole purpose' exemption lists examples such as cookies being used to identify endpoints for a network communication, cookies used to number data packets, or cookies used to detect transmission errors or data loss.[44]

More controversially, cookies were, and still are, allowed where *'strictly necessary* in order to provide an information society service *explicitly requested* by the subscriber or user (my emphasis).[45] This raises the issue of what is 'strictly necessary' as opposed to just easy, quick or cheap. Many websites at present, whether by intent, laziness or technical difficulty, are not designed to work without persistent as well as session cookies. As already noted, it has become common not to allow users access to 'free' (that is, ad-supported) websites, or at least key functionality, without enabling cookies. Therefore, depending on the interpretation of 'strictly necessary', this provision may well be an open invitation to bypass the requirement of consent completely.

Both the Article 29 Working Party and the ICO waded in again to the battlefield to try to provide some consistency. The ICO tried to give an indicative list of what types

---

[40] See the Privacy and Electronic Communications (EC Directive) (Amendment) Regulations 2011/1208.
[41] Document no longer publicly available.
[42] ICO, 'Guidance on the Rules on Use of Cookies and Similar Technologies' (ICO, May 2012, v3 at the time of writing), available at https://ico.org.uk/media/for-organisations/documents/1545/cookies_guidance.pdf. See also 'ICO to Change Cookie Policy to Recognise Implied consent" (*OUT-LAW News*, 28 Jan 2013), available at www.out-law.com/articles/2013/january/ico-to-change-cookie-policy-to-recognise-implied-consent/.
[43] ICO guidance, *ibid*, at 7.
[44] Article 29 Working Party, *Opinion 04/2012 on Cookie Consent Exemption*, WP194, 2012, p 4.
[45] PECD, Art 5(3) and Recital 25.

of cookies might or might not benefit from these exemptions (see Figure 3 below).[46] For example, 'shopping cart' cookies which store your purchases (the first example in the left column) were regarded uncontroversially as both convenient and non-privacy-intrusive. By contrast, the exclusion of analytics cookies in the right hand column was seen as unexpected by commercial norms. Websites can still meet the consent requirements, however, merely by adding a sentence on the use of analytics to their privacy policies and then continuing to use their usual front-page 'informed opt in' formulation; it is clear from a quick web search that this is what many NHS health trusts (to pick up the previous example) have in fact done. It is hard to see how this change particularly protects all but the most vigilant users (or patients).

Figure 3 ICO Guidance on Exceptions to Cookie Consent Requirements

Activities likely to fall within the exception	Activities unlikely to fall within the exception
A cookie used to remember the goods a user wishes to buy when they proceed to the checkout or add goods to their shopping basket	Cookies used for analytical purposes to count the number of unique visits to a website for example
Certain cookies providing security that is essential to comply with the security requirements of the seventh data protection principle for an activity the user has requested – for example in connection with online banking services	First and third party advertising cookies
Some cookies help ensure that the content of your page loads quickly and effectively by distributing the workload across numerous computers.	Cookies used to recognise a user when they return to a website so that the greeting they receive can be tailored

In short, the cookie wars between 2009 and 2013 provide a graphic example of how well-intentioned attempts to give users meaningful control over how their activities are tracked online can not only completely fail to make any real difference, but can at the same time irritate business, consumers and regulators.

D. The Draft e-Privacy Regulation

The EPR re-enacts the basic protection of confidentiality of communications in its new Art 5, and extends the former Art 5(3) into a new and more detailed Art 8. As we shall see below, one of things this article does is more clearly apply the rules on storing

---

[46] See ICO guidance (n 42). See also Article 29 Working Party 2012 Opinion (n 44).

or using information in the terminal equipment of a user to the Internet of Things. Article 8 also introduces a new exception to the need for cookie consent, namely that the cookie is 'necessary for web audience measuring, provided that such measurement is carried out by the provider of the information society service requested by the end user'. This basically allows for web analytics, which are commonly used as noted above, and has been approved by the Article 29 Working Party in principle.[47] The European Data Protection Supervisor (EDPS)[48] has, however, expressed worry this might become a loophole for the long-term storage or reuse of personal data without consent, and has asserted that there should be both notice given and, if possible, an opportunity to opt out. It also remains unclear if it applies to *third-party* analytics services such as those supplied by Google which are overwhelmingly used by small and medium-sized enterprises.

The EPR also recognises that the 'cookie wars' approach requiring informed prior consent has been largely futile, and tries to bring in a new legal approach drawing on a technical protocol called 'do not track'. Instead of expecting users to give real informed prior consent every time they encounter a tracking website, under this new approach the user makes a positive choice to set their browser up to deal with cookies and other trackers according to their preference. This can ideally be done once, perhaps via a 'walkthrough' wizard at first installation of the chosen web browser, and not again (unless the user changes their mind). It can then send signals regarding consent to every website, everywhere; a one-stop, convenient solution for the user.

Article 10 of the draft EPR (as of Council Position, December 2017) attempts to incentivise 'do not track' with the following provision:

1. Software placed on the market permitting electronic communications, including the retrieval and presentation of information on the internet, *shall* offer the option to prevent third or any other parties than the end-user from storing information on the terminal equipment of an end-user or processing information already stored on that equipment.

2. Upon installation or first usage, the software referred to in paragraph 1 *shall* inform the end-user about the privacy settings options and, to continue with the installation or usage, require the end-user to consent to a setting (my emphasis).

'Do not track' has been around as a proposed technical solution for some time (in this form often abbreviated to 'DNT'), but has been considered more or less a failure. This is partly because the US, and standards bodies like the W3C, tried to introduce it as a voluntary, self-regulatory solution, which then failed because websites tracking users simply chose not to respect the DNT signals sent by users' web browsers. Even worse, some websites would regard a negative DNT signal as meaning simply 'do not send ads', as opposed to 'don't collect data about me', which did not deter the use of the information in subsequent profiling and the sharing of those profiles with third parties. It remains to be seen if this *mandatory* approach from the EU will work better – but the usual problems will of course recur around trying to extend the EU rules

---

[47] See Article 29 Working Party, *Opinion 01/2017 on the Proposed Regulation for the ePrivacy Regulation (2002/58/EC)* WP 247, 4 April 2017, p 10.
[48] EDPS 2017/6, p 29.

to a global world of trans-border data controllers, some of whom will have no great intention to comply with EU privacy laws. The cookie wars are likely to continue for some time yet.

III. The Rise of Online Behavioural Advertising (OBA) and Profiling

Despite the amount of legal energy and hot air expelled around them, cookies were only the beginning of the trend towards what is now most often known simply as *profiling*. The volume, and the different types, of data that can now be collected about people browsing the Web or, indeed, interacting with the real world, is remarkable, and has grown exponentially in the last 20 years. Increasingly, furthermore, this data is combined and mined to produce fresh, valuable insights: a process known initially as *text and data-mining* (TDM) and now increasingly facilitated by *machine learning*.

In its initial form, such profiling was done using traditional computing methods, such as sorts in databases, and was used primarily in online commercial environments, mainly by Google[49] and social networks, to target ads at viewers and visitors.[50] Targeted ads, for obvious reasons, were reputed to gain more click-throughs, as well as more eventual purchases, and so they commanded a premium price. Furthermore, since at least 2015, in the UK and most other mature markets, the majority of ad spending has been on digital advertising, and goods and services that would once have charged up-front, such as newspapers, are often now funded entirely, in the case of 'free' competition, by advertising. This adds up to an ecology where profiling to create targeted ads and marketing is the principal means to build and maintain revenue streams in both a variety of mainstream markets including news and entertainment (for example music streaming radio) and in the 'born digital' markets of search and social networking.[51]

Accordingly, we have seen the apparently unstoppable rise of 'online behavioural advertising', or OBA. In 2010, the Article 29 Working Party adopted an *Opinion on Behavioural Advertising*, defining the term as:

> advertising that is based on the observation of the behaviour of individuals over time. Behavioural advertising seeks to study the characteristics of this behaviour through their

---

[49] Google's targeted adverts were (and are) distributed to many websites using the AdSense partnership programme. The technology involved (AdWords) remains Google's own, however.

[50] There is a detailed description of the use of profiling and OBA by Gmail and Facebook, and also the now-defunct Phorm, in the early days of online profiling in Edwards and Hatcher (n 16).

[51] It is also worth noting that profiling as 'microtargeting' is increasingly used for non-commercial purposes such as influencing political and other opinions. Consider, for example, the widespread evidence emerging that microtargeted Facebook adverts were used to influence both the Trump presidential win in the US and the Brexit Leave victory in the UK. These uses raise issues that cannot be fully explored in this chapter, for example the lack of transparency as to who is the advertiser, who receives the ads (specific individuals or the general public), and what ads were actually published ('dark ads'). See the brief account of the Cambridge Analytica political microtargeting scandal of 2018 in Chapter 3 at p 56–57.

actions (repeated site visits, interactions, keywords, online content production, etc.) in order to develop a specific profile and thus provide data subjects with advertisements tailored to match their inferred interests.[52]

OBA involves the pervasive and ambient collection of data, sometimes (realistically, often) without the overt knowledge of the user, in a variety of contexts, by a variety of actors, for a variety of purposes but invariably to make money – an ecology of surveillance capitalism.[53] Actors in this ecology include not just search engines, social networks and other user generated content sites, but ISPs, analytics suppliers, ad networks and general e-commerce sites engaging with social network tracking via 'social plug-ins' such as Facebook's 'Like' buttons.[54] As commercial surveillance has expanded, the types of data that may be gathered and processed into profiles has also multiplied and diversified. Data contributing to OBA and other types of profiling may (non-exhaustively!) include:

- *Explicitly given* data, for example registration profile details, Facebook posts, tweets, photos posted to Instagram.

- *Meta-data*, for example URLs of sites visited, to whom emails have been sent, as well as when, and from what location, and the URLs from which a user was referred to a website.

- *Browser fingerprinting* information, for example the user's browser's unique configuration of language, preferences, plugins, and extensions, and the unique energy consumption pattern of your device (or home or car).[55]

- *Online identifiers*, for example cookies, IP addresses, MAC addresses, IMEI identifiers for phones, Radio Frequency Identification (RFID) chips.

- *'Friends-of-a-friend'* or FOAF data, otherwise known in the context of social networks as the 'social graph'.[56]

- *Location data* (see discussion at section VI. below).

---

[52] Article 29 Working Party, *Opinion 2/2010 on Online Behavioural Advertising*, WP 171, 22 June 2010.

[53] Zuboff (n 8).

[54] See Roosendaal's research which showed that Facebook were tracking site visitors via 'like' widgets, even site visitors who did not click 'like' or were not subscribed Facebook users: A Roosendaal, 'Facebook Tracks and Traces Everyone: Like This!' (2010) *Tilburg Law School Research Paper No. 03/2011*, available at http://ssrn.com/abstract=1717563.

[55] The Article 29 Working Party, *Opinion 9/2014 on the Application of Directive 2002/58/EC to Device Fingerprinting*, WP 224, 25 November 2014, advised that Art 5(3) PECD applied to device fingerprinting. Note that fingerprinting is not limited to web based technologies or protocols, but can also occur with a 'broad range of Internet connected devices, consumer electronics and applications, including those running on mobile devices, smart TVs, gaming consoles, e-book readers, internet radio, in-car systems or smart meters'. A 2010 study found that out of a sample of 500,000 browsers, 83.6% are uniquely identifiable using these kinds of techniques: see P Eckersley, 'How Unique Is Your Web Browser?' (Electronic Frontier Foundation, May 2010). Even if users utilise tools like Ghostery or AdBlock Plus, which block third-party cookies, these will not address these practices because they use elements which are core to web based functionality and cannot be disabled.

[56] This data can typically be publicly scraped from most social network sites by default and is of extreme interest to, for example, police looking for criminal network connections, as well as social marketers.

- *Audio data*, for example voice patterns and entire conversations collected by smart phones and their voice assistants,[57] smart CCTV, smart home hubs like Alexa,[58] or smart TVs.[59]
- *Sensor data*, for example the user's temperature, heart rate and degree of lung exertion when running, collected by a wearable device such as Fitbit or Jawbone; speed of movement of car the user is travelling in collected by software in a connected or autonomous vehicle (CAV); wind strength at a certain location;[60] the degree of footfall in front of a particular shop in a shopping mall.

Note that the list above includes the collection of a great deal of information *covertly*, or at best with notice and/or consent given via largely unread privacy policies. Much modern commercial tracking is done by invisible third-party trackers rather than by the more obvious platform or home website the user actually interacted with. From the occasional DoubleClick advertising cookie with which our discussion started, the profiling infrastructure has spiraled into a vast assemblage of invisible external surveillance. A team of researchers at Princeton, for example, have found that 70 per cent of smartphone apps connected to at least one third-party app, and 15 per cent to five or more trackers.[61] To give an idea of the amount of data collected daily by third-party trackers about the ordinary user, the popular UK newspaper the *Daily Mail* has 19,136 third-party cookies on its site, and the rather more upmarket *Telegraph* has 14,025.[62] Furthermore, this data is collected indiscriminately from children as much as adults, possibly even more intensively: the study above found that out of 111 children's apps tested, 11 of them leaked a unique identifier. Many people assume that tracking of the full content of a communication is more dangerous to our privacy than collection of meta-data; however, this is almost certainly no longer true in a world of profiles assembled by the accumulation of copious data points and classified by machine learning algorithms.[63]

OBA rapidly became the basis of the very successful business models of Google (through its AdWords and AdSense Programmes) and Facebook and other social networks, to the extent that around 90 per cent of online advertising revenue now goes

---

[57] There is a persistent but unproven urban myth that Facebook is collecting all our conversations via its app on mobile phones. Facebook vehemently deny this. See, for example, 'Is Facebook Listening (And So What If They Are)?'(*Forbes*, 17 March 2017), available at www.forbes.com/sites/forrester/2017/03/17/is-facebook-listening-and-so-what-if-they-are/.

[58] For an evocative but non-profiling example of ambient audio gathered by Alexa being used as evidence in a US murder case, see 'A Murder Case Tests Alexa's Devotion to Your Privacy' (*Wired*, 28 February 2017), available at www.wired.com/2017/02/murder-case-tests-alexas-devotion-privacy/.

[59] See the discussion of fears over smart TVs 'listening in' in 'How to Keep Your Smart TV from Spying on You' (*ZDnet*, 8 March 2017), available at www.zdnet.com/article/how-to-keep-your-smart-tv-from-spying-on-you/.

[60] Some of these may not always seem to be personal data in terms of the GDPR. However, this becomes increasingly hard to say in a world of profiling. See the discussion in Chapter 4 at section IV. on anonymous data and 'singling out'. Note also, as discussed above, that the e-privacy legislation, unlike the GDPR, applies to non-personal data.

[61] See '7 in 10 Smartphone Apps Share Your Data with Third-Party Services' (*The Conversation*, 30 May 2017), available at http://theconversation.com/7-in-10-smartphone-apps-share-your-data-with-third-party-services-72404.

[62] See data reported in 'Know Your Cookies: A Guide to Internet Ad Trackers' (*Digiday UK*, 1 November 2017), available at https://digiday.com/media/know-cookies-guide-internet-ad-trackers/.

[63] See discussion in Chapter 7 on data retention and privacy.

to these two entities.[64] Even businesses or websites which still sell goods and services for actual money inevitably see the personal data of its viewers and customers as a potential extra revenue stream monetisable by targeted ads. Many services also claim that they collect data to optimise services, though a secondary purpose may still be monetisation: consider for example Uber, whose drivers and app charge for services but which also clearly mine the personal data of users to maximise its profit.[65]

Concern around OBA and its invasive nature thus quickly gathered in European regulatory circles. Users show continuing dislike for and distrust of OBA and profiling in attitudinal surveys. For example, in the recent 2015 Eurobarometer survey, 53 per cent of Europeans surveyed said they were uncomfortable with Internet companies using their personal information to tailor advertisements. As well as general feelings of 'creepiness',[66] harms caused by OBA may include:

- the loss of *user trust* engendered by what are seen as deceptive and non-transparent practices;

- the uncertain and acontextual mixing of 'new' predictive data with actual data, and the high levels of *error* that might result from such fusion;

- the use of such ads to target users *inappropriately*, for example by targeting alcohol at alcoholics or sugary goods to the obese or diabetic, or perhaps almost anything to children[67]

- the use of such ads to enable *price and service discrimination* online: ie using profiles to offer certain goods or services only to those above a certain salary level, or adjusting prices to what users are calculated to be able or willing to pay at a particular time (as currently happens with airline seating). Such tactics are increasingly common in the algorithmic age[68] and are much disliked, although economists sometimes argue that these practices are in fact sensible and commercially efficient[69]

---

[64] See, eg, 'How Google and Facebook Have Taken Over the Digital Ad Industry' (*Fortune*, 4 January 2017), available at http://fortune.com/2017/01/04/google-facebook-ad-industry/.

[65] A particularly damaging story about Uber's data collection experiments involved revelations that 'walks of shame' – one-night stands – were being tracked in their Big Data. See 'Does Uber Even Deserve Our Trust?' (*Forbes*, 25 November 2014), available at www.forbes.com/sites/chanellebessette/2014/11/25/does-uber-even-deserve-our-trust/#510b871a73f7.

[66] See, eg, O Tene and J Polonetsky, 'A Theory of Creepy: Technology, Privacy, and Shifting Social Norms' (2013) 16 *Yale Journal of Law & Technology* 59.

[67] In the non-commercial domain, even tougher choices are raised. Should it be allowed to microtarget adverts to persuade key voters in swing seats, profiled by, say, income, religion or race, to vote a particular way in elections? This can be distinguished from traditional political advertising by the lack of transparency both to the public and other candidates. Should location data that a mobile phone user is at an abortion clinic be used to target her with pro-choice adverts? See 'Anti-Choice Groups Use Smartphone Surveillance to Target "Abortion-Minded Women" During Clinic Visits' (*Rewire*, 25 May 2016), available at https://rewire.news/article/2016/05/25/anti-choice-groups-deploy-smartphone-surveillance-target-abortion-minded-women-clinic-visits/.

[68] Indeed such dynamic algorithmic pricing can notoriously result in 'battles of bots' on auction sites like Ebay or marketplaces like Amazon where goods are automatically priced up to insane figures: see, eg, 'How A Book About Flies Came To Be Priced $24 Million On Amazon' (*Wired*, 27 April 2011), available at www.wired.com/2011/04/amazon-flies-24-million/.

[69] F Borgesius and J Poort, 'Online Price Discrimination and EU Data Privacy Law' (2017) 40(3) *Journal of Consumer Policy* 347.

- creation of profiles which might be erroneous, biased or acontextual which might then be shared with third parties such as insurers, employers or policing authorities, with unfortunate and unintended consequences.

Accordingly, the Article 29 Working Party demanded in 2010[70] that any tracking of user behaviour for the purposes of OBA should be subject to the user's 'prior explicit consent'. Arguably, since OBA is enabled at least partly by cookies, the requirement of prior informed consent in Art 5(3) of the PECD should also apply to OBA. However, as we have already seen, the cookie consent rules did very little to empower users. As the Article 29 Working Party put it:

> Whilst data protection legislation requires, among other things, obtaining informed consent from individuals to engage in this practice, in reality it is very doubtful whether average individuals are aware of, much less that they consent to, being monitored to receive tailored advertising (p 21).

A. The Draft EPR

The draft EPR appears to confirm that prior consent is necessary for OBA. Article 16 creates a new and wider concept of 'direct marketing communications', introduced to replace the term 'unsolicited communications', and defined, as we noted earlier, as:

> any form of advertising, whether written or oral, sent or presented to one or more identified or identifiable end-users of electronic communications services, including the use of auto-mated calling and communication systems with or without human interaction, electronic messages, SMS, etc.[71]

There has been debate over whether this wider definition includes targeted advertising and OBA, although this is certainly the view taken by the Article 29 Working Party and most commentators.[72] Article 16 requires *opt in consent* to direct marketing communications, just as the PECD already does for spam, as we saw above. This may alert some users more overtly to the dangers of profiling, but does not get us too much further forward, given that cookies, the enabling core technology of OBA, already theoretically require informed opt in consent. As above, it is hoped that the 'Do Not Track' system over time will become a better answer to the problematic nature of behavioural targeting and profiling in the round, than dependence on *ad hoc* website-specific consents.

But a key problem for both cookie and OBA consent, already alluded to above, is the notion of '*tracking walls*': requirements by sites that the user consents (whether automatedly via their browser, or by some human, manual act) to the setting of cookies or the use of profiling technologies before they can proceed to access 'free' but ad-supported online services (for example news, music, video, social networking or

---

[70] Article 29 Working Party 2010 Opinion (n 52).
[71] EPR, Art 4(f).
[72] See discussion in LIBE Report (n 5) at 2.4.1.7, where it is noted that contextual advertising (see below) should probably *not* fall within this definition.

search). These tracking walls are an obvious way to support the dominant ad-supported business model of the Internet when it is under considerable threat from the rise of easy-to-use ad-blocking technologies.[73] Users themselves, unsurprisingly, hate tracking walls: for example, a 2016 survey conducted in Holland found that around 60 per cent of people surveyed did not consider it reasonable that they could not use a site without allowing it to collect their personal data.[74] In the Eurobarometer EU-wide survey of 2015, less than 40 per cent of users agreed that they '[didn't] mind providing personal information in return for free services online'. Of course, such survey results do not really explore how users would feel if the alternative was that these services were simply not available.

Are tracking walls legal? As we saw in the last chapter, the GDPR does now recognise, at least in its recitals, that 'consent to data sharing should not be valid if it is tied as a prerequisite to the provision of a service for which the consent was not necessary' (Recital 43). And it is also explicit in the draft EPR that the standard of consent required for the setting of cookies and the sending of direct marketing messages is now the same as the standard of consent in the GDPR (draft EPR, Art 4a), ie that consent must be

> any freely given specific, informed and unambiguous indication of wishes by which he or she by a statement or by a clear affirmative action signifies agreement to personal data relating to him being processed.[75]

It seems difficult to assert following the GDPR that consent given to repel a tracking wall is 'freely given' – the user's consent is surely necessary for the ads, not the service – and the recommendation of the LIBE committee that tracking walls be banned in the EPR, was accepted by the European Parliament in late 2017. This caused consternation in the online publishing industry, however. How the Council will react in the final stages of the draft EPR remains to be seen.

Borgesius et al suggest interestingly that there are four ways to deal with tracking walls, namely (i) make no new rules, (ii) ban tracking walls in certain circumstances, (iii) ban tracking walls completely, or (iv) ban all web-wide tracking. The second option, as a traditional compromise, seems most likely to succeed, and the question then arises: what types of tracking are considered particularly objectionable? In 2016 the Article 29 Working Party suggested five such circumstances, including:

i.   where sensitive personal data is collected;
ii.   where tracking is performed by 'unidentified third parties for unspecified purposes';
iii.   on government websites;

---

[73] A briefing note found that 37% of Europeans use software to protect them from seeing online adverts (Flash Eurobarometer 443, *Briefing Note: e-Privacy* (December 2016). A fascinating alternative to requiring personal data has emerged from *Salon* magazine, which instead require that readers accessing its free content allow their computer's processor to be used for bitcoin mining. This appears to be more a stunt than a genuine alternative business model. See 'Salon's Monero Mining Project Might be Crazy like a Fox' (*TechCrunch*, 13 February 2018), available at https://techcrunch.com/2018/02/13/salon-coinhive-cryptocurrency-mining/.
[74] See F Borgesius et al, 'Tracking Walls, Take-It-Or-Leave-It Choices, the GDPR, and the ePrivacy Regulation' (2017) *European Data Protection Law Review* 353.
[75] GDPR, Art 4(11).

iv.   in circumstances where the GDPR would make consent invalid; and
v.   in cases of 'bundled consent for multiple purposes'.[76]

A number of possible other approaches can be canvassed, for example prioritising access to news services on grounds of media policy and freedom of expression,
banning trackers from websites where professional confidentiality is expected, as with
lawyers or hospitals, and requiring that a tracking-free alternative version of commercial websites is offered, where users must pay with actual money.

Are subscription models, either alongside or replacing the paid-by-ads model, the
way forward for user privacy? They may be the only way to square the EPR with the
current market. However they run the risk of turning privacy into a luxury only for
those who can pay for it: opposing such a move, the EDPS has said, 'privacy is not a
luxury but a universal right and it should not only be available to those with the means
to pay'.[77] Borgesius et al. themselves recommend a combination of a blacklist of sites
where tracking is not allowed, and a 'greylist' of sites where a presumption of illegality can be rebutted (an approach borrowed from protection against unfair terms in
consumer contracts).

This is a highly complex problem which will be debated for some time to come, but
certainly the success of the streaming music industry (Spotify et al) seems to suggest
that people will pay money to avoid ads (and to protect their privacy) if such an alternative is provided and at a marketable price point.[78] The idea of moving on from the
allegedly free-to-customer business model of social media and other sites may seem
unthinkable: but as Tim Berners-Lee has said:

> Two myths currently limit our collective imagination: the myth that advertising is the only
> possible business model for online companies, and the myth that it's too late to change the
> way platforms operate. On both points, we need to be a little more creative[79]

One further suggestion is that the business model of *behavioural* targeted advertising
may be replaced by the less privacy-invasive *contextual* advertising.[80] This works with
the idea that if a user goes to a website about Volvos (say), she is served a targeted
advert for (say) Saabs. This involves gathering no *personal* data of the user and depends
instead only on the attributes of the *page* the user has visited. Such an approach might
be a better business model for smaller platforms than the usual giants, the former
not having the ability to amass the millions of profiles needed for serious profiling

---

[76] Article 29 Working Party, *Opinion 03/2016 on the Evaluation and Review of the ePrivacy Directive (2002/58/EC)* WP 240, 26 July 2016 at p 17. Borgesius et al note that in a later opinion, the Article 29 Working Party actually decided instead to support a complete ban on tracking walls.

[77] EDPS, 'Opinion on Coherent Enforcement of Fundamental Rights in the Age of Big Data' (23 September 2016) p 16. See also J Angwin, 'Has Privacy Become a Luxury Good?' *New York Times* (3 March 2014), available at www.nytimes.com/2014/03/04/opinion/has-privacy-become-a-luxury-good.html.

[78] It also seems unlikely that advertising alone can continue to fund several markets which used to be paid for primarily by users. For example, traditional journalism is already suffering heavily in the ad-supported age and some leading newspapers, for example *The Times*, have reverted to a paywall experiment, the end result of which is yet to be seen.

[79] See T Berners-Lee, 'The Web is under Threat. Join us and Fight for It' (Medium, 11 March 2018), availa-ble at https://medium.com/@timberners_lee/the-web-is-under-threat-join-us-and-fight-for-it-69cb3408c770.

[80] See the interesting discussion in 'The Other Winner of the EU ePrivacy Regulation – Contextual Targeting' (*Zvelo*, 22 January 2018), available at https://zvelo.com/winner-eu-eprivacy-regulation-contextual-targeting/.

(see below), and who currently mostly depend on partnering with (and paying) an ad network provider like Google AdSense. Interestingly, shortly before the GDPR came into force, Google for the first time offered contextual non-personal advertising as an option to its advertisers.[81]

IV. Big Data, Machine Learning and Algorithms

Everything we have discussed so far is part of the phenomenon of '*Big Data*'.[82] Big Data, like many Internet-hype related words, is a term which is frequently mentioned but has no single clear meaning.[83] It is frequently related to ideas of "volume, velocity and variety", with the emphasis on the first.[84] Big Data has come to the fore for three reasons: the costs of both storage and processing of data have dramatically fallen; algorithms for analysing huge amounts of data have improved ('data analytics'); and, perhaps most importantly, the online data industries – and now the Internet of Things (IoT) industries (see later) – have created incredibly vast pools of data to mine. IoT applications are particularly prodigious in their generation of Big Data. In their 2015 IoT report, the FTC noted that 'the sheer volume of data that even a small number of devices can generate is stunning ... [we heard that] fewer than 10,000 households ... can generate 150 million discrete data points a day'.[85] These massive volumes of granular data generated from IoT systems allow inference of data on a previously unprecedented scale. As Wisman comments, 'Bentham's Panopticon is child's play compared to surveillance in a fully functioning IoT'.[86]

The twin sister or symbiote of Big Data in the information society is *machine learning* by *algorithmic systems*, a concept we introduced in the last chapter. There, we discussed profiling and automated decision making at some length, and referenced issues like anonymisation; pseudonymisation; the GDPR, Art 22 right to object to solely automated decisions; and the alleged 'right to an explanation' which may be

---

[81] See 'Google's Steps toward GDPR Surrounded by Questions" (*Martech*, 23 March 2018), available at https://martechtoday.com/googles-steps-toward-gdpr-surrounded-by-questions-212939.

[82] The UK ICO provides a useful introduction to defining Big Data, relying on the characteristics of velocity, volume and variety: see ICO, 'Big Data, Artificial Intelligence, Machine Learning and Data Protection' (ICO, 2017, v2.2 at time of writing), available at https://ico.org.uk/media/for-organisations/documents/2013559/big-data-ai-ml-and-data-protection.pdf. Douglas Laney is credited with inventing the mantra of the 'three Vs': see '3D Data Management: Controlling Volume, Velocity and Variety' (*Gartner*, 6 February 2001), available at https://blogs.gartner.com/doug-laney/files/2012/01/ad949-3D-Data-Management-Controlling-Data-Volume-Velocity-and-Variety.pdf.

[83] In the US, Big Data was popularised among policymakers by the report *Big Data: Seizing Opportunities, Preserving Values, Executive Office of the President* (May 2014) and the Federal Trade Commission (FTC) report, *Big Data: A Tool for Inclusion or Exclusion?* (January 2016), available at www.ftc.gov/system/files/documents/reports/big-data-tool-inclusion-or-exclusion-understanding-issues/160106big-data-rpt.pdf. Big Data is so overused a term it has in fact been removed from the famous 'hype cycle' issued by Gartner.

[84] See, eg, ICO Big Data guidance (82) at p 6, drawing on work by Gartner Research.

[85] See FTC Staff Report, *Internet of Things: Privacy and Security in a Connected World* (January 2015), available at www.ftc.gov/system/files/documents/reports/federal-trade-commission-staff-report-november-2013-workshop-entitled-internet-things-privacy/150127iotrpt.pdf, p 14.

[86] THA Wisman, 'Purpose and Function Creep by Design: Transforming the Face of Surveillance through the Internet of Things' (2013) 4(2) *European Journal of Technology* at section 3.

mined out of GDPR, Art 22 or Art 15 (section VIII of Chapter 4). In this chapter, we look more deeply into profiling and machine learning.

Machine learning (ML) loosely involves statistically spotting patterns in Big Data, in the form of *training datasets*, building a *model* out of those patterns, and comparing new data inputs to that model to classify them.[87] This is sometimes called 'deep learning'. Two main relevant forms of ML exist. *Supervised learning* takes a training dataset of variables, such as physical symptoms or characteristics, and notes when such a set of inputs leads to what is deemed a 'success', such as a certain medical diagnosis. This success is known as a 'ground truth'. The aim of supervised learning is to accurately predict this ground truth from the input variables, in later cases using the trained model. *Unsupervised learning* is not 'supervised' by the ground truth: ML systems instead simply try to infer structure and groups based on other heuristics, such as proximity. For example, it was recently reported that a ML system developed by DeepMind had taught itself new ways to win at Go using unsupervised learning by studying and playing many millions of games.[88]

Figure 4 'Deep' Learning

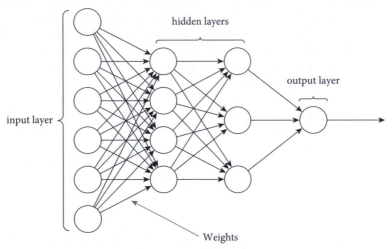

ML can deal with making decisions rapidly and consistently in complex and subtle domains involving hundreds, thousands, or millions of variables, some of which may not be obvious, or even known, to humans. They can automate much more difficult tasks than manually specified rule-based software can, including tasks previously thought to be only possible for humans, like understanding speech and translating it into different languages, machine vision, searching for the most relevant answer to a

---

[87] See explanation in L Edwards and M Veale, 'Slave to the Algorithm? Why a "Right to an Explanation" Is Probably Not the Remedy You Are Looking For' (2017) 16 *Duke Law & Technology Review* 18, 24–27 (hereinafter 'Slave'). The argument in the following three pages is drawn from Slave which should be consulted for full referencing.

[88] See report from DeepMind at https://deepmind.com/blog/alphago-zero-learning-scratch/.

query, manipulating vehicles to drive safely on roads, creating workmanlike business text and, arguably, assessing an appropriate sentence for a crime, or a price for a service.

Accordingly, ML is coming to be used extensively in private sector domains well beyond advertising, including hiring, firing and assessment of employees, algorithmic pricing and distribution of assets, and curation of content on social networks (for example what users see in their Facebook 'News Feed'). In high-stakes public sector areas, such as criminal justice sentencing and risk assessment for bail release, ML is becoming widely used for the promise it brings of low cost and fast results. It is also notorious, however, for the risks attendant in aggregate justice, embedded racism in training data, and ideas of 'pre-crime'. ML uptake is often driven, it should be noted, by business models and political goals. Cheap computation has produced large datasets, often as by-products of digitised service delivery in both private and public sectors, as well as governmental 'open data' programmes, and there has been a visible near-evangelical compulsion to 'mine' or infer insights from these datasets in the hope they might have social or economic value.

ML thus enables inferred, *predictive* data to be created from the Big Data available, giving us inferences like 'if x likes this y probably will too' and 'she's a risk-taker, so don't hire her'. In reality, however, these inferences are based on statistical processes and are wholly dependent on the quality and selection of the training datasets as well as the chosen internal model. Another problem with ML, already discussed in the previous chapter, is that since the correlation between the inputs and the output decision is made by a model which is not built to be understood by humans, ML systems tend to be seen as a 'black box' that is resistant to any requirements of transparency and contestability.[89] One clear issue is that profiling takes data from its original context and turns it into acontextual derivatives which may or may not turn out to be accurate. Predictive analytics involving ML techniques are particularly subject to widespread criticism for potentially unfair and discriminatory results flowing from the classification of data subjects via training datasets in which historic prejudices and assumptions are embedded.[90]

V. Rights to Control Big Data, Profiling and ML

All this raises enormous issues for DP law, where fairness, legitimacy and transparency in processing are key principles of the GDPR.[91] In particular, Big Data:

○ challenges *purpose limitation*,[92] since the key intent is to reuse personal data for unforeseen purposes. As Mayer-Schönberger and Cukier put it pithily, a 'treasure hunt is on';[93]

[89] See at length this argument in Slave (n 87), particularly at 38–43; FR Pasquale, *The Black Box Society: The Secret Algorithms That Control Money and Information* (Harvard University Press, 2015).
[90] See summary of research in Slave (n 87) 27–37.
[91] GDPR, Art 5. See useful discussion in ICO Big Data Guidance (n 82), Ch 2.
[92] *Ibid*, Art 5(1)(b).
[93] V Mayer-Schönberger and K Cukier, *Big Data: A Revolution That Will Transform How We Live, Work and Think* (London, John Murray, 2013) 15.

o   challenges *data minimisation*,[94] since controllers will often want to collect 'all the data', not knowing in advance what data will produce especially interesting or commercial results. Similarly, the *data retention* principle[95] instructs that data should be deleted or anonymised as soon as the purpose for which it is processed is fulfilled. Both of these are clearly fundamentally at odds with the concept of Big Data;

o   challenges the principle of *transparency*, since the 'newly discovered information is not only unintuitive and unpredictable, but also results from a fairly opaque process'.[96] We discussed this in relation to the 'right to an explanation' in Chapter 4;

o   challenges fundamentally the notion of *consent*[97] as either an effective protection for users and as a lawful ground for processing, since it is not known to what purposes of processing the data subject is consenting;

   •   A sub-issue of this problem is that ML may generate *new sensitive personal data* from 'old' inputs of ordinary personal data. This raises very difficult issues as to whether it is lawful to gather the *initial* data other than (in most commercial contexts) by use of specific and explicit consent,[98] when it may be standard practice to apply other grounds such as the legitimate interests of the data controller.

o   above all, ML challenges *fairness*:[99] can opaque systems driven by historic data, which may be partial, biased and discriminatory, ever conceivably produce automated decisions which are not at times unfair?

There are putative solutions to these issues within the existing framework of DP law. Indeed, the Article 29 Working Party has consistently declared, albeit in a somewhat Canute-like way, that DP law can adequately deal with the challenges of Big Data.[100] In terms of lawful grounds for processing, alternatives to consent do of course exist, such as the legitimate interests of the data controller (Art 6(1)(f)) and, in the public sector,

[94] GDPR, Art 5(1)(c).
[95] *Ibid*, Art 5(1)(e).
[96] Quote from Ira S Rubinstein, 'Big Data: The End of Privacy or a New Beginning' (2013) 3 *International Data Privacy Law* 74, 76.
[97] GDPR, Arts 5(1)(a) and 6(1)(a).
[98] See Slave (n 87) 36–38; see also A Cormack, 'A Data Protection Framework for Learning Analytics' (JISC, UK), available at https://community.jisc.ac.uk/system/files/391/Learning%20Analytics%20-%20Legal%20 Framework%20Draft%20Submitted.pdf; JG Canas et al, 'Facebook Use of Sensitive Data for Advertising in Europe' (2018) *arXiv preprint arXiv:1802.05030*, available at https://arxiv.org/pdf/1802.05030v1.pdf which found empirically that Facebook had assigned an ad preference involving sensitive personal data to 73% of EU users, primarily via inferred rather than explicitly shared data.
[99] GDPR, Art 5(1)(a). These problems are of course particularly acute in the public sector where high stakes outcomes like liberty and welfare and health benefits are at stake. Rare empirical evidence on how public sector workers actually try to consider fairness in ML systems can be found in M Veale, M van Kleek and RD Binns, 'Fairness and Accountability Design Needs for Algorithmic Support in High-Stakes Public Sector Decision-Making', *ACM Conference on Human Factors in Computing Systems (CHI'18)* 21–26 April 2018, Montreal.
[100] See Article 29 Working Party, *Opinion 03/2013 on Purpose Limitation*, WP 203, 2 April 2013, particularly section III.2.5; Article 29 Working Party, *Statement of the WP29 on the Impact of the Development of Big Data on the Protection of Individuals with Regard to the Processing of their Personal Data in the EU*, WP 221, 16 September 2014.

that the processing is necessary for the public interest (Art 6(1)(e)). If it is mandatory or desirable to depend on consent, for example for ethical reasons, consent forms may be made very broad and may extend to potential re-uses, but then they run the risk of failing to be 'specific'. Obtaining new, more informed and more specific consents to re-use data for a new purpose may be costly and impractical, especially, perversely, if anonymisation or pseudonymisation has been attempted.[101]

An obvious alternative is to argue that the Big Data used is not 'personal' because it has been anonymised, and this tends to be current industry practice in many contexts such as within marketing and social networking. However, it is now well known that Big Data analytics can potentially lead to the re-identification of individuals from non-personal data.[102] In some cases, such as medical research, there may be a strong agenda to regard Big Data as non-personal, given the likely social benefits of the outcome of the processing, but this can also arouse enormous public concern given the high sensitivity of health data.[103] Exceptions from parts of the GDPR for research, including medical research, do exist, albeit they are limited in scope and are subject to Member State discretion.[104]

An interesting supplementary point is to consider whether the inferences resulting from ML are themselves personal data – or are they merely statistical guesses? One approach to this is to note that frequently – perhaps in up to 10 per cent of cases depending on the training set, the domain and the algorithm – simply wrong. If these inferences are not personal data, then the data subject has no right to rectify them, which seems a priori wrong. Another approach is simply to argue that inferences, whether right or wrong, are 'opinions'; which have always been regarded as personal data (eg in context of 'political opinions') and were named explicitly as such in the UK Data Protection Act 1998, s 1(1) ('includes any expression of opinion about the individual').

Data subjects are entitled under the GDPR to a number of important rights relevant to Big Data and ML, namely:

(i) to object to direct marketing, profiling and automated decision making (Arts 21 and 22[105]);

---

[101] But see Recital 29 which possibly suggests, as an incentive to pseudonymise, that if the original data controller applies pseudonymisation to go on to further analytical use of personal data, this will be deemed a new purpose compatible with the old.
[102] See discussion in Chapter 4 at Section IV.
[103] A good example of the sensitivity of health data and its misuse without adequate user consent can be seen in the DeepMind/Royal Free Trust farrago of 2015–2017. For an excellent analysis, see J Powles and H Hodson, 'Google DeepMind and Healthcare in an Age of Algorithms' (2017) *Health and Technology* 1. See also the work of Michael Birnhack who traced 'Big Medical Data' research practices and found that most studies either ignored DP altogether or assumed an *ex post* position in which use of data was justified by the fact it was eventually de-identified. See M Birnhack, 'A Process-Based Approach to Informational Privacy and the Case of Big Medical Data' (2018) 20 *Theoretical Inquiries in Law* (forthcoming), pre-print available at https://ssrn.com/abstract=3129588.
[104] See GDPR, Art 89(2). Note that Art 5(1)(b) (purpose limitation) does allow some types of archiving for public, research or statistical purposes to be done without further consent where the processing is not considered to be incompatible with the original purpose; but considerable safeguards are required (Art 89(1)).
[105] See important clarifications of the rights to object to automated decision making and profiling in Article 29 Working Party *Guidelines on Automated Individual Decision-Making and Profiling for the Purposes*

(ii) to seek rights to rectify or erase data or links to that data (the 'right to erasure')
      (Arts 16–18)
(iii) and to request both access to, and portability of, their personal data (Arts 13, 15
      and 20).

We discussed these rights in the previous chapter, where we noted in particular how
limited the protection offered by Art 22 is, given the small number of decisions which
will be both 'solely' decided by automatic processes and will have a 'significant' effect
on the user.

Solutions in the GDPR for those *building* Big Data or ML systems which should
always be considered include:

o Using a Data Protection Impact Assessment (DPIA) before building a Big Data
   application, especially one involving sensitive personal data, or one deemed 'high
   risk' (in which case a DPIA is mandatory).[106]

o Anonymisation or deletion/non-retention of as much personal data as possible.

o Encryption.

o Other forms of Privacy by Design (termed 'data protection by design' in the
   GDPR).[107]

o Use of ethical advisory boards or adherence to industry sectoral standards certified
   by an approved body, and potentially evidenced by trust marks and trust seals.[108]

o Continuing audit and adherence to principles of accountability.[109]

The big question then is: can DP law adapt in reality to Big Data? The jury remains
out. There have been various suggestions as to how the accountability of those who
conduct Big Data analytics can be ensured beyond (or instead of – see below) simple
enforcement of the GDPR principles we have surveyed. The use of internal or external
ethics boards for businesses, or the creation of ethical standards or charters for industry or public sectors, are popular suggestions.[110] Of course, ethics lacks the mandatory

---

of Regulation 2016/679 WP251, 3 October 2017, and comment on these in M Veale and L Edwards. 'Clarity,
Surprises, and Further Questions in the Article 29 Working Party Draft Guidance on Automated Decision-
Making and Profiling' (2018) *Computer Law & Security Review* 398.

[106] See GDPR, Art 35.

[107] GDPR, Art 25.

[108] See n 115 below. GDPR, Arts 40–43 also incentivise the creation of sectoral codes of conduct and certification of organisations.

[109] GDPR, Art 5(2). The points discussed in nn 1066–109 are explored in suitable detail in Chapter 13.

[110] See from a very large selection of sources: in the UK, the Royal Society/British Academy report,
Machine Learning: The Power and Promise of Computers that Learn by Example (April 2017), available
at https://royalsociety.org/~/media/policy/projects/machine-learning/publications/machine-learning-report.
pdf. Its recommendations have led to the forthcoming establishment of a Centre for Data and Ethics in
the UK (see for alert comment, 'Another Toothless Wonder? Why the UK.Gov's Data Ethics Centre Needs
Clout' (*The Register*, 24 November 2017), available at www.theregister.co.uk/2017/11/24/another_tooth-
less_wonder_why_the_ukgovs_data_ethics_centre_needs_some_clout/; for the US, see Campolo et al,
AI Now 2017 Report, available at https://ainowinstitute.org/AI_Now_2017_Report.pdf, p 30 *et seq*; in
industry, an ethical Partnership for Artificial Intelligence (AI) has been formed, including many of the
large players, whose work can be found at www.partnershiponai.org/. It is fair to say this is a good time to
be an ethicist.

character of law, and while more flexible, may also be seen as a 'soft' or counter-regulatory option. Another version of this approach is to build ethics into standards for building software (and hardware such as robots) and there is a great deal of activity here right now from ICO, Institute of Electrical and Electronics Engineers (IEEE), British Standards Institute (BSI) and others.[111]

An alternate approach is to argue, as some US commentators do, that Big Data conveys 'the ability of society to harness information in novel ways to produce useful insights or goods and services of significant value'[112] and that therefore we must 'revisit the balance between privacy and information flows in a world of not only vastly more data but also more rapidly changing, valuable uses of that data'.[113] In other words, privacy must give way to generating profit and innovation for the good of society. This suggestion of 'big data exceptionalism[114] – at its most extreme the idea that safeguards on collecting personal data should be abandoned, and only restraints on use survive – may fly in the risk-taking, 'permissionless innovation' campuses of Silicon Valley, but is unlikely to go down well in the EU. Even innovation-friendly countries with short histories of privacy regulation, such as Singapore, Japan and South Korea, are moving more towards the EU 'gold standard' of DP law than away from it.[115] Notably, China, the principal major player lacking DP protections, has recently passed a 'standard' that comes very close to a data protection law.[116] In this climate, it is actually the US which stands out as the principle outlier in resisting strong DP rules. We may find in the new Asian DP world however some pointers towards ways of *balancing* particular areas of public interest in data-driven innovation with individual human rights to respect for privacy. We consider these after our last section on the Internet of Things.

---

[111] At the time of writing, the IEEE is preparing candidate standards for AI and ethical standards across a variety of application areas (P7000-P7003) – this author is on the committee for P7003 *Algorithmic Bias Considerations*. See further discussion in J Bryson and A Winfield, 'Standardising Ethical Design for AI and Autonomous Systems' (2017) 50(5) *Computer* 116.

[112] V Mayer-Schönberger and K Cukier (n 93).

[113] FH Cate and V Mayer-Schönberger, 'Notice and Consent in a World of Big Data' (2013) 3 *International Data Privacy Law* 67, 73. More bluntly, Tene and Polonetsky argue that '[t]he big data business model is antithetical to data minimization ... data minimization is simply no longer the market norm' (see O Tene and J Polonetsky, 'Big Data for All: Privacy and User Control in the Age of Analytics' (2013) 11 *Northwestern Journal of Technology and Intellectual Property* 5).

[114] See H Nissenbaum, 'Deregulating Collection: Must Privacy Give Way to Use Regulation?' (1 May 2017). Available at SSRN: https://ssrn.com/abstract=3092282.

[115] See evidence from G Greenleaf whose life mission has been to survey the rise of DP standards globally and in Asia particularly: see '"European" Data Privacy Standards Implemented in Laws Outside Europe' (2017) 149 *Privacy Laws & Business International Report* 21, which claims that after surveying the 20 highest GDP countries outside Europe that have DP-like laws, the current global standard for data privacy laws is moving closer to the EU DPD's standards than those of the Organisation for Economic Co-operation and Development or the US's Fair Information Processing Principles. Japan and South Korea at the time of writing are vying to achieve adequacy in terms of the EU's GDPR standards: see Chapter 3 at section IV. – and Singapore's DP law is discussed below.

[116] See G Greanleaf, 'China's Personal Information Standard: The Long March to a Privacy Law' (2017) 150 *Privacy Laws & Business International Report* 25. The Standard was officially released on 29 December 2017 and became effective on 1 May 2018.

VI. The Internet of Things

The Internet of Things (IoT), also known as ubiquitous computing (ubicomp), ambient intelligence, or pervasive computing, has a long history in computer science but has only fairly recently come to the attention of lawyers. The Pew Research Center defines the IoT as 'a global, immersive, invisible, ambient networked computing environment built through the continued proliferation of smart sensors, cameras, software, databases, and massive data centres in a world-spanning information fabric'.[117] The number of 'things' connected to the Internet has long exceeded the number of people.[118] Technically, the IoT is made up of billions of 'smart' devices, and is growing at a breathtaking pace, from two billion objects in 2006 to a projected 200 billion by 2020.[119] Historically the IoT has been an industrial concept – used in factories, retail chains, businesses, and transport and tagging of goods as a kind of 'intelligent barcode'. However, the IoT has now very much moved into the domestic and consumer world. Over the last few years we have seen the rise of connected toys,[120] cars,[121] TVs[122] and so on, alongside developments such as smart metering of domestic energy consumption[123] and primitive 'robots'[124] helping vacuum our homes or care for the elderly, thus combining to make 'smart homes' or 'smart workplaces'.[125] The logical end-product of this step-change is the 'smart city' – a connected urban environment where transport, housing, crime surveillance, energy provision and many other aspects of civic life are monitored and integrated. This has tremendous utility for concerns such as improving environmental and energy efficiency, and so is being taken very seriously, especially in emergent economies where whole new smart cities are being built from scratch. It may also be seen, however, to represent the building of new forms of the Panopticon.[126] As the

---

[117] Pew Research Internet Project, 'The Internet of Things Will Thrive by 2025' (14 May 2014), available at www.pewinternet.org/2014/05/14/internet-of-things/.

[118] FTC Report (n 83).

[119] IDC, Intel, United Nations.

[120] For some typical worries here, see J Sheffield, 'Mattel's WiFi Barbie Could be Used to Spy on Children' *The Independent* (18 March 2015), available at www.independent.co.uk/news/business/news/mattels-wifibarbie-could-be-used-to-spy-on-children-10115724.html.

[121] See, inter alia, *Resolution on Data Protection in Automated and Connected Vehicles*, 39th International Conference of Data Protection and Privacy Commissioner, Hong Kong (25–29 September 2017), available at https://edps.europa.eu/sites/edp/files/publication/resolution-on-data-protection-in-automated-and-connected-vehicles_en_1.pdf.

[122] See n 59.

[123] On the privacy implications of smart metering, see I Brown, 'Britain's Smart Meter Programme: A Case Study in Privacy by Design' (2014) 28(2) *International Review of Law, Computers & Technology* 172.

[124] See, for example, R Calo, 'Robots and Privacy' in Lin et al (eds), *Robot Ethics: The Ethical and Social Implications of Robotics* (MIT Press, 2011). On ethical and privacy implications (inter alia) see European Parliament Resolution of 16 February 2017 with recommendations to the Commission on Civil Law Rules on Robotics (2015/2103(INL)).

[125] Surveillance by trackers such as wearables in the smart workplace, is an emerging fascinating area in the already conflicted space of employee monitoring. See discussion in Article 29 Working Party *Opinion 2/2017 on Data Processing at Work*, WP 249, 8 June 2017. Note that Art 88 of the GDPR gives Member States the right and duty to make supplementary rules to protect the privacy of employees.

[126] See discussion in L Edwards, 'Privacy, Security and Data Protection in Smart Cities: A Critical EU Law Perspective' (2016) 2 *European Data Protection Law Review* 28. See also A Townsend,

IoT continues to grow and spread from industrial into domestic and other 'human' environments, the number of privacy and security concerns will inevitably multiply.

Location data, which is the key piece of data collected by the IoT, is an increasingly vital part of the general thrust towards profiling and creation of Big Data. The PECD tried to give users an early legal protection in the form of a right to give or refuse prior informed consent specifically to the collection of location data[127] by electronic communications service providers (primarily, mobile phone operators). There then arose a debate about how far these protections applied to RFID chips, which were the earliest form of the IoT, small and inexpensive passive chips which were used in many retail and domestic systems and basically only gave away their location.[128]

The IoT is now however about much more than just collection of location data. For example, a smartphone will measure its acceleration as it moves, so it can estimate things like the user's speed and time to destination, as well as interpret various types of movement. Wearables like the Fitbit and Jawbone may collect heartrate and 'steps', and perhaps other biometrics such as blood pressure or body heat. Sensors in smart shopping centres may collect pressure of footsteps. (A more low-tech option is simply to measure footfall by the presence of mobile phone identifiers.) Smart CCTV may collect our images and listen to conversations, and these video images may be transformed into intercepted transcripts via ML algorithms that automate lip-reading.[129] Smart fridges may monitor what fresh food we buy (or don't), order new choices and chastise us for our lack of healthy eating.[130] This has sometimes been called the 'internet of stoolpigeons'[131] – a 24/7 surveillance world of ubiquitous sensors which simultaneously has the potential to give us the kind of immersive experience we have only dreamed of in movies like *Minority Report* and *Her*.

Hildebrandt and Koops sum up this contradictory allure in their concept of 'ambient intelligence':

> Ambient Intelligence presents an adaptive environment that 'learns' what time you get up, how you like your coffee, which types of groceries you buy in the course of the week, what kind of news, mail, or calls are relevant for your professional life; it calculates what is important and what is urgent, in order to alter, sort, and prioritise incoming communications for you. Ambient Intelligence is based on proactive computing meant to adapt your

Smart Cities: Big Data, Civic Hackers, and the Quest for a New Utopia (WW Norton & Co, 2014) and R Kitchin, 'The Ethics of Smart Cities and Urban Science' (2016) 374(2083) *Philosophical Transactions of The Royal Society*.

[127] PECD, Art 9. 'Location data' for these purposes was narrowly defined as data 'indicating the geographic position of the terminal equipment of a user of a publicly available electronic communications service' (PECD, Art 2(c) and Recital 14).

[128] For a full discussion of the EU history of governance in respect of RFID chips, see Edwards and Hatcher (n 16) 520–528.

[129] See 'Google's DeepMind AI can Lip-Read TV Shows Better than a Pro' (*New Scientist*, 21 November 2016), available at www.newscientist.com/article/2113299-googles-deepmind-ai-can-lip-read-tv-shows-better-than-a-pro/.

[130] This longstanding researcher dream is now, scarily, coming true: see 'Samsung's New SMART FRIDGE Plays Movies and Music, Learns your Voice, and even Serves up Recipes Based on your Soon-to-Expire Food' *The Sun* (8 January 2018), available at www.thesun.co.uk/tech/5294662/samsung-family-hub-refrigerator-fridge-2018/.

[131] 'Hacked Dog, a Car that Snoops on you and a Fridge Full of Adverts: The Perils of the Internet of Things' *The Guardian* (11 March 2015), available at www.theguardian.com/technology/2015/mar/11/internet-of-things-hacked-online-perils-future.

environment to your preferences before you become aware of them. It organises your life at a subliminal level by seamlessly catering to your needs and desires and thus providing you with personalised opportunities based on a calculated anticipation of what you would have preferred had you known what the smart environment 'knows'.[132]

A. Regulating Processing of Data in the IoT and Ambient Environments

Unless operating in a wholly industrial environment, many IoT systems will process personal data, and thus fall within the GDPR unless steps have been taken to effectively anonymise any personal data gathered. Furthermore, the GDPR makes it clear that personal identifiers can be personal data, and specific reference is made to include RFID tags which are one of the root technologies of the IoT (GDPR, Recital 30). Thus, if personal data is collected or processed by IoT systems, a lawful ground for processing is *prima facie* required.

This troubled the Article 29 Working Party[133] when it came in 2014 to consider how the DP law (under the DPD) regulated the IoT, especially in respect to *consent* to processing of personal data. A significant number of issues were raised, particularly with consent, including the facts that:

- data may be shared automatically machine to machine (M2M), with no transparency to the user, or an opportunity to review;

- the *quality* of any user consent may be poor. For example, there may simply be no opportunity for refusal of consent. As the Article 29 Working Party said, '… [T]he possibility to renounce certain services or features of an IoT device is more a theoretical concept than a real alternative … such situations lead to the question of whether the users consent to the underlying data processing can then be considered as free, hence valid under EU law.' Put simply, in an ambient IoT environment, you are likely to be sharing data (for example with a WiFi hotspot) before you even know you are, let alone have a chance to think about refusing consent;

- IoT devices often simply do not usually have means to display privacy notices and/or to 'provide fine-tuned consent in line with the preferences expressed by individuals', because devices developed for industrial use were usually small, screenless and lacked a user interface.[134]

Consent is, however, as discussed several times above, not the only ground for lawful processing, and nor does it, contrary to popular belief, have any particular priority. Where IoT systems are used to prevent or detect crime (as with most smart CCTV systems) the GDPR may be excluded along with lawful grounds/consent

---

[132] M Hildebrandt and BJ Koops, 'The Challenges of Ambient Law and Legal Protection in the Profiling Era' (2010) 73 *Modern Law Review* 428.
[133] Article 29 Working Party, *Opinion 8/2014 on Recent Developments on the Internet of Things*, WP 223, 16 September 2014 (hereinafter 'A29WP IoT Opinion'). See further on consent, E Kosta, *Consent in European Data Protection Law* (Brill/Nijhoff, 2013).
[134] A29WP IoT Opinion, *ibid* 7.

requirements.[135] Where local or national governmental agencies gather data for e-government systems, e-health, or e-welfare, then a ground of 'public interest' can also sidestep any need for consent (GDPR, Art 6(1)(e)). But for most commercial systems, what we might expect to see is a heavy reliance on the 'legitimate interests' ground of processing under the GDPR (Art 6(1)(f)), which might become a worryingly easy way to circumvent any semblance of user control.

The Article 29 Working Party clearly shared these concerns, and went out of its way in its 2014 Opinion on the IoT to stress that, following *Google Spain*,[136] it was unlikely that processing of data via IoT devices which reveals the 'individual state of health, home or intimacy, his/her location and … his/her private life' could 'be justified by merely the economic interest' of an IoT stakeholder, given the need to balance this against the fundamental rights of the data subject.[137]

B. Enter the e-Privacy Directive

The PECD is *lex specialis* to the GDPR (as will be its successor, the e-Privacy Regulation (EPR)). This means in essence that if both regimes apply – as they do when we are talking about the IoT and personal data – the PECD rules take precedence. The general rules of the GDPR allowing multiple lawful grounds for processing of personal data must therefore be read as restricted in IoT environments by Art 5(3) of the PECD, which requires, since its revision in 2009, that where 'information' is stored on the 'terminal equipment[138] of a user' (or access if given to it when it is already stored there) the user must give *consent* to such storage, having been provided with 'clear and comprehensive information' about the purposes for which that information will be processed. This rule (which is the same one as the notorious 'cookies consent' rule considered above) has had important consequences for the IoT.

Assuming the above applies to the IoT (see below), prior informed consent is the *only* way such storage can be legitimised; there are no alternative grounds. (The same also applies to the consent necessary for the collection of *location* data by communications service providers under PECD, Art 9.) Such consent must be 'informed' but need not be explicit. Strenuous attempts were made during the passage of the draft EPR to add an equivalent to a 'legitimate interests' alternative to consent: so far, as of

---

[135] But note the new DP Policing Directive may apply instead. See Directive 2016/680 on the protection of natural persons with regard to the processing of personal data by competent authorities for the purposes of the prevention, investigation, detection or prosecution of criminal offences of the execution of criminal penalties, and on the free movement of such data, and repealing Council Framework Decision 2008/977/JHA [2016] OJ L119/89.

[136] Case C-131/12 *Google Spain v Agencia Española de Protección de Datos (AEPD) and González* (CJEU, 13 May 2014), cited at A29 WP IoT opinion (n 133) para 4.2.

[137] It should also be noticed that if *sensitive* personal data is processed – as will invariably be the case in a health related IoT system, such as telemedicine for the aged – then processing can in most circumstances only be legitimised by explicit consent and the 'legitimate interests' ground will not suffice (GDPR, Art 9, although note Art 9(2)(c) *in extremis* (vital interests)).

[138] This phrase is undefined in the PECD. The A29 WP IoT Opinion suggested helpfully that it 'be understood in the same manner as that of "equipment" in art 4(1)(c)' (n 133) para 4.1.

January 2018, these have failed.[139] This special requirement of consent is regarded as a key safeguard for protection of the fundamental right to privacy of communications, but given the canvassed difficulties of providing consent in IoT environments, it is also a severe constraint on both industry and e-government (smart cities especially).

But does Art 5(3) *in fact* apply to information collected about users by IoT sensors? This question has dogged the history of IoT regulation. It is currently predicated on two issues:

(i)   whether such information is stored in the 'terminal equipment of the user'; and
(ii) whether the networks to which IoT sensors connect are 'public' enough to fall within the scope of the PECD.

i. When is IoT Data Stored in the 'Terminal Equipment of the User'?

As we have seen, Art 5(3) has been primarily used to control the placing of cookies on a user's computer without her knowledge and consent. It is unclear how far this provision applies to data about users collected from sensors of various kinds in the 'real world'. It is often hard to envisage an IoT environment as the 'terminal equipment of the user', the phrase clearly having been designed to fit the modern computer, laptop or smartphone and not much else. Is a smart fridge terminal equipment? Is a connected car? Furthermore, who is the 'user'? Is it the owner of the connected car (who may not be the usual occupier) – or everyone who rides in it? Since the data of *all* riders is likely to be collected, one would hope the latter.

Attempts were made during the passage of the 2009 amendments to the PECD to amend Art 5(3) to give it a wider and clearer applicability to the IoT, but for political reasons these resulted only in a change in the recitals.[140] Recital 56 of the PECD now reads:

> When such devices are connected to publicly available electronic communications networks or make use of electronic communications services as a basic infrastructure, the relevant provisions of Directive 2002/58/EC, including those on security, traffic and location data and on confidentiality, should apply.

ii. Is IoT Data Collected by Devices Connected to 'Publicly Available Electronic Communications Networks'?

This formulation was intended to extend coverage to *private* networks connected to the *public* Internet (very common with 'smart' products), but it is not without uncertainty. The EDPS criticised the failure to amend this scope restriction in 2009,[141] but

---

[139] Another useful addition might have been a 'domestic purposes' or household exemption akin to that found in the GDPR.

[140] See E Kosta, 'Peeking into the Cookie Jar: The European Approach towards the Regulation of Cookies' (2013) 21 *International Journal of Law and Information Technology* 380, and Recital 65 of the Citizens Rights Directive (Directive 2009/136/EC [2009] OJ L337/11) amending Directive 2002/22/EC (see n 2).

[141] See the EDPS's *Second Opinion on the Review of the PECD* (9 January 2009). See also criticism from the European Commission in 'Radio Frequency Identification (RFID) in Europe: Steps towards a Policy Framework' (P6 COM(2007) 96 final, 15 March 2007).

the alternate proposed formulation that the PECD should apply generally to 'publicly accessible private networks' was unfortunately not added.

One further 'get out of jail' card for IoT developers here is the exception from consent under Art 5(3) where storage is 'strictly necessary in order to provide a service explicitly requested by the subscriber or user' (again we have already considered this exception above, in the context of cookies). It seems fairly logical to assert that, for example, the location of a connected car must be collected for it to work and that that service has been explicitly requested by the passengers ('users'). What is rather less clear is if this is true if the location is used to help navigate *another* connected car, as will happen given M2M communications. The *re-use* of that location data for, say, building a profile to provide targeted ads beamed to the car's internal dashboard, would also not benefit from the exemption.

Requiring consent to legitimise collection and processing of data via IoT systems, with no alternate grounds, should not be the end of the world. Consent is not desperately hard to obtain in situations where there is a contractual nexus (though its quality and freely given nature may still be doubted). The user who buys a connected car or a fitness tracker can be asked to give explicit consent, even to the collection of sensitive personal data, when they buy the product, download the app, etc. However, in situations where there is no obvious contract, for example where the user walks into a shopping mall and her presence is sensed via her smartphone's unique identifier, or where the user's body heat or speed of walking are measured in some other public area by ground sensors, then it will be considerably harder to claim that consent of any kind was given, and surely impossible to claim that *explicit* consent, of the kind required for processing *special* categories of data under Art 9 of the GDPR, was given. (For the former, non-special category of data, attempts may be made at finessing this to find 'consent' via notices, eg at entry to shopping malls. These seem unlikely to be a success given the clear requirement in the GDPR Art 4(11) that consent be shown by 'a clear affirmative action'.)

This is a serious problem for builders of IoT-equipped public spaces. One answer is to claim that data collected will always be anonymised. This removes many commercially-useful purposes of processing, so is a rather partial solution, but could be useful for aggregate marketing uses such as measuring footfall, or social uses such as working out the 'hot spots' of an integrated transport network.[142] The problem is however aggravated by the fact that, as we have noted before, much anonymised data is in fact now quite likely to be re-identifiable using Big Data and ML techniques, which means that under the GDPR it will be regarded as personal data.[143] We may not lament this regulatory obstacle if it stops dubious marketing practices in shopping

---

[142] Remember that data that is only pseudonymised is, under the GDPR, still personal data, albeit with some privileges. The GDPR defines pseudonymisation in Art 4(5) as involving 'the processing of personal data in such a manner that the personal data can no longer be attributed to a specific data subject without the use of additional information, provided that such additional information is kept separately and is subject to technical and organisational measures to ensure that the personal data are not attributed to an identified or identifiable natural person'.

[143] See discussion earlier and in Chapter 4.

malls,[144] but it can make life extremely difficult for those who wish perhaps to build socially beneficial ambient environments. A key issue relates to 'cooperative intelligent transportation systems'.[145] CCAVs will likely automatically send information between, and among themselves, in real time, to maximise speed and safety on the roads and to reduce congestion. Do these M2M communications require consent, and if so whose consent, and when? Can anonymisation be any kind of answer when persistently tracking the location of a CCAV? This is a serious issue for the emerging connected car industry, which lobbied during the process of the draft EPR for a 'legitimate interests' alternate ground for processing.

Finally, there is the problem, already identified in relation to connected cars, that one person – the car owner, say – may have a contractual connection to the IoT data controller whereby they have given consent to the collection of data – but there may be no contract with other riders. If they are family members perhaps the owner can be asked to give *their* consent in advance as part of the contract (though this is dubious in many legal systems on grounds of privity of contract), but if they are friends or even strangers (imagine a smart car being used to share a school run to the local school) then how can their consent practically be obtained every time?[146] And what about capacity to consent in the case of minors?

C. The Draft EPR

Crucially, the EPR, unlike the PECD, is clearly intended to govern the IoT. First, the recitals (which are still very much in flux at the time of the writing) specifically mention M2M communications as within the scope of the draft regulation. Furthermore, Art 5, which re-encodes the basic principle of confidentiality of communications, adds a new paragraph which specifically applies this principle to M2M electronic communications (Art 5(2)). Second, the protection of 'information stored in the terminal equipment of a user' (as previously governed by the PECD, Art 5(3)) is extended in Art 8 of the draft EPR to cover information not only stored in, but also, 'related to or processed by *or emitted by*' (my emphasis) such equipment. This is a radical change which clarifies in particular that the collection of user information via WiFi hotspots[147] – a common method of adding location and frequency of encounters to user profiles – does fall

---

[144] See, eg, 'High Street Shops Secretly Track Customers using Smartphones' *The Telegraph* (27 December 2016), available at www.telegraph.co.uk/science/2016/12/27/high-street-shops-secretly-track-customers-using-smartphones/. An interesting side point is that under their terms and conditions of use some consumer IoT devices, such as the Fitbit, forbid users from using pseudonyms to protect their identity.

[145] Discussed in the Data Protection Commissioners' Resolution (n 121).

[146] This is not just a problem for connected cars but for other types of shared 'connected' resources. For example, a smart thermostat like NEST in a 'smart home' collects information about the movements and activities of all the occupants but it is likely that only one or two householders have agreed to share data in the related contract or via an app, and certainly not their friends or strangers who visit the house. See G Noto La Diega and I Walden, 'Contracting for the "Internet of Things": Looking into the Nest' (2016) 7(2) *European Journal of Law and Technology* in which it is suggested that consent (from anyone) would probably not be necessary as data sharing would be 'necessary for the performance of a contract to which the data subject is a party'. But this simply raises the question of which data subject?

[147] It was not clear in the original version of the EPR that consent would be required for WiFi location data collection, merely notice – see Article 29 Working Party concerns in its *Opinion 01/2017* (n 47) para 17.

under the rules about protection of communications confidentiality. Article 8(2) seeks to ensure in particular that WiFi analytics cannot be employed without the knowledge or consent of the user, except in the controversial case of 'statistical counting', meaning for example processing for the purpose of constructing 'heat maps' of how many people are using transport systems, malls, sports grounds, etc.

Third, the draft EPR replaces the specific concepts of location and traffic data with a general concept of 'electronic communications data' which sub-divides into content and meta-data (Art 4(3)). 'Electronic communications meta-data' is then defined to include:

> data processed in or by means of electronic communications network services for the purposes of transmitting, distributing or exchanging electronic communications content; including data used to trace and identify the source and destination of a communication, data on the location of the device generated in the context of providing electronic communications services, and the date, time, duration and the type of communication.

Again, this fairly clearly applies to a great deal of information collected or processed by IoT systems.

Finally, the EPR deals with the uncertainty observed in the PECD concerning whether IoT systems run on 'publicly available networks'. Draft Recital 13 provides that the EPR applies to 'networks providing access to a group of end-users which is not pre-defined and where end-users get access to the network under the same conditions, e.g. wifi network of a department store open to all customers, [is] regulated by this Regulation'. This clarifies that data collected by IoT sensors such as WiFi or smart TVs in private spaces where users can have access, such as hotels, coffee shops or airports is subject to the PECR; it still leaves uncertain, it seems, what the situation is where a private network collects data from users but they do not themselves have access rights, for example in a supermarket where user interactions are measured via smart CCTV, IoT tags on retail items and footfall sensors.[148]

Article 8 of the draft EPR thus roughly replicates the protections of Art 5(3) of the PECD but with a much clearer application to the IoT. It provides that '[t]he use of processing and storage capabilities of terminal equipment and the collection of information from end-users' terminal equipment, including about its software and hardware, other than by the end-user concerned shall be prohibited', except in certain circumstances (which are the same as those we already looked at above in relation to the updating of the cookies and OBA rules). These include:

- it is *necessary* for the sole purpose of carrying out the transmission of an electronic communication over an electronic communications network; or

---

On WiFi location analytics and DP generally, see the ICO's useful practical guidance in 'Wi-Fi Location Analytics' (ICO, 2016, v1.0 at the time of writing), available at https://ico.org.uk/media/for-organisations/documents/1560691/wi-fi-location-analytics-guidance.pdf.

[148] See, eg, the interesting new phenomenon of Amazon Go – supermarkets without human staff where billing for goods taken from shelves and checkout are completely automated. Of course, even if the draft PECR did not apply, the GDPR still would if personal data was processed (as would seem inevitable). See, eg, 'Amazon Could be Planning to Bring its Checkout-Free Grocery Stores to Europe' (*The Verge*, 20 May 2017), available at www.theverge.com/2017/5/20/15669982/amazon-go-checkout-free-grocery-stores-europe-trademark. It seems to this author there may be DP difficulties with this initiative, given the level of surveillance required.

- the end-user has given his or her *consent*; or
- it is *necessary* for providing an information society service requested by the end-user; or
- if it is *necessary* for web audience measuring, provided that such measurement is carried out by the provider of the information society service requested by the end-user;[149] or
- it is *necessary* for a security update (my emphasis).

As can be seen, all these exemptions are fairly limited by the use of the word 'necessary', except user consent which is thus likely to remain the primary enabler of IoT tracking.

Article 6 of the draft EPR then replaces the provisions of Arts 6 and 9 of the PECD on location and traffic data with wider rules relating to permitted processing of electronic communications data. In relation to both content and meta-data, user data can only be collected if it is necessary to enable the communication or to maintain or restore the security of the communication (including fault detection). In relation to meta-data, including location, in essence consent must be given, but it will only be valid if it is shown that the purpose of processing could not be fulfilled by anonymising their data.

A number of familiar exceptions exist, including that:

- It is necessary for the contract to which the user is party – this includes billing, and detecting fraudulent transactions and abuse of the service.
- It is necessary for compliance with a legal obligation.
- It is necessary to protect the vital interests of the user (ie when consent cannot physically be given).
- It is necessary for scientific research or statistical purposes (but then demands are made for proportionate safeguards such as encryption and pseudonymisation to protect users).

In short, therefore,[150] consent remains at least as significant an issue under the draft EPR as under the PECD, and arguably remains a problem for the development and use of the IoT under the new instrument.[151] While it is true that Art 6 opens up possibilities for processing of communications data, including location data, which are wider than those that existed in the PECD, this may yet be altered before the final version of the EPR and, on the whole, despite the best lobbying efforts of industry, the whole instrument has remained remarkably 'consent centred', resting on the fundamental

---

[149] See discussion above, at n 47 re 'web analytics' and also draft Art 8(2)(c).

[150] A very truncated version of the draft EPR Art 6 has been given here. This is partly because it is quite likely that these rules will substantially alter before the final version is passed.

[151] It is true that compared to the PECD, there are now substantially more grounds for the processing of location data than was true in that instrument. However, these new grounds are very limited by the use of the word 'necessary'. Note that Recital 3, EPR confirms that the rules of the EPR continue as *lex specialis* to take precedence over those of the GDPR: 'Processing of electronic communications data by providers of electronic communications services should only be permitted in accordance with this Regulation'.

sensitivity of communications, both content and meta-data, and respect for the protection given by Art 8 of the ECHR.[152]

Furthermore, the hoped for 'silver bullet' solution to consent issues in respect of cookies and OBA, namely the Do Not Track requirements of draft Art 10, may have some application to the IoT where there is a contractual nexus (for example, a user could set her phone browser not to share data with WiFi hotspots – but she may find this somewhat counter-productive), but it does not get us much further for public collection of data in the IoT where no contract and no applicable user-accessible web or software interface exists.

VII. Where Do We Go Now? Augmenting the Consent Based Paradigm

Above, we have seen a critical battleground emerging in the wake of the discovery of the enormous commercial and societal gains which can be made from unfettered use of Big Data. We have seen the rise of profiling from the early days of cookies to the reality now where it seems that every portion of our lives, however intimate,[153] can theoretically be converted into data points which can be accessed, stored, aggregated, processed, shared and transformed via ML algorithms to classify, sell things to, and socially sort us.[154] This offends and scares many – perhaps most – of us in Europe, who are by no means all privacy fundamentalists. The values involved go beyond privacy and data protection to embrace issues like discrimination, fairness, transparency, access to knowledge, the right to an individual identity and a basic feeling of control over the world we live in.

It is often said that most people want convenience and opportunity, free treats and social benefit, far more than they want privacy, but that is not the correct dichotomy to focus on. People also want to live in a world where they understand why and how decisions are being made about them (especially high risk public sector decisions) and then to have some chance of influencing those decisions, both by planning their future and understanding their past, not living in a capricious bureaucratic cloud of uncertainty. These worries now go far beyond what adverts we see or even what products we are sold: they embrace, in the personal realm, our employment, insurance, credit, education and reputational prospects, and in the societal realm, inter alia the potential degradation of democracy by fake news, the fairness of distribution of welfare and health benefits and the accountability of criminal justice systems. A recent study by UK NGO, doteveryone, pinpointed that, although users may be willing to sacrifice

---

[152] See draft EPR, Recitals 1–2.

[153] See, eg, the rise of connected sex toys, often with unfortunate results – see N Brown, 'Sextech: Sticky Legal Issues?' (2017) *Society for Computers and Law*, available at www.scl.org/articles/3859-sextech-sticky-legal-issues.

[154] D Lyon (ed), *Surveillance as Social Sorting: Privacy, Risk and Automated Discrimination* (Routledge, 2003).

their own privacy for convenience, they are nevertheless worried about what this is doing to *society*:

> The internet has had a strongly positive impact on our lives as individuals, but people are less convinced it has been beneficial for society as a whole. 50% say it has made life a lot better for people like themselves, only 12% say it's had a very positive impact on society.[155]

As we noted above, there are prevalent arguments, especially from the US, that if we are to reap the benefits for society of everything from new health treatments to better security and policing, we must move beyond a focus on consent to *collection* of data, to either consent to a particular *use* of Big Data, or perhaps even removing consent as a pivotal concept altogether. The rise of 'deep learning' and the over-hyped reports on the potential arrival of artificial intelligence (AI) that will solve all our woes via unsupervised learning and some mythical 'singularity' have reinforced these arguments.[156]

But as Nissenbaum astutely notes, there is a problem that the main accumulators and controllers of Big Data are not the state (although governmental data is an increasing force, especially in the form of 'open data') but large companies driven by private profit and shareholder value – and a very restricted, US-centred group of companies at that. So far, the evidence is, she asserts, that those who collect Big Data are the ones who benefit from it and any societal benefit, while possible, is mainly a happy side-effect.

> In reality, there are no assurances that opening the floodgates and relieving these dominant data collectors of accountability will result in celebrated knowledge gains and decisional integrity in service of individual[s] or, for that matter, the common good. Not that it will not serve them at all; only that it is unlikely to be the primary motivation.[157]

Furthermore, accumulation of Big Data without controls on collection or storage prior to use will accentuate the drive to 'stock up' for the 'treasure hunt', with concomitant rises in both insider and outsider attacks on the security of the data stores being likely.

But there can, perhaps, be compromises between the stance dominant in European institutions, that privacy as a fundamental right must be defended at all costs *primarily or exclusively by consent*, and the position of Silicon Valley that Big Data is the new oil[158] and whoever has the least trouble acquiring it becomes the new potentates? Even before Big Data, consent had, as we saw in the last chapter, become an increasingly

---

[155] See doteveryone, *People, Power and Technology: The 2018 Digital Attitudes Report*, available at http://attitudes.doteveryone.org.uk/files/People%20Power%20and%20Technology%20Doteveryone%20Digital%20Attitudes%20Report%202018.pdf. The report also found that 'There is a major understanding gap around technologies. Only a third of people are aware that data they have not actively chosen to share has been collected. A quarter have no idea how internet companies make their money ... People feel disempowered by a lack of transparency in how online products and services operate. 89% want clearer terms and conditions, half would like to know how their data is used but can't find out'.

[156] Although an equally unfounded backlash has arrived in the form of a belief that AI will kill us all via the Singularity: see Nick Bostrom's totemic text *Superintelligence* (Oxford, Oxford University Press, 2014).

[157] Nissenbaum (n 114) 23.

[158] This metaphor is much used and abused: see, eg, S Watson, 'Data is the New "___"' (DIS Magazine, 2018) available at http://dismagazine.com/discussion/73298/sara-m-watson-metaphors-of-big-data/. It has been said that big data to a privacy advocate is not so much the new oil as toxic waste. Brown and Marsden have suggested in their *Regulating Code* (MIT Press, 2013) that data is more like silk than oil in that it is not dug up and inanimate but rather is spun from the life experiences of many individuals.

meaningless and debased concept in the online world; real consent may in fact be the ultimate luxury good of the elite: well-educated, time-rich and with access to various options. Meanwhile, in this chapter, we have seen that the practical difficulties of providing consent in a meaningful way, especially in relation to the IoT, are enormous.

When we turn to ML in particular, this author has in other work pointed out at length that a right to transparency of the logic behind ML algorithms does not inherently empower users or provide them with remedies – this can be described as a 'transparency fallacy'.[159] Understanding is not the same as power, and there are many reasons, already canvassed, why choice may still not be free or real or useful even where 'notice' is available. Substantial evidence from behavioural science[160] has demonstrated that individuals themselves do not, as liberal philosophy has it, make informed and rational choices, but respond to lack of time and resources and cognitive shortcomings which leave them open to 'nudging'[161] and worse. Consent theory places most of the burden of safeguarding privacy and autonomy on data subjects, which is an incomprehensible position when they have neither the resources nor the overall insights of data controllers. Indeed, arguably no one can really predict what happens to their personal data in a modern data-driven ecology.

For all these reasons many commentators have agreed that 'notice and choice', narrowly, and consent more widely, are near-fatally broken.[162] If we are to go on depending on consent, we need at least to find better ways of understanding it, providing it and withholding it. We need also to consider how we can deal with protecting rights and autonomy in other ways, where consent is simply not the best method, or where society may suffer from the poor consent practices of individuals.[163]

Singapore is an interesting example here, being a modern Asian state with some European heritage which exerts semi-paternalistic rule over its citizens but which also thrives and has become extremely wealthy on digital industry. Singapore is also a state that thinks of itself as a smart city as a social experiment,[164] and is thus trying actively to find answers to the huge difficulties of IoT consent. The Singapore DP authority is therefore currently proposing,[165] rather radically, that a new approach to consent in Big Data and IoT environments should be taken. Referring but explicitly to smart environments, it notes:

> … where huge volumes of personal data involving large numbers of individuals are collected at high velocities and from a variety of sources, it may not be practical for organisations to

---

[159] 'Slave' (n 87).

[160] The work of Alessandro Acquisti and his team at Carnegie Mellon in applying behavioural science to privacy has been outstanding over a period of decades: for a recent summary, see A Acquisti et al, 'Privacy and Human Behavior in the Age of Information" (2015) 347 *Science* 509, available at www.cmu.edu/dietrich/sds/docs/loewenstein/PrivacyHumanBeh.pdf.

[161] See C Sunstein and R Thaler, *Nudge* (Yale University Press, 2008).

[162] See recent evidence from R Joergensen, 'The Unbearable Lightness of User Consent' (2014) 3(4) *Internet Policy Review*.

[163] We discussed the idea of privacy as a group value as well as an individual right in Chapter 3 – see n 16.

[164] See 'What the UK can Learn from Singapore's Smart City' (*Wired UK*, 20 June 2017), available at www.wired.co.uk/article/sara-watson-singapore-smart-cities.

[165] See Singapore Personal Data Protection Commission, *Public Consultation for Approaches to Managing Personal Data in the Digital Economy* (27 July 2017), available at www.pdpc.gov.sg/-/media/Files/PDPC/PDF-Files/Legislation-and-Guidelines/publicconsultationapproachestomanagingpersonaldatainthedigital-economy270717f95e65c8844062038829ff000.pdf.

seek individuals' consent in every instance of data collection, or to attempt to identify the individuals in order to seek their consent for every new purpose. In some cases, organisations do not have a means of contacting the individuals to seek their consent. Facilitating withdrawals of consent in some of these situations may also pose a challenge [at para 2.2].

It goes on to say:

The frequent taking of consent and proliferation of verbose consent clauses may unduly burden individuals and cause consent fatigue. An approach that calibrates the balance of responsibilities by holding organisations accountable to act responsibly and adopt pre-emptive preventive measures can meaningfully address consent fatigue [at para 2.3].

And, finally, it notes that debased individual choices about consent can have bad effects for society:

The consent approach also assumes that individuals, in exercising 'informed' choice over their personal data, will weigh the cost to themselves and the benefits to the wider public. Individual consent decisions, however, may not always yield the most desirable collective outcomes for society ... A recalibration of the balance between individual autonomy and corporate responsibility may be necessary, particularly in situations where the use or disclosure is appropriate, is expected to have broader systemic benefits or is unlikely to have any adverse impact on the individual [at para 2.4].

As a result, the Singapore DP authority proposes replacing consent with other mechanisms in 'circumstances where *consent is not feasible or desirable, and where the collection, use or disclosure would benefit the public* (or sections thereof)'.[166] Instead, organisations collecting data in such scenarios would have to

(i)   *Make appropriate notification to the public* (possibly one-to-many) of the purpose of the collection, use or disclosure of the personal data, and where it is feasible for the organisation to allow individuals to opt out of the collection, use etcetera, how the user can do this.

(ii) *Conduct a risk and impact assessment, such as a data protection impact assessment* ('DPIA'), and put in place measures to *mitigate the risks* when relying on notification as above, rather than consent (my emphasis).

This approach is both scary and enthralling to an EU DP lawyer. It echoes GDPR practice in the emphasis on protection impact assessments, privacy by design and *ex post* accountability. But it removes the central plank of European informational self-determination in smart environments, ie consent. Attractively, however, unlike Nissenbaum's 'big data exceptionalism', it makes these concessions not to allow commercial processing which may accidentally spin-off social benefit as a happy by-product, but explicitly only to enable social benefit, perhaps especially in 'smart city' environments.

---

[166] Para 3.3. It should be noted that Singapore DP law is quite different from EU DP law in having no alternatives to consent, but also having a much more restricted scope than the GDPR, for example it does not cover the public sector at all. Thus, the resort to a consent-free approach arises out of a quite different set of problems than those that arise in EU law.

A. Code Solutions

Privacy enhancing technologies are often touted as the best way forward for the failure of 'traditional' consent. As already noted, data protection by design and by default is mandated by Art 25 of the GDPR. However, the details of what this might entail beyond the familiar mantra of impact assessments, encryption, data minimisation and anonymisation, as well as various specific techniques to prevent the collection of personal data,[167] remain vague. Software solutions can arguably do at least two things:

- Provide better or more meaningful ways to give (and withdraw) consent, and
- Predict and perhaps substitute 'imputed' consent where past experience shows that a user would likely have consented (or not).

We have already seen some practical developments relating to the first idea: notably the concept of DNT. Concerning the second, more aspirational, idea, a concept that was burgeoning when this author was writing about smart cities and consent in 2016,[168] was the idea of 'sticky privacy preferences'.[169] The idea here is that the privacy choices the user makes are remembered by smart systems, and applied the next time a choice needs to be made. A single device in a smart home hub could potentially learn a consumer's preferences based on prior behaviour, perhaps using ML predictive algorithms, and apply them to new appliances and new uses. Fully-fledged programmable software agents have been developed which could be used to make 'semi-autonomous' choices for us about our privacy in ambient environments wherever we encounter them.[170] This idea has gained some currency in human-computer interaction (HCI) and computing science research circles,[171] but has as yet not caught on. There seems a strong danger in that an imputed consent might not be relevant to, or accurate in, the new context, or alternately, that prior privacy preferences, even if correctly identified, might be ignored and 'filed off' when data is shared with third parties, unless some kind of fool-proof 'privacy DRM' is invented.[172] Provenance of data for audit and accountability

---

[167] These techniques range from simple cookie cutters and ad-blockers to more advanced ideas, such as browsers which enable anonymous micro-payments, thus preventing collection of profiling data (and eventual OBA) by websites from which the user buys: see, eg, the Brave browser (a web browser, based on the same open source codebase as Google's Chrome, which lets you 'browse faster by blocking ads and trackers that violate your privacy and cost you time and money' (see https://brave.com)). My thanks to Laurence Diver for this reference.

[168] Edwards (n 126).

[169] See S Pearson and M Carassa-Mont, 'Sticky Policies: An Approach for Managing Privacy across Multiple Parties' (2011) 44(9) Computer 60.

[170] See, eg, R Gomer, MC Shraefel and E Gerding, 'Consenting Agents: Semi-Autonomous Interactions for Ubiquitous Consent' *Proceeding UbiComp '14 Adjunct Proceedings of the 2014 ACM International Joint Conference on Pervasive and Ubiquitous Computing* 653. An attempt to show how a consent prediction system in the mobile environment can be operationalised can be seen in B Liu et al, 'Follow My Recommendations: A Personalized Privacy Assistant for Mobile App Permissions', *Symposium on Usable Privacy and Security (SOUPS) 2016* (22–24 June 2016, Denver, Colorado).

[171] And in law and IT circles, Polonetsky for example proposes obtaining consent in advance through profile management portals that would allow consumers to determine what information they agree to share. See J Polonetsky, *Comments of the Future of Privacy Forum on Connected Smart Technologies in Advance of the FTC 'Internet of Things' Workshop* (10 July 2013).

[172] It has been suggested, unsurprisingly, that blockchain might help with this: see A Ramachandran and M Kantarcioglu, 'Using Blockchain and Smart Contracts for Secure Data Provenance Management' (2017) *arXiv preprint arXiv:1709.10000v1 [cs.CR]*. For a discussion of smart contracts, see Chapter 11.

purposes is an active research field,[173] but at root these techniques merely reinforce the centrality of consent, an approach we have come in the narrative so far to distrust.

What else can code solutions do? Two approaches worth noting include *fairness aware algorithms*; and *personal data containers*. The first of these attempts to deal with the problems discussed above that ML algorithms run considerable risk of producing decisions which are not fair, accountable and transparent (now often known under the acronym FAT, or FATML). A number of techniques are being developed[174] to, for example, exclude factors involving sensitive personal data such as race from algorithmic decisions, incorporate fairness constraints into the models built to make these decisions, and provide external audit of systems by trusted third parties. This work presents numerous challenges. For example, simply excluding race as an input factor from ML systems does not mean that they will be race-neutral, as that factor may simply be reconstructed as the system 'learns' from other factors such as postcode and income to create 'proxies' for race. As another example, in unsupervised learning, input factors are not 'labelled' at the start to be vetted, so they cannot be filtered in advance. Nonetheless, this is a highly significant area of work of which lawyers should be aware.

Personal data containers, which were briefly mentioned in the last chapter, rest on the idea that processing of personal data does not need to occur centrally in the servers of the huge companies such as Google and Facebook where data subjects' data is exposed to profiling and the risk of security breaches. Instead, much of the processing can be done locally ('edge computing'), with only the result of the processing shared with the central service, resulting in a far more privacy-protective solution. Research projects trying to implement this approach in the UK include HaT (Hub of all Things)[175] and Databox,[176] the latter a joint Horizon Nottingham/Imperial College, London Cambridge EPSRC-funded project. Both are particularly focused on addressing the problem of consent in the context of the IoT. In relation to Databox, Haddadi et al argue persuasively[177] that if every user had a 'Databox' of their own, they would enjoy numerous benefits, including a reduction in the risk of major security breaches in central datastores, 'legibility' (the ability to understand what data they have and how it is being used), 'agency' (the ability to control and manage 'our' data and access to it), and 'negotiability' ('[t]he ability to continually navigate our way through the ways that data is social in construction and use'.

---

[173] See, eg, R Aldeco-Perez and L Moreau, 'Provenance-Based Auditing of Private Data Use' *BCS International Academic Conference 2008 – Visions of Computer Science*, available at http://www.bcs.org/upload/pdf/ewic_vs08_s5paper1.pdf.

[174] See, eg, S Hajian and J Domingo-Ferrer, 'A Methodology for Direct and Indirect Discrimination Prevention in Data Mining' (2013) 25(7) *IEEE Transactions on Knowledge and Data Engineering* 1445, and general discussion in RD Binns and M Veale, 'Fairer Machine Learning in the Real World: Mitigating Discrimination without Collecting Sensitive Data' (2017) 4(2) *Big Data & Society* 1. There is a huge literature here which this text cannot canvass. Readers are directed towards the FATML (now FAT*) conferences: see https://fatconference.org/.

[175] See https://hubofallthings.com/.

[176] See www.databoxproject.uk/about/. Disclosure: this author is on the advisory board of Databox and her research is partly funded by the Horizon Digital Economy Hub at Nottingham (EPSRC).

[177] See Haddadi et al, 'Personal Data: Thinking Inside the Box' (2015) *arXiv preprint arXiv:1501.04737v1 [cs.CY]*.

This is a very attractive scenario. But an issue which joins the software and the legal strands of this discussion together is what happens to Big Data and ML algorithms, and the promise they have to solve major societal problems, when data is held locally by millions of individual users, rather than centrally. A new solution to this problem is emerging, called 'distributed machine learning analytics', involving the creation of training models and the application of user data as inputs, even when no central huge 'data silo' of millions of examples is available in one place. If such a technique was perfected outside the lab (and we are only at the very beginnings of this[178]) we might find ways to overcome one of the crucial limitations on societal access to the benefits of Big Data and ML, namely the fact that currently they are largely dependent on 'data silos' accumulated and exploited by the familiar GAFAM giants. (Competition law may be another way to attack these oligopolies,[179] but as has been plain in previous European actions against Google and Microsoft, competition law is a very slow, expensive and often in the end futile way to get anything done in the digital world.)

To return to normative law, after our whistle-stop tour round these aspirational technologies, it may be worth taking a 'helicopter-eye' view at what has happened to privacy protection between Warren and Brandeis' seminal 1890 article[180] and now, in 2018, in the era of algorithmic decision making, ambient intelligence and ubiquitous profiling.

Arguably, we have seen a number of stages in user desires and needs for privacy through the last century, driven by the advancements of technology:

- Privacy 1.0 – leave me alone in my domestic sphere (Warren and Brandeis).

- Privacy 2.0 – let me control *what* is known about me outside the domestic sphere (Westin).

- Privacy 3.0 – let me control *how* I am known, ie moving beyond a take-it-or-leave-it choice either to refuse consent and disengage from the digital society, or to engage with it and suffer harms due to pervasive data collection and profiling. The key speaker here in Europe at the time of writing is Mireille Hildebrandt, who has advocated notably for 'a right to co-determine how we will be read'.[181]

---

[178] See, eg, J Zhao et al, 'Privacy-Preserving Machine Learning Based Data Analytics on Edge Devices', *AAAI AIES 2018 Workshop*, available at www.aies-conference.com/wp-content/papers/main/AIES_2018_paper_161.pdf; S Servia-Rodrigues et al, 'Personal Model Training under Privacy Constraints', *IoTSec 2018* (17 April 2018, Orlando, Florida), available at https://arxiv.org/abs/1703.00380. Note this raises very interesting issues about whether trained and transferable models themselves are a kind of personal data: see M Veale, R Binns and L Edwards, 'Algorithms that Remember: Model Inversion Attacks and Data Protection Law', (2018) *Philosophical Transactions*.

[179] The EU has already noted that the new data portability right in the GDPR – see Chapter 4 section VIII. B. iii., – may be seen partly as a competition law remedy to help break down data silos. In relation to non-personal data therefore, they have suggested a need for similar remedies to encourage access to diverse sources of data, extending beyond portability to interoperability and common standards for data – see EC, *Communication on Building a European Data Economy* (COM(2017)9 final, Brussels, 10 January 2017), available at https://ec.europa.eu/digital-single-market/en/news/communication-building-european-data-economy.

[180] See S Warren and L Brandeis, 'The Right to Privacy' (1890) 4 *Harvard Law Review* 193.

[181] M Hildebrandt, *Smart Technologies and the End(s) of Law* (Elgar, 2015). See also discussion in M Hildebrandt, 'Law as an Affordance: The Devil Is in the Vanishing Point(s)' (2017) 4(1) *Critical Analysis of Law* 116, 124.

In Privacy 3.0, we need rights that go beyond the right merely to consent or refuse consent; we need not only a right to *understand* automated decisions, classifications and service provisions in meaningful ways, but a right to *control* our digital lives in more constructive and subtle ways than simply withdrawing into electronic purdah. We need a right to control our *histories* – possibly with a regular 'reset' button from time to time, a sort of 'right to be forgotten' on steroids – and, above all, in the era of Big Profiling, we need a right to be treated as an individual and not as the aggregate of our peers – a right to be a human, not part of a machine.[182]

---

[182] G Leonhard, *Technology v Humanity* (Fast Future, 2016).

6

A Bridge too Far? The Investigatory Powers Act 2016 and Human Rights Law

NÓRA NI LOIDEAIN*

I. Introduction

This chapter examines the legislative framework governing the use of covert surveillance powers within the UK[1] and the related human rights laws that safeguard the individual's right to respect for private life, particularly data privacy. First, the current landscape of how powerful and intrusive covert surveillance powers have become is explored. Second, the conditions and safeguards that these measures should, at a minimum, be meeting in order to be compatible with Art 8 of the European Convention Human Rights (ECHR) and the related rights under the EU Charter of Fundamental Rights are outlined. Third, the main novel provisions of the Investigatory Powers Act 2016 (IPA), the UK's framework governing covert surveillance, recently enacted to replace the Regulation of Investigatory Powers Act 2000 (RIPA) are examined. The focus here is on the new bulk powers of *acquisition* of data as well as *computer interference*. The issues around *retention* of data are reserved for the next chapter by Eleni Kosta although some overlap, as we shall see, is inevitable. In conclusion, the

* Grateful thanks to Graham Smith, Judith Rauhofer and Julian Huppert for comment on final drafts. The chapter states the law as of 22 March 2018. The case of *R (National Council for Civil Liberties (Liberty)) v Secretary of State for the Home Department* [2018] EWHC 975 (Admin) was decided after the chapter was finalised.
[1] 'Covert surveillance' is used in this chapter to indicate state surveillance, including interception and acquisition of communications, undertaken without notification to, or consent by, the target of surveillance. The phrase is not used in UK legislation in this general sense; and should not be confused with the term of art 'covert human intelligence sources' in Ch 2 of Pt 2 of RIPA (still in operation after the IPA) which refers to surveillance in the non-digital world (eg informers).

details of the pending legal challenges before the ECHR to RIPA, in operation before the IPA, but with obvious implications for its legality, are examined, including some reflections on their potential outcome.

II. Covert Surveillance and Privacy: Technical Developments

In the past century, the power to reveal sensitive personal information from monitoring an individual's communications and movements has been dramatically expanded. This is the result of three main factors – the mobility of communication devices, the ubiquitous addition of the Internet to devices and services, and the convergence of the two previous developments through the creation of 'Internet-enabled' or 'smart' mobile devices.[2] For instance, the amount of information that can be derived from the location data of a landline telephone is unquestionably much more limited when compared to that of any of the many mobile devices that are used by much of current society (phone, tablet, smart watch). We are far beyond the time when electronic communications always took place from the same location, typically the caller's home. We are also no longer living in a society where access to the *content* of a communication reveals the most information about the parties involved. Instead 'meta-data' about a communication (known in UK legislation as 'communications data'), such as traffic and location data, which can identify and locate Internet users and the services and devices they use, how often they communicate, and when, has become perhaps the most crucial investigatory tool for public authorities. Consequently, several provisions of the IPA reflect this shift in emphasis in policy and practice towards greater communications data surveillance.[3]

The 'electronic exhaust'[4] left behind from the constant use of Internet-enabled communications devices has led to the development of a 'rich tracking ecosystem'[5] facilitating the collection of unprecedented amounts of data. Today, we live in an era of 'Big Data' collected from smart cities, smart cars, smart homes and a society that is shifting more towards 'life-logging' and the 'quantified self' (self-surveillance) on online social media platforms.[6] Mobile devices are especially valuable to state surveillance. '[M]ore than other types of technology, mobile devices are typically personal

---

[2] See eg, AA Gillespie, 'Regulation of Internet Surveillance' (2009) 4 *European Human Rights Law Review* 552, 560; N Ni Loideain, '*Cellular Convergence and the Death of Privacy* by S.B. Wicker' (2014) 4(3) *International Data Privacy Law* 243.

[3] See discussion of data retention in Chapter 7.

[4] D Omand, 'Intelligence and Security in the Digital Age' (Conference Paper, University of Cambridge, 1 March 2012).

[5] O Bray, 'The App Effect: How Apps are Changing the Legal Landscape' (2013) 19(2) *Computer and Telecommunications Law Review* 66, 68–69.

[6] See discussion of Big Data and profiling in Chapter 5. See also European Network and Information Security Agency (ENISA), *Risks and Benefits of Emerging Life-Logging Applications* (Heraklion, ENISA, 2011).

to an individual, almost always on, and with the user'.[7] Effectively, the combination of traffic and location data can provide what this author would describe as 'narrative data', tracking information generated from every electronic interaction made by an individual, particularly every online communication.

'Developments like 'Big Data', the Internet of Things and data mining have altered state surveillance in several fundamental ways.[8] First, the scale and detail of personal information that can be acquired from the long-term acquisition, retention and subsequent correlation of traffic and location data, makes the collection of *communications data* immeasurably more intrusive than access to the *content* of a single letter, e-mail or a telephone call. Second, digitised data processing today is automated, cheap and collects everything.[9] It has become easier to collect data by default than not to. Furthermore, private data collection, which the State can also obtain to augment its own databases, has exponentially increased as the business model of most online companies has become based on the processing of personal data (otherwise referred to as 'surveillance capitalism'[10]). Third, it is now possible to construct a profile of an individual that may be considered to be invasive of privacy from isolated items of information that would not once have been considered private or personal.[11] The lines between content and communications have also become blurred: a mailing address does not give away much about content but a website URL certainly does. Consequently, the collection and processing of an individual's communications data can provide a level of monitoring that was never attainable previously.

Finally, such profiling and data mining of Big Data, especially communications data, now makes it possible even to (arguably) predict the future conduct of those monitored. 'Predictive policing' has become a norm in many US police forces and is making inroads in other jurisdictions, including the UK and South Africa.[12] Accordingly, we now live in a time of 'dataveillance'[13] and 'digital dossiers',[14] otherwise aptly described as 'badges of the totalitarian state'.[15] The combining of innocuous pieces of information can reveal to the State or the private sector 'new facts' about an individual that could not be expected to be revealed, when the original isolated data was collected.[16]

As a result, this ever-increasing knowledge of the individual's daily activities and private life contributes to a growing imbalance of power between the State and the

---

[7] US Federal Trade Commission (FTC) Staff Report, *Mobile Privacy Disclosures: Building Trust through Transparency* (Washington, DC, FTC, 2013) 2.

[8] N Ni Loideain, 'A Port in the Data-Sharing Storm: GDPR and the Internet of Things' (2018) *Journal of Cyber Law* (forthcoming).

[9] FTC Staff Report (n 7).

[10] S Zuboff, 'Big Other: Surveillance Capitalism and the Prospects of an Information Civilization' (2015) 30 *Journal of Information Technology* 75. See further discussion in Chapter 5.

[11] J Michael, *Privacy and Human Rights: An International and Comparative Study, with Special Reference to Developments in Information Technology* (Paris, Aldershot, 1994) 10.

[12] N Ni Loideain, 'Cape Town as a Smart and Safe City: Implications for Governance and Data Privacy' (2017) 7(4) *International Data Privacy Law* 314.

[13] RA Clarke, 'Information and Technology and Dataveillance' (1988) 31(5) *Communications of the ACM* 498, 499.

[14] DJ Solove, *Understanding Privacy* (London, Harvard University Press, 2008) 13.

[15] *Marcel v Metropolitan Police Commissioner* (1991) 2 WLR 1118, 1130 (Browne-Wilkinson VC).

[16] *Ibid.*

individual. Profiles constructed about an individual's personal and professional relationships, their racial or ethnic origin, political opinions, religious or philosophical
beliefs, trade-union membership or data concerning health or sex life may be used in
both private and public contexts with uneasy alliances and information leaks between
the two.[17] If accessed illegally/hacked by third parties, this information could be used
to cause other harms, including blackmail and fraud through identity theft.[18] Profiling
by non-transparent 'black box' Artificial Intelligence (AI) or machine learning (ML)
algorithms may especially lead to discrimination, bias, and the creation or reinforce-
ment of unequal treatment in society.[19]

Human rights law has a crucial role to play in ensuring that state surveillance
powers only operate within a legal framework that satisfies the principles and safeguards required by the conditions of legality, necessity and proportionality. Article 8
of the ECHR has had considerable influence on UK law governing interception and
surveillance by public authorities and the case law of the European Court of Human
Rights (ECtHR, the Strasbourg Court) has been 'an important driving force' in this
area of UK statute and common law since the 1980s.[20] Furthermore, since 2000, when
the UK Human Rights Act (HRA) 1998 entered into force, statutory law now clearly
mandates that interception and data processing by the State must be compatible with
the ECHR. More specifically, the Act requires all public authorities (including the
national courts) to act in a way that is compatible with ECHR rights. One practical
demonstration of this compliance is the requirement under s 19 of the 1998 Act that
Ministers must make a statement regarding a bill's compatibility with the ECHR. In
this respect, not only was the Investigatory Powers Bill 2015 (enacted in 2016), deemed
to have met the requirements of Art 8 ECHR, the then Secretary of State also promised that the major reforms to the then legal framework would create 'a world leading
oversight regime'.[21]

With respect to Brexit, it would be a risk for the UK Government to substitute a
'British Bill of Rights' for the HRA 1998 should the need for an adequacy decision
arise for the UK (see further discussion in Chapter 4), in matters of compliance with
EU data protection law and EU fundamental rights law more generally. One of the
key reasons underpinning this challenge is the fact that the EU Charter of Fundamental Rights mandates that the ECHR standards provide the very minimum that
must be provided under the EU Charter of Fundamental Rights. Hence, to Art 8

---

[17] Article 29 Data Protection Working Party, *Opinion 5/2009 on Online Social Networking*, WP 163.
[18] FTC Staff Report (n 7).
[19] See discussion in Chapters 3 and 5 and L Edwards and M Veale, 'Slave to the Algorithm? Why a "Right
to an Explanation" Is Probably Not the Remedy You Are Looking For' (2017) 16 *Duke Law & Technology
Review* 18. See also OH Gandy, 'Data Mining, Surveillance, and Discrimination' in KD Haggerty and
RV Ericson (eds), *The New Politics of Surveillance and Visibility* (London, Toronto University Press,
2006) 364.
[20] D Feldman, 'Secrecy, Dignity or Autonomy? Views of Privacy as a Civil Liberty' (1994) *Public Law*
41, 43; J Spencer, 'Telephone-Tap Evidence and Administrative Detention in the UK' in M Wade and
A Maljevic (eds), *A War on Terror? The European Stance on a New Threat, Changing Laws and Human
Rights Implications* (New York, Springer, 2010) Ch 13.
[21] Secretary of State for the Home Department, *Draft Investigatory Powers Bill* (Cm 1952) (London,
HM Stationery Office, 2015).

ECHR scrutiny has been added the relevance of Arts 7 and 8 of the EU Charter of Fundamental Rights, as adjudicated on by the Court of Justice of the EU (CJEU). Following the entry into force of the Lisbon Treaty in 2009, the protection of personal data is now an EU fundamental right, as guaranteed under both primary EU law (as a separate fundamental right under Art 8 of the EU Charter of Fundamental Rights and Art 16 TFEU[22]) and secondary EU law (the EU data protection regulations and directives).

As discussed below, UK surveillance law, in the form of RIPA's targeted interception provisions, has already come before the Strasbourg Court, and has in the past been assessed to have met the requirements of legality under Art 8(2) ECHR. Its bulk interception provisions (subsequently revealed as being 'obscurely' provided for under section 8(4) of RIPA[23]), however, have yet to be assessed at the Strasbourg Court but may be shortly in the forthcoming legal challenges discussed below.

The IPA however contains arguably even more controversial provisions in human rights terms than RIPA. In particular it seeks to 'avow' or put on a firm legal footing several known surveillance practices which have previously been shrouded in secrecy.[24] The IPA also plans to allow a broad range of public authorities to have access of up to a year to any data relating to an individual's web browsing data history, or in fact any data relating to any online communications they make ('Internet Connection Records').[25] Other powers that have raised major concerns with respect to their far-reaching and uncertain scope include allowing the intelligence services to obtain access to information from collections of bulk personal datasets,[26] the mass hacking of computer systems/communication devices ('bulk equipment interference')[27] and the requirement that industry may effectively be mandated to enable access to encrypted communications ('technical capability notices').[28] Given these far-reaching powers, it is essential for ensuring oversight, public trust and accountability, to identify the scope of the privacy-related interests being infringed, and safeguards that should be provided by the Act if it is truly to be described as providing a 'world leading oversight regime'. It is to these standards that this analysis now turns.

---

[22] As Article 16 of the Treaty on the Functioning of the European Union [2012] OJ C 326/47, provides:

1. Everyone has the right to the protection of personal data concerning them.
2. The European Parliament and the Council, acting in accordance with the ordinary legislative procedure, shall lay down the rules relating to the protection of individuals with regard to the processing of personal data by Union institutions, bodies, offices and agencies, and by the Member States when carrying out activities which fall within the scope of Union law, and the rules relating to the free movement of such data. Compliance with these rules shall be subject to the control of independent authorities.

[23] D Anderson, *A Report of the Bulk Powers Review* (August 2016), para 2.6.

[24] As highlighted by the Investigatory Powers Tribunal in *Privacy International v Secretary of State* [2016] UKIPTrib 15_110-CH [13].

[25] See further discussion in Chapter 7 on retention, esp at section V. B. (ICRs). Twelve months relates only to the maximum mandatory retention period. The access provisions are not time limited, so could potentially be used to access data retained *voluntarily* for business purposes beyond 12 months.

[26] IPA, s199.

[27] *Ibid*, s176.

[28] *Ibid*, s 253.

III. State Surveillance, Art 8 of the ECHR and the Approach of the ECtHR

Article 8 ECHR provides:

1.   Everyone has the right to respect for his private and family life, his home and his correspondence.
2.   There shall be no interference by a public authority with the exercise of this right except such as is in accordance with the law and is necessary in a democratic society in the interests of national security, public safety or the economic well-being of the country, for the prevention of disorder or crime, for the protection of health or morals, or for the protection of the rights and freedoms of others.

Since the late 1970s,[29] the Strasbourg Court has progressively developed a general set of principles governing the surveillance of communications that constitute an interference under Art 8(1) and the requirements to be satisfied before a state can justify an interference by reference to the conditions of Art 8(2).[30] Significantly, this means that Art 8 ECHR provides for a qualified right to respect for private life, not an absolute right. The use of surveillance by public authorities invokes the primary duty of the State under Art 8 ECHR not to interfere with the private life and correspondence of the applicant.[31] A challenge brought under Art 8 ECHR where a negative obligation arises (conduct that the State should refrain from) involves a two-stage test.

First, the ECtHR will consider whether the complaint falls within the scope of Art 8(1) (Art 8(1) 'is engaged'). Second, they will consider if the alleged interference by the Contracting State is legal under the conditions of Art 8(2). To do this the Court determines whether the interference was 'in accordance with the law', pursued one of the several legitimate aims identified under Art 8(2) (eg national security) and whether the measure was 'necessary in a democratic society'. If not the State will have violated Art 8. Third, they will consider what safeguards Art 8(2) requires to be put in place to prevent against the arbitrary use of non-transparent surveillance by the State. This may involve positive not merely negative obligations on the State.[32]

A. Engaging Article 8(1)

i. Technologies

In 1978, the ECtHR established that telephone conversations fall within the notions of 'private life' and 'correspondence'[33] and are protected under Art 8(1). Keeping up to

---

[29] Klass v Germany (1978) 2 EHRR 214.
[30] B Emmerson et al, Human Rights and Criminal Justice, 3rd edn (London, Sweet and Maxwell, 2012) 315.
[31] K Starmer, European Human Rights Law (London, Legal Action Group, 1999) 129.
[32] Craxi v Italy (No 2) (2004) 38 EHRR 995 [73].
[33] Klass (n 29) [41]; Malone v United Kingdom (1985) 7 EHRR 14 [64]; Lambert v France (2000) 30 EHRR 346 [21].

date with developments in communications technology and surveillance capabilities, the Strasbourg Court has since expanded this protection to include the monitoring of metadata,[34] communications within the home/business,[35] Internet usage (e-mails, online browsing),[36] mobile phones,[37] and mass surveillance programmes (including signals intelligence).[38] An interception also interferes with the right to respect for private life and correspondence even if no use is subsequently made of the accessed material.[39]

The Strasbourg Court has not considered it possible or necessary to attempt an exhaustive definition of the notion of 'private life'.[40] As a result, this concept has been interpreted broadly and its scope of protection applies to the interests within the inner circle of an individual's private life and extends to the zone of interaction of an individual with others.[41] The interception of communications constitutes a breach of physical and psychological integrity and amounts therefore to a breach of Art 8(1). Even if no physical intrusion into a private place occurs, surveillance can interfere with physical and psychological integrity and the right to respect for private life.[42]

ii. Collection, Storage and Use

The mere *collection* of information that relates to an individual's private life (even if retrieved from public sources) can amount to an interference with Art 8 ECHR. It is irrelevant if this information has not been subsequently used or disclosed. *Access* to this data can constitute a further interference with Art 8.[43] Private-life issues are more likely to arise where there is not just collection of information existing in the public domain but the creation of systematic or permanent records based on this material. For example, files collected by secret intelligence authorities regarding a particular individual will fall within the scope of Art 8(1), even where the information has not been gathered through intrusive or covert surveillance.[44]

---

[34] *Malone* (n 33).

[35] *Niemietz v Germany* (1992) 16 EHRR 97 [29]; *Halford v United Kingdom* (1997) 24 EHRR 523[44]; *Amann v Switzerland* [2000] ECHR 87 [44].

[36] *Copland v United Kingdom* (2007) 45 EHRR 858.

[37] *Zakharov v Russia* Application No 47143/14, 4 December 2015 [163]; *Szabó & Vissy v Hungary* Application No 37138/06, 12 January 2016 [53].

[38] *Liberty v United Kingdom* (2009) 48 EHRR 1; *Centrum_för_Rättvisa v_Sweden_*Application No 35252/08, 19 June 2018.

[39] *Kopp v Switzerland* (1999) 27 EHRR 91 [53].

[40] *Niemietz* (n 35); *Peck v United Kingdom* (2003) 36 EHRR 719.

[41] *Niemietz,* (n 35) [29]; *PG. and JH. v United Kingdom* [2001] ECHR 546 [56].

[42] N Moreham, 'The Right to Respect for Private Life in the European Convention on Human Rights: A Re-Examination' (2008) 3 *European Human Rights Law Review* 44, 53.

[43] *Leander v Sweden* (1987) 9 EHRR 433; *Rotaru v Romania* [2000] ECHR 192 (GC); *Weber and Saravia v Germany* (App 54934/00) 29 June 2006.

[44] *Rotaru, ibid* [43]. This matter becomes crucial in a world where surveillance is often based on material publicly posted on social media sites such as Twitter. See discussion in L Edwards and L Urquhart, 'Privacy in Public Spaces: What Expectations of Privacy Do We Have in Social Media Intelligence?' (2016) *International Journal of Law and Information Technology* 279–310.

Storage of information concerning the private life of an individual by any public authorities may also amount to an interference with private life.[45] Again, the subsequent use of this stored information has no impact on this finding.[46] In determining whether the personal information retained by the State involves any of the private-life aspects mentioned above, the ECtHR will have due regard to the following factors: the specific context in which the information at issue has been recorded and retained; the nature of the records; the way in which these records are used and processed; and the results that may be obtained.[47] Contracting States also have a positive obligation to ensure secure storage of personal information about an individual. Finally, *disclosing* information about an individual will also amount in principle to a breach of Art 8(1).[48]

iii. Knowledge that Art 8(1) is Engaged

An increasingly significant aspect of Art 8 ECHR relates to *bulk surveillance* powers where data is obtained relating to a large category of people who may not individually be suspected with any evidence of any particular crime. Key issues here include whether the data subject has any *notice* they are under surveillance, and the lack of targeted focus. Certain former members of the intelligence agencies have referred to this as bulk collection of data, rather than 'surveillance'.[49] Nevertheless, it is clear an individual may under certain conditions claim to be the victim of a violation of Art 8 ECHR based on the mere existence of secret measures, or of legislation permitting covert measures, without having to allege that such measures were in fact applied to them, which of course is difficult to prove.[50] Hence, the ECtHR held in *Malone v UK* that the existence in England and Wales of laws and practices which permit and establish a system for effecting secret surveillance of communications amounted in itself to an interference.[51]

This addresses the dilemma of *proving* that such measures have taken place[52] given there has historically been no legal requirement in the UK for individuals to be notified if they have in fact been subject to surveillance.[53] If an applicant contends in their complaint that they have actually been subject without notification to measures of surveillance, they will have to show a 'reasonable likelihood' that this has occurred.[54]

Section 231 of the IPA now provides that applicants may only be informed if they have been affected by an *error* discovered by the Investigatory Powers

---

[45] *Amann* (n 35).

[46] *Amann* (n 35 [69].

[47] *Friedl v Austria* (1995) 21 EHRR 83; *Peck* (n 40).

[48] *Z v Finland* (1998) 25 EHRR 371; *Peck* (n 40).

[49] See, eg Omand (n 4).

[50] Omand (n 4) para 41; *Liberty* (n 38) [56].

[51] *Malone* (n 33) [63].

[52] I Brown, 'Regulation of Converged Communications Surveillance' in BJ Goold and D Neyland (eds), *New Directions in Surveillance and Privacy* (Cullompton, Willan, 2009) Ch 3, 69.

[53] See further Chapter 7.

[54] *Halford* (n 35).

Commissioner (IPC). The Commissioner is only permitted to do so, however, if the error meets the high threshold of causing 'significant prejudice or harm' to the individual in question. The last annual report of the former supervisory authority, the Interception of Communications Commissioner (IOCCO), observed that this effectively carries forward the current approach adopted in practice under section 8.3 of the 2015 Code of Practice.[55] Hence, the impact of section 231 of the Act of 2016 'will be difficult to judge'.[56]

Nevertheless, the ability of the Commissioner to inform affected individuals of these miscarriages of justice (intentional or not) as soon as possible is significant as such serious errors do occur and may result in major implications for an individual's liberty and livelihood. One striking example is that of Nigel Lang who was wrongly arrested in 2011 on suspicion of sharing indecent images of children due to an incorrect IP address that was attributed to an Internet account used by him and his partner by the relevant police authorities. Following legal action that lasted several years, including a claim under the Data Protection Act 1998, the police in question settled out of court and Mr Lang was awarded legal costs and £60, 000 in compensation.[57]

B. Conditions for Justifying an Interference with a Right: Article 8(2)

As noted above, there are three requirements to proving that measures by the State which engage Art 8(1) satisfy the condition of legality imposed by Art 8(2).

i. 'In Accordance with law'

First, the interference must be in *accordance with domestic law*. The 'quality' of the law, or the 'legality requirement', governing the exercise of this state power requires that the measure must comply with the rule of law.[58] This means that the domestic law must provide protection against arbitrary interference with an individual's rights under Art 8 ECHR.[59] The legality requirement consists of two key tests: *accessibility* and *foreseeability*. The ECtHR has accepted that common law, or case law, may satisfy the legality test but only if it is sufficiently detailed, clear and precise.[60] The law must be sufficiently accessible and clear in its terms to give individuals an adequate indication to foresee the circumstances and the conditions in which public authorities are empowered to resort to the measure in question.[61] In line with the principle of the rule of law, it is essential that surveillance measures must be based on law that is particularly

---

[55] *Acquisition and Disclosure of Communications Data: Code of Practice* (London, Home Office, 2015), available at www.gov.uk/government/uploads/system/uploads/attachment_data/file/426248/Acquisition_and_Disclosure_of_Communications_Data_Code_of_Practice_March_2015.pdf.

[56] *Ibid*.

[57] A Eley and J Adnitt, 'My Life was Ruined by a Typo' *BBC News* (21 March 2017), available at www.bbc.co.uk/news/uk-39328853.

[58] *Khan v United Kingdom* (2001) 31 EHRR 1016.

[59] *Ibid* [26].

[60] *Huvig v France* (1990) 12 EHRR 547; *Valenzuela Contreras v Spain* (1999) 28 EHRR 483; *Amann* (n 35).

[61] *Malone* (n 33); *Valenzuela Contreras* (n 60) 483.

precise, with clear and detailed rules as the technology used is becoming continually more sophisticated.[62]

Foreseeability, in the 'special context' of covert surveillance, does not mean that an individual should be able to foresee when public authorities are likely to intercept his communications so that he can adapt his conduct accordingly.[63] Instead it demands a level of transparency in the otherwise secret exercise of this power by public authorities. Clearly expressed provisions will have a binding force that will circumscribe the discretion of judges in authorising surveillance.[64]

The first hurdle of Art 8(2) has not been overcome by states where there has been no legal framework governing the covert surveillance of telephone communications.[65] In *Halford v UK,* there was no domestic law in place regulating surveillance by the State of internal communications systems operated by public authorities. Interception of the applicant's telephone conversations in her place of work, police headquarters in this case, had no basis therefore in domestic law and could not be in accordance with the law under Art 8(2). Additionally, the law must indicate with sufficient clarity at the material time the extent of the discretion of the relevant public authorities or the way in which this discretion should have been exercised.[66] A key matter is an institution to effectively scrutinise any errors. The ECtHR has expressed the view that this role is best carried out by the judiciary as independent, impartial and with proper procedure,[67] but it is not essential to involve judges.[68]

ii. 'For Legitimate Purposes'

Satisfying the second condition of Art 8(2), the 'legitimate purposes' hurdle, is rarely a difficulty for states in light of the broad terms in which these legitimate purposes are framed and due to the fact that applicants frequently concede the existence of a legitimate aim in this area.[69]

iii. Proportionality

For the third condition of Art 8(2) ECHR ('necessary in a democratic society'), Contracting States must show that the measure in question is responding to 'a pressing social need' and that the interference with the protected rights is no greater than is necessary to address that need.[70] This requirement is otherwise referred to as the test of *proportionality* and contains four principles.[71]

---

[62] *Huvig* (n 60) [32].
[63] *Leander* (n 43) [51].
[64] *Valenzuela Contreras* (n 60) [60].
[65] *Halford* (n 35).
[66] *Malone* (n 33); *Valenzuela Contreras* (n 60).
[67] *Klass* (n 29) [55]; *Rotaru* (n 43) [59]; *Kennedy v United Kingdom* (2011) 52 EHRR 4 [167].
[68] *Klass* (n 29); *Kennedy, ibid.* See discussion below re RIPA 2000.
[69] J Beatson et al, *Human Rights: Judicial Protection in the United Kingdom* (London, Sweet and Maxwell, 2008) 162.
[70] *Leander* (n 43) [58].
[71] *Silver v United Kingdom* (1983) 5 EHRR 347.

First, the ECtHR has held that the adjective 'necessary' is not synonymous with 'indispensable' or as flexible as 'reasonable' or 'desirable'.[72] In practice, powers allowing for secret surveillance of communications must have adequate and effective guarantees against abuse.

Second, a national 'margin of appreciation' will apply in assessing the existence and extent of such necessity.[73] The concept raises the question regarding how far the ECtHR should defer to a State's interpretation of ECHR rights.[74] In cases concerning covert surveillance by public authorities, the ECtHR has tended to grant a wider margin to Contracting States in matters of national security in light of the sensitive and confidential nature of the information involved.[75]

Third, the phrase 'necessary in a democratic society' implies that there is 'a pressing social need' which must be 'proportionate to the legitimate aim pursued' if the interference is compatible with the ECHR. Fourth, the proportionality test requires that articles under the ECHR which provide for an exception to a right guaranteed are to be narrowly interpreted.[76]

Hence, Art 8(2) is subject to a narrow interpretation on the basis that it may permit an exception to rights guaranteed under Art 8(1).[77] Powers of secret surveillance, characterising as they do the police state, are tolerable under the ECHR only in so far as strictly necessary for safeguarding democratic institutions.[78] Accordingly, States must ensure that *adequate safeguards* govern the use of these surveillance powers to prevent against their abuse or misuse.[79] In the next section we will discuss if such adequate safeguards are provided in the UK's surveillance regime as recently reformed and extended by the IPA. As before, the main emphasis here is on powers of interception and acquisition of communications. Retention of data powers are primarily addressed in the next chapter by Kosta.

IV. Legality of UK Law Governing Investigatory Powers and Oversight

The Regulation of Investigatory Powers Act 2000 (RIPA)[80] which regulated in this area before the IPA was enacted, was examined by the ECtHR for the legality of its targeted interception provisions in the case of *Kennedy v UK*. The key issue was

---

[72] *Ibid* [97].

[73] *Ibid*.

[74] B Rainey et al, *Jacobs, White and Ovey: The European Convention on Human Rights*, 6th edn (Oxford, Oxford University Press, 2014) 325.

[75] *Klass* (n 29); *Leander* (n 43); *Segerstedt-Wiberg v Sweden* (2007) 44 EHRR 14.

[76] *Silver* (n 71) [97].

[77] *Klass* (n 29); *Rotaru* (n 43); *Drakšas v Lithuania* Application No 36662/04, 31 July 2012.

[78] *Klass* (n 29) [42].

[79] *Segerstedt-Wiberg* (n 75) [88].

[80] For further on RIPA, see J Rauhofer, 'Privacy and Surveillance Legal and Socioeconomic Aspects of State Intrusion into Electronic Communications' in L Edwards and C Waelde (eds), *Law and the Internet*, 3rd edn (Oxford, Hart Publishing, 2009) Ch 8.

the lack of requirement of prior authorisation of covert surveillance powers by judges. However, other safeguards enabled the regime to pass the requirements of Art 8 ECHR.[81]

The Strasbourg Court emphasised that these other protections included:

- The 'independent and impartial body' of the Investigatory Powers Tribunal (IPT), which has the power to review the exercise of powers under RIPA. Its members were experienced lawyers or judges who had held high judicial office, and it also reviewed complaints without individual notification.[82]

- The publication of the IPT's judgments to the public.

- The publicly available code of practice which set out in sufficient clarity the procedures for the authorisation and processing of interception warrants, as well as the processing, communicating and destruction of the intercepted materials collected.

- The *ex post* oversight role of the IOCCO, the Commissioner of which had to be independent of the executive and legislature and hold or have held high judicial office.

- The IOCCO's annual report that scrutinised any errors that had occurred in the system.

Perhaps most importantly, the ECtHR's examination showed that there was 'no evidence that any deliberate abuse of interception powers is taking place'.[83] Consequently, the ECtHR came to the conclusion that there were no 'significant shortcomings' in the application and operation of the UK's surveillance regime.

However, revelations since 2013 of far-reaching surveillance programmes and data sharing by the US National Security Agency (NSA), and other intelligence services worldwide including the UK, by Edward Snowden, a former CIA computer analyst and defence consultant to the NSA, have subsequently indicated that this was, at least, not the whole story.[84] Allegations of such programmes' existence were confirmed in one of a number of legal challenges brought by Privacy International (a UK human rights non-governmental organisation (NGO)) before the IPT following the Snowden revelations. One resulting judgment in 2016 (in proceedings that are ongoing and will soon be reviewed by the Court of Justice of the EU as a preliminary reference[85]) has already held that the use of bulk processing of personal data by the intelligence agencies *without the knowledge* of parliament, the public or the IOCCO up until 2015 (or 'pre-avowal') was in violation of Art 8 ECHR.[86]

---

[81] *Kennedy* (n 67) [168]–[170].

[82] RIPA, s 65.

[83] *Ibid*, para 168.

[84] For further information, see N Ni Loideain, 'EU Law and Mass Internet Metadata Surveillance in the Post-Snowden Era' (2015) 3(2) *Media and Communications – Special Issue on Surveillance: Critical Analysis and Current Challenges* 53.

[85] For all documents relating to this preliminary reference, see the IPT website at www.ipt-uk.com/judgments.asp?id=41.

[86] *Privacy International* (n 24) [101].

UK law came significantly under scrutiny, this time before the CJEU not the ECtHR, in the Joined Cases of *Watson and Tele2 Sverige*. *Tele2/Watson*, as it is known, like its predecessor *Digital Rights Ireland*,[87] was undoubtedly influenced by the major concerns raised by privacy advocates following the Snowden revelations and culminated for the first time in the striking down of an entire EU law for its incompatibility with the EU Charter of Fundamental Rights. *Tele2/Watson* dealt primarily with the legal frameworks governing communications data *retention* under Swedish and UK law (in particular the validity of the Data Retention and Investigatory Powers Act 2014 ('DRIPA'), and is examined in full detail in the next chapter, but it also has serious implications for the general questions of legality of surveillance powers, especially the new bulk powers, not just in RIPA and DRIPA but now in the IPA.

In particular, *Tele2/Watson* noted that national data retention legislation should satisfy key minimum safeguards required by the EU Charter of Rights. These safeguards relate to access to the data retained. According to *Tele2/Watson*, these two issues can now not be separated; it cannot be legal to compel retention of data with a view to future access by state authorities unless these safeguards are put in place.[88] First, access to such mandatorily retained data can only be authorised (except in cases of 'validly established urgency') following *prior review by a court, or an independent administrative authority*, of a reasoned request to that body by the relevant public authority.[89] Second, users affected by data access and retention must be *notified as soon as to do so will not prejudice the investigation*.[90] Third, communications service providers (CSPs) must ensure that the relevant data must be subject to a *particularly high level of protection and security* by means of appropriate technical and organisational measures. Accordingly also, the national law should also ensure that the relevant data is retained within the EU, and for the 'irreversible destruction of the data at the end of the data retention period'.[91]

As required by Art 8(3) of the Charter and in line with CJEU's case law, these requirements are 'an essential element of respect' for the protection of individuals in relation to the processing of personal data.[92] As can be seen, these are requirements that go far beyond those asserted against RIPA in *Kennedy*. We will now turn to looking at how these rules might impact on the new provisions of the IPA relating to acquisition of communications including bulk powers and equipment interference. In the final section, we will reconsider how *Tele2* may impact on these new powers and other aspects of the IPA.

---

[87] C-203/15 *Tele2 Sverige/Watson*, (Judgment of the Grand Chamber, 21 December 2016): Joined Cases C-293/12 and C-594/12 *Digital Rights Ireland and Seitlinger*, (8 April 2014).

[88] See Chapter 7, and esp section V. D. of that chapter.

[89] *Tele2/Watson* (n 87) [120].

[90] *Tele2/Watson* (n 87) [121].

[91] *Tele2/Watson* (n 87) [122].

[92] *Tele2/Watson* (n 87) [123].

V. The Investigatory Powers Act 2016 (IPA)

A. Legislative Background

On 4 November 2015, the Home Office published the first draft of the Investigatory Powers Bill. Between January and November 2016, the House of Commons and the House of Lords reviewed and proposed a number of amendments to the proposed legislation. During this period, academics, practitioners, and representatives from the private sector and civil society submitted written evidence[93] to the three parliamentary committees which subsequently published reports that urged for a number of key amendments to be made to this lengthy, and often technically complex, draft bill.[94] These committees put forward nearly 200 recommendations following their review of the draft legislation.[95] The Intelligence and Security Committee (ISC) was particularly critical of the draft bill and observed that 'thus far the Government has missed the opportunity to provide the clarity and assurance which is badly needed'.[96] Concerns were also raised that the publication of the draft bill had been rushed as it 'suffered from a lack of sufficient time and preparation'.[97]

Arguably, these criticisms were to be expected given that the ISC had recently recommended in a prior report to the Government the need for any such future law to be clear and precise in its language, requirements and safeguards.[98] This proposal was underpinned by the ISC's conclusion that the law as it stood governing and constraining the investigatory powers of the security and intelligence agencies was inadequate, 'opaque', and 'unnecessarily complicated'.[99] Any new legislation in this area thereby required much more than mere reform of RIPA, but also needed to address the entire patchwork of relevant statutes concerned with the investigatory powers of the agencies. Such a major recommendation invariably raises questions of the compatibility of the legal framework with the two key requirements of the legality test (accessibility and foreseeability) discussed above. Notably, the concerns expressed by the ISC were consistent with the recommendations of two other key comprehensive reports subsequently published, by David Anderson QC, the then Independent Reviewer of

---

[93] See, eg, Information Law and Policy Centre, *Report of Expert Working Group on Investigatory Powers Bill*, Findings Published in Joint Committee Report on Draft Investigatory Powers Bill (HL Paper 93), 11 February 2016.

[94] Science and Technology Committee, *Investigatory Powers Bill: Technology Issues* (HC 573), 19 January 2016; Intelligence and Security Committee (ISC), *Report on Draft Investigatory Powers Bill* (HC 795), 9 February 2016 ('ISC Report (2016)'); Joint Committee on the Draft Investigatory Powers Bill, *Report: Draft Investigatory Powers Bill* (HL Paper 93, HC 651), 11 February 2016.

[95] Following the publication of the second draft bill, the Joint Committee on Human Rights (JCHR) also published its review and recommendations for reform: *Legislative Scrutiny: Investigatory Powers Bill* (HC 104, HL Paper 6), 2 June 2016.

[96] ISC Report (2016) (n 94) p 2.

[97] ISC Report (2016) (n 94) p 2.

[98] ISC, *Privacy and Security: A Modern and Transparent Legal Framework* (HC 1075), 12 March 2015 ('ISC (2015)').

[99] *Ibid*, 7–8.

Terrorism Legislation (otherwise known as the 'Anderson Report'),[100] and the Royal United Services Institute (RUSI), also drawn on by the Government in its review of the existing law governing investigatory powers.[101]

In response to these criticisms, the Home Office published a revised draft in March 2016 that incorporated some, but rejected most, of the proposed reforms. Although it made a number of recommendations, the Joint Committee on Human Rights (JCHR) nevertheless stated that it considered the second draft as 'a significant step forward in human rights terms' with respect to the Government providing a clear and transparent legal basis 'for investigatory powers already being exercised by the security and intelligence agencies and law enforcement authorities'.[102] The latter part of this statement refers to powers allowing for the use of bulk personal datasets and acquisition of bulk communications data under s 94 of the Telecommunications Act 1984 by the State; these were not made known (or 'avowed') to the public, parliament or relevant oversight authorities for decades until March and November of 2015.[103]

Throughout the pre-legislative stage of the first and revised bill, however, regulators and other commentators raised concerns that the review and pre-legislative scrutiny of the proposed legislation was subject to a 'hasty' and 'aggressive timeline'.[104] It is perhaps then unsurprising that the final bill given royal assent in November 2016 was largely unaffected by the many recommendations made during its pre-legislative scrutiny by parliament and thereby contains the same nine-part structure, and most of the substantive provisions, of the draft bill published in 2015.

B. IPA: Main Provisions and Oversight

The IPA is a lengthy and detailed piece of legislation comprised of nine parts, with more than 270 sections.[105] It updates and expands previous provisions governing the scope, retention and authorisation of access to communications and communications data by public authorities as provided for under RIPA and other statutes. Like its predecessor RIPA, the IPA will only be even vaguely comprehensible with the aid of a number of codes for guidance. Section 241 and Schedule 7 of the 2016 Act set out the requirements that underpin the drafting, revision and oversight of the codes of practice.

---

[100] D Anderson, *A Question of Trust: Report of the Investigatory Powers Review* (June 2015), paras 14.3–14.7; RUSI, *Democractic Licence to Operate: Report of the Independence Surveillance Review* (July, 2015) xv. While these reports called for the adoption of a clearer and comprehensive new law, both disagreed with the ISC recommendation to consolidate all of the current laws relating to the intelligence agencies in a single framework.

[101] Note that the scope of review of the latter two reports extends beyond the powers of the intelligence agencies to the law governing the authorisation and use of investigatory powers by many other public authorities, including law enforcement and local authorities.

[102] JCHR Report (n 95) 3.

[103] *Privacy International* (n 24) [13]–[15].

[104] See, eg, Joint Committee on the Draft Investigatory Powers Bill, Written Evidence: Interception of Communications Commissioner's Office (IPB0101), 2 December 2015, 676; L Woods, 'An Overview of the Investigatory Powers Bill Report by the Joint Committee on Human Rights', *Information Law and Policy Centre Blog,* 10 June 2016.

[105] In contrast, RIPA had five parts and 83 sections.

Many of the powers under the Act of 2016 are not new, such as the interception of communications, the retention and acquisition of communications data.[106] Other powers such as interference with equipment, and the acquisition of bulk data, discussed below, are not technically new (see below) but are only placed for the first time on an open public footing by the IPA.

Our emphasis here is on these 'new' powers. Some of these were unknown to the public, parliament, or the relevant oversight bodies until recently. For instance, the Government only 'avowed' the power of a Secretary of State to authorise a warrant permitting MI5, MI6 and GCHQ to hack into an individual's/group's/organisation's computer system(s) or electronic devices (otherwise known as 'Computer Network Exploitation' (CNE)) on 6 February 2015 when it published the Draft Equipment Interference Code.[107]

The IPA enacts a number of substantive new provisions, introduces some enhanced safeguards, and overhauls the previous system of oversight. It does not, however, consolidate the legal regime governing the authorisation and use of investigatory powers by public authorities within the UK. For example, Part II of RIPA (surveillance and covert human intelligence sources), s 7 of the Intelligence Services Act 1994 (authorisation of acts outside the British Islands by GCHQ/MI6[108]), and Part III of the Police Act 1997 (property interference) continue in operation. A patchwork regime thus remains in place as the legal basis for certain investigatory powers still exists under other pieces of legislation. At the time of writing, aside from sections relating to the retention of communications data (Part 4), oversight arrangements (Part 8), and general provisions (Part 9), most of the major powers under the IPA have not yet come into force.[109]

C. The 'New' Powers

i. Equipment Interference

Part 5 of the IPA allows a Secretary of State to authorise a targeted equipment interference warrant application from the security and intelligence authorities, the army, or from law enforcement.[110] This broad power entails any interference with

---

[106] For discussion of the pre-existing RIPA regime on interception and on access to communications data see Rauhofer (n 80).

[107] Home Office, Equipment Interference: Code of Practice (Draft for Public Consultation), available at www. gov.uk/government/uploads/system/uploads/attachment_data/file/401863/Draft_Equipment_Interference_ Code_of_Practice.pdf. This first draft has subsequently been updated and is one of five codes of practice related to powers under the Investigatory Powers Act 2016 that are currently still being reviewed by the Government (as of 17 March 2018) following a short public consultation in December 2017. Home Office, Draft Equipment Interference Code of Practice (February 2017), available at www.gov.uk/government/ uploads/system/uploads/attachment_data/file/668940/Draft_code_-_Equipment_Interference.pdf.

[108] Referred to as the 'James Bond clause' in the ISC (2015) (n 98) (para 236) and Anderson (n 100) (para 6.27) reports.

[109] IPA 2016, s 272, SI No 1233 of 2016, SI No 137 of 2017, and SI No 143 of 2017; see also SI No 341 of 2018 which for the first time introduced powers where the oversight of Judicial Commissioners was required.

[110] IPA 2016, ss 102–106.

equipment, 'conducted for the purposes of gathering intelligence, or manipulating the equipment, in order to establish control, compromise functionality or gather further intelligence'.[111] The wide scope of the equipment concerns anything that could contain any 'communications', 'equipment data', or 'any other information'.[112] Hence, equipment interference could include accessing or tampering with personal computers, mobile phones, tablets, smart cars, any Internet-enabled home devices/systems (eg thermostats, an AI assistant, baby monitors, alarms), or large communications systems owned by the private sector. Although equipment interference encompasses hacking, its broad definition provides scope for allowing other activities which would not be traditionally considered as hacking, such as spreading malware or otherwise disrupting computer systems, grids or databases.

Under the updated draft equipment interference code of practice, a number of public authorities may apply to a Secretary of State to authorise a targeted equipment interference warrant.[113] However, it is significant to note that a targeted equipment interference warrant is *not*, despite the name, limited to a specific individual. It may apply to an organisation, a group of individuals who share 'a common purpose' or 'particular activity', or many groups or organisations if the conduct authorised by the warrant is for a single investigation or operation.[114] Applications to a Secretary of State for *bulk* equipment interference warrants are, by contrast, limited to the heads of the security and intelligence authorities and are only permitted for large-scale operations for the obtaining of overseas-related communications, overseas-related information, or overseas-related equipment data.[115]

It is important to note, as already mentioned, that the security and intelligence agencies have been carrying out equipment interference for some time, and well before the IPA was drafted. Section 5 (for acts within the British Islands by MI5, MI6, GCHQ) and section 7 (for acts outside of the British Islands by MI6, GCHQ) of the Intelligence Services Act 1994 have long provided that a Secretary of State may authorise a warrant application from the security and intelligences authorities to enter on, or interfere with, 'property' or 'wireless telegraphy'. The IPA is, however, the first time this power has been explicitly set out in an accessible way within the main statutory framework. Both the Joint Committee on the Investigatory Powers Bill and the Joint Committee on Human Rights welcomed the fact that these powers and techniques have now been 'properly addressed in legislation'.[116] Note also that the powers under the 1994 Act remain in operation as they have been updated, but not repealed, by the IPA.[117]

These powers of 'legalised hacking' were the subject of much contention during the drafting of the IPA. The Home Office has argued that it must deal with an increasing number of circumstances where information is being communicated

[111] Joint Committee on Draft Investigatory Powers Bill (n 104), para 266.
[112] IPA 2016, s 99(2).
[113] Home Office, *Draft Equipment Interference Code of Practice* (December 2017), para 4.5.
[114] IPA 2016, s 101(2).
[115] Home Office, *Draft Equipment Interference Code of Practice* (December 2017), para 4.6.
[116] Joint Committee on Draft Investigatory Powers Bill (n 104), para 267; JCHR Report (n 95), 3.
[117] IPA 2016, s 251(3).

'in an impenetrable blanket from sender to receiver', leaving interception impossible or ineffective.[118] Equipment interference was already said to be used regularly for tracing vulnerable missing persons. Representatives from civil society have however described equipment interference 'as potentially far more intrusive than any other current surveillance technique, including the interception of communications'.[119] While a case can be made for *targeted* equipment interference, *bulk* equipment interference warrants (as provided for under Part 6 of the Investigatory Powers Act 2016) may be possibly excessive unless very tight controls are applied in practice. As one leading commentator has observed,

> [t]he right way to get round encryption is targeted equipment interference, and that is hack the laptop, the phone, the car, the Barbie doll or whatever of the gang boss you are going after, so that you get access to the microphones, to the cameras and to the stored data. The wrong way to do it is bulk equipment interference.[120]

The threat to private life and data protection posed by such intrusive interference is unquestionably magnified with respect to the use of *bulk* equipment interference in large-scale operations by the security and intelligence authorities. Any implantation of malware into major communications systems/networks could have tremendously serious implications for affected people, not just those suspected of wrongdoing, such as patients by inadvertently-hacked computer facilities in hospitals. In Germany, such approaches have in the context of state-sponsored spreading of viruses, been declared unconstitutional.[121] Without strict compliance to the principles of legality, necessity and proportionality, such mass hacking could create major vulnerabilities in the security of personal data and communications that third parties, such as criminals, could exploit. These risks will become all the more prevalent with the rise of connected cars, CCTV, lighting systems, and sensors and other Internet-enabled systems that will underpin future smart cities and smart homes, particularly developments such as the Internet of Things which ambitiously seeks to connect all smart devices and systems.

ii. Bulk Warrants[122]

Parts 6 and 7 of the IPA provide for a Secretary of State to authorise applications from the heads of security and intelligence authorities for

- bulk interception warrants,
- bulk acquisition warrants,

---

[118] Joint Committee on Draft Investigatory Powers Bill (n 104), para 276.

[119] *Privacy International v Secretary of State for Foreign and Commonwealth Affairs and GCHQ and others*, Case No IPT/14/85/CH, Statement of Grounds, [4], available at <www.privacyinternational.org/sites/default/files/PI%20Hacking%20Case%20Grounds.pdf.

[120] Science and Technology Committee Report (n 94), para 46 (evidence from Professor Ross Anderson).

[121] See discussion in B Schafer and W Abel, 'The German Constitutional Court on the Right in Confidentiality and Integrity of Information Technology Systems' (2009) 6 *SCRIPTed* 106.

[122] Again, guidance will eventually be found in codes: see drafts as of December 2017 consultation at www.gov.uk/government/consultations/investigatory-powers-act-2016-codes-of-practice on bulk acquisition of communications data and bulk personal datasets.

- bulk equipment interference warrants, and
- bulk personal dataset warrants.

Bulk warrants for interception, acquisition and equipment interference may only be granted if considered necessary in the interests of national security (on its own, or in conjunction with the prevention and detection of serious crime, or the economic well-being of the UK).[123]

There is a broader scope of permitted purposes for the authorisation of (class or specific) *bulk personal datasets* as these may be authorised in the interests of national security *or* for the purposes of preventing or detecting serious crime, even if these purposes have no relevant link to the interests of national security.[124]

Authorisation of any of these bulk warrants (like targeted warrants) is subject to approval by a Judicial Commissioner who has reviewed the Secretary of State's decision. The determination of this approval must involve the same principles that a court would apply in a judicial review application, and must also consider human rights law and privacy requirements. These factors include whether the conduct being permitted is proportionate to achieve the relevant aim of the operation and the public interest of ensuring the protection of data security.[125] If a Judicial Commissioner refuses to approve the decision, the Secretary of State in question may seek to have this overturned by the IPC.[126]

Bulk interception warrants may only be authorised under the IPA[127] if two conditions are met.[128] First, their main purpose must be limited to the interception of *overseas* communications (with at least one 'end' of the communication sent or received outside the UK) or obtaining secondary data from those communications. The latter may include the identity of the parties, method/device/system of communication, time, duration, location, web browsing history and login passwords. The Intelligence and Security Committee observed in its report that the latter (in other words, the context of the communications) was of 'primary value to GCHQ', rather than reading the content of communications.[129]

Second, the warrant authorises/requires the person to whom it is addressed to intercept the communications set out in the warrant and/or obtain the secondary data, select for examination and disclose the relevant data from the communications. Bulk interception involves three stages of collection, filtering and selection for examination. For collection, of the 100, 000 'bearers' that the Internet currently consists of,[130]

---

[123] IPA 2016, ss 138, 158, 178.

[124] IPA, ss 204–205.

[125] IPA 2016, ss140, 159, 179, 208. See in particular the 'General duties in relation to privacy' requirements mandated by s 2 of the Act.

[126] For more detailed discussion of the very significant introduction of 'Judicial Commissioners', see section iv, entitled 'Oversight' below.

[127] The (very broadly interpreted) legal basis currently drawn on by the Government for this power is RIPA, s 8(4). This provision will not be repealed by the new Act.

[128] IPA 2016, s136.

[129] ISC Report (2016) (n 94), para 80.

[130] ISC Report (2016) (n 94), para 55: One transatlantic cable currently contains 47 bearers, each operating at 10 giga (one thousand million) bits per second. Some evidence contradicts the assertion that filtering is always carried out on intercepted metadata, as opposed to content. See, eg, ISC (2015) (n 98), which refers to 'all' communications data being extracted.

GCHQ selects which bearers will be accessed based on the likely intelligence value of the communications they are carrying. The filtering process is then applied to the traffic on these bearers which then selects communications of potential intelligence value and discards the remainder. Finally, the selected communications are then subject to searches which may include using 'strong selectors' such as a telephone number or e-mail address. Communications that are highlighted through these search results are then automatically retained, any other communications are automatically 'discarded'. If a considerable amount of communications are retained, analysts will then determine which of these should be examined based on what is 'most likely to be of intelligence value'.[131] When communications are collected between persons in the UK (but eg from a server outside of the UK) under a bulk interception warrant, a targeted examination warrant (containing further safeguards) must be authorised before the content of those communications can be examined.[132]

Again these practices were and are ongoing long before the IPA was drafted or passed. They came to light in the main during the aftermath of Snowden. Section 94 of the Telecommunications Act 1984 currently provides the legal basis for warrants authorising bulk *acquisition* which permit the obtaining of traffic data/communications data, not the content of communications, from CSPs. The pre-IPA basis for bulk *interception* was s 8(4) RIPA. (It is worth noting that s 8(4) bulk interception, not s 94, was GCHQ's principal source of metadata (ISC (2015) report). Section 8(4) was not secret, even if it was obscure.)

The IPA equivalent of RIPA s 8(4) is Pt 6, Ch 1; while s 94 is replaced by Pt 6, Ch 2. Once in force, Pt 6 of the IPA will provide a more precise and clear legal basis for this intelligence data gathering power. This acquisition of data is not limited to foreign-focused operations and also significantly allows for aggregation of many databases of information. The latter factor has been described as 'a key element in the added value of bulk acquisition power' and one which will 'plainly have to be kept under review' given the high level of intrusiveness posed by applying a search filter through all of these connected databases.[133] This call for stringent oversight and clear safeguards of bulk acquisition powers echoes concerns raised in a highly critical report by the IOCCO which reviewed the use of s 94 in 2015 (once the use of powers were no longer secret).[134]

In responding to these criticisms, the draft Bulk Acquisition Code of Practice (updated in December 2017) sets out requirements governing the authorisation, modification and cancellation of warrants, general safeguards with respect to the storage, transfer, and destruction of data, and special selection procedures for examining communications data concerning legal professional privilege.[135] For instance, any

[131] Anderson (n 22), paras 2.15–2.18.
[132] Anderson (n 22), para 2.26. This does not apply to metadata acquired under the interception warrant.
[133] Anderson (n 22), para 2.34.
[134] IOCCO, *Review of Directions Given under Section 94 of the Telecommunications Act (1984)*, HC 33, SG/2016/67, July 2016.
[135] Home Office, *Bulk Acquisition of Communications Data: Draft Code of Practice* (December 2017), available at www.gov.uk/government/uploads/system/uploads/attachment_data/file/668935/Draft_code_-_Bulk_Acquisition_of_Communications_Data.pdf.

major modifications to a bulk acquisitions warrant (eg where its operational purpose is extended – addition of a name of description) now require approval from both a Secretary of State *and* a Judicial Commissioner.[136]

Given the enormity of the data already being collected by the security and intelligence authorities under the three bulk warrant powers, and that these were only set out explicitly for the first time in statute under the IPA, pressure was put on the Government to provide a detailed operational case showing the necessity of these provisions. This review was subsequently assessed by the then Independent Reviewer of Terrorism Legislation in August 2016. Notably, especially in light of several pending legal challenges against the bulk powers, the scope of this assessment did *not* extend to examining whether the powers comply with the legality, necessity, or proportionality conditions mandated by ECHR or EU law, or what safeguards should apply to them (see above).[137]

Overall, the Independent Reviewer concluded in his report that the Government had provided a proven operational case for the three bulk powers already in use and that there was a 'distinct' but ultimately 'not yet proven' operational case for the 'strikingly broad' powers provided by bulk equipment interference.[138] Although these are not classified as bulk warrants, they could be as broad in scope given that a targeted equipment interference warrant could apply to any 'equipment belonging to, used by or in the possession of a group of persons who share a common purpose or who carry on, or may carry on, a particular activity'.[139]

iii. Other Key Provisions: Technical Capability Notices and Impact on Encryption

The 'Miscellaneous and General Provisions' section of the IPA (Part 9) also contains significant power whereby a Secretary of State may, subject to Judicial Commissioner approval, issue a 'technical capability notice' to a CSP (an 'operator'). This notice allows a Secretary of State to require any number of tasks within a broad range of conduct to be undertaken by the latter, including any 'obligations relating to the removal by a relevant operator of electronic protection applied by or on behalf of that operator to any communications or data'.[140] In other words, this duty could be interpreted as requesting CSPs to remove, or refrain from using, any form of encryption used to ensure the confidentiality, integrity, or security of their customers' communications, eg e-mails, instant messaging services, telephone calls.

Leading industry representatives (including Apple and Facebook) have expressed concern regarding whether the 'removal of electronic protection' will entail requiring companies operating in the UK to adopt weaker standards of encryption or prevent the use of 'end-to-end encryption', thereby endangering the security of any electronic communication devices and systems ubiquitously used by individuals,

---

[136] *Ibid*, para 5.8.
[137] On some of these points however see the JCHR Report (n 93) 34.
[138] Independent Reviewer of Terrorism Legislation, *Report of the Bulk Powers Review* (August 2016), paras. 2.12, 9.14(c).
[139] IPA 2016, s 101(1).
[140] IPA 2016, s 253(5).

companies and public authorities.[141] During its pre-legislative scrutiny, the Home Office informed Parliament that the legal requirement under the IPA would be the same as that currently provided for under RIPA. Hence, a technical capability notice would not apply to content that is encrypted end-to-end before being passed to the communications provider for transmission, only to 'the electronic protection that the service-provider itself has put on the message'.[142] However, recent statements by the Home Secretary with respect to requiring industry to limit the use of end-to-end encryption for the content, or communications data, from everyday communications, have made it difficult to clearly establish the Government's policy position on this matter.[143] These powers were brought into force in March 2018[144] and merely repeat the rubric that 'The Regulations also include an obligation to ensure that electronic protection applied by the operator to communications can be removed, where reasonably practicable'.[145]

iv. Oversight

Part 8 of the IPA provides for the establishment of a single body of oversight to replace and carry out the duties of the three previous oversight institutions, the IOCCO, the Office of Surveillance Commissioners (OSC), and the ISC.[146] In an unprecedented reform, the IPC, and other Judicial Commissioners, will have an oversight role in the authorisation of warrants by a Secretary of State.[147] Furthermore, in response to calls from previous oversight bodies for greater resources,[148] the explanatory notes accompanying the Investigatory Powers Bill[149] highlighted that the IPC would have 'significantly greater powers and resources compared to the current oversight regime' and 'will be a more visible [public] body'.[150] In order to be eligible for the position of IPC, and of Judicial Commissioner, an individual must hold, or have previously held high judicial office.[151] Lord Justice Fulford, who will remain a judge of the Court of Appeal, was appointed as IPC in March 2017 (with immediate effect) for a term of three years and the Judicial Commissioners were appointed on 18 October 2017.[152]

---

[141] Science and Technology Committee Report (n 94) para 37.

[142] Science and Technology Committee Report (n 94) para 41.

[143] D Lee, 'Message Encryption a Problem – Rudd' BBC News (1 August 2017).

[144] See The Investigatory Powers (Technical Capability) Regulations 2018 (SI 2018/No 353).

[145] See explanatory memorandum at www.legislation.gov.uk/uksi/2018/353/pdfs/uksiem_20180353_en.pdf.

[146] IPA 2016, s 240.

[147] IPA 2016, s 229. Guidance on how the IPC and Judicial Commissioners will review matters under the IPA was issued in March 2018: see IPCO Advisory Notice 1/2018: Approval of Warrants, Authorisations and Notices by Judicial Commissioner 8 March 2018 at www.ipco.org.uk/docs/20180308%20IPCO%20 Advisory%20Notice%2012018%20v1.1.pdf.

[148] See, eg, OSC, Annual Report for 2014-2015, HC 126 (SG/2015/56), paras 3.19, 6.2.

[149] Home Office, Draft Investigatory Powers Bill (November 2015) 237, available at www.gov.uk/ government/uploads/system/uploads/attachment_data/file/473770/Draft_Investigatory_Powers_Bill.pdf.

[150] These statements have not been repeated in the Home Office, IPA 2016: Explanatory Notes.

[151] IPA 2016, s 227(2).

[152] See Home Office Press Release, 18 October 2017 at www.judiciary.gov.uk/wp-content/uploads/2017/10/ jc-announcement-13-new-commissioners-oct2017.pdf; Home Office Press Release, 'Investigatory Powers Commissioner Appointed: Lord Justice Fulford', 3 March 2017.

The IPC, and his Judicial Commissioners, will be tasked with a number of functions as part of the office's dual role in both authorising and overseeing (via audit, inspection and investigation of a public authority or CSP[153]) the use of investigatory powers by public authorities. These functions will also include carrying out reviews, subject to request by the Prime Minister, of any aspect of the functions of the intelligence services, or of the defence authorities or any other public authorities in so far as they are engaging 'in intelligence activities'.[154] The Parliament's Intelligence and Security Committee may also refer a matter to the IPC for inspection, investigation or audit.[155]

Second, the IPC is also responsible, as examined above, for informing individuals of any 'serious error' arising from the use of investigatory powers that has caused 'significant prejudice or harm' to them. Notably, the Act of 2016 makes clear that a breach of an individual's rights under the Human Rights Act 1998 does not by itself constitute such a 'serious error'.[156]

Third, the IPC must provide any materials, assistance or opinion, to the Investigatory Powers Tribunal for any investigation, or to assist in the determination of any matter, by the Tribunal.[157] Fourth, the IPC must provide an annual report concerning the exercise of his office to the Prime Minister (which will subsequently be published and made available to Parliament following any necessary exclusions). The scope of this report will include statistics on the use of investigatory powers kept under review by the IPC, such as the number of warrants issues given, considered and approved, information on their use, their impact and on the operation of the Act's safeguards (such as materials subject to legal privilege or confidential journalistic material).[158] This report must also provide details on the activities of the new 'Technology Advisory Panel' which will provide advice to the IPC on the implications of technological developments for the investigatory powers exercised under the Act and how such powers can be used 'while minimising interference with privacy'.[159]

Overall, the establishment of the IPC has been welcomed by commentators and other public authorities for ending the long-established authorisation of warrants purely by the executive. Nevertheless, some have been rightly critical of the fact that the new oversight body is still not strictly independent either operationally or functionally. For instance, the staffing of the IPC and its resources (eg accommodation, equipment, facilities) will be provided by the Secretary of State (not Parliament), subject to approval by the Treasury.[160] Furthermore, there has been some debate regarding the effectiveness in practice of the IPC's function of providing prior approval for the authorisation of warrants by a Secretary of State (with the exception of urgent cases). This system, requiring *both* IPC and executive consent, has become referred to as the '*double-lock*' mechanism. The former Intelligence Services Commissioner commended

---

[153] IPA 2016, s 235.
[154] IPA 2016, s 230.
[155] IPA 2016, s 236.
[156] IPA 2016, s 231.
[157] IPA 2016, s 232.
[158] IPA 2016, s 234.
[159] IPA 2016, s 246.
[160] IPA 2016.

the scope of the judge's role as it takes into account the lack of experience that judges from the IPC will have in matters of national security but still provides the judge a 'vital role' in assessing 'whether the necessity test and whether the proportionality test has been applied' and ensuring that an 'improper use of powers' does not occur.[161] Civil society, however, have been highly critical of the double-lock regime for effectively being a diluted form of independent judicial oversight, describing the mechanism as 'impractical' and a 'rubber-stamping exercise'.[162] The former Deputy Prime Minister has also questioned the independence of the prior oversight regime on the similar basis that 'judges will have very little discretion' in the decision-making process.[163] Ultimately, it remains to be seen how effectively the oversight role of the IPC and the Judicial Commissioners will be exercised within the double-lock system in practice, in addition to all of their other key functions.

VI. Conclusion and Future Developments

A. Implications of *Watson* for the IPA

During its pre-legislative stage, the then Home Secretary, Rt Hon Theresa May MP, stated that the IPA would represent 'a signature departure' from past attempts to reform the prior regime.[164] According to the former Home Secretary, this new legislative framework would be 'clear and understandable', 'strengthen safeguards' and 'introduce world-leading oversight arrangements'. The expressed intention to fulfil these three key commitments was welcomed, particularly following the unsuccessful Communications Data Bill 2012[165] (otherwise known as the 'Snoopers' Charter' for its far-reaching scope), the loss of public trust following the Snowden revelations, and the roundly criticised[166] emergency legislation of DRIPA which was held to be incompatible with EU law by the CJEU in *Tele2/Watson*.

Following its decision in *Tele2*, the CJEU referred the case back to the UK Court of Appeal to determine how its assessment affected the now repealed 2014 legal regime governing data retention under DRIPA.[167] These proceedings, though superficially

---

[161] Interview with Sir Mark Waller, 'A Threat to Justice?' *BBC Law in Action* podcast (12 November 2015).

[162] Big Brother Watch Press Release, 'Reaction to the Draft Investigatory Powers Bill' (4 November 2015), available at https://bigbrotherwatch.org.uk/all-media/reaction-to-the-draft-investigatory-powers-bill/; Liberty Press Release, 'Tracking, Hacking, and Lip Service to Safeguards', 4 November 2015, available at www.liberty-human-rights.org.uk/news/press-releases-and-statements/tracking-hacking-and-lip-service-safeguards-liberty's-analysis.

[163] P Wintour, 'Only "Tiny Handful" of Ministers Knew of Mass Surveillance, Clegg Reveals' *The Guardian* (5 November 2015).

[164] House of Commons, 'Meeting', 4 November 2015, available at <http://parliamentlive.tv/event/index/a5075dd3-5742-4651-b91d-243b76ba4478?in=12:39:29.

[165] 'Draft Communications Data Bill to be Redrafted-No 10' *BBC News* (11 December 2012).

[166] J Kiss, 'Academics: UK DRIP Data Law Changes are "Serious Expansion of Surveillance"' *The Guardian* (15 July 2014).

[167] For further information on the 2016 CJEU Grand Chamber judgment in the Joined Cases of *Tele2/Watson* (n 87), see also the next chapter.

only relevant to the past, in fact attracted great interest for how they affected the relevant provisions of the IPA, and (critically) the new oversight arrangements of that Act.

The Court of Appeal delivered its response in January 2018.[168] Much of the discussion related primarily, as might be expected, to the legality and scope of national data *retention* legislation, which are discussed at length in the next chapter in relation to future ramifications for the IPA Part 4. The Court deferred making any determination on the minimum safeguards stipulated in *Watson* that: the very measure of 'general and indiscriminate' retention of communications data itself is incompatible with EU law; that national law must provide that any data retained for the purpose of 'fighting serious crime' must be retained within the EU; and that individuals affected by data retention measures should be informed after the fact (provided the notification will not undermine ongoing investigations). Strikingly, the Court of Appeal also sidestepped any examination of the minimum safeguard in *Watson* ([122]) that mandates national law to also provide for the 'irreversible destruction' of the relevant data at the end of the data retention period.

The Court did so primarily on the basis that the CJEU had already been asked to further clarify the scope of their application with respect to matters of national surveillance in a pending preliminary reference submitted by the IPT (as discussed above).[169] The CJEU is being asked to clarify whether the domestic law of EU Member States that governs *national security* falls within the scope of EU law and is thus subject to the scrutiny of the CJEU. This may result in yet another radical and landmark judgment for the increasingly expansive reach of CJEU scrutiny.[170] In addition, the question of whether a general data retention regime is invalid under EU law will be the subject of review in a separate legal challenge to the IPA before the High Court in 2018.

Adding to this regulatory briar patch, given the considerable delay between the Court of Appeal's judgment and that of the CJEU judgment of *Watson* in 2016, there have been a number of further legal and policy developments that have taken place in the interim.[171] The High Court heard in February 2018 a legal challenge against the legality of the data retention provisions of the IPA by Liberty, a UK-based civil liberties advocate organisation.[172] The outcome of this judicial review will be yet another preliminary reference to the CJEU.[173]

B. After the IPA: Still an Unconsolidated Surveillance Regime

It is significant to note that although the IPA updates current powers, enacts a number of new substantive powers, and overhauls the previous system of oversight, the new

---

[168] *Secretary of State for the Home Department v Watson and Others* [2018] EWCA Civ 70.

[169] See note to the *Privacy International* case at n 24.

[170] N Ni Loideain, C Kuner, C Millard, F Cate, O Lynskey and D. Svantesson, 'An Unstoppable Force and an Immoveable Object? EU Data Protection Law and National Security' (2018) 8(1) *International Data Privacy Law* 335.

[171] See summary in *Watson* (n 168) [6].

[172] See www.libertyhumanrights.org.uk/news/press-releases-and-statements/people-vs-snoopers%E2%80%99-charter-high-court-hear-first-part-liberty%E2%80%99s.

[173] Case C-314/85 *Foto-Frost v Hauptzollamt Lübeck-Ost* [1987] ECR 4199.

statute still does not consolidate the legal regime governing the authorisation and use of investigatory powers by public authorities within the UK: this is a serious missed opportunity. Furthermore, this patchwork regime may still be open to further challenge for not complying with the accessibility and foreseeability requirements mandated by the legality condition of Art 8(2) ECHR and the proportionality principle of Arts 7 and 52(1) of the EU Charter of Fundamental Rights. Only time will tell whether the IPA will avoid the fate of RIPA which one leading commentator has described as 'obscure since its inception' and 'patched up so many times as to make it incomprehensible to all but a tiny band of initiates'.[174]

C. More Challenges before the Strasbourg Court

On top of the aforementioned pending judgments to the CJEU and High Court from *Liberty* and *Privacy International*, three further applications are currently pending before the ECtHR: *Big Brother Watch and Others v United Kingdom*; *Bureau of Investigative Journalism and Alice Ross v United Kingdom*; and *10 Human Rights Organisations v United Kingdom*.[175]

The first of these, *Big Brother Watch*, was lodged with the ECtHR in September 2013[176] but was later adjourned by the ECtHR in April 2014 pending three other challenges before the IPT brought by other NGOs. The ECtHR concluded the adjournment in November 2015 (following the delivery of the Tribunal's judgments[177]) and a new deadline (March 2016) was set for the UK Government to provide its response submission to the Court. At the time of writing, the Government's submission is still pending. *Big Brother Watch* now proceeds in parallel with two subsequent applications lodged with the ECtHR in September 2014 and May 2015. All applicants highlight in their submissions to the ECtHR that their legal challenges were prompted by the surveillance programmes identified in the Snowden revelations and claim that they are likely to have been subjects of surveillance by the UK intelligences services given the nature of their advocacy work.

The claimants in all three applications contend that their right to respect to private life, under Art 8 ECHR, has been unjustifiably interfered with on the ground that the surveillance regimes in question have not met the requirements of the legality condition under Art 8(2) ECHR. These legal challenges concern two systems of monitoring. The first involves the framework governing the receipt, and use, by the UK intelligence services of communications (and communications data) obtained from foreign governments, such as the US, via the PRISM and UPSTREAM programmes made public by the Snowden revelations. The other system before the review of the ECtHR

---

[174] Anderson Report (n 100), 8.

[175] *Big Brother Watch and Others v United Kingdom* Application No 58170/13; *Bureau of Investigative Journalism and Alice Ross v United Kingdom* Application No 62322/14; *10 Human Rights Organisations v United Kingdom* Application No 24960/15.

[176] *Big Brother Watch, ibid*, 'Timeline of Events', available at www.privacynotprism.org.uk/assets/files/privacynotprism/Timeline%20of%20Events.pdf.

[177] See, eg *Liberty and Others v Secretary of State for Foreign and Commonwealth Affairs* [2015] UKIPTrib 13_77-H.

comprises the acquisition of worldwide and domestic communications (and communications data) by GCHQ for intelligence agencies within the UK and aboard, via the TEMPORA programme.

Both the *Bureau of Investigative Journalism* and *10 Human Rights Organisations* applications also claim that their right to freedom of expression, as guaranteed under Art 10 ECHR, has been violated by these monitoring systems, particularly in light of the chilling effect that knowledge of these unlawful programmes has had on their work and consequently their role as a public watchdog of government activities. Furthermore, the latter application also claims that the IPT's decision to hold closed hearings was a violation of their right to a fair trial, as guaranteed under Art 6 ECHR. Finally, the same application also submits that the granting of additional safeguards to those known to be in the British Islands subjects to these programmes, but not those elsewhere, constitutes indirect indiscrimination and therefore amounts to a violation of Art 14 ECHR.

It is difficult to see how the broad scope of the relevant provisions under RIPA, especially s 8(4), that have been relied on in the past as a legal basis for the granting of warrants authorising the bulk interception of internal and external communications by UK intelligence agencies, meet the accessibility and foreseeability requirements stipulated under the legality condition of Art 8(2) ECHR. The ECtHR has clearly established in its case law since 2009 (*Liberty v UK*)[178] that the same principles concerning the accessibility and foreseeability tests under the legality condition of Art 8(2) that apply to the monitoring of individuals, apply equally to mass surveillance programmes. As discussed above, the two key tests of accessibility and foreseeability require that domestic law must be sufficiently accessible and clear in its terms to give individuals an adequate indication to foresee the circumstances and the conditions in which public authorities are empowered to resort to the measure in question. In line with the principle of the rule of law, it is essential that covert surveillance measures must be based on law that is particularly precise with clear and detailed rules as the technology used is continually becoming more sophisticated.

The ECtHR has already held once that UK surveillance legislation (the Interception of Communications Act 1985) was without 'sufficient clarity', and thus failed to provide adequate protection against state abuse of power. Based on previous case law of the ECtHR (especially *Liberty* and *Kennedy*), it seems likely that the impugned provisions of RIPA may go the same way as the Act of 1985.

This conclusion would be significant for two reasons. First, such an examination by the ECtHR would demonstrate that both the scope of Art 8(1) and the conditions of Art 8(2) are keeping pace with modern technological and regulatory developments in the area of covert surveillance, particularly with respect to mass surveillance programmes. Second, this conclusion would make clear that the use of new technology, or surveillance methodologies, for the purposes of national security will not evade

---

[178] *Liberty* (n 38). Reference to these standards was previously made by the ECtHR in its admissibility decision, ultimately held to be inadmissible, of *Weber and Saravia* (n 43), which concerned the interception of international communications.

the 'classic concerns' and robust scrutiny to be found in the well-established case law of the ECtHR.[179]

Furthermore, the Snowden revelations have also arguably played a role in prompting the ECtHR to consider the adequacy of its current interpretation of Art 8(2) ECHR. The ECtHR has admitted that current guarantees 'need to be enhanced' in order to address the issue of States' 'present-day capabilities for sophisticated and invasive surveillance, as well as to their ability to build a detailed profile of any individual's activities and relationships' using intercepted content and metadata. Indeed, as the ECtHR itself has traditionally warned, adequate and efficient safeguards are essential as the abuse of *any* form of covert monitoring is 'potentially so easy in individual cases and could have such harmful consequences for democratic society as a whole'.[180] These concerns may play a considerable role in the outcomes of the forthcoming legal challenges to the UK's surveillance regime now before the Strasbourg Court. Certainly all of the above pending cases will have enormous significance within the UK and EU, and in other Contracting States to the ECHR with similar legal frameworks.[181]

---

[179] T Murphy and GO Cuinn, 'Works in Progress: New Technologies and the European Court of Human Rights' (2010) 10(4) *Human Rights Law Review* 601, 636.
[180] *Klass* (n 29) [56]; *Kennedy* (n 67) [167].
[181] *Big Brother Watch*; *Bureau of Investigative Journalism*; *10 Human Rights Organisations* (n 175).

7

The Retention of Communications Data in Europe and the UK

ELENI KOSTA*

I. Introduction and Chronological Background

In the last chapter, we began to examine the state surveillance landscape that has evolved, diversified and expanded over the almost two decades since 9/11 and the rise of the 'war on terror'. In that, and previous chapters, we also highlighted the controversy and disquiet that has followed the whistleblowing revelations from Edward Snowden in 2013 of mass blanket surveillance of Internet users, in the EU and elsewhere, by a number of US and EU intelligence agencies.[1] In the backlash and loss of public trust that has followed these disclosures, the European Court of Human Rights (ECtHR) at Strasbourg and the Court of Justice of the European Union (CJEU) have played a major role in Europe in attempting to rein in unconstitutional powers used by state law enforcement and intelligence agencies to investigate crime and terrorism, using Art 8 of the European Convention of Human Rights (ECHR) and Arts 7 and 8 of the Charter of Fundamental Rights of the European Union (CFR) as tools to restore confidence in fundamental rights.

In the last chapter, we focused on looking at the developing human rights scrutiny of state surveillance in these courts, notably the need for incursions into Art 8 of the ECHR in the name of security to be in accordance with law; undertaken for legitimate purposes; and 'necessary in a democratic society', ie proportional to the social need. Following this rubric, a number of far-reaching cases have effectively limited state powers of interception of the *content* of communications and access to *meta-data*

---

* The author would like to thank Magda Brewczyńska for her assistance in the collection of the material for the writing up of this chapter, as well as Judith Rauhofer, who authored the relevant chapter for a previous edition of the book, and the editor, Lilian Edwards, for her invaluable feedback, insightful comments, assistance and guidance. Very helpful comments on a final draft were also received from Graham Smith of Bird and Bird. This chapter was completed before the decision in *Liberty v UK* [2018] EWHC 975 (Admin) on 27 April 2018.

[1] See further Ni Loideain in Chapter 6 of this volume.

connected to communications. In particular, in the last chapter, we highlighted the recent and crucial case of *Tele2/Watson*[2] in the CJEU which lead (inter alia) to the UK Data Retention and Investigatory Powers Act (DRIPA) being declared invalid.

In this chapter, we focus on laws concerning *data retention* as opposed to interception or access. Communications data[3] (meaning *not* content, but data *about* communications, such as the time a call was made and from where, or to whom an email is sent) has historically been collected by those who provided communications services, ie telecommunications operators (fixed line and mobile) and Internet service providers (ISPs). More recently, other types of service providers, using the Web and the Internet as a medium for both text and voice communications (eg Facebook Messenger, WhatsApp, Skype) have become significant loci for private communications.

Historically, telecoms providers and ISPs only retained customer data for long enough to fulfil billing and complaints functions. There was no business case to do more, and storage costs. As a result, European governments, especially the New Labour UK Government lead by Tony Blair from 1997 to 2007, began to feel the need for laws to compel such providers to retain communications data longer, so it could be accessed by law enforcement agencies (LEAs) and intelligence agencies as this became necessary, eg when a terrorist incident occurred. Such data retention laws, were (and are), however, directly opposed to the data protection (DP) laws we studied in previous chapters which assert as a key principle that personal data should not be retained for longer than is necessary for the original purposes of processing. This patent conflict was partly resolved in Art 15 of the Privacy and Electronic Communications Directive 2002 (PECD)[4] which is discussed further below. The Madrid bombings in 2004 and the London subway bombings in 2005 then helped create a political environment which drove a pathway to a harmonised data retention law for the EU, and this new Data Retention Directive (DRD) was proposed as part of a package of measures during the UK presidency of the EU, at the end of 2005.[5]

The DRD[6] was adopted in 2006 and placed an obligation on providers of publicly available electronic communications services and of public communications networks (communication service providers or 'CSPs') to retain certain communications data for law enforcement purposes. The Directive regulated the retention of traffic and location data, as well as data necessary to identify the subscriber or registered user by CSPs, while making it clear that no *content* data should be retained under its provisions.

---

[2] Joined Cases C-203/15 and C-698/15 *Tele2 Sverige AB v Post- och telestyrelsen and Secretary of State for the Home Department v Tom Watson and Others* (hereinafter '*Tele2/Watson*') [2016] ECLI:EU:C:2016:970, Judgment of 21 December 2016.

[3] See further below for discussion of the exact meaning of this term and its equivalents in UK legislation.

[4] European Parliament and the Council of the European Union, Directive 2002/58/EC of 12 July 2002 concerning the processing of personal data and the protection of privacy in the electronic communications sector (Directive on privacy and electronic communications) [2002] OJ L201/37 (PECD) (31 July 2002). See also Chapter 5 of this volume.

[5] European Parliament and the Council of the European Union, Directive 2006/24/EC on the retention of data generated or processed in connection with the provision of publicly available electronic communications services or of public communications networks and amending Directive 2002/58/EC [2006] OJ L105/54 (DRD) (15 March 2006). A draft framework Decision on Data Retention had been proposed in 2004, suggesting retention periods of one to three years, but this was rejected by the European Parliament.

[6] DRD, *ibid*.

Article 15 of the PECD[7] allowed Member States, even before the adoption of the DRD (and still does), to adopt legislative measures for the retention of traffic and location data when such measures 'constitute [...] a necessary, appropriate and proportionate measure within a democratic society to safeguard national security [...], defence, public security, and the prevention, investigation, detection and prosecution of criminal offences or of unauthorised use of the electronic communication system'.[8] These conditions under which data retention measures may be adopted significantly resemble the exceptions to the right to privacy laid out in Article 8(2) of the ECHR.[9]

The DRD met significant resistance during its adoption process by human rights organisations, privacy advocates and citizens regarding its compatibility with fundamental rights, and more specifically with the rights to privacy and data protection. After its adoption, numerous national courts declared unconstitutional specific provisions of the national laws transposing the Directive on the basis that they violate the rights to privacy and data protection.[10]

In April 2014, in the case *Digital Rights Ireland*, discussed in detail below, the CJEU marked a turning point in the debate by invalidating the DRD.[11] The CJEU ruled that the DRD entailed a serious interference with the fundamental rights to privacy and data protection as protected in the CFR and that the EU legislature exceeded 'the limits imposed by compliance with the principle of proportionality in the light of Articles 7, 8 and 52(1) of the Charter'.[12] Mandatory safeguards were enumerated to protect privacy in any case of data retention legislation by the EU. The judgment of the CJEU did not automatically result in the invalidation of national implementations of the DRD. However, in some countries (such as the UK – see below) such laws were indeed open to challenge for loss of the empowering authority of the DRD after *Digital Rights Ireland*.[13]

In the UK, the main Act authorising UK authorities to carry out surveillance and investigation at the time of *Digital Rights Ireland* (and interestingly, promulgated even before 9/11) was the Regulation of Investigatory Powers Act 2000 (RIPA). RIPA was a complex Act which had to be read with many other existing legislative acts, in

---

[7] PECD (n 4).

[8] Article 15(1) PECD. However, while the Directive was in force, a new Article 15(1a) – now defunct – effectively exhausted that right with regard to the retention of communications data for crime prevention purposes. That right therefore only resurged on the part of the Member States after the Directive was declared invalid in Case C-293/12 and C-594/12 *Digital Rights Ireland and Seitlinger and others* ECLI:EU:C:2014:238, CJEU Judgment of 8 April 2014.

[9] Article 8 ECHR: '1. Everyone has the right to respect for his private and family life, his home and his correspondence. 2. There shall be no interference by a public authority with the exercise of this right except such as is in accordance with the law and is necessary in a democratic society in the interests of national security, public safety or the economic well-being of the country, for the prevention of disorder or crime, for the protection of health or morals, or for the protection of the rights and freedoms of others.'

[10] Some of the early court decisions include judgments issued by the Bulgarian Supreme Administrative Court, the Romanian Constitutional Court, the German Constitutional Court, the Czech Constitutional Court and the Supreme Court of Cyprus.

[11] *Digital Rights Ireland* (n 8).

[12] *Digital Rights Ireland* (n 8) [65] and [69].

[13] For eg the Austrian Constitutional Court, the Constitutional Court of the Republic of Slovenia, the District Court of The Hague and Constitutional Court of the Slovak Republic ruled on (provisions of) the national data retention laws in light of the CJEU *Digital Rights Ireland* judgment.

particular, the Intelligence Services Act 1994, the Police Act 1997 and the Human Rights Act 1998.[14] RIPA dealt with both *interception* of the content and metadata of communications, and powers to *access communications data* (metadata) as well as the *grounds* for such access by various state agencies, were not always limited to LEAs or intelligence agencies.[15] Notably, under RIPA, the authorisation of interception was by executive power alone, with no judicial warrant needed; this was also the case in relation to authorising access to communications data, and indeed, in respect of some data, access was automatically permitted for a large number of state bodies including local authorities, health and safety authorities, etc. By many Continental standards, this was a highly permissive regime for the executive, with a very low degree of independent oversight, although as we noted in the last chapter it passed muster in the pre-Snowden days of *Kennedy v UK*[16] by virtue of having independent *post factum* review by the Investigatory Powers Tribunal (IPT).

RIPA did *not* deal with mandatory retention by telcos. At the time of, and prior to, the passing of the DRD, interception and access to data were seen as powers not delegated by states to the EU and part of their vital domestic security apparatus. As a result they were not harmonised across the EU and varied considerably among Member States. Retention on the other hand became, as a result of the above initiative and justified by the connection to EU PECD in Art 15 (see Chapter 5), part of the corpus of EU law. In the UK, the DRD was implemented by a series of delegated statutory instruments, most notably the Data Retention Regulations 2009 (DRR 2009).[17] The 2009 Regulations required any public communications provider generating or processing communications data in the UK to retain the specific categories of data pertaining to its type of network or service[18] for up to 12 months.[19]

Historically, literature in the UK has thus tended to treat the issues of *retention* of data and *access* to data, as separable to some extent. However, as we saw in the last chapter, and will see further below, following *Tele2/Watson*, access and retention rules have become inextricably connected; and readers will have to decide if the separation of the topics in this book remains useful (arguably so, at least for UK readers, as access and retention are still dealt with in separate chapters of RIPA's successor, the Investigatory Powers Act 2016 (IPA)). Notably, the IPA now includes interception of communications, access to communications data *and* retention of such all in one instrument for the first time.

Following the annulment of the DRD by the CJEU in *Digital Rights Ireland*, confusion briefly reigned as to the status of national transpositions of the DRD. The UK initially maintained that the DRR 2009 might be independently viable[20] but fairly quickly plugged the gap by passing new emergency legislation, DRIPA in July 2014.

---

[14] Explanatory notes to RIPA, para 5.

[15] Explanatory notes to RIPA, Ch 23, para 4. It also dealt with a number of non-digital investigative powers such as covert human intelligence sources and these parts of RIPA remain in force to this day – see discussion in Chapter 6.

[16] *Kennedy v UK* (2011) 52 EHRR 4. See discussion in Chapter 6.

[17] Data Retention (EC Directive) Regulations 2009 (SI 2009/No 859).

[18] *Ibid*, reg 4. But see exemption in reg 10.

[19] *Ibid*, reg 5.

[20] Hansard HC Deb, 16 June 2014, c445W.

The Act, confusingly, also took the opportunity to amend some parts of RIPA relating to interception and access to data which had become particularly sensitive (ie possibly illegal) in the light of the Snowden revelations and the *Digital Rights Ireland* case. Most of RIPA however at this point remained in force along with a plethora of various codes and guidance which had been developed alongside it.

In December 2014, Members of the UK Parliament (MPs) Davis and Watson challenged the new 2014 UK data retention legislation in the courts.[21] The High Court issued a seminal decision declaring s 1 of DRIPA void on the basis, following *Digital Rights Ireland*, that it violated the mandatory safeguards laid down in that case, ie that (a) use of data retained was not restricted to purposes relating to *serious crime* only, and (b) access to data retained was not dependent on *prior review* by a court or independent body.[22]

On appeal, the Court of Appeal disagreed to some extent with the Divisional Court and felt there was room for doubt that *Digital Rights Ireland* had been intended to lay down mandatory rules for *national* legislation on access, as opposed to merely EU legislation (such as the DRD). It referred this and other questions to the CJEU, which were dealt with alongside similar questions relating to Swedish legislation, in December 2016, in *Tele 2/Watson*. Here, the CJEU took the position that the legality of mandatory data retention was dependent in part on the safeguards around *access* to data retained, which was not a matter harmonised by EU law. National data retention laws had to lay down 'clear and precise rules' about when access to retained data could be granted.[23] Such laws could not therefore be legal unless the important safeguards on access, which had been foreshadowed by the CJEU in *Digital Rights Ireland*, were in place.[24] This raised clear questions on the compatibility of the UK DRIPA with rights to privacy and data protection.

DRIPA, as emergency legislation, was set to expire on 31 December 2016.[25] At the end of 2016, on 29 November, in the nick of time before this 'sunset' clause cut in, an updated framework for the use of investigatory powers for interception, access and retention requirements was enacted in IPA.[26] Only a month later however, on 21 December 2016, the CJEU decided *Tele2/Watson* which, to the dismay of the UK Government, immediately made precarious the already controversial new rules of the IPA. The validity of the IPA, which in many parts replicated what had already been law in RIPA and DRIPA and in many places expanded further state power, has thus been controversial from day one.

---

[21] *Davis & Ors, R (on the application of) v Secretary of State for the Home Department & Ors* [2015] EWHC 2092 (Admin), [2015] WLR(D) 318, Interveners' submissions, CO ref: CO/3794/2014, available at www.openrightsgroup.org/assets/files/legal/Intervention%20submissions%20ORG%20and%20PI%20in%20 DRIPA%20case%2023.12.14.pdf.

[22] *Davis & Ors v Secretary of State for the Home Department* [2015] EWHC 2092 (Admin) [83], available at www.judiciary.gov.uk/judgments/david-davis-and-others-v-secretary-of-state-for-the-home-department; L Woods, 'High Court Strikes Down Data Retention Laws in Ruling on DRIPA' (2015)1 *European Data Protection Law Review* 236.

[23] *Tele2/Watson* (n 2) [109].

[24] *Tele2/Watson* (n 2). See discussion in Chapter 6.

[25] DRIPA, s 8(3).

[26] IPA 2016.

The IPA received Royal Assent on 29 November 2016. The Investigatory Powers Act 2016 (Commencement No 1 and Transitional Provisions) Regulations 2016 (IPA Regulations 2016)[27] specified a number of provisions of IPA which would enter into force on 30 December 2016. Timing was critical here if a gap was not to be left in which data retention had no legal basis, in the eyes of the UK Government. Retention of communications data by CSPs in Part 4 of the IPA was thus in the main brought into force on 30 December 2016,[28] thus plugging the gap before DRIPA expired.[29]

Meanwhile, other parts of the IPA have been and are being brought in at a slower pace, as considerable work is involved, eg setting up and training the new Judicial Commissioners (see below). Chapter I of Part 1 of RIPA concerning *interception of communications* was replaced by Part 2 of IPA and Chapter I of Part 6 thereof. Acquisition of (access to) communications data from CSPs previously regulated by Chapter II of Part 1 of RIPA, is replaced by Part 3 of IPA. As of 8 March 2018, four delegated instruments[30] bringing into force parts of the IPA have been passed, including, on that date, the first provisions requiring 'double lock' oversight by Judicial Commissioners (see below). As we shall discuss later, the challenges, which killed the DRD and then the UK's DRIPA, are still very much alive, and may yet invalidate parts of the UK's new IPA.

II. The Data Retention Directive

Following a vigorous debate on whether the retention of traffic and location data was an issue that should be regulated under the first pillar, as an internal market instrument, or under the third pillar, as an instrument relating to justice and home affairs,[31] the DRD was finally adopted on 15 March 2006.

The main aim of the DRD was the harmonisation of national laws on CSPs' obligations to retain communications data generated or processed by them so that they would be available for the purpose of investigation, detection and prosecution of serious crime.[32] The DRD itself did not include a definition of the term 'serious crime', which was left to the Member States to regulate in their national legislation. However the Council urged the Member States to have due regard to the criminal offences listed

---

[27] The Investigatory Powers Act 2016 (Commencement No 1 and Transitional Provisions) Regulations 2016 (SI 2016/No 1233) (C 85).

[28] See n 25.

[29] Accordingly there is no need to refer to any non-mandatory codes on data retention which existed before RIPA or DRIPA such as the Voluntary Code on data retention made under Part 11 of Anti-terrorism, Crime and Security Act 2001 (ATCSA). Interestingly however, that Voluntary Code only required retention for 6 months, half the length of time the subsequent IPA regime can demand.

[30] SI 2017/No 137; SI 2017/No 859; SI 2018/No 341.

[31] See *inter alia* Project de décision cadre sur la conservation des données – Analyse juridique' – (SEC(2005) 420) (March 22, 2005) and Commission Staff Working Document 'Annex to the: Proposal for a Directive of the European Parliament and of the Council on the retention of data processed in connection with the provision of public electronic communication services and amending Directive 2002/58/EC Extended Impact Assessment' COM(2005) 438 final, available at http://eur-lex.europa.eu/legal-content/EN/TXT/HTML/?uri=CELEX:52005SC1131&from=EN (21 September 2005).

[32] DRD, Art 1(1).

in Article 2(2) of the Framework Decision on the European Arrest Warrant[33] and crime involving telecommunications.[34]

The data to be retained were traffic data, location data and data necessary to identify the subscriber or registered user.[35] The content of a communication was specifically excluded from the retention requirement.[36] Crucially, traffic data relating to web browsing were *not* to be retained, as this invoked concerns that content not metadata was being retained. With regard to Internet traffic, the Directive only covered data relating to Internet access, Internet email and Internet telephony. The Directive provided that the data should be retained for a period between six months and two years from the date of the communication, with discretion left to Member States as to what period they chose within these bounds and for what type of data.[37]

The DRD required that retained data were to be provided only to the competent national authorities and in accordance with national law. Notably, the Directive left it to the Member States to specify the procedures to be followed and the conditions to be fulfilled in order for the competent national authorities to gain *access* to retained data.[38] These procedures and conditions had to be defined by Member States in accordance with the requirements of necessity and proportionality, in the light of the ECHR as interpreted by the ECtHR.[39]

A. Invalidation of the Directive

The controversy over the European law of data retention was apparent from the start with an early challenge in July 2006 from Ireland to the CJEU asking for the annulment of the DRD on the grounds that it had not been adopted on an appropriate legal basis for 'law-enforcement purposes'.[40] The Court however ruled that Article 95 of the Treaty of the Functioning of the European Union (TEC) was indeed the right legal basis for the data retention instrument and dismissed the case.[41]

National laws transposing the DRD were challenged in several Member States and in a number of cases from 2008 onwards, national courts declared them unconstitutional.[42] Eventually, the CJEU was requested to deliver preliminary

---

[33] Council Framework Decision 2002/584/JHA on the European Arrest Warrant and the surrender procedures between Member States [2002] OJ L190/1.

[34] Council of the European Union, Proposal for a Directive of the European Parliament and of the Council on the retention of data processed in connection with the provision of public electronic communication services and amending Directive 2002/58/EC, [first reading] – Statements, 5777/06 ADD 1, 10 February 2006.

[35] A detailed list with the categories of data to be retained is contained in Article 5 of the DRD.

[36] DRD, Art 5(2).

[37] DRD, Art 6.

[38] DRD, Art 4.

[39] *Ibid.*

[40] ECJ, Case C-301/06, ECR 2009 p I-593 *Ireland / Parliament and Council* ECLI:EU:C:2009:68, Judgment of 10 February 2009 [91].

[41] *Ibid* [93] and [94].

[42] Some of the early Court decisions include judgments issued by the Bulgarian Supreme Administrative Court, the Romanian Constitutional Court, the German Constitutional Court, the Czech Constitutional Court and the Supreme Court of Cyprus.

rulings on data retention by the High Court of Ireland and the Austrian Constitutional Court. The CJEU summarised the main questions referred to it by the national courts as 'asking the Court to examine the validity of Directive 2006/24 in the light of Articles 7, 8 and 11 of the Charter'[43] and on 8 April 2014 delivered a seminal judgment that invalidated the DRD, commonly known as *Digital Rights Ireland*.[44]

The CJEU found that the obligation to *retain* the data already constituted interference with the right to privacy in itself[45] and that the data that could be retained under the Directive were very detailed, allowing for the drawing of significant information about the citizens' habits and activities[46] including 'the habits of everyday life, permanent or temporary places of residence, daily or other movements, the activities carried out, the social relationships of those persons and the social environments frequented by them'.[47] The Court found that the *access* of the competent national authorities to the retained data constituted a further interference with the right to privacy.[48] It thus found a *prima facie* interference with Articles 7 (private life) and 8 (processing of personal data) of the CFR, and then looked to see whether the interference with these could be justified under Article 52(1) CFR which allows interference where 'necessary and genuinely meet[s] objectives of general interest recognised by the Union or the need to protect the rights and freedoms of others'.[49] However this interference also has to be proportional.

The CJEU found that the objective of the DRD, ie to contribute to the fight against serious crime and consequently to public security, was indeed an objective of general interest.[50] Proportionality was assisted by the requirement that retention of data was to be used only for fighting serious crime.[51]

However, the DRD as a whole resoundingly did not meet the standards of necessity and proportionality. First, the DRD provided for the *blanket retention* of the data of all citizens.[52] The Directive covered:

> … in a generalised manner, all persons and all means of electronic communication as well as all traffic data without any differentiation, limitation or exception being made in the light of the objective of fighting against serious crime.[53]

It thus inevitably applied to some individuals whose conduct was not linked by any evidence to serious crime, and provided none of the exceptions that might be expected, eg for communications subject to an obligation of professional secrecy such as between lawyer and client.[54]

Second, it facilitated *unlimited access* of competent national authorities that could further use the data 'for the purposes of prevention, detection or criminal prosecutions'[55]

---

[43] *Digital Rights Ireland* (n 8) [23].
[44] *Digital Rights Ireland* (n 8).
[45] *Digital Rights Ireland* (n 8) [34].
[46] *Digital Rights Ireland* (n 8) [27].
[47] *Digital Rights Ireland* (n 8) [26]–[27].
[48] *Digital Rights Ireland* (n 8) [35].
[49] *Digital Rights Ireland* (n 8) [38].
[50] *Digital Rights Ireland* (n 8) [41] and [44].
[51] *Digital Rights Ireland* (n 8) [49].
[52] *Digital Rights Ireland* (n 8) [59].
[53] *Digital Rights Ireland* (n 8) [57].
[54] *Digital Rights Ireland* (n 8) [58]–[59].
[55] *Digital Rights Ireland* (n 8) [60].

restricted only by the notion of serious crime. As that concept was not defined in the DRD, this left dubiety as to whether national rules would be proportionate.

Third, the CJEU criticised the fact that substantive or procedural conditions for *access to* and *use of* retained data were left to the national competent authorities and not mandatorily laid down by the DRD.[56] A crucial point in the CJEU judgment was the *absence of a requirement for a prior review* by a court or an independent administrative body before the competent authorities gain access to the data or use them.[57]

Fourth, the CJEU stressed the lack in the DRD of *'objective criteria* in order to ensure that [the retention period was] limited to what is strictly necessary'.[58] Instead, states were given an unfettered discretion to set a data retention period without making any distinction between categories of data, based on either their potential value for the purposes pursued, or on the basis of the type of person involved.[59]

Fifth, the CJEU criticised the fact that the level of protection and security of the data could be compromised due to economic considerations and in particular the lack of an obligation to irreversibly destroy the data at the end of the retention period.[60] Finally, the CJEU criticised the lack of a requirement for data to be retained within the EU, which might involve consequent lack of oversight.[61]

Following this reasoning, the CJEU concluded that 'the EU legislature has exceeded the limits imposed by compliance with the principle of proportionality in the light of Articles 7, 8 and 52(1) of the Charter'[62] and declared the DRD invalid. The DRD was declared retrospectively invalid from the date when it entered into force.[63] This did not directly or automatically affect the validity of all national data retention legislation,[64] but led to such invalidation following national court decision.[65]

III. UK Reaction to the *Digital Rights Ireland* Case

In the aftermath of the *Digital Rights Ireland* judgment, as outlined in the Introduction, the UK Government after a bare four days of Parliamentary process adopted in July 2014 DRIPA and its secondary legislation, the Data Retention Regulations 2014

---

[56] *Digital Rights Ireland* (n 8) [61].
[57] *Digital Rights Ireland* (n 8) [62].
[58] *Digital Rights Ireland* (n 8) [64].
[59] *Digital Rights Ireland* (n 8) [63].
[60] *Digital Rights Ireland* (n 8) [67].
[61] *Digital Rights Ireland* (n 8) [68].
[62] *Digital Rights Ireland* (n 8) [69].
[63] This was also confirmed in the Press Release of the Court on the cases: Court of Justice of the European Union, Press Release No 54/14, Luxembourg, 8 April 2014, Judgment in Joined Cases C-293/12 and C-594/12, Digital Rights Ireland and Seitlinger and Others, n 2. See J Rauhofer and D Mac Sithigh, 'The Data Retention Directive Never Existed' (2014) 11 *SCRIPTed*; available at http://script-ed.org/?p=1480.
[64] Council of the European Union, 'Note from Eurojust to Council delegations on "Eurojust Analysis of the EU Member Stated" Legal Framework and Current Challenges on Data Retention', Brussels, 26 October 2015, 13085.
[65] *Ibid* p 4: The data retention legislation, or specific provisions of it, was invalidated in Austria, Belgium, Bulgaria, Germany, Lithuania, The Netherlands, Poland, Romania, Slovenia, Slovakia and the UK.

(DRR 2014).[66] Two MPs, Davis and Watson, challenged DRIPA in the courts, claiming that DRIPA failed to meet the clear requirements of *Digital Rights Ireland*. Special attention was drawn to the width of the powers in DRIPA and the lack of concern for the confidentiality of communications with solicitors and constituents.[67]

On 17 July 2015, the High Court of Justice (Divisional Court of the Queen's Bench Division) declared[68] that as DRIPA was 'an identically worded domestic statute' to the repealed Regulations made under the DRD for the UK, it must be found, like the DRD, invalid.[69] Like the DRD, it did not meet the safeguards laid down by the CJEU in *Digital Rights Ireland*, particularly in relation to access, especially the lack of restriction to serious crimes, and the lack of independent prior review.[70] The High Court thus issued an order disapplying section 1 DRIPA from 31 March 2016.[71]

The UK Secretary of State for the Home Department appealed to the Court of Appeal[72] which decided to stay the proceedings and refer the case to the CJEU for a preliminary ruling. The CJEU was requested to answer whether the *Digital Rights Ireland* judgment laid down 'mandatory requirements of EU law applicable to a Member State's domestic regime governing access to data retained in accordance with national legislation, in order to comply with Articles 7 and 8' of the EU Charter of Fundamental Rights.[73] This resulted in the next crucial CJEU judgment in this story, the *Tele2/Watson* judgment of December 2016, where the questions sent by the UK Court of Appeal were conjoined with a similar application from the Administrative Court of Appeal of Stockholm in Sweden.

IV. The *Tele2/Watson* Judgment

The questions the CJEU thus eventually examined asked in the round if *national* data retention legislation had to abide by the safeguards laid down in *Digital Rights Ireland* or whether they only restricted *EU* legislation.

The CJEU concluded that the list of objectives listed in Article 15(1) of PECD is exhaustive and that only the objective of fighting serious crime is capable of justifying access to retained data to safeguard 'the prevention, investigation, detection and prosecution of criminal offences'.[74] Any legislative measures taken to meet this objective should not exceed the limits of what was strictly necessary, in accordance

---

[66] Data Retention Regulations 2014 (SI 2014/No 2042).
[67] *Davis* (n 22) [1].
[68] *Davis* (n 22).
[69] *Davis* (n 22) [83].
[70] *Davis* (n 22) [83].
[71] *Davis* (n 22) [122].
[72] *Secretary of State for the Home Department v Davis MP & Ors* [2015] EWCA Civ 1185, [2016] HRLR 1, [2016] 1 CMLR 48.
[73] *Ibid* [118]. The UK Court of Appeal asked a second question on the relation between Articles 7 and 8 CFR and Article 8 ECHR and in particular whether the *Digital Rights* judgment expands the scope of Articles 7 and/or 8 CFR beyond that of Article 8 ECHR, as established in the jurisprudence of the ECtHR. However, the CJEU in its 21 December 2016 judgment found the second question inadmissible.
[74] *Tele2/Watson* (n 2) [115].

with the principle of proportionality[75] and should contain specific rules on the circumstances and the conditions for access to retained data by competent national authorities.[76]

In particular, in *Tele2/Watson*, the CJEU clearly held that *national* legislation that permits *access* to mandatorily retained communications data must satisfy key minimum safeguards required by the EU Charter of Fundamental Rights.[77] We examined these in part in the last chapter in relation to access and acquisition of data[78] but to recapitulate, *Tele2/Watson* addressed the issues of whether national legislation must:

- Require prior review by a court, or an independent administrative authority before access to or use of retained data can be made.[79]

- Only allow access to retained data in relation to individuals that are 'suspected of planning, committing or having committed a serious crime or of being implicated in one way or another in such a crime'.[80]

- Require notification to affected persons as soon as such notification will not jeopardise the investigation.[81]

- Provide for a high level of protection of the retained data; providers shall take appropriate technical and organisational measures to ensure the effective protection of retained data against risks of misuse and against any unlawful access to that data. Furthermore, data has to be retained within the EU and be destroyed at the end of the retention period.[82]

After *Tele2/Watson*, it became clear that DRIPA s 1 was effectively dead and that there would also be grave resulting challenges to the new IPA. In January 2018, the Court of Appeal formally declared that DRIPA s 1 was inconsistent with EU law, but explicitly only on the grounds that it did not restrict access to data to fighting serious crime, and that access was not subject to prior review by a court or an independent authority. As Ni Loideain noted in the previous chapter,[83] both of these findings left no doubt that Part 4 of the IPA on retention would now need to be urgently amended.[84]

Meanwhile in November 2017, after a year's intense work and consultation after *Tele2/Watson*, the UK Home Office published a package of suggestions for reform of the IPA to meet the *Tele2/Watson* requirements along with a draft statutory instrument and an evidence case for the need for, and productivity of, retention of communications data.[85] A plethora of applications to national courts, the CJEU and the Strasbourg

[75] *Tele2/Watson* (n 2) [116].
[76] *Tele2/Watson* (n 2) [117].
[77] *Tele2/Watson* (n 2) [125].
[78] See Chapter 6.
[79] *Tele2/Watson* (n 2) [120] and [123].
[80] *Tele2/Watson* (n 2) [119].
[81] *Tele2/Watson* (n 2) [121].
[82] *Tele2/Watson* (n 2) [122].
[83] See Chapter 6.
[84] *Secretary of State for the Home Department v Tom Watson MP & Others* [2018] EWCA Civ 70.
[85] See www.gov.uk/government/consultations/investigatory-powers-act-2016.

court, as detailed in the last chapter, are still to come. There is no doubt at all that the whole concept of a blanket national data retention law is massively under siege in the post-Snowden world.

However, some commentators would assert that the Court of Appeal did not go as far as one would expect following *Tele2/Watson*, in that it did not declare the blanket retention of data intrinsically unlawful, nor did it establish a requirement that retained data should remain in the EU or that such data should be destroyed at the end of the retention period. As Ni Loideain pointed out in the last chapter, these questions were quite notably sidestepped. We wait now to see which existing challenges come to the CJEU and indeed what the impact of Brexit will be on all this, which may remove the CJEU as a determining final court from the table and may in time even exclude the jurisdiction of the ECtHR. In the meantime however, we turn to the last question, which is, post-DRIPA, how the IPA now attempts to regulate requirements for retention of data for the benefit of UK authorities.

V. Retention of Communications Data under the IPA 2016

Part 4 of IPA regulates the mandatory retention of communications data.[86] Part 4 was in the main brought into force on 30 December 2016 to replace DRIPA.[87] Graham Smith has commented that this part, controversially, considering the demise of the DRD, actually 'extends existing powers under [DRIPA] and revives elements of the draft Communications Data Bill on which the pre-2015 Coalition government was deadlocked'.[88]

A. Purposes for the Retention of Communications Data

Section 87 of IPA provides that the Secretary of State has the power to give retention notice to telecommunications operators[89] to retain relevant communications

---

[86] As well as the main text, six new Codes of Practice are being drafted to deal with the IPA – see summary of responses to consultation issued December 2017 with revised draft Codes, *Investigatory Powers Act 2016: Response to Home Office Consultation on Investigatory Powers Act Codes of Practice*, available at www.gov.uk/government/uploads/system/uploads/attachment_data/file/668943/Response_to_the_IPA_codes_consultation.pdf. However, the *Code of Practice on Access to Retained Communications Data* made under s 71(4) of RIPA and adopted in March 2015, which previously related to the powers and duties conferred or imposed under Part 1 of DRIPA and the DRR 2014, remains currently in force. See p 3 of December 2017 document.

[87] Investigatory Powers Act 2016 (Commencement No. 1 and Transitional Provisions) Regulations 2016 (SI 2016/No 1233).

[88] See https://www.twobirds.com/en/news/articles/2016/uk/what-the-investigatory-powers-bill-would-mean-for-your-business.

[89] The provisions on the retention of communications data apply also to postal operators and postal services: IPA, s 96.

data. In particular, CSPs may be required to retain relevant communications data for the same purposes for which these data may be obtained, which are specified in section 61(7) IPA:[90]

a)   In the interests of national security.
b)   For the purpose of preventing or detecting crime or of preventing disorder.
c)   In the interests of the economic well-being of the United Kingdom.
d)   In the interests of public safety.
e)   For the purpose of protecting public health.
f)   For the purpose of assessing or collecting any tax, duty or levy.
g)   For the purpose, in an emergency, of preventing death or of preventing or mitigating injury or damage to a person's physical or mental health.
h)   To assist investigations into alleged miscarriages of justice.
i)   Where a person ('P') has died or is unable to identify themselves because of a physical or mental condition, to assist in identifying P, or to obtain information about P's next of kin or other persons connected with P or about the reason for P's death or condition.
j)   For the purpose of exercising functions relating to the regulation of financial services and markets or to financial stability.

The above list of purposes is not a novelty of the IPA. It is based on RIPA, s 22(2), which contained the first seven grounds, and was extended in the IPA with the addition of grounds (h), (i) and (j). The IPA tries to justify the inclusion of the interests of the economic well-being of the United Kingdom by explaining that such interests should also be relevant to the interests of national security.[91]

Fairly obviously, these purposes seem to go way beyond the notion of serious crime as a hard threshold for retention requirements which was specified as far back as the DRD itself and reviewed approvingly in *Digital Rights Ireland* and *Tele2/Watson*. In the Home Office's consultation on needed amendments to the IPA after *Tele2/Watson* of November 2017 (discussed in more depth below at section V. D.), this was somewhat grudgingly acknowledged and a new required definition of 'serious crime' was proposed.

> In its present form, the IPA permits the retention of and access to data for 10 purposes. The Government considers that communication data should not be retained or acquired for trivial matters, and the important tests of necessity and proportionality in the Act prevent data being retained or acquired where it is not appropriate to do so. Nevertheless, the Government proposes to amend the Act to impose a serious crime threshold in relation to the retention and acquisition of events data for criminal purposes.[92]

---

[90] *Ibid*, s 87(1)(a).
[91] *Ibid*, s 61(7)(c).
[92] See Home Office *Investigatory Powers Act 2016: Consultation on the Government's proposed response to the ruling of the Court of Justice of the European Union on 21 December 2016 regarding the retention of communications data* November 2017, available at www.gov.uk/government/uploads/system/uploads/attachment_data/file/663668/November_2017_IPA_Consultation_-_consultation_document.pdf at para 102, p 15 (consultation closed on 18 January 2018).

B. Scope of Retention Requirements: Relevant Communications Data and Telecommunications Operators

The IPA, in section 261(5), provides that:

'Communications data', in relation to a telecommunications operator, telecommunications service or telecommunication system, means **entity data** or **events data**—

a)   which is (or is to be or is capable of being) held or obtained by, or on behalf of, a telecommunications operator and—

(i)   is about an **entity** to which a **telecommunications service** is provided and relates to the provision of the service,

(ii)   is comprised in, included as part of, attached to or logically associated with a **communication** (whether by the sender or otherwise) for the purposes of a telecommunication system by means of which the communication is being or may be transmitted, or

(iii)   does not fall within sub-paragraph (i) or (ii) but does relate to the use of a telecommunications service or a telecommunication system,

b)   which is available directly from a telecommunication system and falls within sub-paragraph (ii) of paragraph (a), or

c)   which—

(i)   is (or is to be or is capable of being) held or obtained by, or on behalf of, a telecommunications operator,

(ii)   is about the architecture of a telecommunication system, and

(iii)   is not about a specific person,

but **does not include any content of a communication** or anything which, in the absence of subsection (6)(b), would be content of a communication".[93]

Effectively, according to the Home Office, 'entity data' corresponds roughly to what was subscriber data in RIPA and 'events data' to what RIPA described as traffic or location data.[94]

Section 87(11) of the IPA provides that only 'relevant communications data' can be required to be retained. This is defined as

communications data which may be used to identify, or assist in identifying, any of the following

(a)   the sender or recipient of a communication (whether or not a person),

(b)   the time or duration of a communication,

(c)   the type, method or pattern, or fact, of communication,

(d)   the telecommunication system (or any part of it) from, to or through which, or by means of which, a communication is or may be transmitted, or

(e)   the location of any such system, and this expression therefore includes, in particular, **internet connection records**.[95]

Internet connection records are a controversial novelty of the IPA. The explanatory notes define them as a 'record of the internet services that a specific device connects

---

[93] IPA, s 261(5) (emphasis added).
[94] See Home Office *Investigatory Powers Act 2016* (n 91) at p 11.
[95] IPA, s 87(11) (emphasis added).

to – such as a website or instant messaging application – captured by the company providing access to the internet'.[96] According to many press reports, this meant that 'as the Investigatory Powers Bill passes into law, Internet providers will be required to keep a full record of every site that each of its customers have visited'.[97] This looks somewhat like content as opposed to the metadata that the retention regime is designed for and some non-governmental organisations such as Liberty and BigBrotherWatch have thoroughly protested this. On the other hand the Government assert that:

> An ICR is not a person's full internet browsing history. It is a record of the services that they have connected to, which can provide vital investigative leads. It would not reveal every web page that they visit or anything that they do on a web page.[98]

Like many other aspects of the IPA, this is likely to end up in court. The actual utility of ICRs is also contested: a similar scheme ran the Danish Internet Session Logging legislation but was reportedly scrapped for lack of effectiveness, although the UK Government purports that they studied the Danish model to learn lessons from it and increase the effectiveness of Internet connection records.[99]

C. Retention Notices

IPA section 87(1) provides that the Secretary of State is empowered, subject to Judicial Commissioner approval, to give a retention notice to a telecommunications operator to retain relevant communications data. The Secretary of State can only issue such a notice if it is necessary and proportionate to the purposes for which communications data may be obtained, in accordance with IPA section 61(7), as discussed above.

Who can be obliged to retain data? This is significantly wider than it was in RIPA. Most of the Act's powers apply to 'telecommunications operators'. Telecommunications operators are defined as persons who offer or provide a telecommunications service to persons in the UK or control or provide a telecommunication system which is (wholly or partly) in the UK, or controlled from the UK.[100] This broad definition includes not just traditional telcos or network providers, but any provider of a service that facilitates the creation, management or storage of communications transmitted, or that may be transmitted, by means of a telecommunication system. This definition is intentionally broad, as can be seen from the draft Codes of Practice, which claimed that Internet-based services such as web-based email, messaging applications and cloud-based services were covered. Social media companies, such as Facebook or Twitter, will also intentionally be in scope.[101] One of the Government's repeated justifications

---

[96] Explanatory Notes to IPA, para 265.

[97] *The Independent* (24 November 2016).

[98] See factsheet at www.gov.uk/government/uploads/system/uploads/attachment_data/file/530556/Internet_Connection_Records_factsheet.pdf.

[99] See 'Comparison of Internet Connection Records in the Investigatory Powers Bill with Danish Internet Session Logging Legislation at www.gov.uk/government/uploads/system/uploads/attachment_data/file/504189/Comparison_of_ICRs_with_Danish_Session_Logging.pdf.

[100] IPA, s 261(1).

[101] See, eg, Interception Code of Practice at 2.6.: 'The Act makes clear that any service which consists in or includes facilitating the creation, management or storage of communications transmitted, or that may be transmitted, by means of a telecommunication system is included within the meaning of "telecommunications service". Internet based services such as web-based email, messaging applications and cloud-based services are, therefore, covered by this definition.'

for the reshuffle of the IPA was that criminals and terrorists were increasingly using facilities such as WhatsApp or Facebook Messenger to send private messages, often encrypted, rather than traditional CSPs, and thus putting themselves beyond the interception, access and retention powers of RIPA and the DRRs.

Section 87(8) of the IPA lists obligatory elements of retention notices, which are identical with those formerly contained in DRIPA. For instance, the notice must specify the operator to whom it relates; the data which is to be retained; the period for which the data is to be retained; other requirements, or any restrictions, in relation to the retention of the data. The maximum retention period, specified in the retention notice, must not exceed 12 months.[102]

Section 88 of the IPA enumerates the matters which need to be taken into account by the Secretary of State prior to issuing a retention notice to a CSP. These include among others: the likely benefits of such a notice; the likely number of users of the telecommunications service concerned; the technical feasibility of complying with the notice; the likely costs of compliance; and any other impact that the notice may have on the CSP.[103] The Secretary of State is also obliged to take reasonable steps to consult a telecommunications operator before giving it a notice.[104]

D. Safeguards under IPA

Unlike the previous data retention regime under DRIPA and clearly with the attention of averting further challenge under *Digital Rights Ireland* and *Tele2/Watson*, Part 4 of the IPA contains an extensive list of safeguards which are here correlated to the mandatory safeguards enumerated after *Tele2/Watson*.

i. Prior Independent Review

Arguably the most crucial change in the IPA is that a retention notice must not only be approved by the executive but also by a Judicial Commissioner (JC),[105] who must review the Secretary of State's conclusions about the necessity and proportionality of the notice.[106] This 'double lock' approach is an explicit attempt to meet the 'prior independent review' requirements of *Digital Rights Ireland* and *Tele2/Watson* without passing the matter entirely to the capricious hands of ordinary judges, who might cause undue delay where national security was at stake.

What is the role of the JCs? They must 'apply the same principles as would be applied by a court on an application for judicial review' but also 'consider the matters … with a sufficient degree of care' so as to safeguard the rights of privacy of targets.[107] There was some doubt as to exactly what this meant. However recently

---

[102] IPA, s 87(3).
[103] *Ibid*, s 88(1).
[104] *Ibid*, s 88(2).
[105] *Ibid*, s 87(2).
[106] *Ibid*, s 89(1). See further discussion of the novel introduction of the Judicial Commissioners and their value or otherwise as independent reviewers, at Chapter 6, section V.
[107] *Ibid*, s 89(2).

issued guidance on the role and powers of JCs[108] makes it clear that the JCs will adopt the standard a court would if the decision came to them as a fresh case, *not*, as is the norm in administrative judicial review, only deny the request if they feel that no reasonable Secretary of State would have made it (known in English law as *Wednesbury*[109] unreasonableness); this would be clearly too limited a role to meet the requirements of *Tele2/Watson* in policing the discretion of the executive.

However if a JC issues a negative decision, the Secretary of State may ask the Investigatory Powers Commissioner (IPC) to decide whether to approve the decision.[110] In addition, any telecommunications operator who receives a notice may refer the retention notice (in its entirety or with regard to any aspect of it) back to the Secretary of State for a review.[111] Furthermore, although the Secretary of State is required under section 90(6) of IPA to consult both the Technical Advisory Board and a Judicial Commissioner in this kind of case, it is still the Secretary of State's own decision whether to withdraw, vary or confirm the effect of the notice. In these cases, approval of the IPC is also mandatory.[112]

These review provisions may potentially be seen as eating into the independent power of the JCs and reducing their role below the standard required by the CJEU.[113]

ii. Provide for a High Level of Protection of the Retained Data

In more attempts to meet the standards of *Digital Rights Ireland* and *Tele2/Watson*, the IPA contains rules on data integrity and security, including obligations for the destruction of data,[114] as well as an obligation to protect retained data against any unlawful disclosure.[115] Notably, however, it does not require that retained data be stored in the EU. In its November 2017 Consultation, the Home Office refused to give way entirely on this point on the ground that data retention requests might be made to overseas telecommunications operators, causing various problems if data had to be transported to the UK, but conceded that:

> we have nevertheless included additional proposed requirements in the code of practice which will ensure that where data is held outside the EU, it is retained to an adequate level of protection, comparable to that required by EU data protection laws.[116]

---

[108] See IPCO *Advisory Notice 1/2018: Approval of Warrants, Authorisations and Notices by Judicial Commissioner* 8 March 2018, available at www.ipco.org.uk/docs/20180308%20IPCO%20Advisory%20 Notice%2012018%20v1.1.pdf.

[109] See *Associated Provincial Picture Houses Ltd v Wednesbury Corporation* [1948] 1 KB 223 and *ibid* at para 19. 'The purpose of the so-called "double lock" provisions of the Act are to provide an independent, judicial, safeguard as to the legality of warrants, in particular to their necessity and proportionality. In cases engaging fundamental rights, the Judicial Commissioners will not therefore approach their task by asking whether a Secretary of State's decision that a warrant is necessary and proportionate is *Wednesbury* reasonable, as this would not provide the requisite independent safeguard.'

[110] IPA, s 89(4).

[111] *Ibid* s 90(1)(2).

[112] *Ibid*, s 91(1). The IPC needs to take the same matters into account as the JC, when approving the initial retention notice under s 89(2).

[113] See a more detailed discussion of the independence of the IPC and Judicial Commissioners, and the worth of *double-lock* in Chapter 6 at section V. C. iv.

[114] IPA, s 92.

[115] *Ibid*, s 93.

[116] See Home Office *Investigatory Powers Act 2016* (n 91) p 18.

This leaves a number of crucial areas where the safeguards mandated by *Tele2/Watson* are still not apparently met by the IPA. As noted above, the Home Office produced a Consultation document in November 2017, which closed in January 2018, incorporating concrete suggestions for amendments to the IPA by statutory instrument.

iii. Notification after the Fact of the Affected Individuals

A key unresolved issue is the requirement in *Tele2/Watson* for notification of the affected individuals as soon as 'that notification is no longer liable to jeopardise the investigations being undertaken by those authorities'.[117] This matter was discussed by the UK Investigatory Powers Tribunal (IPT)[118] in the context of *Privacy International v Secretary of State for Foreign and Commonwealth Affairs.*[119] In its September 2017 judgment[120] the UK IPT acknowledged the notification requirement established in *Tele2/Watson*, finding it however to 'be very damaging to national security'.[121] The notification requirements would be especially difficult to enforce in relation to bulk data collection and retention requirements.[122] The Home Office's response on this matter in their November 2017 Consultation remained fairly obdurate: 'a general requirement to notify an individual that their data has been accessed would unnecessarily inform criminals, suspected criminals and others of the investigative techniques that public authorities use'. A safeguard for the fear that powers had been misused already existed in the shape of an application to the UK IPT. Simply because an investigation had ceased or an individual was ruled out of a particular investigation did not mean that notification would not be operationally damaging. Interestingly, the response did not explicitly refer to *bulk* powers as presenting any especial challenges.

E. Reimbursement of Costs of Telecommunications Operators

One of the many controversial aspects of the DRR 2014, made under DRIPA, was that it allowed, but did not require, the Home Secretary to reimburse any expenses incurred by public telecommunications operators in complying with retention notices.[123] Telcos and ISPs have with some reason long felt aggrieved about being asked to shoulder even part of the cost of defending national security which is not exactly part of their core

---

[117] *Tele2/Watson* (n 2) [121].
[118] *Privacy International v Secretary of State for Foreign and Commonwealth Affairs* [2016–2017] UKIPTrib IPT_15_110_CH.
[119] A request for a preliminary ruling in this case was sent by the IPT to the CJEU, but the main point referred relates to whether national security is excluded from CJEU competence. Order for reference to the Court of Justice of the European Union issued in case [2017] UKIPTrib IPT_15_110_CH www.ipt-uk.com/docs/IPT%20BULK%20DATA%20ORDER%20FOR%20REFERENCE%20TO%20CJEU.pdf.
[120] Judgment of 8 September 2017 [2017] UKIPTrib IPT_15_110_CH.
[121] *Ibid* [63].
[122] *Ibid* [64]. See discussion of these bulk powers in Chapter 6.
[123] DRR 2014 reg 13 with reference to s 1(1) to (6) DRIPA.

business model.[124] The IPA stipulates that '[t]he Secretary of State *must ensure* that arrangements are in force for securing that telecommunications operators (…) receive an appropriate contribution in respect of such of their relevant costs as the Secretary of State considers appropriate'.[125]

In contrast to the former regime, furthermore, such reimbursement is no longer conditional on the expenses having been notified to the Secretary of State and agreed in advance.[126] Instead, a retention notice given to a telecommunications operator must already specify the level of contribution the Secretary of State has determined in respect of the costs incurred, or likely to be incurred.[127] The Secretary of State may also require providers to comply with any audit that may be reasonably required to monitor the claim for reimbursement.[128]

F. Extra territorial Application

Extra territorial jurisdiction is an extremely sensitive area in the IPA, not only in relation to interception but also access and retention. Similar to DRIPA, the IPA makes provision that most of the retention notice regime in Part 4 'may relate to conduct outside the United Kingdom and persons outside the United Kingdom'.[129] Similarly, the IPA provides for the extra territorial application of Part 3 of IPA relating to authorisations for obtaining communications data.[130]

VI. Conclusions

The UK has traditionally been a strong proponent of telecommunications data retention, being one of the initiators on the European initiatives for the adoption of a European data retention legal instrument and by reintroducing data retention legislation at national level, despite the scrutiny of the CJEU. This chapter aimed at sketching the complicated landscape on the European and UK data retention legislation and raising questions on the compliance of the European and in particular the UK rules on data retention with fundamental rights and the safeguards introduced by the CJEU in a number of court cases, which is expected to become longer and longer.

---

[124] Similar complaints surfaced, with possibly less inherent justice, during the 'graduated response' phases of the copyright wars when service providers were also asked to take part of the financial burden of defending the interests of copyright holders. See Chapter 9.

[125] IPA, s 249(1) (emphasis added).

[126] DRR 2014, reg 13(2)(a).

[127] IPA, s 249(7).

[128] IPA, s 249(4). (The same as it was according to DRR 2014, reg 13(2)(b).)

[129] IPA 2016, s 97(1).

[130] IPA 2016, s 85. For a lengthier discussion of the difficulties with RIPA, s 8(4)'s use of foreign intelligence data, and its current challenge in the Strasbourg court, see Chapter 6.

Following the recent UK IPT's request for a preliminary ruling, the CJEU will have the opportunity to discuss the application in a national security context of the requirements it developed in *Tele2/Watson* and the safeguards established by the ECtHR, and to reflect on the upcoming judgment of the ECtHR on the secret surveillance activities of the UK intelligence agencies. The CJEU is explicitly requested to answer the question

> how and to what extent do those requirements apply, taking into account the essential necessity of the SIAs [Security and Intelligence Agencies] to use bulk acquisition and automated processing techniques to protect national security and the extent to which such capabilities, if otherwise compliant with the ECHR, may be critically impeded by the imposition of such requirements.[131]

In essence, this request for a preliminary ruling requires the CJEU to clearly take a position towards the stance of the ECtHR in surveillance cases. Will the two courts align their positions in the UK bulk surveillance cases or will they each establish their own system of requirements? The cross-references between the case law of the two courts in the last cases relating to secret surveillance allow me to hope that the two courts will join forces and deliver coherent judgments that will establish a robust system of checks and balances in cases of secret surveillance.

It should be borne in mind that Article 52(3) CFR requires that

> In so far as this Charter contains rights which correspond to rights guaranteed by the Convention for the Protection of Human Rights and Fundamental Freedoms, the meaning and scope of those rights shall be the same as those laid down by the said Convention. This provision shall not prevent Union law providing more extensive protection.[132]

This provision facilitates the CJEU to interpret the relevant European legislation in line with the case law of the ECtHR and could be the basis for judicial cross-fertilisation.[133]

In the recent consultation, the UK Government clarified that the consultation leaves out all issues related to national security, as they fall outside the scope of EU law. However, the continuous attempts of the UK Government to avoid introduction of strict safeguards in the regulation of powers of Security and Intelligence Agencies in the context of national security are a clear illustration of the unwillingness of the UK Government to follow the CJEU requirements. However, this situation may radically change depending on the impact of Brexit on the issue, as the CJEU may not be competent for UK cases anymore.

---

[131] Order for reference to the CJEU issued in case [2017] UKIPTrib IPT_15_110_CH, 22.

[132] EU Charter of Fundamental Rights, Art 52(3).

[133] 'These provisions may constitute a sound basis to interpret EU law in accordance with the model of protection underlying the ECHR': Oreste Pollicino and Marco Bassini, 'Bridge is Down, Data Truck Cannot Get Through … A Critical View of the *Schrems* Judgment in the Context of European Constitutionalism' in Giuliana Ziccardi Capaldo (ed), *The Global Community – Yearbook of International Law and Jurisprudence* (Oxford, Oxford University Press, 2016) 260.

8

Regulation of Privacy and Freedom of the Press from 2004–2018: From *Campbell* to Fake News

LACHLAN D URQUHART*

I. Introduction

In this chapter, we assess developments in the English law of breach of confidence since the seminal *Campbell v MGN*[1] case in 2004. We document the growth of the action of 'misuse of private information' and provide doctrinal analysis of the case law that maps the complex, fragmented range of principles and tests established by the UK courts. These are situated against the backdrop of regulation of the UK print press, reflecting how this system is changing through the Leveson Inquiry, European Court of Human Rights (ECtHR) jurisprudence and the Royal Charter on Self-Regulation of the Press. Regulatory challenges emerging from new technologies used for news collection and distribution are also considered, with specific attention to the role of social media for super-injunctions and fake news, and to the use of drones in newsgathering.

The chapter structure is as follows:

First, we outline what the action of misuse of private information (MOPI) is, noting how it relates to 'traditional' notions of breach of confidence.

Second, we analyse the two-stage test from *McKennitt v Ash*[2] for determining if a MOPI action exists. This requires assessing the existence of a 'reasonable expectation to privacy' and how the freedom of the press and the privacy of the individual is balanced. At this point, we also reflect on regulatory challenges of drone use in newsgathering.

---

* Funded by RCUK Grant No EP/G037574/1.
[1] *Campbell v MGN* [2004] UKHL 22 (hereinafter '*Campbell v MGN 2004*').
[2] *McKennitt v Ash* [2008] QB 73 CA (hereinafter '*McKennitt*') [11].

Third, we assess the case law to observe how this test plays out in practice, focusing on approaches for determining the public interest in such stories.

Fourth, we look to the regulatory role of the UK Data Protection Act 1998, particularly the exemption for journalistic activity. This also involves considering the provisions on damage and why these have not been used greatly in practice. The new 2016 EU General Data Protection Regulation[3] is mentioned briefly too.

Fifth, we consider the importance of injunctions as the only effective remedy in this domain and the practical challenges these bring.

Sixth, we reflect on several changes in press regulation, namely:

- The interaction of social media and super injunction cases through case law, including findings of the Neuberger Report on super-injunctions and the Joint Committee Report on Privacy and Injunctions.

- Outcomes of the Leveson Report into the Culture, Practices and Ethics of the Press. We examine progress since the Report's release and on finding a new regulator that meets accreditation requirements of the Royal Charter on Self-Regulation of the Press. We also consider debates from 2017 about enacting the controversial s 40 Crime and Courts Act 2013.

- Future challenges for press regulation posed by fake news.

II. Introducing the Action of Misuse of Private Information

Although the UK lacks an express right of privacy[4] or a right to one's own image,[5] the combination of the Human Rights Act (HRA) 1998 and judicial 'shoe-horning' of Articles 8 and 10 of the European Convention on Human Rights (ECHR) into the law of confidence has led to the emergence of a complex patchwork of privacy protection under English common law.[6] The extent to which ECtHR jurisprudence guides English breach of confidence actions is extensive,[7] and in *McKennitt* it was noted:

> to find the rules of the English law of breach of confidence we now have to look in the jurisprudence of articles 8 and 10 ... they are now not merely of persuasive or parallel effect but ... those articles are now the very content of the domestic tort that the English court now has to enforce[8]

---

[3] Regulation (EU) 2016/679 of the European Parliament and of the Council of 27 April 2016 on the protection of natural persons with regard to the processing of personal data and on the free movement of such data, and repealing Directive 95/46/EC (General Data Protection Regulation or GDPR) [2016] OJ L119/1.

[4] *Wainwright v Home Office* [2003] 3 WLR 1137 (no general tort of invasion of privacy); *Kaye v Robertson* [1991] FSR 62.

[5] *Campbell v MGN 2004* (n 1) *per* Lady Hale at [154].

[6] 'Shoe-horning' terminology from *Douglas v Hello!* [2005] EWCA Civ 595 [53], cited in *McKennitt* (n 2) at [8]; *Coogan and Phillips v News Group* [2012] EWCA Civ 48 [48].

[7] Lord Woolf CJ stated in *A v B Plc* [2003] QB 195 that Arts 8 and 10 are the 'new parameters' for court decisions in breach of confidence actions; this was reasserted by Lord Nicolls in *Campbell v MGN* [2004] 2 All ER 995 at [17].

[8] *McKennitt* [2007] 3 WLR 194 at 11.

Importantly, these values are not restricted to disputes between individuals and public authorities, but instead have horizontal validity for individual complaints against non-governmental bodies, like newspapers.[9]

In England and Wales, a distinct common law action of MOPI has spawned from the traditional breach of confidence. It provides the framework for balancing individual privacy interests and freedom of the press. 'Traditional' breach of confidence is ordinarily used in commercial relationships[10] and is predicated on satisfaction of the following tripartite test:[11]

- Information must have the necessary quality of confidence about it.

- Information must have been imparted in circumstances importing an obligation of confidence.

- There must be an unauthorised use of that information to the detriment of the party communicating it.

However, building on earlier suggestions from *Attorney General v Guardian Newspapers No 2 (Spy Catcher)*[12] and *A v B Plc*,[13] Lord Nicolls in *Campbell v MGN* acknowledged that breach of confidence has changed, and the second requirement, a need for an initial confidential relationship, has now been 'firmly shaken off'.[14] Instead, a duty of confidence can arise when 'someone receives information they know or ought to know is fairly and reasonably to be regarded as confidential'.[15] Importantly, the language of confidence and confidentiality was deemed no longer apt, leading to the growth of the MOPI action. As was held in *Campbell*, 'the more natural description today is that such information is private. The essence of the tort is better encapsulated now as misuse of private information'.[16]

Despite these changes, 'traditional' breach of confidence actions continue to exist, and the two actions protect different interests, namely privacy and secret, 'confidential' information.[17] MOPI is based not on breach of good faith, as confidence actions are, but instead on protecting human autonomy and dignity by controlling 'dissemination of information about one's private life'.[18] This shift to framing the action in terms of human autonomy and dignity should expand legal protection for the kind of information entitled to protection, the extent and form of publication that attracts a remedy, and the circumstances in which publication can be justified.[19]

Back in 2012, Moosavian highlighted the lack of consistency in how courts named the new action.[20] Sometimes it is called 'the action formerly described as breach of

---

[9] *Campbell v MGN 2004* (n 1) *per* Lord Nicolls at [17] and [18].

[10] T Aplin, 'Commercialising Privacy and Privatising the Commercial: The Difficulties Arising from the Protection of Privacy via Breach of Confidence' in N Lee et al, *Intellectual Property, Unfair Competition and Publicity – Convergences and Development* (Cheltenham, Edward Elgar, 2014).

[11] *Coco v AN Clark (Engineers) Ltd* [1969] RPC 41, 47–48.

[12] *Attorney General v Guardian Newspapers No 2 (Spy Catcher)* [1990] 1 AC 109 [281].

[13] *A v B Plc* [2002] EWCA Civ 337; [2003] QB 195 at [11] (ix).

[14] *Campbell v MGN 2004* (n 1) [14]; also, Lord Hoffman at [47]–[48] and Lord Hope at [85].

[15] *Campbell v MGN 2004* (n 1) [14].

[16] *Campbell v MGN 2004* (n 1) [14].

[17] *Douglas v Hello! Ltd* [2007] UKHL 21; [2007] 4 All ER 545 at 255.

[18] *Campbell v MGN 2004* (n 1) *per* Lord Hoffman at [50]–[51].

[19] *Campbell v MGN 2004* (n 1) *per* Lord Hoffman at [52].

[20] R Moosavian, 'Charting the Journey from Confidence to the New Methodology' (2012) 34(5) *European Intellectual Property Review* 324–335 at 326.

confidence',[21] sometimes 'breach of privacy',[22] 'purloining of private information',[23] and sometimes it is not named at all.[24] By 2014, *Vidal Hall and Ors v Google Inc*[25] settled that 'misuse of private information' is a tort.[26] Whilst it had been referred to in this way in prior cases,[27] this unequivocal confirmation settled its place as a distinct action.[28] Concurrent claims for 'old fashioned' breach of confidence and MOPI were seen in post *Campbell* cases such as *Mosley v News Group Newspapers*,[29] *LNS v Persons Unknown*,[30] and *Ferdinand*.[31] In *Mosley*, for example, an old fashioned breach of a confidence arose from the confidence in Mosley's sexual relationship with prostitutes. The MOPI action developed from a reasonable expectation of privacy in the covert video recording of the activity.[32]

III. Procedural Requirements of MOPI

We now turn to the nuts and bolts of a MOPI action. Buxton LJ in *McKennitt*[33] outlined the process:

> the court has to decide two things. First, is the information private in the sense that it is in principle protected by article 8? If 'no' that is the end of the case. If 'yes', the second

---

[21] *Douglas v Hello!* (n 6) [53].

[22] *Prince of Wales v Associated Newspapers Ltd* [2006] EWCA Civ 1776 [28]; see also recently the release of the Prince of Wales 'Black Spider Memos' (*The Guardian*, 13 May 2015), available at www.theguardian.com/uk-news/prince-charles-letters.

[23] Buxton LJ in *McKennitt* (n 2) at [8] and [15].

[24] *ETK v News Group Newspapers* [2011] EWCA Civ 439 (hereinafter referred to as '*ETK*').

[25] *Vidal Hall and Ors v Google Inc* [2014] EWHC 13 (QB) (see [1]). In this case, claimants raised actions against Google, including one for misuse of private information (see [35]), because Google tracked and collated information on their Internet usage from Apple's Safari browser without their consent or knowledge.

[26] See para 3.1(9)(b) of CPR Practice Direction 6B procedural requirements for applicability of the case, ie 'a claim was made in tort where a) damage was sustained within the jurisdiction or b) the damage sustained resulted from an act committed within the jurisdiction'.

[27] *Vidal Hall* (n 25) *per* Tugendhat J at [66]–[68]: 'It would not be correct to say that the specific tort of misuse of private information is unknown in English law … I conclude that the tort of misuse of private information is a tort within the meaning of ground 3.1(9)'. See [67] for list of cases he mentions in justification of this statement, including *Walsh v Shanahan* [2013] EWCA Civ 411; See *Campbell v MGN 2004* (n 1) at [14] – 'the essence of the tort is better encapsulated now as misuse of private information'.

[28] *Tchenguiz & Ors v Imerman* [2010] EWCA Civ 908 showed the two actions are options, depending on satisfactions of requirements in a particular case. Breach of Confidence is not a tort, unlike Misuse of Private Information.

[29] *Mosley v News Group Newspapers* [2008] EWHC 1777 (QB); [2008] EMLR 20 at [3] (hereinafter '*Mosley v NGN 2008*').

[30] *LNS v Persons Unknown* [2010] EWHC 119 (QB) (hereinafter '*Terry*')[48] for breach of confidence discussion and [54] for misuse of private information; *Prince of Wales v Associated Newspapers Ltd* [2007] 2 All ER 139 at [29], where the Court discusses the old law of confidence (contrasted with the new misuse of private information tort).

[31] *Ferdinand v MGN Limited* [2011] EWHC 2454 (QB) (hereinafter '*Ferdinand*') at 1.

[32] *Mosley v NGN 2008* (n 29); the old and new actions can influence each other too. In *McKennitt v Ash* a relationship of confidentiality arose due to a pre-existing friendship, irrespective of contractual confidence obligations. The friendship was not *directly* related to the misuse of private information action, but it informed the reasonable expectation of privacy, because to ignore it would create a 'distorted outcome'. Buxton LJ in *McKennitt* (n 2) at [15]; this was followed by Sir Anthony Clark MR in *Lord Browne of Madingley v Associated Newspapers* [2007] EWCA Civ 295; [2008] QB 103 (hereinafter '*Madingley*') at [26] and [31].

[33] *McKennitt* (n 2) at [11].

question arises: in all the circumstances, must the interest of the owner of the private information yield to the right of freedom of expression conferred on the publisher by article 10? The latter inquiry is commonly referred to as the balancing exercise ...

Our analysis below follows this structure, starting with 'is the information private?' and then engaging with 'the balancing exercise'.

A. Is the information private?

We need to question the nature of what it means for information to be 'private'. Certain classes of information will obviously be private, as can be seen from their nature or form.[34] Details on health,[35] business affairs,[36] diary entries[37] or, as *Douglas v Hello!* showed, even information destined for widespread circulation and commercial gain,[38] can all be private. Importantly, information cannot be private if it is already in the public domain, as we discuss further below. The ECtHR provided an illustrative definition of 'private life' in *Peck v UK*, stating it is:

> gender identification, name, sexual orientation and sexual life ... a right to identity and personal development, and the right to establish and develop relationships with other human beings and the outside world and it may include activities of a professional or business nature.[39]

Campbell later settled that 'the touchstone of private life is whether in respect of the disclosed facts the person in question had a reasonable expectation of privacy'.[40]

A more subjective 'highly offensive'[41] test for what 'a reasonable person of ordinary sensibilities would feel if she was placed in the same position as the claimant and faced with the same publicity'[42] was dismissed as the threshold test, due to its narrower application.[43] Nevertheless, it remains useful when information is not obviously private.[44] We now enquire further into what it means to have a 'reasonable expectation of privacy' (REoP).

The REoP test has been fine tuned in case law since *Campbell*, although it remains highly circumstantial and underpinned by many factors.[45] *Murray v Big Picture* was key in establishing the range of circumstances underpinning a REoP. These included:

> attributes of the claimant, the nature of the activity in which the claimant was engaged, the place at which it was happening, the nature and purpose of the intrusion, the absence of

---

[34] *Douglas v Hello (No 3)* [2006] QB 125 [83].
[35] *McKennitt* (n 2) at [23], where it is said a person's health is in any event a private matter. *Campbell* too showed details about therapy for drug addiction were private.
[36] *Madingley* (n 32) at [34] and [50].
[37] *Prince of Wales v Associated Newspapers* [2008] Ch 57 [36].
[38] *OBG v Allan* [2008] 1 AC 1 [118].
[39] *Peck v UK* [2003] EMLR 15 at 57 (hereinafter '*Peck*').
[40] *Campbell v MGN 2004* (n 1) [21].
[41] Lenah Test from *Australian Broadcasting Corp v Lenah Game Meats Pty Ltd* [2001] HCA 63.
[42] *Campbell v MGN 2004* (n 1) *per* Lord Hope at [99].
[43] *Campbell v MGN 2004* (n 1) *per* Lord Nicolls at [21]–[22].
[44] *Murray v Big Picture* [2008] EWCA Civ 446 (hereinafter '*Murray*') [39]; *Campbell v MGN 2004* (n 1) *per* Lord Hope at [94].
[45] *Madingley* (n 32) [109].

consent and whether it was known or could be inferred, the effect on the claimant and the circumstances in which and the purposes for which the information came into the hands of the publisher.[46]

Some of these are considered below:

i. Attributes of the Claimant: Celebrity

Although celebrities have a symbiotic relationship with the press, there remain limitations on the information that can be published, irrespective of celebrity status. In *Campbell*, Baroness Hale stated that because Naomi Campbell made a living being photographed as a supermodel, she could not complain that readers wanted to see what she looked like while going about her daily life, unless she was engaged in private activity.[47] This notion contradicts the position in *Von Hannover*, where it was held, 'the Court considers that anyone, even if they are known to the general public, must be able to enjoy a "legitimate expectation" of protection of and respect for their private life'.[48] Publishing information about daily activities will engage the Article 8 ECHR right to respect for private and family life,[49] irrespective of whether the activity engaged in is private.[50]

ii. Nature and Place of Activity

a. General Nature

In *Campbell*, it was the nature of private activity that was critical in determining a REoP. As noted, this narrowed position is at odds with *Von Hannover*, especially when the distinction between private and official functions is introduced. Photos exclusively of Princess Caroline of Monaco's private life, not taken in the scope of any official function, triggered Article 8.[51] The legitimacy of press publishing information about an official person's private life is considered in the balancing stage, but the case indicates limitations on publishing information on private activities of well-known figures at all, if they lack any 'official' capacity.[52]

Although lower UK courts are bound by the House of Lords'[53] *Campbell* decision, subsequent case law has narrowed the gap between the two cases. The Court of

---

[46] *Murray* (n 44) [36].
[47] *Campbell v MGN 2004* (n 1) [154], namely attending Narcotics Anonymous and the associated indication of an underlying health issue that created.
[48] *Von Hannover v Germany* [2005] 40 EHRR 1 (hereinafter '*Von Hannover*') [69].
[49] Full Text from the ECHR:

'Article 8 – Right to Respect for private and Family Life:

1) Everyone has the right to respect for his private and family life, his home and his correspondence.
2) There shall be no interference by a public authority with the exercise of this right except such as in accordance with the law and is necessary in a democratic society in the interests of national security, public safety or the economic wellbeing of the country, for the prevention of disorder or crime, for the protection of health or morals, or for the protection of the rights and freedoms of others'.

[50] *Von Hannover* (n 48) [67].
[51] *Von Hannover* (n 48) [53].
[52] *Von Hannover* (n 48) [76].
[53] *Kay v Lambeth LBC* [2006] 2 WLR 570; [2006] UKHL 10, *per* Lord Bingham at [43]–[44].

Appeal in *Murray v Big Picture* held that activities like going to the shops or riding a bus *may* attract a reasonable expectation of privacy in certain circumstances.[54] This case concerned photos taken of JK Rowling's child, David Murray, whilst in public in Edinburgh. The Court held REoP in public for the child should exist when the procurer or photographer of the image would know there would be objections on behalf of the child, in order to stop such 'intrusive media attention'.[55] The Court limited their consideration to the child, David, not acknowledging if Rowling would equally have such an expectation, merely stating it '[a]ll depends upon the circumstances. The position of an adult may be very different from that of a child.'[56] To an extent the former Press Complaints Commission (PCC) Editors' Code of Practice attempted to protect children, when it stated 'Editors must not use the fame, notoriety or position of the parent or guardian as sole justification for publishing details of a child's private life'.[57] This was carried over into the Independent Press Standards Organisation (IPSO) Code of Practice.[58]

Buxton LJ in *McKennitt* further narrowed the gap between the cases, stating the principles from *Von Hannover* that 'fairly banal' daily activities falling into the zone of private life, even in public, are not merely made as a result of a media campaign of intrusion.[59] As *Von Hannover* has been applied more generally by the ECtHR outside press harassment context, notably in *Sciacca v Italy*,[60] he felt English courts must also apply this ECHR case law when determining the reasonable expectation to privacy.[61] This appears to provide a route for greater consistency between English cases.

b. Sexual Nature

As many 'kiss and tell' cases involving footballers lead to legal action,[62] it is worth briefly mentioning the REoP for sexual activity. Whilst the public interest may tip the balance in favouring publication of such information, sexual behaviour is one of the most intimate aspects of life, and as such there must be strong reasons for interfering with it.[63] If the activity is on private property and between consenting adults, whether with prostitutes or not, that will be deemed private.[64] Furthermore, there is no general rule against an expectation of privacy for adulterous relationships.[65] Importantly, despite activities being immoral, unsavoury or depraved in the eyes of the public or the judiciary, judges cannot allow their judgments to be 'coloured' by personal attitudes or prejudices.[66] If publishing sexual content is in the public interest, there are

---

[54] *Murray* (n 44) [56].
[55] *Murray* (n 44) [57].
[56] *Murray* (n 44) [56].
[57] Former PCC Editors' Code of Practice, cl 6.
[58] IPSO Code of Practice, cl 6(v).
[59] *McKennitt* (n 2) [37]–[41].
[60] *Sciacca v Italy* (2006) 43 EHRR 400.
[61] *Ibid* [40]–[41].
[62] See Rio Ferdinand, Ryan Giggs, etc.
[63] *Dudgeon v UK* (1981) 4 EHRR 149 (hereinafter 'Dudgeon').
[64] *Mosley v NGN 2008* (n 29) [99].
[65] *CC v AB* [2006] EWHC 3083 (QB) [30].
[66] *CC v AB* [2007] EMLR 11 [26], cited in *Mosley v NGN 2008* (n 29) [129].

still limitations on sexual information. For example, every salacious detail need not be disclosed, and the court may restrain publication of a photo but there can still be description of the information provided.[67]

c. Place of Activity

When a camera intrudes into a private place, even if nothing embarrassing is happening, this could be an infringement of privacy.[68] *Douglas* highlighted that telephoto lenses can give access to scenes where the subject would not reasonably expect their appearance or actions to be brought to public attention.[69] This is reflected in the former PCC Code of Practice, which stated that 'it is unacceptable to photograph individuals in private places without their consent. Private places are public or private property where there is a reasonable expectation of privacy'.[70] Importantly, when famous people are in public, lack of consent to being photographed is in itself not enough to constitute a wrongful invasion of privacy.[71] Photographs can be 'much more intrusive and informative than words', hence why they get special protection.[72] However, whilst being photographed in a public place should be 'taken to be one of the ordinary incidents of living in a free community', equally 'the fact that we cannot avoid being photographed does not mean that anyone who takes or obtains such photographs can publish them to the world at large'.[73]

In *Peck v UK* it was held that monitoring an individual in a public place with photographic equipment, but not recording, does not interfere with that individual's private life,[74] although it may do if it is recorded or permanently stored.[75] The private life considerations will depend upon who is the 'true subject' of the photograph, not just other people in the background, irrespective of the public setting.[76] In *Peck*, Mr Peck was not participating in any public event, was not a public figure, and no crime was committed or charged, although he attempted to kill himself. The issue was that the footage was circulated far wider than he could possibly have foreseen.[77] Reflected in *Campbell*, Lord Hoffman acknowledged widespread publication of a photo where someone is in a severely embarrassing or humiliating photo, even in public, might infringe privacy.[78]

---

[67] *Douglas v Hello* [2003] EWHC 55 (Ch) [85], citing *D v L* [2004] EMLR 1, *per* Waller LJ at [23]; see also *Mosley v NGN 2008* (n 29) [23] citing *Theakston v MGN Ltd* [2002] EWHC 137(QB) [78] on the impact on personality and humiliating nature of disclosure of photos being the basis for preventing publication.

[68] *Campbell v MGN 2004* (n 1), *per* Lord Hoffman at [75].

[69] *Douglas v Hello* (n 6) *per* Lord Phillips at [84]–[87].

[70] PCC Code of Practice, cl 3(i); IPSO Code of Practice, cl 3(iii).

[71] *Douglas v Hello* (n 6) [73].

[72] *Douglas v Hello* (No 3) (n 34) at [56].

[73] *Campbell v MGN 2004* (n 1) *per* Lord Hoffman at [74].

[74] *Peck* (n 39) [59]; in *Murray* (n 44) it was stated at [67] that 'in the absence of distress caused when the photograph is taken, the mere taking of a photograph in the street may well be entirely unobjectionable'.

[75] *PG and JH v UK* (2001) (App No 44787/98) [58]; *Rotaru v Romania* (App No 28341/95), [2000] ECHR 192 [43]–[44]; *Amann v Switzerland* (2000) 30 EHRR 843 [65]–[67].

[76] *Campbell v MGN 2004* (n 1) at 122.

[77] *Peck* (n 39) [62]–[63]; the Council had legitimate aims, using footage to indicate CCTV benefits for public safety and prevention of crime. The Court held inadequate steps were taken to protect his interests, such as masking his face or identifying him to seek his consent ([80]).

[78] *Campbell v MGN 2004* (n 1) [75].

Von Hannover expanded *Peck* further, acknowledging that private life includes, *inter alia*, *physical and psychological integrity*, including a 'zone of interaction of a person with others, even in a *public context*'.[79] Thus, the photos of Princess Caroline whilst she was in public restaurants or at the beach still carried a legitimate expectation of privacy, because protecting development of human personality exists beyond the private family circle and into a social dimension.[80]

Drone Journalism

As a brief aside, we will consider the emergence of a new technology with scope to impact privacy rights through photography in public spaces: flying drones. The impact of flying unmanned aerial vehicles (UAVs) on newsgathering needs to be assessed. The paparazzi have long used telephoto lenses to obtain images from intimate or hard to reach settings. We already have examples of UAVs being used to collect images of celebrities, participation in protests and sports matches.[81] Goldberg, Corcoran and Picard are optimistic around the growth of 'drone journalism',[82] noting that 'the costs of aerial photography will go down, allowing more media outlets to use it and the simplicity and size of some systems will allow a single journalist to operate them'.[83] Equally, however, they note the risks of drone usage, such as in covert journalism, and the accompanying obligation on news providers to address privacy and safety concerns.[84] They are wary of scope for trespass cases, nuisance actions or blanket bans on use.[85]

In recent years, Goldberg's advocacy of drones in newsgathering has strengthened, coining the term 'dronalism' to describe use of drones in newsgathering. He is concerned that regulatory restrictions on drone use could infringe part of the right to freedom of expression, namely the right to receive ideas and information. Accordingly, he argues that overly general restrictions on the use of drones limit the methods of newsgathering and thus only in limited circumstances should another right (like privacy) trump this right to freedom of expression. Softening the point, he argues that 'at the very least, in the absence of carrying out an explicit exercise balancing the competing interest involved, any restriction would be challengeable as procedurally flawed'.[86]

In contrast, Finn et al focus primarily on privacy and data protection risks of drone journalism. They are concerned about the exemption for responsible journalism in the Data Protection Directive (as enacted in UK legislation by section 32 of the Data Protection Act 1998) and how it might lead to 'irresponsible practices', especially on

---

[79] *Von Hannover* (n 48) [50]–[51] (my emphasis).

[80] *Von Hannover* (n 48) [69].

[81] See Drone Journalism Lab available at www.dronejournalismlab.org; BBC News, 'California Bans Paparazzi from Operating Drones on Private Property' (BBC News, 7 October 2015) available at www.bbc.co.uk/news/world-us-canada-34460441.

[82] D Goldberg, M Corcoran and RG Picard, *Remotely Piloted Aircraft Systems & Journalism Opportunities and Challenges of Drones in News Gathering* (Oxford, Reuters Institute for the Study of Journalism, 2013).

[83] *Ibid*, Conclusions.

[84] *Ibid*, Section 5.

[85] *Ibid*.

[86] D Goldberg, 'Dronalism: Journalism, Remotely Piloted Aircraft, Law and Regulation' (2015) *FIU Law* 10(2) 409.

the part of the paparazzi.[87] Similarly, Calo argued in a US context that 'Drones may help restore our mental model of a privacy violation. They could be just the visceral jolt society needs to drag privacy law into the twenty first century'.[88] Back in the UK, the 2015 UK House of Lords Inquiry into Regulation of RPAS (remotely piloted aircraft systems[89]) highlighted that there is a tension between using drones to 'enhance the reporting of important events' and invading people's privacy, thus they recommend a public consultation by media regulators to formulate guidelines.[90]

From a UK regulatory perspective, drones are analogous to CCTV,[91] and recently the UK surveillance Camera Commissioner has expressed concerns about their increasing use.[92] The UK Information Commissioner's Office (ICO) has released public advice around keeping images safe, or thinking before sharing images on social media.[93] In the context of the media, they would not be covered by the CCTV Code of Practice due to journalistic exemptions in data protection law, mentioned above, but any other individuals or organisations which provide footage to the press would be.[94] Guidance on drones in the CCTV Code of Practice applies to the whole system, from collection of images from the air to storage approaches and how long footage is retained.[95] Those providing images to the press would therefore need to consider these issues.

Given the growing use of drones, often by hobbyists, interesting questions around the crowdsourcing of drone images also raises questions about safety, provenance of information, and legitimacy of use in reporting. For example, if images highlight that the user contravened rules laid down by the Civil Aviation Authority by flying too close to protected installations such as nuclear submarine facilities,[96] can such images legitimately be used by the press?[97]

---

[87] R Finn, D Wright, L Jacques, P De Hert, *Study on Privacy, Data Protection and Ethical Risks in Civil Remotely Piloted Aircraft Systems Operations* (Brussels, European Commission, 2014). See Scenario 'Sensationalist Journalism' at para 8.4.2.

[88] R Calo, 'Drone as Privacy Catalyst' (2011) *Stanford Law Review Online* available at www.stanfordlawreview.org/online/the-drone-as-privacy-catalyst/.

[89] The more precise terminology of RPAS is often preferred to drone or UAV and it originated from the European Commission (see http://ec.europa.eu/enterprise/sectors/aerospace/uas/). Paragraph 15 of the House of Lords European Union Committee Report, *Civilian Use of Drones in the EU* (HL 2014-2015, HL 122 defines them as 'RPAS are controlled by a pilot, normally on the ground, who may directly control or intervene in the management of the flight. The basic components of an RPAS are the aircraft which flies in the air, the pilot station (ground station), and the command and control link (C2) connecting the two. The command and control link is a radio data link between the pilot station and the aircraft, which enables the pilot to give commands to, and download data from, the aircraft along radio waves on a selected frequency'.

[90] House of Lords Report 122, *ibid*. However, ICO Deputy Commissioner David Smith stated, 'If RPAS are being used to investigate matters of serious public concern and to comply with the data protection law would stand in the way of that, there is an exemption' (para 190).

[91] L Urquhart, 'The Aerial Gaze: Regulating Domestic Drones in the UK' (2013) *Computers and Law*, available at www.scl.org/articles/2759-the-aerial-gaze-regulating-domestic-drones-in-the-uk.

[92] See www.gov.uk/government/uploads/system/uploads/attachment_data/file/598774/NSCS-strategy-post-consultation.pdf.

[93] See https://ico.org.uk/for-the-public/drones/.

[94] 'The use of conventional cameras (not CCTV) by the news media or for artistic purposes, such as for film making, are not covered by this code as an exemption within the DPA applies to activities relating to journalistic, artistic and literary purposes. However, this code does apply to information collected by surveillance systems that is then provided to the media', available at https://ico.org.uk/media/1542/cctv-code-of-practice.pdf (p 8).

[95] ICO CCTV Code of Practice, available at https://ico.org.uk/media/1542/cctv-code-of-practice.pdf p 30.

[96] *Ibid*, p 30–31.

[97] 'First Conviction for Illegal Use of an Unmanned Aircraft' (Civil Aviation Authority, 2 April 2014), available at www.suasnews.com/2014/04/first-conviction-for-illegal-use-of-an-unmanned-aircraft/.

iii. Impact on Subject

Whilst the law of privacy does not exist to protect the 'unduly sensitive',[98] courts should respond to what reasonable people of ordinary sensibilities might feel if exposed to the same publicity as high profile claimants. *Campbell* indicates the harm to an individual caused by a publication is a factor for determining whether information is private. In relation to Naomi Campbell's drug therapy, Lord Hope noted:

> the assurance of privacy is an essential part of the exercise. The therapy is at risk of being damaged if the duty of confidence which the participants owe to each other is breached by making public. I would hold that these details are obviously private.[99]

Lady Hale reflected this further, stating potential harm can be exacerbated 'by making her [Naomi Campbell] think that she was being followed or betrayed, and deterring her from going back to the same place again'.[100] In *Ferdinand*, it was held that simply photographing two people who were in a private room but who were not engaging with each other would not cause additional harm in the *Campbell* sense.[101]

iv. Public Domain

In the pre Human Rights Act 1998 *Spycatcher* case, Lord Goff established that once information is *generally* accessible by the public, that information can no longer be confidential.[102] This has been followed in *McKennitt v Ash*[103] and *OBG v Allan*,[104] where confidentiality was held still to subsist despite the existence of an exclusive high-value agreement to publish wedding photos, and also in the 2010 Top Gear 'Stig' case.[105] In *Lord Browne of Madingley v Associated Newspapers*, it was held that whilst limited disclosure of information to people in close proximity does not equate to disclosure into the public domain, it remains a question of degree in each case.[106] Relevant for online dissemination of content, in *Mosley* an interim injunction for a video of Mosley's sex party was refused because its wide online circulation meant the injunction would serve no purpose.[107] Expressing this, Eady J stated, '[t]he Court should guard against slipping into playing the role of King Canute'.[108] This can be contrasted with the 2011 *Ryan Giggs* case,[109] where despite the Court acknowledging widespread disclosure on Twitter, the interim injunction remained to restrict the print media.[110] This reflects the judicial observation in *Goodwin* that '[o]nce a person's name

---

[98] *Campbell v MGN 2004* (n 1) *per* Lord Hoffman at [70].

[99] *Campbell v MGN 2004* (n 1) *per* Lord Hope at [95].

[100] *Campbell v MGN 2004* (n 1) *per* Lady Hale at [155].

[101] *Ferdinand* (n 31) [102].

[102] *A-G v Guardian Newspapers No 2* [1990] 1 AC 109 at 282.

[103] *McKennitt* (n 2) [53].

[104] *OBG* (n 38) [122].

[105] *BBC v Harper Collins Publishers Ltd* [2010] EWHC 2424 (Ch). Newspapers revealed the identity of a masked racing driver on the BBC programme *Top Gear* who had previously been known as 'the Stig'. As the information was then in the public domain, the BBC could not stop it spreading further.

[106] *Madingley* (n 32) at 61.

[107] *Mosley v NGN (No 1)* [2008] EWHC 687 (QB) [34].

[108] *ibid* [34]; K Westcott, 'Is King Canute Misunderstood?' (*BBC Magazine*, 26 May 2011), available at www.bbc.co.uk/news/magazine-13524677.

[109] *CTB v News Group Newspapers Ltd* [2011] EWHC 1334 (QB) (hereinafter '*Ryan Giggs*') at 3.

[110] See discussion below.

appears on a newspaper or other media archive, it may well remain there indefinitely. Names mentioned on social networking sites are less likely to be permanent.'[111] In *Ferdinand v MGN*, the defender argued that Ferdinand's prior openness in the media about previous sexual indiscretions removed his REoP with respect to information showing extra-marital affairs. Lord Nicolls rejected this argument,[112] following the position from *McKennitt* that a REoP is not forfeited when information from certain zones of life are publicly disclosed.[113]

B. The Balancing Exercise

The second part of the test outlined in *McKennitt* is 'having established an individual has a reasonable expectation to privacy, how is this interest balanced against the freedom of the press to publish a story relating to that person'. This requires the 'ultimate balancing test'[114] underpinned by the so-called 'new methodology'[115] summarised by Lord Steyn in *Re S (FC) (a Child) (Appellant)*.[116] It is used to balance interests between the conflicting Article 8 and Article 10 rights of the ECHR. *Dudgeon v United Kingdom* has long established that the more serious the aspects of an individual's life that are being interfered with, the more serious the justifying reasons must be in order for that interference to be deemed legitimate.[117] Accordingly, this assessment is very important, and four considerations underpin it:

> Firstly neither article [8 or 10] has as such precedence over the other. Secondly, where the values under the two articles are in conflict, an intense focus on the comparative importance of the specific rights being claimed on an individual case is necessary. Thirdly, the justifications for interfering with or restricting each right must be taken into account. Finally, the proportionality test must be applied to each'.[118]

The merits of each aspect (lack of precedence, intense focus, justifications for interference and the proportionality test) are examined briefly below.

i. Lack of Precedence

As Moosavian has stated, '[a]rticles 8 and 10 enjoy a reciprocal structural summary; each contains potential allowance for the other'.[119] Similarly, Resolution 1165 of the Parliamentary Assembly of the Council of Europe states that Article 8 and Article 10 are neither absolute nor hierarchical, because they are equally valued in a

---

[111] *Goodwin v NGN* [2011] EWHC 1437 (QB) (hereinafter '*Goodwin*') at 124–125.

[112] *Ferdinand* (n 31) [56].

[113] *McKennitt* (n 2) [53].

[114] See discussion of balancing metaphor in R Moosavian, 'A Just Balance or Just Imbalance? The Role of Metaphor in Misuse of Private Information' (2015) *Journal of Media Law* 7(2).

[115] *Mosley v NGN (No 1)* (n 107) at 28.

[116] *Re S (FC) (a Child) (Appellant)* [2004] UKHL 47.

[117] *Dudgeon* (n 63) [52].

[118] *Re S (FC) (a Child) (Appellant)* (n 116) at 17 (my emphasis).

[119] R Moosavian, 'Charting the Journey from Confidence to the New Methodology' (2012) 34(5) *European Intellectual Property Review* 331.

democracy.[120] Yet, confusingly, section 12(4) of the Human Rights Act 1998 (herein-after 'HRA') requires courts to give 'particular regard to the importance of freedom of expression'. In practice, this legislative provision has not given Article 10 any prec-edence over Article 8. Sedley LJ in *Douglas v Hello!* held that section 12(4) HRA would require equal 'particular regard' to Article 8 because, *inter alia*, section 3(1) HRA requires that the HRA itself is interpreted compatibly with the ECHR. To give Article 10 presumptive priority would not be in line with ECHR jurisprudence.[121] Instead, section 12(4) requires the court to consider the limitations on Article 10(1) imposed by Article 10(2), which brings 'into the frame the conflicting right to respect for privacy' where the limitations of the respective rights are balanced through propor-tionality considerations.[122]

ii. Intense Focus

Eady J clarified in *Mosley* the notion of 'intense focus', highlighting that each case should be considered on its own facts and circumstances in order to determine if there was a 'public interest' in the intrusion.[123] It is no longer valid to allude to generalisa-tions that public figures should expect less privacy, or that they must be upstanding 'role models', as justifications for an intrusion into their private lives.[124]

iii. Justifications for Interfering with the Respective Rights

As mentioned above, Articles 8 and 10 of the ECHR are not absolute: they already contain extensive limitations. Article 10(2) allows necessary limitations on 10(1) to prevent disclosure of information received in confidence. Similarly, Article 8(2) can limit Article 8(1) in respect of protecting rights and freedoms of others (including, for example, the press). Within this structure, ECtHR case law can enlighten court deci-sions on such justifications.

iv. Proportionality Test

Lord Hope noted in *Campbell* that where the press published private material, allegedly in the public interest, deference to editorial and presentation decisions is not justifiable. Instead, the courts must consider first whether publication pursues legitimate aims, and second the issue of proportionality with respect to the benefits and harms that flow from limiting either right.[125] Conducting a proportionality test for each right is essential when they represent a pressing social need, and limiting one could adversely

---

[120] Resolution 1165 (1998), para 11.
[121] *Douglas v Hello! Ltd* [2001] 1 QB 967 1004 at [133]–[137]. The ECHR 'jurisprudence does not – and could not consistently with the Convention itself – give article 10(1) the presumptive priority which is given for example to the First Amendment in the jurisprudence of the United States' courts.'
[122] *Ibid* [137].
[123] *Mosley v NGN 2008* (n 29) [12].
[124] *Mosley v NGN 2008* (n 29) [12].
[125] *Campbell v MGN 2004* (n 1) [113].

impact the other.[126] Even if a public interest for disclosure can be established, if this is not proportionate then the correct balance has not been obtained. Recognising practicalities of press freedom and necessity in reporting, Lord Hoffman stated in *Campbell* that '[t]he practical exigencies of journalism demand that some latitude must be given. Editorial decisions have to be made quickly and with less information than is available to a court'.[127] Nevertheless, in the same decision Lord Hope stated that 'decisions about the publication of material that is private to the individual raise issues that are not simply about presentation and editing'.[128]

This conflict is illustrated in *Campbell*, where the Lords unanimously agreed with the Court of Appeal[129] that there was a public interest in the press correcting a false image projected by the public figure Naomi Campbell.[130] What they disagreed on was the level of detail the press disclosed in so doing. In particular, the covertly-obtained photos and details about Narcotics Anonymous treatment[131] led the majority to deem this an unjustifiable infringement of Article 8.[132]

C. The Public Interest Defence

The 'public interest' is a multifaceted notion, not easily defined, but it remains a concept at the core of the press' ability to establish legitimacy in its publishing decisions. A 2014 UK ICO guide *Data Protection and Journalism: A Guide for the Media* affirms there is no definitive 'public interest test'. Instead, case-by-case assessments are necessary, guided to an extent by facts in industry codes of practice and the impact of publication on privacy interests of the story subject. As it states:

> any consideration of what is in the public interest must involve an element of proportionality – it cannot be in the public interest to disproportionately or unthinkingly interfere with an individual's fundamental privacy and data protection rights. If the method of investigation or the details to be published are particularly intrusive or damaging to an individual, a stronger and more case-specific public interest argument will be required to justify that, over and above the general public interest in freedom of expression.[133]

Equally, Leveson did not want to define public interest, but instead stated that any new standards code should reflect:

> the importance of freedom of speech, the interest of the public (including the public interest in detecting or exposing crime or serious impropriety, protecting public health and safety and preventing the public from being seriously misled) and the rights of individuals.[134]

---

[126] *Campbell v MGN 2004* (n 1) [140].
[127] *Campbell v MGN 2004* (n 1) [67].
[128] *Campbell v MGN 2004* (n 1) [113].
[129] *Campbell v MGN* [2003] QB 633 [43].
[130] *Campbell v MGN 2004* (n 1) [82].
[131] *Campbell v MGN 2004* (n 1) [23].
[132] *Campbell v MGN 2004* (n 1) [36].
[133] ICO, *Data Protection and Journalism: A Guide for the Media* (Wilmslow, ICO, 2014) (hereinafter 'ICO 2014') 34.
[134] Leveson LJ, *An Inquiry into the Culture, Practices and Ethics of the Press Report*, Volume 4 (London, The Stationery Office (TSO), 2012) 1763.

We return to factors from case law in the public interest below, but first we tackle the long-standing aphorism[135] that what is 'interesting to the public' is not necessarily in the 'public interest'.[136] As this division is complex and oft-cited, we use Moosavian's work on distinguishing between each as they have emerged in MOPI actions.[137] Legitimate 'public interest' claims have largely aligned with one of three character-istics in the courts. First there is 'contribution to a democratic debate', which goes beyond just political speech to include 'that which stimulates wider social or moral debate'.[138] Second, there is 'preventing the public from being misled' and revealing truth when public figures present a false image.[139] Third there is 'revealing crime or serious misdeeds' which combines the previous two as '... by their very nature, crime and corruption will invariably involve deceit or surreptitious activity, and thus reveal-ing such activity will disclose the true position to the wider public ... this ground serves general democratic ideals by fostering accountability'.[140]

When defining what is 'interesting to the public', Moosavian looks at the constitu-ent elements of the term. For something to be 'interesting', it is 'entertaining rather than empowering, entirely inconsequential or even pernicious. For this reason, trivia or tittle tattle ... has low value in the balancing process'.[141] We explore this more below in terms of case law doctrine. Second, for defining who is the 'public', the judiciary often characterise the public interested in tabloids as an unrepresentative minority and thus 'it forms a select social group; a group narrower than the broad, civic, ideal total-ity represented in "public interest". In this context, the term "public" shifts in meaning from its use in public interest proper'.[142] Third, the commercial context is important, as 'newspapers' commercial sales rely directly upon their ability to interest the public', and thus this justification is often central to arguments in favour of publishing.[143]

Although Lord Woolf in *A v B*[144] suggested that the public had a legitimate inter-est in trivial facts about the private lives of celebrities, partly because this sells papers and continuation of newspapers is in the public interest, Lord Phillips discredited this interpretation when *Campbell* was heard in the Court of Appeal. He stated:

> We would observe that the fact that an individual has achieved prominence on the public stage does not mean that his private life can be laid bare by the media. We do not see why

---

[135] *British Steel Corp v Granada Television Ltd* [1981] AC 1096, *per* Lord Wilberforce; *Rocknroll v News Group Newspapers Ltd* [2013] EWHC 24 (Ch) [30].

[136] *Prince of Wales* (n 22) [51]; *Mosley v NGN 2008* (n 29) [114]; *Goodwin* (n 111) [2]; *Mosley v UK* [2012] EMLR 1 (48009/08 Judgment 10th May 2011) [114].

[137] R Moosavian, 'Deconstructing the Public Interest in the Article 8 vs Article 10 Balancing Exercise' (2014) 6(2) *Journal of Media Law* 234–68, 243–49; Also see Media Lawyer, 'Case Report: Sir Cliff Richard v BBC, Day 10. BBC had "Public Interest Responsibility" over Coverage of Search' (*Inforrm Blog*, 26 April 2018).

[138] *McClaren v News Group Newspapers Ltd* [2012] EWHC 2466 (QB) [19]: extra marital affairs of role models enabling criticism and 'as a result of public discussion and debate ... public opinion develops' (see also Moosavian, *ibid*, 246).

[139] Moosavian, *ibid*, 247–48.

[140] Moosavian, *ibid*.

[141] Moosavian, *ibid*, 253; as she notes from *Von Hannover v Germany (No 1)* [2004] EMLR 21 [25], this difference should not be overstated as 'the formations of opinions and entertainment are not opposites. Entertainment also plays a role in the formation of opinions. It can sometimes even stimulate or influence the formation of opinions more than purely factual information'.

[142] Moosavian, *ibid*, 254.

[143] Moosavian, *ibid*, 255.

[144] *A v B* (n 13) [48].

it should necessarily be in the public interest that an individual who has been adopted as a role model without seeking this distinction, should be demonstrated to have feet of clay.[145]

As a brief aside on the topic of the role model, in *Ferdinand* it was shown that as a voluntary role model the England football captain assumes a position where the public can have high expectations of him both on and off the pitch.[146] This puts him alongside headmasters, clergyman, politicians, senior civil servants, surgeons and journalists.[147] This is distinct from involuntary role models, like folk singer Loreena McKennitt, whom the public could not legitimately hold to such a higher standard.[148]

Buxton LJ in *McKennitt* further rejected Lord Woolf's position, primarily because 'the rights given to the media by *A v B* cannot be reconciled with *Von Hannover*'.[149] As such, although domestic courts have obligations to apply English precedent,[150] *A v B* did not take account of ECtHR jurisprudence, and Buxton LJ concluded it could not be binding on the *content* of balancing Articles 8 and 10 of the ECHR. Instead, English courts should look to *Von Hannover* and its more privacy protective provisions for public figures.[151]

Von Hannover introduced the test of the contribution published material makes to a 'general debate of public interest'. This is shaped by the distinction between legitimacy in publishing information about an individual's official public functions, but not their private affairs.[152] For public officials like politicians, there can be a legitimate public interest, but for celebrities, such as Princess Caroline, the ECtHR held that 'the publication of the photos and articles, the sole purpose of which was to satisfy the curiosity of a particular readership regarding the applicant's private life, *does not contribute to any debate of general interest*'.[153]

This rather narrow interpretation of the public interest in celebrity affairs challenges the tabloid press, and their business model predicated on exposing details of celebrities' private lives. It is however in line with the ECtHR vision of the press as a 'democratic watchdog'.[154] In *Jameel*, the House of Lords held that 'vapid tittle tattle' about footballers' wives and girlfriends, despite being of intrigue to many members of the public, does not carry any real public interest in its disclosure.[155]

The type of speech is also critical, and in *Campbell* three types of expression were acknowledged – political, artistic and commercial. There, Lord Hope stated that political or democratic values and a pressing social need would influence the restriction on the press, indicating political speech will be most highly protected.[156]

---

[145] *Campbell v MGN* [2002] EWCA Civ 1373 [41].
[146] *Ferdinand* (n 31) 90.
[147] *McKennitt v Ash* [2006] EWCA Civ 1714, [65], where Buxton LJ outlines these categories of role model.
[148] *Ibid.*
[149] *Ibid* [61].
[150] *Kay v Lambeth* (n 53) *per* Lord Bingham at [43]–[45].
[151] *McKennitt v Ash* (n 147) [63]–[64].
[152] *Von Hannover* (n 48) [66] and [76].
[153] *Von Hannover* (n 48) [65] (my emphasis).
[154] *Von Hannover* (n 48) [46].
[155] *Jameel v Wall Street Journal Europe Sprl* [2006] UKHL 44, *per* Baroness Hale at 147.
[156] *Campbell v MGN 2004* (n 1) [117].

This approach has persisted, as the relevant judicial considerations in the recent *ETK* case indicated:

the organisation of the economic, social and political life of the country, so crucial to democracy, is not enhanced by publication. The intellectual, artistic or personal development of members of society is not stunted by ignorance of the sexual frolics of figures known to the public.[157]

Nevertheless, whilst the private lives of politicians can be very much in the public interest, the level of detail provided is key. Lord Hoffman recognised in *Campbell* that whilst there may be a public interest in the disclosure of sexual relations between a politician and someone in public office, the 'addition of salacious details or intimate photographs is disproportionate and unacceptable. The latter, even if accompanying a legitimate disclosure of the sexual relationship would be too intrusive and demeaning.'[158] The 2012 case of *Trimingham v Associated Newspapers Ltd* showed that whilst details of the existence of UK politician Chris Huhne's affair were in the public interest, the extent and intimacy of details about the nature of the activities were less so.[159]

However, determining the extent of detail is also a complex exercise. The public interest in the President of the F1 Association Max Mosley's unconventional sexual practices was disputed in *Mosley v NGN*. Here it was held just because an individual's 'tastes are unconventional or "perverted", does not give the media *carte blanche*'.[160] Eady J held that:

it is not for the state or for the media to expose sexual conduct which does not involve any significant breach of the criminal law. That is so whether the motive for such intrusion is merely prurience or a moral crusade. It is not for journalists to undermine human rights, or for judges to refuse to enforce them, merely on grounds of taste or moral disapproval.[161]

Importantly, the accusations that he was 'parodying Holocaust horrors' during a 'Nazi sex orgy' could have established legitimate public interest, if they had been proven, as they would have questioned his suitability for a job dealing with people of all races and religions, and undermined his comments regarding the tackling of racism in F1.[162]

Further to this point of correcting false representations, *Campbell* showed the press *can* claim public interest in correcting a falsely projected image, within bounds of proportionality.[163] However, in *McKennitt*, Eady J held that a very high degree of misbehaviour must be demonstrated to justify an infringement of privacy or a breach of confidence in the course of correcting inaccurate information.[164] In this regard, press disclosure of Rio Ferdinand's sexual indiscretions contributed to a debate surrounding

---

[157] *ETK* (n 24) [21]; Similar comments were given by Lady Hale in *Campbell* [2004] 2 AC 457 at [148]–[149]: '[the] political and social life of the community, and the intellectual, artistic or personal development of individuals are not obviously assisted by poring over the intimate details of a fashion model's private life'.

[158] *Campbell v MGN 2004* (n 1) [60].

[159] *Trimingham v Associated Newspapers Ltd* [2012] EWHC 1296 (QB).

[160] *Mosley v NGN 2008* (n 29) [128].

[161] *Mosley v NGN 2008* (n 29) [127].

[162] *Mosley v NGN 2008* (n 29) [122].

[163] *Campbell v MGN 2004* (n 1) *per* Lord Hoffman at [58].

[164] *McKennitt v Ash* [2005] EWHC 3003 (QB) [97].

his suitability for the role of England's football captain. This was especially relevant given that his predecessor John Terry also lost his role as England football captain in the wake of an extra marital affair with another player's girlfriend.[165] In *Ferdinand*, evidence of private life contributed to press correction of the plaintiff s' false public relations campaign[166] in which he portrayed himself as a reformed and responsible family man.[167]

Having outlined the English common law principles, we now consider what statutory controls exist in the Data Protection Act 1998 with respect to privacy and freedom of the press. At time of writing, the Data Protection Act 1998 was replaced by the new UK Data Protection Act 2018/EU General Data Protection Regulation 2016. The following section now provides historic analysis around the journalism exemption and remedies as they were in the Data Protection Act (1998).

IV. Data Protection Act 1998

The Data Protection Act 1998 (hereinafter 'DPA') had a relatively narrow impact on the relationship between the press and data subjects, due to the journalism exemption contained in section 32. The following will consider both section 32 and the provisions around damages from harm contained in section 13.

A. Section 32 Public Interest Exemption for Journalism, Literature and Art

Section 32 of the DPA exempted data controllers from, *inter alia*,[168] all but one of the data protection principles[169] when (i) certain conditions were met, and (ii) the data processing was for 'special purposes' of journalism, literature or art. Importantly, the processing had to be 'with a view' to publication to the wider public, and the data controller must have reasonably believe publication 'would be' in the public interest. The Information Commissioner had powers to determine application of the exemption, when it appeared data were not being processed *only* for special purposes or were *not* being processed with a view to publication.[170] This distinction between protection for pre-publication processing and subsequent publication was considered whilst *Campbell* was at the Court of Appeal.[171] The Court held publishing hard copies still

---

[165] *Ferdinand* (n 31) [75] and [80].
[166] Taking the form of various newspaper reports and an autobiography.
[167] *Ferdinand* (n 31) [84].
[168] Scope of this exemption is outlined in s 32(2), including reprieve from s 7 subject access provisions, s 10, s 12 and s 14(1)–(3).
[169] Except the seventh principle: 'Appropriate technical and organisational measures shall be taken against unauthorised or unlawful processing of personal data and against accidental loss or destruction of, or damage to, personal data.'
[170] DPA, s 45(1); the Court stayed proceedings against a data controller prior to publication or within 24 hours of first publication until the ICO decision or the claim is withdrawn. See s 32(5)(a) and (b).
[171] *Campbell v MGN* (n 145) [85].

fell within the remit of processing, and thus the section 32 exemption.[172] Furthermore, it was not limited to the moment of publication,[173] instead applying to subsequent publication too, because it would be 'totally illogical to exempt the data controller from the obligation prior to publication ... but to leave him exposed to a claim for compensation under s13 the moment that the data have been published'.[174]

In *Douglas v Hello!*, Lindsay J discussed section 32 and noted that unauthorised photos taken by *Hello!* soon to be legitimately released by *OK* magazine were not in the public interest. He warned against confusing the public interest, with what interests the public.[175] Section 32(3) provided guidance as to the relevance of compliance with Codes of Practice in assessing the reasonable belief of publishing in the public interest.[176] These used to include, amongst others, the former PCC Code of Practice, in which the definition of public interest is stated as detecting or exposing crime or serious impropriety, protecting public health and safety, or preventing the public being misled by an individual or organisation.[177]

It is interesting to consider the extent of the section 32 exemption in the context of private journalism. Flanagan's analysis considering the PCC noted that the publication by 'any person' in section 32 would include bloggers. When considering the reasonable belief, he said if they complied with the former PCC Code the exemption could apply.[178] The PCC stated:

> It is the responsibility of editors and publishers to apply the Code to editorial material in both printed and online versions of publications. They should take care to ensure it is observed rigorously by all editorial staff and external contributors, including non-journalists.[179]

The PCC's successor, the Independent Press Standards Organisation (IPSO), retains virtually identical text in its Editors' Code of Practice.[180]

New ICO guidance provided, *inter alia*, a bit more clarity on the s 32 DPA exemption, specifically regarding what constitutes journalism. It also reflected on citizen bloggers and non-media journalists.[181] As journalism is not defined in the DPA,

---

[172] *Campbell v MGN* (n 145) [97]–[107], in order to give effect to Art 23 of Directive 95/46/EC of the European Parliament and of the Council of 24 October 1995 on the protection of individuals with regard to the processing of personal data and on the free movement of such data.

[173] *Campbell v MGN* (n 145) [108]–[128], informed by Art 9 and Recital 37 of Directive 95/46/EC.

[174] *Campbell v MGN* (n 145) [120].

[175] *Douglas v Hello!* [2003] EWHC 786 [231].

[176] Defined in Data Protection (Designated Codes of Practice) (No 2) Order 2000/1864, which listed relevant codes such as Ofcom Standards Code; The Independent Television Commission Programme Code and the BBC Producers Guidelines.

[177] The new IPSO Code retains similar provisions, see www.ipso.co.uk/IPSO/cop.html.

[178] A Flanagan, 'The Blogger as Journalist under UK Law" (2005) 10 *Communications Law* 125–29, 126–27.

[179] The concept of 'journalism' in s 32 was explored by Lord Walker in *Sugar v BBC* [2012] UKSC 4 at [70], albeit from the perspective of a Freedom of Information Act 2000 claim. It meant coverage of news, current affairs and sport. The broader 'journalism, art or literature' exemption considered as a whole includes all BBC output, with the remit of informing, educating and entertaining the public. (As defined in Art 5 of the BBC Royal Charter.)

[180] Introduction to the IPSO Code: 'It is the responsibility of editors and publishers to apply the Code to editorial material in both printed and online versions of publications. They should take care to ensure it is observed rigorously by all editorial staff and external contributors, including non-journalists, in printed and online versions of publications.'; on IPSO, see N Duffy, 'IPSO One Year On' (2015) 7(2) *Journal of Media Law* 116–29.

[181] ICO 2014 (n 133).

the ICO took a broad interpretation, following case law.[182] They stated that it clearly covered

> all output on news, current affairs, consumer affairs or sport. Taken together with art and literature, we consider it is likely to cover everything published in a newspaper or magazine, or broadcast on radio or television – in other words, the entire output of the print and broad-cast media, with the exception of paid-for advertising.[183]

Citizen bloggers, and non-traditional media bloggers could also claim protection of the exemption if the information they were posting was information, ideas and opinions for public consumption online, even if they were not professional or paid journalists.[184]

Importantly for bloggers, the opinion of Eady J in *Author of a Blog v Times Newspapers Ltd*[185] showed blogging is essentially a public activity, and there can be no reasonable expectation to privacy in terms of maintaining a pseudonym. This case related to *The Times* disclosing the identity of the police officer who ran the *Night Jack* blog, which discussed social and political aspects of policing and justice. Although no claim for breach of the DPA was raised, Brimsted argued that if *The Times* tried to rely on section 32 it might have failed, because unmasking an anonymous author could not reasonably be said to be in the public interest.[186] As an aside, a claim under Article 10 of the ECHR of entitlement to tell one's own story of shared experiences, at the cost of intrusion on the privacy of the other party, has not found favour with the courts. In *McKennitt*, the defendant had shared experiences, but she had no story of her own to tell. Any interest came from unjustifiably disclosing private details about the famous country singer, Loreena McKennitt.[187] This may create limitations for private journalism.

In terms of changes flowing from the EU GDPR, which comes into force from May 2018, Article 85 declares:

> Member States shall by law reconcile the right to the protection of personal data pursuant to this Regulation with the right to freedom of expression and information, including processing for journalistic purposes and the purposes of academic, artistic or literary expression.

Whilst the UK Government has brought the GDPR into post-Brexit Britain, through the new UK Data Protection Act 2018, the reliance of this provision on Member States legally reconciling rights to personal data and freedom of expression in the context of journalism will introduce uncertainty as to the future UK approach.[188]

---

[182] See n 172; CJEU Case C-73/07 *Satamedia* (2008).
[183] ICO 2014 (n 133) 29; see also 30: 'The exemption can potentially cover almost all information collected or created as part of the day to day output of the press and broadcast media, and comparable online news or current affairs outlets. However, advertising revenue, property management, financial debt, circulation, or public relations would not usually be considered as journalism.'
[184] ICO 2014 (n 133) 30–31; see also *The Law Society and Others v Kordowski* [2011] EWHC 3185 (QB) on the nature of journalism.
[185] *Author of a Blog v Times Newspapers Ltd* [2009] EWHC 1358 (QB).
[186] K Brimsted, 'Author of a Blog v Times Newspapers Ltd: Privacy – Blogging and Anonymity' (2009) 31 *European Intellectual Property Review* 86–87, 87.
[187] *McKennitt v Ash* (n 147) [52]–[54].
[188] Data Protection Act 2018 s 124 requires the ICO to prepare a code on Data Protection and Journalism.

B. Section 13 Compensation for Failure to Comply with Certain Requirements

Section 13(2) of the DPA allowed compensation claims by a data subject when there had been 'damage' or 'distress' caused by contravention of the Act. Damage meant pecuniary loss[189] and not general loss of reputation.[190] Distress could be claimed, provided it was in conjunction with damage, or standalone when contravention of DPA was for the special purposes of journalism, art or literature.[191] A limiting factor with section 13 claims was identifying if the financial loss was directly attributable to a breach of the DPA, or instead from something broader. In *Douglas v Hello!*, for example, the section 13 action was predicated on *Hello!* journalists not seeking the subject's consent. However, Lindsay J held that even if they had done so, *Hello!* would still have published the photos, and as such any distress and damage was not due to disregard of the DPA rules.[192]

Similarly, in *Murray v Express Newspapers and Others*, despite a breach of section 17 of the DPA arising from Big Picture Ltd not being registered as a data controller,

> the failure to register was not causative in itself of the damage. What (if anything) caused the damage was the publication of the photograph but this loss (for the reasons set out earlier) would have resulted even if BPL had been registered as required.[193]

Even if he was entitled to section 13 compensation due to the section 17 contravention, the Court held there had to be proof David Murray suffered distress or damage due to the photo and publication. It held that there was not and consequently the claim was struck out.[194] Despite Express Newspapers profiting from such photographs, a claim for market value restitutionary damages under the DPA was held as inappropriate. It would have provided property rights in the data contrary to the role of the DPA, which 'does not purport to give the data subject any property in his personal data but merely regulates the way in which it can be processed'.[195]

Black has criticised the adequacy of this judicial approach, and civil rights generally under the DPA, whereby controllers could decide if they wanted to comply with the Act, failing which they were made only to pay nominal compensation.[196] Due to a lack of prescriptive guidelines, compensation levels varied greatly. For example, in

---

[189] *Johnson v Medical Defence Union* [2007] EWCA Civ 262 [74].

[190] *Johnson v Medical Defence Union* [2006] EWHC 321 (Ch) [218].

[191] DPA, s 13(2)(a) and (b).

[192] *Douglas v Hello!* (n 175) [239].

[193] *Murray v Express Newspapers Plc & Another* [2007] EWHC 1908 (Ch) [88], and see generally [69]–[92].

[194] *Ibid* [89] and [93]; the Court did not accept that the photo of David Murray was sensitive personal data in terms of s 2(e) of the DPA. Despite showing his skin and hair colour, it provided no information on his physical or mental condition, and to be sensitive there would have to be a clearly identifiable physical condition exposed ([80]); See also *Weller & Ors v Associated Newspapers Ltd* [2014] EWHC 1163 (QB) Although in *Campbell v MGN* [2002] EWHC 499, Morland J held that although the pursuer's race was evident from photos, it was not sensitive personal data, although he also clarified that this was not a general rule ([80]–[90]).

[195] *Murray* (n 193) [92].

[196] G Black, *Data Protection – Stair Memorial Encyclopaedia* (The Law Society of Scotland, 2010) 113, para 224.

Douglas v Hello!,[197] each party received a mere £50, and in *Campbell v MGN*,[198] part of £2500. Comments made *obiter* by the Court of Appeal in *Johnson v Medical Defence Union* indicated £5000 was too much compensation for a 'modest level of distress', but defined neither what would be an appropriate sum nor 'modest'.[199]

Change in this area has however been ushered in by *Vidal Hall & Ors v Google Inc*, where the meaning of 'damage' was clarified.[200] Unlike in *Johnson v Medical Defence Union*, it was held that pecuniary/financial loss need *not* be proven in order to claim damages caused by distress (for example moral damage of stress/anxiety).[201] This is to be welcomed. With damages more generally, a couple of other recent developments are worthy of note. One of Leveson LJ's recommendations, for example, was that 'exemplary' punitive damages 'should be available in actions for breach of privacy, breach of confidence and similar media torts'.[202] Tomlinson highlighted that these do not pose a threat to freedom of speech to journalism carried out genuinely in the public interest, and instead would be reserved for extreme cases like phone hacking that may meet the high threshold of conduct by defendants showing 'deliberate or reckless disregard of an outrageous nature for the claimant's rights' whereby they should be punished to an extent beyond that available from other remedies.[203]

This is interesting, when considered against the backdrop of the responses to phone hacking. On the one hand, police operations were uncovering the large number of phone voicemail hacking victims linked to private investigator Glenn Mulcaire and others and directed by News Group Newspapers (NGN).[204] In response, NGN[205] set up a compensation scheme to deal with claims. This was a streamlined adjudication process overseen by former High Court Judge Sir Charles Grey, and was intended to avoid the need for slower and costlier litigation. The process benefited from costs being paid for by NGN, as well as confidentiality provisions, but claimants lost the right to appeal, and waived their rights to claim through other channels.[206] It was used

---

[197] *Douglas v Hello!* (n 6).

[198] *Campbell v MGN 2004* (n 1).

[199] *Johnson* (n 189) [77].

[200] *Vidal Hall* (n 25) *per* Tugendhat J at [103]: 'my preliminary view of the question is that Mr Tomlinson's submissions are to be preferred, and so that damage in s. 13 does include non-pecuniary damage' where Mr Tomlinson argues '"moral damage" is a recognised EU concept connoting the right to compensation for breach of individual rights where the rights are non-pecuniary or non-property based' ([95]).

[201] 'What they claim damages for is the damage they suffered by reason of the fact that the information collected from their devices was used to generate advertisements which were displayed on their screens' (*Vidal Hall* (n 25) [23]). As these adverts displayed information deduced about them, the issue was other people seeing what was on their screens. 'What each of the Claimants claims in the present case is that they have suffered acute distress and anxiety. None of them claims any financial or special damage' (*Vidal Hall* (n 25) [25]).

[202] Leveson Report (n 134) Vol 4, p 1512, para 5.12.

[203] H Tomlinson, 'Why Extending Exemplary Damages is the Best Approach for Public Interest Journalism' (*Inforrm*, 27 March 2013), available at https://inforrm.wordpress.com/2013/03/27/why-extending-exemplary-damages-is-the-best-approach-for-public-interest-journalism-hugh-tomlinson-qc.

[204] Operation Weeting in particular, but others which were related to phone hacking were Pinetree, Golding and Tuleta. See D Casciani, 'Hacking Probes: What Happens Next?' (*BBC News*, 25 June 2014), available at www.bbc.co.uk/news/uk-28027911.

[205] *The Sun* and the now defunct *News of the World*, owned by News UK (formerly News International).

[206] S Heffer, 'The Future of Phone Hacking Claims: Details of News Group Compensation Scheme' (*Inforrm*, 4 November 2011), available at https://inforrm.wordpress.com/2011/11/04/the-future-of-phone-hacking-claims-details-of-the-news-group-compensation-scheme-steven-heffer/.

by a few hundred applicants, with most claims eventually settled by late 2014 for between £10,000 and £60,000.[207] The scheme was closed in 2013, with remaining claimants being left to pursue their case through traditional judicial channels.[208]

By contrast, in 2015, court proceedings against Mirror Group Media for phone hacking[209] resulted in uniquely large damages of £1.2m across eight claimants.[210] In *Gulati and Others v MGN*, damages of between £72,500 and £260,250 were awarded to each individual, 'compensating'[211] them not just for distress or injury to feelings, but also for loss of privacy/autonomy and damage/aff ront to dignity and standing.[212] The sustained nature of the privacy invasions (near daily), coupled with regular resulting news stories distinguished these cases from previous cases where low damages were awarded, in addition to acknowledgments that in any event the awards of damages in those earlier cases were too low.[213] As Tomlinson and Mansoori have stated, the damages in *Gulati* were more comparable to those awarded in defamation actions, and in future we may see similarly higher damages data protection breaches and harassment cases.[214]

V. Remedies

Having looked at the remedies that existed under the DPA, we now look more broadly to injunctions and super injunctions. We consider general aspects of injunctions as the only real remedy to protect privacy, and the factors that courts consider when granting them such as pre-notification requirements. We look in detail at deliberations made in specific cases, namely *LNS v Persons Unknown*, *CTB v News Group Newspapers* and *Goodwin v News Group Ltd* to unpack how these remedies work in practice, and their limitations. An emerging consideration in the *CTB* case was the role of social media in defying injunctions. As such we look at the recommendations of the subsequent Neuberger report that was, in part, prompted by the *LNS* case.

---

[207] S Heffer, 'Phone Hacking, Corruption and Remedies' (*Inforrm*, 7 November 2014), available at https://inforrm.wordpress.com/2014/11/07/phone-hacking-corruption-and-remedies-steven-heffer.

[208] L O'Carroll, 'News International to Close Phone Hacking Compensation Scheme' *The Guardian* (4 February 2013), available at www.theguardian.com/media/2013/feb/04/news-international-phone-hacking-compensation.

[209] *The Daily and Sunday Mirror*, and *The People*.

[210] S Heffer, 'Mirror Phone Hacking Judgment: A Turning Point in the Phone Hacking Litigation' (*Inforrm*, 22 May 2015), available at https://inforrm.wordpress.com/2015/05/22/mirror-phone-hacking-judgment-a-turning-point-in-phone-hacking-litigation-steven-heffer/.

[211] Not vindicatory but truly compensatory. See *Gulati and Others v MGN* [2015] EWHC 1482 (Ch) [132].

[212] *Ibid* . See [13] for details of claims, and [108] for details of what they are being compensated for.

[213] *Ibid* [184].

[214] H Tomlinson and S Mansoori, 'Case Law: *Gulati v MGN Ltd*, A Landmark Decision on the Quantum of Privacy Damages' (*Inforrm*, 22 May 2015), available at https://inforrm.wordpress.com/2015/05/22/case-lawgulati-v-mgn-ltd-a-landmark-decision-on-the-quantum-of-privacy-damages-hugh-tomlinson-qc-and-saramansoori; see also N Moreham, 'Liability for Listening: Why Phone Hacking is an Actionable Breach of Privacy' (2015) 7 (2) *Journal of Media Law* 155–69.

A. Injunction as the *Only* Remedy

Article 13 of the ECHR dictates there must be an effective remedy at national level for Convention rights. Phillipson has argued that injunctions are the *only* effective remedy for privacy actions, necessary especially in the UK where the tabloid press 'openly declares its hostility to the European Convention and judicial protection of privacy and exhibits a very clear pattern of publishing grossly invasive stories'.[215] This point has found support in UK case law,[216] for example in *Douglas v Hello!*, where it was held that granting an interlocutory injunction was the only way to satisfactorily protect the Douglas's rights.[217] In *Mosley v NGN*, Eady J stated that 'whereas reputation can be vindicated by an award of damages … once privacy has been infringed the damage is done and the embarrassment is only augmented by pursuing a court action'.[218] When *Mosley* was appealed to the ECtHR, the Court acknowledged his high non-pecuniary damages of £60,000, but said that 'no sum of money awarded after disclosure of the impugned material could afford a remedy in respect of the specific complaint advanced by the applicant'.[219]

With prior restraint measures, the ECtHR has recognised the inherent dangers requiring most careful scrutiny by courts, because 'news is a perishable commodity and to delay its publication, even for a short period, may well deprive it of all value and interest'.[220] In English law, the HRA itself seeks to establish domestic remedies and, critically for prior restraint of the press, section 12(3) requires any relief that stifles freedom of expression, for example interim injunctions, must show it 'is more probable than not' that the petitioner will succeed in obtaining an injunction at trial.[221] With a MOPI action, for example, the two stage test from *Campbell* will be considered, establishing the reasonable expectation of privacy and considering the proportionality in balancing ECHR Article 8 against Article 10. The Court then should decide what action provides an effective remedy under Article 13. Importantly, injunctive relief may not always be the only option, with damages also being a possibility.[222] Tugendhat and Christie assert a differentiation in privacy cases between intimate use of information, and information that is objectionable because it represents unwanted attention, but is otherwise harmless. For the latter, 'it is arguable that damages are an adequate remedy, because they do not involve irreversible loss of privacy'.[223]

---

[215] G Phillipson, 'Max Mosley goes to Strasbourg: Article 8, Claimant Notification and Interim Injunctions' (2009) 1 *Journal of Media Law* 73–96, at 74–75 and at 96.

[216] *Greene v Associated Newspapers* [2005] QB 972 at 78.

[217] *Douglas v Hello! (No 3)* (n 34) at 257–59.

[218] *Mosley v NGN 2008* (n 29) [230].

[219] *Mosley v UK* (2011) 53 EHRR 30 (hereinafter '*Mosley v UK*') [72].

[220] *Observer and Guardian v UK* [1991] ECHR 49 [60]; see also Resolution 1165 Parliamentary Assembly of Council of Europe (26 June 1998), para 14.

[221] Eady J in *Mosley v NGN (No 1)* (n 107) at 27; see also *Cream Holdings Ltd v Banerjee* [2004] UKHL 33 [22], discussing sufficiently favourable prospects of success where the 'general approach should be that courts will be exceedingly slow to make interim restraint orders where the applicant has not satisfied the court he will probably ("more likely than not") succeed at the trial'.

[222] As opposed to only in commercial confidence cases.

[223] J Price, I Christie and D Hirst, 'Remedies' in M Warby, N Moreham and I Christie (eds), *Tugendhat and Christie: The Law of Privacy and the Media*, 2nd edn (Oxford, Oxford University Press, 2011), para 13.62.

i. Pre-notification Requirement

Despite these recognitions, legally requiring the press to provide prior notice to the subject so they can seek an injunction, has not found favour at Strasbourg. In *Mosley v UK*, the ECtHR held the UK has no obligation under Article 8 to demand the press provide advance notification before publishing a story which interferes with the subject's right to private life.[224] This was primarily justified to prevent a chilling effect on real journalism, particularly political and investigative reporting. Threatening the press with criminal sanctions and punitive fines, although potentially effective, could be deemed incompatible with Article 10 on the basis it would be 'a form of censorship prior to publication'.[225] Any pre-notification requirement would also require a public interest exception, but there were significant risks that this could be too narrowly defined.[226] Furthermore, pre-notification does not exist in any other jurisdiction, and the ECtHR acknowledged that the UK system already has many regulatory measures in place to protect privacy[227] and is sufficiently compliant with Council of Europe resolutions on media and privacy.[228] Nevertheless, although there is no statutory duty to pre-notify subjects of publication, the Joint Select Committee on Privacy and Injunctions has stated that in the UK, the relevant code of practice should include such a duty, and any negligence to carry it out must have compelling justification.[229]

ii. Considerations in Granting Injunctions

Deliberations in granting interim injunctions vary greatly, and can be seen most clearly in case law.[230] A good example is *LNS v Persons Unknown*[231] where former England Captain John Terry, a self-styled family man with many lucrative sponsorship deals, sought a super injunction to stop the disclosure of his affair with the girlfriend of a teammate. To clarify, super injunctions differ from conventional injunctions in that they often apply to third parties in the media, and the proceedings are normally anonymised and heard in private.[232] Their key feature is that they prohibit any publicising of the existence of the order and proceedings.[233] Ultimately Terry's application

---

[224] *Mosley v UK* (n 219) [132].

[225] *Mosley v UK* (n 219) [129].

[226] *Mosley v UK* (n 219) [126].

[227] PCC Editors' Code; furthermore, the flexible approach of UK courts to balancing Arts 8 and 10, derived largely from *Campbell v MGN*, was considered in *MGN v UK* [2011] ECHR 66. There the ECtHR considered the principles that MGN publishing photos of Naomi Campbell leaving Narcotics Anonymous unjustified did not violate Art 10 (see paras 150–56).

[228] *Mosley v UK* (n 219) [124]; Resolution 1165 (1998) on the right to privacy focusing on public figures, Resolution 1636 (2008) indicators for media in a democracy; Resolution 428(1970) declaration on mass communication media and human rights.

[229] House of Lords and House of Commons Joint Committee on Privacy and Injunctions, *Privacy and Injunctions HL Paper 273 HC 1443* (London, TSO, 2012) (hereinafter '*Privacy and Injunctions* Report') para 127.

[230] See generally Price et al (n 223).

[231] *Terry* (n 30) [32].

[232] Master of the Rolls, *Report of the Committee on Super Injunctions: Super Injunctions, Anonymised Injunctions and Open Justice* (Master of the Rolls, London 2012) (hereinafter 'Super Injunctions Report') paras 2.9 to 2.16.

[233] *Ntuli v Donald* [2010] EWCA Civ 1276 (hereinafter '*Ntuli*') [43].

was refused for a number of reasons.[234] Most importantly, the Court doubted if this was even a privacy claim, feeling instead that Terry was more concerned with loss of his sponsorship through adverse publicity.[235] As such, Tugendhat J noted it was unnecessary and disproportionate to gag the press when the impact on his private life was minimal.[236] Neglecting to inform parties with an interest in the application, and the likelihood of legitimate public interest in his actions, as discussed above, were also influential.

In *CTB v News Group Newspapers*,[237] the 'Ryan Giggs' case, the conflict between court orders and online social media became apparent. Following widespread speculation on Twitter that Ryan Giggs had obtained a super injunction to cover up an affair with model Imogen Thomas, NGN requested the anonymised element of his injunction was removed. NGN felt it unjust that the order against it reporting the facts stood, while simultaneously the same information was circulating on Twitter in direct contempt of the order. However, Eady J opined

> should the court buckle every time one of its orders meets widespread disobedience or defiance? In a democratic society, if a law is deemed to be unenforceable or unpopular, it is for the legislature to make such changes as it decides are appropriate.

He differentiated this case from *Mosley*, where he refused to play the role of King Canute, because Imogen Thomas could have provided much more information to the press beyond the identity of the claimant, and therefore the order did, in his view, serve a purpose.[238] He also rejected the claim that the information was in the public domain, thus rendering the injunction pointless, noting 'the modern law of privacy is not concerned solely with information or "secrets": it is also concerned importantly with intrusion'.[239] As such, by maintaining the order, it still serves a purpose of preventing him and his family being subjected to a 'cruel and destructive media frenzy'.[240]

This case developed further. Later the same day, John Hemming MP used his Parliamentary privilege to name Ryan Giggs, despite the injunction still being in force.[241] Following this, NGN once again applied to remove the enforced anonymisation of Giggs, but Eady J held again that the injunction continued to stand, stating:

> it is obvious that if the purpose of this injunction were to preserve a secret, it would have failed in its purpose. But in so far as its purpose is to prevent intrusion or harassment, it has not failed ... The order has not protected the claimant and his family from taunting on the Internet. It is still effective to protect them from taunting and other intrusion and harassment in the print media.[242]

---

[234] It was granted for a week whilst a judgment was reached.
[235] *Terry* (n 30) [95].
[236] *Terry* (n 30) [149] (viii).
[237] *CTB v News Group News* [2011] EWHC 1326 (QB) [15].
[238] *Ibid* [19].
[239] *Ibid* [23].
[240] *Ibid* [26].
[241] Bill of Rights 1688 (c 2) s 1; Art IX confirmed by the Crown and Parliament Recognition Act 1689; for an in-depth discussion of parliamentary privilege and injunctions, see P Johnson, 'What Can the Press Really Say? Contempt of Court and the Reporting of Parliamentary Proceedings" (2012) *Public Law* 491.
[242] *Ryan Giggs* (n 109) [3].

Lastly, we look at *Goodwin v News Group Ltd*. There, Sir Fred Goodwin had remained an anonymous party on an injunction, until Lord Stoneham named him in Parliament.[243] Whilst he did not object to the injunction being amended to name him,[244] he did not want his adulterous colleague being named. In a subsequent judgment, it was held that publishing her name would be disproportionate and an unnecessary intrusion into her privacy.[245] However, publishing her job description was allowed, and although her name may circulate online, the point of injunctions is not merely to maintain confidentiality,[246] but also protect against intrusion. Many people would not actively seek her name online, but would know it by reading it in the daily papers. The Court highlighted that 'the degree of intrusion into a person's private life which is caused by Internet publications is different from the degree of intrusion caused by print and broadcast media'.[247]

B. The Neuberger Report

In his *Super Injunctions, Anonymised Injunctions and Open Justice Report*, Master of the Rolls Lord Neuberger made several observations about super injunctions.[248] This was in part a response to apparent 'gagging' of the press by the injunctions in *Trafigura*[249] and *Terry*.[250] However, contrary to press depictions at the time, it was shown that super injunctions were rarely applied for, and rarely granted. At the time of the Report, the only time one had been granted for protecting private information was to prevent tipping off in a blackmail case.[251] Furthermore, they were normally granted only for a short period, and extended only in very narrow circumstances.[252] The rules for granting injunctions have been clarified in the *Practice Guidance: Interim Non-Disclosure Orders* derived from the Neuberger Report,[253] which came into effect in August 2011.

---

[243] Regarding this parliamentary privilege, the Select Committee Report on Privacy and Injunctions (n 229) noted the presumption should be court orders are respected in Parliament, only being disregarded when in demonstrable public interest (para 219).

[244] *Goodwin* (n 111) [22]. Tugendhat J noted 'Lord Stoneham was frustrating the purpose of the court order and thus impeding the administration of justice, but he was doing so under the protection of Parliamentary privilege. If he had identified Sir Fred Goodwin in words spoken outside Parliament he would have been interfering with the administration of justice, or committing a contempt of court, as it is called'.

[245] *Goodwin* (n 111) [120].

[246] *Goodwin* (n 111) [124].

[247] *Goodwin* (n 111) [125].

[248] For a summary of recent super injunction case law, see Super Injunctions Report (n 232) paras 2.27–2.30.

[249] *RJW & SJW v The Guardian Newspaper & Person or Persons Unknown* (Claim no HQ09). *The Guardian* was prevented, by super injunction, from reporting on a Parliamentary question about oil trader Trafigura dumping toxic waste in the Ivory Coast. See 'How UK Oil Company Tarfigua Tried to Cover up African Pollution Disaster' *The Guardian* (16 September 2009), available at www.guardian.co.uk/world/2009/sep/16/trafigura-oil-ivory-coast.

[250] Guidance Note for Interim Non-Disclosure Orders 2011.

[251] *DFT v TFD* [2010] EWHC 2335 (QB).

[252] *Ntuli* (n 233) [54].

[253] Ten key observations on anonymity and publishing restraint orders were made by Lord Neuberger in *JIH v News Group Newspapers* [2011] EWCA Civ 42 [21].

The Guidance reaffirms the importance of the open justice principle by clarifying that judgments and orders should be public,[254] with applications for interim non-disclosure orders being no different.[255] Any derogations must be in wholly exceptional circumstances, and strictly necessary.[256] There is 'no general exception to open justice where privacy or confidentiality is an issue' and when it is strictly necessary for justice, anonymity will only be granted to the extent necessary.[257] Section 12(2) of the HRA requires advance notice to the persons whom the order impacts, parties[258] and non-parties,[259] and applicants must show the court that they have taken all reasonable and practical steps to do so.[260] Justification for failure to notify has to be on clear and cogent evidence with compelling reasons, for example if notification defeats the order's purpose, or in blackmail cases.[261] If an interim non-disclosure order has been obtained, applicants have a duty to inform respondents and non-parties of developments, including when it ceases to have effect.[262] Furthermore, anonymised injunctions and super injunctions must contain return dates, an omission that contributed to the refusal of the application in *Terry*.[263] Neuberger requests that anyone aware of a super injunction without a return date raise this with the applicant's solicitors.[264]

Regarding the future of super and anonymised injunctions, Lord Neuberger stated that 'a super injunction should never in practice become permanent, and it is now practically inconceivable that this should happen again'.[265] Interestingly, since the flurry of injunctions and super injunctions publicised in 2010–11, numbers started to fall. Indeed, some proclaimed the death of super injunctions,[266] and between January 2013[267] and December 2014 no privacy injunctions were granted, with one against the *Sun on Sunday* being the first to break that pattern.[268] Nevertheless, Neuberger

---

[254] ECHR, Art 6(1); Civil Procedure Rules 39.2; *Scott v Scott* [1913] AC 417 [463]: open justice is 'on the whole, the best security for the pure, impartial and efficient administration of justice, the best means for winning the public confidence and respect'.

[255] *Ntuli* (n 233) [50].

[256] Master of the Rolls (2011) *Practice Guidance: Interim Non-Disclosure Orders* (hereinafter 'Practice Guidance') para 10.

[257] *Ibid*, para 12.

[258] Direct respondents to proceedings.

[259] Those with an existing interest in the information to be protected (*X & Y v Persons Unknown* [2007] EMLR 290 [10]–[12]).

[260] Practice Guidance (n 256) para 20.

[261] See *RST v UVW* [2009] EWHC 2448 (QB) [7] and [13] (Defeat the orders purpose), and *ASG v GSA* [2009] EWCA Civ 1574 [3] (Blackmail).

[262] Practice Guidance (n 256) para 36.

[263] *Terry v Persons Unknown* [2011] 1 FCR 659 [141] (the lack of return date would have effectively made the order permanent).

[264] Super Injunctions Report (n 232) para 2.36, in accordance with guidance on doing so in *Goldsmith v BCD* [2011] EWHC 674 (QB) [60]–[61].

[265] Super Injunctions Report (n 232) para 2.37.

[266] 'Privacy Law: The Super-Injunction is Dead' (*Inforrm*, 27 April 2011), available at https://inforrm.word-press.com/2011/04/27/privacy-law-the-super-injunction-is-dead, discussing cases showing the high threshold for 'super injunctions' and where they were not granted, for example *DFT v TFD* (n 251) and *Ntuli* (n 231).

[267] *Rocknroll v News Group Newspapers* [2014] EWHC 24 (Ch) (injunction granted on 17 January 2013); see 'Privacy Injunction Granted Against "Sun on Sunday", First against the Media for Nearly 2 Years' (*Inforrm*, 7 December 2014), available at https://inforrm.wordpress.com/2014/12/07/news-privacy-injunction-granted-against-sun-on-sunday-first-against-the-media-for-nearly-two-years.

[268] *AMM v News Group Newspapers* [2014] EWHC 4063 (QB).

does acknowledge any derogation from open justice must be strictly necessary to ensure administration of justice. A final injunction, for example, could be made to secure permanent secrecy or anonymity regarding private information after trial and judgment, if necessary to protect substantive rights.[269] The Guidance differentiates between traditional media organisations and online organisations, tweeters and bloggers. For the former, there will rarely be justifiable grounds for not providing advanced notice on urgency or secrecy grounds, although for the latter it merely notes there may be different circumstances.[270]

The negative impact of online social networks, particularly Twitter, for maintaining injunctive relief has been significant. Both *Goodwin* and the Giggs case highlighted the courts' willingness to restrict print media, despite ease of access to private information online, with the intent of limiting further distress to subjects. However, Smart asks, when protected private information spreads 'virally' on Twitter, '[i]s there still something to be achieved by these super injunctions to stop kiss and tell stories being revealed in the press by the rich and famous?'.[271] A few years on, the recent *PJS v NGN* Supreme Court case[272] brought the question of online versus print distribution back into consideration. Despite the fame of the claimants there was limited public interest in the alleged threesome, which was reported online and in the United States, Scotland and Canada. Furthermore, it was held that the loss of the injunction would lead to additional harm to their family.[273] Here, the medium of publication matters. Despite online sharing occurring in certain jurisdictions, there is still value in preventing print releases to stop unnecessary details being documented in the press.[274] They do consider the claimants may have a right to be forgotten claim, and that despite online sharing, the injunction should enable online content be geo-blocked from view in England and Wales.[275]

Of use in this context is the 2012 *Privacy and Injunctions* Report of the Joint Committee on Privacy and Injunctions.[276] The Committee recommend interim injunctions granted in one UK jurisdiction should apply across all, as with final injunctions.[277] Currently, section 18(5)(d) of the Civil Jurisdiction and Judgments Act 1982 states that an interim measure obtained in one UK legal system is not enforceable in other UK jurisdictions. This was spectacularly highlighted when the front page of the *Sunday Herald* on 22 May 2011 showed Ryan Giggs to be the claimant of an anonymised injunction, whilst English and Welsh Newspapers were still subject to the injunction.

Recognising jurisdictional issues and practical costs in protecting material distributed across social networking sites and hosted overseas,[278] the Committee recommend

[269] *Ibid* [2.37].

[270] *Ibid* [22].

[271] U Smart, 'Twitter Undermines Superinjunctions' (2012) 16 *Communications Law* 135–39, 137. She derives this question from a quote by C Brooker, 'Winning a Superinjunction no Longer Guarantees Super-Anonymity. In Fact, it Delivers the Opposite' *The Guardian* (16 May 2011).

[272] *PJS v News Group Newspapers Ltd* [2016] UKSC 26.

[273] *Ibid* [21]–[24]

[274] *Ibid* [35].

[275] *Ibid* [63].

[276] Privacy and Injunctions Report (n 229).

[277] Privacy and Injunctions Report (n 229) para 74.

[278] Privacy and Injunctions Report (n 229) para 95, discussing Ryan Giggs' disclosure on Twitter and that 'Max Mosley spent £500,000 on actions in 23 different countries to try to remove offending material from

that the Attorney General should be more willing to bring actions for contempt of court where injunctions are breached online. Although the Attorney General would in any event intervene if the breach endangered an individual's life or welfare, or if there was a 'systematic conspiracy to undermine the ability of civil courts to carry out their work', the Committee held that that approach was too narrow.[279] Broader use would allegedly provide a useful deterrent.[280]

The Committee advocates greater use of notice and take down procedures against social media providers too.[281] Twitter's censorship policy, which blocks content on receipt of a court order in one country but leaves it visible in others, is highlighted and acknowledged as recommended practice.[282] Perhaps more concerning, the Committee foresees a greater role for intermediaries, such as search engines, in blocking access to content. Google is reluctant to do this, as it sees it potentially censoring political commentary, and legally it should not have to pro-actively monitor content in order to comply with the law.[283] Nevertheless, the Committee stated that search engines should develop technology for filtering offending content, mandated by legislation if necessary.[284] Clearly, more aggressive tactics are being sought to ensure online campaigns cannot frustrate court orders, such as in the Giggs case.

VI. The Future

In concluding we look to the future, and the recurring question of the efficacy of press regulation.[285] We conclude this chapter by considering the Leveson Report into the Culture, Practices and Ethics of the Press and the Royal Charter on Self-Regulation of the Press. We look at challenges in establishing a new post PCC regulator, and the emerging challenges of regulating fake news.

---

the Internet. Nonetheless the offending material can still be found on the Web'; see discussion around social media in J Rowbottom, 'A Landmark at a Turning Point: *Campbell* and the Use of Privacy Law to Constrain Media Power' (2016) 7(2) *Journal of Media Law* 170–95.

[279] Privacy and Injunctions Report (n 229) para 103.

[280] Privacy and Injunctions Report (n 229) para 104.

[281] They should also be served the injunction notice; Privacy and Injunctions Report (n 229) para 109.

[282] D Meyer, 'Twitter to Censor Posts by Country' (*ZDNet*, 27 January 2012), available at www.zdnet.com/article/twitter-to-censor-posts-by-country.

[283] CJEU Case C-70/10 *Scarlet v SABAM* (2011) (no requirement on intermediaries like ISPs and search engines to filter illegal content to comply with Directive 2000/31/EC of the European Parliament and of the Council of 8 June 2000 on certain legal aspects of information society services, in particular electronic commerce, in the Internal Market ('Directive on electronic commerce' or 'e-Commerce Directive') [2000] OJ L178/1). Note that despite this reluctance Google do operate a takedown by notice service for defamation in the UK and do not require a court order: see https://inforrm.org/2018/05/12/defamation-take-down-requests-to-google-max-campbell/amp/?__twitter_impression=true.

[284] Privacy and Injunctions Report (n 229) paras 112–115.

[285] Interested to consider the impact on MOPI if the HRA is repealed, as the current UK Government has discussed doing. See H Tomlinson, 'Will the Tort of Misuse of Private Information Disappear of Human Rights Act is Repealed?' (*Inforrm*, 11 May 2015), available at https://inforrm.wordpress.com/2015/05/11/will-the-tort-of-misuse-of-private-information-disappear-if-the-human-rights-act-is-repealed-hugh-tomlinson-qc.

A. Leveson, the Royal Charter and Press Reform

The revelations in summer 2011 that the tabloid press were hacking phone voicemails of celebrities, crime victims and their families[286] led to widespread public questioning (again)[287] of the efficacy of press regulation in the UK.[288] The Government quickly established a formal inquiry into press ethics and practices, which ran from 2011–12 and was headed by Lord Justice Leveson.[289] Following extensive hearings and evidence from both press and observers of the industry, the inquiry's report was released with a number of recommendations on how to address the regulatory shortcomings.

The key recommendation was the creation of a new independent self-regulatory body, following concern at the failings of the Press Complaints Commission. As Leveson LJ concluded, 'I unhesitatingly agree with the Prime Minister, the Deputy Prime Minister and the Leader of the Opposition who all believe that the PCC has failed and that a new body is required'.[290] The pre-Leveson 2012 Privacy and Injunctions Report of the Joint Committee on Privacy and Injunctions had similar concerns. It recommended extensive PCC reform, with a new body independent of industry and government[291] that could command sufficient public confidence and which would cover all major newspapers and online publishers.[292] Furthermore, the Committee argued that if industry could not create such a body, the Government should establish statutory oversight, by for example giving Ofcom a role in press regulation.[293]

The Leveson Inquiry's recommendations for press regulation reform involved establishing a new body which audits any industry-established self-regulatory body. After much political wrangling,[294] in October 2013 the Press Recognition Panel (PRP)

---

[286] L O'Carroll, '300 Alleged Phone Hacking Victims: From Prince Charles to Milly Dowler' *The Guardian* (29 November 2012), available at www.theguardian.com/news/datablog/2012/nov/29/leveson-inquiry-list-victims-phone-hacking.

[287] As Leveson LJ states in *An Inquiry into the Culture, Practices and Ethics of the Press: Executive Summary and Recommendations* (London, TSO, 2012) (Executive Summary), 'For the seventh time in less than 70 years, a report has been commissioned by the Government which has dealt with concerns about the press. It was sparked by public revulsion about a single action – the hacking of the mobile phone of a murdered teenager.' (p 1).

[288] News of the World famously shut down; there were high profile trials of employees, including former editors Rebekah Brooks and Andy Coulson; Rupert Murdoch, owner of News Corporation – the parent company of News International, appeared before the Leveson Inquiry – see detailed time line in I Chandrasekhar et al, 'Phone Hacking: Timeline of the Scandal' *The Telegraph* (23 July 2012), available at www.telegraph.co.uk/news/uknews/phone-hacking/8634176/Phone-hacking-timeline-of-a-scandal.html.

[289] L O'Carroll, 'Phone Hacking Scandal: Timeline' *The Guardian* (24 June 2014), available at www.theguardian.com/uk-news/2014/jun/24/phone-hacking-scandal-timeline-trial; see also the Leveson Inquiry website, archived at http://webarchive.nationalarchives.gov.uk/20140122145147/http:/www.levesoninquiry.org.uk.

[290] Leveson LJ also stated that '[t]he PCC has not monitored press compliance with the Code and the statistics which it has published lack transparency. Even what the organisation undoubtedly was able to do well, namely complaints handling and anti-harassment work, was restricted by a lack of profile and a reluctance to deal with matters that were the subject of civil litigation. That latterly high profile complainants almost invariably turned to the courts instead of using the PCC speaks volumes.' (para 46).

[291] Privacy and Injunctions Report (n 229) para 170.

[292] Privacy and Injunctions Report (n 229 para 180; some bloggers make a lot of revenue from advertising. Requiring a kite mark system indicating support for press regulation principles could become a prerequisite demanded by advertisers.

[293] Privacy and Injunctions Report (n 229) para 188.

[294] The type of instrument used by the Privy Council to establish universities, etc to avoid using legislative regulation of the press. See P Wintour and D Sabbagh, 'Leveson Report: David Cameron Refuses to

was established to carry out this task by the Royal Charter on Self-Regulation of the Press.[295] The PRP reviews applications from industry self-regulators[296] to determine if they match 'recognition criteria' that ensure regulation remains independent and effective.[297] This includes criteria like fair committee appointments, principles that need to underpin a code of journalistic standards,[298] and even establishing a whistle-blowing hotline.[299]

Industry replaced the PCC with the Independent Press Standards Organisation (IPSO) in summer 2014. Despite incentives like a free arbitration service for claims against publishers, which would save on the cost of litigation,[300] in 2014 IPSO announced it did not intend to apply for recognition, instead working to its own remit.[301] At the time of printing, IPSO has yet to be approved by the PRP, and its head has publicly stated that it will not go for accreditation as it would not be deemed an approved regulator due to its '(i) absence of a compulsory arbitration scheme; and (ii) the absence of a power to require newspapers to publish an apology (as distinct from a correction).'[302]

Debates around the Government's 2016 consultation on enacting s 40 of the Crime and Courts Act 2013 show how little things have moved forward since the Leveson Inquiry.[303] Section 40 was designed to incentivise sign-up to the PRP by making a news organisation defending a privacy or defamation action liable for both sides' fees,[304] *unless* they were signed up to an approved regulator. Campaigns by the press, from tabloids[305]

"Cross Rubicon" and Write Press Law' *The Guardian* (29 November 2012), available at www.theguardian.com/media/2012/nov/29/david-cameron-refuses-to-write-press-law.

[295] Royal Charter on Self-Regulation of the Press (2013), available at www.gov.uk/government/uploads/system/uploads/attachment_data/file/254116/Final_Royal_Charter_25_October_2013_clean__Final_.pdf; as MacSithigh has stated, the Royal Charter was used as 'Government and others have spent energy crafting a legal form that would be enforceable and meaningful without being labeled as "statutory".' In D MacSithigh, 'Beyond Breach of Confidence: An Irish Eye on English and Scottish Privacy Law' (2014) *Juridical Review* 27–36, 27.

[296] Functions of Panel, Section 4: 'a) Determining applications for recognition from Regulators; b) reviewing whether a Regulator which has been granted recognition shall continue to be recognised; c) withdrawing recognition from a Regulator where the Recognition Panel is satisfied that the Regulator ceases to be entitled to recognition; and d) reporting on any success or failure of the recognition system.'

[297] See H Tomlinson, 'The New UK Model of Press Regulation' *LSE Media Policy Project Series, Media Policy Brief 12* (London, LSE, 2014) (hereinafter 'Tomlinson 2014').

[298] Section 8 Sch 3 Royal Charter on Nature of the Code; See Schedule 3 of Charter for Recognition Criteria and full details.

[299] Royal Charter, Sch 3, s 8D.

[300] Tomlinson 2014 (n 297) 13.

[301] G Phillipson, 'Leveson, The Public Interest and Press Freedom' (2013) *Journal of Media Law* 220–40, 222: 'when the press denounces the Royal Charter as a fatal blow to a "free press", what it is relying on is a simple, almost literal notion of press freedom as freedom from restraint; parts of the press want to be free of any effective regulation and able to operate with as much impunity as possible, relying on the inability or unwillingness of most people to use the expensive legal remedies in privacy and libel that are theoretically open to them.'

[302] S Carne, "The Section 40 Debate Shows Just How Much our Press Needs a Proper Regulator' (*Inforrm*, 13 January 2017), available at https://inforrm.wordpress.com/2017/01/13/the-section-40-debate-shows-just-how-much-our-press-needs-a-proper-regulator-simon-carne.

[303] *Ibid.*

[304] See www.legislation.gov.uk/ukpga/2013/22/section/40.

[305] J Beattie, 'Stop the Snowflake Press that the Cheats, Charlatans and Corrupt Want You to Read" *The Mirror* (5 January 2017), available at www.mirror.co.uk/news/uk-news/stop-snowflake-press-cheats-charlatans-9504327.

to broadsheets,[306] however argued vigorously that this might stifle their freedoms to report, especially in the case of small, local papers.[307] As a result, s 40 has never been brought into force and PRP for the mainstream press has remained largely a dead letter.

IPSO is largely favoured by major players in the press, and indeed is funded by them through the Regulatory Funding Company.[308] Accordingly, it can be criticised as being actually a worse solution than its predecessor the PCC, as it may be deemed not adequately independent. Only one alternative self-regulation body has sought and been granted accreditation by the PRP, IMPRESS, which in 2016 was approved as complying with Royal Charter standards.[309] IMPRESS is primarily financed by the Independent Press Regulation Trust, which in turn is funded by Max Mosley, who as we saw earlier had had many privacy-related run-ins with the mainstream press.[310] It has many safeguards such as having an independent board and being incorporated as a charity, and was commended by PRP in its 2017 second annual report,[311] but the link to Max Mosley makes it unlikely that any mainstream titles will ever join its ranks.[312]

The press argues accreditation by the PRP is tantamount to state regulation, and frame s 40 as an attempt to force news organisations to sign up to IMPRESS, or for IPSO to become accredited by the Royal Charter process. Supporters of the PRP on the other hand argue it would make it easier for the public to challenge illegality by unregulated news publishers. Tambini, a supporter of change, nonetheless feels that if reforms under s 40 are rejected it may have to be accepted that:

> real reforms of press accountability, even when they are delivered by an independent judge-led inquiry, are not possible, as the press themselves hold too much power and they will use it in pursuit of their own narrow interests. If this is the case, the press should be considered beyond reform, and it should be acknowledged that they are likely to worsen as the industry becomes more focused on the bottom line, and more likely to engage in more and more intrusive and unethical behaviour in pursuit of popular stories.[313]

Reform is important, and 2017 analysis showed public support for stronger press regulation – with 59 per cent of respondents to a YouGov survey stating they have no

---

[306] R Greenslade, 'Hacked Off Punches above its Weight, but it Will Not – and Should Not – Win' *The Guardian* (13 January 2017), available at www.theguardian.com/media/greenslade/2017/jan/13/hacked-off-punches-above-its-weight-but-it-will-not-and-should-not-win.

[307] See a contrary view from P Wragg, 'Don't Believe What You Read: Section 40 Will Protect the Local Press, Not Kill it' (*Inforrm*, 14 January 2017), available at https://inforrm.wordpress.com/2017/01/14/dont-believe-what-you-read-section-40-will-protect-the-local-press-not-kill-it-paul-wragg.

[308] S Barnett, 'IMPRESS vs IPSO: A Chasm, Not a Cigarette Paper' (*LSE Media Policy Project Blog*, 31 October 2016), available at http://blogs.lse.ac.uk/mediapolicyproject/2016/10/31/impress-vs-ipso-a-chasm-not-a-cigarette-paper.

[309] F Mayhew, 'Press Recognition Panel Gives Alternative Press Regulator Impress Royal Charter Backing' (*PressGazette*, 25 October 2016), available at www.pressgazette.co.uk/press-recognition-panel-gives-alternative-press-regulator-impress-royal-charter-backing.

[310] In terms of differences between the two, see Barnett (n 308); Duffy (n 180); J Heawood, 'Independent and Effective? The Post-Leveson Framework for Press Regulation' (2015) 7(2) *Journal of Media Law* 130–44.

[311] See Press Recognition Panel, 'Annual PRP Report on the Recognition System 2017' (29 November 2017) at https://pressrecognitionpanel.org.uk/annual-report-on-the-recognition-system-2017/.

[312] J Doward, 'Max Mosley, the 56-year-old Fascist Leaflet, and a Battle for the Press' *The Guardian* (3 March 2018).

[313] D Tambini, 'Where Now for Media Reform in the UK?' (*Inforrm*, 11 January 2017), available at https://inforrm.wordpress.com/2017/01/11/where-now-for-media-reform-in-the-uk-damian-tambini.

faith in IPSO.[314] As Barnett argues, this is the latest in a 30-year-long process from the Calcutt Inquiry to the phone hacking scandal, and attempts at reform should not be abandoned.[315]

Despite this clear need, the Conservative Government announced after the 2017 election its intent to implement its Manifesto pledge not to proceed with the second part of Leveson's Inquiry, and to repeal s 40.[316] The second inquiry would have focused on wrongdoing by the police and press.[317] Following one of the largest government consultations ever,[318] Part II was deemed unnecessary. This is in part due to the number of police investigations already undertaken into phone hacking, that policing practices have since changed, as has press self-regulation, since Leveson's original findings. With respect to s 40, the 'chilling effect' on press freedom was the primary justification for repeal.[319] Understandably, many commentators and campaigns view this as a retrograde step.[320] Leveson himself has stated the work is not fully done and that this has implications for victims.[321] With the loss of momentum as a result of this consultation, meaningful change, as Leveson envisaged, seems unlikely.[322]

B. Fake News

We conclude by briefly reflecting on a growing challenge for press regulation: fake news. The industry[323] around the creation of factually incorrect news stories has risen

[314] 'YouGov Poll: 57% Favour Tougher Press Regulation, 59% Have No Confidence in Press Regulation Established by the Newspapers' (*Inforrm*, 10 January 2017), available at https://inforrm.wordpress.com/2017/01/10/yougov-poll-57-favour-tougher-press-regulation-59-have-no-confidence-in-press-regulation-established-by-the-newspapers.

[315] S Barnett, 'Press Regulation: Three Reasons Why a 30 Year Old Campaign Must Continue' (*Inforrm*, 19 January 2017), available at https://inforrm.wordpress.com/2017/01/19/press-regulation-three-reasons-why-a-30-year-old-campaign-must-continue-steven-barnett.

[316] The Conservative Party Manifesto (2018), available at www.conservatives.com/manifesto.

[317] P Magrath, 'Press Regulation: The End of the Road for Leveson Reforms' (*Inform*, 5 March 2018) available at https://inforrm.org/2018/03/05/press-regulation-the-end-of-the-road-for-leveson-reforms-paul-magrath/.

[318] Department for Digital, Culture, Media & Sport (DCMS)/Home Office, *Government Response To The Consultation On The Leveson Inquiry And Its Implementation* (London, TSO, 2018) 6, available at www.gov.uk/government/uploads/system/uploads/attachment_data/file/684678/GOVERNMENT_RESPONSE_TO_THE_CONSULTATION_ON_THE_LEVESON_INQUIRY_AND_ITS_IMPLEMENTATION_.pdf.

[319] *Ibid*, 14.

[320] N Fenton, 'Government's Leveson Announcement A Sorry Betrayal of the Victims of Press Abuse' (*Inforrm*, 6 March 2018), available at https://inforrm.org/2018/03/06/governments-leveson-announcement-a-sorry-betrayal-of-the-victims-of-press-abuse-natalie-fenton/; B Cathcart, 'The Guardian's Betrayal Line by Line' (*Inforrm*, 2 March 2018), available at https://inforrm.org/2018/03/02/the-guardians-leveson-betrayal-line-by-line-brian-cathcart/.

[321] DCMS/Home Office, 'Correspondence with Sir Brian Leveson' (2017), available at www.gov.uk/government/uploads/system/uploads/attachment_data/file/684967/DCMS_and_Home_Office_Correspondence_with_Sir_Brian_Leveson.pdf where Leveson LJ states 'there is still a legitimate expectation on behalf of the public and, in particular, the alleged victims of phone hacking and other unlawful conduct, that there will be a full public examination of the circumstances that allowed that behaviour to develop and clear reassurances that nothing on the same scale could occur again: that is what they were promised'.

[322] As of 15 May 2018, the future of Levenson Part II was still being debated and promoted by the House of Lords as part of the progress of the Data Protection Bill. Its future remains however precarious. A useful summary of these developments can be found at https://researchbriefings.parliament.uk/ResearchBriefing/Summary/CBP-7576.

[323] D Tambini, 'How Advertising Fuels Fake News' (*Inforrm*, 26 February 2017), available at https://inforrm.wordpress.com/2017/02/26/how-advertising-fuels-fake-news-damian-tambini.

to prominence in recent years, primarily due to its role in the shock UK vote to leave the European Union, and the election of reality TV personality Donald Trump as President of the United States.[324] Defining fake news is complex, but largely refers to the spreading of false stories that masquerade as legitimate news, often through social media channels.[325] How fake news differs from or intersects with marketing, public relations communications and propaganda remains contested.[326] Nevertheless, the importance of the digital world to news uptake has become apparent as more news is viewed via social media platforms, especially for younger demographics and this in turn changes the capacity of readers to interrogate its validity.[327]

A related issue is that how content is served to individuals on their social media feeds is determined by algorithmic curation processes.[328] Individuals are profiled by social media platforms to identify their preferences, and then algorithms tailor delivery of content to match those perceived political and ideological viewpoints. As a result, individuals are often said to be living in a 'filter bubble' where they only ever read content that matches their existing perceptions of the world.[329] This enhances rather than combats existing biases and reduces access to pluralistic content which is supposed to underpin true democratic values and processes.[330] Emotions are also increasingly targeted in algorithmic journalism, drawing on tools from digital advertising and affective computing to catch viewer attention and optimise content to fit emotive states or even to manipulate reader sentiment.[331] The political impact of fake news in this setting is even more powerful, as individuals are often being served content that matches to their preconceptions, without their awareness. Accordingly, in an age of 'post truth' and 'alternative facts',[332] trust in digital media is sorely tested.

In responding to fake news, questions are being asked around the extent to which social media platforms are now taking the same role as traditional publishers or news organisations, and therefore whether they should not be regulated as such.[333]

---

[324] 'The Facebook "Fake News" Scandal is Important – but Regulation isn't the Answer' *The Independent* (15 November 2016), available at http://www.independent.co.uk/voices/editorials/the-facebook-fake-news-scandal-is-important-but-regulation-isnt-the-answer-a7419386.html. The Cambridge Analytica story broke after this chapter was completed, with wide ranging implications on themes considered here. See *The Guardian* Resource Page at www.theguardian.com/news/series/cambridge-analytica-files. The scandal is outlined briefly in this volume in Chapter 3.

[325] See H Allcott and M Gentzkow, 'Social Media and Fake News in the 2016 Election' (2017) 31(2) *Journal of Economic Perspectives* 211–36.

[326] V Bakir, E Herring, D Miller, P Robinson, 'Organized Persuasive Communication' (2018) *Critical Sociology*.

[327] M Flintham, C Karner, H Creswick, K Bachour, N Gupta, S Moran, 'Falling for Fake News: Investigating the Consumption of News via Social Media' (2018) *Proceedings of ACM CHI Conference on Human Factors in Computing Systems*.

[328] The EPSRC Unbias Project is currently researching these issues, particularly around perceptions of algorithmic bias. See https://unbias.wp.horizon.ac.uk/about-us/.

[329] E Pariser, *The Filter Bubble: What the Internet is Hiding from You* (Penguin, 2012).

[330] Algorithms, their governance and how to create algorithmic transparency are addressed multiple times in this volume. See especially the discussion of algorithmic content moderation in Chapter 9 as well as the discussion through the preceding data protection chapters on inter alia 'the right to an explanation' (Chapter 4, p 101) and targeted marketing (Chapter 5, p 134).

[331] V Bakir and A McStay, 'Fake News and the Economy of Emotions' (2017) *Digital Journalism* 6(1).

[332] SI Strong, 'Alternative Facts and the Post-Truth Society: Meeting the Challenge' (2017) 165(1) *University of Pennsylvania Law Review*.

[333] See, eg, 'Ofcom Chair Raises Prospect of Regulation for Google and Facebook' *The Guardian* (10 October 2017) at www.theguardian.com/media/2017/oct/10/ofcom-patricia-hodgson-google-facebook-fake-news.

This raises considerable difficulties however, not only because online intermediaries have since around 2000 mainly been treated as neutral platforms rather than publishers with editorial responsibility,[334] but also because of jurisdictional issues – platforms are often US-based – and because if 'editorial control' is exercised by such bodies it is at least partially automated and algorithmic, making it harder to understand how content is being curated. Deeper ethical questions also stem from what the nature is of 'true' and 'false' news in reporting, and to what extent social media platforms have responsibilities to filter and edit content.

Responding to risks of algorithmic bias and fake news[335] requires new strategies: for example 'popping' the social media filter bubble by presenting individuals with random content they disagree with in order to challenge their views; or requiring social media platforms to increase algorithmic accountability and transparency around what content readers are served.[336] In the future, the roles of online actors in the dissemination of news will be considered alongside traditional media outlets, as is already beginning to happen with the controversies around Twitter and the publicisation of injunctions.

One interesting and surprising global trend in the midst of the rise of fake news has been increased subscriptions to newspaper outlets.[337] In this context, bolstering trust in traditional press media is increasingly important. Press regulator IMPRESS has already argued (after addressing the Leveson Inquiry recommendations) that a framework to address fake news is necessary, utilising kite marks for accredited news.[338] The UK Government has also shown interest in addressing fake news, running an initial Parliamentary Inquiry in 2017,[339] and opening another one until 2019 after the first concluded.[340] The European Commission has also addressed fake news, particularly in the context of its work against illegal content and hate speech, promoting effective removal within specific timeframes, the use of trusted flaggers and automatic

---

[334] See discussion concerning the 'safe harbours' given to online service providers, especially under the e-Commerce Directive Arts 12–15 in the EU, in Chapter 9 where there is also a brief discussion of how fake news, alongside other factors such as hate speech, may have created a climate for reassessment of these protections of online intermediaries.

[335] E Goodman, 'How Has Media Policy Responded to Fake News?' (*Inforrm*, 17 February2017), available at https://inforrm.wordpress.com/2017/02/17/how-has-media-policy-responded-to-fake-news-emma-goodman.

[336] N Newman, 'Journalism, Media, and Technology Trends and Predictions 2017' (*Reuters Institute for Journalism*, 2017); E Hunt, 'Facebook to Change Trending Topics after Investigation into Bias Claims' *The Guardian* (24 May 2016), available at www.theguardian.com/technology/2016/may/24/facebook-changes-trending-topics-anti-conservative-bias.

[337] S Bond and D Bond, 'Newspapers Welcome More Digital Subscribers in Time of Fake News' *Financial Times* (15 February 2017), available at www.ft.com/content/d97bef40-f19b-11e6-8758-6876151821a6.

[338] 'IMPRESS Highlights Need for Post-Leveson Framework in Fight against Fake News' (*Inforrm*, 14 March 2017), available at https://inforrm.wordpress.com/2017/03/14/impress-highlights-need-for-post-leveson-framework-in-fight-against-fake-news.

[339] House of Commons Culture, Media and Sport Select Committee, '"Fake News" Inquiry Launched' (30 January 2017), available at www.parliament.uk/business/committees/committees-a-z/commons-select/culture-media-and-sport-committee/news-parliament-2015/fake-news-launch-16-17.

[340] Digital, Culture, Media and Sport Inquiry on Fake News available at www.parliament.uk/business/committees/committees-a-z/commons-select/digital-culture-media-and-sport-committee/inquiries/parliament-2017/fake-news-17-19/.

detection and removal techniques as well as steps to prevent the reappearance of dubious content.[341]

Bakir and McStay conducted extensive analysis of submissions to the Inquiry, focusing on proposed solutions to fake news challenges. They found that for established media organisations, building up reader trust is a key challenge. This requires greater use of fact checking (economically challenged by staffing shortages and decline of print media); transparency of sources (balancing deception and bias against protecting sources); and regulating for media pluralism and encouraging truth-telling in journalism. Other aspects include increased education, critical thinking and digital literacy around news; digital intermediaries performing fact checking, flagging, downgrading or blocking of fake content; advertisers policing their networks to cut fake news sites out of the ecosystem; addressing how persuasion is leveraged in political campaigning (whilst being conscious of censorship risk); and tackling security implications of propaganda and information warfare.[342] Some of these strategies have now been taken up by Facebook and Google in the wake of the fake news and Cambridge Analytica political micro-targeted ads scandals (see Chapter 3) including notably the adoption of a greater use of trusted flaggers, the hiring of a large number of humans to supplement or override the automated processes and a greater degree of transparency around (especially) political targeted advertising.[343]

Whether dealing with real news or fake news, effective regulation of the press will need to overcome many hurdles in the years ahead.[344]

---

[341] See European Commission Recommendation of 1 March 2018 on measures to effectively tackle illegal content online (C(2018) 1177 final); European Commission Communication on tackling illegal content online, towards enhanced responsibility of online platforms COM(2017) 555 final, adopted on 28 September 2017.

[342] V Bakir and A McStay, 'Combatting Fake News: Analysis of Submissions to the Fake News Inquiry' (*Three D*, 3 June 2017) available at www.meccsa.org.uk/news/three-d-issue-28-combatting-fake-news-analysis-of-submissions-to-the-fake-news-inquiry/.

[343] See, eg, R Goldman, 'Making Ads and Pages More Transparent' (Facebook news Blog, 6 April 2018), available at https://newsroom.fb.com/news/2018/04/transparent-ads-and-pages/.

[344] J Rodgers, 'Good News in an Era of Fake News: The Public is Becoming Wiser about How the Media Works' (*Inforrm*, 7 March 2017), available at https://inforrm.wordpress.com/2017/03/07/good-news-in-an-era-of-fake-news-the-public-is-becoming-wiser-about-how-the-media-works-james-rodgers.

Part III

Online Intermediaries, e-Commerce and Cybercrime

9

'With Great Power Comes Great Responsibility?': The Rise of Platform Liability

LILIAN EDWARDS*

I. Introduction and Historical Development

The potential liability of Internet intermediaries for the content and activities of their users – known in the early days as 'Internet Service Provider (ISP) liability' – was one of the earliest legal problems to demand real attention in the fledgling development of Internet law.[1] The problematic content may be originated by a party with whom the intermediary has a contractual relationship, eg a blog posted on a host site such as WordPress; provided by a third party with no contractual nexus, eg where a defamatory comment is left on a newspaper website; or content arguably originated by the intermediary itself but pointing at content held elsewhere, eg Google search results. The different issues of policy raised by these different classifications of authorship, responsibility, control and types of content were largely not teased out systematically in the early pre-2000 jurisprudence (mostly of US origin), leading to widely differing regimes being imposed both in different legal systems, and within the same legal system but in differing scenarios, depending perhaps on the type of content or the type of 'publisher' or 'host'.[2]

---

* My thanks to Ian Brown for helpful comments on a draft of this work.

[1] For historical context, see earlier discussion of these issues by this writer in 2009 ('The Rise and Fall of Online Intermediary Liability' in L Edwards and C Waelde (eds), *Law and the Internet*, 3rd edn (Hart Publishing, 2009)); 2005 ('Defamation and the Internet' and 'Pornography and the Internet', both in L Edwards and C Waelde (eds), *Law and the Internet: A Framework for Electronic Commerce* (Hart Publishing, 2000)); and 1997 ('Defamation and the Internet' in L Edwards and C Waelde (eds), *Law and the Internet: Regulating Cyberspace* (Hart Publishing, 1997)). The topic is also known following copyright style as 'secondary liability of ISPs': see GB Dinwoodie (ed), *Secondary Liability of Internet Service Providers* (Springer, 2017). A useful text for UK practitioners is J Riordan, *The Liability of Internet Intermediaries* (Oxford University Press, 2016).

[2] Notable early US cases included *Cubby v CompuServe* 766 F Supp 135 (SDNY, 1991) where an early ISP was held to be the distributor only of defamatory comments and hence not liable; and *Stratton Oakmont,*

Online intermediaries have changed a lot in the last 20-odd years. Nowadays they are better known perhaps as platforms and most of us deal with them every day. The importance of platforms and their regulation can be seen in the flood of enquiries and consultations on their power in the last few years.[3] The Digital Single Market strategy of the EU has drawn special attention to the power of platforms noting that they play 'an ever more central role in social and economic life: they enable consumers to find online information and businesses to exploit the advantages of e-commerce'.[4] The main legal tool to date with which platforms and intermediaries have been regulated has been the threat of liability for the content they host, and this is the main thread of this chapter. It is important to note however that platform power is now also being substantially addressed by topics dealt with elsewhere in this volume, notably data protection (Chapters 3–5), consumer protection law (Chapter 11), and competition and net neutrality (Chapter 2).

Content often carries with it legal liability, which may be civil or criminal. A text (or a video or a song or a picture or an executable file) may be defamatory. It may contain illegal images of child sexual abuse ('child abuse material' or CAM[5]). It may infringe the copyright of the owner thereof, if the host (or the publisher or the reader or listener) has made an unauthorised copy. It may incite racial hatred or 'hate speech' or promote pro-jihadi ideas.[6] It may infringe laws on truthful advertising, or reveal facts which are embargoed by laws of confidence[7]; or contempt of court

Inc v Prodigy Services Co, 1995 NY Misc LEXIS 712 where a similar ISP was held by virtue of its partial editorial control to have made itself into a publisher. See also *Religious Technology Center v Netcom On-Line Communication Services, Inc*, 907 F Supp 1361 (ND Cal 1995) where the Court decided an 'Internet access provider' had not infringed copyright by giving access to copyright works of the Church of Scientology.

[3] From the UK see notably: HL *Online Platforms and the Digital Single Market*, Select Committee on EU, 10th Report of Session 2015–16 (20 April 2016); HL Select Committee House of Lords *Enquiry into the Regulation of the Internet* (ongoing 2018) (see call for evidence at www.parliament.uk/documents/lords-committees/communications/InternetRegulation/Internet-regulation-call-for-evidence.pdf); in the EU, *Public Consultation on the Regulatory Environment for Platforms, Online Intermediaries, Data and Cloud Computing and the Collaborative Economy* (24 September 2015) at https://ec.europa.eu/digital-single-market/en/news/public-consultation-regulatory-environment-platforms-online-intermediaries-data-and-cloud; *A Clean and Open Internet: Public Consultation on Procedures for Notifying and Acting on Illegal Content Hosted by Online Intermediaries* (4 June 2012) at http://ec.europa.eu/internal_market/consultations/2012/clean-and-open-internet_en.htm; and many more (see also n 4), some referenced below, specifically dealing with platforms and copyright, illegal and obscene content, machine learning and artificial intelligence, hate speech and fake news, et al.

[4] Communication from the Commission, *A Digital Single Market Strategy for Europe*, COM(2015) 192. This was followed in 2016 by the *Communication on Online Platforms and the Digital Single Market Opportunities and Challenges for Europe*, COM/2016/0288 final, which proposed, alongside revision of the Audio-Visual Media Services Directive (AVMS – addressed to some extent in the next chapter), changes addressing lack of a level playing field in digital services, rules to ensure online platforms acted responsibly in relation to harmful speech rules to foster trust and transparency in users of platforms including in the business to business (B2B) environment. The first two are dealt with in this chapter; for the third see n 175.

[5] See section V. below for an account of 'notice and take down' (NTD). For full discussion of intermediary filtering of CAM and other related types of illegal material such as extreme pornography in the UK, see Chapter 10.

[6] *Ibid* for full discussion of hate, extremist and terror-related speech in the UK.

[7] See, eg, the *Estelle Halliday* case, Tribunal de Grande Instance de Paris, 9 June 1998. Note that the ECD excludes from its scope data protection liability: see ECD, Art 1(5)(b) and updating in the General Data Protection Regulation at Art 2(4) (Regulation (EU) 2016/679 of the European Parliament and of the Council of 27 April 2016 on the protection of natural persons with regard to the processing of personal data and on the free movement of such data, and repealing Directive 95/46/EC (General Data Protection Regulation or GDPR) [2016] OJ L119/1).

rules.[8] It may even be blasphemous.[9] In all these (and many more) cases, a crucial issue arises which is: how far should online intermediaries be responsible for this content, or contrarily, how far should responsibility stay with the original content author or provider?

Connectedly, if the intermediary is deemed even partially responsible, what acts should the law demand it takes to *remove* this content, or perhaps even to prevent it being made available in the first place (the notions of *ex ante blocking, filtering and stay down*)? Alternately, if only the content provider, not the intermediary, is deemed liable, will it be practical for the law to control the dissemination of the undesirable content (or abuse of legitimate content, as in the copyright example)? If liability *is* placed on online intermediaries, what will the impact be on their business models and economic survival, given their aforementioned importance to the Internet economy? And finally, what are the societal impacts on values like free speech and privacy if unlimited filtering, blocking or monitoring obligations are placed on intermediaries (or these actions taken voluntarily by them to avoid liability or regulation)?

Uncertainty as to the answers to these questions and lack of global harmonisation on liability lead to calls from industry for help in the form of special statutory regimes of immunity – 'safe harbours' as the US calls them – from as early as the mid-1990s. The EC Electronic Commerce Directive 2000 (or E-Commerce Directive or ECD)[10] alongside the Digital Millennium Copyright Act (DMCA) in the USA effectively established the ideas of limited liability and 'notice and take down' (NTD) as the template for intermediary responsibility, a solution which had remarkable reach for over a decade and remains the pattern of many Organisation for Economic Co-operation and Development (OECD) laws.[11]

However, this compromise was not to last. New types of intermediaries appeared whose peculiar qualities had not been anticipated by the ECD or the DMCA: search engines, cloud service providers, social media sites, price comparison and aggregator sites, and most devastatingly, peer to peer (P2P) torrent sites and other types of sites supporting unauthorised uploading, downloading and streaming of copyright

---

[8] See *R v Barnardo* [1995] Ont CJ Lexis. In 2001, the ISP Demon successfully asked the English courts to grant it an exemption from strict liability for contempt of court in advance, in relation to the 'Jamie Bulger' Thompson and Venables murder trial. But note *Mosley v News Group Newspapers* [2008] EWHC 687 (QB), where Eady J refused to grant an injunction preventing publication of an 'intrusive and demeaning' sex video of Max Mosley, since the material had already been widely published on the Internet. This precedent has probably substantially diminished the risk for ISPs and hosts of being held liable for contempt of court in cases where there is little they can do to stop circulation of material already 'out' on the Internet. See further Chapter 8.

[9] See unreported 1997 UK case involving gay poem found illegal as blasphemous in the UK courts; a host in the UK subsequently linked to that poem (which was hosted physically on a server abroad) and was reported to the police for so doing. A police investigation followed but no charges were ever brought. Details can be found at www.xs4all.nl/~yaman/linkpoem.htm.

[10] Directive 2000/31/EC of the European Parliament and of the Council of 8 June 2000 on certain legal aspects of information society services, in particular electronic commerce, in the Internal Market (Directive on electronic commerce) [2000] OJ L178/1.

[11] See OECD, *The Role of Internet Intermediaries in Advancing Public Policy Objectives* DSTI/ICCP(2010)11/FINAL (2011) at www.oecd.org/internet/ieconomy/48685066.pdf. A useful global reference for online intermediary laws can be found at the World Intermediary Liability Map, supported by Stanford University at http://wilmap.law.stanford.edu/.

works. As will be discussed in some detail below, these new intermediaries especially destabilised the balance set by the ECD between the interests of platforms, and the needs for redress and action by victims, governments and rights-holders, during what became known as the online 'copyright wars'.[12] More recent pressures have included the ascending desire, in a post 9/11, post-recession and increasingly xenophobic society, for digital platforms to help police the Internet against terror, hate speech and extremism; and the rise of 'fake news' and associated fears that targeted advertising, the revenue stream of choice of the largest platforms, has been 'weaponised' to destabilise democracy.

Underneath it all, perhaps, lies the feeling, among both users and traditional state governments, that the giant 'GAFAM' platforms (Google Amazon Facebook Apple Microsoft) now exert power greater than any prior private companies and possibly than some elected governments.[13] In this 'perfect storm', the question of how far online intermediary liability, once a relatively technical area of the law, should be used to leverage the power of platforms for social as well as commercial goals, has become one of the most crucial and controversial areas of Internet law: drawing on elements of many long-running debates around child protection, state control over morality, extraterritorial law enforcement, innovation promotion, self- versus state regulation and 'net neutrality', as well as traditional content liability, all in one tangled mess. A better title for this chapter might now simply be 'How the Internet is Regulated'.[14]

We begin therefore by attempting to tease out the policy factors which lead to the current status quo in intermediary liability paradigms with some looking ahead to the factors which may have caused them to no longer apply.

II. Policy Factors and the Development of the 'Limited Liability' Paradigm

Online intermediary liability is a complex ecology involving many different types of content. In the earliest reported cases, issues mostly arose around the hosting and transmission of CAM and other types of obscene or criminal content; these were particularly pressing as rules on possession of CAM often commanded strict liability and jail terms as well as social opprobrium.[15] Defamation and libel cases have also

[12] See an excellent account of the European legal struggles relating to copyright enforcement in S Schmitz, *The Struggle in Online Copyright Enforcement* (Hart/Nomos, 2014).

[13] This may not actually be true. In the Lobbying Spending Database as updated at 24 April 2018, the top spending lobbying industries were pharma, insurance and electronics manufacturing, with the Internet industry very far down the list. See www.opensecrets.org/lobby/search.php. On the other hand there are very few industries which support ambassador positions: see, eg, the Danish appointment of an ambassador to Silicon Valley discussed in '"Techplomacy": Denmark's Ambassador to Silicon Valley' (Politico.eu, 20 July 2017), at www.politico.eu/article/denmark-silicon-valley-tech-ambassador-casper-klynge/.

[14] It is notable that the 2018 HL enquiry into the regulation of the Internet (n 3) despite its expansive title, in the main asks questions falling into the traditional remit of online intermediary liability as discussed in this chapter.

[15] In Europe, considerable angst was caused by the prosecution of Felix Somm, Chief Executive Officer of Compuserve in Europe in 1998 for distribution of child pornography (Local Court, Munich, 12 May 1998).

played a significant part, partly because of the prevalent theory that those who repub-
lish a libel are as culpable as those who originate it, a doctrine seemingly tailor made
to terrify Internet platforms.[16]

Once the Napster[17] era dawned, issues around material which infringed IP rights
began to dominate the discourse; especially copyright, but also sometimes trademarks.[18] The combination of music and film piracy, P2P networks and the rise of
user generated content (UGC) sites such as YouTube, where users could upload and
download content without effective gate keeping, exposed ISPs and hosts to potential
risk in a volume and manner quite different from that anticipated in the early cases on
'publication' liability. Finally, in the post 9/11 period, and especially since around 2015,
substantial emphasis has been placed on the control of 'hate speech',[19] including pro
terror and jihadi speech (eg ISIS videos).

Thus, by virtue of their obvious role as the gatekeepers to Internet publication, the
emerging industry sector of ISPs quickly became aware of their potential high risk
status in content liability cases sometime in the middle to early Nineties. As a result,
ISPs plead a case for immunity from content liability around the world, which heavily
informed the development of the limited liability regimes in the US DMCA and the
ECD.

This ISP plea is still worth considering, over 15 years later, when intermediary
'safe harbours' have become normalised. It rested mainly on three factors:

- lack of effective legal or actual control;
- the *inequity* of imposing liability upon a mere intermediary ('shooting the
  messenger');
- and in Europe especially, *consequences* for the public interest if unlimited liability
  was, nonetheless, imposed.

On the first point, ISPs argued forcibly that they could not conceivably check manually
the legality of all the material which passed through their server, without impossible
amounts of delay and expense,[20] nor was it desirable or possibly legal for them to
do so without invading the privacy and confidentiality of their subscribers. Furthermore, while conventional publishers, such as newspapers or book publishers could
limit their risk contractually, by, for example, issuing acceptability guidelines to its
employees, or putting indemnity clauses into contracts with freelancers, ISPs and hosts
were exposed to risk as a result of content authored by parties with whom they most
often had no contractual nexus. Their aim was thus ideally to legally be classified not
as publishers who carried the risk of the content they made available to the public but

---

[16] See in the US, n 2; in the UK, n 43.

[17] See the landmark case of *A&M Records, Inc v Napster, Inc*, 239 F3d 1004 (2001).

[18] See Joined Cases C-236/08 to C-238/08, *Google France v Louis Vuitton and others* (CJEU, 23 March
2010); *Cartier International and Others vs BSkyB and others* [2016] EWCA Civ 658.

[19] The landmark early case on this kind of content dates from 2000 – *LICRA and UEJF v Yahoo!Inc and
Yahoo! France,* Tribunal de Grande Instance de Paris (Superior Court of Paris, 22 May 2000) and TGI de
Paris, Ordonnance de refere du 20 November 2000.

[20] BT Internet estimated, even in 1999, that just to effectively monitor news-group traffic alone, they would
have to hire 1500 new employees working 24 hours a day. See *WIPO Workshop on Service Provider Liability*
(Geneva, 9–10 December 1999), paper by Janet Henderson, Rights Strategy Manager, BT Internet.

as common carriers, akin to the postal service and phone companies in the United States, or distributors such as libraries or bookshops, institutions which carried no or at least limited liability for content.[21]

One obvious way forward to circumvent the problem of filtering massive amounts of information was via automation, but content classification and filtering technologies in the late Nineties were highly unsatisfactory and tended to radically under and over-block. In areas like libel and hate speech, where semantic meaning is hugely dependent on human interpretation, automated blocking was regarded as entirely impractical. In the significant 2000 turning point of the *France v Yahoo!* case, however, the French Court, presented with the defence that it was technically impossible for Yahoo! US to block access to pages on its site selling Nazi memorabilia items to *all persons from France*, remitted the question of automated filtering of requests from a particular *location* to a technical sub-committee to investigate. They reported back that, in fact, Yahoo! had the capacity (already used to serve up adverts in the relevant language to users from whatever country of origin) to identify and thus block access to 90 per cent of French citizens.[22] Accordingly, Yahoo! was instructed to block access. Note however that the question here only involved determining a *location* to which to apply filtering – not a semantic analysis of *content*.

Since 2000, as we shall see below, automated content curation has become steadily more sophisticated and prevalent, especially in relation to copyright 'take downs', and with the rise of machine learning (ML), automated blocking has begun to look more feasible, even in heavily contextual and cultural areas, such as 'fake news' and indecency, albeit with more successful application to images than text.[23]

Second, ISPs argued that they were mere messengers, not content providers, and thus that it would be inequitable to hold them liable.[24] The model typically contemplated before 2000, long before the rise of social media, was probably that of a subscriber, business or domestic, who used his ISP, or an online host like Geocities or Hotmail or a corporate server farm, to store his web pages, documents or emails; perhaps also of a university or school where large numbers of students stored files on central servers for free. In such a scenario, the host is easy to see as both morally 'innocent' – ISPs charged flat fees generally regardless of the type of content

---

[21] In fact the US courts confusingly entertained both distributor and publisher paradigms in two influential early decisions (n 2). One of these cases, *Prodigy*, was finally overruled by the US Supreme Court in a subsequent case, *Lunney v Prodigy Services Co* 94 NY 2d 242 confirming that an ISP is not a publisher at common law in US law for defamation. A similar decision was reached in the UK in the defamation case of *Tamiz v Google* though only at first instance (see n 51). Note that the common carrier doctrine also contains the idea of universal service, ie that any local user should be able to access the services of the carrier without discrimination. ISPs have never fitted into this part of the metaphor.

[22] See *LICRA et UEJF vs Yahoo! Inc and Yahoo France* (20 November 2000, Tribunal de Grande Instance de Paris, Superior Court of Paris) 14. Around 70% of users' country of origin could be established from IP address and the remaining 20% or so could be made up by asking users to fill in a form declaring country of origin. Some degree of evasion would always be possible however because of use of foreign ISPs, proxy servers and anonymising services.

[23] See detailed discussion of filtering in the context of child abuse images, extreme porn and terrorist/hate speech material in Chapter 10. On 'fake news' see Chapter 8.

[24] See adoption of this metaphor in G Sutter, 'Don't Shoot the Messenger? The UK and Online Intermediary Liability' (2003) 17 *International Review of Law, Computers and Technology* 73.

stored – and factually devoid of actual or constructive knowledge of illegal or unwelcome content, unless specific notice was given.

This claim of innocence and neutrality has however suffered considerably since 2000 as a result of the rise of 'for free' business models, driven by the monetisation of user data and attention. In the hands of the CJEU (see section V.D. below), this awareness of economic complicity by platforms has morphed into a complex legal debate about when intermediaries can be said to be 'neutral'. In practice, a sense of 'common enterprise'[25] between the online intermediary and the user was not readily apparent at the stage of industry development which formed the backdrop to the drafting of the ECD and DMCA. But even by 2000, the music industry was prepared to regard service providers as less than angelic, with Jack Valenti, former President of the Motion Picture Industry Association of America, notoriously describing downloading as the ISP industry's 'dirty little secret' during hearings prior to the passing of the US DMCA.[26] Over the next 15 years both the profits made by the giant GAFAM platforms from putting ads next to hosted UGC or searches, and the failure of these same platforms to curtail the circulation of damaging types of content, further weakened the 'innocent messenger' narrative.

Finally around 2017–2018, the public has arguably begun to comprehend that algorithms used by platforms to distribute, moderate and filter content can and do incorporate value-judgements and inherent bias, and can be used to apparently modify public emotions[27] and opinions.[28] The dawning horror at this covert manipulation of everything from buying choices to democratic decision making may have finally killed off once and for all the notion of platforms as innocent intermediaries. Kohl pointed out astutely as early as 2013 that platforms and search engines had incentives to promote 'the idea that automated processes are inherently neutral, thus releasing the actor behind it from legal accountability. This idea accords with popular consciousness according to which automated decision-making appears impartial'.[29] After Cambridge Analytica, however, it is hard to regard Facebook – and its social media stablemates – as at all innocent or non-complicit in what it does with other people's content.[30]

Finally, the fledgling ISP industry of the late 90s argued that its emergent business sector could not withstand the burden of full liability for content authored by others.

---

[25] A test proposed by C Reed, 'Policies for Internet Immunity' [2009] 19 (6) *Computers and Law* 20, the full version is available online at www.scl.org/site.aspx?i=kc189.

[26] See On-Line Copyright Liability Limitation Act and WIPO Copyright Treaties Implementation Act: Hearing on HR 2280 and HR 2281 Before the House Judiciary Committee, Courts and Intellectual Property Subcommittee, 105th Cong (1997) (statement of Jack Valenti, President, Motion Picture Industry Association of America). Valenti claimed that around 80% of ISP bandwidth was devoted to P2P traffic.

[27] See, eg, the infamous 'Facebook contagion' paper which showed that Facebook (FB) had modified the newsfeed to certain users to include more or less 'happy' news to see if it could alter the emotional response of users: first exposed outside the scientific press in 'Even Online, Emotions Can be Contagious' (*New Scientist*, 25 June 2014). Notably in this as in other 'social manipulation' cases, no ethical approval or consent was sought either from an advisory board or the users affected.

[28] See the Cambridge Analytica/FB political adverts micro-targeting scandal of 2018 discussed in detail in Chapter 3. It is interesting to wonder if the adverse reaction to the 'right to be forgotten' in data protection law also arose from the realisation it provoked of how access to content could be manipulated online.

[29] U Kohl, 'Google: The rise and Rise of Online Intermediaries in the Governance of the Internet and Beyond (Part 2)' (2013) 21 *International Journal of Law and Information Technology* 187.

[30] See n 28.

Since the promotion of e-commerce and the information society depended on a reliable and expanding Internet infrastructure, an immunity regime was seen as in the public interest. Without it, the ISP industry might be rendered uneconomic. Furthermore, future innovation which brought with it prosperity required a feeling of safety against future liability. This was a particularly effective claim in Europe, which lagged behind the US in the development of the Internet industry, since servers were easily moveable, online commerce was still a fringe activity, and the European ISP industry had largely not yet been absorbed into the concentrated global market of cross-media conglomerations.[31]

Again, this argument has suffered in recent years as it has seemed less and less plausible that US service providers would desert the second biggest global market for online services, and as Europe has developed its own service provider, social media and cloud host industries. On the other hand, sites like Google, Amazon and Facebook still dominate European online activities, and confrontational European legislation has been known to cause industry to pack up its bags and go home. For example, in 2014 the Spanish Government chose to impose a 'link tax' on Google News to protect its local media industry, in response to which Google simply closed Google News to Spanish readers, with apparently negative effects for Spanish publishers.[32] In 2018, with the arrival of the General Data Protection Regulation (GDPR) imposing severe restraints on online behavioural marketing and monetisation of user data, a number of businesses are also aggressively declaring they are no longer open for business from Europeans.[33]

However, if we retrench back to the mid-1990s, this narrative was largely successful. Claims that ISPs should be exempted from liability on the basis of some kind of 'innocent dissemination' defence, a term borrowed from the law of defamation, were heard sympathetically in a world keen to get ahead in the information revolution. Against this plea in Europe, however, was the European Commission's strong interest in ISPs, as the only effective gatekeepers, taking up the role of 'cleaning up the Internet', ie ridding it of pornography, spam, libel and other forms of undesirable content. This was a policy goal not only for the obvious reasons, such as child protection, but also as

---

[31] In the UK, the main broadband providers are now BT, Virgin Media, TalkTalk and Sky providing services to c 95% of subscribers (Ofcom's December 2016 figures). This concentration of Internet access delivery has been used advantageously by UK Government regulators when enrolling ISPs to combat obscene material and P2P file-sharing.

[32] See 'Google News Quits Spain in Response to New Law' (*The Verge*, 11 December 2014) at www.theverge.com/2014/12/11/7375733/google-news-spain-shutdown. The 'link' or 'publishers' tax is back on the agenda of the European Commission at the time of writing; see section VI.C. below. The net effect, quixotically, was that smaller Spanish media publishers suffered due to the loss of traffic driven by Google. Note also the figure from the Commission Communication on Online Platforms, 2016 (n 4) that only 4% of the market capitalisation of the largest platforms is in the EU (p 3) as opposed to the app market where the EU represents 30% of global revenue.

[33] Or, alternately, imposing special paywalls, or providing more limited services. Unroll is a Twitter based business which declared it was out of the EU: see 'Unroll.me to Close to EU Users Saying It Can't Comply with GDPR' (TechCrunch, 6 May 2017), at https://techcrunch.com/2018/05/05/unroll-me-to-close-to-eu-users-saying-it-cant-comply-with-gdpr/. Contrast the 'Premium EU GDPR' service offered by the *Washington Post* as of May 2018, which allows subscribers in the EU access only by buying a subscription to no-tracking no-ads content, for 50% extra, because the *Post* felt it could not otherwise comply with the GDPR. See discussion in 'U.S. News Outlets Block European Readers Over New Privacy Rules' *The New York Times* (25 May 2018) at www.nytimes.com/2018/05/25/business/media/europe-privacy-gdpr-us.html.

part of a general drive to improve public trust and confidence in the Internet as a safe space for economic activity.[34]

By the year 2000 or so, a rough consensus had thus emerged in both Europe and the US that ISPs should in principle be left free from liability for content authored by third parties, *so long as* they were prepared to cooperate when asked to *remove or block access* to identified illegal or infringing content (though the US was sometimes prepared to go even further and declare intermediaries entirely immune from liability). This 'limited liability' paradigm, implemented in Europe in the ECD, and in the US in the DMCA (as regards IP infringing material only) was to prove of incalculable benefit to the ISP, e-commerce and fledgling UGC industries.

We shall examine this solution below, and then ask: how did these immunity regimes work out and what happened next?

III. National and Transnational Regimes for Online Intermediary Liability

A. USA Regimes

In the USA, a combination of historical accident[35] and the desire to preserve free speech and innovation online but, subsequently, domestic pressure to crack down on Internet piracy in music and films, lead to the creation of two quite separate regimes of immunities for intermediary liability, one (in broadbrush[36]) relating to all types of liability except IP and federal crimes, but especially, 'publication torts' such as defamation and false advertising; and the other only in respect of material infringing IP rights, especially copyright. The first regime was s 230(c) of the Communications Decency Act (CDA),[37] which provides total immunity to service providers in respect of all kinds of liability bar that relating to IP,[38] so long as the content in question was provided by a party other than the service provider. Section 230(c)'s breadth was intended not only to preserve freedom of speech from arbitrary censorship by platforms but also, by providing safe harbour to new emergent business models, to promote innovation and growth surrounding UGC. (The secondary stated intention

---

[34] See recently, EU Commission consultation, *A Clean and Open Internet* (n 3).

[35] See discussion of the demise of the Communications Decency Act in L Edwards, 'Pornography, Censorship and the Internet' in Edwards and Waelde, *Law and the Internet*, 3rd edn (n 1) 644–56. The immunity granted service providers for moderating or removing content as 'Good Samaritans' had been intended to mollify the liability they suffered under the CDA as hosts of pornographic material which was accessible by children (including legal adult pornography). However, those parts of the CDA were struck down as unconstitutional restraints on freedom of speech for all (*Reno v ACLU (No1)* 521 US 844 (1997)) leaving the immunity provisions without context. Section 230 (c) thus remains, slightly by accident, as one of the most extensive protections of online intermediaries in Western legal systems.

[36] Section 230 (c) is excluded in relation to Federal criminal law and intellectual property claims.

[37] Technically, Title V of the Telecommunications Act of 1996.

[38] See detailed discussion of the very wide scope of this immunity in M Lemley, 'Rationalising Safe Harbors' (2007) 6 *Journal on Telecommunications and High Technology Law* 101, 102–105.

of Congress, to encourage online platforms to voluntarily develop responsible community standards, has however been less successful.)[39] Section 230 (c) is often regarded
outside the US as unbalanced in protecting platforms at the expense of users or rights-
holders and has been described as a highpoint of utopian 'Internet exceptionalism'[40]

By contrast, the US DMCA, Title 512, gives service providers exemptions from
liability for hosting copyright infringing material only if they follow what has become
known as a 'limited liability' paradigm. It sets out a series of immunities relating to
certain functions of service providers, but only on certain terms, such as the disclosure
of the identity of infringers on request, subscription to a detailed code of practice
relating to notice, 'take-down' and 'put-back', and the banning of identified repeat
infringers from access.[41]

B. EU

In Europe, as we shall see in detail below, a harmonised 'horizontal' regime exists in
the ECD for liability for all kinds of content. This regime has strong similarities to the
DMCA, thus establishing limited liability and notice and take-down as the dominant
global paradigms for online intermediary liability.

C. UK

In the UK, pornography and defamation were the early drivers for the local development of intermediary law and policy. From 1995 on, the UK police began a series
of investigations into distribution of pornography via the Internet which lead to the
delivery of an ultimatum to the then ISP/hosting industry: self-regulate or face prosecution.[42] This in its turn led to the creation of an industry self-or co-regulatory body,
the Internet Watch Foundation (IWF) which runs a blacklist of sites known to host
CAM. This blacklist has proved both successful at restraining the hosting of such
material by UK hosts, as well as constraining delivery from foreign sites into the UK,
albeit with some controversy as to its impact on due process and freedom of speech,
and has become something of a global model.[43]

---

[39] See discussion in J Kosseff, 'Twenty Years of Intermediary Immunity: The US Experience' (2017)
14 *SCRIPT-ed* at https://script-ed.org/article/twenty-years-of-intermediary-immunity-the-us-experience/.
See also the excellent volume of papers edited by Eric Goldman and Jeff Kosseff on the 20th anniversary of *Zeran v AOL* 129 F3d 327, cert denied, 524 US 937 and available at law.com (20 November 2017):
'Commemorating the 20th Anniversary of Internet Law's Most Important Judicial Decision' at www.law.
com/therecorder/sites/therecorder/2017/11/10/commemorating-the-20th-anniversary-of-internet-laws-
most-important-judicial-decision/.

[40] See E Goldman, 'The Third Wave of Internet Exceptionalism' (11 March 2009) at https://
blog.ericgoldman.org/archives/2009/03/the_third_wave.htm.

[41] See section III.A.

[42] See discussion in Y Akdeniz, 'The Regulation of Pornography and Child Pornography on the Internet'
(1997) (1) *Journal of Information Law and Technology* at https://warwick.ac.uk/fac/soc/law/elj/jilt/1997_1/
akdeniz1/.

[43] See the next chapter; and earlier discussion in L Edwards, 'Pornography, Censorship and the Internet' in
Edwards and Waelde, *Law and the Internet*, 3rd edn (n 1) at 651ff.

Meanwhile the 1999 case of *Godfrey v Demon Internet*[44] raised for the first time the issues of what the liability of ISPs might be in relation to publication of defamatory material provided by users. A later case, *Bunt v Tilley*, provided guidance on how both the Defamation Act 1996 and the ECD Regulations[45] applied to internet access providers. Few major cases have since been heard in the English or Scottish courts, perhaps because the basic paradigm of NTD quickly became universally known as how to avoid hoisting liability, but a number of interesting decisions against Facebook have come out of Northern Ireland, seeking action by Facebook to remove material such as the identifying details of alleged paedophiles.[46]

A few interesting English cases specific to defamation have involved Google in different roles. In the first UK case on *search engine* liability, *Metropolitan International Schools Ltd v Designtechnica Corporation*,[47] the Court held that Google (as search engine), could not be considered a publisher at English law, as the search was performed entirely automatically, without any human interference.[48] However, Eady J also held that, if he *had* found Google to be a publisher, it would not have been able to rely on s 1 of the Defamation Act 1996's defences on innocent dissemination, because Google 'is not in a position to "take down" the offending words in the way that Demon Internet could have done'.[49] According to Eady J, the hosting provisions of the ECD Regulations 2002 would not be applicable in this case either. The judge referred to the UK Government's refusal to include search engines within the scope of this protection, and concluded that for Google 'to be classified as or deemed a "host", statutory intervention would be needed'.[50]

In *Tamiz v Google*, the Court of Appeal[51] finally resolved uncertainty as to whether Google was a publisher in its capacity as the *host* of user generated content, rather than as a search engine, after skirmishes at High Court level. In *Tamiz*, the plaintiff, a local politician, sued Google for defamation in respect of eight anonymous comments posted on 'London Muslim' blog (hosted by Google's hosting service, Blogger) in late April 2011 (c 28–30 April). Tamiz notified Google of these comments straightaway and asked for their removal. Google, as was its policy, attempted to broker a resolution on this between the blog owner and the complainant rather than intervening itself to take down. In the end, on 14 August, the blog owner removed the blog post and its comments. Thus around three and a half months elapsed before the comments were removed.

Prior to *Tamiz*, in *Davison v Habeeb*,[52] the High Court had held that Google was a common law publisher (although, on the facts, exculpated from liability by the defences in the ECD, discussed below in section IV.C.). HHJ Parkes QC drew an

---

[44] *Godfrey v Demon Internet* [1999] 4 All ER 342.
[45] See, eg, *Bunt v Tilley* [2006] EWHC 407 (QB). The ECD was implemented in the UK in the Electronic Commerce (EC Directive) Regulations SI 2002/No 2013.
[46] See *CG v Facebook Ireland Ltd* [2015] NIQB 11.
[47] *Metropolitan International Schools Ltd v Designtechnica Corporation* [2009] EWHC 1765 (QB).
[48] *Ibid* [50]–[52]. Note that in light of the later Court of Appeal case of *Tamiz* (n 51)) this conclusion may be seen as vulnerable.
[49] *Ibid* [79].
[50] *Ibid* [112].
[51] *Tamiz v Google* [2013] EWCA Civ 68.
[52] *Davison v Habeeb* [2011] EWHC 3031 (QB).

analogy comparing the Google Blogger site to a gigantic notice board on which others could post comments.[53] Google had control over the noticeboard, and appeared to assume a degree of responsibility for what was published, given its ability to remove offending matter in accordance with its own content policy. It could thus not be simply considered a passive provider.

By contrast in *Tamiz v Google* at first instance,[54] Eady J took an opposite approach. Noting that the Blogger.com platform contained more than half a trillion words, with 250,000 new words added every minute, he held that accepting the responsibility to notify the offending bloggers did not necessarily change Google's status from neutral to publisher, nor did the technical ability to remove content. 'In these circumstances, it is virtually impossible for the corporation to exercise editorial control over content.' He adopted briefly a competing metaphor: rather than owning a notice board under its control, Google 'owned a wall on which various people had chosen to inscribe graffiti. It does not regard itself as being more responsible for the content of these graffiti than would the owner of such a wall'.[55] Google's role was 'purely passive' and thus it was not a common law publisher, whether it had been notified of a complainant's objection or not.

This was quite a remarkable decision which would have given Google (and presumably, similar giant platforms hosting a huge amount of UGC) a complete immunity as publishers of libellous material. The Court of Appeal struck a compromise. Google *could* indeed be considered a common law publisher. However – and it is a big however – per *Byrne v Deane*,[56] liability as a publisher could only be possible *after* Google had received notification that defamatory comments were posted to its 'notice board'. Thus on the facts of *Tamiz*, Google had only been a publisher for a short while, and the comments in question had by the time of notification been submerged by later additions. Thus it was held that the likely damage was minimal and the action was dismissed.

The *Tamiz* wars,[57] though something of a footnote to the pan-European regime of the ECD and relevant only, or mainly, to libel cases, are fascinating for the way they clearly replay parts of the policy wars which were summarised in the last section. Eady J especially reprises the claim so common in the early 2000s that the volume of material hosted by Google was too great to practically police, with a strong smidgeon of respect apparent for the economic and social utility of having Google active in the UK.

Finally, the Defamation Act 2013, s 5 (applicable in England and Wales only) now gives a special defence to website operators in relation to defamatory content posted by others on their website. The aim is to strike a balance between providing websites,

---

[53] Analogy drawn from the pre Internet case of *Byrne v Deane* [1937] 1 KB 818, involving a noticeboard at a golf club open to members to post messages on.

[54] *Tamiz v Google* [2012] EWHC 449 (QB).

[55] *Ibid* [10] and [38].

[56] *Byrne v Deane* (n 53); see *Tamiz* (n 51) at [42]: 'Notification is plainly of cardinal importance'.

[57] Mr Tamiz made a final stab at a remedy by taking his case to the European Court of Human Rights (*Tamiz v UK*, Application No 3877/14, 12 October 2017) claiming infringement of his Art 8 right to private life. His application was declared inadmissible on the grounds that the national legal process had struck an acceptable balance between protection of reputation (Art 8) and freedom of expression (Art 8), especially given the applicant was a budding politician.

especially online newspapers, with a way to allow comments on their sites, in the interests of freedom of speech, without feeling unduly at risk – while still allowing due protection to victims of libellous comments.

The intention therefore was that those who claimed to be victims of defamation should primarily sue the commenter, not the website. Accordingly, the website is exculpated if it can show that it was a third party who posted the statement on the website. This defence can be defeated however if the claimant shows that it was not possible for them to identify the person posting the statement, the claimant notified the operator regarding that statement and the operator did not respond in accordance with The Defamation (Operators of Websites) Regulations.[58] As a result, s 5 has effectively led to the closing of many websites to anonymous comments – which is arguably a diminution of freedom of speech!

IV. The European E-Commerce Directive Regime

A. ISSPs – definition

Articles 12–15 of the EC E-Commerce Directive[59] (ECD) introduced throughout Europe a harmonised regime on the liability of online intermediaries. The regime affects not 'ISPs' but 'ISSPs', ie 'information society services providers'[60] or, as the title of Section 4 of the ECD also calls them, 'intermediary service providers'. An 'information society service' is defined[61] as 'any service normally provided for remuneration, at a distance, by means of electronic equipment for the processing (including digital compression) and storage of data, and at the individual request of a recipient of a service'. 'Recipient of a service' is defined[62] as 'any natural or legal person who … uses an information society service …'.

Thus, broadly, the ECD liability regime covers not only the traditional ISP sector, but also a much wider range of actors who are involved in selling goods or services online, offering online information, providing search tools, etc. However the requirement that an information society service be offered 'at the individual request of the recipient' means that TV and radio broadcasters do not fall within the remit of the ECD liability regime, although sites which offer individually on-demand services such as video-on-demand or email are included. In particular spammers and other 'providers of commercial communications'[63] are included as providers of information society services.

---

[58] SI 2013/No 3028. Note this defence is *in addition* to the immunities offered by the ECD as incorporated into UK law.

[59] 2000/31/EC, passed 8 June 2000. The ECD was implemented in the UK via the Electronic Commerce (EC Directive) Regulation 2002 (SI 2002/2013) (hereafter the 'UK ECD Regs') largely taken verbatim from the European English text.

[60] ECD, Art 2(b). These providers can be natural or juristic persons.

[61] *Ibid*, Art 2(a) refers back to the definition in Art 1(2) of Directive 98/34/EC as amended by Directive 98/48/EC. The definition is discussed further in Recitals 17 and 18 of the ECD.

[62] *Ibid*, Art 2(d).

[63] See further *Ibid*, Recital 18.

Importantly, Recital 18 of the ECD notes explicitly that although a service may be free to the recipient, this does not mean the provider of that service need fall outside the scope of the ECD if the service broadly forms part of an 'economic activity'. Given that one of the dominant successful models of e-business is to give away a major product or service but then make money out of it in lateral ways, this issue has still caused some debate.[64]

The matter was partly resolved by the CJEU in *Papasavvas v O Fileftheros Dimosia Etairia and Others*[65] in which the plaintiff in the Cypriot courts sought damages for libellous remarks both against a Cypriot newspaper and two websites the newspaper maintained where the same content was provided free of charge but with income generated by ads posted on that site. On reference to the CJEU, that Court held without hesitation that the concept of 'information society services' included such free websites.[66] In *McFadden v Sony*,[67] a shop offered free wireless internet access to its customers as part of its general business, but did not charge *or* monetise it via external placed advertising. The WiFi was used by a customer to download a music file without permission and thus infringe copyright. The first question was whether the WiFi operator (McFadden) qualified as an ISSP to take advantage of the 'mere conduit' immunity in Art 12. The CJEU held, as per Recital 18, that despite the lack of any explicit revenue model, it nonetheless formed part of an 'economic activity', in this case as ancillary advertising for the shop owner's own general business.

But these two cases do not solve all problems. What about e-government sites, which provide a service and do not normally charge, or act as advertising, in either online or offline form? Do they form part of an 'economic activity'? What about non-profit sites such as Wikipedia or Wikileaks, which do not charge or monetise user data but do ask for donations from users? Since the EU broadly only regulated economic activities at the time the ECD was passed, the exclusion of non-commercial sites is deliberate; but in terms of social benefit and freedom of speech, these may be the kind of sites that most need immunities.

The ECD also excludes certain activities from its remit,[68] including taxation, competition law, the activities of notaries and gambling. Some activities are further excluded by Recital 18 as not provided wholly 'at a distance': eg a doctor is not a provider of such a service even if he bills his private clients and sends them their prescriptions by email, so long as his advice even partially requires the 'physical examination of a patient'.

The most controversial classification problems have arisen recently in the context of the so-called 'sharing' or 'gig' economy. In two recent cases,[69] the CJEU has held

---

[64] See, in the UK, obiter discussion in *Bunt v Tilley* (n 45) [43]–[45] and in *Metropolitan International Schools* (n 47).

[65] Case C-291/13 *Papasavvas v O Fileftheros Dimosia Etairia and Others* (CJEU, 27 March 2013).

[66] *Ibid* [45]. However, there was a sting in the tail: since the newspaper had posted its own libellous content to those sites, it could not possibly have known about their content: it had 'in principle, knowledge about the information which it posts and exercises control over that information'. Accordingly the immunities granted by Art 14 did not apply to immunise the websites.

[67] Case C-484/14 *McFadden v Sony* (CJEU, 15 September 2016).

[68] See Art 1(5). See also n 7 on the apparent exclusion by the ECD of immunity for liability arising from data protection. This was implicitly upheld in Case C-131/12 *Google Spain v Costeja* (13 May 2014) where the CJEU found that (a) Google as a search engine was a data controller under DP law and (b) this meant it was liable to comply with DP law.

[69] Case C-320/16 *Uber France v Bensalem* (CJEU, 10 April 2018) where Case C-434/15 *Asociacion Profesional Elite Taxi v Uber Systems Spain, SL* (CJEU, 20 December 2017) ('*Uber Spain*') was followed: see [22].

that Uber, the popular ride-sharing or taxi-hire app, is not an ISSP for the purposes of the ECD. In *Uber Spain*,[70] the CJEU found, on the evidence, that the 'intermediation service' Uber provided also exercised a 'decisive influence' over the selection of the drivers, the conditions under which that service is provided by those drivers, the maximum fare and the division of the fare between driver and Uber, as well as 'a certain control over the quality of the vehicles, the drivers and their conduct, which can, in some circumstances, result in their exclusion'.[71] All this led the Court to determine that, although Uber did offer an information society service at a distance by electronic means, it formed an 'integral part of an overall service whose main component is a transport service'. Accordingly, it had to be classified not as 'an information society service' but as a conventional service subject to regulation by the Member State.[72]

This leaves wide open the issue of how the very many *other* services should be classified, which include elements of both digital service and 'real world' delivery: for example, hotel booking apps like Booking.com, plane travel apps like Kayak, online sales of physical goods as supplied by Amazon, etc. The AG Opinion, but not the Court, devoted some thought to this,[73] arguing that the answer turned on whether the two elements were 'economically independent' of each other. If they were, it was then necessary to identify the *main* component of the supply envisaged, ie the component which gave it meaning in economic terms. For a service to be classified as an information society service, this main component had to be performed by electronic means. So for a site like Amazon, the main elements of the service – contract formation, and payment – are usually done online and so Amazon is an ISSP.[74] For Uber, on the other hand, as the subsequent judgment upheld, the main elements related to the real-world transportation service, not the electronic service. This case by case approach – as opposed to, say, a bright line that the overriding question is who owns the 'key assets' (taxis, in the case of Uber[75]) – looks likely to provoke further litigation.

B. Division of Immunities by Function

The ECD takes a horizontal approach to ISSP liability – in other words it deals with all kinds of content issues, whether intellectual property, criminal obscenity, libel, et al – rather than focusing on a single area, as the US DMCA does with copyright. Furthermore, rather than giving a blanket immunity to ISSPs in all circumstances, as the US CDA s 230(c) does, it takes a more subtle approach in which the various functions of intermediaries are addressed separately.

---

[70] *Uber Spain, ibid.*

[71] *Uber Spain, ibid* [39].

[72] The political background to this is the struggle by taxi drivers in Barcelona and many other global cities to insist that Uber be regulated like ordinary taxi services, ie subject to licensing, vetting, etc as opposed to operating in a regulatory vacuum. This commercial battle has also been positioned as a fight to avoid a degradation of consumer protection after reports of unvetted Uber drivers assaulting passengers. See also the London decision to withdraw Uber's license to offer taxi services: see Transport for London, 'Licensing Decision on Uber London Limited' (22 September 2017) at https://tfl.gov.uk/info-for/media/press-releases/2017/september/licensing-decision-on-uber-london-limited.

[73] Case C-434/15, Opinion of AG Szpunar (CJEU, 11 May 2017) [29]–[36].

[74] See C-108/09 *Ker-Optika* (CJEU, 2 December 2010) (online sale of contact lenses fell within E-Commerce Directive).

[75] Compare approach taken by European Commission Communication, *A European Agenda for the Collaborative Economy*, COM (2016) 356 final.

Where ISSPs act as a *'mere conduit'* – ie, solely transmitting content originated by and destined for other parties – the ECD, in the form of Art 12, regards them as basically absolved from all liability. To maintain immunity, the ISP must not initiate the transmission, select the receiver of the transmission or modify the information contained in the transmission.[76] This is very much in line with the common law position in England developed for neutral carriers such as the post office and the phone company.[77]

In *McFadden*,[78] having confirmed that a free provider of WiFi qualified as an Art 12 mere conduit, the CJEU went on nonetheless to consider what injunction to prevent copyright infringement might be ordered against such an intermediary. (As discussed below, even where an immunity operates, an injunction to prevent infringing activity can still be made, in this case under Art 12(3).) After considering the options of banning WiFi access or constant monitoring of all traffic exchanged via such a hotspot, the CJEU held the most proportionate option was to require the operator to implement password protection. The decision has been criticised for possibly jeopardising access to public WiFi without ceding privacy rights.

Where ISPs *cache* material, they will not be liable for it subject to the same conditions as in Art 12 above.[79] Caching is a ubiquitous technical process whereby local copies of remote web pages are made by hosts in order to speed up delivery of those pages on subsequent request. It was initially uncertain if such activity would be construed as making unauthorised copies of copyright work. This has mainly been resolved by the InfoSoc Directive though some clashes between it and the ECD may remain.[80] Since the effect of caching is to speed up the Web for all users and reduce transmission costs for access providers, it is important that caching not be legally discouraged. As with the 'mere conduit' provision, immunity is subject to the requirement the information not be modified by the ISSP, and also that the cached copy be updated regularly according to industry practice. Immunity is also subject to the ISSP taking down cached copies once they obtain actual knowledge that the original source of the information has been removed or access to it disabled, or removal or blocking of access has been ordered by a competent court or authority.[81]

---

[76] ECD, Art 12. Transmission includes automatic, intermediate and transient storage. Presumably 'information' excludes header information which ISPs routinely and automatically add to through traffic they forward. Such header information is vital to the routing of packets through the Internet to their destination, but does not form part of the message information actually read by the recipient.

[77] This was confirmed in *Bunt v Tilley* (n 45) [37ff], where the Court held there was no binding authority at common law which deemed a 'passive mode of communication' such as an ISP acting as 'mere conduit' a publisher at common law for defamation purposes.

[78] *McFadden* (n 67).

[79] ECD, Art 13 actually refers in full to 'automatic, intermediate and temporary storage of that information, performed for the sole purpose of making more efficient the information's onward transmission to other recipients of that service'.

[80] See in Europe, EC Copyright Directive 2001/29/EC of the European Parliament and the Council of 22 May 2001, Art 5(1) which includes as an exemption from the exclusive right of reproduction of the author, 'temporary acts of reproduction which are transient or incidental and part of a technological process whose sole purpose is to enable (a) a transmission in a network between third parties by an intermediary and (b) a lawful use of a work or other protected material).

[81] See further discussion on NTD in relation to Art 14 below. Immunity for caching is most obviously relevant to content copied by an ISP *prima facie* in breach of copyright. However it is conceivable that a

An issue left out of the ECD is the question of *linking liability*. This is a particularly crucial matter to consider for search engine sites, which as their *raison d'etre* create automated links to material provided by third parties. 'Hosting' as dealt with in Article 14 requires storage, undefined in either the ECD or the UK Regulations, which seems to imply that merely making a hyper-link to content cannot constitute 'hosting' – therefore Art 14 immunities (see below) should not apply. The US DMCA by contrast expressly grants immunity[82] under certain conditions where a link is made to infringing material.

Although the Commission was specifically instructed to investigate linking liability on an ongoing basis by Article 21(2) of the ECD, so far, only a few EU states have chosen to create special linking immunities, creating an unhelpful cross-Europe disharmony.[83] Linking is of ever greater significance as the Internet becomes manageable only via search engines. Since the drafting of the ECD, aggregators have also become important online intermediaries – eg news aggregators like Google News, or price comparison engines for utilities like gas or water, or consumer services such as airline fares or hotel rooms. What all such aggregators are doing is in essence making links to a wide variety of 'upstream' content where they may or may not have technical control to remove individual items, depending on how the software is implemented. Aggregator sites, alongside search engines, are generally seen as a public good in terms of promoting access to knowledge, information management, consumer choice and competition.[84] It would seem logical therefore, both for reduction of business risk, harmonisation within Europe and harmony with the US DMCA scheme, to incorporate immunity from linking liability into the ECD intermediary scheme – however this now seems unlikely given the reluctance to move to a full scale overhaul of the ECD (see below).

C. Hosting

The main controversy in the EU regime has centred on the hosting provisions in Art 14, which deals with circumstances where ISSPs host or store more than transient content originated by third parties. Under Article 14(1)(a), ISSPs are exempt from criminal liability in respect of the 'storage' of information provided by a recipient of their services, so long as they have no 'actual knowledge' of 'illegal activity or information'; and are immune from civil liability as long as they have no such actual knowledge *and* are not aware of 'facts and circumstances from which the illegal activity or information is apparent'. Art 14(1)(b) provides however that if such knowledge or

cached copy of a page containing libellous or obscene material might be deemed to be 'published' by an ISP or host since it can still be retrieved by other subscribers to that ISP seeking that particular page until the cache is purged.

[82] Information Location Tools, s 512 (d).

[83] See *Consultation Document on the Electronic Commerce Directive: The Liability of Hyperlinkers, Location Tool Services and Content Aggregators – Government Response and Summary of Responses* (DTI, December 2006). The UK chose not to pursue a separate exemption for linkers and aggregators.

[84] The 'important role' played by search engines is specifically acknowledged in *Google Spain* (n 68) [50] (see full discussion in Chapter 4).

awareness is acquired, then liability is still avoided if the provider acts 'expeditiously' to remove or disable access to the information. This creates the standard paradigm where most platforms put in place a team whose job it is to take down on notice so as to avoid any potential liability.[85]

Art 15 provides furthermore that EC Member States are not to impose any general monitoring requirement on ISSPs, especially 'a general obligation actively to seek facts or circumstances indicating illegality' and this was generally taken when the ECD was passed to mean that ISSPs could not be instructed to proactively look for and filter out illegal content on an ongoing basis, since this would drive a coach and horses through the NTD paradigm. Recital 48 provides however that it is still possible for states to require ISSPs 'to apply duties of care which can reasonably be expected from them and which are specified by national law, in order to detect and prevent certain types of illegal activities'. Importantly also, regardless of Art 14 immunity from liability, ECD Art 14(2) still allows national courts to issue injunctions to terminate or prevent an infringement, 'nor does it affect the possibility for member states of establishing procedures governing the removal or disabling of access to information'. As we shall see below, these provisions set up a battlefield over intermediary immunities between IP rights-holders, governments and online platforms as to how far intermediaries can be 'enrolled' to protect commercial rights and prevent societal harms.

V. Problems with the ECD Hosting Immunity Regime

A. 'Expeditious' Take Down

Article 14(1)(b) provides that so long as an ISSP 'acts expeditiously to remove or to disable access to the information' they host, immunity is retained, even after notice. No guidance is given in the Directive as to what 'expeditious' means, however, and whether it allows enough time to, eg, check facts, consult an in-house lawyer, find an external lawyer or request counsel's opinion. In the UK *Mumsnet* case,[86] for example, the defendants, who moderated an online child care forum, were forced to settle even though they might well have had arguable defences to the claim of defamation,

---

[85] It is worth noting however the unfortunate and still partly unresolved conflict set up between the ECD and European Court of Human Rights (ECtHR) jurisprudence on platform liability, in the heavily criticised *Delfi v Estonia* ECtHR, 2015, 64669/09. In this case the Strasbourg Court held an Estonian court was *not* in breach of Art 8 (freedom of expression) in holding a website liable for the defamatory comments of its readers – even though many felt the Estonian Court itself was in breach of the ECD. The 'Delfi mess' (see G Smith, 'Who Will Sort Out the Delfi Mess?' (Cyberleagle, 16 October 2013) at www.cyberleagle.com/2013/10/who-will-sort-out-delfi-mess.html) was not fixed by an appeal to the Grand Chamber on 16 June 2015, but was to some extent glossed by the ECtHR in its subsequent decision in *MTE v Hungary*, 22947/13, 2 February 2016, where the Court confirmed that *Delfi* was restricted to hate speech comments. Most recently, in *Pihl v Sweden*, 9 March 2017, the ECtHR agreed that the Swedish courts had *not* been in breach of the Art 8 private life rights of a user by *failing* to find a website where defamatory comments had been left liable for them, ie by complying with the ECD. However again it is possible the *Pihl* decision is restricted only to 'small and non-profit' websites.

[86] See OUT-Law News, 11 May 2007, at www.out-law.com/page-8040.

apparently because they were uncertain if even removal of comments within 24 hours constituted 'expeditious' removal. The UK implementation of the ECD gives no further guidance than the Directive, although the specialised Electronic Commerce Directive (Terrorism Act 2006) Regulations 2007, which provide specific immunities for ISPs from offences under the Terrorism Act 2006, do prescribe that take down must take place within two days.[87]

However, an increasing trend is towards imposition of hard time limits to meet social goals, notably in the area of hate speech, including racist and anti-semitic speech. Notoriously, in 2017, the German *Netzwerkdurchsetzungsgesetz* (NetzDG) law demanded that platforms with more than 2 million users (aimed, obviously, at Facebook, Instagram, et al) removed 'obviously illegal' hate speech posts within 24 hours or be fined up to 50 million Euros.[88] Germany's law can be understood in a historical context of zero tolerance of post-Holocaust racism but more worrying is the current favourable uptake and widening of scope of this approach by the European Commission, whose *Code of Conduct on Countering Illegal Hate Speech Online*[89] was issued in May 2016 and agreed with four major IT companies, Facebook, Twitter, YouTube and Microsoft. The Code set a target for the removal of notified hate speech within 24 hours.

In June 2017, the Commission reported that some progress had been made on this target, but not enough: an increase in removals of content on take down was reported from 28 per cent to 59 per cent over a six month period, but with important variations across platforms; furthermore 28 per cent of removals still only took place after a week or more. It then issued, in September 2017,[90] a set of proposals for voluntary action by social media platforms in relation to the removal of 'illegal content inciting hatred, violence and terrorism online'. These included the requirement that illegal content be removed as fast as possible, with the strong implication that regulation along the German model would follow if better progress was not made.

Most recently, in March 2018, the Commission issued a series of 'operational procedures'.[91] These included, radically, the demand that all companies should remove 'terrorist' content within one hour from its referral as a general rule. The need for progress on targets for general hate speech was reiterated, with the statistic emphasised that 'in more than 80% of these cases, the removals [of hate speech] took place within 24 hours'.[92] This hard line attitude to the removal of illegal content within 24, or even sometimes 1 or 2 hours has been picked up on in the UK, where government ministers have made a series of speeches through 2017 and 2018 threatening regulatory action

---

[87] Article 14, furthermore, seems to imply that once notice has been given and the expedient period of grace expired, liability is strict even if take down presents technical or administrative problems. A better alternative might be, as the German Multimedia Act provides, for liability to arise only after the ISSP has failed to take some kind of 'reasonable steps'.

[88] See 'Verboten: Germany's Risky Law for Stopping Hate Speech on Facebook and Twitter' (*New Republic*, 3 April 2018) at https://newrepublic.com/article/147364/verboten-germany-law-stopping-hate-speech-facebook-twitter.

[89] *Commission Recommendation of 1 March 2018 on Measures to Effectively Tackle Illegal Content Online* Brussels, 1.3.2018 C(2018) 1177 final.

[90] European Commission Communication, *Tackling Illegal Content Online – Towards an Enhanced Responsibility of Online Platforms* Brussels, 28.9.2017 COM(2017) 555 final.

[91] See http://europa.eu/rapid/press-release_IP-18-1169_en.htm.

[92] See press release at http://ec.europa.eu/newsroom/just/item-detail.cfm?item_id=54300.

against social media sites, both in relation to terrorist and hate speech content, and more worryingly, 'fake news' (discussed below).[93]

These developments look good to a public (and electorate) horrified by the rise and ease of access to racism and xenophobia online, especially in easily digestable forms such as professionally edited IS videos promoting radicalisation. However, they also show a number of worrying trends. First, there is an emphasis, to enable speed, on automated take down via algorithmic systems, which, as discussed both below, and earlier in this volume in Chapters 4 and 5, show worrying tendencies towards high rates of error, discrimination and bias and are often opaque and difficult to audit or challenge. Artificial intelligence (AI) is not the 'magic bullet' here: it may even make a bad situation worse. Second, enforcement is being pushed on to the private sector, largely in the form of the traditional scapegoats, the large US social media platforms, and away from local governance and community enforcement where local cultural concerns might be better implemented. Third, the combination of private platform governance and automated management of take downs leads inevitably (as has been empirically shown in the case of copyright take downs, see below) to a failure to consider defences or mitigations in respect of the content – most notably, whether freedom of speech, or religion and perhaps of political discussion and assembly are being bulldozed in the rush to meet removal targets and avoid regulation or fines. Fourth, these rules (or 'suggestions') are established in the vacuum of an EU wide definition of terms like 'hate speech' or 'terrorist material' as these are subject to local definitions. This may very strongly affect the harmonisation, efficacy and justice of resulting action.

The hate speech experience also illustrates that we are seeing a sudden and very definite trend towards fragmentation of the cohesive intermediary immunity regime the ECD tried to establish in 2000.[94] This may be inevitable when dealing with emotive topics like hate speech and fake news, but it also has downsides for one of the key underlying goals of the ECD: to promote innovation and competition across a Single Market by reducing risk and increasing predictability for service providers.

B. Notice and Take Down: Due Process and Free Speech Concerns and the Rise of Automation

The ECD in its current form rests, as we have discussed, principally on a 'notice and take down' paradigm. This has the advantage of cutting down the risk exposure of platforms handling large volumes of material to a (more) manageable level. But it also exerts a potential chilling effect on freedom of speech. This dichotomy has exercised critics since the early 2000s, especially in the US in relation to the DMCA.

NTD has so far only been explored to a very limited extent in UK case law, the first reported case being *Godfrey v Demon Internet*.[95] The case involved allegations by a British physicist, Lawrence Godfrey, that an anonymous hoax message posted

---

[93] See, eg, 'Tech Firms Must Remove Extremist Content within Two Hours' (Politico.eu, 19 September 2017) at www.politico.eu/article/theresa-may-tech-firms-must-remove-extremist-content-within-two-hours/.
[94] See, insightfully, an early paper by D MacSithigh on this: 'The Fragmentation of Intermediary Liability in the UK' (2013) 8 *Journal of Intellectual Property Law and Practice* 521.
[95] *Godfrey v Demon Internet* (n 44).

in a newsgroup in 1997 was libellous. Godfrey asked the ISP Demon, who carried the newsgroup in question, to remove the offensive posting. When Demon did not comply, Godfrey sued it for libel as the publisher. Demon plead s 1 of the Defamation Act 1996, which provided that an ISP was not liable if it 'did not know and had no reason to believe what [it] did contributed to the publication of a defamatory statement'.[96] Because Demon *had* been notified and not removed it, the judge held it clearly could not take advantage of the s 1 defence, and Demon subsequently settled the case.

An issue which has haunted ISPs ever since the US case of *Prodigy*)[97] is whether taking proactive steps to moderate content rather than merely responding to notices – and therefore potentially becoming generally aware of illegality – means that the site may come under the second leg of Art 14 ('constructive' knowledge). This has been said to discourage intervention and encourage a 'head in sand' approach. The Commission has recently promised in its 2017 Communication on Illegal Content (see discussion above) that guidelines would clarify that such 'Good Samaritan' action would not attract liability.

One problem with the ECD is that, as a Directive designed to be transposed differently across the Member States, the rules for take down are very vague, with no firm requirements on key matters such as identification of the person requesting take down, right (where relevant, as in IP) to request take down, format of take down, notification to original author or publisher of content, etc. In reality however many Member States, including the UK, simply transposed the ECD with little annotation. The E-Commerce Regulations, reg 22, do specify that for 'actual knowledge' a number of factors may be taken into account, such as the name and address of the notifier, the location of the offending content (if the ISSP cannot find the content, how can they remove it?), and details of the illegality.[98]

By contrast, the US DMCA, designed for one country and one set of rights (copyright) can be much more definite, and has strict rules that the person demanding take down must properly identify themselves as the relevant rights-holder (using digital signature identification if requesting take down by email). It also specifies details enabling offending content to be easily located: both of these discourage spurious complaints and over-broad or unauthorised take down. Indeed, a knowingly false request for take down under the DMCA is perjury[99] and can be subject to damages for consequential loss.

The DMCA builds in a number of further due process safeguards against ill-founded or deceptive take down requests. When a take down request is sent a notification must be supplied to the original provider. If they then resist the take down via a 'put back' counter-notice, the matter can be moved to dispute resolution in court, with, hopefully,

---

[96] Defamation Act 1996, s 1(1)(c).

[97] See *Prodigy* (n 2).

[98] More such details can also be found in relation to defamation take downs in the Defamation Act 2013, s 5(6).

[99] DMCA, s 512(g)(i). See summary from US Copyright Office at https://www.copyright.gov/legislation/dmca.pdf. The most famous win here involved the 'dancing baby' case, *Lenz v Universal Music Corp*, 137 S Ct 2263, where the Ninth Circuit held that, given fair use considerations, a take down notice was wrongfully sent relating to a 29 second clip of a Prince song used as the background to a video of the plaintiff's baby dancing to the song. Leave to take the case to the Supreme Court was however refused.

full opportunity for due process and fairness considerations. During this process, the service provider is protected if it keeps the content up. This 'put back' procedure in principle sounds like a huge advance on the ECD which provides few remedies against knee-jerk take down. In practice however, put back has been little used and even then, largely ineffective. Urban et al reported that it was a 'dead letter – impractical and rarely used'[100], mainly because of user ignorance of their rights; their fear of ignoring typically threatening cease and desist letters; and the lack of time to make a counter-notice given automated immediate take down.

But the biggest problems relating to NTD revolve around 'chilling effects', which have been proven empirically in a number of classic studies. In research carried out at Oxford known as the 'Mystery Shopper' test,[101] a major UK ISP was asked to take down a web page alleged to be copyright infringing. In fact the web page contained an extract from Mill's 'On Liberty', published in 1869 and long in the public domain. Nonetheless the web page was removed without demur.[102] More robust empirical studies have followed since. Urban and Quilter[103] (subsequently, Urban, Karaganis and Schofield[104]) in a series of projects have analysed, over time, all the take down notices received by the search engine Google, which have been voluntarily posted on the Chilling Effects website (now known as Lumen).[105] Their 2016 report draws some fascinating conclusions about the complex ecology which has emerged around take down. They identified three types of take downs:

1. 'DMCA Classic': take downs received by small sites or platforms for which the volume of notices has remained relatively infrequent and substantial human review of notices is still the norm. These remained the majority of respondents.
2. 'DMCA Auto': take downs received by sites which receive very large numbers of notices generated by automated systems, and have experienced a steep increase in volume in each of the past several years. These sites have shifted to more automated notice-processing practices.
3. 'DMCA Plus': take downs received by sites which have adopted procedures that go beyond measures required by the DMCA s 512, including filtering systems, direct take down procedures for trusted rights-holders, hash-matching based 'stay-down' systems, and contractual agreements with certain rights-holders that set forth additional protections and obligations for both parties. A considerable overlap was observed between Auto and Plus categories.

[100] JM Urban, J Karaganis and BL Schofield, *Notice and Takedown in Everyday Practice* (BerkeleyLaw, 2016) 44.
[101] See C Ahlert, C Marsden and C Yung, 'How Liberty Disappeared from Cyberspace: The Mystery Shopper Tests Internet Content Self-Regulation' ('Mystery Shopper') at http://pcmlp.socleg.ox.ac.uk/wp-content/uploads/2014/12/liberty.pdf.
[102] Similar results were found in a Dutch experiment carried out shortly after by Sjoera Nas at Bits of Freedom, in the Netherlands.
[103] J Urban and L Quilter, 'Efficient Process or "Chilling Effects"? Takedown Notices under Section 512 of the Digital Millennium Copyright Act' (2006) *Santa Clara Computer and High Technology Law Journal* 22.
[104] Urban et al (n 100).
[105] See www.lumendatabase.org. Lumen, formerly Chilling Effects, is a collaborative archive created by Wendy Seltzer and founded along with several law school clinics and the Electronic Frontier Foundation. The site hosts take down notices voluntarily submitted by private parties and participating ISPs and sites such as Google.

These classifications crystallise significant and observable, but previously anecdotal, trends. Much of the discussion about NTD, prior to 2010, revolved around the issue of 'privatised justice'[106] and though conscious that companies were not likely to make decisions in a style akin to a court, still relied on the expectation that humans would review take down requests. Although this might be done by abuse teams or content moderators with little time or legal training, working globally rather than with respect for local laws, and possibly with conflicting commercial motivations (such as risk avoidance, PR or target-hitting), a space still existed to consider matters such as legal defences (eg journalistic privilege, fair dealing in copyright), the truth of, or the rigour of evidence backing, the complaint, and most importantly, freedom of expression. But increasingly, this is no longer true and instead content moderation is increasingly carried out by automated algorithmic systems, sometimes known as 'bots'.

The canonical case here is Google, which receive not thousands but millions of (usually) automated requests to take down allegedly copyright infringing material every day – an 'automated onslaught'.[107] As documented in successive transparency reports,[108] Google received over 20 million requests for copyright take down every day in July 2016 and this had risen from 1 million a day in July 2012. Such numbers cannot conceivably be handled manually. Instead, Google created an automated system known as 'Content ID', designed specifically for YouTube (a video sharing site bought by Google in 2006 and featuring large amounts of infringing as well as original content), which depends on copyright owners to 'claim their content'. Rights-holders submit files (such as songs, or videos) which they assert to be their intellectual property, and these are entered into the system as mathematical hashes. When users subsequently upload material which matches these hashes, the system detects it as proof of unauthorised infringement, and gives the rights-holders a choice. They can either block the file from being run or watched (essentially, take down); mute the audio that matches the video; track the viewing statistics; or, most cleverly, monetise the video, by running placed adverts next to it. This revenue is then split between the rights-holder and Google.

Content ID is the outstanding example of the new field of automated 'censorship machines'.[109] For Google, it was a stroke of absolute brilliance in simultaneously allowing it to reduce their risk of being sued for complicity in copyright

---

[106] See L Edwards, *Redress & Alternative Dispute Resolution in Cross-Border E-commerce Transactions Briefing Note* (IP/A/IMCO/IC/2006-206).

[107] Urban et al (n 100) 81.

[108] According to Google's own timeline, its first transparency report was launched on 21 September 2010, see https://transparencyreport.google.com/about. An overview of the multiple reports now available can be found at https://transparencyreport.google.com/?hl=en. By far the majority of take downs received related to copyright, though Google also report on requests from governments for take down, and requests under the GDPR right to be forgotten (see Chapter 4). Google no longer seem to give easy graphical access to the number of copyright take downs received per day, month or year (as of May 2018) though full raw data is available as Excel download; Google do state as of 9 May 2018 that over 3 billion URLS have been requested to be taken down (copyright only), presumably since 2010. The second largest requester of take downs is the UK's own BPI.

[109] Phrase probably coined by MEP Julia Reda – see https://juliareda.eu/eu-copyright-reform/censorship-machines/ – as part of the debate on the draft EU copyright proposal still outstanding as of May 2018 – see *Proposal for a Directive of the European Parliament and of the Council on copyright in the Digital Single Market*, Brussels, 14.9.2016, COM(2016) 593 final.

infringement[110] and to create a new and very lucrative revenue stream, effectively licensing copyright properties to create advertising revenue at low cost and on their own terms. For rights-holders, it was something of a Pyrrhic defeat: on the one hand they had a quick, cheap and mostly effective way to police misuse of their IP; but on the other hand, they had to surrender the control of their property that copyright law had historically given them – and instead of them setting royalty terms for Google's use of their asset, the reverse had occurred. The resulting 'value gap'[111] – between what the rights-holder could have bargained for as a return on their asset in an open market, and what they got from Google (or other platforms such as Facebook or Apple) – become a running grievance in the music, film and publishing industries which has spilled over, as we shall see later, into the ongoing process of EU copyright reform.

Returning for now to 'chilling effects' however, studies such as those by Urban et al have shown huge problems with automated systems such as Content ID in terms of accuracy, bias and due process. Nearly a third of take down requests raised clear questions about their validity. Of requests, four per cent were flawed in that the take down request did not match the work taken down. Some requests were for subjects outside the DMCA's scope, or in respect of content from outside the US. In terms of due process, it was apparent to researchers that potential claims for fair use had been ignored in at least seven per cent of cases.

These issues do not only apply to copyright and YouTube. Similar observations have been made about algorithmic moderation of content on other sites (eg Facebook, Twitter) and in other content domains (eg obscenity, hate speech, fake news). Classification of semantically or contextually ambiguous material such as breastfeeding pictures or 'satirical' racist jokes is extremely difficult. Machine learning (ML) specialists anecdotally reckon that an automated system will probably have around a 90 per cent success rate, depending on the training set and the case being classified. Both false negatives and false positives are inevitable. Historic training set data which does contain bias may simply transfer that bias to new automated systems but in more opaque fashion.

A huge problem in interrogating and challenging such algorithms is not just the known opacity of ML 'black box' algorithms and the general difficulty of challenging or explaining their decisions,[112] but the veil of secrecy that has traditionally enclosed the content moderation practices of large players such as social media platforms. Not only do we not know the breakdown between human and automated content moderation, we also do not know how (or where) the system was initially 'trained' and whether the human raters who provided data were standardised, biased or appropriate.[113] One of the more positive spin-offs of the 'fake news' and political micro-targeting scandals

---

[110] See the long running *Viacom v YouTube* litigation in the US courts, now settled (No 07 Civ 2103, 2010 WL 2532404 (SDNY 2010) – a good account can be found at www.eff.org/cases/viacom-v-youtube.

[111] Similarly, a campaigning phrase for publishers coined in the course of draft Copyright Directive debates (see n 109).

[112] See further L Edwards and M Veale, 'Slave to the Algorithm? Why a "Right to an Explanation" Is Probably Not the Remedy You Are Looking For' (2017)16 *Duke Law & Technology Review* 18.

[113] See discussion in R Binns et al, 'Like Trainer, Like Bot? Inheritance of Bias in Algorithmic Content Moderation', 5 July 2017 at doi: 10.1007/978-3-319-67256-4_32.

of 2017–2018 has been the bursting, or at least, pricking, of the algorithmic bubble. Google and Facebook especially have felt compelled to reveal (some) details of both their human and automated moderation practices,[114] both by legislative subpoena at multiple hearings, and by the demands to assuage a public relations disaster.[115]

It seems obvious that what is needed is a combination of automated and human discretion, with enough checks and balances to provide both guarantees of accuracy, fairness, transparency and due process. Yet requests for take down within two hours, or 24 hours; drives to reduce costs and sack staff in competitive markets[116]; and snake-oil promises that 'AI will sort everything out' under threats of regulation,[117] all mitigate in the other direction.

The vast lobbying power of the rights-holder industries has also been involved. In the latest draft of the new EU copyright legislation, one requirement is that for certain intermediaries, automated take down systems ('censorship machines') must be installed to protect rights-holders.[118] This runs in the teeth of Urban et al's conclusion that 'We would strongly recommend avoiding statutory changes that would expand automated practices without much better control against mistake or abuse, or raise the costs of compliance for the vast majority of [smaller service providers].'[119]

C. 'Neutral Intermediary' and the Rise of Data and UGC Monetising Business Models

As discussed above, the ECD was drafted in a world before Facebook, Google, et al and before the rise of the 'free but supported by ads' business model. These models have made these and other companies some of the richest companies in the world. As we have seen, on YouTube, Google brilliantly took advantage of copyright content provided illegally by users to generate revenue through ads, not just for rights-holders but themselves. Alternative models include that of eBay, Amazon Marketplace and similar (known in EU lingo as 'online marketplaces') where consumers sell goods to

---

[114] See Facebook's blog post at and revelation of their detailed content moderation rules after a year of pressure from *The Guardian*: 'Facebook Releases Content Moderation Guidelines – Rules Long Kept Secret' *The Guardian* (24 April 2018) at www.theguardian.com/technology/2018/apr/24/facebook-releases-content-moderation-guidelines-secret-rules; YouTube's release of the 'flags' it uses to take down videos at https://transparencyreport.google.com/youtube-policy/overview.

[115] See T Gillespie, 'Facebook and YouTube Just Got More Transparent. What Do We See?' (NiemanLab, 3 May 2018) at www.niemanlab.org/2018/05/facebook-and-youtube-just-got-more-transparent-what-do-we-see/. Remarkably, industry have even begun attending and making disclosures at a series of public Content Moderation and Removal at Scale conferences run by universities including UC Santa Clara, which issued on 2 February 2018 the Santa Clara Principles on Transparency and Accountability of Content Moderation (http://globalnetpolicy.org/research/the-santa-clara-principles-on-transparency-and-accountability-of-content-moderation-practices/).

[116] Another important issue beyond the scope of this chapter is that moderation is increasingly carried out by piece-time workers in developing countries under poor conditions, both financially and in terms of support for emotionally stressful work. It was been suggested we need the equivalent of 'fair trade' content moderation certification.

[117] See 'Why AI Isn't Going to Solve Facebook's Fake News Problem' (*The Verge*, 5 April 2018) at www.theverge.com/2018/4/5/17202886/facebook-fake-news-moderation-ai-challenges.

[118] See n 109, Art 13. Response to this proposal from academics has been highly critical, see, eg, C Angelopoulos, *On Online Platforms and the Commission's New Proposal for a Directive on Copyright in the Digital Single Market* (CIPIL, University of Cambridge, January 2017. At the time of writing (May 2018) it is still unclear if this very controversial proposal will survive or in what form to become EU law.

[119] Urban et al (n 100) 4.

other consumers (the 'C2C' model) and a commission is taken from sellers. It is anec-dotally known that on such sites a large amount of products are sold which break rules of copyright or trademark, especially in relation to counterfeit luxury goods where protection of brand is crucial.

As these platforms have grown to dominate global markets, it becomes harder (especially for IP rights-holders) to see them as merely passive and innocent intermedi-aries, as opposed to a financial beneficiary of illegal or infringing content. Who should bear the cost of policing IP rights on sites like eBay and YouTube or within Google adverts? The most obvious answer is the IP owner, since they most proximately make profits from enforcement activity. Platforms argue without fail that they are merely intermediaries which facilitate the legal and sometimes illegal activities of users trans-acting with each other. Yet the costs of enforcement might arguably be less for the platforms which should have the facilities to automatedly search, monitor and remove their content. These issues came to a head in relation to Art 14 in two landmark CJEU cases: *Google France v Louis Vuitton*[120] in 2010 and *L'Oreal v eBay*[121] in 2011.

In *Google France*, the question was whether Google was liable for trademark infringement because it allowed companies to advertise on its site using trademarks owned by competitors. The Court held that Google was entitled to claim immunity under Article 14 of the ECD only if Google's role was 'neutral in the sense that its conduct is merely technical, automatic and passive, pointing to a lack of knowledge or control of the data which it stores'.

Crucially however it then stated that

> the mere facts that the referencing service is subject to payment, that Google sets the payment terms or that it provides general information to its clients cannot have the effect of depriving Google of the exemptions from liability provided for in Directive 2000/31.[122]

The issue of 'neutrality' was thus clearly restrained to knowledge or awareness of infringing activity, as per the original intent of Art 14(1), rather than being expanded to some presumption of complicity via proof of financial gain. 'Neutrality' seemed in fact a rather unnecessary gloss on the pre-existing rules of Art 14. As an exam-ple of non-neutrality however, the Court suggested that if Google had generated an automatic advertising message for a trademark infringer that might be evidence of sufficient control to remove immunity.

In *L'Oreal v eBay*,[123] the CJEU added more detail to this new concept. Here the case was brought by a number of luxury goods trademark holders, which argued that because eBay listed (and made commission from) sales of counterfeit goods which infringed its trademarks, eBay bore responsibility for *preventing* such infringement. By contrast, eBay said that it took down such infringing posts when notified – indeed, it had a 'fast track' take down service for major trademark names – and so fell firmly within the hosting immunity since it met Art 14(1)(b). This left open however

---

[120] Case C-236/08 *Google France v Louis Vuitton* (CJEU, 23 March 2010).
[121] Case C-324/09 *L'Oreal v eBay* (CJEU, 12 July 2011).
[122] *Google France* (n 120) [116].
[123] *L'Oreal v eBay* (n 121).

the question if an injunction might still be made requiring eBay to prevent future infringements under Art 14(1)(a), on the basis of the second branch of 'facts and awareness' – essentially based on the idea that eBay had enough access to have known its site was full of counterfeit listings. Art 15, however, as noted earlier, provides that ISSPs are not required to monitor to actively seek this awareness.

This question thus morphed into that of whether eBay was a sufficiently 'neutral' intermediary to benefit from Art 14. The CJEU repeated, following *Google France*, that it was 'necessary to examine whether the role played by that service provider was neutral, in the sense that its conduct is merely technical, automatic and passive, pointing to a lack of knowledge or control of the data which it stores'.[124] It added similarly that the mere fact that eBay took money for displaying listings of goods (some of which might infringe trademarks), set the terms of service and was renumerated for these did not render them 'non-neutral', although it might if they provided *active* assistance, such as optimising sales listings or promoting those offers (eg 'bargain of the week!').[125]

More interestingly though, the CJEU also spoke about the test the national courts should apply to determine if an operator had 'awareness' under Art 14. An operator would be denied immunity, the Court said, if it was 'aware of facts or circumstances on the basis of which a *diligent economic operator should have identified the illegality in question* and acted in accordance with Article 14(1)(b)'.[126] This test was for the national court to apply, so the CJEU did not venture further, except to add, tellingly, that such awareness could come not just from notice by an external party, but also as a result of an 'investigation undertaken on its own initiative'.[127]

Finally the CJEU confirmed, following the previous AG Opinion, that an injunction to restrain not just current but *future* infringements was possible under Art 14(3). This was regarded as a serious blow for eBay, effectively implying that 'notice and stay down' was now a possibility (and has become the norm since in countries like Germany). However, such an injunction could only be made[128] if it was effective, proportionate, dissuasive, not excessively costly on the platform, and did not create barriers to legitimate trade.

In the particular case of an online marketplace like eBay, that last proviso meant an injunction could not demand that no one except a trademark holder was ever allowed to sell goods bearing their trademark. On the other hand it could be reasonable to demand a marketplace insisted on its users being 'clearly identifiable' at least if they operated in the course of trade not as purely private persons. Finally, the Court reiterated that all this was subject to Art 15 which required that an injunction against future infringements could still not require active monitoring of all the data of customers just to prevent future violation of IP rights.[129]

---

[124] *L'Oreal v eBay* (n 121) [113].
[125] *L'Oreal v eBay* (n 121) [116].
[126] *L'Oreal v eBay* (n 121) [120] (emphasis added).
[127] *L'Oreal v eBay* (n 121) [122].
[128] *L'Oreal v eBay* (n 121) [139]–[142].
[129] *L'Oreal v eBay* (n 121) [139].

D. Filtering

L'Oreal v eBay opened the possibility that an order for *ex ante* filtering, phrased as an injunction to prevent future infringements, might be legitimate under Art 14, even despite the limiting influence of Art 15 which had seemed drafted explicitly to prevent such infringement. This idea was first tested in the CJEU in *Scarlet Extended v SABAM*,[130] another case involving IP rights-holders, in this case a Belgian collecting society, which sought to compel a leading ISP, Scarlet, to block all of its subscribers from accessing infringing content on P2P torrent sites by putting in place wholesale monitoring of all traffic and blocking of key sites. Scarlet argued this was a general monitoring obligation in breach of Art 15 and furthermore that it benefitted from the Art 12 'mere conduit' immunity.

Scarlet was something of an extreme test case. The CJEU held firmly that the injunction as sought was not lawful. It breached numerous fundamental rights (privacy of communications; freedom of expression); it was far too wide and expansive an order, applied indiscriminately to all customers, guilty or not, and so constituted 'general monitoring';[131] it dictated how the filtering should be done, and so was in breach of the freedom of Scarlet to conduct its own business;[132] furthermore it insisted all the costs of blocking should fall on the ISP, and that blocking was for an unlimited period; and thus it quite manifestly did not strike a viable balance between the rights of the copyright owners and the ISP.[133]

Nonetheless, *Scarlet* still upheld the principle that a filtering injunction *might* be possible if properly tailored and constrained. The question was, what would that kind of order look like? Some answers were found in the next case, *Telekabel*.[134] This involved a 'pirate' site kino.to which gave access to multiple copyright works such as films without the authorisation of rights-holders. These IP holders sought an injunction against an Austrian ISP, Telekabel Wien, to prevent access to kino. to to their subscribers. This injunction was tailored to be far more limited than in *Scarlet* and was a success. The ISP was given freedom how it chose to block/filter, thus with less incursion into its right to do business. The filtering was 'strictly targeted' to one site so the rights of non-infringing users were not affected. The Court agreed that a block might not be totally effective against some users, but it would still 'seriously discourage' access. Thus the Court held it was possible to make an injunction that did not breach fundamental rights and the matter was passed back to the national court.

---

[130] Case C-70/10 *Scarlet Extended v SABAM* (CJEU, 24 November 2011).

[131] *Ibid* [40].

[132] *Ibid* [48].

[133] *Ibid* [49]. A similar result was reached in a parallel case against a host, Netlog, which claimed benefit of the Art 14 hosting exemption: see Case C-360/10 *SABAM v Netlog* (16 February 2012). Note that a blanket blocking order by the Turkish Government preventing all users in Turkey from accessing YouTube in its entirety, regardless of what particular content they sought to see, was also declared a breach of Art 8 (freedom of expression) by the ECtHR in *Cengiz and others v Turkey*, Application Nos 48226/10 and 14027/11, judgment of 1 December 2015.

[134] C-314/12 *UPC Telekabel Wien v Constantin* EU:C:2014:192, judgment of 27 March 2014.

VI. More Influences from the P2P Wars: From NTD to Graduated Response and Website Blocking

It is not the place of this chapter[135] to contain a detailed account of the battle of the last 18 years against P2P filesharing by music, film, video and e-book rights-holders. Famously, lawsuits launched against centralised P2P sites such as *Napster*[136] and decentralised ones such as *Grokster*[137] and latterly torrent sites such as the notorious Pirate Bay,[138] although successful on legal points, made limited headway in practice against the growth of unauthorised filesharing and downloads. What these sites had in common was that they did not host infringing files, but merely pointed to (usually parts of) such files held by other filesharers. Thus, even where a P2P site was taken down, many others could immediately spring up to provide the same connectivity function, especially when protocols like BitTorrent were made open source. Napster at least had a centralised database index; modern decentralised protocols make it impossible to find a critical central chokepoint intermediary to sue. Thus, rights-holders have had to turn to methods other than the liability or NTD paradigms examined so far to prevent filesharing. The obvious way forward was to abandon trying to sue filesharing sites directly (which in any case often ignored court orders and moved their servers successively to out-of-reach jurisdictions) and to attempt instead to persuade or force ISPs to block access to these sites to their subscribers – turning ISPs into 'copyright cops'.[139]

A. Graduated Response

A variety of roles were proposed for ISPs in the copyright wars c 2009, such as disclosing the identities of filesharers, with[140] or without a court order; warning filesharers

---

[135] For a full discussion, see L Edwards, *The Role and Responsibility of Internet Intermediaries in the Field of Copyright and Related Rights* (WIPO, 2010) at www.wipo.int/publications/en/details.jsp?id=4142& plang=EN. A fascinating meta analysis of empirical economic and psychological literature on the P2P and filesharing wars can be found in SJ Watson et al, *Determinants and Welfare Implications of Unlawful File Sharing: A Scoping Review* (CREATe Working Paper 14/5, 2014) at www.create.ac.uk/publications/determinants-and-welfare-implications-of-unlawful-file-sharing-a-scoping-review/.

[136] *A&M Records, Inc v Napster Inc* 239 F3d 1004 (9th Cir 2001).

[137] *MGM v Grokster* 545 US 913 (2005).

[138] The Pirate Bay was sued in many jurisdictions. See one of the earliest cases in Sweden at *Sony and Ors v Neij*, Stockholm District Court, Division 5, Unit 52, VERDICT B 13301-06, 17 April 2009 handed down in Stockholm, Case no B 13301-06.

[139] See L Edwards, 'Should ISPs be Compelled to become Copyright Cops?' (2009)(6) *Computers and Law* 29, also available at www.scl.com.

[140] See the important ECJ decision in C-275/06 *Promusicae v Telefonica* Judgment (OJ) OJ C64 of 08.03.2008, 9 in which the Court asserted firmly that although copyright enforcement was a goal backed by EC law, it could nonetheless not overrule the rights to privacy of alleged filesharers, and instead a balance had to be struck according to human rights jurisprudence. The case itself concerned whether it was legitimate under EC law for a national Spanish court to demand that identifying data be handed over to rights-holders claiming infringement; in the UK, it was already clear this was possible via a *Norwich Pharmacal* order ([1974] AC 133) – see *Totalise v Motley Fool* [2001] EWHC 706 (QB).

that their illegal downloading had been observed[141]; filtering out copyright material acquired via suspicious activity such as downloading from P2P sites; traffic management (ie, slowing of traffic to a user, classified by type, volume or origin perhaps); and at the most draconian, operating a policy of 'notice and disconnection' to users.

The last of these was pioneered by the French Government under the presidency of Sarkozy as a policy of 'graduated response', although better known internationally as 'three strikes and you're out'.[142] The basic idea was that warnings that a subscriber was known to have illegally shared files, based on information collected by the music industry, were passed by an ISP to that subscriber; when three (or however many) warnings were accumulated, the ISP disconnected the subscriber. Graduated response, driven by extensive rights-holder lobbying, was taken up with some enthusiasm by a number of jurisdictions as a way to 'educate' filesharers into reforming, including the UK, in the Digital Economy Act 2010 (DEA 2010) ss 3–18, as well as in South Korea, New Zealand, Chile, Ireland, Australia, the US and others.[143]

Many legal challenges were aimed at 'graduated response' and especially disconnection, as a fundamental attack on freedom of access to the Internet, with varying degrees of success.[144] It was clear that arguments could be made that graduated response infringed freedom of expression by under- or over-blocking; infringed rights of privacy by collecting personal data without permission and using it for unnamed purposes; as well as more hazy rights such as the 'right to the Internet' asserted in some countries.[145] However in the end it was not these civil liberties arguments that saw off graduated response, but three pragmatic matters: it cost a great deal, which ISPs were unwilling to swallow whole and had fought successfully to argue should be mainly the lot of rights-holders[146]; it was easily avoided by the many users who had learnt to use Virtual Private Networks (VPNs) and similar IP-masking technologies; and perhaps most importantly, just as suing users individually had been, it was deeply unpopular with the industry's own customers.

Graduated response might have survived as a least worst option had two other important developments not occurred: first, the arrival of a successful legitimate alternative to filesharing in the form of streaming sites like last.fm and then Spotify, which combined an ad-supported business model with an increasingly successful flat rate subscription model; and second, the legitimisation of website blocking orders in the

---

[141] This policy was trialled under a Memorandum of Understanding struck between the six largest ISPs in the UK and the music industry, for six months in 2008 prior to the passing of the Digital Economy Act 2010.

[142] French *Loi Olivennes*, or 'HADOPI' law, passed on second attempt by the French legislature on 13 May 2009.

[143] Legislative solutions such as those found in France and the UK tended to give way to less controversial 'voluntary' schemes set up by agreement or after court actions against ISPs – such as the six-strikes system in the US (which was formally abandoned in January 2017 – see www.bbc.co.uk/news/technology-38808719).

[144] See in the UK, the failed attempt by a number of ISPs to have the DEA 2010 annulled by judicial review: see *BT et al v Secretary of State for BIS, BPI et al* [2011] EWHC 1021 (Admin).

[145] See, eg, the assertion of Costa Rica that Internet access was a fundamental right: see A Guadamuz, *Technollama* blog (2 October 2010).

[146] In fact the only successful part of the UK judicial review case was the reduction of the financial burden borne by ISPs to keep the DEA scheme afloat.

EU after *eBay* and *Telekabel*. Thus, graduated response is effectively vanishing as a phenomenon[147] and has largely been replaced in terms of legal strategy by use of filtering and blocking court orders against ISPs.

B. UK Website Blocking Orders

The lead nation pushing use of web-blocking orders to control access to 'pirate' sites has been the UK. In the landmark case of *Twentieth Century Fox and others v BT*,[148] Arnold J held that an order could be made under s 97A of the Copyright Designs and Patents Act 1998 against the ISP BT instructing it to block access to Newzbin, a site which had in previous litigation[149] been found to be hosting and giving access to predominantly copyright infringing material (mainly films). Section 97A provided that a Court 'shall have power to grant an injunction against a service provider, where that service provider has actual knowledge of another person using their service to infringe copyright'. This had long been thought to raise numerous problems in terms of compliance with the ECD as well as other parts of EU law and the ECHR, which was why it took over 20 years to bring a test case.

One question was whether an ISP like BT had 'actual knowledge' of every infringement its customers had or were likely to commit. Arnold J held however ([116]–[149]) that although the service provider must have *actual* knowledge of one or more persons using its service to infringe copyright, it is not essential to prove actual knowledge of a *specific* infringement of a *specific* copyright work by a *specific* individual [emphases added]. A second hurdle which was seen off was whether a customer of BT was 'using its services' to infringe copyright, as opposed to the services of the intermediary they were trying to access; Arnold J answered in the affirmative.

Finally on the crucial assessment of whether it was proportional to make a web-blocking order, which did intrinsically represent an infringement of both the Art 8 privacy and Art 10 free expression rights of users (and of Newzbin itself), Arnold J came down firmly after a comprehensive analysis, on the side that the order was proportionate. The property interests of the rights-holders in this case outweighed the other interests affected. As in *Telekabel* later, the order sought did not breach Art 15 of the ECD because it did not involve monitoring in *general* the data of each subscriber, but merely packets going to and from one *specific* site, Newzbin, which had conveniently already been found to be in breach of copyright. Accordingly the order was 'narrow

---

[147] The DEA 2010 scheme was, as a cardinal example, never in fact brought into force, mainly because the rights-holders involved were unconvinced it would pay its way in reduction of filesharing losses and also because web-blocking orders arrived as a more effective approach. The attempt to set up a voluntary 'notice and warning' system to replace it (Voluntary Copyright Alert Programme or VCAP in 2014) also seems to have disappeared into oblivion (see, interestingly, 'Nobody Wants to Talk About UK ISP Internet Piracy Alert Emails' (ISPreview, 18 April 2018) at www.ispreview.co.uk/index.php/2018/04/nobody-wants-to-talk-about-uk-isp-internet-piracy-alert-emails.html. Even the flagship French HADOPI scheme has been effectively neutered by the reduction of its funding and the removal of the disconnection option in 2013. Australia, bucking the trend, did bring a new three strikes scheme into force in 2015.

[148] *Twentieth Century Fox and others v BT* [2011] EWHC 1981 (Ch) ('*Newzbin 2*').

[149] *Twentieth Century Fox Film Corp v Newzbin Ltd* [2010] EWHC 608 (Ch) ('*Newzbin 1*').

and targeted'. Furthermore, interestingly, the scheme was affordable for the ISP, as BT already had content filtering software in place to deal with blocking child sexual abuse material. Finally, and very significantly, Arnold J refused to consider whether easy circumvention of blocking orders might render them ineffective, asserting both in this case, and quoted in many subsequent cases, that 'the order would be justified even if it only prevented access to Newzbin2 by a minority of users' ([198]).

After *Newzbin 2*, the floodgates opened. First, actions were initiated successfully against other websites giving access to pirate AV material, eg the Pirate Bay[150]; against other ISPs; then against whole new classes of site, such as sites streaming live football matches.[151] Finally, web-blocking became so normalised that in *Cartier v BskyB*,[152] a power other than s 97A was found to extend blocking orders to cover sites which hosted material in breach of trademark rather than copyright.[153] It is hard to say how many websites have been blocked in the UK by IP related orders, as new URLs or addresses can be added to orders without further court process to prevent avoidance, but it is clearly regarded by the copyright industries as a highly successful strategy and the UK is often touted as a 'world leader' in copyright-related blocking.[154]

One point which seems worth emphasising in this rising swell of blocking orders, is that although it may be proportional to impose these burdens on intermediaries to protect rights-holders, there is a worrying precedent being created for the populist extension of automated and largely invisible blocking – or censorship – infrastructure to other forms of content and thus to imperil freedom of expression generally. Although the level of scrutiny and analysis in these s 97A test cases was extremely high, as blocking has normalised, due process has become less visible. The blocked site is rarely available to defend, so the free speech and privacy rights of users are left in essence to be defended by the ISPs, who themselves now rarely defend now that their costs and risk worries have been sorted out. As noted, new URLs can be added to existing orders without scrutiny. The dangers of over blocking are under explored and most importantly the efficacy of the orders is basically irrelevant. Effectively the UK, already a leader in blocking and filtering in areas like child abuse material and terrorist material (see next chapter), has now taken that role on also in respect of copyright and trademark infringement. As we shall explore in the conclusion, this has lead inexorably to more and more pressure being put on once 'neutral' intermediaries to act as enforcers in a wide range of social problems.

---

[150] *Dramatico Entertainment Limited & Ors v British Sky Broadcasting Limited & Ors* [2012] EWHC 1152 (Ch).

[151] *FA Premier League v BT and others* [2017] EWHC 480 (Ch). See also the 'Popcorn Time' case, Twentieth Century Fox Film Corporation & Ors v Sky UK Ltd & Ors [2015] EWHC 1082 (Ch) which involved a site facilitating downloads of an application which then ran on the users' home machine rather than a conventional website.

[152] *Cartier v BskyB* [2014] EWHC 3354(Ch), upheld by Court of Appeal in [2016] EWCA 658.

[153] Senior Courts Act 1981, s 37(1) and IP Rights Enforcement Directive (IPRED) 2004/48/EC [2004] OJ L195/16, Art 11.

[154] See, eg, 'The UK is One of the Global Leaders of Anti-Piracy Blocking, Says MPA Canada' (Gizmodo, 11 April 2018) at www.gizmodo.co.uk/2018/04/the-uk-is-one-of-the-global-leaders-of-anti-piracy-blocking-says-mpa-canada/. In it the MPA asserts that in the UK, 171 sites and 2,215 domains have been blocked on copyright grounds, the largest amount of blocking orders in the EU. See also useful data at https://torrent-freak.com/mpa-reveals-scale-of-worldwide-pirate-site-blocking-180410/.

C. 'Censorship Machines'

In the latest round of the copyright wars, the EU has again come under heavy lobbying pressure to place obligations on intermediaries to protect the content industries. As noted above, the latest proposal for a new EU copyright directive makes reference to automated take down systems, dubbed aggressively 'censorship machines' by their opponents.[155] Draft Article 13 aims to address the 'value gap' identified above, by forcing platforms which 'provide public access to' 'large amounts' of copyright works (both legally and semantically vague terms) to make agreements with rights-holders for the use of these works. Alternately, platforms are to prevent access to such uploaded work by the use of technologies such as 'content recognition technologies' which involve cooperation between service providers and rights-holders. Even more confusingly, draft Recital 38 then asserts however that the licensing obligation under Art 13 does not apply if the platform is immunised by Art 14 of the ECD, which itself depends on where the platform goes beyond neutrality by playing 'an active role' – but that the second obligation persists.

The political intent here is to restrain the profits made by sites like YouTube, Vimeo and Dailymotion which rely on copyright content provided by users, while not upsetting 'legitimate' sites like Netflix and Spotify which only provide access to copyright properties after licensing agreements have been concluded. But Art 13 is legally a complete mess, attempting to reduce the protection offered by Arts 12 and 14 of the ECD while not saying so in actual words, and setting conditions for 'large' sites like YouTube while not saying how this distinction is to be evaluated. In part this was because the 2016 Communication on Online Platforms had declared after consultation that the E-Commerce Directive was fit for purpose and would not be revised. Angelopoulos argues convincingly in relation to the 'large amounts' criterion, that there is no clear way to tell 'David' from 'Goliath', and that Art 13 is incompatible with current copyright law, Art 15 of the ECD prohibiting general monitoring, and the EU Charter of Fundamental Rights.[156] Despite this, and despite a militant fightback from a coalition of academics, intermediaries and some software providers, it is still quite possible that Art 13 may yet become law.[157]

VII. The End of Online Intermediary Immunities? Hate Speech and the 'Fake News' Era

Near the beginning of this chapter, I described the three factors which won the day for the emergent ISP industry in securing regimes of immunity from liability around

---

[155] See n 109.
[156] Supra n 118.
[157] Article 13 (and Art 11 on the link tax) were accepted by the lead JURI committee of the European Parliament in June 2018 in a close and very controversial vote. However on 5 July 2018, the European Parliament in plenary voted to delay progress on Art 13 by requiring a full debate on it in September 2018. The saga thus goes on.

the turn of the millennium. ISPs, it was claimed, could not practically exercise effective control over the volume of content provided by users; were not morally responsible for the content or acts of others; and if they were held so liable, the Internet intermediary industry and hence the information society might collapse or at least withdraw from Europe.

In the 2009 version of this chapter, I argued that the foundations of this narrative had been almost entirely deconstructed as a result of the copyright wars. In 2017, they lie in shreds. YouTube/Google's invention of Content ID has been appropriated by the copyright industry to repel the volume argument in the form of mandated 'censorship machines'. Meanwhile, regulators, platforms and the media all seem conjoined in selling the narrative of the magic 'AI bullet' which will allow perfect filtering and moderation of all types of content, at minimal cost, at great speed, with no errors, no biases and no societal downsides. As explored above, this is simply, at least at the moment, an illusion, and at that, probably a harmful one.

On the second point, the rise of the 'free but ad-supported' business model, and more recently, the dawning societal sense that many intermediaries are not only in some way financially complicit in the distribution and upload of illegal material but also actively intent on collecting the personal data of, and thereby manipulating the opinions and actions of, users, has diluted almost to nothingness the moral core of the adage not to 'shoot the messenger'. On the third and most instrumental point, we are perhaps no longer so much concerned to protect the emergent Internet industry, as we are fearful of its power over citizens, consumers and governments alike.

Into this landscape, as we began to discuss above, came two new horsemen of the infocalypse: hate speech and fake news. As we have seen above,[158] targets for removal of hate speech within 24 hours, or two hours, or less, however vital they seem to social cohesion and minority protection, will have perverse consequences in making unfettered prior automated content moderation the norm: done by private hands, cheaply, non-transparently and without safeguards. More generally, hate speech, like CAM before it, seems to fix the minds of regulators inexorably on the idea that only technology can 'improve online safety for all users'[159] and that intermediaries who claim things are not as easy as all that are merely being recalcitrant. Theresa May's major speech at Davos in January 2018 carried some of this tone of bemused frustration in its invocation that: 'These companies have some of the best brains in the world … They must focus their brightest and best on meeting these fundamental social responsibilities.'[160]

Fake news raises even more difficult issues.[161] Once, the EU drew a bright line between *illegal* content, which should properly be subject to regulation and top down filtering; and *harmful* content, which was in principle to be only subject to voluntary control and self-regulation, eg by users adopting their own home filters for their

[158] See section V.A.
[159] See HM Government, *UK Internet Safety Strategy – Green Paper* (October 2017).
[160] 25 January 2018: whole speech at www.weforum.org/agenda/2018/01/theresa-may-davos-address/.
[161] A good summary of global legal responses to fake news can be found in Kremlin Watch Report 'Making Online Platforms Responsible for News Content' (25 July 2017) at www.europeanvalues.net/wp-content/uploads/2017/07/Making-online-platforms-responsible-for-news-content-3.pdf.

children.[162] This idea, already mostly forgotten, has now vanished.[163] Fake news may be vile, xenophobic, right wing, left wing, misogynistic, inaccurate and possibly destabilising of elections, but it is not, in the main, actually illegal.[164] Yet in the furore post Cambridge Analytica, Brexit and Trump, the ether is awash with suggestions for forcing intermediaries, somehow, to take steps to ensure its suppression. In Malaysia, fake news has been made actively illegal and punishable by up to six years in jail.[165] In more constitutionally minded countries, what is apparent is a rising tide of demands that the powerful platforms, the Googles and Facebooks, be treated as publishers with editorial responsibility.[166] The appeal of this idea is obvious but it probably involves outright destruction of the core principles of the ECD designed to protect speech, Internet access and innovation. Other wilder ideas are also being explored: suggestions that Google and Facebook be treated as equivalent to public utilities with public duties of some kind; or broken up by competition law, or even nationalised outright.[167] One way or another, regulation to reduce intermediary immunity is in the air. Matt Hancock, Minister for Digital Matters at DCMS, summed up this increasing frustration with traditional self-regulation in April 2018:

> Social media companies are not above the law and will not be allowed to shirk their responsibilities to our citizens. We will do what is needed to ensure that people's data is protected and don't rule anything out – that includes further regulation in the future.[168]

The move towards greater platform regulation and the decline of special immunities is of course not only a European phenomenon. Even in the US, home of the CDA s 230(c), the first cracks in this bulwark of 'internet exceptionalism' have appeared in the form of SESTA (the Stop Enabling Sex Traffickers Act 2018), an Act which amends s 230(c) to allow platforms to be held liable for content promoting sex-trafficking. Is this for the US 'the beginning of the end of the Internet's legal immunity' as

---

[162] See European Parliament Communication of 16 October 1996 *Illegal and Harmful Content* COM (1996) 487.

[163] Again most notably in the UK experience in David Cameron's introduction of 'family-friendly' filters for non-illegal content such as adult erotic material from which broadband accountholders had to make an 'unavoidable choice' to opt out. See 'Ofcom Report on Internet Safety Measures: Strategies of Parental Protection for Children Online' (Ofcom, 16 December 2015) 3–6, available at http://stakeholders.ofcom.org.uk/binaries/internet/fourth_internet_safety_report.pdf.) See detailed discussion of the UK's network of voluntary filters relating to porn, terror and similar content in the next chapter.

[164] Of course it does not help that there is absolutely no consistency in definitions of 'fake news'. An exception would be where fake news was defamatory of a living person, incited racial hatred or clearly constituted misleading advertising. Often however none of these categories apply.

[165] The first person was convicted under the law in April 2018: see 'First Person Convicted under Malaysia's Fake News Law' *The Guardian* (30 April 2018) at www.theguardian.com/world/2018/apr/30/first-person-convicted-under-malaysias-fake-news-law. Malaysia's new Government has however said it will review but not necessarily revoke the law: see BBC News, 14 May 2018 at www.bbc.co.uk/news/world-asia-44104879.

[166] See 'Ofcom Chair Raises Prospect of Regulation for Google and Facebook' *The Guardian* (10 October 2017) at www.theguardian.com/media/2017/oct/10/ofcom-patricia-hodgson-google-facebook-fake-news.

[167] See, eg, D Tambini, 'What Should be Done with Facebook – Break it up, or Regulate it?' *The Guardian* (27 April 2018) at www.theguardian.com/commentisfree/2018/apr/27/facebook-regulate-tech-platforms. See also the recommendations of the HL Online Platforms Report (n 3) regarding competition remedies at Chs 5 and 9.

[168] 'Act on Data Privacy or we'll Regulate, UK Minister tells Facebook' *The* Guardian (April 2018) at www.theguardian.com/technology/2018/apr/11/digital-secretary-threatens-facebook-with-regulation-over-data-breaches.

one commentator has already claimed?[169] It is easy and tempting to ask platforms to clean up messes which they have to some extent created, to some extent arguably profit from, and which they seem to have the best ability to fix. But these solutions often involve inadvertent consequences.

Vague and overbroad laws restricting non illegal speech run the risk of being co-opted by power; 'fake news', for example, may soon become any story that Donald Trump does not like. (There is of course a long history of protective laws such as libel being used to silence the less empowered.) Furthermore, requiring more privatised governance of content, especially automated moderation, without thinking through safeguards, transparency and audit first is also quite probably an unhappy path to take. The Manila Principles on Intermediary Liability[170] suggest that take down should only be legal when authorised by court order; nowadays, this seems beyond imagination but it does remind us how far we have moved from the traditional idea that censorship was once a public matter, for legislators and judges. Finally, there is an irony in placing more power to control content in the hands of the same platforms whose opaque and trade-secret protected algorithms, based on maximising attention and profit, have created the very problems we are trying to solve.

The deceptively simple rules of the ECD were actually the result of hard-fought compromise on a regime which would simultaneously promote Internet innovation, and balance the interests of users, rights-holders, victims and platforms, while not disregarding the societal value of freedom of expression. We should be slow to throw this consensus away in the rush to put liability on platforms to deal with admittedly pressing new threats like hate speech and fake news online. As Graham Smith has put it, defending the 'phantom demon' of the ECD:

> .. the Directive adapts to changes in behaviour and operates across business models. It is technology-neutral and business sector-agnostic ... The fact that the ECD encompasses simple and complex platforms alike leads to a final point: the perhaps underappreciated variety of activities that benefit from hosting protection. They include ... online games and virtual worlds ... collaborative software development environments such as GitHub. Cloud-based word processor applications, any kind of app with a user-generated content element, website discussion forums, would all be within scope. By focusing on activities defined in a technology-neutral way the Directive has transcended and adapted to many different evolving industries and kinds of business.[171]

Another commentator, William Echikson, gives a good flavour of the US business view looking in:

> A grown-up internet no longer deserves a liability free pass. The unanswered question remains just how far to compel ... proactive action. Many of the justifications for the original safe harbour remain valid: to promote free speech and to foster innovation. Kill the

---

[169] A Rozenshtein, 'It's the Beginning of the End of the Internet's Legal Immunity' (*Foreign Policy*, 13 November 2017) at http://foreignpolicy.com/2017/11/13/its-the-beginning-of-the-end-of-the-internets-legal-immunity/. Note the suggestion from respected US academics D Citron and B Wittes in 2017 that s 230(c) should be amended to allow Facebook to be held liable for illegal content hosting: 'The Internet Will Not Break: Denying Bad Samaritans § 230 Immunity' (2017) 86 *Fordham Law Review* 401.

[170] EFF, 24 March 2015. See www.eff.org/files/2015/10/31/manila_principles_1.0.pdf.

[171] 'The Electronic Commerce Directive – a Phantom Demon?' (Cyberleagle, 30 April 2018) at www.cyberleagle.com/2018/04/the-electronic-commerce-directive.html.

E-Commerce Directive and you may kill the magical power of all of us to reach a global audience with a few keystrokes. Kill the E-Commerce Directive and today's internet giants have the resources to cope. But what about tomorrow's giants? They would never escape the liability threat. If for this reason only, regulators should proceed with care.[172]

If we want to curtail the power of platforms – and I think we do – we should look more to the structural solutions of competition law as well as to data protection and consumer protection than to dismantling the ECD and its kin. As discussed in detail in Chapter 5, social media companies tend by nature to become monopolies; remedies drawn from data protection such as data portability, expanded to become true rights of data interoperability, would help to create a more competitive marketplace.[173] Stronger data protection rules in the GDPR and forthcoming e-Privacy Regulation may incentivise a move from data-driven business models to subscription-based models, reducing the acquisition of user data and the consequential power of platforms to surveille and profile us. Developments in decentralised or 'edge' computing may also reduce platform lock-in. From consumer protection law, user rights against platforms need to be strengthened, as does due process in private content moderation and curation: it is possible that a regulator to oversee social media in some form needs to be appointed. Perrin and Woods have suggested that this role might be taken by Ofcom pro tem, but there is a danger that a regulator might not recognise the crucial differences between a platform and a traditional publisher and rely too much on media law solutions.[174] An Ombudsman able to get remedies for users which exceed the scope or ability of the Information Commissioner might be better.

As this book went to press, the EU announced a package of measures designed to address exactly some of these points. The proposals relate to B2B use of platforms rather than the more familiar consumer issues, but still make very interesting reading. The draft Platform Regulation proposed would: (a) increase transparency around platform terms of service, especially concerning removal or delisting of other businesses; (b) require better internal complaint-handling systems; and (c) set up an EU Observatory to monitor the impact of the new rules. These rules are evidently designed to improve competition and allow small businesses a greater equality of arms with the giant platforms – but some of them would also very much benefit consumers.[175]

We are in the middle now, not the beginning or the end, of the debate about platform power and liability, and the most obviously appealing answers may turn out to be neither practical nor helpful; it will be intriguing to see what happens in another eight years.

---

[172] 'Limited Liability for the Net? The Future of Europe's E-Commerce Directive' (Huffington Post, 13 April 2017) at www.huffingtonpost.com/entry/58ecd2cfe4b0145a227cb846.

[173] I am indebted for these ideas to I Brown and C Marsden, *Regulating Code* (MIT Press, 2013). See further in this volume, Chapter 5.

[174] W Perrin and L Woods, *Harm Reduction in Social Media – A Proposal* (Carnegie Trust, 2018) at www.carnegieuktrust.org.uk/blog/social-media-regulation/.

[175] See https://ec.europa.eu/digital-single-market/en/news/regulation-promoting-fairness-and-transparency-business-users-online-intermediation-services (26 April 2018).

10

Internet Censorship in the United Kingdom: National Schemes and European Norms

TJ McINTYRE*

I. Introduction

The United Kingdom (UK) has been at the vanguard of online censorship in democracies from the beginning of the modern internet.[1] Since the mid-1990s the Government has developed distinctive patterns of regulation – targeting intermediaries, using the bully pulpit to promote 'voluntary' self-regulation, and promoting automated censorship tools such as web blocking – which have been influential internationally but raise significant issues of legitimacy, transparency and accountability.[2] This chapter examines this UK experience in light of the European Convention on Human Rights (ECHR) and EU law, arguing that in key regards current censorship practices fail to meet European standards.

There is already an extensive literature in this field: authors such as Akdeniz, Edwards, and Laidlaw have examined the fundamental rights implications of UK policy from a number of legal and regulatory perspectives.[3] The current chapter

---

*This chapter draws on material from 'Internet Blocking Law and Governance in the United Kingdom: An Examination of the Cleanfeed System' (University of Edinburgh, 2014) and 'Content, Control and Cyberspace: The End of Internet Regulatory Forbearance in the United Kingdom?', a paper presented at 'Governance of New Technologies' (SCRIPT Centre, University of Edinburgh School of Law, 29–31 March 2009). Disclosure: the author is Chair of civil liberties group Digital Rights Ireland.

[1] The term 'censorship' is a loaded one, but it is used here neutrally as a catch-all to describe state actions which aim to prevent the distribution or viewing of certain types of material. Censorship in this sense is narrower than 'content regulation' – it refers to schemes which aim to suppress certain material entirely, rather than merely regulating aspects such as how it is published, whether children can see it, or whether it meets the terms of use of a particular service.

[2] See, eg, B Wagner, *Global Free Expression – Governing the Boundaries of Internet Content* (Cham, Springer International Publishing, 2016) Ch 4.

[3] See, eg, Y Akdeniz, *Internet Child Pornography and the Law: National and International Responses* (Aldershot, Ashgate, 2008) Ch 9; L Edwards, 'Pornography, Censorship and the Internet' in

builds on that work in two main ways. First, it assesses emerging censorship practices in the area of terrorist material and extreme pornography. Second, it considers how recent EU legislation and European Court of Human Rights (ECtHR) case law might constrain the freedom of the UK Government and force a move towards different models of censorship.

The chapter starts by outlining the regulatory context. It then takes three case studies – child abuse material (CAM), terrorist material and pornography/extreme pornography under the Digital Economy Act 2017 – and traces how censorship has evolved from one context to the next. These systems are then evaluated against the standards set by Articles 6 and 10 ECHR, the Open Internet Regulation,[4] and the Directives on Sexual Abuse of Children[5] and on Combating Terrorism.[6] The chapter concludes by considering what lessons we can learn from the UK experience.

II. UK Censorship Schemes

A. UK Regulatory Context

UK government policy towards internet content has been very different from that applied to media such as television, cinema and video games. In those areas the norm has been sector-specific legislation overseen by statutory regulators.[7] For the Internet, however, successive governments have opted for 'legislative forbearance': application of the general law rather than sector-specific legislation, overseen by industry self-regulation rather than statutory bodies.[8] Until recently, internet content regulation in the UK has largely been carried out through a patchwork of government promoted self-regulatory systems. To summarise the most important examples:

- The Internet Watch Foundation (IWF) has operated a notice and takedown system for CAM since 1996, a URL blocking list[9] since 2004, and more recently a range of

---

L Edwards and C Waelde (eds), *Law and the Internet*, 3rd edn (Oxford, Hart Publishing, 2009); E Laidlaw, 'The Responsibilities of Free Speech Regulators: An Analysis of the Internet Watch Foundation' (2012) 20 *International Journal of Law and Information Technology* 312.

[4] Regulation (EU) 2015/2120 of the European Parliament and of the Council of 25 November 2015 laying down measures concerning open internet access and amending Directive 2002/22/EC on universal service and users' rights relating to electronic communications networks and services and Regulation (EU) No 531/2012 on roaming on public mobile communications networks within the Union [2015] OJ L310/01.

[5] Directive 2011/93/EU of the European Parliament and of the Council of 13 December 2011 on combating the sexual abuse and sexual exploitation of children and child pornography, and replacing Council Framework Decision 2004/68/JHA [2011] OJ L335/01.

[6] Directive (EU) 2017/541 of the European Parliament and of the Council of 15 March 2017 on combating terrorism and replacing Council Framework Decision 2002/475/JHA and amending Council Decision 2005/671/JHA [2017] OJ L88/06.

[7] See, eg, G Robertson and A Nicol, *Media Law*, 4th edn (London, Penguin, 2002) Chs 15 and 16.

[8] D Currie, 'The Ofcom Annual Lecture 2008'.

[9] See, eg, TJ McIntyre, 'Child Abuse Images and Cleanfeeds: Assessing Internet Blocking Systems' in I Brown (ed), *Research Handbook on Governance of the Internet* (Cheltenham, Edward Elgar, 2013).

other responses including worldwide proactive searches[10] and an image hash list[11] to enable intermediaries to detect and block uploads of files.

- Under the Mobile Operators' Code of Practice, mobile operators have age-rated and blocked certain content accessed on mobile phones since 2004, using a framework developed by the British Board of Film Classification (BBFC).[12]

- Since 2008, several filtering software companies have blocked web pages which police identify as illegally terror-related, under a confidential agreement with the Home Office.[13]

- Since 2010, the Counter Terrorism Internet Referral Unit (CTIRU) has notified sites such as Facebook and YouTube of material which it deems to be illegally terror-related, for voluntary takedown as a violation of their terms of use.[14]

- Since 2013, all major fixed line internet service providers (ISPs) have presented subscribers with an 'unavoidable choice' whether to activate 'family friendly filters', blocking access to content unsuitable for children.[15] The main providers of public Wi-Fi – covering over 90 per cent of the market – have also agreed to impose these filters on all users of their public networks.[16]

- Since 2014, the .uk domain registry Nominet has policed new registrations to prevent use of domain names which appear to 'promote sexual offences'.[17]

There has been little co-regulation or statutory regulation. The most significant is the regulation from 2009 onwards of on-demand audiovisual media services ('TV-like' services) by the Authority for Television on Demand (ATVOD) and Ofcom.[18]

---

[10] T Prosser, 'United Kingdom: New Proactive Approach to Seek Out Child Pornography' (IRIS Legal Observations of the European Audiovisual Observatory, 2013), available at http://merlin.obs.coe.int/iris/2013/8/article22.en.html (last accessed 5 July 2018).

[11] Internet Watch Foundation (IWF), 'Image Hash List', available at www.iwf.org.uk/our-services/image-hash-list (last accessed 5 July 2018).

[12] Unless a subscriber verifies that they are an adult. See Mobile UK, 'Codes of Practice', available at www.mobileuk.org/codes-of-practice.html (last accessed 5 July 2018); C Marsden, *Internet Co-Regulation: European Law, Regulatory Governance and Legitimacy in Cyberspace* (Cambridge, Cambridge University Press, 2011) 139–46.

[13] J Fae, 'The Internet Censorship Programme You're Not Allowed to Know About' (politics.co.uk, 2014), available at www.politics.co.uk/comment-analysis/2014/03/27/the-internet-censorship-programme-you-re-not-allowed-to-know (last accessed 5 July 2018).

[14] Association of Chief Police Officers (ACPO), 'CTIRU Factsheet' (March 2010).

[15] 'Ofcom Report on Internet Safety Measures: Strategies of Parental Protection for Children Online' (Ofcom, 16 December 2015) 3–6, available at http://stakeholders.ofcom.org.uk/binaries/internet/fourth_internet_safety_report.pdf (last accessed 5 July 2018).

[16] 'The Internet and Pornography: Prime Minister Calls for Action' (GOV.UK, 22 July 2013), available at www.gov.uk/government/speeches/the-internet-and-pornography-prime-minister-calls-for-action (last accessed 5 July 2018).

[17] 'Nominet Formalises Approach to Tackling Criminal Activity on .Uk Domains' (Nominet, 3 April 2014), available at www.nominet.uk/nominet-formalises-approach-to-tackling-criminal-activity-on-uk-domains (last accessed 5 July 2018).

[18] Initially by ATVOD under a co-regulatory agreement with Ofcom, until Ofcom took the function fully in-house in 2015. See J Metzdorf, 'The Implementation of the Audiovisual Media Services Directive by National Regulatory Authorities: National Responses to Regulatory Challenges' (2014) 5(2) *Journal of Intellectual Property, Information Technology and E-Commerce Law* 88; 'Ofcom Brings Regulation of "Video-on-Demand" In-House' (Ofcom, 2015), available at www.ofcom.org.uk/about-ofcom/latest/media/media-releases/2015/1520333 (last accessed 5 July 2018).

It is telling that this was not a domestic initiative but was forced on a reluctant government by the Audiovisual Media Services (AVMS) Directive.[19] As Petley notes, historically 'British governments generally do not like to appear to be playing the censor and are far happier when they can instigate apparently "self-regulatory" systems in which they play a key role, albeit very much behind the scenes'.[20]

Why has self-regulation been so dominant? In part the UK is simply reflecting a global consensus on the expediency of this approach; in 2001 the Cabinet Office adopted the principle that internet self-regulation 'generally provide[s] a more rapid and flexible means of responding to changing market needs, and achieving international consensus, than is possible through legislation'.[21] However, there are also significant domestic factors at play.

Since the early years of the Thatcher Government, trends such as privatisation, outsourcing and deregulation have led to a 'contracting state' – 'contracting' in the sense of shrinking, contracting out functions to the private sector, and also using contracts as a tool of governance.[22] The result has been a 'post-regulatory state' in which more emphasis is placed on approaches such as self-regulation, soft law and non-state rulemaking.[23] Against this background the preference for self-regulation online is not an outlier but exemplifies a wider UK tendency.[24]

Structural conditions have also played a part.[25] A highly centralised government with dominance over parliament means that the state can make credible threats of legislation and prosecution unless internet firms implement government policy.[26] This has been helped by the concentrated market for internet access, which enables the Government to achieve outcomes that cover almost all subscribers by dealing with only a small number of internet service providers (ISPs).[27]

There are, however, some developments pointing to a greater use of statutory regulation in future. The Conservative/Liberal Democrat coalition of 2010–15 continued

---

[19] Directive 2010/13/EU of the European Parliament and of the Council of 10 March 2010 on the coordination of certain provisions laid down by law, regulation or administrative action in Member States concerning the provision of audiovisual media services [2010] OJ L95/1.

[20] J Petley, 'The Regulation of Pornography on Video-on-Demand in the United Kingdom' (2014) 1 *Porn Studies* 276, at 294.

[21] Office of the e-Envoy, 'E-Policy Principles: A Policymakers Guide to the Internet', available at http://webarchive.nationalarchives.gov.uk/20040722012403/http://e-government.cabinetoffice.gov.uk/assetRoot/04/00/60/79/04006079.pdf (last accessed 5 July 2018).

[22] See, eg, J Freeman, 'The Contracting State' (2000) 28 *Florida State University Law Review* 155.

[23] C Scott, 'Regulation in the Age of Governance: The Rise of the Post-Regulatory State' in J Jordana and D Levi-Faur (eds), *The Politics of Regulation: Examining Regulatory Institutions and Instruments in the Age of Governance* (Cheltenham, Edward Elgar, 2004).

[24] R Collins, 'Networks, Markets and Hierarchies: Governance and Regulation of the UK Internet' (2006) 59 *Parliamentary Affairs* 314.

[25] For a comparative empirical analysis of structural factors shaping internet censorship, see P Theiner, Y Breindl and A Busch, 'Internet Blocking Regulations: A Comparative Analysis of 21 Liberal Democracies' (Paper presented at the U4 Cluster Conference 'Governance of a Contemporary Multilateral Institutional Architecture', Groningen, November 2015).

[26] Wagner (n 2) 80.

[27] For example, in 2015, four firms (counting BT and EE as one entity following the agreed merger) held 92% of the retail fixed broadband market: see 'Communications Market Report 2016' (Ofcom, 2016), 149, available at www.ofcom.org.uk/__data/assets/pdf_file/0024/26826/cmr_uk_2016.pdf (last accessed 5 July 2018).

to use self-regulatory tactics, but was also marked by an increased use of legislation, including a contentious widening of the online material censored by ATVOD/Ofcom.[28] Continuing this trend, the Digital Economy Act 2017 has put in place a new statutory scheme requiring pornography websites to introduce age verification, with blocking of sites which do not apply age verification or which host extreme pornography.

As described later in this chapter, developing EU and ECHR norms on freedom of expression and net neutrality[29] will also increasingly constrain self-regulatory controls on internet content and may force greater use of legislation – assuming, of course, that these standards continue to apply given the on-going uncertainty about the effects of Brexit and possible withdrawal from the ECHR.[30]

B. Child Abuse Material (CAM) and the Internet Watch Foundation (IWF)

In this area the best-known UK initiative is the Internet Watch Foundation (IWF), which was established by the Internet industry in 1996 following government pressure on ISPs, including a threat of prosecution should self-regulation not be put in place.[31] The IWF is a charitable body which has been funded by industry and the EU through successive Safer Internet Programmes. It describes its remit as being 'to remove child sexual abuse content hosted anywhere in the world [and] non-photographic child sexual abuse images hosted in the UK',[32] and the ways in which it implements this remit have expanded significantly over the two decades it has been in existence.

i. Notice and Take Down

The IWF began by establishing an internet hotline to receive and adjudicate on complaints from the public.[33] This operates using a notice and take down model which is mandatory for members under the Code of Practice; if the IWF issues a take down notice then members must remove items which they host.[34]

---

[28] D Mac Síthigh, 'Computers and the Coalition: Legislation on Law and Information Technology, 2010–2015' (2015) 12(2) *SCRIPTed* 141; D Haley, 'Dirty Laws: A Critique of the Audiovisual Media Services Regulations 2014 and Section 63 of the Criminal Justice and Immigration Act 2008' (2015) 22 *Cardozo Journal of Law and Gender* 493.

[29] Swiss Institute of Comparative Law, 'Comparative Study on Blocking, Filtering and Take-Down of Illegal Internet Content' (Council of Europe, 2017) 24–25.

[30] See, eg, T Lock et al, "Brexit and the British Bill of Rights" (Edinburgh, University of Edinburgh, 2017), available at https://papers.ssrn.com/abstract=2913566 (last accessed 5 July 2018).

[31] 'DTI Press Release P/96/636' (DTI, 14 August 1996), available at www.mit.edu/activities/safe/cases/demon/minister-statement.txt (last accessed 6 July 2018); J Carr, 'A Brief History of Child Safety Online: Child Abuse Images on the Internet' in J Brown (ed), *Online Risk to Children: Impact, Protection and Prevention* (John Wiley & Sons, 2017).

[32] 'Our Remit and Vision' (IWF), available at www.iwf.org.uk/what-we-do/why-we-exist/our-remit-and-vision (last accessed 6 July 2018). The IWF had previously (reluctantly) taken on functions in respect of criminally obscene adult content, extreme pornography, and hate speech; however by mid-2017 it had succeeded in divesting itself of these responsibilities.

[33] 'Our History' (INHOPE), available at www.inhope.org/gns/who-we-are/Ourhistory.aspx (last accessed 6 July 2018).

[34] 'FC Code of Practice' (IWF), available at www.iwf.org.uk/what-we-do/who-we-are/governance/funding-council/fc-code-of-practice (last accessed 6 July 2018).

Initially the IWF dealt mainly with complaints about individual Usenet posts. However, following pressure from the Home Office in 2003, the IWF controversially widened its policy to require members to remove entire Usenet newsgroups if it found that the newsgroups 'regularly contained' CAM, or had 'names judged to support or condone paedophilic activity'. As critics pointed out, this resulted in the suppressing of newsgroups in which the overwhelming majority of content was perfectly legal.[35]

ii. Web Blocking

The focus on newsgroups became less effective as CAM began to spread from Usenet to websites. These were mostly hosted outside the UK and for that reason beyond the reach of the IWF.[36] From 2001 onwards, ISPs came under pressure from the Home Office to introduce network level blocking of child pornography on the web, including a threat to introduce legislation unless the entire industry did so 'voluntarily'.[37] Though some smaller ISPs have refused to implement blocking, all major ISPs have acquiesced and in 2009 the Home Office eventually shelved plans to legislate when an Ofcom survey confirmed that over 98 per cent of home connections were subject to blocking.[38]

The scheme developed by the IWF – popularly but inaccurately known as 'Cleanfeed'[39] – provides members with a list of URLs to block; unlike compliance with take down notices, however, blocking is not a condition of membership and members have discretion as to whether and how they will block. The list is updated twice daily and contains about 500 URLs at any time.[40] The list is limited to 'child sexual abuse images', by which the IWF means indecent images of children that are prohibited under the Protection of Children Act 1978.[41] This does not include all forms of 'child pornography' prohibited by UK law – non-photographic images of children ('virtual child pornography') have not been included by the IWF, due to fears that their inclusion would flood the blocking system and undermine popular support.[42]

---

[35] Akdeniz (n 3) 256–57; W Grossman, 'IWF: What Are You Looking At?' *The Independent* (25 March 2002), available at www.independent.co.uk/news/business/analysis-and-features/iwf-what-are-you-looking-at-9206884.html (last accessed 6 July 2018).

[36] J Carr, *Child Abuse, Child Pornography and the Internet* (London, NCH, 2004) 18–19.

[37] S Hargrave, 'Surfing with a Safety Net' *The Guardian* (29 June 2006), available at www.guardian.co.uk/technology/2006/jun/29/guardianweeklytechnologysection (last accessed 6 July 2018); J Merrick, 'Internet Providers Face Child Porn Crackdown *The Independent* (6 September 2009), available at www.independent.co.uk/news/uk/crime/internet-providers-face-child-porn-crackdown-1782530.html (last accessed 6 July 2018).

[38] C Williams, 'Home Office Backs down on Net Censorship Laws' (*The Register*, 16 October 2009), available at www.theregister.co.uk/2009/10/16/home_office_iwf_legislation (last accessed 6 July 2018).

[39] For the history of the Cleanfeed name, see the appendix to TJ McIntyre, 'Internet Blocking Law and Governance in the United Kingdom: An Examination of the Cleanfeed System' (PhD thesis, University of Edinburgh, 2013), available at www.era.lib.ed.ac.uk/handle/1842/17971 (last accessed 6 July 2018).

[40] 'URL List Policy' (IWF), available at www.iwf.org.uk/become-a-member/services-for-members/url-list/url-list-policy (last accessed 6 July 2018).

[41] 'FAQs Regarding the IWF's Facilitation of the Blocking Initiative' (IWF), available at www.iwf.org.uk/become-a-member/services-for-members/url-list/url-blocking-faqs (last accessed 6 July 2018).

[42] 'Board Minutes 29 September 2009' (IWF, 29 September 2009), available at www.iwf.org.uk/what-we-do/who-we-are/governance/board-minutes (last accessed 6 July 2018).

iii. Blocking – Transparency and Remedies

Decisions to add a URL to the list are taken in almost all cases without notice to the site involved.[43] The URL list itself is not publicly available, nor is there a requirement of notice at the point of blocking. Although the IWF recommends that members use block pages[44] to tell users that a page has been blocked, ISPs are free to disregard that recommendation and many have used fake error messages instead.[45] Similarly, while the IWF recommends that ISPs block only the exact URL on the list, a number of ISPs have used the cheaper and cruder methods of IP address blocking or Domain Name System (DNS) poisoning instead, resulting in the blocking of unrelated pages or in some cases even completely unrelated sites.[46]

Following recommendations in a 2014 human rights audit,[47] the IWF has introduced a new appeal system which can be invoked by any person who believes that a URL has been wrongfully assessed.[48] This provides for internal review, review by police, and ultimately a formal appeal to an independent inspector (a retired High Court judge). This appeal mechanism has yet to be used.[49]

iv. Blocking as a Surveillance Tool

Should web blocking be used to identify and prosecute users who attempt to view CAM? At the outset, the industry opposed this. When the IWF established the URL list it did so in close partnership with BT, which was the first ISP to introduce blocking. When news of that blocking system emerged, BT responded to criticism by stressing that it did not log the IP addresses of computers which had attempted to reach a blocked URL.[50] There had been some police interest in using the system to identify users. This was made impossible, however, by a deliberate design choice on the part of BT to prevent the system becoming a means of surveillance.

---

[43] In exceptional cases the IWF may seek takedown at source first. See 'URL List Policies Procedures and Processes' (IWF, 11 August 2015), available at www.iwf.org.uk/sites/default/files/inline-files/URL%20List%20Policies%20Procedures%20and%20Processes%2011.8.15.pdf (last accessed 6 July 2018).

[44] Also known as 'stop pages' or 'splash pages'.

[45] 'Administrators' Noticeboard/2008 IWF Action' (Wikipedia), available at http://en.wikipedia.org/wiki/Wikipedia:Administrators%27_noticeboard/2008_IWF_action (last accessed 6 July 2018).

[46] S Lahtinen, 'Be Unlimited Causes Stir in Effort of Blocking Child Abuse Images' (Think Broadband, 11 October 2007), available at www.thinkbroadband.com/news/3235-be-unlimited-causes-stir-in-effort-of-blocking-child-abuse-images.html (last accessed 6 July 2018); J McNamee, 'Blocking of Innocent Websites by O2 Ireland' (EDRi, European Digital Rights, 14 July 2010), available at https://edri.org/edrigramnumber8-14o2-blocking-websites-ireland (last accessed 6 July 2018).

[47] K Macdonald, 'A Human Rights Audit of the Internet Watch Foundation' (2014) 24, available at www.iwf.org.uk/sites/default/files/inline-files/Human_Rights_Audit_web.pdf (last accessed 6 July 2018).

[48] 'Content Assessment Appeal Process' (IWF), available at http://iwf.org.uk/content-assessment-appeal-process (last accessed 6 July 2018); 'Content Assessment Appeal Flow Chart Process' (IWF), available at www.iwf.org.uk/sites/default/files/inline-files/Content%20assessment%20appeal%20flow%20chart%20process.pdf (last accessed 6 July 2018).

[49] M Hedley et al, 'Independent Inspection Report 2017' (IWF), available at www.iwf.org.uk/sites/default/files/inline-files/Approved%20amended%20INTERNET%20WATCH%20FOUNDATION%20Hotline%20report%20-%202017.pdf (last accessed 6 July 2018).

[50] M Hutty, 'Cleanfeed: The Facts' (LINX Public Affairs, 10 September 2004).

In 2006, however, South West Grid for Learning (SWGfL) began to use the URL list explicitly as a surveillance tool.[51] This was done as a pilot project in 2,500 schools in the South West, under Home Office supervision and with the permission of the IWF.[52] Under this system, attempts to visit blocked URLs were automatically reported to police. In the decade from 2006 to 2016 this resulted in 12 reports being generated; of these, two were false positives, one resulted in a criminal charge, one in a caution, and for the remainder there was either insufficient evidence to bring charges or it was not in the public interest to do so.

Following this pilot, the system has been commercialised and can now be bought by schools in the UK as a self-contained network device under the brand name ICAlert.[53] As well as the IWF URL list, the device also uses the CTIRU blacklist (discussed further in the next section of this chapter) and automatically reports to police any attempts to visit URLs on either list. The Metropolitan Police has expressed an interest in rolling the device out to all schools across the UK.[54]

This use of the IWF URL list illustrates the issues of function creep and the convergence of censorship and surveillance which recur throughout this chapter – in this case, a system initially developed to protect users against inadvertent access to CAM has been repurposed to presumptively criminalise such users. The school setting complicates the assessment of proportionality, as staff and students will have a reduced expectation of privacy in their internet use at school. However, it is hard to see how a system which monitored the Internet use of all students and staff at 2,500 schools for a decade but resulted in only one criminal charge could be said to be proportionate, much less one that should be replicated nationwide.

v. Proactive Searching

In 2013 the then-Prime Minister, David Cameron, launched an initiative on internet safety and children,[55] including a 'cyber-summit' focusing specifically on CAM.[56] As part of this, the Government asked the IWF to begin proactively searching the web for material to takedown and block and the IWF has developed that role since 2014, with the help of significantly increased industry funding.[57]

---

[51] 'ICAlert Pilot Project' (SWGfL, August 2016), available at http://swgfl.org.uk/magazine/ICAlert-launches-to-safeguard-schools-against-onli/PilotProjectReport.aspx (last accessed 6 July 2018).

[52] 'Board Minutes 16 January 2007' (IWF, 16 January 2007), available at www.iwf.org.uk/what-we-do/who-we-are/governance/board-minutes (last accessed 23 May 2018).

[53] C Heal, 'ICAlert: Safeguard Schools against Online Child Abuse' (SWGfL, 17 February 2017), available at http://swgfl.org.uk/magazine/ICAlert-launches-to-safeguard-schools-against-onli (last accessed 6 July 2018).

[54] 'ICAlert Related Agreements with Police and Other Organisations – a Freedom of Information Request to South West Grid for Learning Trust' (What Do They Know?, 12 April 2017), available at www.whatdotheyknow.com/request/icalert_related_agreements_with (last accessed 6 July 2018).

[55] D Cameron, 'The Internet and Pornography: Prime Minister Calls for Action' (London, NSPCC, 22 July 2013), available at www.gov.uk/government/speeches/the-internet-and-pornography-prime-minister-calls-for-action (last accessed 6 July 2018).

[56] S Gibbs, 'UK's Top Tech Executives Meet for Summit against Online Child Abuse' *The Guardian* (18 November 2013), available at www.theguardian.com/technology/2013/nov/18/uk-top-tech-executives-online-child-abuse (last accessed 6 July 2018).

[57] 'IWF Ready to Step up the Fight against Online Child Sexual Abuse Content' (IWF, 18 June 2013), available at www.iwf.org.uk/about-iwf/news/post/360-iwf-ready-to-step-up-the-fight-against-online-child-

Proactive search addresses a long-standing criticism of the IWF – that by relying on *ad hoc* reports from the public it works in a reactive and haphazard way. A proactive approach has the potential to significantly increase the amount of material taken down and the number of URLs blocked and perhaps, therefore, the overall effectiveness of the system in its expressed aim of limiting inadvertent and casual access to CAM. However, this change marks a significant move towards a policing role, particularly as the IWF will be sharing intelligence with law enforcement, and risks taking the IWF further away from its core functions.[58] The IWF has taken on this new role cautiously: it limits proactive searches to the public web, and has not implemented proactive searches of peer to peer services. This reflects concern that peer to peer searches would involve more intrusive surveillance aimed at individual users with significantly greater privacy implications.[59]

vi. Image Hash List

Another result of the Cameron initiative was the creation of an IWF Image Hash List containing hashes of CAM, which serve as 'digital fingerprints' and which hosting providers can use to automatically block uploads of identical or nearly identical images.[60] This contains in excess of 200,000 unique hashes and incorporates hashes from the Government Child Abuse Image Database (CAID) project, which compiles images seized by UK police.[61] It uses Microsoft PhotoDNA signatures as well as MD5 hashes, and so can be used to detect either exact matches of images or modified variants – albeit at some risk of false positives in the latter case.[62] The list is already used by Facebook, Google, Microsoft, Twitter and Yahoo to screen images, and the IWF is also seeking to roll it out to other firms.[63]

The IWF has described this technology as a 'game-changer', a description which has some force: hash matching offers new opportunities for censorship at scale.[64] Hash matching systems could completely change the dynamic of regulation, enabling automated detection and take down of CAM which is already available, and restricting new distribution by blocking images at the point of upload. The technology will allow for

sexual-abuse-content (last accessed 6 July 2018); 'IWF to "Proactively" Search for Illegal Content' (LINX Public Affairs, 20 June 2013).

[58] 'Police' (IWF), available at www.iwf.org.uk/partnerships/police (last accessed 6 July 2018).

[59] See the discussion of this point in Macdonald (n 47) s 8.3.

[60] L Clark, 'Child Sexual Abuse Hash Lists Shared with Internet Giants' (*WIRED UK*, 10 August 2015), available at www.wired.co.uk/article/iwf-hash-lists-child-abuse-images (last accessed 6 July 2018).

[61] 'Child Abuse Image Database' (GOV.UK, 16 November 2015), available at www.gov.uk/government/publications/child-abuse-image-database (last accessed 6 July 2018).

[62] A Microsoft researcher has stated that the false positive rate will be approximately one in two billion images. R Richmond, 'Facebook's New Way to Combat Child Pornography' *New York Times* (19 May 2011), available at http://gadgetwise.blogs.nytimes.com/2011/05/19/facebook-to-combat-child-porn-using-microsofts-technology (last accessed 6 July 2018).

[63] 'Tech Breakthrough Announced on the 20th Anniversary of IWF's First Child Sexual Abuse Imagery Report' (IWF, 21 October 2016), available at www.iwf.org.uk/news/tech-breakthrough-announced-on-20th-anniversary-of-iwfs-first-child-sexual-abuse-imagery (last accessed 6 July 2018).

[64] 'Hash List Could Be Game-Changer in the Global Fight against Child Sexual Abuse Images Online' (IWF, 10 August 2015), available at www.iwf.org.uk/news/hash-list-could-be-game-changer-global-fight-against-child-sexual-abuse-images-online (last accessed 6 July 2018).

an image to be categorised once and once only, eliminating a repetitive aspect of the workload of IWF analysts and allowing for more time to be devoted to new images and proactive searching.

From a fundamental rights perspective, however, hash matching presents new threats to privacy. Since 2004, similar hash value systems have been used in the United States[65] in a way which goes beyond scanning publicly available materials to include the scanning of private emails and files.[66] For example, Microsoft scans all files on its OneDrive service[67] using PhotoDNA and Google scans all emails sent through Gmail,[68] and there have been numerous cases of individuals arrested as a result.[69] This form of indiscriminate surveillance is disproportionate in itself and is also prone to function creep – being readily co-opted for other types of content. There is a risk that scanning of private communications and files is being normalised in the context of CAM as a prelude to its use in other areas.

vii. Public Law Status and Governance

The IWF is neither a statutory body nor publicly funded. However, it came into being at the behest of the state, was reorganised in 2000 on the basis of a review[70] carried out for central government, and carries out its functions on the basis of a memorandum of understanding between the Association of Chief Police Officers (ACPO) and the Crown Prosecution Service (CPS).[71] Significantly, in that document the IWF is described by ACPO and the CPS as carrying out functions for the state:

> The IWF is ... supported by UK law enforcement and CPS and *works in partnership with the Government* to provide a 'hotline' for individuals or organisations to report potentially illegal content and to seek out illegal content online. *It then assesses and judges the material on behalf of UK law enforcement agencies.*[72]

At an operational level we can also see this in the close working arrangements between the IWF and the police. UK police forces direct complaints of online illegality in the first instance to the IWF, and in assessing those complaints IWF analysts rely on

---

[65] It is not clear whether hash matching is being used against the private emails and files of European users in the same way; if so, this will raise significant questions regarding the application of data protection law.

[66] See, eg, TJ McIntyre, 'Blocking Child Pornography on the Internet: European Union Developments' (2010) 24 *International Review of Law, Computers & Technology* 209, s 5.6.

[67] Microsoft, 'About Our Practices and Your Data', available at https://blogs.microsoft.com/datalaw/our-practices (last accessed 6 July 2018); L Kelion, 'Microsoft Alerts Police to Child Porn' (*BBC News*, 6 August 2014), available at www.bbc.com/news/technology-28682686 (last accessed 6 July 2018).

[68] R McCormick, 'Google Scans Everyone's Email for Child Porn, and It Just Got a Man Arrested' (*The Verge*, 5 August 2014), available at www.theverge.com/2014/8/5/5970141/how-google-scans-your-gmail-for-child-porn (last accessed 6 July 2018).

[69] See, eg, S Gibbs, 'Microsoft Tip Led Police to Arrest Man over Child Abuse Images' *The Guardian* (7 August 2014), available at www.theguardian.com/technology/2014/aug/07/microsoft-tip-police-child-abuse-images-paedophile (last accessed 6 July 2018).

[70] KPMG Peat Marwick and Denton Hall, 'Review of the Internet Watch Foundation' (London, 1999).

[71] Crown Prosecution Service and Association of Chief Police Officers, 'Memorandum of Understanding Between Crown Prosecution Service (CPS) and the Association of Chief Police Officers (ACPO) Concerning Section 46 Sexual Offences Act 2003', available at www.iwf.org.uk/sites/default/files/inline-files/CPS%20ACPO%20S46%20MoU%202014%202.pdf (last accessed 6 July 2018).

[72] *Ibid*, emphasis added.

training from police and apply standards of legality which reflect the criminal law.[73] In 2010 the IWF formalised this relationship further by entering into a 'Service Level Agreement' with ACPO which 'provide[s] a protocol for the management of investigations into criminal content' hosted in the UK and to guide the interactions between the IWF and its law enforcement partners.[74]

This close integration with the work of the police means that the IWF is in many ways operating as a *de facto* public body, and to its credit it has recognised this point: in 2001 it accepted that it is 'acting in a quasi-regulatory role on matters of great public interest' and therefore that it should commit to higher standards of governance and transparency.[75] Also in 2001, the IWF board declared itself to be bound by the Human Rights Act 1998, stating that:

> The IWF accepts the principles of the European Convention on Human Rights and undertakes to be governed subject to the Human Rights Act on the basis that it should be treated as a public body.[76]

This is an important concession which opens the door to litigants who wish to challenge its decisions. As Walden puts it, '[t]he IWF, in accepting that it is subject to the Human Rights Act, is essentially telling a future court that they would be susceptible to judicial review'.[77]

That said, the concession of public body status is at best only a partial response to criticism that the IWF exercises considerable power in a way which is largely unchecked.[78] While judicial review will allow challenges to particular acts of the IWF, it still leaves the IWF outside the scope of other public law oversight mechanisms, such as the Freedom of Information Act 2000.[79] As Cane has pointed out, 'judge made administrative law is only the tiny tip of a huge iceberg of norms by which the performance of public functions is framed, influenced, guided, and regulated'.[80]

Another limitation is that the concession applies only to the IWF, but the systems it has established include many other entities whose actions will not be subject to judicial review. For example, an ISP may choose to use a technology which over-blocks, to provide a deceptive error message to users instead of a stop page, or to monitor users' private emails against the IWF Hash List. These actions by ISPs will have significant effects in their own right, but being outside the control of the IWF would escape judicial scrutiny.

---

[73] 'FAQs Regarding the IWF's Facilitation of the Blocking Initiative' (n 41).

[74] Internet Watch Foundation and Association of Chief Police Officers, 'Service Level Agreement between the Association of Chief Police Officers (ACPO) and the Internet Watch Foundation (IWF)', available at www.iwf.org.uk/sites/default/files/inline-files/SLA%20ACPO%20IWF%20FINAL%20OCT%202010.pdf (last accessed 6 July 2018).

[75] R Darlington, 'Chairing the Internet Watch Foundation', available at www.rogerdarlington.co.uk/iwf.html (accessed 23 May 2018).

[76] See Akdeniz (n 3) 264.

[77] I Walden, 'The Future of Freedom of Speech' (SCL 6th Annual Policy Forum: 'The New Shape of European Internet Regulation', London, 15 September 2011), sound recording available at www.scl.org/files/scl_policy_forum_2011/The_Future_of_Freedom_of_Speech_-_Professor_Ian_Waldren.mp3 (last accessed 6 July 2018).

[78] See, eg, Laidlaw (n 3).

[79] D Mac Síthigh, 'Datafin to Virgin Killer: Self-Regulation and Public Law' (9 April 2009), available at https://papers.ssrn.com/abstract=1374846 (last accessed 6 July 2018).

[80] P Cane, *Administrative Law*, 4th edn (Oxford, Oxford University Press, 2004) 8.

C. Terrorist Material

i. Background

Since the Internet became a mainstream technology there has been concern that it can be used to promote terrorism.[81] Initially the focus was on its use as an organisational tool for terrorist groups, but in the 2000s the dominant narrative – particularly in relation to jihadi terrorism – shifted to one of 'radicalisation' and the use of the Internet to indoctrinate and recruit.[82] The main concern now is that the Internet can foster a decentralised type of terrorism: an 'autonomous radicalisation', in which individuals or small groups are influenced by online material but otherwise act to plan and carry out an attack under their own initiative.[83]

The result has been a strong emphasis in UK and European counter-terrorist policy on internet censorship, though this has not gone unchallenged. The concept of radicalisation itself has been condemned as simplistic and reductionist.[84] Stevens and Neumann have been critical of the focus on censorship and technical solutions, describing strategies which rely on reducing the availability of content online as necessarily 'crude, expensive and counterproductive'.[85] Most fundamentally, while it is plausible that internet content may promote violence, there is little evidence as to whether or how it actually does so.[86]

Whatever the merits of internet censorship as a counter-terrorism strategy, it is now firmly cemented in the UK and Europe. Following the 7 July 2005 London bombings the UK adopted an offence of 'encouragement of terrorism' which criminalises not just direct incitement to violence but also speech which might indirectly promote terrorism.[87] This fits into a wider trend by which European states have adopted laws which criminalise 'glorification', 'apology for', 'encouragement' and 'public promotion' of terrorism.[88] At a European level this was matched in 2005 by the Council of Europe Convention on the Prevention of Terrorism, which requires states to criminalise 'public provocation to commit a terrorist offence',[89] and also most recently by the Directive on Combating Terrorism.[90] The Directive, agreed in March 2017, requires Member States to criminalise 'public provocation' including 'glorification of terrorist acts'[91]

---

[81] IO Lesser et al, *Countering the New Terrorism* (Rand Corporation, 1999) 66.

[82] J Ryan, *Countering Militant Islamist Radicalisation on the Internet: A User Driven Strategy to Recover the Web* (Dublin, Institute of European Affairs, 2007) Ch 1.

[83] The term 'lone wolf' is often used but is misleading as in many cases attackers have some contact with or support from the terrorist group. See, eg, R Pantucci, *A Typology of Lone Wolves: Preliminary Analysis of Lone Islamist Terrorists* (London, International Centre for the Study of Radicalisation and Political Violence London, England, 2011).

[84] A Kundnani, 'Radicalisation: The Journey of a Concept' in C Baker-Beall, C Heath-Kelly and L Jarvis (eds), *Counter-Radicalisation: Critical Perspectives* (Routledge, 2014).

[85] T Stevens and PR Neumann, *Countering Online Radicalisation: A Strategy for Action* (London, International Centre for the Study of Radicalisation and Political Violence, 2009) 1.

[86] M Conway, 'Determining the Role of the Internet in Violent Extremism and Terrorism: Six Suggestions for Progressing Research' (2016) 40 *Studies in Conflict & Terrorism* 77, 78.

[87] Terrorism Act 2006, ss 1 and 2 cover publication and dissemination of statements likely to be understood as encouraging terrorism.

[88] D Banisar, *Speaking of Terror* (Strasbourg,Council of Europe, 2008) 20.

[89] Convention on the Prevention of Terrorism, Art 5.

[90] Directive (EU) 2017/541.

[91] *Ibid*, Art 5.

and 'to ensure the prompt removal of online content' which amounts to public provocation.[92] It also permits Member States to 'take measures to block access to such content' where removal is not feasible.[93]

These glorification offences have been controversial due to their vague terms, remoteness from any completed offence, and fears that they will chill legitimate discussion.[94] There is an extensive literature assessing the extent to which they are compatible with freedom of expression.[95] In this section, however, we focus not on the content of these offences but rather the procedures by which they are policed in the UK. How, in practice, is this type of speech suppressed, and what implications does this have?

ii. Take Down Notices under Section 3 of the Terrorism Act 2006, and Voluntary Take Downs

Section 3 of the Terrorism Act 2006 provides a mechanism for police to serve notices on service providers that material is 'unlawfully terrorism-related', requiring that the material be removed. Failure to do so means that the service provider will be treated as having endorsed it, giving rise to possible criminal liability.

The section was criticised at the time as effectively delegating decisions on legality to police, with no judicial oversight, but it was defended by the Government on the basis that this was necessary to avoid delay. Despite that claim, it has never been used.[96] Instead, it has been deliberately kept in reserve as a fall-back in case 'negotiations with industry falter'.[97] Guidance from the Home Office requires police to use voluntary arrangements where possible, on the basis that these give:

> greater flexibility to discuss how to ensure the material is removed, how further publications can be prevented, whether there is other similar material, whether evidence identifying those involved in publishing the material can be obtained, whether the accounts responsible for the publications can be terminated, timescales, etc.[98]

This emphasis on voluntary cooperation is significant. As with child abuse images, a reliance on informal cooperation with industry is seen by the state as more effective and as lending itself to outcomes, such as preventing republication and terminating user accounts, which are not provided for by law.

---

[92] *Ibid*, Art 21(1).

[93] *Ibid*, Art 21(2).

[94] B Emmerson, 'Report of the Special Rapporteur on the Promotion and Protection of Human Rights and Fundamental Freedoms While Countering Terrorism, A/HRC/31/65' (New York, United Nations General Assembly, 2016) 14–16.

[95] See, eg SC Ekaratne, 'Redundant Restriction: The UK's Offense of Glorifying Terrorism' (2010) 23 *Harvard Human Rights Journal* 205.

[96] 'Memorandum to the Home Affairs Committee: Post-Legislative Scrutiny of the Terrorism Act 2006' (UK Home Office) 6–7, available at www.official-documents.gov.uk/document/cm81/8186/8186.pdf (last accessed 6 July 2018).

[97] *Ibid*.

[98] 'Guidance on Notices Issued under Section 3 of the Terrorism Act 2006' (WhatDoTheyKnow, 2 May 2010) 6, available at www.whatdotheyknow.com/request/implementation_of_terrorism_act (last accessed 6 July 2018).

The take down function is administered by the specialist police Counter Terrorism Internet Referral Unit (CTIRU), established in 2010 by ACPO.[99] The CTIRU has followed the model of the IWF in relation to child abuse images by encouraging individuals to make anonymous reports about online material. The CTIRU prioritises English language websites, and has massively increased the numbers of take down requests it issues: from 1,527 in 2010 and 2011 to 121,151 in 2016 – over 2,000 per week.[100]

This is an opaque process, but a recent glimpse behind the curtain suggests that it is of variable quality: in evidence before the House of Commons Home Affairs Committee Google has said that the accuracy rate of requests from the CTIRU in relation to YouTube is only 80 per cent.[101] It is remarkable that one in every five take down requests from a specialist police unit is rejected on the basis that the video in question is neither illegal nor contrary to YouTube's own 'community standards'. The implications are unappealing: either the CTIRU and/or YouTube are at fault in making inconsistent decisions, the assessment of this material inherently involves an undesirable level of subjectivity, or perhaps both.

The CTIRU has been influential in a European context, and in July 2015 Europol launched the European Union Internet Referral Unit (EU IRU) which, as the name suggests, was largely modelled on the CTIRU. The revised Europol Regulation provides for this by conferring power on Europol to refer internet content 'to the online service providers concerned for their voluntary consideration of the compatibility of the referred internet content with their own terms and conditions'.[102] As with the CTIRU, the voluntary nature of the scheme is being relied upon to insulate it from a requirement for procedural safeguards or judicial oversight. Europol has asserted that:

> Referral activities will not constitute an enforceable act, thus the decision and related implementation of the referral is taken under full responsibility and accountability of the concerned service provider … The overall process of the EU IRU reporting terrorist and extremist online content to the online service provider is no different from any citizen flagging content for removal by the respective online service provider.[103]

iii. Automating Take Down and Preventing Uploads

While European, as distinct from national, measures are beyond the scope of this chapter, it is worth noting that the UK has been active in promoting the use of hash

---

[99] ACPO (n 14).

[100] '250,000th Piece of Online Extremist/Terrorist Material to Be Removed' (Metropolitan Police, 23 December 2016), available at http://news.met.police.uk/news/250000th-piece-of-online-extremist-slash-terrorist-material-to-be-removed-208698 (last accessed 6 July 2018).

[101] 'Oral Evidence: Hate Crime and its Violent Consequences' (House of Commons Home Affairs Committee, 2017), available at http://data.parliament.uk/writtenevidence/committeeevidence.svc/evidence-document/home-affairs-committee/hate-crime-and-its-violent-consequences/oral/48836.pdf (last accessed 6 July 2018).

[102] Regulation (EU) 2016/794 of the European Parliament and of the Council of 11 May 2016 on the European Union Agency for Law Enforcement Cooperation (Europol) and replacing and repealing Council Decisions 2009/371/JHA, 2009/934/JHA, 2009/935/JHA, 2009/936/JHA and 2009/968/JHA, Article 4(1)(m). Emphasis added.

[103] C Jones, 'Policing the Internet: From Terrorism and Extremism to "Content Used by Traffickers to Attract Migrants and Refugees"' (Statewatch, March 2016) 2, available at www.statewatch.org/analyses/no-290-policing-internet.pdf (last accessed 6 July 2018).

value matching and other automated censorship tools through the EU Internet Forum, drawing on the experience of the IWF in relation to CAM. The Minister for Internet Safety and Security, Baroness Shields, describes the aim as being:

> to improve solutions that classify the language of extremism, automate the identification and removal of dangerous content at scale, and create tools that better tackle automated bots and other techniques that support these propaganda machines.[104]

The main result of this initiative has been a December 2016 agreement to establish an industry database of hash values for images and videos, with a view to pre-emptively blocking uploads.[105] Facebook, Microsoft, Twitter, and YouTube are the initial partners, but the intention is also to make the database available to other firms. Rather than assessing legality, the firms will add material to the database on the basis that they are 'hashes of the most extreme and egregious terrorist images and videos we have removed from our services – content most likely to violate all of our respective companies' content policies'.[106] Regarding procedures, the firms have stated that:

> each company will independently determine what image and video hashes to contribute to the shared database. No personally identifiable information will be shared, and matching content will not be automatically removed. Each company will continue to apply its own policies and definitions of terrorist content when deciding whether to remove content when a match to a shared hash is found. And each company will continue to apply its practice of transparency and review for any government requests, as well as retain its own appeal process for removal decisions and grievances.[107]

This leaves a number of questions unanswered. Will the database be used to scan private messages? Could it be used to detect and report users to law enforcement if they email or upload particular material? Both of these developments have already taken place in the context of CAM, where blocking and hash matching have both rapidly become prosecution tools, and it would not be surprising if the use of this database were to evolve in the same way.

Indeed, the database may already be used for these purposes. A June 2017 story in the *Guardian* indicates that Facebook has established a 'counter-terrorism unit' which has the power to 'carry out investigations into user accounts if they are suspect of having links to terrorist groups'.[108] Moderators are given '[f]ull account access ... to any profile once it has been flagged by algorithms looking for certain names, images

---

[104] J Shields, 'Countering Online Radicalisation and Extremism' (George Washington University Centre for Cyber and Homeland Security, 7 April 2017), available at www.gov.uk/government/speeches/countering-online-radicalisation-and-extremism-baroness-shields-speech (last accessed 6 July 2018).

[105] 'EU Internet Forum: A Major Step Forward in Curbing Terrorist Content on the Internet' (European Commission, 8 December 2016), available at http://europa.eu/rapid/press-release_IP-16-4328_en.htm (last accessed 6 July 2018).

[106] 'Partnering to Help Curb the Spread of Terrorist Content Online' (Twitter Blog, 5 December 2016), available at https://blog.twitter.com/2016/partnering-to-help-curb-the-spread-of-terrorist-content-online (last accessed 23 May 2018).

[107] *Ibid.*

[108] O Solon, 'Counter-Terrorism Was Never Meant to Be Silicon Valley's Job. Is That Why It's Failing?' *The Guardian* (29 June 2017), available at www.theguardian.com/technology/2017/jun/29/silicon-valley-counter-terrorism-facebook-twitter-youtube-google (last accessed 6 July 2018).

or hashtags associated with terrorist groups' and may then 'access the individual's private messages, see who they are talking to and what they are saying, and view where they have been'. In a remarkable passage, the story describes how this results in users routinely being referred to police:

> The team's highest priority is to identify 'traveling fighters' for Isis and Al-Qaida. Someone would be categorized as such if their profile has content that's sympathetic to extremism and if they had, for example, visited Raqqa in Syria before traveling back to Europe. When a traveling fighter is identified – which according to one insider takes place at least once a day – the account is escalated to an internal Facebook team that decides whether to pass information to law enforcement.

It would take another chapter to discuss all the issues presented by this form of privatised policing (not least the data protection issues involved in profiling users and routinely accessing private messages in this way) but the story is significant for the way in which it again highlights the intersection between censorship and surveillance. As the CJEU recognised in *Scarlet (Extended) v SABAM*,[109] filtering systems which scan communications are an inherent threat to the fundamental rights to privacy and data protection, as well as the right of freedom of expression.

iv. Blocking

a. Enlisting the IWF?

In addition to take down, the UK Government has long sought ISP-level blocking of terrorist web pages. In 2008 and again in 2011, the Home Office floated the idea that terrorist material should be incorporated into the IWF list so that ISPs would block access in the same way as they do for CAM, using the Cleanfeed system.[110] The 2015 Counter-Extremism Strategy again addressed ISP blocking, but took a different tone, talking instead about 'learning from' the IWF rather than directly using its structures.[111] This change in emphasis is significant. The IWF has resisted expanding its remit to new categories of material, largely due to fears of reputational damage and increased costs which might undermine its child protection role.[112] It seems that the Government has, for the time being, abandoned any intention to enlist the IWF in relation to terrorist material.

---

[109] C-70/10 *Scarlet (Extended) v SABAM* EU:C:2011:771 (Judgment of 24 November 2011).

[110] H Mulholland, 'Government Targets Extremist Websites' *The Guardian* (17 January 2008), available at www.theguardian.com/politics/2008/jan/17/uksecurity.terrorism (accessed 23 May 2018); C Williams, 'Jacqui's Jihad on Web Extremism Flops' (*The Register*, 13 February 2009), available at www.theregister.co.uk/2009/02/13/jacqui_smith_web_extremism (last accessed 6 July 2018); Home Office, *Prevent Strategy* (London, Her Majesty's Stationery Office (HMSO), 2011) 79; J Fae, 'Gov and ISPs Clash over Informal Policing of Net' (*The Register*, 16 March 2011), available at www.theregister.co.uk/2011/03/16/self_regulation (last accessed 6 July 2018).

[111] Home Office, *Counter-Extremism Strategy* (London, HMSO, 2015) 25.

[112] For example, in relation to extreme pornography and non-photographic images, see 'Board Minutes 25 November 2008' (IWF, 25 November 2008), available at www.iwf.org.uk/what-we-do/who-we-are/governance/board-minutes (last accessed 6 July 2018); 'Board Minutes 29 September 2009' (IWF) (n 42).

b. CTIRU Blacklist

In a parallel programme, however, the UK Government has proceeded with its own URL list system, compiling a blacklist of terrorist-related URLs which it makes available under direct agreements with companies which provide filtering software.[113] From November 2008 to February 2011 the Labour Government ran this as a pilot project, and following a pause for evaluation it restarted it in July 2011, and it has been in place since then.

There is little transparency about the system, but if we piece together material in the public domain and responses to several Freedom of Information Act requests[114] it appears to operate as follows:

- The CTIRU identifies URLs relating to material which breach the Terrorism Acts 2000 and 2006 but which is hosted overseas and cannot be taken down.

- That material is (in some cases at least) considered for legality by specialist prosecutors in the CPS.[115]

- The URLs assessed as relating to illegal material are passed under a confidentiality agreement to filtering companies that restrict access to those URLs in their software.[116]

- There is no notification made to website owners, nor is there an opportunity to make representations about the blacklisting before or after the fact. There is no mechanism to appeal against a decision to blacklist.

- There is no information as to whether or how the list is checked periodically to determine whether URLs should remain blocked.

- Individuals who attempt to view a blacklisted URL will see a stop screen indicating that it has been blocked, but not that the CTIRU was responsible for blacklisting it.

- As of 2013, approximately 1,000 URLs were on the list.[117]

The blacklist was rolled out initially to companies that supply filtering products across 'the public estate', including locations such as schools, colleges and libraries. In December 2013 the Report of the Prime Minister's Task Force on Extremism indicated an intention to use the blacklist more widely, saying that the Government would 'work

---

[113] See generally Fae (n 13).
[114] 'Filtering of Terrorist Material – a Freedom of Information Request to Home Office' (WhatDoTheyKnow, 13 November 2010), available at www.whatdotheyknow.com/request/filtering_of_terrorist_material (last accessed 6 July 2018); 'Filtering of Terrorist Material – a Freedom of Information Request to Home Office' (WhatDoTheyKnow, 31 July 2011), available at www.whatdotheyknow.com/request/filtering_of_terrorist_material_2 (last accessed 6 July 2018); 'Current Status of Terrorist Internet Filtering – a Freedom of Information Request to Home Office' (WhatDoTheyKnow, 9 May 2013), available at www.whatdotheyknow.com/request/current_status_of_terrorist_inte (last accessed 6 July 2018).
[115] 'CPS Role in Internet Filtering of Terrorist Material – a Freedom of Information Request to Crown Prosecution Service' (WhatDoTheyKnow, 3 July 2013), available at www.whatdotheyknow.com/request/cps_role_in_internet_filtering_o (last accessed 6 July 2018).
[116] 'Current Status of Terrorist Internet Filtering – a Freedom of Information Request to Home Office' (n 114).
[117] HC Deb 19 June 2013, vol 564, col 687W.

with internet companies to restrict access to terrorist material online which is hosted overseas but illegal under UK law'.[118]

Following pressure from the Prime Minister, in November 2014 the major UK ISPs (BT, TalkTalk, Virgin Media and Sky) agreed to adopt the blacklist.[119] Unlike the IWF URL list, however, the blacklist is currently only used in their 'family friendly' internet connections – it is not used for connections where the subscriber has chosen to disable parental filters. Nevertheless, this still covers a significant portion of UK internet users: depending on the ISP between 6 per cent of subscribers (BT) and 30–40 per cent of subscribers (Sky) have these network level filters active.[120]

The Home Office has stated that there is no statutory underpinning for the blacklist, saying that it is done 'on a voluntary basis'.[121] The only formal basis appears to be contracts with the firms which receive the blacklist, which require them to keep the list confidential.[122] The Home Office has refused to release copies of these contracts, and in particular has refused to confirm how the contracts deal with liability for wrongful blocking – though the context suggests that the Home Office has agreed to indemnify the firms against any liability.[123]

The criteria and procedures used for blocking are set out by internal guidelines. These are not publicly available, but have been partially disclosed in response to a Freedom of Information Act request.[124] The test applied is whether the publication of material breaches section 57 or 58 of the Terrorism Act 2000 (information useful in commission of act of terrorism; eg bomb-making manuals) or sections 1 or 2 of the Terrorism Act 2006 (eg encouragement to commit acts of terrorism and glorification). Guidance for the decision makers includes the question 'Does the context of material demonstrate that it is aimed primarily at an extremist audience?', explaining that '[f]or instance, a video on a mainstream media web site is likely to be aimed at a different audience to one in an extremist chat forum'.

This guidance illustrates that the decision to block involves a complex assessment of whether material is 'likely to be understood' as encouraging terrorism, including the context in which it is published and its target audience – the same video may be blocked if it appears on an extremist chat forum but not if it appears on a mainstream news site – making it particularly inappropriate that the decision should be carried out by the executive in secret, without any notification or appeal mechanism.

The decision to blacklist has no direct legal effect. However, it is significant that the filtering companies do not exercise any discretion in deciding whether to block the URLs provided by the CTIRU: unlike the referral of videos to YouTube,

---

[118] Prime Minister's Task Force on Tackling Radicalisation and Extremism, *Tackling Extremism in the UK* (London, Cabinet Office, 2013) 3, available at www.gov.uk/government/uploads/system/uploads/attachment_data/file/263181/ETF_FINAL.pdf (last accessed 6 July 2018).

[119] A Hern, 'ISPs Criticised over Deal to Filter Extremist Material Online' *The Guardian* (14 November 2014), available at www.theguardian.com/technology/2014/nov/14/isps-filter-extremist-material-internet (last accessed 6 July 2018).

[120] Ofcom, 'Ofcom Report on Internet Safety Measures (n 15) 25–28.

[121] 'Filtering of Terrorist Material' (n 114).

[122] Filtering of Terrorist Material' (n 114).

[123] Filtering of Terrorist Material' (n 114).

[124] Filtering of Terrorist Material' (n 114).

for example, there is no independent assessment of compliance with terms of use which might distance the state from the censorship taking place. In this context, an official and effectively binding determination that particular material amounts to a criminal offence certainly appears to be a direct 'interference by public authority' with the right to freedom of expression so as to ground an action under section 7 of the Human Rights Act 1998.

This remedy is, however, largely theoretical, given that the individual will have no notification that the Home Office has blacklisted a particular URL, and the filtering companies are contractually precluded from revealing this fact. In these circumstances, there is an argument to be made that the secret nature of the system also means that there is no 'adequate and effective remedy' as required by Article 13 ECHR.

D. Pornography and Extreme Pornography under the Digital Economy Act 2017

i. Background

Part 3 of the Digital Economy Act 2017 creates a general obligation to introduce age controls on online pornography as well as wide-ranging statutory powers to block pornographic material including, but not limited to, extreme pornography.[125] As such it is a significant departure from the self-regulatory models used to date, and also a break from Western European norms in providing for extensive blocking of legal material.[126] By setting out to regulate the behaviour of websites based outside the UK, it is also an ambitious attempt to compel firms to abide by national law even though they may have no connection with the UK.

The background to the 2017 Act is a longstanding public concern (many have said moral panic[127]) about the availability of pornography to children. This has developed against a wider background where puritanical views of the right have been matched by a swing on the left from libertine to censorious, leaving pornography with few friends on either side of the UK political spectrum.[128] The result has been cross party consensus on a need for greater controls, initially expressed by pressuring ISPs to adopt family-friendly filters, followed by an aggressive expansion of the implementation of the AVMS Directive,[129] and culminating in the 2017 Act, which implements the following 2015 Conservative Party manifesto pledge: '[W]e will stop children's exposure to harmful sexualised content online, by requiring age verification for access to all sites containing pornographic material'.[130]

---

[125] Though age verification was previously in place for the narrow category of TV-like material regulated by the AVMS Directive, and statutory blocking powers in the context of intellectual property infringement.

[126] Putting the UK in the company of the Russian Federation and Turkey: Swiss Institute of Comparative Law (n 29) 14.

[127] J Greer, 'Children and Internet Pornography: A Moral Panic, a Salvation for Censors and Trojan Horse for Government Colonisation of the Digital Frontier' in VE Cree, G Clapton and M Smith (eds), *Revisiting Moral Panics* (Bristol, Policy Press, 2015).

[128] J Barnett, *Porn Panic! Sex and Censorship in the UK* (John Hunt Publishing, 2016) Ch 5.

[129] Petley (n 20).

[130] 'The Conservative Party Manifesto 2015', p 35.

ii. Age Verification

The main aim of Part 3 of the 2017 Act is to reduce availability of pornography to children by requiring commercial sites to implement age verification. It applies to any person, anywhere in the world, regardless of whether they target the UK, establishing a general rule that they shall not 'make pornographic material available on the internet to persons in the United Kingdom on a commercial basis' unless they ensure that 'the material is not normally accessible by persons under the age of 18'.[131] The restriction is not limited to websites: it prohibits any form of 'making available on the internet' which would also appear to include apps and peer to peer services.[132] 'Pornographic material' is defined in some detail, but broadly speaking means material 'produced solely or principally for the purposes of sexual arousal'.[133]

a. Enforcement

Enforcement is the responsibility of an age-verification regulator to be designated by the Secretary of State and confirmed by both Houses of Parliament.[134] In February 2018 the Department for Digital, Culture, Media & Sport designated the BBFC – a private company, albeit one that is already embedded in a number of co-regulatory schemes for UK media regulation.[135]

The age-verification regulator can impose financial penalties (up to £250,000 or five per cent of 'qualifying turnover'), or seek an injunction against a person who fails to comply with the age verification requirement.[136] The regulator also has two powers to indirectly enforce age-verification, designed with overseas websites in mind.

b. Blocking

First, the regulator is empowered to block sites which do not age-verify, by giving a notice to an ISP requiring them to 'prevent persons in the United Kingdom from being able to access the offending material'.[137] The ISP is then obliged either to take 'steps specified in the notice', or to implement 'arrangements that appear to the [ISP] to be appropriate' to give effect to the blocking – a formula which gives the regulator power to specify the blocking technology to be used.

The section explicitly permits over-blocking by specifying that the blocking measures may 'have the effect of preventing persons in the United Kingdom from

---

[131] Digital Economy Act 2017, s 14(1).
[132] N Brown, 'Age Verification and Online Pornography under the DEA 2017: Whose Fine Is It Anyway?' (July 2017), available at www.scl.org/articles/3920-age-verification-and-online-pornography-under-the-dea-2017-whose-fine-is-it-anyway (last accessed 6 July 2018).
[133] See Digital Economy Act 2017, s 15.
[134] *Ibid*, ss 16 and 17.
[135] 'Notice of Designation of Age-Verification Regulator' (Department for Digital, Culture, Media & Sport, 21 February 2018), available at www.gov.uk/government/uploads/system/uploads/attachment_data/file/683354/BBFC_Designation_Notice.pdf (last accessed 6 July 2018).
[136] Digital Economy Act 2017, s 19.
[137] *Ibid*, s 23.

being able to access material other than the offending material'.[138] The implication is that the regulator does not have to block at the level of the individual URL but may block, for example, all content hosted on a particular site. This will be significant given the move towards websites offering secure (HTTPS) connections: blocking of individual pages becomes impossible where a website is served in this way, leaving blocking of the full site as the all-or-nothing option.[139]

There is no requirement of proportionality regarding either the decision to block or the manner of its implementation (such as the collateral damage it might cause, or the cost it might impose on the ISP). The regulator may, but is not required to, specify that a blocking notice (stop page) be used to tell individuals why the material is not available.[140]

c. Notices to Payment and Ancillary Service Providers

The second indirect enforcement power permits the regulator to issue a notice to payment service providers (such as credit card processors) and ancillary service providers (others providing services to the site, including advertisers and, crucially, platforms such as Twitter[141]), specifying that a person has failed to comply with the age verification duty.[142] The Act does not require these providers to take any specific action on receipt of such a notice,[143] but the expectation is that they will choose to cut off dealings with sites which are 'named and shamed'[144] – in effect resulting in a form of state-directed boycott, intended to have extraterritorial effect by targeting firms such as Visa, MasterCard and PayPal. Again, there is no requirement that this be a proportionate response.

d. Procedures

The procedures to be followed by the regulator differ as between the fining, blocking, and notice of non-compliance powers, without any obvious justification. In the case of fines the regulator must give the person to be fined prior notice and an opportunity to be heard.[145] In the case of blocking, the regulator must give the non-complying person prior notice but, surprisingly, is not required to give them an opportunity to be heard.[146]

---

[138] *Ibid*, s 23(3).
[139] 'Internet Society Perspectives on Internet Content Blocking' (Internet Society, 2017) 15, available at www.internetsociety.org/resources/doc/2017/internet-content-blocking (last accessed 6 July 2018).
[140] Digital Economy Act 2017, s 23(4).
[141] The Government position was set out in the Lords as being that 'services, including Twitter, can be classified by regulators as ancillary service providers where they are enabling or facilitating the making available of pornographic or prohibited material'. See Brown (n 132).
[142] Digital Economy Act 2017, s 21.
[143] Though it may be that a notice might put a platform or hosting provider at risk of accessorial liability if they failed to act, on the basis that they would have actual knowledge of publication of obscene material or extreme pornography to persons within the UK. See eg S Frances, 'Digital Economy Bill Contains Mandatory Age-Verification, but Avoids Blocking' (*LINX Public Affairs*, 7 July 2016); Brown (n 132).
[144] B Schafer, 'No Data Protection Please, We Are British – Privacy, Porn and Prurience in the Digital Economy Bill' (2017) 41 *Datenschutz und Datensicherheit-DuD* 354, 357.
[145] Digital Economy Act 2017, s 19(3).
[146] *Ibid*, s 23(10).

For a notice of non-compliance to payment service providers and ancillary service providers, only notification after the fact is required[147] – remarkably so, given the reputational and business damage such a notice is intended to cause. The regulator must make arrangements for appeals against these enforcement decisions, by a person who is 'sufficiently independent of' the regulator.[148]

Each of these enforcement powers is discretionary. Section 26(1) provides that the regulator may choose to target 'persons who make pornographic material … available on the internet on a commercial basis *to a large number of persons* [or] *generate a large amount of turnover* by doing so'.[149] This gives considerable freedom as to how enforcement will take place, and the BBFC has indicated that it plans to aim at a relatively small number of high profile sites, those most visited by children, and then 'moving down the list'.[150]

Significantly – in light of *Scarlet (Extended) v SABAM*[151] and the potential cost of implementing blocking – the ISP as well as the non-complying person may appeal against a blocking notice.[152] However, there is no provision for appeal by individual web users, notwithstanding that their Article 10 rights will also be implicated by a decision to block.[153]

e. Privacy

Privacy was one of the most contentious issues during the passage of the 2017 Act, with fears that age verification requirements would mean 'databases of the UK's porn habits' as well as collections of identity documents would be open to misuse.[154] Despite this, Part 3 of the Act does not contain the terms 'privacy' or 'data protection'. The age verification regulator is obliged to publish guidance as to the types of age verification systems it will treat as being compliant with the Act, but there is no provision that the regulator have regard to the need to protect privacy in doing so and (despite some obfuscation on this point from government) the regulator has no power to insist on any privacy requirements. The scheme of Part 3 will force the regulator to recognise systems such as credit card authentication as effective notwithstanding that the systems may collect details of individuals' identity as well as their age.[155]

---

[147] *Ibid*, s 21(3).
[148] *Ibid*, s 16(5).
[149] Emphasis added.
[150] David Austin, Chief Executive of the BBFC, in parliamentary testimony on 11 October 2016, discussed in Brown (n 132).
[151] *Scarlet (Extended) v SABAM* (n 109).
[152] Digital Economy Act 2017, s 16(6).
[153] See in particular *Cengiz and others v Turkey*, Application Nos 48226/10 and 14027/11, judgment of 1 December 2015.
[154] See, eg J Grierson, 'Privacy Campaigners Criticise UK Plan for Age Checks on Porn Websites' *The Guardian* (17 July 2017), available at www.theguardian.com/technology/2017/jul/17/age-checks-introduced-porn-websites-uk-credit-card-details (last accessed 6 July 2018).
[155] J Killock, 'A Database of the UK's Porn Habits. What Could Possibly Go Wrong?' (Open Rights Group, 18 October 2016), available at www.openrightsgroup.org/blog/2016/a-database-of-the-uks-porn-habits-what-could-possibly-go-wrong (last accessed 6 July 2018); J Killock, 'Fig Leafs for Privacy in Age Verification' (Open Rights Group, 19 October 2016), available at www.openrightsgroup.org/blog/2016/fig-leafs-for-privacy-in-age-verification (last accessed 6 July 2018).

The response of the Government on the privacy issue has been to leave the issue to the Information Commissioner's Office (ICO) as a matter of general data protection law. The Department for Digital, Culture, Media & Sport has published draft guidance to the regulator which provides that the regulator's guidance should include information about the data protection obligations of pornography providers and age verification services – but does not provide for any concrete requirements on providers. Instead, the guidance includes a bare statement that the regulator should 'inform the ICO where concerns arise'.[156]

The privacy risks are significant, particularly in light of recent large-scale data breaches. Data on individuals' sexual preferences is sensitive by definition, and especially so in the case of sexual minorities, but this scheme is likely to force users to link their identity to that information. In this, it highlights the recurring theme that internet censorship schemes, which often require monitoring of users' activity, must be assessed for their impact on privacy as well as on freedom of expression.

iii. Extreme Pornography

The 2017 Act also provides for the age verification regulator to take enforcement action against sites containing 'extreme pornography', which is a relatively recent concept in the UK.[157] Until 2008, violent pornography was dealt with by the law in the same way as other forms of pornography (excluding CAM), with publication, but not simple possession, of 'obscene articles' prohibited by the Obscene Publications Act 1959.[158] The expansion of the law can be traced to the 2003 strangulation of Jane Longhurst by a man obsessed with violent pornography, including images of sexual asphyxiation and rape.[159] Following her death, a campaign to criminalise the possession of violent pornography received considerable media and political support, resulting in the Labour Government criminalising possession of 'extreme pornographic images' (for example depictions of bestiality, necrophilia and acts which threaten serious harm or death) in 2008.[160] In 2015 the Conservative/Liberal Democrat coalition widened the scope of the offence to include images of rape.[161]

While the merits of the extreme pornography offence are beyond the scope of this chapter, it should be noted that it has been extremely controversial from the outset, with many arguing that it is overbroad and largely motivated by unfounded views of a

---

[156]'Guidance to the Age Verification Regulator' (Department for Digital, Culture, Media & Sport, January 2018), available at https://assets.publishing.service.gov.uk/government/uploads/system/uploads/attachment_data/file/673425/Guidance_from_the_Secretary_of_State_for_Digital__Culture__Media_and_Sport_to_the_Age-Verification_Regulator_for_Online_Pornography_-_January_2018.pdf (last accessed 6 July 2018).

[157]See generally AK Antoniou and D Akrivos, *The Rise of Extreme Porn: Legal and Criminological Perspectives on Extreme Pornography in England and Wales* (London, Palgrave Macmillan, 2017).

[158]Obscene Publications Act 1959, s 2(1), as amended by the Obscene Publications Act 1964. Section 1(1) defines 'obscene' in the following terms: 'an article shall be deemed to be obscene if its effect ... is taken as a whole, such as to tend to deprave or corrupt persons who are likely, having regard to all relevant circumstances, to read, see or hear the matter contained or embodied in it'.

[159]A Murray, 'The Reclassification of Extreme Pornographic Images' (2008) 72 *Modern Law Review* 73.

[160]Criminal Justice and Immigration Act 2008, s 63.

[161]Criminal Justice and Courts Act 2015, s 37.

causal relationship between fantasy and sexual violence.[162] Murray points out that it criminalises material featuring consenting adults, making it a crime to video something which it is legal to do and creating a risk that 'police will use [the offence] as a Trojan Horse to regulate the underlying activity'.[163] Jackman suggests that it has been abused as a 'consolation prize' offence where a defendant has their phone or computer seized on an unrelated matter in respect of which they are acquitted or face no charges.[164]

a. Powers of the Age-Verification Regulator over Extreme Pornography

As already mentioned, the focus of Part 3 of the Digital Economy Act 2017 is to prevent children from accessing pornography. The provisions in relation to extreme pornography were an afterthought: as originally introduced, the Bill did not address extreme pornography at all. The legislative history is complex, but these provisions are watered down from an earlier government amendment to the Bill which aimed to block any 'prohibited material', ie pornographic material which would be refused classification by the BBFC.[165] Following opposition in the House of Lords, the Government replaced that provision with a narrower one limited to extreme pornography, acknowledging that 'as this measure is about protecting children, we do not want to create a new threshold for what adults can or cannot see'.[166]

The 2017 Act therefore creates additional censorship powers in respect of 'extreme pornographic material'.[167] These piggyback on the age-verification enforcement powers, and in respect of extreme pornography the regulator has the same powers to require ISPs to block, and to issue notices of non-compliance to payment service providers and ancillary service providers, subject to the same notice and appeal mechanisms. Significantly, these powers apply against any person 'making extreme pornographic material available on the internet to persons in the United Kingdom', whether or not they are doing so on a commercial basis – something which greatly increases the possible scope of blocking. As with the age-verification powers there is no requirement of proportionality in enforcement – on the face of it, the Act would permit an entire domain to be blocked if necessary to prevent access to a single image – raising the same questions as to whether these powers are compatible with Article 10 ECHR.

---

[162] See in particular N Cowen, 'Nothing to Hide: The Case against the Ban on Extreme Pornography' (Adam Smith Institute, 2016), available at www.adamsmith.org/s/Nicholas-Cowen-Nothing-to-hide-FINAL.pdf (last accessed 6 July 2018).

[163] Murray (n 159) 90.

[164] Cowen (n 162) 2; contrary to some claims that the offence would be largely symbolic, prosecutions for extreme pornography are increasingly common and in most cases will be based on possession of material downloaded from the Internet. In 2009–10 (the first full year of the extreme pornography offence being in force) 270 prosecutions were brought, rising to 1,740 in 2015–16. See 'Violence against Women and Girls Crime Report 2015–16' (CPS, 2016) 89, available at www.cps.gov.uk/publications/docs/cps_vawg_report_2016.pdf (last accessed 6 July 2018).

[165] This would have included material depicting acts such as face sitting, watersports, and fisting. See, eg, D Gayle, 'UK to Censor Online Videos of "non-Conventional" Sex Acts' The Guardian (23 November 2016), available at https://www.theguardian.com/technology/2016/nov/23/censor-non-conventional-sex-acts-online-internet-pornography (last accessed 6 July 2018).

[166] Lord Ashton of Hyde, HL Deb 20 March 2017, vol 782.

[167] Defined in s 22 by reference to the offence in s 63(7) or (7A) of the Criminal Justice and Immigration Act 2008.

iv. Effectiveness

Even on its own terms Part 3 seems likely to have little effect in preventing access to pornography. It does nothing, for example, to prevent access to non-commercial material, and the BBFC have already indicated that it will be targeting only a small number of high profile sites. Ample alternatives will be available. Quite apart from those structural problems, at best blocking is likely to be only a minor obstacle to users who have become increasingly familiar with circumvention tactics such as virtual private networks (VPNs) and the use of alternative DNS providers. In 2011 Ofcom concluded (in the context of filesharing) that '[f]or all blocking methods circumvention by site operators and internet users is technically possible and would be relatively straightforward by determined users'.[168] As Schafer points out, it is difficult to see why blocking should be expected to work any better in this context.[169]

III. Identifying European Legal Standards and Analysing the Case Studies

A. Fundamental Rights Scrutiny

To what extent do our three case studies meet fundamental rights standards? In this section we summarise the main requirements for internet censorship under the ECHR and identify some areas where each system appears to fall short.

i. Article 10 ECHR

a. 'Prescribed by Law'

Article 10 ECHR requires that interferences with freedom of expression be prescribed by law. The best-known treatment of this concept was given in *Sunday Times v United Kingdom*[170] where the ECtHR held that in addition to requiring a legal basis it also imposes requirements regarding the quality of the law. First, 'the law must be adequately accessible: the citizen must be able to have an indication that is adequate in the circumstances of the legal rules applicable to a given case'. Second,

> a norm cannot be regarded as a 'law' unless it is formulated with sufficient precision to enable the citizen to regulate his conduct: he must be able – if need be with appropriate advice – to foresee, to a degree that is reasonable in the circumstances, the consequences which a given action may entail.[171]

---

[168] '"Site Blocking" to Reduce Online Copyright Infringement: A Review of Sections 17 and 18 of the Digital Economy Act' (London, Ofcom, 2011) 5–6.

[169] Schafer (n 144) 355.

[170] *Sunday Times v United Kingdom* Series A No 30 (1979–80) 2 EHRR 245.

[171] *Ibid* [47] and [49].

The *Sunday Times* approach has been supplemented in *Ekin Association v France*[172] which held that in relation to prior restraints 'a legal framework is required, ensuring both tight control over the scope of bans and effective judicial review to prevent any abuse of power'.[173] In that case a French law which gave the Minister of the Interior a wide-ranging power to ban foreign publications by administrative action was held to be contrary to Article 10. Central to this finding were the facts that bans took place prior to any hearing, the criteria for bans could produce results which were 'surprising' or which 'verge on the arbitrary', while the only judicial review available was limited in its scope (it did not provide for a full review of the merits) and was not automatic but required the publisher to apply to the courts.[174] Consequently, the ECtHR took the view that the judicial review procedures in place provided 'insufficient guarantees [against] abuse'.

The decision in *Ekin Association* has been applied to the Internet in *Yıldırım v Turkey*,[175] in which the ECtHR considered for the first time the question of internet blocking. *Yıldırım* concerned a decision of a Turkish court which issued an order blocking access to the entirety of the Google Sites service, in an attempt to prevent access to a single site critical of Atatürk. The Court had initially issued an order which was limited to the offending website. That order was sent to the state Telecommunications and Information Technology Directorate (TİB) for execution. The TİB however lacked the technical capability to block this particular site, and advised the Court that it would be necessary to block all material hosted on the domain sites.google.com. The Court varied the order accordingly.[176]

The blocking order therefore blocked a vast number of unrelated sites, including one belonging to a Turkish PhD student who found himself unable to access his own site. He claimed that this measure breached his right to freedom to hold opinions and to receive and impart information and ideas under Article 10.

The ECtHR found at the outset that this over-blocking constituted an interference with his rights, notwithstanding that his site was collateral damage from an order intended to target a third party.[177] Consequently the ECtHR considered whether the measure could be said to be 'prescribed by law'.

Turkish law provided that a court could order the blocking of access to 'Internet publications where there are sufficient grounds to suspect that their content is such as to amount to ... offences'[178] and specified the eight classes of offences for which such orders could be issued.[179] The ECtHR nevertheless found that the blocking was not prescribed by law in that the law had 'no provision for a wholescale blocking of access such as that ordered in the present case' and did not expressly permit 'the blocking of an entire Internet domain like Google Sites which allows the exchange of

---

[172] *Ekin Association v France*, Application No 39288/98, judgment of 17 July 2001.
[173] *Ibid* [58].
[174] *Ibid* [58]–[65].
[175] *Yıldırım v Turkey*, Application No 3111/10, judgment of 18 December 2012.
[176] *Ibid* [8] to [12].
[177] *Ibid* [53] to [55].
[178] *Ibid* [61].
[179] *Ibid* [15].

ideas and information'.[180] The ECtHR was also critical of the role of the TİB as an administrative body in widening the blocking order, stating that 'the TİB could request the extension of the scope of a blocking order even though no proceedings had been brought against the website or domain in question and no real need for wholesale blocking had been established'.[181]

The ECtHR then referred to *Ekin Association* in reiterating the need for 'tight control' and 'effective judicial review' in the case of prior restraints, and found that these elements were missing. In relation to judicial review of prior restraints the Court held that this required 'a weighing-up of the competing interests at stake … designed to strike a balance between them' and also 'a framework establishing precise and specific rules regarding the application of preventive restrictions on freedom of expression'. Both were absent in Turkey, where national law did not provide for any balancing test and where the domestic courts had simply acted on the recommendation of the TİB without considering the proportionality of the blocking measure and its collateral impact on internet users. Consequently, the ECtHR held that the measure 'did not satisfy the foreseeability requirement under the Convention and did not afford the applicant the degree of protection to which he was entitled by the rule of law in a democratic society'.[182]

Yıldırım is a judgment of fundamental importance for internet censorship, and particularly for its treatment of over-blocking. By identifying internet blocking as a form of prior restraint, the ECtHR subjects blocking to a particularly stringent set of criteria for legality as well as proportionality. Not only blocking, but also any collateral damage in the form of over-blocking must be explicitly authorised by law, and that law must in turn build in safeguards to ensure that the extent of the blocking is both necessary and proportionate. Otherwise, the collateral damage caused by a blocking order will not be 'prescribed by law'.[183]

Applying the reasoning in *Ekin Association* and *Yıldırım* to the CTIRU and IWF blocking schemes, it seems clear that both fall at the first hurdle: in each case there is a system giving rise to prior restraint with no legal basis, no criteria for assessing proportionality of the interference with Article 10 rights, and no judicial review. It should be stressed that in both *Ekin Association* and *Yıldırım* there was underlying legislation, albeit that it was lacking in some regards – by contrast, the CTIRU and IWF blocking practices have no legal basis whatsoever. The 'voluntary' nature of those blocking systems would not appear to change this assessment – in each case the ISPs and filtering companies cannot look behind the determination that the relevant URLs contain illegal content. By making determinations of legality which are directly applied by the filtering firms, the state is going beyond mere support for voluntary action carried out by the firms themselves.

There are also question marks over the legality of Part 3 of the 2017 Act when measured against these standards. The power of the age-verification regulator to make

---

blocking orders without any requirement of proportionality would not seem to be 'prescribed by law' in so far as it permits prior restraints and over-blocking without any right to be heard or 'a framework establishing precise and specific rules regarding the application of preventive restrictions on freedom of expression'.

b. Necessity, Proportionality, and Over-Blocking

For restrictions on freedom of expression to meet the requirements of Article 10(2) ECHR they must also be 'necessary in a democratic society'. This involves a proportionality test which considers whether there is a 'pressing social need'[184] for the interference and whether the interference goes further than is 'proportionate to the legitimate aim pursued'.[185] As part of this, we must ask whether an outcome could be achieved by less restrictive means than those actually used.[186] In the context of online censorship this test requires us to consider whether there is over-blocking of unrelated content and whether more granular blocking might be used.[187]

There is as yet no consensus on what degree of collateral damage will make a restriction disproportionate under Article 10(2). In an offline context we can look to comparators such as *Ürper and others v Turkey*,[188] where the ECtHR held that orders banning the future publication of entire periodicals went beyond any restraint which might be necessary in a democratic society and therefore amounted to impermissible censorship. By analogy it seems unlikely that filtering systems which block at the level of an entire website or domain would be acceptable where there is significant legitimate content on that site or domain.[189] This is supported by the decision in *Yıldırım*, where the ECtHR appeared to take the view that the blocking – in addition to lacking a legal basis – was in any event disproportionate because it 'produced arbitrary effects and could not be said to have been aimed solely at blocking access

---

[184] *Handyside v United Kingdom,* Application No 5493/72, judgment of 7 December 1976 [48].

[185] *Ibid* [49].

[186] See, eg, *Campbell v United Kingdom*, Application No 13590/88, judgment of 25 March 1992, where the Court held that the routine reading of correspondence from lawyers to prisoners could not be justified where the legitimate needs of the prison authorities could be achieved by the less invasive method of opening (but not reading) letters suspected of containing contraband.

[187] Cost of implementation may also be a factor: see *Twentieth Century Fox v British Telecommunications* [2011] EWHC 1981 (Ch); *Twentieth Century Fox v British Telecommunications (No 2)* [2011] EWHC 2714 (Ch); and *EMI Records Ltd & Ors v British Sky Broadcasting Ltd & Ors* [2013] EWHC 379 (Ch). In those cases BT has estimated its costs in complying with blocking injunctions at £5,000 for the initial implementation and £100 for each injunction notified to it thereafter.

[188] *Ürper and others v Turkey*, Application Nos 55036/07, 55564/07, 1228/08, 1478/08, 4086/08, 6302/08 and 7200/08, judgment of 20 October 2009 [44].

[189] Compare the analysis in General Comment 34: 'Any restrictions on the operation of websites, blogs or any other internet-based, electronic or other such information dissemination system, including systems to support such communication, such as internet service providers or search engines, are only permissible to the extent that they are compatible with paragraph 3. Permissible restrictions generally should be content-specific; generic bans on the operation of certain sites and systems are not compatible with paragraph 3'. United Nations Human Rights Committee, 'General Comment No. 34 – Article 19: Freedoms of Opinion and Expression' (2011) para 43, available at www2.ohchr.org/english/bodies/hrc/docs/gc34.pdf (accessed 23 May 2018).

to the offending website, since it consisted in the wholesale blocking of all the sites hosted by Google Sites'.[190]

Under the Charter of Fundamental Rights, the judgment of the CJEU in *UPC v Constantin*[191] sets a similarly stringent standard by holding that

> measures adopted by the internet service provider [to implement a blocking injunction] must be strictly targeted, in the sense that they must serve to bring an end to a third party's infringement of copyright or of a related right but without thereby affecting internet users who are using the provider's services in order to lawfully access information. Failing that, the provider's interference in the freedom of information of those users would be unjustified in the light of the objective pursued.[192]

What this means for the technical implementation of blocking measures remains to be seen, but the language of 'strict targeting' would seem to require, at a minimum, that the most granular form of blocking available should be used.

At a domestic level, the judgment of Arnold J in *Newzbin2* has held that an order requiring blocking of an entire site was proportionate, notwithstanding that not all of the content on that site would infringe copyright, on the basis that non-infringing use of the site was *de minimis*.[193] Later intellectual property blocking cases have not elaborated on this; while the courts have developed safeguards against *accidental* over-blocking, they do not appear to have assessed whether *deliberate* over-blocking is permissible, and if so to what degree.[194]

This issue of over-blocking will be important in the context of the powers of the age-verification regulator under Part 3 of the Digital Economy Act 2017. The regulator is expressly given power to over-block, and from the outset the Government has promoted the legislation on the implicit assumption that whole sites will be blocked.[195] That may be appropriate for sites such as PornTube.com which are dedicated to pornographic content. But it will be problematic in relation to sites which mix pornography with other material – for example, a video streaming site which mixes pornography with mainstream content. The judgments in *Constantin* and *Newzbin2* suggest that blocking of such sites in their entirety would not be permissible if the non-pornographic content is more than merely *de minimis*.

ii. Article 6 ECHR

Is a decision by a public body to block a particular URL or to require take down of particular material a 'determination of … civil rights and obligations' within the

---

[190] *Yıldırım* (n 175) [68]. Though compare *Akdeniz v Turkey*, Application No 20877/10, decision of 11 March 2014, which held that the applicant was not a 'victim' of a block ordered against an entire music service where he could access the same music by other means and services ([25]). This reasoning would suggest that a deliberate degree of over-blocking might be permissible if the same material remains available elsewhere.

[191] C-314/12 *UPC Telekabel Wien v Constantin* EU:C:2014:192, judgment of 27 March 2014.

[192] *Ibid* [56].

[193] *Twentieth Century Fox v British Telecommunications* [2011] EWHC 1981 (Ch) [186].

[194] See the discussion in J Riordan, *The Liability of Internet Intermediaries* (Oxford University Press, 2016) 492–93.

[195] 'New Blocking Powers to Protect Children Online' (GOV.UK, 20 November 2016), available at www.gov.uk/government/news/new-blocking-powers-to-protect-children-online (last accessed 6 July 2018).

meaning of Article 6 ECHR so as to trigger the entitlement to a 'fair and public hearing' before 'an independent and impartial tribunal established by law'?

a. 'Civil Rights and Obligations'

Early jurisprudence gave the concept of 'civil rights and obligations' a restrictive interpretation, applying to private law obligations only, and leaving most public law matters outside its scope.[196] More recently, however, the trend in the judgments of the ECtHR has been to widen the scope of the concept to ensure greater protection for individuals.[197] Consequently, while there is no authority expressly on this point, there is a strong case to be made that censorship decisions made by national authorities would fall within Article 6[198] – either on the basis that freedom of expression must be regarded as a 'civil right'[199] or else on the basis that the result of a blocking decision is decisive for private rights and obligations[200] by interfering with the commercial operation of a site.[201] The Council of Europe Recommendation on Internet Filtering supports the view that Article 6 applies by stating that content blocking should only take place if:

> the filtering concerns specific and clearly identifiable content, a competent national authority has taken a decision on its illegality and the decision can be reviewed by an independent and impartial tribunal or regulatory body, in accordance with the requirements of Article 6.[202]

b. Requirements Imposed by Article 6

Assuming that Article 6 applies in the context of internet censorship decisions, it will trigger the requirements identified in *Belilos v Switzerland* that such decisions must be made by a tribunal which 'determin[es] matters within its competence on the basis of rules of law and after proceedings conducted in a prescribed manner' with safeguards of 'independence, in particular of the executive; impartiality; duration of its members' terms of office; [and] guarantees afforded by its procedure'.[203]

---

[196] See generally D Harris et al, *Law of the European Convention on Human Rights*, 2nd edn (Oxford, Oxford University Press, 2009) Ch 6.

[197] See, eg *Ferrazzini v Italy*, Application No 44759/98, judgment of 12 July 2001.

[198] Though compare OJ Settem, *Applications of the 'Fair Hearing' Norm in ECHR Article 6(1) to Civil Proceedings* (Cham, Springer International Publishing, 2016) s 4.1.3, where the author argues that the French text and case law require a dispute between parties in order for Art 6 to apply.

[199] Compare *Reisz v Germany*, Application No 32013/96, decision of 20 October 1997.

[200] *Ringeisen v Austria*, Application No 2614/65, judgment of 16 July 1971.

[201] M Husovec, 'Injunctions against Innocent Third Parties: The Case of Website Blocking' (2013) 4 *Journal of Intellectual Property, Information Technology and E-Commerce Law* 116, at 123.

[202] Committee of Ministers of the Council of Europe, 'Recommendation CM/Rec(2008)6 of the Committee of Ministers to Member States on Measures to Promote the Respect for Freedom of Expression and Information with Regard to Internet Filters' (March 2008), available at https://wcd.coe.int/ViewDoc. jsp?Ref=CM/Rec(2008)6 (last accessed 6 July 2018).

[203] *Belilos v Switzerland*, Application No 10328/83, judgment of 29 April 1988 [64].

This is not a requirement for an independent tribunal at the initial stage in every case.[204] In the interests of 'flexibility and efficiency'[205] the ECtHR will allow decisions which affect fundamental rights to be made administratively at first instance, provided that there is 'subsequent control by a judicial body that has full jurisdiction and does provide the guarantees of Article 6(1)'.[206] The case law on this point, however, makes it clear that 'full jurisdiction' requires the existence of an appeal on the merits: a mere review of legality is insufficient.[207] Consequently, judicial review in the narrow sense of domestic law would not be sufficient: for a state blocking system to be compatible with Article 6 a statutory appeal mechanism would have to be established.

Some form of notification – either before or after an initial decision is made – will also be required by Article 6, which establishes a right to an adversarial trial that includes 'the opportunity for the parties to a civil or criminal trial to have knowledge of and comment on all evidence adduced or observations filed with a view to influencing the Court's decision'.[208] This applies a fortiori where one party has not been notified and is therefore entirely unaware of the existence of proceedings. Indeed, quite apart from Article 6 the failure to provide any notice of a censorship decision seems likely to provide the basis for judicial review on traditional procedural grounds.[209]

Who should be notified? National internet censorship procedures sometimes provide for notice to an intermediary – such as an ISP, host, or social network – but not to the person responsible for the content. However, the logic of Article 10 as a right which extends to both publishers and intermediaries suggests that in all cases notification should be made to the person responsible for the material as well as the intermediary, to the extent that this is practicable.[210] In the case of blocking, this should also include a blocking notice (stop page) which indicates to the intended viewer why material was blocked, and how to challenge that decision.

Applying Article 6 to our case studies, it again seems clear that the IWF and CTIRU blocking systems would fall at the first hurdle: in each case there is neither any notice nor possibility of appeal to an independent tribunal.[211]

The procedures under Part 3 of the Digital Economy Act are better, as one would expect from a statutory regime, and do provide for an independent appeal mechanism.

---

[204] Harris (n 196) 228–32.
[205] *Le Compte, Van Leuven and De Meyere v Belgium,* Application Nos 6878/75 and 7238/75, judgment of 23 June 1981 [51].
[206] *Albert and Le Compte v Belgium*, Application Nos 7299/75 and 7496/76, judgment of 24 October 1983 [29].
[207] Harris et al(n 196) 228–32.
[208] *Vermeulen v Belgium*, Application No 19075/91, judgment of 22 January 1996 [33].
[209] Particularly following the decision in *Osborn v The Parole Board* [2013] UKSC 61 which stressed that human rights protection is not a distinct area of law limited to ECHR obligations but permeates the legal system as a whole.
[210] See the discussion in P Mysoor, 'A Pirate Too Needs to Be Heard: Procedural Compromises in Online Copyright Infringement Cases in the UK' (2014) 3 *Laws* 553, at 559–60.
[211] In France, by comparison, administrative blocking (of CAM and now terrorist material) has been upheld by the Conseil d'État where the law provides for oversight of the blocking system by the Commission Nationale de l'Informatique et des Libertés (CNIL) and the possibility of a judicial remedy against blocking. See, eg, M Lacaze, 'Latest Developments in the Repression and Prevention of Terrorism under French Criminal Law' [2015] *Montesquieu Law Review* 2; W Maxwell, 'CNIL's New Role: Overseeing Website Blocking' (*Lexology*, 26 May 2016), available at www.lexology.com/library/detail.aspx?g=2632d9f2-27bd-4485-9092-33f326fc473d (last accessed 6 July 2018).

Nevertheless, some of those procedures are still of questionable legality. As we have noted already, there is no entitlement to be heard before the regulator makes a blocking order against a site, while a notice of non-compliance to payment service providers and ancillary service providers can be issued without any prior notification to the affected site. In each case there is a likelihood of significant economic harm to a site, as well as an impact on Article 10 rights, making it surprising that prior notice and a right to be heard are not the norm.

B. EU Law Standards

In parallel with the ECHR, EU law establishes a number of standards which may limit censorship by Member States. This section identifies the most important EU instruments applying to these case studies and considers the ways in which they may impose obligations going further than the ECHR.

i. Directive on Sexual Abuse of Children and Directive on Combating Terrorism

Internet censorship has been addressed at EU level in the context of both CAM[212] and public provocation to commit a terrorist offence, and the result in both the 2011 Directive on Sexual Abuse of Children[213] and the 2017 Directive on Combating Terrorism[214] is a compromise as to how such censorship should be implemented: under each Directive, Member States (i) *must* take measures to ensure the prompt removal of material hosted in their territory, (ii) *must* endeavour to obtain the removal of such material hosted outside their territory, and (iii) *may* take measures to block access to such material.[215]

At first glance, each Directive appears to impose significant safeguards, including a requirement of judicial redress. Article 25(2) of the 2011 Directive requires these in the case of blocking measures only:

> Member States may take measures to block access to web pages containing or disseminating child pornography towards the Internet users within their territory. These measures must be set by transparent procedures and provide adequate safeguards, in particular to ensure that the restriction is limited to what is necessary and proportionate, and that users are informed of the reason for the restriction. Those safeguards shall also include the possibility of judicial redress.

---

[212] For background, see McIntyre (n 66).

[213] Directive 2011/93/EU.

[214] Directive (EU) 2017/541.

[215] In the case of child pornography, approximately half of all Member States have introduced blocking. Of these, half have done so on a legislative basis, half on a voluntary basis. See 'Report from the Commission to the European Parliament and the Council Assessing the Implementation of the Measures Referred to in Article 25 of Directive 2011/93/EU of 13 December 2011 on Combating the Sexual Abuse and Sexual Exploitation of Children and Child Pornography" Brussels, 16 December 2016 COM(2016) 872 final, available at www.europarl.europa.eu/RegData/docs_autres_institutions/commission_europeenne/com/2016/0872/COM_COM(2016)0872_EN.pdf (last accessed 6 July 2018).

Article 21(3) of the 2017 Directive goes further, specifying safeguards which must apply to both removal and blocking:

> Measures of removal and blocking must be set following transparent procedures and provide adequate safeguards, in particular to ensure that those measures are limited to what is necessary and proportionate and that users are informed of the reason for those measures. Safeguards relating to removal or blocking shall also include the possibility of judicial redress.

In each case, however, the effect of these safeguards is limited by the fact that they apply only to measures taken by Member States themselves. The Recitals to both Directives expand on this by excluding 'voluntary' action by the Internet industry, and Member State support for such action. Recital 47 of the 2011 Directive provides that:

> The measures undertaken by Member States in accordance with this Directive in order to remove or, where appropriate, block websites containing child pornography could be based on various types of public action, such as legislative, non-legislative, judicial or other. In that context, this Directive is *without prejudice to voluntary action taken by the Internet industry to prevent the misuse of its services or to any support for such action by Member States*. Whichever basis for action or method is chosen, Member States should ensure that it provides an adequate level of legal certainty and predictability to users and service providers.[216]

Recital 22 of the 2017 Directive goes further again by specifically excluding situations where Member States themselves detect and flag terrorist content:

> The measures undertaken by Member States in accordance with this Directive in order to remove online content constituting a public provocation to commit a terrorist offence or, where this is not feasible, block access to such content could be based on public action, such as legislative, non-legislative or judicial action. In that context, *this Directive is without prejudice to voluntary action taken by the internet industry to prevent the misuse of its services or to any support for such action by Member States, such as detecting and flagging terrorist content*. Whichever basis for action or method is chosen, Member States should ensure that it provides an adequate level of legal certainty and predictability for users and service providers and the possibility of judicial redress in accordance with national law. Any such measures must take account of the rights of the end users and comply with existing legal and judicial procedures and the Charter of Fundamental Rights of the European Union.[217]

The remaining language in each Recital about ensuring 'legal certainty', 'predictability' and 'end user rights' is aspirational – using the term 'should' rather than 'must' – and reflects the position of Member States such as the UK which already had self-regulatory systems and were unwilling to agree to rules which would have required them to put in place a domestic legislative basis. The result is that these safeguards are of little practical significance. Any removal/blocking measures taken directly by public bodies would in any event be subject to the equivalent requirements of Articles 10 and 6 ECHR,[218]

---

[216] Emphasis added.
[217] Emphasis added.
[218] J McNamee and MF Pérez, 'Net Neutrality: An Analysis of the European Union's Trialogue Compromise' in L Belli and P De Filippi (eds), *Net Neutrality Compendium* (Cham, Springer, 2016) 187.

while voluntary/self-regulatory measures are beyond their scope.[219] For these systems the language in the Recitals provides only the veneer of legality, rather than the reality.

ii. The EU Open Internet Regulation

The developing legal framework on net neutrality offers more potential for applying fundamental rights to internet censorship, even in relation to genuinely voluntary and self-regulatory actions. While net neutrality has often been narrowly framed as an issue of economics, innovation policy, and consumer choice,[220] more recent work highlights how it promotes freedom of expression and privacy in communications, and in this sense it has the potential to disrupt internet censorship implemented through ISPs.[221]

At an EU level, net neutrality provisions have been in force since April 2016 under the Open Internet Regulation.[222] The key provision for blocking is Article 3(3) which provides that:

> Providers of internet access services ... shall not block ... specific content ... except as necessary, and only for as long as necessary, in order to ... comply with Union legislative acts, or national legislation that complies with Union law, to which the provider of internet access services is subject, or with measures that comply with Union law giving effect to such Union legislative acts or national legislation, including with orders by courts or public authorities vested with relevant powers.

Recital 13 elaborates on this by explaining that:

> The requirement to comply with Union law relates, inter alia, to the compliance with the requirements of the Charter of Fundamental Rights of the European Union ('the Charter') in relation to limitations on the exercise of fundamental rights and freedoms. [A]ny measures liable to restrict those fundamental rights or freedoms are only to be imposed if they are appropriate, proportionate and necessary within a democratic society, and if their implementation is subject to adequate procedural safeguards in conformity with the European Convention for the Protection of Human Rights and Fundamental Freedoms, including its provisions on effective judicial protection and due process.

By requiring that blocking be carried out on the basis of legislative acts, and that they must include effective judicial protection and due process, these provisions sound the death knell for purely self-regulatory blocking systems by providers of

---

[219] In a 2016 report on the implementation of the 2011 Directive, the Commission noted, but did not criticise, the fact that the UK does not offer judicial redress but merely a non-statutory appeals process in relation to IWF decisions. See 'Report from the Commission (n 215) p 11.

[220] C Marsden, 'Network Neutrality: A Research Guide' in I Brown (ed), *Research Handbook on Governance of the Internet* (Cheltenham, Edward Elgar, 2013).

[221] See, eg, M Mueller, 'Net Neutrality as Global Principle for Internet Governance' (November 2007), available at www.internetgovernance.org/wp-content/uploads/NetNeutralityGlobalPrinciple.pdf (last accessed 6 July 2018); C Marsden, *Net Neutrality: Towards a Co-Regulatory Solution* (London, Bloomsbury Academic, 2010) 18–19 and 105–31.

[222] Regulation (EU) 2015/2120.

internet access services.[223] Article 10(3) of the Regulation confirms this by identifying self-regulatory schemes as violating Article 3 and requiring that existing schemes be brought to an end by 31 December 2016.[224]

a. Impact on the IWF URL List and Family-Friendly Filters

This prohibition on self-regulatory censorship is particularly significant in the UK context where it precludes both main forms of ISP censorship – use of the IWF URL list and family-friendly filters. This does not seem to have been fully appreciated by the UK Government as an inevitable consequence of the Regulation – in October 2015 then-Prime Minister David Cameron told the House of Commons that he 'spluttered over his cornflakes' on reading a *Daily Mail* story stating that the newly adopted Regulation would prevent ISPs from using family-friendly filters.[225] Cameron went on to promise legislation to permit such filters, and this was eventually adopted as section 104(1) of the Digital Economy Act 2017, which provides:

> A provider of an internet access service to an end-user may prevent or restrict access on the service to information, content, applications or services, for child protection or other purposes, if the action is in accordance with the terms on which the end-user uses the service.

Section 104(1) is quite a remarkable piece of drafting. It goes well beyond the IWF URL list or family-friendly filters and permits any form of blocking, for child protection or any 'other purposes', without any legislative basis or user consent, provided only that it is 'in accordance with the terms on which the end-user uses the service'. Since terms of use are set by ISPs on a take it or leave it basis, this guts the Open Internet Regulation by allowing ISPs to dictate their own blocking policies.

A narrowly tailored provision confirming that ISPs can block material at the request of subscribers would have been permissible: despite some uncertainty in this area, the Commission has taken the position that filters blocking pornography can be used by ISPs if they respect 'the basic principle in the new Regulation that end-users – in this case, parents of minors – should be able to choose freely the content, applications and services to which they wish to have access'.[226] As is, however, the section is in clear breach of EU law by displacing Article 3(3) and purporting to permit blocking without the judicial protection and procedural safeguards required by the Regulation.

In ordinary circumstances, one might have expected this section eventually to be challenged on these grounds. In light of Brexit, however, it seems likely that the

---

[223] Swiss Institute of Comparative Law (n 29) 24–25.
[224] Regulation (EU) 2015/2120, Art 10(3) provides that 'Member States may maintain until 31 December 2016 national measures, including self-regulatory schemes, in place before 29 November 2015 that do not comply with Article 3(2) or (3). Member States concerned shall notify those measures to the Commission by 30 April 2016'.
[225] A Phippen, *Children's Online Behaviour and Safety* (London, Palgrave Macmillan UK, 2017) 26.
[226] 'Answer to a Written Question – Impact of Telecoms Regulation upon Opt-in Porn Filters Online', available at www.europarl.europa.eu/sides/getAllAnswers.do?reference=E-2015-014433&language=EN (last accessed 6 May 2018).

section will survive until the UK leaves the EU. The Open Internet Regulation will be important in governing internet censorship elsewhere in the EU – in Germany, for example, the telecoms regulator has already taken steps to prohibit ISP blocking without legal basis.[227] In the UK, however, this aspect of the Regulation has effectively been negated.

iii. EU Consumer Law

A common complaint about self-regulatory censorship measures is that they may evade both vertical and horizontal accountability norms: vertical in that the actions of private firms cannot be attributed to the state, and horizontal in that a firm's terms of use will invariably be drafted so widely as to prevent a user from having a remedy in cases of abuse.[228] Might it be possible to address this as a consumer rights issue?[229]

In March 2017 the European Commission and a number of European consumer authorities adopted a common position which challenges the censorship practices of Facebook, Google and Twitter as part of a wider review of their compliance with consumer law.[230] The core argument is that provisions which permit removal of content on vague and discretionary grounds, without any form of notice or redress, constitute unfair terms within the meaning of the Unfair Contract Terms Directive.[231] For example, while each firm already has appeals in place for certain issues, such as account suspensions, only Twitter allows appeals against removal of individual items.[232] According to the common position:

> The criteria on the basis of which social media operators can refuse to display or remove content generated by the consumer cannot remain general or unspecified. Standard terms and conditions should contain a sufficiently detailed indication of the main grounds on which content can be removed and possibly of how consumers are informed and can appeal to the removal of content … This however, should not prevent social media operators from providing in their standard terms very clearly that user generated content can be removed without notice, when this is needed to stop rapidly illegal conducts [sic].[233]

---

[227] 'Net Neutrality in Germany Annual Report 2016/2017' (Bundesnetzagentur, 2017) 11.

[228] See, eg, L DeNardis and A Hackl, 'Internet Governance by Social Media Platforms' (2015) 39 *Telecommunications Policy* 761.

[229] For a general analysis of the application of consumer law to social media terms of use, see E Wauters, E Lievens and P Valcke, "Towards a Better Protection of Social Media Users: A Legal Perspective on the Terms of Use of Social Networking Sites" (2014) 22 *International Journal of Law and Information Technology* 254.

[230] 'The European Commission and Member States Consumer Authorities Ask Social Media Companies to Comply with EU Consumer Rules' (European Commission, 17 March 2017), available at http://europa.eu/rapid/press-release_IP-17-631_en.htm (last accessed 6 July 2018); 'EU Increases Pressure on Facebook, Google and Twitter over User Terms" (*Reuters*, 25 July 2017), available at www.reuters.com/article/us-social-media-eu-consumers-idUSKBN1A92D4 (last accessed 6 July 2018).

[231] Council Directive 93/13/EEC of 5 April 1993 on unfair terms in consumer contracts [1993] OJ L95/29, specifically as a term within Annex 1.m which prohibits 'Terms which have the object or effect of: giving the seller or supplier the right to determine whether the goods or services supplied are in conformity with the contract, or giving him the exclusive right to interpret any term of the contract'.

[232] 'How to Appeal' (Online Censorship), available at https://onlinecensorship.org/resources/how-to-appeal (last accessed 6 July 2018).

[233] European Commission (n 230).

In short, the consumer authorities have demanded that the firms put in place detailed rules regarding what content is permissible, along with notification prior to removal of content (except in cases of urgency) and some form of appeal mechanism after the fact. These procedures have the potential to address some of the criticisms around otherwise opaque systems such as the CTIRU take down function.

How have the firms responded? As of February 2018, Google has accepted these criticisms and agreed to clarify the grounds on which content can be removed, to introduce notification before removal, and to put in place a general appeal procedure against removal.[234] Facebook and Twitter, however, have resisted these demands – in particular, neither is willing to notify users before content is removed. Furthermore, Facebook has refused to introduce appeals against content removal, and Twitter has refused to modify terms of use which give it unfettered discretion to remove content.

The application of consumer law in this area has potential, but is still very much at a preliminary stage. It remains to be seen how hard national consumer authorities will push and whether the courts will uphold this use of the Unfair Contract Terms Directive. The possible impact is also limited by the common position of the consumer protection authorities, which is limited to procedural, rather than substantive, guarantees of freedom of expression. Terms of use which ban lawful speech would not be affected, provided that they are clearly set out and provide minimum procedural fairness. At best, consumer law might help to promote transparency as to *what* and *how* social media firms censor – but it will not itself require these private spaces to be governed as though they were public forums.

IV. Conclusion

It is difficult to offer an overall assessment of internet censorship in the UK. There is no single model of censorship but rather a patchwork of individual schemes, and the three case studies chosen for this chapter differ greatly in relation to core elements such as their legal basis, procedural safeguards and accountability mechanisms. Nevertheless, these case studies do share some common themes and illustrate several wider issues.

At the outset, we can identify a direct evolution of UK policy from CAM to terrorist material. While the Government has not succeeded in its aim of adding terrorist material to the IWF URL list it has nevertheless drawn heavily on tactics previously developed in the context of CAM: crowd sourcing the process of detection by encouraging users to report content they consider to be illegal, matching images by using hash value databases to automate the process of identification and take down, and relying on voluntary cooperation with industry rather than statutory processes.

---

[234] 'Social Media Companies Need to Do More to Fully Comply with EU Consumer Rules' (European Commission, 15 February 2018), available at http://europa.eu/rapid/press-release_IP-18-761_en.htm (last accessed 6 July 2018).

Unfortunately, in borrowing from the censorship of CAM the Government has neglected the strengths of the IWF system, while replicating its failings. Although the IWF has often been criticised as operating a form of privatised censorship,[235] it has nevertheless demonstrated a level of transparency in its activities which far outstrips that of the Home Office in relation to the CTIRU's functions. The IWF has also shown much greater willingness to examine its own practices against human rights standards, most notably in 2014 by commissioning Ken Macdonald QC (Lord Macdonald) to carry out a human rights audit, prompted largely by criticisms expressed by an academic author in a journal article.[236]

The experience in relation to CAM and terrorism also illustrates a dangerous trend towards convergence of censorship and surveillance. Both the IWF and CTIRU blocking lists are being used, with the cooperation of the state, to identify individual internet users visiting blocked web pages, echoing the US experience of the PhotoDNA system being used extensively to scan private emails and files. In each case this is a form of indiscriminate surveillance, taking place in close coordination with the state but without any prior suspicion or legal basis. This is an under-examined area: there is little written on this from a European perspective,[237] with the bulk of the literature on this point coming from the United States, where privacy rights against private firms are much weaker.[238] However, it is difficult to see that these systems would survive legal challenge when fully assessed against Article 8 ECHR, the General Data Protection Regulation,[239] and the standards elaborated by the CJEU in *Schrems*.[240] (A particularly disturbing development in this context is the Commission recommendation of 1 March 2018 on tackling illegal content online which recommends that service providers 'in the context of their activities for the removal ... of access to illegal content' should be obliged to report any 'evidence of alleged serious criminal offences' to police.[241] If implemented, this would have the effect of unifying censorship and surveillance across all service providers, requiring user information to be handed over without any legal process.)

This overlap between censorship and privacy recurs in a slightly different way in the context of age verification under the Digital Economy Act 2017. Age verification

---

[235] Edwards (n 3) 657–58.

[236] Laidlaw (n 3); 'Board Minutes 16 October 2012' (IWF, 16 October 2012), available at www.iwf.org.uk/what-we-do/who-we-are/governance/board-minutes (last accessed 6 July 2018); Macdonald (n 47).

[237] See C Angelopoulos et al, 'Study of Fundamental Rights Limitations for Online Enforcement through Self-Regulation' (Amsterdam, Institute for Information Law (IViR), University of Amsterdam, 2016) s 4, available at https://openaccess.leidenuniv.nl/bitstream/handle/1887/45869/IVIRStudyOnlineenforcementthroughself-regulation.pdf (last accessed 6 July 2018).

[238] See, eg AL Mitter, 'Deputizing Internet Service Providers: How the Government Avoids Fourth Amendment Protections' (2011) 67 *New York University Annual Survey of American Law* 235.

[239] Regulation (EU) 2016/679 of the European Parliament and of the Council of 27 April 2016 on the protection of natural persons with regard to the processing of personal data and on the free movement of such data, and repealing Directive 95/46/EC.

[240] C-362/14 *Maximillian Schrems v Data Protection Commissioner*, ECLI:EU:C:2015:650, Judgment of 6 October 2015.

[241] European Commission, 'Commission Recommendation of 1. 3. 2018 on Measures to Effectively Tackle Illegal Content Online' C(2018) 1177 final para 24, available at https://ec.europa.eu/digital-single-market/en/news/commission-recommendation-measures-effectively-tackle-illegal-content-online (last accessed 6 July 2018).

systems have the potential to record and expose sensitive information about the sexual preferences of individuals, and it is disappointing that the Act does not take any steps to minimise these risks.

More generally, all three case studies indicate that the application of fundamental rights standards to UK internet censorship is still at a nascent stage. This is, perhaps, unsurprising in relation to the IWF and CTIRU schemes, where the lack of a legal obligation to filter or take down material contributes to the traditional view that 'voluntary' measures are not subject to fundamental rights standards. It is more surprising to see that the Digital Economy Act 2017 still does not take full account of ECHR obligations in relation to even basic matters, such as the right to be heard before a blocking order is made, or the requirement of proportionality in blocking.

Turning to the EU law issues which arise from these case studies, this chapter highlights a tension between different legal instruments. On one side, there is an EU framework which can be used to ensure freedom of expression rights against internet intermediaries, even in schemes where there is no state involvement. The Open Internet Regulation requires a legislative framework for blocking measures; similarly, the Commission and national consumer authorities have made creative use of the Unfair Contract Terms Directive in a way which will ensure greater procedural protections for users against removal of their content. On the other side, the Directive on Sexual Abuse of Children and Directive on Combating Terrorism have been drafted with a view to facilitating self-regulation, and both envisage state involvement in voluntary blocking and take down schemes without the need for a legislative basis or procedural safeguards.

This tension reflects a wider trend in Brussels where the Commission has increasingly moved towards weakening intermediary immunities and encouraging or requiring greater policing by internet intermediaries.[242] Most recently we see this in the Commission's communication of 28 September 2017[243] and Recommendation of 1 March 2018[244] on tackling illegal content online, which call for 'an enhanced responsibility of online platforms', to include proactive searches for potentially illegal content, automated hash value matching for preventing uploads and removal of content, and systems of 'trusted flaggers' to report and remove allegedly illegal content more easily – with these measures to take place on a voluntary basis. As with the EU IRU, this approach follows the informal UK model rather than national schemes such as the German Network Enforcement Law (the Netzwerkdurchsetzungsgesetz/ 'NetzDG') which provides for legislative frameworks.[245] It is ironic that

---

[242] L Belli and C Sappa, 'The Intermediary Conundrum: Cyber-Regulators, Cyber-Police or Both?' (2017) 8(4) *Journal of Intellectual Property, Information Technology and E-Commerce Law* 183. See discussion generally about the decline of intermediary immunities in the previous chapter.

[243] European Commission, 'Communication from the Commission of 28. 9. 2017 on Tackling Illegal Content Online: Towards an Enhanced Responsibility of Online Platforms' C(2017) 555 final, available at https://ec.europa.eu/digital-single-market/en/news/communication-tackling-illegal-content-online-towards-enhanced-responsibility-online-platforms (last accessed 6 July 2018).

[244] Commission Recommendation of 1. 3. 2018 (n 241).

[245] For an initial analysis of the NetzDG, see A Kuczerawy, 'Phantom Safeguards? Analysis of the German Law on Hate Speech NetzDG' (CITIP blog, 30 November 2017), available at www.law.kuleuven.be/citip/blog/phantom-safeguards-analysis-of-the-german-law-on-hate-speech-netzdg (last accessed 6 July 2018).

the UK model appears to influence EU policy here even as the UK itself heads for the door.

Speaking of Brexit brings us to the somewhat dispiriting conclusion that fundamental rights protections in this area, as in other areas, will be substantially weakened by the UK's departure from the EU.[246] The most visible loss will be the Charter of Fundamental Rights, but the Open Internet Regulation will also be a significant casualty which is unlikely to be replaced by comparable domestic legislation. In addition, Brexit may have the effect of dis-entrenching the ECHR, making it possible for the Conservative Party to proceed with its reported plan of campaigning in the next election on a commitment to leave the Convention.[247] UK governments have not been notable for their respect for fundamental rights online; one wonders how they might behave if freed entirely from oversight by either the Strasbourg or Luxembourg courts.

[246] See, eg, T Lock, 'Human Rights Law in the UK after Brexit' (2017), available at https://papers.ssrn.com/abstract=3046554 (last accessed 6 July 2018).

[247] C Hope, 'Theresa May to Fight 2020 Election on Plans to Take Britain out of European Convention on Human Rights after Brexit Is Completed' *The Telegraph* (28 December 2016), available at www.telegraph.co.uk/news/2016/12/28/theresa-may-fight-2020-election-plans-take-britain-european (last accessed 6 July 2018).

11

Making Contracts Online: Old Wine in Smart Bottles?

FRANCIS DAVEY*

I. Introduction

The law of electronic contracts sounds deceptively simple; after all, today's users transact online all the time without a second thought. What is there new to say that has not already been learnt in a first or second year contract class?[1] Many will already appreciate that the most frequent lie told in cyberspace is the following: 'Yes, I have read and understood the terms and conditions', as users routinely click away without ever considering what was agreed to. The British retailer, GameStation, highlighted the futility of this statement when 7,500 online customers agreed to 'sell their souls' to the company after GameStation sneaked an unusual and largely unnoticed clause into its online terms and conditions in 2010 as an April Fool:

> By placing an order via this Web site on the first day of the fourth month of the year 2010 Anno Domini, you agree to grant us a non-transferable option to claim, for now and for ever more, your immortal soul. Should We wish to exercise this option, you agree to surrender your immortal soul, and any claim you may have on it, within 5 (five) working days of receiving written notification from gamesation.co.uk or one of its duly authorised minions.[2]

Such a clause is almost certainly unenforceable, for a host of reasons. However it highlights neatly one aspect of entering into contracts in cyberspace; the general lack of scrutiny by and bargaining power of, the consumer; and the tendency to opacity of

---

* Extra research assistance was supplied by Mark Leiser, now Lecturer, University of Leicester; and the editor.
[1] The title is a derivation of the frequent aphorism about online contract law that it is 'old wine in new bottles': see, eg, H Deveci, 'Consent in Online Contracts: Old Wine in New Bottles' (2007) 13 *Computer and Telecommunications Law Review* 223.
[2] See 'Nobody Reads Terms and Conditions: It's Official' (OUT-Law News, 19 April 2010), available at www.out-law.com/page-10929.

terms and conditions. Other less obvious questions also arise when contracting online which are frequently discussed in textbooks. When is the contract actually formed? Where is it formed? These things matter, for issues like liability, amendment of terms and jurisdiction, although perhaps less than one might expect, especially in the context of professionally drafted commercial contracts. For consumers, imbalances of power may only become obvious long after the contract is made so remedies relating to information rights and unfair terms become of interest.

Many e-contract questions do indeed resolve to variations on familiar conundrums relating to formation, interpretation and fairness of contractual terms. Can one conclude a contract by email? Was an acceptance 'communicated' if the email is incorrectly directed into the spam folder of the recipient and never read? Is it unfair to demand that online disputes involving UK consumers are resolved in the courts of California or by mandatory arbitration? As this chapter aims to set out, the law of contract has managed to cope fairly well with many technological changes over the years. Legally binding contracts were after all being formed before the invention of the printing press, or indeed, paper.

On the other hand some new technological developments do indeed seem to have the potential to offer genuine challenges to traditional doctrine. Among them may be the recent emergence of the 'smart contract', a kind of automated process based on the distributed ledger technology (DLT) or blockchain which also provides the underpinning to cryptocurrencies such as bitcoin.[3] Alternately, as others have said,[4] such devices may actually be neither smart, nor contracts (nor indeed very useful) and fall from attention as the hype cycle moves relentlessly on.

Possible and continuing challenges for the law of online contracts include:

- *International commerce.* E-commerce engages far more individuals, and particularly consumers, in cross-border commerce than in the pre-internet era. Rules of international private law, such as those on jurisdiction and conflict of law, are more likely to play a role in even relatively minor commercial purchases.

- *Trust.* While remote contracting – and indeed remote consumer contracting – dates back to antiquity, there has always a problem of trust in dealing with someone at a distance. The relative anonymity that is afforded by the Internet exacerbates this. How are consumers meant to know who they are transacting with when the most professional of websites can be produced by fraudsters for relatively little cost? How are they to have confidence that their consumer remedies will be enforced abroad?

- *Formal validity.* While contracts have been formed in many ways, the paradigmatic commercial contract has until recently been a signed document or set of counter-part documents embodied in a physical object and handled physically by the parties. The Internet allows contracts to be formed in ways such as clicking on web links that are entirely new. How can 'clicking' replace an actual signature on a physical document?

---

[3] See Chapter 12, section VIII. Bitcoin and its ilk are discussed in the next chapter.
[4] See Ed Felten, 'Smart Contracts: Neither Smart nor Contracts?' (Freedom to Tinker, 20 February 2017), available at https://freedom-to-tinker.com/2017/02/20/smart-contracts-neither-smart-not-contracts/.

As mentioned briefly above, numerous questions arise in the law of contract that need reconsideration in the context of e-commerce. These include:

- Was there a contractual offer?
- Is there a contract (contract formation)?
- When was the contract formed?
- Where was the contract formed?
- What are the terms of the contract?

There may also be a concern that certain contracts must obey specific rules as to form. Would e-contracts obey those rules? For example, in English law, a contract for the assignment of copyright must be made 'in writing'.[5] Can copyright be validly assigned electronically?

II. Formation of Contracts

A. Academic Obsession

The common law theory of contract formation – shared by both English and Scots[6] law – is that a contract is formed by an offer followed by an acceptance that meets the terms of that offer. Contract formation also sets up interesting conceptual questions. Sometimes contracts are formed without even saying a word. One goes into a shop, picks up a bottle of milk, notes the price, takes it to the counter, and puts down the bottle and the cashier rings the item up and displays the cost of the milk. When the customer hands over the money, a contract is formed. Sometimes a contract is formed by a machine; for example, when one buys sweets from a vending machine or takes a ticket for entry into a short-term car park. These pose theoretical questions that academics and students often encounter, usually as to the implications of agreeing to the terms and conditions on a contract of sale or a contract of service when contracting with a machine.

The reality of most machine-based contracting is rather different: the practice of commerce rarely creates any doubts about the formation of a contract, and questions such as the time and location of its formation are rarely of relevance. One reason for this is that a well-advised commercial actor will make sure that they answer all these questions in advance in suitably-drafted terms and conditions. For example, the

---

[5] Copyright, Designs and Patents Act 1988, s 90(3).
[6] The Scottish Law Commission's (SLC) Discussion Paper on Formation of Contract (DP 154) has a very thorough account on the Scots law of contract formation as part of its work on 'contract formation for the digital age'. See www.scotlawcom.gov.uk/news/contract-formation-for-the-electronic-age/. SLC COM No 252 *Report on Review of Contract Law: Formation, Interpretation, Remedies for Breach, and Penalty Clauses* followed on 29 March 2018 with draft Bill attached.

UK based supermarket Tesco offers an internet ordering facility through its website. Its terms and conditions include the following:[7]

> At all times our acceptance of an order takes place on despatch of the order, at which point the purchase contract will be made and you will be charged for your order.

Under these terms, then, it is clear at what point an order submitted by a customer becomes a contractually-binding contract on the parties: the moment of despatch. This also tells us where the contract is formed, which may be of relevance to questions of jurisdiction.

Most modern judicial attempts to define rules about contract formation have been triggered by situations where contracting parties – increasingly only those with the significant financial resources necessary to litigate in a court with sufficient seniority to create judicial precedent – have failed to deal with these questions. In very rare cases that failure may even be deliberate (see *Apple Corps v Apple Computer*[8]).

B. Offer and Acceptance

The common law has developed a conceptual framework for the formation of contracts[9] centred on the concepts of:

- an offer, made by one party, the 'offeror', to another, the 'offeree'; and
- An acceptance of that offer by the offeree.

This simple model could be complicated by other factors, for example:

- There may be multiple parties (several offerors and/or offerees);
- An offer might be made to the whole world which could be accepted by multiple offerees (forming several contracts). For example, an offer to pay £100 to anyone who contracts flu after using a particular medical product designed to prevent this, as happened in *Carlill v Carbolic Smoke Ball Company*;[10]
- Common law systems (but not Scots law) require that each party get something out of a contract, a doctrine known as 'consideration'.[11] An agreement between a lender and a debtor that the lender will reduce the debtor's indebtedness if they pay a part of what is owed does not create a contract in English law, on the basis that the lender does not get anything out of it to which they were not already entitled;[12] or

---

[7] See www.tesco.com/help/terms-and-conditions/.
[8] *Apple Corps v Apple Computer* [2004] EWHC 768 (Ch).
[9] D Ibbetson, *A Historical Introduction to the Law of Obligations* (Oxford University Press, 2002).
[10] *Carlill v Carbolic Smoke Ball Company* [1893] 1 QB 256.
[11] M Chen-Wishart, *Contract Law*, 5th edn (Oxford University Press, 2015) Chs 2 and 3. Continental systems may have functional equivalents such as in the French system, *cause*.
[12] Although frequently doubted in the academic literature, this doctrine has been affirmed several times by courts at the highest level. See, eg, *Pinnel's Case* [1602] 5 Co Rep 117a and *Jordan v Money* (1854) 5 HLC 185.

- The offer may be an invitation to tender, with a promise to take the lowest bid. This could be analysed as kind of two stage agreement: the offeror agrees to enter into a contract with the highest bidder, but that obligation is owed to all those submitting a bid.[13]

C. Is There an Offer? Offers Versus Invitations to Treat

The first question that arises is: was there an offer in the first place or was there merely an invitation to treat?

It is generally accepted in English and Scots[14] law that the display of goods in a shop window, priced or unpriced, is not an offer to sell but merely an invitation to treat.[15] It is the customer who makes the offer to the shopkeeper. The authorities cited in support of this proposition are not as conclusive for the online environment has might have been expected. The only directly relevant authorities, *Pharmaceutical Society of Great Britain v Boots Cash Chemists (Southern) Ltd*,[16] and *Fisher v Bell*,[17] concerned the interpretation of criminal statutes as to whether, respectively, drugs were sold without a licensed pharmacist at the 'point of sale' when they were left for customers to pick up from shelves and only pay for later at the till; and whether knives were 'offered for sale' when they were in a shop window display. In each case, the Court answered no thus repelling criminal liability. From these cases has been derived a general rule that the display of items in a supermarket is an invitation to treat. One suspects that the original decisions were however mainly pragmatic. Had the *Boots* case gone the other way, would supermarket 'chemists' have been next to impossible to run?

Shop windows and supermarket displays are rather different from the display of goods on an e-commerce website, because in the former cases there will be an actual physical good displayed which may be purchased. A website displaying prices is more akin to a price list or advert. An unfettered obligation to supply goods at the advertised price risks the e-commerce supplier of not only being unable to fulfil the order because they have run out of stock, but obligated to sell stock at far below market value when there is a pricing error displayed on the webpage.[18] These errors are actually quite common. In January 2012 Argos offered a television and DVD player normally priced at £350 for 49p.[19] Argos refused to fulfil these orders. In March 2012 consumers started a petition to force Tesco to honour purchases of a 64GB third generation iPad presented for sale at £49.99 instead of £659,[20] while in January 2014

---

[13] *Harvela Investments Ltd v Royal Trust Co of Canada (CI) Ltd* [1986] 1 AC 207.

[14] *Stair Memorial Encyclopaedia* (LexisNexis Butterworths) (Vol 15) 621.

[15] *Fisher v Bell* [1961] 1 QB 394

[16] *Pharmaceutical Society of Great Britain v Boots Cash Chemists (Southern) Ltd* [1953] 1 QB 401.

[17] *Fisher v Bell* (n 15).

[18] No cases on pricing errors in England have resulted in reported cases but there is an interesting Singapore case: see *Chwee Kin Keong v Digilandmall.com Pte Ltd* [2005] 1 SLR(R) 502.

[19] See http://news.bbc.co.uk/1/hi/uk/4204002.stm.

[20] See www.thisismoney.co.uk/money/news/article-2114797/iPad-3-49-99-Tesco-Direct-refuses-honour-price-glitch-customer-revolt-e-petition.html.

hardware seller Screwfix suffered a technical glitch which reduced all items to £34.99.[21] Except those orders already delivered or collected, Screwfix cancelled all orders. After an online petition, Kodak fulfilled orders for a digital camera sold for £100 instead of its intended price of £329. Customers argued that had Kodak held out against customer complaints, it may have been committing an offence under the Consumer Protection Act 1987 which makes it a criminal offence to give a misleading price indication. Furthermore, Kodak's terms and conditions stated at the time that the contract would be concluded when it sent the order confirmation email, not the later dispatch confirmation stage. Also in January 2012, Marks & Spencer honoured sales of a £599 television wrongly priced at £199 following a petition.[22] However it is believed few orders were made as the error was in the early hours of Sunday morning.

D. Time of Acceptance

Having decided that a contract is formed upon acceptance, it becomes important in many circumstances to know when precisely that acceptance took place, because at that instant the parties become bound by their respective obligations under the contract. The time when a contract was formed may be important because:

- The offeror may want to withdraw their offer. They cannot do so if their offer has already been accepted;

- Some aspect of the performance of the contract (for example the exchange rate between two currencies) may vary rapidly and so the nature of the parties' obligations may depend on the exact time the contract was formed; or

- If the contract transfers property from one party to the other, it may be vital to know who is the owner of the property at a particular time because the property may have been stolen, damaged or fallen into the estate of an insolvent vendor, and thus the exact time of the contract's formation may be crucially important.

Where the parties make an agreement in each other's presence by shaking hands, signing a document or by oral agreement, there is usually no problem with the time of acceptance. Things become more difficult, however, when a contract is formed at a distance.

The failure of an offeror to properly state their address led the Court in *Adams v Lindsell*[23] to find that a late acceptance by the offeree was acceptable because its misdirection in the post was the fault of the offeror. From this unpromising beginning has developed what in English jurisprudence is known as the 'postal rule', which states that if an offer is made which, expressly or impliedly, may be accepted by post, the time of the acceptance is when the letter of acceptance is *posted*, and not when it *arrives*.[24]

---

[21] See www.theguardian.com/money/2002/feb/02/jobsandmoney.

[22] See www.thisismoney.co.uk/money/bills/article-2089372/Marks--Spencer-Panasonic-50-inch-3D-TV-glitch-Petition-forces-M-S-honour-orders-199.html.

[23] *Adams v Lindsell* (1818) B & Ald 681.

[24] *Dunlop v Higgins* (1848) 1 HL Cas 381 (Scots law); for England and Wales see the Court of Appeal cases of *Household Fire Insurance Company v Grant* (1879) 4 Ex D 216 and *Henthorn v Fraser* [1892] 2 Ch 27.

The rule is relatively narrow. For example, the handing of a letter to a postal worker who is not authorised to receive letters will not be sufficient to take advantage of the rule.[25] The courts have been reluctant to extend the rule to new technologies, instead holding that the contract is made when (and where) the acceptance is received. In *Entores v Miles Far East Corp*,[26] the Court of Appeal (E&W) was reluctant to apply the rule to the now long-defunct technology of the telex. The Court was strongly influenced by the fact that the telex was to all intents and purposes instantaneous, operating as if the parties were talking by telephone. The fact that a receiving telex machine sends and accepts confirmation to the sending machine was also an important factor in Lord Denning's reasoning.

Brinkibon v Stahag Strahl[27] also concerned the telex. There the House of Lords affirmed that the postal rule did not apply to the technology. Lord Wilberforce said:

> Since 1955 the use of Telex communication has been greatly expanded, and there are many variants on it. The senders and recipients may not be the principals to the contemplated contract. They may be servants or agents with limited authority. The message may not reach, or be intended to reach, the designated recipient immediately: messages may be sent out of office hours, or at night, with the intention, or on the assumption that they will be read at a later time. There may be some error or default at the recipient's end which prevents receipt at the time contemplated and believed in by the sender. The message may have been sent and/or received through machines operated by third persons. And many other variants may occur. No universal rule can cover all such cases; they must be resolved by reference to the intentions of the parties, by sound business practice and in some cases by a judgement where the risks should lie.

The statement that there is no universal rule means that attempts to decide whether the postal rule applies to email, web contracts and so on may be misguided, since the Court has said that it would examine a number of context-dependent factors in deciding the question. In other words, then, the Court in *Brinkibon* adopted a technology-neutral policy.

In *Olivaylle Pty Ltd v Flottweg GMBH & Co KGAA* (No 4),[28] the Federal Court of Australia held that an email acceptance occurred when the email was received by the offeror. Numerous and contradictory reasons have been used to justify the postal rule.[29] An English court, forced to consider the question afresh, should probably hold that the rule does not apply to email, for reasons given below.

E. A Technical Note on Email

One difficulty with legal analysis of electronic mail is that most authors writing on the topic often seem not to understand exactly how email works, and are therefore confused about whether or not the sender of an email is (ever) aware that their email

---

[25] *Re London & Northern Bank ex p Jones* [1900] 1 Ch 220.
[26] *Entores v Miles Far East Corp* [1955] 2 QB 327.
[27] *Brinkibon Ltd v Stahag Stahl und Stahlwarenhandels-Gesellschaft* [1983] 2 AC 34.
[28] *Olivaylle Pty Ltd v Flottweg GMBH & Co KGAA* (No 4) (2009] FCA 522.
[29] See Edwin Peel, *The Law of Contract*, 13th Revised edn (London, Sweet & Maxwell 2011) 2–031.

has arrived. The system used for email on the Internet is known as the Simple Mail Transfer Protocol (SMTP). Other systems are used internally by some organisations and as part of some computer systems (such as Microsoft Exchange) but between institutions and internet service providers, SMTP is the standard. The first step in sending an email is the conversion of the addressee's email address into the Internet Protocol (IP) address of one or more mail servers. Where – as is the norm – the email address is written as a Domain Name System (DNS) name, the DNS is interrogated to find one or more IP addresses. For example, if sending an email to contact@francisdavey.co.uk, the user's email application will query the DNS for the domain francisdavey.co.uk, and receive the following response, known as the domain's 'records':

; ->>HEADER<<- opcode: QUERY, status: NOERROR, id: 35682

;; flags: qr rd ra; QUERY: 1, ANSWER: 9, AUTHORITY: 0, ADDITIONAL: 0

;; QUESTION SECTION:

;francisdavey.co.uk.   IN   ANY

;; ANSWER SECTION:

francisdavey.co.uk.   86400 IN   SOA   ns2.mythic-beasts.com.
Hostmaster.mythic-beasts.com. 2010000220 21600 7200 604800 3600

francisdavey.co.uk.   86400 IN   A   93.93.131.18

francisdavey.co.uk.   86400 IN   MX   5 alt1.aspmx.l.google.com.

francisdavey.co.uk.   86400 IN   MX   5 alt2.aspmx.l.google.com.

francisdavey.co.uk.   86400 IN   MX   10 aspmx2.googlemail.com.

francisdavey.co.uk.   86400 IN   MX   10 aspmx3.googlemail.com.

francisdavey.co.uk.   86400 IN   MX   1 aspmx.l.google.com.

francisdavey.co.uk.   3600   IN   NS   ns1.mythic-beasts.com.

francisdavey.co.uk.   3600   IN   NS   ns2.mythic-beasts.com.

Figure 1

The five records labelled 'MX' are all machines that are willing to accept email addressed to the domain francisdavey.co.uk. The user agent is entitled to choose any of these. A further query for an IP address associated with aspmx.1.google.com will reveal an IP address of 173.194.66.26. The mail user agent then contacts that IP address, and delivers the email to it. If the email is received correctly, the server at aspmx.1.google.com will give a positive indication to the mail user agent at the end of the communication. SMTP is designed around the idea that at any given time one particular machine will take responsibility for email. In the above example, once the server whose address is aspmx.1.google.com has accepted responsibility, the mail user agent has no further

responsibility to deliver the message. In practice it is likely that a user's email application will first deliver the message to another server (known as a mail transfer agent)
which is responsible for delivering their email on to aspmx.1.google.com (rather like a
delivery courier).

Ideally, SMTP's idea of 'responsibility' should inform any rigorous legal analysis,
but sadly it appears that so far it has not. At any given time, the protocol dictates
that either a machine chosen by the sender (their email application or mail transfer agent) or one chosen by the recipient is responsible for the message. One of the
sender's machines will therefore know for certain whether the recipient's machine has
accepted responsibility. This is more reliable than technologies like telex, which are not
designed around this idea of responsibility. Because of this idea of servers accepting
responsibility for a message, it is reasonable to think of email as being 'instantaneous',
even though in practice some time may elapse before the recipient actually receives the
message.

This is where many legal authors are mistaken. They confuse the receipt of the email
with its being read by the intended recipient. Of course, the sender has no idea whether
an email is ever read (there are protocols for sending 'read receipts' but they are not
widely used outside the legal profession and are not particularly reliable). But this is
also true of telex or any other communication other than one made to the offeror's face
(for example delivering an acceptance through the door of the offeror). The offeror
may not in the end receive an acceptance email, but the law may treat it as received, as
it does with posted letters. The fact that email is 'split into packets' and 'may be sent
via several different routes'[30] should be irrelevant. The same is true of, for example,
many modern forms of voice telephony which may also be sent over IP networks. The
splitting of data into packets and their routing across the network happens at a lower
level than the SMTP protocol, and as such is invisible to it.

All of this is a rather theoretically moot point anyway, considering the postal rule
can be seen as a kind of *sui generis* rule limiting the scope of delivery of acceptance to
an actual posting.[31] While one could spend a lot of energy arguing that sending email
is instantaneous communications, the Electronic Commerce Directive ('e-Commerce
Directive' or 'ECD'),[32] however, suggests that it is not. Article 11(1), given effect by
reg 11(2)(a) of the Electronic Commerce (EC Directive) Regulations ('e-Commerce
Regulations'),[33] states 'the order and the acknowledgement of receipt will be deemed
to be received when the parties to whom they are addressed are able to access them'.
Regulation 11(2) (a) is a strict rule. It only applies to the offer (termed here the order)
and the acknowledgement of receipt of that offer, not to the acceptance that normally
occurs much later when goods are dispatched.

[30] See, eg, A Murray, 'Entering into Contracts Electronically: The Real W.W.W.' in L Edwards, and
C Waelde (eds), *Law and the Internet: A Framework for Electronic Commerce* (Oxford, Hart Publishing,
2000) 25.
[31] This was affirmed in the House of Lords case of *Brinkibon Ltd v Stahag Stahl* (n 27).
[32] Directive 2000/31/EC of the European Parliament and of the Council of 8 June 2000 on certain legal
aspects of information society services, in particular electronic commerce, in the Internal Market ('Directive
on electronic commerce') [2000] OJ L178/ 1.
[33] Electronic Commerce (EC Directive) Regulations 2002 (SI 2013/2002).

III. Incorporation of Terms

Contracts made orally or by conduct are notoriously difficult to pin down to their exact terms. If the contract is at all complicated the parties may have very different ideas about what they agreed. The solution – to record the parties' agreement in writing – appears to be about as old as writing itself.[34] In order to avoid a situation where one party claims not to have read the details of a written contract, English courts have developed what is known as the parole contract rule.[35] If you sign a written agreement, you are deemed to have read it. The problem is that e-commerce agreements are rarely made in the form of signed documents agreed by the parties. The question for an e-commerce provider – particularly a business-to-consumer (B2C) provider – is how to ensure that a contract is made pursuant to particular written terms of business.

A considerable amount of litigation in the US has been generated around the validity of so-called 'shrink-wrap' agreements. Software was once usually sold on physical media of various kinds that were shrink-wrapped in cellophane. On the outside of this packaging there might be a notice saying something like 'by opening this package, you agree to be bound by the terms and conditions contained inside'. In other situations, the software itself might require the acceptance of terms and conditions upon installation – that is, after the product had been purchased and the shrink-wrapping opened.

The logical difficulty of binding a person to contractual terms they have not read is obvious. The purchaser could not read the terms inside the packet, let alone those contained in the software installation, until it was too late for it to be practical to refuse them. That logical conundrum might be solved by, for example:

• Reasoning that the purchaser knows there will be *some* conditions on the use of the software, and they could contact the supplier to discover what these are before making the purchase; or

• Implying a right for the purchaser to refuse the terms and return the product for a refund.

The validity of shrink-wrap licences has not been considered in English law. In Scots law, the Court in the first instance decision of *Beta Computers (Europe) Ltd v Adobe Systems (Europe) Ltd*[36] held that the contract was formed upon the purchaser reading the licence conditions and accepting them. That case is odd because the licence conditions were imposed by a third party (Informix, the owner of the copyright in the supplied software) and the Court's analysis depended on the Scots law principle of *jus quaesitum tertio*, which did not at that point exist in English law.[37]

---

[34] Many early Sumerian cuneiform tablets are contracts.
[35] See *L'Estrange v F Graucob Ltd* [1934] 2 KB 394.
[36] *Beta Computers (Europe) Ltd v Adobe Systems (Europe) Ltd* 1996 SLT 604.
[37] The decision has been doubted; see S Robertson, 'The Validity of Shrink-Wrap Licences in Scots Law: *Beta Computers (Europe) Ltd v. Adobe Systems (Europe) Ltd*' [1998] (2) *Journal of Information, Law & Technology*.

If anything, the situation is easier for the e-commerce provider, who is able to link to terms and conditions, than it was for the software vendor who could not offer the purchaser a copy of the terms until after they had opened the box. In some e-commerce situations there need not be a problem – a customer can be given a link to terms and conditions at the point of sale (or other form of contracting) and told that those terms will apply to the contract. Now the customer is able – at least in theory – to check the terms of the contract before agreeing to it.

E-commerce providers may try to strengthen this approach by, for example:

• including some means by which the customer must affirmatively indicate their consent to the terms – for example by checking a box (sometimes called 'click-wrap'[38]); or

• Presenting a scrollable text box containing the terms, which must be scrolled through in its entirety before the possibility of agreeing to the terms is made available.

But in some cases these methods will be awkward. This is particularly true of e-commerce providers who wish to bind visitors to a website to terms and conditions without requiring them to sign up for an account, or otherwise take some form of positive action. In such cases, there have been attempts to argue that a contract can be formed by so-called 'browse-wrap'. These contracts are alleged to be formed merely by the customer browsing a website rather than clicking on any particular terms of acceptance or other positive action. The theory is that browsing forms acceptance of the terms of the website by conduct.

In the US, a number of cases have considered these, with varying degrees of approval[39], while in the EU the theory has been tested especially by Ryanair, the Irish budget airline, which have tried vigorously to prevent price comparison sites scraping their site by, inter alia, complaining they are breaching the terms and conditions of the site even though no ordinary contract for services was sought.[40] Many contract theorists have found these cases to adopt unreasonably broad notions of classic offer and acceptance rules, and 'browse-wrap' is best advised against in favour of adopting a click-wrap approach.

A. Incorporation and Unusual Terms

Note that there is a difference between incorporation of terms as a general rule, and whether unusually onerous terms – such as those in *Thornton v Shoe Lane Parking*[41] – are

---

[38] 'Click-wrap' has been 'officially' approved by the CJEU as a method of validly concluding a contract in Case C-322/14 *El Majdoub v CarsOnTheWeb.Deutschland* GmbH, 21 May 2015 (the case actually concerned jurisdiction).

[39] See, eg, *Specht v Netscape* 306 F.3d 17; *Register.com Inc v Verio Inc* 356 F3d 393;

[40] See, eg, Irish case of *Ryanair Ltd v Billigfluege.de GMBH* [2010] IEHC 47 (2010); in the CJEU, Case C-30/14 *Ryanair Ltd v PR Aviation BV*.

[41] *Thornton v Shoe Lane Parking* [1971] 2 QB 163.

enforceable. Even if a term would normally form part of a contract, there might be some rule that prevents it from operating without it first being drawn to the particular attention of a contracting party. In *J Spurling Ltd v Bradshaw*, Denning LJ said:

> the more unreasonable a clause is, the greater the notice which must be given of it. Some clauses which I have seen would need to be printed in red ink on the face of the document with a red hand pointing to it before the notice could be held to be sufficient.[42]

English common law held that clauses of an unusual kind that exclude liability should be drawn to the attention of the party against whom they would operate.[43]

B. E-Commerce Directive (ECD)[44] Rules Affecting Contract Formation

The ECD is one of the prime pieces of European legislation attempting to harmonise the rules regulating e-commerce suppliers which we have already looked at in detail in Chapter 9 in relation to the liability of online intermediaries and in Chapter 5 in relation to spam. The ECD also deals with electronic contracting. The ECD does not (and at the time of enactment, probably could not) harmonise the substantive domestic contract law of EU Member States. However it did, in the interests of certainty and consumer protection, go some way to introducing a harmonised regime for e-contracts in relation to information requirements, and the placing of the order for a contract.

Article 10 of the ECD provides that a minimum set of information must be supplied to the recipient of an internet society service before they place an order, which must be provided 'clearly, comprehensibly and unambiguously' and comprises:

- the different technical steps to follow to conclude the contract;
- whether or not the concluded contract will be filed by the service provider and whether it will be accessible;
- the technical means for identifying and correcting input errors prior to the placing of the order; and
- the languages offered for the conclusion of the contract.

An Information Society Service Provider (ISSP) must also indicate any relevant codes of conduct to which the ISSP subscribes, as well as information on how those codes can be consulted electronically. The purpose of Article 10 seems to be to make sure that a prospective user of an ISSP understands the contracting process. Article 10 does

---

[42] *J Spurling Ltd v Bradshaw* [1956] EWCA Civ 3. See Mark Anderson's blog post, 'Three Cheers for the Manicule' for an amusing discussion of this point http://ipdraughts.wordpress.com/2012/02/10/three-cheers-for-the-manicule/.

[43] *Parker v South Eastern Railway* (1877) 2 CPD 416.

[44] Directive 2000/31/EC.

not, importantly, apply to contracts formed by exchange of emails, and non-consumer parties can agree otherwise. It is aimed at web-based automated contract formation processes, as are typical in dealings with Amazon and other online B2C e-commerce vendors, not at the bespoke transactions more typical of the business-to-business (B2B) world.

Article 11 of the ECD deals with 'placing the order'. There is confusion here when this is combined with national laws, because as seen above, an 'order' may sometimes be construed as a legal offer, and other times as merely an invitation to treat. This has led to considerable academic concern.[45] The phrase 'order' is replicated in the UK incorporation of these rules in the e-Commerce Regulations.

The ISSP must:

- **prior** to the placing of the order, make available to the recipient of the service appropriate, effective, and accessible technical means allowing them to identify and correct 'input errors' (Art 11(2)); and

- **after** the placing of the order, acknowledge receipt of the order by electronic means (Art 11(1)) and without undue delay.

As with Art 10, neither of these requirements apply if (i) non-consumer parties agree otherwise, or (ii) the contract is concluded exclusively by exchange of electronic mail or equivalent individual communications. Article 11(1) includes the deeming provisions regarding receipt of the order and the acknowledgement as discussed earlier.

Finally, Art 5 of the ECD sets out a minimal set of information that must be provided by all ISSPs.[46] The information must be 'easily, directly and permanently accessible'. This appears not to require that this information be provided using the same medium as that used to access the ISSP. For example, it would be very difficult for a mobile service to do so, given the character limits of an SMS. It is not clear whether making the information available on a website is enough, or whether 'permanently' requires some kind of immutable historical record. The information must be made available to recipients of the service, and any relevant competent authorities. Information required includes the name, address, email address, location and VAT number, if relevant, of the trader, as well as any relevant details of professional accreditation. In addition, where information society services refer to prices, these are to be indicated clearly and unambiguously, including in particular whether or not they are inclusive of tax and delivery costs.

As we shall see below, in section VI, these requirements are often added to or duplicated by laws relating specifically to information which must be supplied to consumers.

---

[45] See discussion in C Reifa and J Hornle, in L Edwards and C Waelde (eds), *Law and the Internet*, 3rd edn (Oxford, Hart Publishing, 2009) Ch 2, 106–109.

[46] See Chapter 9 on some of the difficulties around defining an ISSP. Articles 6 and 7 dealing with commercial communications are addressed within the discussion of spam in Chapter 5.

IV. Formalities

Very few contracts in English law[47] have either to be in writing or to be evidenced by writing. 'Evidenced by writing' means that although the contract may be made orally, there must be some written evidence of it. Examples include:

- most contracts for the sale of land,[48] and
- contracts of guarantee.[49]

As such, many of these situations are of only minor interest in the e-commerce sphere. In most cases 'writing' will have the definition given to it by the Interpretation Act 1978, which states that writing 'includes typing, printing, lithography, photography and other modes of representing or reproducing words in a visible form, and expressions referring to writing are construed accordingly'. The requirement of visibility might cause difficulty since not all electronic information can reasonably be said to be in a 'visible form', a point with which the Law Commission for England and Wales have concurred.[50]

An assignment of copyright, important in some e-commerce activities, must be made in writing and signed by the assignor (the person assigning).[51] Here, the Act contains its own definition of writing as 'any form of notation or code, whether by hand or otherwise regardless of the method by which or medium in or on which it is recorded'.[52] An agreement to assign may not therefore be implied. The operator of a user-contributed content site will also need to ensure that any agreement is 'signed' – a question that will be dealt with later in this chapter.

A requirement that a contract be written is much more common in jurisdictions based on the civil law tradition, such as France, than it is in those based on the common law (and in this case Scots law). This divergence reflects different approaches to contractual intention in the two traditions,[53] and means that the question of whether any particular form of electronic contract involves 'writing' is accordingly more important in civil law jurisdictions.

Various efforts to reform the law in order to put beyond doubt the validity of electronic contracts have included:

- UNCITRAL Convention On The Use Of Electronic Communications In International Contracts;

---

[47] For a summary of the state of Scots law on formal probativity of electronic contracts and a suggestion for an electronic document depository, see 'Report on Formation of Contract: Execution and Counterpart' (Scot Law Com No 231, 2013).

[48] Law of Property (Miscellaneous Provisions) Act 1989, s 2.

[49] Statute of Frauds 1677, s 4.

[50] Law Commission, 'Electronic Commerce: Formal Requirements in Commercial Transactions, Advice from the Law Commission' (December 2001) see in particular p 7 *et seq.*

[51] Copyright, Designs and Patents Act 1988, s 90.

[52] *Ibid*, s 178.

[53] See M Thomas Arceneaux, 'Writing Requirements and the Authentic Act in Louisiana Law: Civil Code Articles 2236, 2275 and 2278' (1975) 35 (4) *Louisiana Law Review* 764.

- UNCITRAL Model Law on Electronic Commerce, Article 11(1); and
- EU e-Commerce Directive.[54]

A. Signatures in Electronic Contracts

A place to start when discussing electronic signatures is to ask what signatures are for. There are many approaches to this. One of the most useful considers whether the function of the signature is evidential or formal. The most instinctive approach to the function of a signature – and, as we shall see, that taken by many legislators and those in the cryptography profession – is evidential. Because (most) people's signatures are hard to copy, if one is present on a document it is taken as evidence that that person signed it. The quality of a signature may then be judged by how well it acts as evidence.

However, a moment's thought demonstrates that this cannot be the only role of a signature. Signatures have been used since before the common law came into existence, at a time when many people were illiterate. It was common for people to sign many documents with a mark such as a cross. Clearly a simple cross has much less evidential value than a handwritten signature. Because signing a document is a formal step, requiring a person to sign a document can force them to consider whether they genuinely wish to be bound by it and, if they do sign, we may assume that they have accepted the contract in its entirety. This is the basis of the *parole* contract.

Here the requirement for a signature is purely formal. The formality of a signature has many purposes. For example, in commercial negotiations towards a signed contract, the parties to the contract will know that once it is signed, they have concluded an agreement. As you will have read, UNCITRAL identifies three main purposes of signatures:[55]

1. to identify a person;
2. to provide certainty as to the personal involvement of that person in the act of signing; and
3. to associate that person with the content of a document.

In their list of other uses, they note one of importance to e-commerce:

4. to attest to the intent of a party to be bound by the content of a signed contract.

The primary legal focus is on use of a security procedure – particularly digital signatures and on procedures for verifying that a message is that of a specified person or detecting error in the content of the message. You may notice that these are actually rather disparate aims. For example, the second purpose is about evidence, whereas the fourth concerns the mental state of the signer. Chris Reed suggests a heading of

---

[54] Directive 2000/31/EC.
[55] See, eg, UNCITRAL Model Law on Electronic Commerce: Guide to Enactment.

'consumer protection',[56] where a signature has the formal role of alerting a consumer to the fact that what they are doing may have legal consequences.

B. Lawyers Versus Cryptographers

Lawyers and cryptographers often talk at cross-purposes about signatures. Cryptographers tend to focus on the evidential nature of signatures. For them the value of a signature is reflected in its resistance to forgery. To a cryptographer, 'authentication' means providing evidence that someone is who they claim to be or, in the case of a signature, that a document was signed by the claimed signer. As we will see, it is technically possible to create 'electronic signatures' which are very difficult to forge.

Lawyers have traditionally been much more interested in the formal role of the signature and, in particular, on its effect on the mental state of the signer. In practice, surprisingly few parties to litigation deny having signed a relevant document. Forensic arguments about the identity of the signer are very rare, particularly in civil litigation, and thus in legal practice the evidential value of a signature is much less important than it might appear to be. Much confusion was caused in the early development of e-signature law by what Winn describes as the 'facile equation of two different types of signatures'.[57]

C. Validity of Electronic Signatures

In e-commerce, signing an email or other electronic document is clearly not entirely straightforward. In the early days of e-commerce, much attention was diverted to creating 'electronic signatures' which combine aspects of making a message secure with reliably authenticating the sender. A message can be transformed using public key encryption (PKE) so that the recipient can verify the message's authenticity and integrity. There are two forms of this: symmetric, single key, and asymmetric, two keys: one public, one private. A symmetric key only provides confidentiality, while a public key provides confidentiality and is used as a form of digital signature authenticating the sender. The 'keys' are numbers generated by software or hardware and come in pairs – the private pair must be kept secret and the public key is freely disclosed. There are two important characteristics of key pairs; (i) they are mathematically related, but use number sets so large that one can't calculate the private key even if the public key is known; and (ii) either key can encrypt, but only the other will decrypt.

Despite the availability of PKE, and its promotion by legislators globally (see below), many electronic documents or emails are in fact signed by much more low-tech methods such as typing in a signature, or pasting in a scan of a manual

---

[56] C Reed, 'What is a Signature?' (2000) (3) *Journal of Information, Law & Technology*.

[57] J Winn, 'Signature Standards: Competing US and EU Legislative Approaches to the Problem of Online Authentication' (Austin, Texas, International Academy of Commercial and Consumer Law, 12 August 2006).

signature. As seen below, the English courts have found it fairly easy to recognise these as signatures, making the apparatus of electronic signatures, certification authorities, etc not always necessary and arguably somewhat over-complex for purposes required.

i. England and Wales

The common law has long treated the primary function of a signature as being evidence of authentication that is that the signer intends to adopt the signed document. This reflects that a signature is an evidentiary tool used to reduce reliance on post-agreement oral evidence which attempts to deny the apparent accuracy of a document or explain its true meaning. The form taken by the signature is of secondary importance – no reported English decision has ever found the requirement for a signature not to be met on the basis only of the form of the signature. This is, in part, because common law courts have focussed on the function of a signature, rather than its form. Reed[58] correctly argues that the primary function of a signature consists of three 'sub-functions':

- the identity of the signatory;
- that the signatory intended the 'signature' to be his signature; and
- that the signatory approves of and adopts the contents of the document.

In *Jenkins v Gaisford*[59] the engraving of the deceased's name was used on his behalf by a person acting under his direction to sign a codicil to a will. The High Court of Admiralty held that it was a valid signature because it 'was intended to stand for and represent the signature'.

Similarly, in *Goodman v J Eban Ltd*,[60] a rubber stamp facsimile signature was used by a firm of solicitors to sign a bill of costs. The Court of Appeal held this was a good signature. Denning LJ dissented, but his dissent also focussed on the mental state of the signer. In his view the problem with a rubber stamp was not that it offered poor evidence as to the identity of the signer, but that it could be easily used by someone other than the person whose signature it was and, importantly, without their having considered its use.

The position of a signature is also important. In *Caton v Caton*[61] the House of Lords held that, depending where it was placed, a signature could theoretically affirm only a *part* of a document.

This focus on function led Laddie J to accept that a faxed form was signed in *Inland Revenue v Conbeer*.[62] In *Mehta v J Pereira Fernandes*[63] the Court accepted that the adding of an email address to an email could, if added with intent to sign, constitute a valid signature. The difficulty with electronic acts is that they are easily automated.

---

[58] *Reed* (n 56).
[59] *Jenkins v Gaisford* (1863) 3 Sw & Tr 93.
[60] *Goodman v J Eban Ltd* [1954] 1 QB 550.
[61] *Caton v Caton* (1867) LR 2 HL 127.
[62] *Inland Revenue Commissioners v Conbeer* [1996] 2 All ER 345.
[63] *Mehta v J Pereira Fernandes* [2006] EWHC 813 (Ch).

An e-signature may be applied without the user of a computer realising. That is a difficulty which may be resolved by a court depending on the circumstances of the case, which will usually be clear. For example, this was the point in issue in *Mehta*, where the alleged signature was added automatically at the start of every email. The Court found that in those circumstances there was no evidence of it being used as a signature.

But this is not a problem peculiar to electronic signatures, in *Birmingham City Council v Hosey*[64] a statement of truth was rubber stamped with the name of a council employee who had not read the statement. Addressing Denning LJ's dissent in *Eban*, the Court held that the document had not been properly signed.

Thus, there is no reason in principle why English common law should not be able to encompass electronic signatures using exactly the same set of principles as it has already applied to other forms of signature. In principle any form of electronic addition to a document (or any other action) should be capable of providing evidence of mental state – a conclusion which the Law Commission has supported.[65]

A note of caution was sounded in *Firstpost Homes v Johnson*.[66] There it was held that the cases on signatures may be context-specific: different criteria could apply depending on the particular statutory (or common law) rule being interpreted. There might therefore be a role for new legislation to put beyond doubt the validity of electronic signatures in all situations.

A similar situation is likely to obtain in the United States and in other common law jurisdictions. For example, in the Australian case of *The Anemone*,[67] it was held for the purposes of the Statute of Frauds 1677 that the response of the sender of a telex would constitute a valid signature.

ii. Within the EU

The English approach is not the only one taken by jurisdictions of EU Member States. For example, French jurisprudence has taken a narrow approach to the question of what constitutes a signature. The Court of Cassation (1st Civil, 15 July 1957) rejected the use of a cross as a valid signature, while the Court of Appeal of Limoges rejected an email document (18 March 1999). The French approach, echoed in other civil law countries, represented an obstacle to electronic commerce, making it difficult for signatures to be used over the Internet. That problem was exacerbated by the wider Civil Code requirements for the use of signatures in ordinary consumer contracts. Reform was therefore necessary, and on the interests of harmonisation within the EU, an early EU instrument, the Electronic Signatures Directive 1999,[68] was promulgated to achieve this in Article 5(2), which requires that an e-signature must not be denied legal effectiveness and admissibility solely on the grounds that it is in electronic form.

---

[64] *Birmingham City Council v Hosey* 2002 *Legal Action* 20.
[65] Law Commission (n 50).
[66] *Firstpost Homes v Johnson* [1995] 1 WLR 1567.
[67] *The Anemone* [1987] 1 Lloyd's Rep 546.
[68] Directive 1999/93/EC of the European Parliament and of the Council of 13 December 1999 on a Community framework for electronic signatures [1999] OJ L13/12.

V. Digital Signatures

There are known technical solutions to the problem of creating an electronic artefact which can provide strong evidence that a document has originated from a particular individual. In cryptography, these are known as 'digital signatures'. Most known solutions to this problem rely on one or more 'one-way' mathematical functions. These are functions that take little computational effort in one direction but are computationally very difficult in the other. A simple example is the multiplication of two prime numbers. With enough paper and patience, one can calculate the product of two 40 digit numbers, for example:

$$2425967623052370772757633156976982469681$$

$$\text{X} \qquad\qquad 1451730470513778492236629598992166035067$$

$$3521851118865011044136429217528930691441965435121409905222808922963363310303627$$

Figure 2

But reversing the process starting with the answer is much, much more difficult. Indeed, this characteristic (factorisation is hard, multiplication is easy) is the basis for a very popular form of cryptography known as RSA public-key encryption, which can be used to create digital signatures.

For digital signatures, PKE works as follows:

○ The signer has two 'keys' (either numbers, or collections of numbers) which are uniquely connected to one another:

  • the 'public key' which is publicised, and
  • The 'private key' which is kept secret by the signer.

○ The signer uses the two keys together to encrypt[69] a document. Only the signer can do this, because only she knows both keys.
○ Anyone can decrypt the document using the public key.
○ If someone receives an encrypted document and successfully decrypts it using the public key, they know that it must have been someone who had both keys that encrypted it. Because of the relationship between the public and private keys, then assuming all is otherwise well, only the signer can have encrypted the document, and therefore she must have 'signed' it.

---

[69] In popular language this is sometimes called 'encoding', but 'code' has a technical meaning to cryptographers.

There are numerous refinements on this theme, but this is the basic idea. PKE may seem like a magic solution, but it clearly has a number of drawbacks, of which two have particular importance for e-commerce. First, while the signer may 'publish' her public key, how does the other party know it was *she* who published it? This fundamental problem is known to cryptographers as 'key distribution'. For communication between individuals who know each other a public key could be distributed by hand. Business partners with a strong need for highly secure forms of signature might meet physically to hand over public keys.

This is impractical for a lot of e-commerce, and so PKE tends to rely on an infrastructure of trusted third parties that form part of a Public Key Infrastructure (PKI). The HTTPS protocol used by web browsers to allow secure communication between a user's web browser and a web server relies on the fact that a set of 'certificates' (which are essentially forms of public key) are distributed with the browser. If the user does not trust the web browser, then the question of secure communications is already moot. If she does trust the web browser, then she can trust the browser's bundled set of public keys.[70]

The second difficulty with digital signatures for an e-commerce lawyer is that they are sufficiently complicated that they will almost certainly need to be applied by computer. It will usually be impossible to tell, from a digital signature, that the signer was actively involved personally in applying it, rather than just her computer. Thus digital signatures solve an evidential problem as to identity and origin, but they do not really help with formal validity.

A. Attempts to Regulate

The first attempt to regulate the use of electronic signatures was the Utah Digital Signature Act 1996, which gave digital signatures equivalent validity to handwritten signatures. The Act was technology-specific, assuming public key encryption and a PKI that included state-licensed certification authorities. Some European countries adopted similar technology-specific approaches (for example Germany[71] and Italy). Clearly there are advantages with state regulation of certification providers for the benefit of e-commerce, but licensing on a per-state basis is much less useful than it might seem because of the global reach of e-commerce. Technology-specific laws risk inflexibility and short-term obsolescence. The Utah law had nothing to say about systems of electronic signatures outside the state-licensed system.

By contrast, the UNCITRAL Model Law on Electronic Commerce adopted a technologically neutral 'functional equivalence' test. Article 7 provides that where the law requires a person's signature, if any method is used either to identify the person or to indicate their approval of the information contained in a data message then, provided that the method is as reliable as was appropriate for the purpose for which the data message was generated or communicated, the method will be treated as the

---

[70] See K Thompson, 'Reflections on Trusting Trust' (1984) 27 *Communications of the ACM* 761.
[71] German Digital Signature Act 1997 (*Signaturgesetz*, SIG).

equivalent of a handwritten signature. In other words, if it quacks like a signature it should be accepted as a signature. This is of course akin to the approach already taken in most of the common law cases.

Functional equivalence laws were adopted in some states, such as the UK, Australia, and New Zealand, and in the United States at the federal level in the Federal Electronic Signatures in Global and National Commerce Act 2000 (rendering obsolete the Utah law).

The Electronic Signatures Directive takes a two-tier approach. It defines two types of signature:

1. Electronic signatures (adopting a functional approach).
2. Advanced electronic signatures (a technology-neutral approach requiring a higher evidential standard than an electronic signature).

Although 'advanced electronic signature' is fairly neutral as to the technology used, the Directive is principally concerned with advanced electronic signatures which are also based on (i) a 'qualified certificate', and (ii) that are created by a secure-signature-creation device. These requirements are highly prescriptive in form.

B. Liability of Certification Providers

A system of electronic signatures that relies on certification providers (as does one of the tiers of the Electronic Signatures Directive) raises two questions of liability:

1. If a certification provider's negligence means that a signature is falsely signed, does anyone who relies on that signature have recourse against the certification provider?
2. Do users of electronic signatures, who may have their own private keys, have any responsibility to prevent their own signatures being misused?

Some forms of e-signature regulation have tried to impose liability on certification providers and, more rarely, on the users of electronic signatures. Of course, the possibility of liability for a certification provider may discourage a service provider from allowing its service to be used for authentication in other contexts.[72]

VI. Consumer Protection

A. Introduction

Consumer protection is usually justified in two ways. First as a way in which the law may intervene to protect a party (the consumer) which is presumed to be weaker than

---

[72] See s 3.3.2 of the 'Report from the Commission to the European Parliament and the Council – Report on the Operation of Directive 1999/93/EC on a Community Framework for Electronic Signatures' COM/2006/0120 final.

the business with which they deal, although there are clearly unusual situations in which the reverse is true. However, there is a second, and indirect, justification for legal intervention, namely that if consumers are not protected, they may be discouraged from entering into otherwise economically valuable activity to the detriment of businesses with which they deal and the economy as a whole. This latter rationale tends to be assumed by legislators, and sometimes courts, without evidence. Actual evidence for the proposition seems to be weak.[73]

In e-commerce, a consumer is likely to have a greater transactional distance from the trader and the trader may be unknown to them or even if known, may be located geographically far from them. A consumer may be discouraged by that distance, for example because they are less likely to trust a trader they do not know; or they are less likely to feel they are able to bring to bear social or legal pressure against a trader based far from their own location. In the purchase of goods, consumers may be used to visiting a trader to return faulty or unwanted goods – something which is not possible in the same way for the sale of goods over the Internet, where the trader may not only be far away, but may have no physical presence at all.

The EU has sought to protect consumers in a number of ways. Some of these, such as rules on product liability, impact on e-commerce only via the possibility that harmonising the law between Member States will improve cross-border trade and hence perhaps cross-border forms of e-commerce. However, some forms of consumer protection bear more directly on the e-commerce situation. In particular:

o Fairness, in two particular ways:

    a. fair behaviour by traders when dealing with consumers; and
    b. fairness in the form of contract terms between traders and consumers.

o Information – requiring that consumers be given clear information by traders both before and after the conclusion of a contract.
o Provisions addressing the geographical separation of consumer and trader, in particular a right to cancel or return.

The main EU legislative act in this area is now the Consumer Rights Directive (CRD) 2011[74] which replaces a number of prior instruments such as the Distance Selling Directive (DSD).[75] The CRD is implemented in the UK in the Consumer Contracts Regulations (Information, Cancellation and Additional Charges) Regulations 2013[76]

---

[73] C Twigg-Flesner, 'Does the Codification of Consumer Law Improve the Ability of Consumers to Enforce Their Rights? – A UK-Perspective' in B Heiderhoff, R Schulze (eds), *Verbraucherrecht und Verbraucherverhalten, Consumer Law and Consumer Behaviour* (Nomos Verlagsgesellschaft bilingual edition, 2016) 211–30.

[74] Directive 2011/83/EU of the European Parliament and of the Council of 25 October 2011 on consumer rights. [2011] OJ L304/64. See extensive guidance at https://ec.europa.eu/info/sites/info/files/crd_guidance_en_0.pdf. See further, European Commission, 'Results of the Fitness Check of Consumer and Marketing Law and of the Evaluation of the Consumer Rights Directive' (2017) at http://ec.europa.eu/newsroom/just/item-detail.cfm?item_id=59332.

[75] Directive 97/7/EC of the European Parliament and of the Council of 20 May 1997 on the protection of consumers in respect of distance contracts [1997] OJ L144/19.

[76] Consumer Contracts (Information, Cancellation and Additional Charges) Regulations 2013 (SI 2013/3134).

and in the Consumer Rights (Payment Surcharges) Regulations 2012.[77] Other
EU consumer instruments relevant to e-commerce include those on misleading
advertising[78] the Unfair Terms in Consumer Contracts Directive (UTCCD),[79]
implemented in the UK by the Unfair Terms in Consumer Contracts Regulations
1999; the Directive on Consumer goods and Guarantees[80] implemented in the UK by
the Sale and Supply of Goods to Consumers Regulations 2002[81] and the Price Indications Directive 1998.[82] The rules on distance selling and unfair terms are discussed in
detail below in the context of the UK legal system. A new Directive to deal with the
problems specific to digital contracts to replace or subsume some of the above has been
in the pipeline for a very long time[83]: see discussion below.

B. Fairness

The principle of freedom of contract is the idea that two contracting parties should
be free to make any bargain they choose, subject perhaps to principles of legality and
public policy, has never been an absolute one. This principle was never absolute and
has over time allowed exceptions to protect a weaker party, such as a consumer. In the
context of online trading, where a trader will often supply a set of terms and conditions, few if any consumers actually read the contract to which they are adhering. One
solution found by the common law is to require the existence of the terms to be drawn
to the attention of the consumer and in the case of unusual terms, the existence of
the unusual terms.[84] But a more general solution is to disallow some or all classes of
term which are in some sense unfair. Fairness is not confined solely to the terms of a
contract. A trader can mislead a consumer in numerous ways – for instance in advertising or in the information supplied to the consumer. Legislative rules against unfair
practices in general have also developed over recent years.

i. EU UTCCD

Rather than outlawing specific forms of unfair term, the UTCCD starts with a general
rule that contract terms should not be unfair to the consumer, together with an

---

[77] Consumer Rights (Payment Surcharges Regulations 2012 (SI 2012/3110).

[78] Directive 2006/114/EC of the European Parliament and of the Council of 12 December 2006
concerning misleading and comparative advertising (codified version) [2006] OJL376/21.

[79] Council Directive 93/13/EEC of 5 April 1993 on unfair terms in consumer contracts [1993]
OJ L95/29.

[80] The Unfair Terms in Consumer Contracts Regulations 1999 (SI 1999/2083); Directive 1999/44/EC of
the European Parliament and of the Council of 25 May 1999 on certain aspects of the sale of consumer
goods and associated guarantees [1999] OJ L171/12.

[81] Sale and Supply of Goods to Consumers Regulations 2002 (SI 2002/3045).

[82] Directive 98/6/EC of the European Parliament and of the Council of 16 February 1998 on consumer
protection in the indication of the prices of products offered to consumers [1998] OJ L80/27.

[83] See below section VII.B.

[84] eg Thornton v Shoe Lane Parking Ltd [1971] 2 QB 163.

indicative and non-exhaustive list of unfair terms. An unfair contract term is defined as follows:

> A contractual term which has not been individually negotiated shall be regarded as unfair if, contrary to the requirement of good faith, it causes a significant imbalance in the parties' rights and obligations arising under the contract, to the detriment of the consumer.[85]

A contract supplied in advance, such as a website's terms and conditions, will contain terms that have 'not been individually negotiated'. If a contract term is unfair, it is not binding on the consumer, although the contract will continue in existence if it is capable of doing so without any unfair terms it contains.

ii. UK Law

In the UK there have long been general rules, applying to B2B as well as B2C agreements, limiting certain classes of unfairness, for example the Unfair Contract Terms Act 1977 (UCTA) prevents an exclusion clause found in a standard form agreement from taking effect unless it is fair and reasonable.[86]

From this era, there were also specific protections for consumers. For example UCTA also prevented indemnities given by consumers from taking effect unless they were fair and reasonable[87] and extended the protection against unreasonable exclusion clauses to consumers whether the underlying agreement was in standard form or not. Specific protection for consumers is found in other legislation. For example, the Sale of Goods Act 1979 implied a condition into any sale of goods in the course of business that the goods are of merchantable quality.[88] Any provision that attempts to exclude that implied condition is void in a consumer sale.[89]

From 1994, under the influence of the Unfair Terms in Consumer Contracts Directive 1993 (UTCCD), the UK adopted a more generalised approach in the form of the Unfair Terms in Consumer Contracts Regulations 1994, followed by the Unfair Terms in Consumer Contract Regulations 1999.[90] All these provisions – general ones found in the UCCR 1999 and specific rules found in UCTA and other legislation – have been codified in the Consumer Rights Act 2015. It goes slightly further in that:

- There is now no requirement that a term has not been individually negotiated.
- The rule against unfairness also applies to 'consumer notices' as well as consumer contracts.

iii. Distance |Selling

As noted above, these rules are now found in the Consumer Contracts (Information, Cancellation and Additional Charges) Regulations 2013[91] made under the CRD,

---

[85] UTCCD, Art 3(1).
[86] UCTA, s 17.
[87] *Ibid*, s 18.
[88] Sale of Goods Act 1979, s 14.
[89] *Ibid*, para 11, Sch 1.
[90] SI 1999/2083.
[91] SI 2013/ 3134.

and themselves are similar to the rules once found in the DSD. The rules governed, inter alia, the contracts to which the rules applied in full or in part; the information that needed to be supplied in connection with distance selling (these supplement the rules in the ECD already examined, and, to some extent, the General Data Protection Regulation (GDPR),[92] Arts 12–15); and the rules which concerned the right to cancel the contract.

Initially, the cases concerning the distance selling rules focused on whether or not the rules applied to the contract in question (see for example *easyCar (UK) Ltd v Office of Fair Trading*,[93] and the German *eBay Case*[94]) rather than the specific requirements of the Directive. However, there has been growing judicial scrutiny of substantive elements, like the right of cancellation.

The DSD and now the CRD provide for a right of withdrawal, which may apply to some e-contracts. The principle behind the right of withdrawal was that a consumer should have some time after delivery to ascertain whether the goods met their requirements.

In *Pia Messner v Firma Stefan Krüger*,[95] the Court found that while a provision of national law cannot in general provide for a seller's right of compensation for value of the use of the goods upon withdrawal by the customer within the withdrawal period, the DSD did not preclude a provision of national law allowing for a compensation claim for use of goods by the customer that is incompatible with the principles of contract law. Furthermore, the CJEU has found that these provisions do not preclude domestic laws from providing stronger consumer protection than that in the Directive. The case of *Lodewijk Gysbrechts and Santurel Inter BVBA*,[96] for example, concerned a prohibition on sellers requiring payment of a deposit during the withdrawal period. The respective liabilities of supplier and consumer after cancellation were also considered in *Handelsgesellschaft Heinrich Heine GmbH v Verbraucherzentrale Nordrhein-Westfalen eV*.[97] There the Court confirmed that the cost of the goods plus any delivery charge had to be reimbursed, holding that the Directive was clear that only the cost of returning the goods and not the costs of delivering them in the first place could be charged by the supplier in the event of a withdrawal by the purchaser.

These cases led to calls for the right of cancellation to be clarified. The European Parliament insisted that there should be some protection for traders to prevent unfair advantage being taken of the right of cancellation.[98] The argument is that principles

---

[92] Regulation (EU) 2016/679 of the European Parliament and of the Council of 27 April 2016 on the protection of natural persons with regard to the processing of personal data and on the free movement of such data [2016] OJ L119/1.

[93] Case C-336/03 *easyCar (UK) Ltd v Office of Fair Trading* [2005] ECR I-01497.

[94] *eBay Case* VIII ZR 375/03 (3 November 2004). The decision (in German) can be found at http://juris. bundesgerichtshof.de/cgi-bin/rechtsprechung/document.py?Gericht=bgh&Art=en&nr=30855&pos=0& anz=1.

[95] Case C-489/07 *Pia Messner v Firma Stefan Krüger* [2009] ECR I-07315.

[96] Case C-205/07 *Lodewijk Gysbrechts and Santurel Inter BVBA* [2008] ECR I-09947.

[97] Case C-511/08 *Handelsgesellschaft Heinrich Heine GmbH v Verbraucherzentrale Nordrhein-Westfalen eV* [2010] ECR I-03047.

[98] See, www.europarl.europa.eu/RegData/etudes/IDAN/2015/565904/EPRS_IDA(2015)565904_EN.pdf.

of good faith should apply and therefore that limitations should be placed on how long the right of cancellation can still operate after the goods have been delivered. The CRD[99] clarified these elements and reshaped the approach to the right of withdrawal. In particular changes were made to the prior information requirements in Article 6(1)(h)–(k), Article 6(4) (model instructions on withdrawal), Article 10 (the effect of omission), and Article 11 on exercising the consumer's rights, particularly the optional use of the model form of cancellation. The CRD also extends the cancellation period from seven to 14 days.

VII. Digital Content[100]

Implied terms relating to contracts for goods or services have a long history. As well as being firmly established in national laws, many are embodied in international agreements, such as the 1980 UN Convention on the International Sale of Goods and the 1964 Uniform Law on the International Sale of Goods. Whether terms will be implied will be a matter first of determining what the applicable law is for the particular contract, and second of looking to that jurisdiction's contract law as well as any international agreements which that law embodies.

In UK law there has long been a distinction between contracts for the supply of goods and contracts for the supply of services. Both categories of contract may have terms implied by statute, for example in relation to the fitness for purpose.[101] The distinction between goods and services has also applied in the EU e-commerce regulatory rules, such as in the former distance selling rules prior to the Consumer Rights Directive, where the rules on cancellation varied between goods and services.

The difficulty for e-commerce, however, is that e-commerce contracts are not easy to classify as either goods or services. In the English Court of Appeal case of *St Albans City and District Council v ICL*,[102] Glidewell LJ thought that customised packaged software was not 'goods' and therefore the implied statutory term as to quality, found in the Sale of Goods Act 1979, did not apply (although he did imply such a term at common law).

Subsequent authorities have not been particularly clear. In *Thunder Air Ltd v Hilmar Hilmarsson*,[103] the Court accepted the parties' agreement that software on a hard disk was not 'goods' for the purposes of the Torts (Interference with Goods) Act 1977. At first instance the English High Court held, based on the wording of a contract for the supply of software in the form of object code, that in that context

---

[99] 2011/83/EU.

[100] See generally Special Issue on Contracts on Digital Goods and Services (2017) *Journal of Intellectual Property, Information Technology and Electronic Commerce Law* 8(1).

[101] Sale of Goods Act 1979; Supply of Goods and Services Act 1982.

[102] *St Albans City and District Council v ICL* [1995] FSR 686.

[103] *Thunder Air Ltd v Hilmar Hilmarsson* [2008] EWHC 355 (Ch).

the contract was not one for the supply of goods.[104] Yet in *Southwark LBC v IBM UK Ltd*[105] the judge thought that software could be 'goods', although that could depend on the terms of the contract.

In the Scottish case of *Beta Computers v Adobe*,[106] the Court held that the sale of software constituted a unique type of contract, rather than a sale of goods. For example, the implied term that delivery should be made within a reasonable time may not be specific enough for electronic delivery, which is often measured in seconds or minutes rather than hours or days. Electronic commerce often requires payment before delivery, so that an implied term could require delivery within a reasonable time of payment. Implied terms from the Sale of Goods Act 1979 ('satisfactory quality' and 'fitness for purpose') – or, for non-goods, earlier Scots law's implied terms or historical English law's implied terms of 'merchantable quality' – do not adapt well to electronic deliverables, where the quality of what is downloaded may be hard to measure, and implied terms of reasonable skill and care in providing services seem ineffectual.

A. Reform

The CRD introduces a new category, alongside goods and services, known as 'digital content', defined as 'data which are produced and supplied in digital form',[107] but, after considerable debate, it did not actually introduce any new legal regime peculiar to digital content. However the EU has now proposed such a regime, discussed below, which is proving controversial and thus very slow to pass.

In the UK, the Consumer Rights Act 2015 adopts the same definition of digital content as the CRD. Chapter 3 of Part 1 of the Act attempts to create a similarly protective regime for consumer contracts for the supply of digital content as that which exists for goods and services, for example, by imposing statutory conditions of satisfactory quality, fitness for purpose and conformity with description backed up by remedies including a right to repair, replacement, a price reduction or refund as the case may be.

B. Proposed EU Directive on the Sale of Digital Content

The European Union has proposed a directive on the sale of digital content,[108] which imposes obligations of conformity with description and so on. It has a number of

---

[104] *Horace Holman Group Ltd. v Sherwood International Group Ltd* (Technology and Construction Court, unreported 12 April 2000).

[105] *Southwark LBC v IBM UK Ltd* [2011] EWHC 549 (TCC).

[106] *Beta Computers (Europe) Ltd v Adobe Systems (Europe) Ltd* [1996] FSR 367.

[107] Art 2(11), given effect in UK law by the Consumer Rights Act 2015, s 2(9).

[108] Progress on this has been protracted. Proposal for a Directive of the European Parliament and of the Council on certain aspects concerning contracts for the supply of digital content was published in 2015 (Brussels, 9.12.2015 COM(2015) 634 final). On 8 June 2017, the Council adopted its position on the proposal

features that, at this stage, seem odd. First, it covers contracts in which data is given by the consumer as 'counter-performance'. It seems this is intended to cover services like Facebook and possibly even Google where personal information about the user is valuable to the service provider, in return for which they provide a service. The proposal includes rules about the deletion or provision of that personal data to the customer. Regarding data as counter-performance is however disquieting from a data protection perspective. The European Data Protection Supervisor has pointed out[109] that the use of personal data, including rights to its return and a right to portability, are already found in the GDPR so that there would be a risk of duplication and confusion as to the rights of data subjects.

The definition of 'digital content' is also broad, including the provision of a service allowing individuals to share their data with others. This sort of service is very unlike digital services, such as the provision of videos, music, software or literature that are digital analogues of non-digital services. It is not at all clear what, for instance, 'conformity' means in such a context.

The proposal is a maximum harmonisation so that Member States may not provide for more enhanced protection. While harmony is often presented as a desirable situation that will encourage consumer participation, there is little evidence that this is the case. What is more, there is very little experience of legislation directed specifically at the supply of digital content in the Member States – the UK have only recently legislated for example. It might be argued that it is rather early to be setting a maximum standard of protection across Europe.

In parallel, the European Commission has proposed[110] a new consumer protection directive[111] including an extension of information and cancellation rights to 'free' digital services, for example cloud storage services, social media and email accounts. The confusing overlap of information requirements between the ECD and CRD would be simplified. The proposal also includes provisions which would permit traders to offer alternative means of electronic communication other than electronic mail to consumers. It is too early to assess the effect these changes may have.

---

for a directive on contract rules on the supply of digital content. The European Parliament then began work on both the proposal for a directive on contract rules on the supply of digital content and on the proposal for a directive on contract rules for the online and other distance sales of goods. The Parliament is due to hold a first reading on 28 November 2018.

[109] *Opinion 4/2017 on the Proposal for a Directive on certain aspects concerning contracts for the supply of digital content* (14 March 2017). On the continuing controversy in this area, see A Metzger et al, 'Statement: Data-Related Aspects of the Digital Content Directive' (2018) *Journal of Intellectual Property, Information Technology and Electronic Commerce Law* 9(1).

[110] 'A New Deal for Consumers: Commission Strengthens EU Consumer Rights and Enforcement' (European Commission, Press Release, Brussels, 11 April 2018).

[111] 'Proposal for a Directive of the European Parliament and of the Council amending Council Directive 93/13/EEC of 5 April 1993, Directive 98/6/EC of the European Parliament and of the Council, Directive 2005/29/EC of the European Parliament and of the Council and Directive 2011/83/EU of the European Parliament and of the Council as regards better enforcement and modernisation of EU consumer protection rules' COM/2018/0185 final, 11 April 2018.

VIII. Smart Contracts

'Smart contract'[112] is a term originally defined by Nick Szabo[113] to mean 'a set of promises, specified in digital form, including protocols within which the parties perform on these promises'. From context he appears to have had in mind contracts that were embodied in either or both of software or hardware, so that their operation should not require human intervention.

So far, that does not seem a particularly revolutionary idea, even in 1996 when Szabo was writing. Machines that automatically dispense a product on the insertion of coins are at least 2,000 years' old. Hero of Alexandria describes the design of a machine that dispensed holy water on insertion of a five-drachma piece.[114]

The execution of contracts electronically was not a new idea, but Szabo appears to have had in mind a more revolutionary idea. A vending machine is able to operate, at least most of the time, without human intervention. The contract of sale inherent in the machine does not require the vendor to be involved. The machine works provided it is given the money.

Szabo appears to have wanted to achieve a similar degree of objectivity in software, rather than hardware, but at the same time to allow transparency so that the operation of the contract would be observable publicly rather than, as in the case with a vending machine, entirely opaque.

Bitcoin is the best-known successor to Szabo's ideas. It allows agreements for payment from one individual to another to be carried out using a technology known as the blockchain. The details of the blockchain are dealt with in the chapter on payment (Chapter 12), but for our purposes it has two significant properties:

- Execution is transparent: everyone can observe all payments and verify that they have been executed correctly.

- There is not, or at least there is not supposed to be, any central authority that ensures payments are made. They happen 'automatically' as a result of the consensus based system that makes the blockchain work.

While the blockchain is best known as a system for operating a distributed ledger – in other words only being suitable for payment obligations – it contains a rudimentary

---

[112] For a useful discussion paper on commercial uses of distributed ledger technology (DLT); the technology which underlies both smart contracts and bitcoin, see Financial Conduct Authority *Discussion paper on distributed ledger technology*, DP17/3, April 2017. An excellent technical introduction to blockchain and smart contracts can be found in J Bacon et al, 'Blockchain Demystified!', Queen Mary School of Law Legal Studies Research Paper No 268/2017 at https://papers.ssrn.com/sol3/papers.cfm?abstract_id=3091218##.

[113] Originally in Extropy #16, a partial rewrite of which is available from www.fon.hum.uva.nl/rob/Courses/InformationInSpeech/CDROM/Literature/LOTwinterschool2006/szabo.best.vwh.net/smart_contracts_2.html.

[114] Hero, *Pneumatics* 1.21, see, eg, JW Humphrey, JP Oleson and AN Sherwood, *Greek and Roman Technology: A Sourcebook. Annotated Translations of Greek and Latin Texts and Documents* (Routledge Sourcebooks for the Ancient World. London and New York, Routledge, 1998) 64.

programming language. It is possible to use blockchain to execute very simple programs.

Running programs using a distributed cryptographic system like blockchain is very inefficient and slow, but the logic of any normal contract is relatively simple in computational terms. It ought to be possible to construct a distributed contract system that was specifically designed to allow the transparent and automatic execution of contracts.

A system designed for this purpose is Ethereum.[115] In short, the Ethereum system introduces a new cryptocurrency ('ether', represented as ETH) together with a more expressive programming language which allows the Ethereum system to execute more complicated forms of 'smart contract'. It is this kind of entity – a program run on a cryptocurrency system with contract-like qualities – that has come to be the core meaning of 'smart contract'.

The first obvious weakness of a system like Ethereum is that a smart contract written within the system can access only properties contained within the system. Such a smart contract cannot be made to depend on any outside event or occurrence. That would rule out the vast majority of most forms of commercial agreement.

But a pure smart contract is not entirely disembodied. It can have cryptocurrency allocated to it and can make and receive payments. A smart contract could, for example, pay interest on a loan made to it without any need to know about the state of the world outside the system. A smart contract may also communicate with the holders of cryptocurrency and in particular take instructions from them. This would allow the construction of a smart contract which held cryptocurrency to be paid out at the direction of a group of individual investors by some form of voting between them.

The DAO (short for 'Decentralised Autonomous Organization') was set up using such a contract. It raised some $120 million in Ether by crowdfunding. The idea was to allow investors to vote on investment proposals, which would then disperse cryptocurrency held by the smart contract. It was marketed as offering complete transparency and autonomous governance. Even here a certain amount of impurity was introduced by the creation of a Swiss company (DAO.Link) to act as a real-world interface to the DAO.

What then happened to the DAO serves as an object illustration of some of the conceptual problems with smart contracts. The contract itself, that is the program that was written to embody the DAO, contained a significant security flaw. The contract permitted investors to withdraw sums of money if they had not yet been committed, but it was written so that it paid the Ether to the investor before updating its own internal balance and such a request could be executed in a way that the contract made multiple payments to the investor.

On 18 June 2016, one investor used this flaw to withdraw Ether worth some $70 million from the DAO but not, at that time, to deal with the Ether (eg to pay to an exchange and therefore realise it as cash in normal currency) because there was a

---

[115] G Wood, 'Ethereum: A Secure Decentralised Generalised Transaction Ledger' (EIP-150 (Ethereum Yellow Papers)), available from http://gavwood.com/paper.pdf.

built-in delay. Before the investor was able to cash in on their investment, the leaders of the Ethereum community – many of whom had invested heavily in the DAO and were therefore highly prejudiced by what had happened – proposed what is known as a 'hard fork'. That is that Ethereum be altered so that the investor's transaction was undone. This happened with the agreement of roughly 89 per cent of holders of Ether creating effectively two versions: Ethereum and Ethereum Classic.[116]

As is explained in Chapter 12 on payments, a problem with majority voting cryptocurrencies is precisely that a majority may take control over what happens and can even force the cryptocurrency to behave in ways it was not intended to. The history of the DAO shows that this is a very real possibility. It is therefore not entirely true to represent cryptocurrencies and smart contracts as entirely 'automatic'. As we see, human intervention is possible.

A second point is that smart contracts may not be as reliable as has been supposed. One author writes:

> the precision of the programming language is much greater than that of written human language; in particular, warranties and conditions can be formulated with much greater accuracy, and contracts can be treated and processed in data formats. Hence, it is argued, smart contracts make transacting considerably less expensive owing to certainty of execution and the near-zero risk of litigation in court.[117]

Such a statement must be questionable in the light of what happened to the DAO. A better characterisation of the situation would be that smart contracts exchange the uncertainties of the use of contract language and interpretation, with the uncertainties of the behaviour of code. A legal drafting problem is replaced by a programming one, but the problem does not disappear. Sklaroff goes further and argues that smart contracts are likely to create more problems than they solve, making them unlikely to be widely used.[118]

What of litigation? Was there, in fact, any contract concerning the DAO? No litigation arose, so we do not know how courts would address the question. On the one hand, one might argue that the smart contract underpinning DAO was written in a particular way that was objectively agreed to behave as it did. All participants in Ethereum/DAO could be understood to have agreed that 'code is law'. That is that the effect of running Ethereum was the agreed outcome. Would the hard fork be objectionable then as a breach of contract or even as some form of fraud?

A counter-argument would be that it was clear to everyone that the outcome was not the shared intention of the investors, whatever the code might say. It is likely that many courts would want to come to this conclusion, but what then? What if there had been no hard fork? Would courts force repayment of Ether that had been taken?

Neither conclusion seems entirely satisfactory. Worse would be a situation where different courts came to different conclusions. This seems to be a situation where

---

[116] For an account, see www.cryptocompare.com/coins/guides/the-dao-the-hack-the-soft-fork-and-the-hard-fork/.

[117] P Paech, 'The Governance of Blockchain Financial Networks' (2017) 80(6) *Modern Law Review* 1073–110.

[118] J Sklaroff, 'Smart Contracts and the Costs of Inflexibility' (2017) 166 *University of Pennsylvania Law Review*, available at https://papers.ssrn.com/sol3/papers.cfm?abstract_id=3008899.

international agreement and then regulation would be desirable. The large sum of money raised by the DAO illustrates that there is already a real risk to investors in an area of law that is almost entirely unregulated.

Returning to the question of the interaction between smart contracts and the outside world, it would clearly be much more useful if smart contracts could be made to depend on real world events (eg the behaviour of stock markets, a change of government of a particular state, weather patterns or the death of an individual). Such smart contracts related to the 'Internet of Things' (see further Chapter 5) are already being touted as the next big thing and legal interest is already engaged.[119] To do so however would require the creation of trusted external input and an infrastructure that supported that trust. An example of such a project is Mattereum.[120] It is too early to tell whether such smart contract/legal hybrids will be significant in the future and if so, to what extent.

IX.   Conclusion

We contract online almost daily, whether we realise it or not. Users have historically been wary of transacting online, and regulators have responded in kind: contracting is now one of the most legally regulated areas of cyberspace. Whereas real world contracting, at least for B2C, can be done informally and face-to-face, and so the consumer can assess the trustworthiness of the trader and formality is not crucial, in cyberspace, the user often has no idea who they are trading with, what the terms of the contract are, or even where the transaction takes place. The ECD and EU-driven consumer rights laws have gone some way to ensure consumer protection guarantees in the online world. However, much work remains to be done with domestic laws, where the substantive content of copyright law is still primarily determined. The future of e-contracts law in the UK after Brexit will be interesting, given that the homegrown legislation in the CRA 2015 on digital content has leapfrogged that of the EU and that uptake of any future Digital Content Directive will probably be optional.

In other future developments, the blockchain and smart contracts loom large. Regulators must not be complacent as cryptocurrencies (discussed further in the next chapter) and the underlying distributed ledger technology will no doubt raise thorny legal issues. Smart contracts may, of course, not be regarded as part of e-contract law: one current aphorism we have already mentioned is that they are somewhat misnamed as neither smart nor contracts. O'Hara, a technical commentator, has renamed them 'dumb contracts', arguing that 'the best contracts are fallible and human'. The apparent idealised vision of distributed ledger contracts is that they constrain human behaviour perfectly (though we have seen above how wrong that can be) and cannot be challenged by law or lawyers. O'Hara suggests that the ability to break the law is

---

[119] See H Lovells' paper at http://f.datasrvr.com/fr1/416/66238/2.pdf; K Christidis and M Devetsikiotis, 'Blockchains and Smart Contracts for the Internet of Things' (2016) 4 *IEEE Access* 2292.
[120] See http://internetofagreements.com/assets/MattereumDraftforPublicComment.pdf.

important in a world where we balance liberty with social efficiency.[121] The alleged immutability of smart contracts and blockchain applications may also be incompatible with some laws: there has been concern recently that the GDPR 'right to be forgotten' under Art 17 may not be possible in a blockchain environment.[122] Whatever we think of smart contracts however, there is commercial and technical interest in them, and problems will arise that are familiar to contract lawyers, including authentication and the applicable legal jurisdiction. Interesting times lie ahead, more than at any time in perhaps the last two decades, for commercial and consumer contract lawyers.

[121] K O'Hara, 'Smart Contract – Dumb Idea' (IEEE Xplore, March/April 2017) at https://ieeexplore.ieee.org/document/7867719/.
[122] M Finck, 'Blockchains and Data Protection in the European Union', Max Planck Institute for Innovation & Competition Research Paper No 18-01, last revised 7 February 2018, available at https://papers.ssrn.com/sol3/papers.cfm?abstract_id=3080322.

12

From Barter to Bitcoin? Online Payments and Electronic Money

FRANCIS DAVEY

I. Introduction

This chapter is primarily concerned with online payment systems, but any consideration of payment must also consider the object of the payment: money.[1] This is especially called for in light of the increasing use of new online payment systems which claim to be a new form of money, for example Bitcoin.

As we will see, the concept of money creates a number of legally interesting reactions:

- In many situations money is either treated differently from other forms of property or has special status. This is because the law has attempted to adapt itself to commercial practice.

- States frequently use the regulation of money as a tool of economic policy.

- States also find money a useful point of articulation for the indirect control of other activities, such as criminality or copyright infringement, by controlling the flow of funds to those engaged in undesirable activities.

The law has tended to understand 'money' in terms of a means of payment and not as a first class entity in its own right. At first this was expressed by focussing on the *physical* objects used in payment (for example coins and bank notes) and only later did it begin to encompass other abstractions. This focus on the means of payment has created a number of conceptual challenges in situations where the law does not reflect

---

[1] For a reasonably up-to-date academic work on payment systems, see Rhys Bollen, *The Law and Regulation of Payment Services: A Comparative Study* (Kluwer Law International, 2012). The UK standard work is Michael Brindle and Raymond Cox (eds), *Law of Bank Payments*, 5th Revised edn (London, Sweet & Maxwell, 2016).

the popular understanding of 'money', for example in its analysis of money transfers. This may in turn have implications for the way that newer conceptions of money, such as Bitcoin, are treated by the law.

II. Money

A. The Origin of Money

The usual explanation given for the development of money is that it originated with a system of barter, perhaps in early agricultural society. Goods and services were exchanged for other goods and services. This process was inconvenient because parties may not have desired the items that the other was offering or because certain goods (such as livestock) might have been hard to subdivide. Some commodity, such as a precious metal, was then settled upon as a means of exchange, allowing individuals to exchange goods and services in return for that commodity.

It is certainly the case that in modern barter economies, commodity money does seem to arise naturally. For example, Radford describes the growth of economic activity in the closed communities of Italian prisoner of war (POW) camps during the Second World War. After an early barter stage, the cigarette rapidly came to be used as a measure of value (sales and purchases were priced in cigarettes) and also as a de facto medium of exchange.[2] As a result of the use of cigarettes as a medium of exchange, prices were quoted in 'cigarettes'. Radford says that purchases on credit were the norm.[3] The 'cigarette' was then used as a way of keeping track of the debtor/creditor relationship. Economists would describe the cigarette used in this way as a 'unit of account'.

The anthropologist David Graeber is sceptical, on historical grounds, that barter predates money.[4] He argues that the earliest money, at least in a form that we would understand it, arose as a way of keeping track of debts owed to and by large palace and temple complexes in the ancient Near East.[5] The original 'money' was primarily a unit of account. This makes sense. In the kind of mythical agricultural society in which barter is supposed to have originated, a typical farmer's problem with barter is not likely to be a mismatch between what they have to offer and what someone they are trading with wants in return, but rather that there will be periods of the year when they have a surplus of products, for example at harvest. In this situation they would need some method of time-shifting their ability to trade with others. The only way to do this on a systematic scale would be to use a system of accounting, for which a unit of account is necessary.

---

[2] Robert A Radford, 'The Economic Organisation of a POW Camp' [1945] *Economica* 189.
[3] *Ibid* 194.
[4] David Graeber, *Debt : The First 5000 Years*, 2nd Revised edn (Melville House Publishing, 2014).
[5] *Ibid* 2 (the 'Myth of Barter').

If this is right, it means that money began as an abstract concept. In turn this means that the law ought, having had 6,000 years to get used to the idea of money as an abstraction rather than a physical token or commodity, to have no difficulty dealing with the various forms of 'money' used on the Internet, including electronic currency. As we shall see, the Internet has not left money entirely alone but, as a legal concept, it has undergone much less modification than other concepts which rely on the physical embodiment of their subject matter, such as copyright.

B. Money as an Abstraction

For the sake of brevity, it is not intended to engage in a lengthy debate as to the nature of money. Instead this chapter will adopt the definition favoured by the post-Keynesian Modern Monetary Theorists,[6] which is broadly speaking 'Chartalist'.[7]

Money arises because some organisation, typically a state, is able to impose an obligation to pay on a large number of people. In the case of a state, this would take the form of impositions such as taxes and fines. The dominant position of the state means that it is able to require that it is paid in the form of its choosing. A monetary system works because sufficient numbers of people will need the money in order to meet their obligations to the organisation in question.

In this analysis, the pound sterling is valuable, not because the possession of a pound gives the legal right to obtain something else of value – as we shall see, it does not – but because the Government of the UK will accept that pound as payment for a tax obligation. There is a demand for pounds, because there is a need to pay tax.

As we shall see, a monetary system may arise, even without the existence of a central government, in circumstances where an organisation has considerable and unavoidable power. For example, the restaurant in Radford's POW camp was able to introduce its own currency, 'bully marks', which became the only means with which food could be bought at the restaurant.[8]

Although a monetary system is generally underpinned by a nation state, in the modern world most money is not created by the state, but by the banking system. A bank creates money whenever it creates a debt obligation. The inter-bank framework means that banks can move money, usually abstractly. Thus the debt created by banks is also 'money'. The debt is the bank's debt. The 'amount' of money that banks create is not determined by the state, but by the commercial considerations of the banks, although those considerations may be influenced by the state.[9]

Since banks create the majority of money in the economy, they also represent a significant point of failure. As a result, governments take steps to ensure that banks

[6] LR Wray, *Modern Money Theory: A Primer on Macroeconomics for Sovereign Monetary Systems* (Palgrave Macmillan, 2012).

[7] LR Wray, 'From the State Theory of Money to Modern Money Theory: An Alternative to Economic Orthodoxy' (2014) at www.levyinstitute.org/pubs/wp_792.pdf.

[8] Radford (n 2).

[9] M McLeay, A Radia and R Thomas, 'Money Creation in the Modern Economy' [2014] *Bank of England Quarterly Bulletin* Q1.

are regulated and, in particular, that they are able to meet their financial obligations, such as being able to pay depositors on demand. One approach is to require that banks retain a sufficient ratio of capital assets to the amount they lend, in other words that the ratio of the money they create to the totality of their capital assets does not go beyond a certain point. This sort of regulation, as we shall see, does not tend to apply where new 'cryptocurrencies', such as Bitcoin, are created by non-bank entities but then function rather like money.

C. The Importance of Money in UK Law

Later in this chapter, we will examine the specific ways in which UK law deals with the concept of money, but two examples should illustrate the widespread importance of the concept of money in UK law.

The concept of 'money' is essential to the UK law on the sale of goods because (i) 'goods' are defined so as to exclude money,[10] and (ii) a 'sale of goods' requires a transfer of goods in return for money.[11] This distinction is a long-standing one, dating back in codified form to the Sale of Goods Act 1893, itself codifying existing practice.[12] Another example is found in the Bills of Exchange Act 1882, which defines a bill of exchange, such as a cheque, as an order to pay a sum of money.[13] An order requiring payment of something other than money is therefore not a bill of exchange.

In neither statute is there a definition of 'money', but the requirement for 'money' may create difficulties if alternative units of account, such as Bitcoin, start to be used for online payments. For example, a purchase of goods using Bitcoin will not engage the usual protections of the Sale of Goods Act.

III. Physical Payment Systems

A. Types of Money: Tokens, Commodities and Cash

One of the essential features of money is that it circulates. Money would be of no use if it could not be transferred from person to person. As with money, the earliest history of payment systems is complicated and not well understood and so the following account should not be understood as historical.

One option is for the issuer of the money to create a *physical token*, not easy to counterfeit, to represent the money itself. This token would be accepted by the issuer in

---

[10] Sale of Goods Act 1979, s 61.
[11] *Ibid*, s 2(1).
[12] Sir M Chalmers, *The Sale of Goods Act, 1893 : Including the Factors Acts, 1889 & 1890*, 2nd Revised edn (William Clowes and Sons Ltd, 1894) 111.
[13] Bills of Exchange Act 1882, s 3.

payment and would be treated by its users as being as good as money. Familiar modern examples are the sterling notes issued by the Bank of England. Despite bearing the words 'I promise to pay the bearer on demand the sum of ...', sterling notes have not been convertible into gold since 1914[14] and prior to that were also not convertible from 1797–1821.[15],[16] Earlier examples of monetary tokens include tally sticks,[17] issued by the English (but not Scottish) Government, and the 'bully marks' used in Radford's POW camp, mentioned above.

An alternative to using a token is to use a valuable commodity as a means of exchange, for example, by allowing payment in gold or silver or, in the case of POW camps, cigarettes. If the commodity is accepted in payment of debt in the same way as a monetary token, then it would count as 'money'. Most commodities used as money have some inherent value. A good example is gold. In the third quarter of 2014, out of a total of 929.3 tonnes of gold traded internationally, only 92.8 tonnes represented a net purchase by central banks, although a further 204.4 tonnes was bought for its investment value. The majority was bought for its use in jewellery and in technology.[18]

Commodities have a tendency to fluctuate in value, more so than money. That uncertainty might make commerce based on payment using commodities difficult. Again, this is a feature we have recently seen replicated in cryptocurrencies such as Bitcoin which have become the subject of furious speculation and often ill-informed investment. The other difficulty with commodity money is that the total amount of money available is limited, but the total amount of money required by commerce may be increased beyond the amount of commodity available.

In practice, most societies have created a hybrid between tokens and commodities: coinage. Coins were made of a valuable commodity, for example gold, silver or copper, but also acted as tokens, acceptable by the issuer of the coins. The fact that coins had an inherent value presumably increased trust in their use – and made them more expensive to fake – but their status as tokens also meant that, in principle, they could be used in the settlement of debts without the holder having to be concerned about the exact metal content of the cash they held.

The *Case of Mixt Monies*[19] is a well-known example of this principle, technically known as 'nominalism'. Brett had entered into an obligation to pay Gilbert a sum in 'Sterling, current and lawful money of England'. After entering into the obligation, but before the date on which payment was due, Queen Elizabeth I's government debased the Irish currency. Brett tendered payment in the new, debased currency. Gilbert sued on the basis that he should be paid an increased sum in the new currency that was equivalent to the value of the debt in the old currency. The Privy Council disagreed and held that the debt could be paid in the currency prevailing at the time payment was due.

---

[14] Glyn Davies, *A History of Money: From Ancient Times to the Present Day* (Paperback edn, with revisions and postscript 1996, reprint, University of Wales Press, 1997) 370.

[15] Bank Restriction Act 1797.

[16] Davies (n 14) 298.

[17] Davies (n 14) 147.

[18] David Graeber, 'Chapter 2: The Myth of Barter' in Graeber (n 4).

[19] *Gilbert v Brett* (1604) Davis 18, translated in English at (1605) 2 Howells State Trials 114.

An unusual, but deliberate, exception to the principle of nominalism is that of the *Krugerrand* – a South African minted gold coin defined to contain a particular volume of gold.[20] A *Krugerrand* may be tendered in payment at the sum that, on that day, the South African Reserve Bank would be prepared to purchase it.[21] The impracticality of making payment in a currency the value of which fluctuates with the value of gold meant that, in practice, *Krugerrands* appear to have been used as a mechanism for trading gold while avoiding many of the international restrictions on gold trading by 'pretending' to be coinage.

Coinage represents a very small proportion of the total money in use in the UK. Even including banknotes, most money is held in the form of bank deposits.

i. Redeemable Tokens

Another alternative to money is the issue of tokens that are redeemable – ie tokens which the issuer will swap for 'money' (whatever form that might take). As discussed above, the current sterling bank notes issued by the Bank of England used to be of this kind.

US Federal Reserve notes are in principle redeemable, but only in 'lawful money',[22] which of course could be other US Federal Reserve notes[23] or coins. They have not been redeemable in gold since 1934.[24] Their value comes from the fact that the United States is obliged to accept them in payment of taxes.[25] As an interesting side note, Scottish bank notes are and always have been redeemable.

IV. Payment

A. Principles of payment

Most payments (outside those made to banks by their customers) are made because one person (the debtor) owes a specific sum of money to the other (the creditor). The first step in making a payment will usually be for the debtor to take some step, known as a 'tender' of payment, that, if accepted by the creditor, would result in payment. An example would be offering cash to a shop assistant. The debtor and creditor may have agreed that one or more forms of payment will be permitted. If not, the debtor will usually be permitted to pay in the subset of cash known as 'legal tender', discussed in the next section.

---

[20] South African Reserve Bank Act 1989, Sch 1.
[21] *Ibid*, s 17(2)(a).
[22] 12 US Code § 411.
[23] *Milam v US*, 524 F.2d 629 (9th Cir 1974).
[24] 48 Stat 337.
[25] 12 US Code § 411.

If a creditor refuses to accept a valid tender from a debtor, the payment obligation remains outstanding (so the debtor will still have to pay at some point) but if the creditor sues the debtor for non-payment, the debtor is likely to be able to recover their costs from the creditor. The creditor may also be unable to recover any (further) interest payable on the debt.

The next question, once a tender has been accepted, is when does the payment take effect? This could be determined by agreement between the parties, for example where payment is for a debt arising under a contract. In the absence of a prior agreement, the law has developed a practice of distinguishing two situations. The first, where acceptance by a creditor of a particular means of payment is presumed to be treated as payment of the debt, is known as an 'absolute payment'.

In the second case, the acceptance is not treated as constituting payment unless and until some condition is met, hence the act of presentation and acceptance is known as a 'conditional' payment. As Goode points out, this is misleading because there is, strictly speaking, no payment.[26]

A cheque is an example of a payment that is presumed to be 'conditional'.[27] Where a cheque is accepted, if the cheque is subsequently honoured, payment is treated as having taken place on the date the cheque was accepted.[28]

On the other hand, payment with a credit card is presumed to be an absolute payment, even if the credit card company subsequently fails to honour its obligation.[29] Presumably the same presumption would apply to payment by a debit card. For many modern means of payment it is unclear whether there is a presumption that payment is absolute or conditional and when payment is to be treated as having taken place.

i. Legal Tender

In English and Scots law, 'legal tender' is a sub-category of cash (and therefore of 'money'). In theory, unless the parties have agreed otherwise, the offer of legal tender is always a valid tender. A creditor who refuses it suffers the consequences explained in the preceding sections.

What the status of legal tender does not confer is a right to use it as a form of payment prior to the formation of a contract under which the payment obligation will arise. For example, the presentation of cash to a shop assistant is analysed in both English and Scots law as a contractual offer. The offer presumably includes a condition that payment may be made in the form of the cash presented. The shop assistant may refuse to agree to accept payment using, for example, a note of a particularly large denomination.

The decreasing use of cash for commercial purposes other than retail purchases means that the role of legal tender as a concept is in practice minimal.

---

[26] Royston Miles Goode and Ewan McKendrick, *Goode on Commercial Law*, 4th edn (Penguin, 2010) 499.
[27] *Sayer v Wagstaff* (1844) 14 LJ Ch 116.
[28] *Homes v Smith* [2000] Lloyd's Rep Bank 139.
[29] *In re Charge Card Services Limited* [1989] 1 Ch 197 (CA).

V. The Law, Money and Physical Payment

A. Legal Concept of Money

As with most legal terminology, 'money' does not have a single consistent meaning throughout statute and common law, even in a single jurisdiction such as England and Wales or Scotland. The contextual nature of 'money' means that debate about its meaning is, as Goode points out, 'rather sterile'.[30] Nevertheless, Mann categorises the following conceptions of money:[31]

1.   a medium of exchange;
2.   as a measure of value or as a standard for contractual obligations;
3.   as a store of value or wealth; or
4.   as a unit of account.

There is a clear distinction between the first of these, which treats money as an entity, and the second and fourth, which treat money as simply a unit of measurement. We discussed this in section III. A. above.

The third concept is based on the idea that money 'stores' value between its original receipt and its subsequent utilisations by a holder as a means of payment. In this sense money is still an entity that confers some right or value on the holder, rather than a unit of account in which money is measured.

If a chattel (or moveable property in Scots terminology) is used as a means of payment and is also 'money', then the law accords it special treatment in a number of ways – many of which may be important when looking at new forms of online money, because of the courts' willingness, in their approach to intangible money, to draw on analogies to physical money.

Goode lists five ways in which physical money is special:[32]

1.   The intrinsic value of the money itself is generally uninteresting (see discussion of the *Case of Mixt Monies* in section III. A. above);
2.   It is impossible to 'buy' or 'sell' money[33];
3.   Money is 'fully negotiable', in other words it is an exception to the principle *nemo dat quod non habet* (see below);
4.   Unless otherwise agreed, a creditor may not demand, nor be forced to accept, anything other than the payment of money in satisfaction of a debt; and
5.   Money is fungible: where money is loaned, there is no need to return identical notes and coins.

---

[30] Goode and McKendrick (n 26) 488.
[31] Charles Proctor (ed), *Mann on the Legal Aspect of Money*, 7th edn (Oxford University Press, 2012).
[32] Goode and McKendrick (n 26) 486.
[33] See Case C-7/78 *R v Thompson* (21 November 1978) where the European Court of Justice (now CJEU) held that means of payment that 'circulated as money' were not 'goods' for the purposes of the European Community principle of the freedom of movement of goods.

Point 3 is important. Money is an exception to the normal English legal rule that no-one can pass title to property they do not own, summed up in the maxim *nemo dat quod non habet*. Thus if property has been stolen, as a general rule, title in that property cannot be acquired by someone else, even innocently.[34] But money is different. Money is designed to be negotiable – to circulate without a need to check on its provenance – and so even if of stolen origin can be owned by someone who receives it from the thief. An English case illustrating this is *Moss v Hancock*,[35] in which the plaintiff kept a £5 gold piece, of sentimental value to himself, on display in a cabinet in his drawing room. The coin was stolen. The Court held that the coin was not 'money', because of its particular value to the plaintiff, and therefore an order for the return of it was possible. If the coin had not had individual significance to the plaintiff, it could not have been the subject of a specific recovery.

Thus, even within the same legal context, whether a particular physical object is 'money' will depend on external factors, including the way in which it is treated by an individual or society as a whole. It is reasonable to conclude that, for many purposes, the law treats 'money' as an additional characteristic that may subsist in physical objects, depending on the context.

B. Can Money be Stolen?

Despite these different conceptions of money as a physical thing or an item of account, etc, in principle, the practical answer is of course yes. For example in English law the Theft Act 1968 s 4(1) makes it clear that '"Property" includes money'. However problems have arisen with money *transfers*. Difficulties arose in *R v Preddy*,[36] a case involving mortgage fraud. Section 15 of the Theft Act 1968 created an offence of 'obtaining property by deception', which required, as part of the factual matrix, the obtaining of 'property belonging to another'. It was held that the fraudsters did not obtain 'property belonging to another', and hence were not guilty of theft.

The courts analysed the 'transfer' of money from one bank account to another as follows. A bank account is simply a statement that a particular sum of money is owed by the bank to its customer or, in the case of an overdraft, by the customer to the bank. This debt is known in English law as a '*chose in action*'. When money is transferred from account A to account B, there are two different *choses in action* – one for each account. The transfer simply alters or extinguishes the first chose and either creates, or alters, the second chose. No property is involved and a particular sum of the destruction of one item of property passes. This principle meant that the fraudsters in *Preddy* never obtained property 'belonging to another'. Instead, they caused the creation of a new item of property (a bank account), which was owned by them.

This reasoning also applies in a situation where a defendant fraudulently obtains cheques made out in his name and pays the money into his own bank account. There is

[34] *Stair Memorial Encyclopaedia*, vol 18 (Butterworth LexisNexis, 1987).
[35] *Moss v Hancock* [1899] 2 QB 111.
[36] *R v Preddy* [1996] AC 815.

no intention to steal the cheques (which in any case are returned to the drawer through the interbank system).[37]

This caused concern. The Theft Act was clearly intended to cover the theft of intangible property, including money. In response, Parliament created a specific offence 'obtaining a money transfer by deception'.[38] Even this was problematic, however, because 'deception' was then understood as being impossible with respect to a machine, and so for example where a money transfer was obtained fraudulently through the use of a co-worker's password, there was a s 15A defence.[39]

The solution eventually adopted was for an offence of this kind to be subsumed into a general offence of dishonesty under the Fraud Act 2006.[40] The nature of the property obtained is no longer an element of the offence and so the 'theft' of immaterial things, including accounting abstractions, now potentially involves an offence of fraud, if not theft, if they were obtained dishonestly.

Students and scholars may like to consider as an exercise if this means that Bitcoins (say), which are in essence only entries in a distributed virtual ledger (a kind of database), can nonetheless be 'stolen'.[41] This problem can usually be avoided (even if the fraud offence discussed above is not available) as most 'thefts' of Bitcoins will involve unauthorised access to someone's account (or 'hacking').

States have increasingly recognised such unauthorised access to, and damage of, computer systems as a criminal offence: see, eg, the Budapest Convention on Cybercrime,[42] or in the UK the Computer Misuse Act 1990, s 1.

However returning to theft proper, English law (and most common law) normally holds that there is no property in information, for obvious policy reasons. Lavy and Khoo hazard however that although there are conceptual difficulties, Bitcoins may be owned, and thus stolen, following the example of carbon credits as property upheld in *Armstrong DLW GmbH v Winnington Networks Ltd*.[43]

The difficulty with this approach is that in *Armstrong* a carbon credit was associated with a legally enforceable right, albeit one recorded in electronic form. Such rights are treated by most legal systems as a form of immaterial property (in common law analysis, a thing in action). The holder of a Bitcoin does not appear to gain, thereby, an enforceable right against any other person.

Inherent in the philosophy underlying Bitcoin is that, in principle, it is not subject to any central control nor, crucially, is it underpinned by any national authority. It is intended to be self-sustaining. It is difficult to find, in this philosophical approach, anything that might look legally enforceable. For example, it would seem to be hard to argue that there was some kind of *convention* between Bitcoin users that they would behave in a certain way.

---

[37] *R v Clark (Brian James Hemmings)* [2002] 1 Cr App R 14.

[38] Theft Act 1968, s 15A, now subsumed in the general offence of fraud in the Fraud Act 2006 pursuant to para 1(a)(ii) of Sch 1 to the Fraud Act 2006.

[39] *Holmes v Governor of Brixton Prison* [2004] EWHC 2020 (Admin).

[40] Fraud Act 2006, para 1 of Sch 1.

[41] See further *Fortune* magazine at http://fortune.com/2017/12/08/bitcoin-theft/.

[42] Council of Europe, European Treaty Series – No 185.

[43] *Armstrong DLW GmbH v Winnington Networks Ltd* [2013] Ch 156. See M Lavy and D Khoo, 'Who Owns Blockchains? An English Legal Analysis' (Society for Computers and Law, 2016) at www.scl.org/articles/3675-who-owns-blockchains-an-english-legal-analysis.

This is of particular relevance where any 'theft' or diversion of Bitcoin happens due to a design feature of the system. For example, if a group of Bitcoin miners obtained more than 50 per cent of the blockchain at some point and used that dominance to gain financial advantage, where is the wrong? The diversion of Ethereum currency from a 'virtual corporation' because of a bug in the underlying 'virtual contract' is an example of how a feature of the system may permit something that to some will look like a 'theft'. There are clearly challenges here.

VI. Account-Based Payment

Money, thought of as a form of debt, moves by accounting. The general form such payment takes is for one party (the payer) to maintain an account of some kind, whether credit or debit, with a service provider of some kind. In order to make a payment the payer may either instruct the service provider to make the payment on their behalf (for example BACS and CHAPS payment), or give the person who is to be paid (the payee) some evidence that will ultimately be presented to their service provider for payment (for example a cheque).

A. Cheques and Negotiable Instruments

A cheque is a request made by the 'drawer' (the person who writes the cheque) that their bank (the 'paying bank') should pay money to the payee. The paying bank may refuse to pay ('honour') the cheque if there are insufficient funds in the drawer's account, or if paying out would exceed any overdraft facility the drawer might have.

In the past, cheques were normally transferable (or 'negotiable'). A payee could assign the right to be paid under the cheque to someone else. That is prevented by 'crossing' the cheque with the words 'account payee only'.[44] At first it would seem that the cheque has no place in Internet payments. There would appear to be nothing to recommend it over other forms of direct electronic payment, such as credit or debit cards (discussed in the next section). Indeed, in many countries the cheque has essentially disappeared as a form of payment.[45]

Electronic versions of cheques, however, rather bizarrely, persist if only perhaps as a transitional measure. A process known as 'cheque imaging' is used to create an authenticated, electronically-scanned image of a cheque. It allows a payer to write a cheque but the payee to scan it in and submit it to the clearing system in electronic

---

[44] Bills of Exchange Act 1882, s 81A.

[45] In the UK, the industry Payments Council set a deadline in 2009 to eliminate the use of cheques. However in 2011 after widespread public resistance, the industry was persuaded to change its mind. In 2015, more than 500 million cheques were still written in the UK: see www.bbc.co.uk/news/business-36345676.

form. Such a system has been in use for some time in the United States, but is a relatively recent innovation in the United Kingdom.[46]

B. Credit Cards

Historically, in many societies many commercial transactions were carried out on credit, particularly consumer purchases made in local shops or transactions between suppliers. Traders would have a long-term relationship with individuals and businesses in their community and would be able to judge whether they were creditworthy or not. 'Out of town' customers were more difficult. A trader would not necessarily know whether a stranger had good credit, and so would either demand cash, potentially losing the customer, or take the risk of extending credit.

Credit cards solved this problem by involving a third party with a direct and on-going relationship with the customer. The third party will take responsibility for paying the trader and recover the expenditure from the customer, thus taking on the credit risk. There is a number of different ways in which credit cards may operate.

One of the earliest widespread systems was Diners Club.[47] In a Diners Club trans-action there are three parties: Diners Club, the trader and the customer. Diners Club issues its card to a customer, who uses it to pay a trader. The trader then periodically (for example monthly) requests payment from Diners Club for all payments made on their cards. Diners Club then debits those sums from its customer accounts.

Most current leading credit card systems involve four parties. VISA,[48] for example, works by the customer having a relationship with one VISA member (typically a bank) that issues them with a card. The trader will have a relationship with another VISA member (typically a merchant bank) that issues them with equipment for reading credit cards. The trader's bank will pay the trader and then recover those payments from the card issuing bank through the VISA system.

Although VISA and similar systems are referred to as 'credit card' payment systems and make use of physical cards, when used for e-commerce, the card is used only as a reminder of the card number. The fact that a physical token is used is in fact irrelevant. This was realised as early as the 1970s by Dee Hock, the founder of VISA, who later said:

> 'Credit card' was a misnomer based on banking jargon. The card was no more than a device bearing symbols for the exchange of monetary value. That it took the form of a piece of plastic was nothing but an accident of time and circumstance.[49]

Since credit cards in effect offer dematerialised payments, suitable for online transactions, their dominance of online payment systems is unsurprising.

---

[46] Small Business, Enterprise and Employment Act 2015, s 13.
[47] Martha L Olney, 'The Credit Card Industry: A History. By Lewis Mandell' (Boston, Twayne Publishers, 1990).
[48] David L Stearns, *Electronic Value Exchange: Origins of the VISA Electronic Payment System*, 1st edn (London, Springer, 2011).
[49] Cited in *ibid*.

i. Legal Implications of Credit Cards

Credit cards in principle involve substantial risks for consumers. Cards may be stolen and the numbers used to illicitly buy goods and services. Merchants who received payment by card at a distance (eg phone or email) might take payment but not send the goods. A critical lack of trust might have developed. Accordingly in the UK (and the EU generally) statute intervened to create consumer protection remedies. The Consumer Credit Act (CCA) 1974 introduced two new consumer remedies.

First, s 75 of the CCA applies to any 'debtor-creditor-supplier' agreement, which will include purchases made by credit card. The creditor – the card issuer – is made jointly and severally liable with the supplier (the merchant) for any misrepresentation or breach of contract, for typical purchases between £100 and £30,000.

In the context of the Internet, this means that a consumer need only trust their card issuer to feel confident in making a reasonably large purchase from a supplier, possibly located in another country.[50] If the supplier defaults or supplies inferior products, the consumer can claim from their credit card company without having to worry about the identity, location or creditworthiness of the supplier. The card issuer acts as guarantor. This plays a significant role in the successful operation of e-commerce.

Second, ss 83 and 84 of the CCA give the card holder some protection against fraud by putting the risk, in most cases, again on the card issuer. Where a 'credit token' (the credit card) is misused by someone who is not acting as the debtor's (consumer's) agent, the debtor is not liable for any loss arising from the action. There are two exceptions:

1.   The debtor is still liable for the first £50 of loss while the credit token is out of their possession (for example because it was stolen); and
2.   Where the credit token is misused by someone (for example a family member) who had possession of the credit token with the debtor's consent.

However, neither of these exceptions applies for the period after the debtor has informed the creditor of the loss, or if the creditor is at fault. In practice therefore, telling your card issuer as soon as possible will usually protect you from misuse of your card. These two protections of the CCA are remarkably powerful consumer protection weapons.

C. Debit Cards

Debit cards operate, from a trader's point of view, very much like credit cards. Customers present a card in order to make payment. The trader will be compensated through the debit card system for that payment.

The difference between debit and credit cards comes from the customer perspective. Debit cards are associated with a user's account in a bank or similar institution.

---

[50] See *Office of Fair Trading (Respondents) v Lloyds TSB Bank Plc* [2007] UKHL 48 settling earlier doubts that s 75 protection applied to purchases from foreign merchants.

That account may well be in credit. If so, any payments made are debited directly from the card holder's account although there may be some delay.

The debit card system is not predicated on an underlying extension of credit by the issuing bank and so the CCA may often not apply. A debit card linked account may sometimes be in debt however, for example through an agreed overdraft, in which case payments by debit card may be based on credit.

(Note that sometimes the term 'debit card' is used to describe cards not associated with an account, for example ones on which 'digital cash' can be stored – these are really a different kind of payment system that will be dealt with below. Sometimes a debit card and a stored value card may both be functions of the same piece of plastic.)

i. Legal Protection of Debit Cards

Debit card transactions will not usually be protected by s 75 of the CCA 1974 because electronic funds transfer from an account is not an 'arrangement'.[51] Furthermore, where a debit card holder's account is in credit, any misuse of that card would not fall under s 83. Thus these vital protections are in principle lost. However in practice similar protection is given by the banking industry under a voluntary code of practice. Most debit card schemes in the UK operate a system known as 'chargeback' which permits the card's issuer, in certain circumstances, and at the customer's request, to reverse a payment made to a merchant. The precise operation of chargeback will depend upon the scheme's rules.[52]

The fact that the UK banking system has adopted a non-statutory scheme, the effect of which is similar to the statutory regime of the CCA, might suggest that the former was superfluous. Alternatively, it might be argued that the existence of credit card protection meant that debit cards – in many cases competing with credit cards – had to offer similar protection in order to compete.

D. PayPal

PayPal is the main other, account based, system by which consumers make online payments. Interestingly it also unilaterally adopted consumer protection mechanisms at an early stage of its development to improve consumer trust. As with debit cards, PayPal will not generally be covered by protections in the 1974 Act, but instead it has two key voluntarily offered protections: first, its own dispute resolution service, which allows paying parties to challenge transactions in various circumstances; and second, a guarantee, which in certain circumstances means PayPal will reimburse in cases of fraudulent non or partial performance.[53]

---

[51] CCA 1974, ss 12 and 187(3).
[52] See www.financial-ombudsman.org.uk/publications/technical_notes/disputed-transactions.htm under 'complaints about chargebacks'.
[53] See details for PayPal US as of 23 April 2018 at www.paypal.com/uk/webapps/mpp/paypal-safety-and-security.

E. Internal Payment Systems (BACS, CHAPS)

Rather than using a cheque, a customer could just instruct their bank to make a direct payment. There are several systems for doing this, such as Bankers' Automated Clearance Services (BACS) and the Clearing House Automated Payment System (CHAPS).

These systems provide very little protection to their customers, in contrast to credit and debit cards. For example, account and beneficiary names are not checked for compatibility in CHAPS transfers. If a customer accidentally mistypes an account number, they bear the loss, rather than the bank, even if it was clearly a number that did not correspond to the customer name.[54]

F. Hawala and Trust Based Systems

Rather than using a centralised system for making payments between institutions, it is possible to use a decentralised network that relies on trust between pairs of actors in the network. Such systems have a long history.

The Hawala systems operating in East Africa and South Asia, involve networks of individuals with bilateral trust relationships.[55] A payment may be made from one Hawala operator to another by tracing a path through the network. Hawala systems are attractive because they are used in areas with expensive banking systems and can avoid currency conversion costs.

Hawala systems inspired the peer-to-peer payment system Ripple,[56] which makes use of a distributed ledger in the same way as cryptocurrencies[57] in order to keep track of transactions. Transactions may use the internal currency (XRP) of Ripple, but may also be denominated in other currencies or commodities. Exactly as is the case for the Hawala system, the network seeks a path between two parties who wish to trade where adjacent nodes trust one another.

VII. Electronic Cash

In 1990 David Chaum and others began to suggest that an electronic analogue of cash was possible, using existing cryptographic technology. Such a payment system would have the advantage of privacy (no-one would be able to trace payment) over the use of existing payment methods, in particular credit cards, where every payment

---

[54] *Tidal Energy Ltd v Bank of Scotland Plc* [2014] EWCA Civ 1107 (Floyd LJ dissenting).
[55] Mohammed El Qorchi and Samuel Munzele Maimbo, *Informal Funds Transfer Systems: An Analysis of the Informal Hawala System* (International Monetary Fund, 2003) Vol 222.
[56] David Schwartz, Noah Youngs and Arthur Britto, 'The Ripple Protocol Consensus Algorithm', available at https://ripple.com/files/ripple_consensus_whitepaper.pdf.
[57] See section VIII. below.

would be visible, at a minimum, to the credit card company.[58] The term electronic cash (or sometimes 'digital cash' or 'e-money'; the terminology has yet to settle) is used to refer to some form of electronic stored value, under the control of its owner, that behaves much like cash.

The key property of cash such as notes and coins is that if the stored value is lost or erased in some way, the owner has no way to recover the lost value. At the same time however no central authority can track where or how it is being spent; nor can they intervene, at least remotely, to stop it being spent or remove its value. Electronic cash has typically been modelled to copy these properties. There is no financial institution keeping track, in an account, of the balance, but also therefore no-one in a position to restore lost cash.

Some systems of electronic cash may allow exchange to take place freely between all users of the system (for example Mondex, discussed below). Other systems will only allow the use of the cash for payments to third parties who have a relationship with the money issuer (for example if a special console is issued to receive payment).

A. Mondex and Other E-Money Schemes

A pioneering early example of electronic cash was the physical card system known as Mondex.[59] Mondex used a smart card system to store value, denominated in the local currency. Consumers could transfer money from their card to a merchant, holding a 'merchant card', or to another consumer's 'consumer card'. Banks would hold 'bank cards' which could transfer money to or from consumer cards so that consumers could store value on, or remove value from, their cards.

Mondex was trialled between 1997 and 2001 in a number of local communities in Canada and the UK. It proved a failure and was eventually withdrawn.[60] The same fate appears to have befallen every other analogous electronic cash system, including:

- VISA Cash, trialled in Leeds (UK) and Trondheim (Norway) in 1997.

- Dexit, trialled in Canada between 2003 and 2006.

The most successful system was the Proton system, which flourished in Belgium between 1995 and 2014. The same technology was used in the Chipknip system in the Netherlands from 1996 to 2015, achieving its highest transaction volume of 171.7 million in 2011.

The reasons for the general early failure of electronic cash are not very hard to spot. Few people want to go to the bother of specially transferring value on to cards which will be lost forever if the card is lost, or similarly, the hardware where the value

---

[58] David Chaum, Amos Fiat and Moni Naor, 'Untraceable Electronic Cash' in *Proceedings on Advances in Cryptology* (New York, Springer-Verlag Inc, 1990).
[59] See www.mondex.org for historical information about Mondex.
[60] For an analysis of the reasons for failure, see Felix Stalder, 'Failures and Successes: Notes on the Development of Electronic Cash' (2002) 18 *The Information Society* 209.

is stored (such as a wallet on a smartphone). Another worry would be that the system, if electronic, might be hacked and value somehow extracted or 'stolen'. Furthermore, use of such electronic cash does not carry the consumer protections of the CCA 1974 or equivalent voluntary protection afforded debit cards. Another worry might be the possible insolvency of the e-cash issuer (originator). Regulatory requirements such as high capital reserves compared to debts applied to banks would almost certainly not apply to e-money issuers (EMIs).[61]

The only advantage to compensate for these problems is anonymity which is of relatively little interest to most of the public, unless they are engaging in illegal or unethical business. Consumers are in general reluctant to risk their money, especially for so limited an advantage, and, compared to familiar high street bank names, a multi-plicity of unknown brands selling e-money did not make much of a dent on them.

The only successful early e-money system, the Proton/Chipknip system, seems to have owed its advantage over similar credit or debit card schemes primarily due to the speed of transactions at retailers; because there was no need to contact the bank system, all transactions could take place locally and therefore more quickly. Furthermore, its use only for low value retail transactions made hacking less likely and also made the loss of a token less serious. As network delays on banking systems have generally reduced, even this advantage to merchants has decreased and the competitive advantage of such systems has appeared to vanish, which would explain their lack of success.

The most successful form of electronic cash is that based on Octopus, which was developed in Hong Kong and which spawned the successful Oyster system used in and around London in the UK. Octopus cards are like Proton/Chipknip in that they store relatively small values on cards, they may be used for payment much like cash, and they are widely accepted. The success of systems like these appears to be because they are strongly linked to a widely used public transportation system, which means:

- Users will be used to carrying a token (for example a ticket or season pass) so having a card to carry is never more awkward and often easier.

- Users of both Octopus and Oyster are given advantages over users of cash (for example discounts, and a cap on the total fare), or in some cases the card is the only acceptable method of payment (on the London bus network, for example).[62]

There are therefore strong incentives to hold and use the card while using public trans-port. This means that using the same card as a stored value card, charged with some currency, is very convenient for much of the relevant audience.

Even here, however, contactless debit and credit cards are likely slowly to displace these remaining e-money schemes. 'Contactless' was introduced to the London Oyster system in September 2014 and has obvious advantages such as no need to keep it 'topped up' or charged and no need to carry an extra card at all times. Existing fare

---

[61] See text at n 63 below.

[62] In London's Oyster system, however, the discount/capping of fares given to users of Oyster cards is now also applied to those using contactless credit and debit cards. See https://tfl.gov.uk/fares-and-payments/contactless/is-contactless-for-me.

capping was retained.[63] There is little obvious advantage to the user of having a purely 'cash' card, which they can then lose and which if not registered, will mean the loss of all its held value.

Given the few advantages of existing electronic money/cash systems, and the serious downsides, it is unsurprising that no serious equivalent system has appeared on the Internet, despite the early best efforts of the EU with its Electronic Money Directive 2000 which was explicitly intended to promote 'e-money' by placing e-money issuers on a firmer but still supportive regulatory footing.[64] All significant Internet payment systems that have a central issuer (ie unlike Bitcoin or other cryptocurrencies) are now account-based.

These issues with electronic cash are however very closely replicated, as we shall see, in the new cryptocurrencies such as Bitcoin. If stored Bitcoins are lost – perhaps because a computer or smartphone is thrown away by mistake[65] – then the value is lost forever.

Anonymity is an alleged advantage, but again seems to have been of interest mainly to those seeking to trade in illegal matters such as drugs or child pornography. As will also be explained, Bitcoin are inherently public, only the identities of the endpoints of a transaction are anonymous. This makes Bitcoin easier to track than cash.

The technical complexity of Bitcoin also requires the use, by most, of exchanges, which themselves have proven sometimes to be of shady reputation, and the Initial Coin Offering (ICO) schemes often crash and burn.[66] There is little or no obvious consumer protection, nor the usual kinds of financial institution regulation. Given these parallels, is it surprising that Bitcoins seem quickly to have become more a speculative commodity, or just a trendy fad, rather than a working currency?

B. Legal Responses to Electronic Cash

Electronic money is regulated in the EU by the E-Money Directive 2009.[67] It defines 'electronic money' in Article 2(2) as:

> electronically, including magnetically, stored monetary value as represented by a claim on the issuer which is issued on receipt of funds for the purpose of making payment transactions as defined in point 5 of Article 4 of Directive 2007/64/EC, and which is accepted by a natural or legal person other than the electronic money issuer.

---

[63] See https://tfl.gov.uk/info-for/media/press-releases/2014/july/contactless-payments-set-to-launch.

[64] Directive 2000/46/EC, now repealed. See discussion below in section VII. B.

[65] See the well-known story of James Howells: 'This Man's Lost Bitcoin Are Now Worth $75m – and under 200,000 Tonnes of Garbage' (*Wired*, 1 December 2017) at www.wired.co.uk/article/bitcoin-lost-newport-landfill.

[66] Note comment by Guadamuz (n 94): 'large amounts of BTC [Bitcoins] are held by shady characters and criminals, as well as anonymous people who do not respond to anyone. Call me crazy, but investing in a currency that is controlled by so many obscure interests does not fill me with confidence of it being a sound store of value.'

[67] Directive 2009/110/EC of the European Parliament and of the Council of 16 September 2009 on the taking up, pursuit and prudential supervision of the business of electronic money institutions [2009] OJ L267/7.

This definition assumes a number of things:

- that there is someone, ie an 'issuer', responsible for the money;
- that the possession of electronic money represents a claim against the issuer – it would be possible to require the issuer to pay money represented by the electronic money;
- that it is accepted by parties other than the issuer; and
- that it is issued on receipt of payment.

The regulation of electronic money institutions (EMI) in the EU began with the EMI Directive.[68]

This Directive, now repealed, had attempted to bolster public confidence in e-money by placing financial requirements on such issuers in a way akin to, though lesser than those placed on banks, notably to hold certain levels of capital funds and to have investments equivalent to their outstanding liabilities. The aim was to make EMIs passably stable and liquid, like banks, without making them go through the stringent regulatory trauma of actually becoming banks as they were thought more likely to be small incoming businesses.

In fact these new requirements made it nearly impossible for an EMI to actually make any money and very quickly the numbers of European e-money issuers dwindled. At the same time account based systems, notably PayPal, were emerging and showing themselves to have most of the advantages of conventional credit and debit payments but with the flexibility and confidentiality as to details desirable for online e-commerce transactions with strangers. Moreover, a new type of digital payment was emerging: micropayments made from smartphones (eg for in-game assets or ringtones) and it was unclear if these meant that mobile operators fell within the EMI Directive or not.[69]

The EMI was reviewed in 2004 and in 2009 a new Directive was passed.[70] One of its key objectives was to allow mobile operators to be classified as Electronic Money Institutions without financial implications sufficient to deter them as entrants, and in this it has generally been deemed successful. Meanwhile a new Payment Services Directive[71] was passed which was revised in 2017 as 'PSD2',[72] this time claiming

---

[68] Directive 2000/46/EC of the European Parliament and of the Council of 18 September 2000 on the taking up, pursuit of and prudential supervision of the business of electronic money institutions [2000] OJ L275/39 (now repealed).

[69] See further, A Guadamuz and J Usher, 'EC Electronic Money Directive 2000 Electronic Money: The European Regulatory Approach' in L Edwards (ed), *The New Legal Framework for E-Commerce in Europe* (Oxford, Hart Publishing, 2005); A Murray, *Information Technology Law*, 3rd edn (University of Warwick, 2016) Ch 19. Reed notes especially the difficulty for possible new providers of e-money which were not traditional financial institutions such as mobile operators: see C Reed, 'The Law of Unintended Consequences – Embedded Business Models in IT Regulation' (2007) *Journal of Information, Law and Technology* (2) at https://warwick.ac.uk/fac/soc/law/elj/jilt/2007_2/reed/ at 72–73.

[70] Directive 2009/110/EC.

[71] Directive 2007/64/EC of the European Parliament and of the Council of 13 November 2007 on payment services in the internal market. [2007] OJ L319/1.

[72] Directive (EU) 2015/2366 of the European Parliament and of the Council of 25 November 2015 on payment services in the internal market. [2015] OJ L337/35 ('PSD2'). This entered into force on

ambitiously its intent to 'modernise Europe's payment services to the benefit of both consumers and businesses, so as to keep pace with this rapidly evolving market'. In the UK, one of the first impacts has been the opening up of high street banking services to new innovators via compulsory open Application Programming Interfaces (APIs).

It is not the aim of this chapter to explain the intensely complicated web of modern EU electronic transactions and finance law after PSD2. What it has done so far however is to demonstrate that the history of e-money to 2009, and the reasons for lack of consumer uptake of e-money, are very likely to be mirrored in the field of cryptocurrencies; and that in consequence they are unlikely to succeed as true currencies rather than merely or mainly as speculative commodities. We now finally turn to this topic.

VIII. Cryptocurrencies

Cryptocurrencies are a new system used for, though not restricted to, online payments.[73] They are a form of account-based money, in the sense that ownership is determined by recorded transactions, with the innovation that the record of transactions is *decentralised*. This decentralised record, known as a 'distributed ledger', is created using algorithms that permit agreement between parties in a network, without the need for trust between them.[74] Early crypto currencies such as Bitcoin were designed for 'trustless' environments[75] and thus involve 'proof-of-work', a computational process designed to make everyone on the network agree when a change has been made to it. 'Proof-of-work' has been heavily criticised as very wasteful of computing resources and energy to no great effect (see below).

However, later cryptocurrencies or blockchain developments may operate in environments where there is a degree of trust between a limited number of participants ('permissioned') and possibly some degree of centralisation. These may not require proof- of-work, which has benefits in terms of energy use but also some dilution of the original vision of an 'unpermissioned' and entirely decentralised currency.

Other details vary considerably. Most cryptocurrencies are not denominated using any national currency unit (such as the pound) and have no central issuer (and are thus not 'electronic money' as defined in the E-Money Directive).

---

13 January 2018. In the UK it has been implemented by the Payment Services Regulations 2017 (SI 2017/No 752). See further UK consultations (now closed) at www.gov.uk/government/consultations/ implementation-of-the-revised-eu-payment-services-directive-psdii.

[73] J Bonneau, A Miller, J Clark, A Narayanan, JA Kroll and E Felten, 'Research Perspectives and Challenges for Bitcoin and Cryptocurrencies' at https://courses.csail.mit.edu/6.857/2015/files/BMCNKF15-IEEESP-bitcoin.pdf.

[74] See J Bacon et al, *Blockchain Demystified* (20 December 2017). Queen Mary School of Law Legal Studies Research Paper No 268/2017. Available at SSRN: https://ssrn.com/abstract=3091218.

[75] Satoshi Nakamoto, 'Bitcoin: A Peer-to-Peer Electronic Cash System' (2009) 1, at https://bitcoin.org/bitcoin.pdf.

A. Bitcoin

The first cryptocurrency, and to date the most successful, is Bitcoin,[76] which illustrates many of the significant issues affecting cryptocurrencies. Currencies other than Bitcoin will be discussed after a detailed description of the operation of Bitcoin.

Bitcoin, famously, is built up on a *distributed ledger technology* (DLT) known as the blockchain. Although the blockchain has subsequently been suggested as suitable for many other use cases, Bitcoin remains its most famous implementation. A block-chain can simply be regarded as a special sort of decentralised database. Among the recognised special features however are:

- *Data integrity* – the blockchain is public and through the use of hashes (see below) effectively tamperproof.

- *Identity authentication* – users are identified by their private keys, although externally they may still remain anonymous.[77]

As its name would suggest, the blockchain consists of a series of blocks. Each block contains a reference to the previous block, a list of transactions to be included in the new block, and proof that it is a valid block. The state of the distributed ledger – the distribution of all existing Bitcoins – can then be determined by analysing in turn the transactions contained in each block.

The proof that a new block is valid is generated by a process known as 'mining', which works as follows.

1. A number is generated from the list of transactions to be included in the new block combined with those contained in the previous block (which in turn will contain information about all previous transactions).
2. Add another arbitrary number (the 'number-used-once', or 'nonce'), and generate a 'hash' from the combination of the two. The hash is a string of 64 characters that is unique to the particular combination of the new block, the preceding block, and the added nonce number.
3. If the calculated hash begins with a number of zeros the same or less than the target defined by the Bitcoin algorithm, there is a valid proof. If not, a different nonce is used, and a new hash generated.
4. Once a proof is discovered, it is then announced to the rest of the network.
5. Miners are rewarded with 12.50 Bitcoins for each new block, and potentially with additional fees paid by those who wish their transactions to be included in the block. Miners may therefore prioritise those offering higher transaction fees.
6. The target is adjusted by the Bitcoin algorithm so that, on average, there will be only one new block every 10 minutes from all the miners in the world, regardless of how much computational power is being used to generate blocks at any given moment.

---

[76] Satoshi Nakamoto, 'Bitcoin: A Peer-to-Peer Electronic Cash System' (2008) 1 *Consulted* 28.
[77] *Ibid* at 1.

This technique is known as a *'proof-of-work'* and requires miners to invest in a computationally intense activity – the hashing calculation – in order to mine. The process is costly, making it difficult to trick the system – and crucially making it vanishingly unlikely to be able to trick the system on multiple successive occasions.

It is possible for more than one new block to be added to the blockchain, for example if two miners produce a new block at roughly the same time. This is known as a 'fork'. The design of the protocol means that everyone in the network will be aware of the fork, and some miners will subsequently start work on different branches of it.

However, it is almost certain that one branch will become longer than the other very quickly because the probability of a fork at any one block is low. Once this happens, miners automatically switch to mining the longest chain. The shorter chain then becoming invalid and the transactions in it will not have a long term effect.

The Bitcoin protocol suggests therefore that anyone carrying out a Bitcoin transaction should wait for six blocks to be been added to the chain before confirming their transaction. The design of the protocol means that it is essentially impossible to change blocks once they have settled beyond a certain threshold, and so at that point it is safe to confirm the transaction.

If a transaction was unwound, however, it would be possible for the person transferring the Bitcoin to make two transactions to different recipients on different branches, one of which would fail, with that recipient receiving no Bitcoins. Such a situation is known as a 'double spend'.

On 11 March 2013, due to an error in an upgrade to the Bitcoin software, some miners continued to mine the shorter block chain and a fork continued to exist for over six hours, creating the risk of transactions being accepted but later invalidated. In that period one double spend was reported.

On 13 June 2014, Ghash (a mining consortium operated by CEX.io) acquired 51 per cent of the processing power in the Bitcoin network. In theory this would have meant that, given sufficient time, it could have forced the network to accept an alternative blockchain preferred by it, which would have enabled it to make money by double spending, or rewarding itself with additional Bitcoins. Had it tried to do so, the remaining miners in the network would have almost certainly taken steps to prevent it, so it is unclear how real this risk is. Since then Ghash has taken steps to ensure that it does not dominate the network.

i. Analysis

Bitcoin comes with numerous disadvantages from the point of view of both owner/investor and society. To summarise:

One analysis of Bitcoin is that it is a form of artificial *commodity*, which may be used as money, in much the same way as gold. It suffers as commodities do from fluctuations in price caused by speculation and falls and rises in demand.

It also suffers from the same problem as *cash*, in that there is no way to return 'stolen' cash to an owner and, unlike payment by debit or credit card, there is no way to undo a transaction because of a mistake or because of mis- or non-performance by the recipient (although in turn this makes Bitcoin very attractive to online vendors).

As we have seen, Bitcoin exchanges such as MtGOX may also be weak points for fraudulent or negligent behaviour with very serious consequences for owners/investors of cryptocoins.

Bitcoin is even less attractive than cash in one respect. Bitcoin is often perceived, like cash, as anonymous and untraceable. In fact this is not true. All transactions in the blockchain are visible to all users of the network. This permits the authorities to trace transactions from one Bitcoin wallet (account) to another. Provided they are able to identify the endpoints (for example, by seizing physical devices on which the wallets are or were stored) they may be able to prove that Bitcoins were transferred between two particular points.[78]

In practice, Bitcoin wallets are difficult to manage. A great deal of Bitcoin is traded through exchanges, which in some cases (for example MtGOX) held accounts in Bitcoin larger than they held Bitcoin reserves – much as do banks, but without being regulated. This undermines many of the advantages of decentralisation and also promotes opacity, and possibly fraud: a possibility that became reality in the case of MtGOX in 2014[79] where approximately 850,000 bitcoins belonging to customers and the company went missing and likely stolen, an amount valued at more than $450 million at the time.

From a societal point of view, cryptocurrencies such as Bitcoin which require proof-of-work are extremely environmentally unfriendly.

B. Proof-of-Stake Cryptocurrencies

The consensus protocol of currencies like Bitcoin and Ethereum requires miners to demonstrate proof-of-work for each new block. A disadvantage of proof-of-work schemes is that they consume a great deal of energy while generating hashes. This, it could be argued, is wasteful, since hashing is not, of itself, a useful activity.[80] Morgan Stanley, for example, has estimated that the blockchain could consume more energy than the current population of Argentina in 2018.[81] It is conceivable that mining in proof-of-work systems could be used to solve more obviously useful problems, but few examples exist to date.[82]

As a result, attempts are being made to move away from proof-of-work. Ethereum is rolling out its new public blockchain, running on an algorithm called proof-of-stake,

---

[78] There is technology (known as a 'tumbler') that may be able to reduce the chance of re-identification. See 'What is a bitcoin tumbler?' (Bitcoin Stack Exchange), at https://bitcoin.stackexchange.com/questions/17807/what-is-a-bitcoin-tumbler.

[79] At this time MtGOX controlled over 70% of all bitcoin ('BTC') transactions worldwide, as the largest bitcoin intermediary and the world's leading bitcoin exchange. See 'The Inside Story of Mt. Gox, Bitcoin's $460 Million Disaster' (*Wired*, 3 March 2014) at www.wired.com/2014/03/bitcoin-exchange/.

[80] There are exceptions to this. Primecoin is something of a counter-example because the work involved in the proof-of-work entails solving prime number problems which may have some interest to pure mathematicians: Sunny King, 'Primecoin: Cryptocurrency with Prime Number Proof-of-Work' (Tech Rep, July 2013), available at http://primecoin.org/static/primecoin-paper.pdf.

[81] See CNBC, 23 Feb 2018 at www.cnbc.com/2018/02/23/bitcoin-blockchain-consumes-a-lot-of-energy-engineers-changing-that.html.

[82] Gridcoin uses BOINC for scientific projects such as SETI.

over the course of 2018. Proof-of-stake rejects solving cryptographic riddles as in proof-of-work. Instead, the next computer to validate a block of transaction data and collect new coins is chosen based on a lottery system. The more coins you own, the better your chances of being chosen. Ben Laurie[83] described such a possible system in some detail in 2011.

The first implementation of proof-of-stake was in PPCoin[84] (now Peercoin) in 2012. Peercoin is a hybrid system with proof-of-work miners alongside proof-of-stake, but it is so designed that the importance of mining steadily declines, and with it the related energy inefficiencies. In PPCoin, 'stake' is based not merely on the number of coins owned but also on their age, such that assignment of transaction processing is weighted by the number of coin days accumulated by an individual.

C. Issuer Backed Cryptocurrencies

There is no reason why a distributed blockchain may not be used by states for issuing money or bonds. The Bank of England has flagged up central bank issuance of digital currency as part of its research agenda, although they have since declared as of 2018 that 'We are not planning to create a central bank-issued digital currency. But we want to understand better the implications of a central bank issuing a digital currency'.[85]

In 2014, Yanis Varoufakis, then the Finance Minister of Greece, suggested that a distributed blockchain could be used to support a parallel currency issued by the Greek currency that would be redeemable for Euros by the Greek Government but could also be exchanged for tax liabilities, at a premium, after being held for two years.[86] The advantages that he saw in the use of a blockchain would be (i) to reduce transaction costs, and (ii) to provide an alternative to a banking industry in which there was little confidence. It would also have allowed the currency to be maintained in an entirely transparent fashion.

D. Other Variations

There are many competing alternative cryptocurrencies, many of these beginning as straight copies of Bitcoin.

---

[83] B Laurie, 'Decentralised Currencies Are Probably Impossible (but Let's at Least Make Them Efficient)' (2011) 100 *Practice* 1.

[84] Sunny King and Scott Nadal, 'Ppcoin: Peer-to-Peer Crypto-Currency with Proof-of-Stake' (2012) at http://wallet.peercoin.net/assets/paper/peercoin-paper.pdf.

[85] 'One Bank Research Agenda' (Bank of England, 2015) 31. See current research agenda at www.bankofengland.co.uk/research/digital-currencies. This includes a document of key current questions at www.bankofengland.co.uk/-/media/boe/files/research/cbdc.pdf?la=en&hash=27D6074B68121BCAA5E2B B50693C031CCE9F8658.

[86] Yanis Varoufakis, 'BITCOIN: A Flawed Currency Blueprint with a Potentially Useful Application for the Eurozone' (15 February 2014) at http://yanisvaroufakis.eu/2014/02/15/bitcoin-a-flawed-currency-blueprint-with-a-potentially-useful-application-for-the-eurozone.

One difference concerns their attitude to the total supply of Bitcoin. Proponents of Bitcoin are often attracted to the fact that the total supply of Bitcoins is limited – although Bitcoins continue to be produced, the number of new Bitcoins progressively falls and a maximum number of 21 million Bitcoins is the limit that its algorithm will permit the creation of.[87]

It is often claimed that Bitcoin is in this respect superior to fiat currency issued by national governments because governments may increase the supply of their currency and thereby cause inflation. As we have seen earlier, however, governments do not in fact have a direct control over the quantity of currency in modern economies. Instead the quantity of money in the economy is determined by the lending choices of banking institutions. (This is of course affected by government policies such as capital ratio requirements or the price set for government bonds). The key point is that most transactions (measured by financial value) do not involve currency (as in coins or notes, usually issued by a state bank). It is hard to see why Bitcoin should be any different in terms of eliminating account-based payment, should it become widespread.

Other differences between cryptocurrencies include block processing time and total capitalisation. For example, Litecoin has a target block processing time of 2.5 minutes (four times as fast as Bitcoin) and a cap of 84 million Litecoins (four times as many).

E. Regulatory Reactions to Cryptocurrencies

Regulatory institutions have begun to recognise the existence of cryptocurrencies, in particular Bitcoin, and in many cases have not found it too hard to find sufficient existing ways to categorise them. Initially the UK's tax authority (HMRC) treated Bitcoins as a single-purpose face-value voucher (on which VAT would be payable), but it subsequently changed its position. Since 2014, VAT has been chargeable on Bitcoin services (such as exchanges), but not on the Bitcoin itself. For capital gains tax, Bitcoin transactions are treated in much the same way as transactions in foreign currencies, and for other taxes Bitcoin is treated as would any other form of value.[88]

There is no bespoke UK regulation of cryptocurrencies to date. Unfortunately, this lack of current regulation means a lack of certainty as to future regulation which may deter investment in genuine innovation as opposed to short term speculation and hype-driven projects.[89]

In the US, FinCEN has given guidance on the treatment of Bitcoin for the purposes of regulation under the Bank Secrecy Act. Mere users of Bitcoin are not 'money transmitters', but someone who creates Bitcoins and sells them for real currency or its equivalent (as would be the case with many miners) is a money transmitter.[90]

---

[87] On the other hand, some cryptocurrencies, such as Dogecoin, put no limit on their total issue.

[88] HM Revenue & Customs, 'Revenue and Customs Brief 9 (2014): Bitcoin and Other Cryptocurrencies – GOV.UK' (2014) at www.gov.uk/government/publications/revenue-and-customs-brief-9-2014-bitcoin-and-other-cryptocurrencies/revenue-and-customs-brief-9-2014-bitcoin-and-other-cryptocurrencies.

[89] 'Project Innovate: Call for Input, Feedback Statement' (Financial Conduct Authority, 2014) Feedback Statement FS14/2 para 2.21.

[90] FinCEN, 'Application of FinCEN's Regulations to Persons Administering, Exchanging, or Using Virtual Currencies' (US Department of the Treasury, Financial Crimes Enforcement Network,

Obviously someone (such as an exchange) who transmits Bitcoins from one person to another, or who exchanges Bitcoins for money, is also an exchanger and/or transmitter.

One potential loophole likely soon to be plugged is the use of Bitcoins for money laundering, with amendments agreed to the 4th revision of the EU Anti-Money Laundering Regulations in Brussels in December 2017.[91]

IX. Conclusions

This chapter has traced the development of the concept of money from physical tokens or commodities, to cash and coins; then to dematerialised, account-based payment systems such as credit and debit cards; electronic payment systems such as PayPal; electronic money or 'digital cash'; and finally cryptocurrencies. As we have seen, as we become a more digital society we also become more innovative with financial technology (or 'fintech') which is now seen as a key driver of economic growth in the UK.[92]

Yet consumers have remained resistant to real innovation in payment mechanisms, even online, generally preferring on the whole to rely on the well-known brands of high street banks and card issuers, or those backed by serious consumer protection guarantees, such as PayPal, rather than delve into e-money and mobile wallet payments,[93] except in certain circumstances such as in-game payments. The recent Bitcoin bubble of 2017–2018 has arguably far more to do with a new commodity for speculation, than any advance into new forms of viable online currencies.[94]

Key legal questions remain to be solved. Much legal energy has gone into what might be called the macro or public law questions, such as whether crypto needs to be regulated further to prevent inflation, consumer fraud, tax avoidance or money laundering; or debates on whether it is a curse for enabling covert criminality and

18 March 2013), available at www.fincen.gov/resources/statutes-regulations/guidance/application-fincens-regulations-persons-administering.

[91] Directive 2015/849/EU of the European Parliament and of the Council of 20 May 2015 on the prevention of the use of the financial system for the purposes of money laundering or terrorist financing [2015] OJ L141/73. See Reuters, 'EU Agrees Clampdown on Bitcoin Platforms to Tackle Money Laundering' (15 December 2017) at https://uk.reuters.com/article/uk-eu-moneylaundering/eu-agrees-clampdown-on-bitcoin-platforms-to-tackle-money-laundering-idUKKBN1E928M.

[92] See UK *FinTech Census 2017* commissioned by HM Treasury, EY and Innovate at www.ey.com/Publication/vwLUAssets/EY-UK-FinTech-Census-2017/$FILE/EY-UK-FinTech-Census-2017.pdf. 'Smart contracts' are covered in Chapter 11 on electronic contracts.

[93] Part of this may be due to limited acceptance of mobile wallet payments (including smart watches, etc): a January 2018 report from the US says 'only 16 percent of U.S. consumers have completed a digital wallet transaction, probably because only 36 percent of U.S. merchants currently offer this payment option'. See 'Mobile Wallets: Apple Pay vs Samsung Pay vs Google Pay' (tom's guide, 17 January 2018) at www.tomsguide.com/us/mobile-wallet-guide,news-20666.html.

[94] See comment from A Guadamuz on 21 January 29018: 'While Bitcoin has been in existence since 2009, the number of places which accept it as a means of payment has remained limited, and on the contrary, some corporate adopters have stopped taking it altogether, such as Dell and Steam' ('Confessions of a Bitcoin Sceptic' (*Technollama* blog, 2018), at www.technollama.co.uk/confessions-of-a-bitcoin-sceptic). Guadamuz also notes that transaction confirmation times have lengthened and transaction fees gone up as the bubble has expanded.

fraud in new forms, or a blessing for promoting innovation.[95] Yet many more traditional private law questions remain under-explored. Some of these have been raised in passing throughout this chapter. For example, are cryptocurrencies 'money' for the purposes of the law of the sale of goods? If not, the purchase of goods using cryptocurrencies falls outside of the existing legal protections. Courts have shown themselves willing to adapt to changes in mercantile practice, but will they be ready in this case?

Another question is how the 'theft' of Bitcoins should be dealt with. If an attacker masquerades as a particular Bitcoin wallet and the victim transfers her Bitcoins into the attacker's wallet, what offence(s) has the latter committed? For such a scenario to arise, the attacker need not have gained unauthorised access to a computer system, which would otherwise be an offence.[96] The difficulties the courts have had in their treatment of intangible property, evidenced by *R v Preddy*,[97] make it unlikely that any form of theft would be chargeable in these circumstances.

Furthermore, will courts consider that use of the Bitcoin protocol implies a representation that the originator of a transaction is also the 'lawful' owner of a wallet? If so, the requirements of the offence of fraud might be met. However, the anonymity inherent in Bitcoin would be an obstacle to the finding of an implied claim of identity, and therefore to a finding of fraud. Civil remedies may also be problematic. There are no goods involved so as to sustain a claim for trespass to goods. In a sense the attacker is 'passing off' herself as the victim, but generally not in the narrow sense in which passing off is understood at common law.

Is a payment by Bitcoin absolute or 'conditional'? It is entirely possible for blocks to be added to the blockchain independently in different parts of the network – allowing in principle a double payment to take place, so that one wallet has made two payments. Eventually, the Bitcoin algorithm will favour one transaction and the other will, retrospectively, become invalid (the rule of thumb being six blocks).

Thus, merely receiving payment does not mean that payment is certain for a period of time. This appears to be similar to the situation of cheque payment discussed earlier in this chapter. With cheques, English courts treated the payment as having been made at the date the cheque was presented, but which could later be invalidated if the cheque did not clear – a 'conditional' payment.

Will courts take the same approach to Bitcoins? Or will they choose to treat a payment of Bitcoin as not having been made until some number of further blocks have been mined?

These and many other questions remain to be answered if Bitcoin or similar systems are to play an important role in the future of e-commerce.

---

[95] See, eg, A Guadamuz and C Marsden, 'Blockchains and Bitcoin: Regulatory Responses to Cryptocurrencies' (2015) 20 *First Monday* 12.
[96] Computer Misuse Act 1990, s 1.
[97] *R v Preddy* (n 36).

13

Exploring Cybersecurity and Cybercrime: Threats and Legal Responses

LACHLAN D URQUHART

'The only way to patch a vulnerability is to expose it first ... the flip side being that exposing the vulnerability leaves you open for an exploit'

Elliot Alderson, *Mr Robot*, season 2, episode 4, 14m25s

I. Introduction

Cybersecurity is a complex domain to study, filled with acronyms, esoteric terminology and an ever-shifting roster of actors and threats. We can begin by thinking about the contested term 'hacker' to get a sense of the diversity.[1] Hackers could be framed as sitting somewhere on the spectrum between law abiding 'white hats' and criminal 'black hats', but that would neglect the richness of the various tribes who mix and overlap. The spectrum includes:

1. traditional cyber criminals organising campaigns to infect laptops or smartphones with remote access tools which allow them to record victims in precarious acts via their webcams with a view to extorting them to prevent release of the footage;[2]

---

[1] To see the history of the term hacker, and associated terms, see S Levy, *Hackers: Heroes of the Computer Revolution 25th Anniversary Ed* (Newton, O'Reilly Media, 2010).

[2] RS Portnoff et al, 'Somebody's Watching Me?: Assessing the Effectiveness of Webcam Indicator Lights' (2015) 1 *Proceedings of the ACM CHI'15 Conference on Human Factors in Computing Systems* 1649–58.

2.   organised crime groups running peer-to-peer marketplaces on the 'dark net' enabling trade of drugs, people, or extreme pornography;[3]
3.   loose hacker collectives, like Lulzsec or Anonymous, which use hacking for social justice purposes, retaliating against organisations for their perceived immoral acts;[4]
4.   state sponsored hackers attacking foreign infrastructure in so-called advanced persistent threats or patriotic campaigns to spread propaganda, steal military secrets, or interfere with foreign elections;[5] and
5.   solitary characters hacking from their bedrooms into US military or national security infrastructure, seeking to prove existence of UFOs, and subsequently spending years fighting extradition.[6]

Popular culture plays with many of these stereotypes, from the recent and critically acclaimed TV series *Mr Robot*, back to the 1980s and 1990s cult classic movies *War Games* and *Hackers*. Unpacking the diversity of hacker communities (an interesting anthropological and criminological topic of inquiry)[7] helps us to get a sense of the multitude of actors, trends, motivations, threats and practices that cybersecurity regulation must contend with.

The types of crime being committed online vary from traditional crimes enabled by IT infrastructure, for example tax evasion, to true cybercrimes that would not exist but for the Internet, for example bitcoin fraud. There are also hybrid crimes which sit somewhere in the middle of this spectrum.[8] Criminal laws in jurisdictions across the globe largely follow the distinctions developed by the UN Office of Drugs and Crime:

1.   acts against confidentiality, integrity and availability of data or systems, for example illegal access to a computer, interception, or acquisition of data;
2.   acts for personal or financial gain or harm, for example computer fraud, identity theft, spam, or child grooming; and
3.   computer content related acts, for example hate speech, distribution of extreme or illegal pornography, or cyber terrorism.[9]

Effective regulation in this setting is complicated by the convergence of IT and the blurring between physical and online lives caused by mobile and embedded computing.

---

[3] J Bartlett, *The Dark Net: Inside the Digital Underworld* (London, Heinemann, 2015).
[4] P Olson, *We Are Anonymous: Inside the Hacker World of LulzSec, Anonymous, and the Global Cyber Insurgency* (Back Bay Books, 2013).
[5] D Alperovitch, 'Revealed: Operation Shady RAT', *White Paper*, 2011.
[6] 'Gary McKinnon Resource Page' *The Guardian* (2017), available at www.theguardian.com/world/gary-mckinnon.
[7] R Jones, 'Cybercrime and Internet Security: A Criminological Introduction' in L Edwards and C Waelde (eds), *Law and the Internet* (Oxford, Hart Publishing, 2009) 1566; M Yar, *Cybercrime and Society* (SAGE, 2013).
[8] D Wall, *Cybercrime: The Transformation of Crime in the Information Age* (Polity, 2007); Ross Anderson et al, 'Measuring the Cost of Cybercrime: A Workshop' (Workshop on the Economics of Information Security (WEIS), 2012) 1–31.
[9] These have similarities to the classes of crimes in the Convention on Cybercrime (discussed below); UN Office on Drugs and Crime, *Comprehensive Study on Cybercrime* (New York, 2013) (hereinafter 'UNODC Report') 16.

Wearable health devices and smart home appliances are becoming increasingly common.[10] This occurs at the macro level too, with computation and sensing being embedded in the urban built environment to manage transport or energy infrastructure.[11]

Legitimate and illegitimate economies associated with cybersecurity involve security vendors, consultants and IT firms trying to patch or address threats, as well as organised crime groups trying to find the vulnerabilities and exploit them, for example by stockpiling and trading 'zero day' attacks.[12] In addressing these challenges, law enforcement agencies (LEAs) need to contend with skillset or resource deficits and procedural challenges of cooperating across borders to address heterogeneous, transnational cybercrimes.

As we explore in this chapter, regulating cybersecurity risks requires ways of cutting through the surrounding fear, uncertainty and doubt (FUD) to find measured and balanced responses. However, the fast pace of technological change is as ever ahead of the patchwork of regulatory and policy frameworks that attempt to regulate them.

In this chapter we explore some of the complexities around regulating cybersecurity in the UK, Europe and internationally. We analyse both legal and technical literature to provide a balanced picture of both the threats and responses, with attention given to novel contemporary challenges of regulating cyberwarfare and building a secure Internet of Things. Cybersecurity risks from emerging technologies cannot be solved with a purely legal approach; instead cooperation and participation between many stakeholders is necessary. Technologists, regulators, industry and the public all have a role to play.

II. Navigating the Diversity of Cybersecurity Threats

Getting a sense of the landscape of cyber threats means turning to a range of stakeholders.[13] Commercial security vendors like Symantec,[14] law enforcement agencies like the UK National Crime Agency (NCA),[15] UK Government[16] and

---

[10] M Weiser, 'Some Computer Science Issues in Ubiquitous Computing' (1993) 7 *Communications of the ACM* 75–84; E Aarts and S Marzano, *The New Everyday: Views on Ambient Intelligence* (Rotterdam, 010 Publishers, 2003).

[11] L Edwards, 'Privacy, Security and Data Protection in Smart Cities' (2016) 1(2) *European Data Protection Law Review* 28–58.

[12] L Bilge and T Dumitras, 'Before We Knew It: An Empirical Study of Zero-Day Attacks in the Real World' (Proceedings of the 2012 ACM Conference on Computer and Communications Security – CCS'12, 2012) 833–44.

[13] Reflecting the fast pace of change in this area, most organisations release a threat landscape report each year.

[14] Symantec Corporation, *Internet Security Threat Report 2018* (March 2018) (hereinafter 'Symantec Report').

[15] NCA/NCSC, *The Cyber Threat to UK Business* (2018), available at www.ncsc.gov.uk/cyberthreat (hereinafter 'NCA Report '18');

[16] HM Government, *Cyber Security Breaches Survey 2018* (2018) https://assets.publishing.service. gov.uk/government/uploads/system/uploads/attachment_data/file/702074/Cyber_Security_Breaches_ Survey_2018_-_Main_Report.pdf (hereinafter 'UK Breach Survey').

international bodies like the European Network and Information Security Agency (ENISA)[17] or the UN Office on Drugs and Crime can all assist in this domain.[18]

A. Threats and Actors

Currently, the traditional cybercrime infrastructure of botnets and exploit kits continues to be put to work spreading malware like Trojans, viruses, worms, key loggers and remote access tools (RATs).[19] Malware remains the dominant contemporary cybersecurity threat,[20] driven overwhelmingly by financial motivations, eg use of ransomware and extortion campaigns.[21] 2017's WannaCry is a prominent example of a major ransomware attack.[22] Exploiting vulnerabilities in legacy Windows XP systems, it removed user access by encrypting files and demanding payment to regain access. It spread far and wide, with the UK National Health Service, Spanish telecoms giant Telefonica and US courier firm FedEx all being affected.[23] In general, such campaigns often target both individuals and organisations, whilst utilising other technological trends like anonymous cryptocurrencies and online social media to support both payment of ransoms and the sourcing of sensitive information that can be used to target individuals.[24] NCA argues social engineering attacks on employees through professional social media sites on employer machines can be as big a risk as opening phishing mails.[25]

Mobile malware is on the increase in 2018, according to Symantec,[26] and in general, malware has become more targeted. Financial sector focused trojans, for example, were used in a Bangladesh Bank heist where $81m was stolen through fraudulent transactions.[27] This fits with wider trends towards monetising crime in more efficient ways. The notion of 'cybercrime as a service' has grown, with criminals offering to hire both their services and toolkits to users to leverage attacks.[28] Relatively unskilled actors, like so-called script kiddies, have easy access to hacking tools.[29] However, LEAs are responding, and the UK NCA's Operation Vulcanalia targeted and arrested users of a DDoS-for-hire tool.[30]

Cybersecurity threats come from everyone from script kiddies to nation states. ENISA argue that the most active threat group are cybercriminals, especially in relation

---

[17] ENISA, *Threat Landscape Report 2017* (Heraklion, 2018) (hereinafter 'ENISA Report').
[18] UNODC Report (n 9).
[19] ENISA Report (n 17) p 21.
[20] It is the top threat in the ENISA Report (n 17); UK Breach Survey (n 16) p 36 for breakdown of breaches and attacks suffered by businesses and charities.
[21] NCA Report '18 (n 15) 7.
[22] ENISA Report (n 17) 28.
[23] NCA Report '18 (n 15) 8, case study on WannaCry.
[24] ENISA Report (n 17) 55.
[25] NCSC/NCA, *The Cyber Threat to UK Business* (2017) (hereinafter 'NCA Report '17'), available at www.nationalcrimeagency.gov.uk/publications/785-the-cyber-threat-to-uk-business/file.
[26] Symantec Report (n 14).
[27] NCA Report '17 (n 25) 7.
[28] NCA Report '17 (n 25) 23.
[29] NCA Report '17 (n 25) 22–23.
[30] NCA Report '17 (n 25) p 6.

to extortion and blackmail. In the UK, cybercrime largely stems from organised crime groups in Russian-speaking Eastern European countries.[31] Other particularly active groups include insider threats (who pose a significant challenge for organisations as they involve legitimate employees abusing IT access privileges for financial gain, espionage, sabotage or IP theft) and those driven by ideological goals like hacktivists, cyber spies, cyber fighters and cyber terrorists.[32]

Finding vulnerabilities and patching them before threat agents exploit them is a complex process. Many stakeholders, from state security services to cybercriminals or IT security vendors, have an interest in finding so-called 'zero day' vulnerabilities (unpatched software security flaws), although of course their motives differ. Cybercriminals may find them and keep them hidden in order to sell the information to the highest bidder, while security services stockpile them for use in cyber-attacks or surveillance and security vendors may look to patch them to protect individual and organisational customers.

The UK Cybersecurity Strategy argues that general vulnerability results from the growing number of systems going online which in turn create more threat vectors. Poor cyber hygiene practices by the ordinary users, such as not using antivirus software, the lack of security skills across society and the continued use of unpatched legacy IT systems are all concerns.[33] The NCA echo the latter point, and are concerned that despite widespread publicity, many vulnerabilities, like Heartbleed, have not been fully patched.[34] This enables hackers to take advantage of these older vulnerabilities, utilising less sophisticated approaches to leverage hacks in order to steal intellectual property (IP) or state secrets, and leaving more sophisticated tools only for when truly necessary.[35]

Exploring the extent of UK cybersecurity threats, the 2018 Crime Survey for England and Wales shows fraud and computer misuse crimes were the most common in the survey, with one in 10 adults being a victim in the previous 12 months.[36] The UK Cyber Security Breaches Survey 2018 (CSBS)[37] shows that 43 per cent of the businesses surveyed experienced cyber security breaches or attacks in the last 12 months, growing to 72 per cent when limited to large firms.[38] Overall, the mean cost for all businesses of all identified breaches or attacks in 12 months of the survey is £1230, rising to £3,100 when there is loss of data or an asset. For larger firms it goes from £9,260 to £22,300 for the same circumstances.[39]

In general, though, the UN Office on Drugs and Crime argue that estimating the full scale and cost of cybercrime is complicated to measure, in part due to

---

[31] NCA Report '17 (n 25) s 3.3.

[32] ENISA Report (n 17).

[33] HM Government, *National Cyber Security Strategy* (2016) 22–23.

[34] NCA Report '17 (n 25) 9.

[35] NCA Report '17 (n 25) 7.

[36] Office for National Statistics, *Crime in England and Wales: Year Ending September 2017* (London, 2018) 6.

[37] The UK Breach Survey (n 16) surveyed 1,519 UK businesses and 569 UK registered charities from 9 October 2017 to 14 December 2017.

[38] UK Breach Survey (n 16) 1.

[39] UK Breach Survey (n 16) 42.

under-reporting.[40] In any case, measures to fight cybercrime are often inefficient and may add more costs than they save, as argued by Anderson et al: 'the botnet behind a third of the spam sent in 2010 earned its owners around US$2.7m, while worldwide expenditures on spam prevention probably exceeded a billion dollars.'[41]

B. Botnets and DDoS

We now consider botnets, the workhorses of the cybersecurity threat economy, in more detail. IT devices around the world can be compromised by malware, turning them into infected 'zombie' units, enslaved to a command and control server which remotely controls their behaviour on demand. These distributed systems are put to work, often for hire, to conduct distributed denial of service attacks (DDoS) and spam campaigns.[42] The major UN Office on Drugs and Crime Comprehensive Study on Cybercrime estimated around one million botnet command and control servers globally, with high volume clusters in Eastern Europe, Central America and the Caribbean.[43] We will consider these two applications in more detail.

In DDoS attacks, servers are targeted with high volumes of legitimate packet requests until the traffic consumes resources like bandwidth or memory and the targeted servers cannot respond anymore. Services hosted on these servers are knocked offline temporarily, but DDoS attacks are not permanent, and impacts are often resolved once servers are brought back online.[44] Nevertheless, downtime can cause significant economic, safety or political costs. Higher-risk targets may include critical IT infrastructure like hospitals, banks and air traffic control systems, or services delivering time-critical political or safety information, for example in relation to natural disasters or terrorist attacks. DDoS attacks can be as a distraction technique to mask more targeted hacks too, such as social engineering attacks which take advantage of the chaos during server downtime.[45]

Spam levels fell from all-time highs in the early 2000s to sit at 55 per cent of all email volume in 2016, but are on the rise again.[46] The average number of emails in 2017 per user rose from 63 to 67.[47] Spam is a primary mechanism for delivering malware and malicious URLs (ie those that execute code when clicked) to targets.[48] Despite increasingly sophisticated spam filters, more intelligent spam campaigns can still evade these and are able to fool their targets upon delivery, now moving more heavily to social networks too.[49] We now look at two contemporary cybersecurity challenges: Internet of Things (IoT) security and cyberwarfare.

---

[40] UNODC Report (n 9) 21.
[41] Anderson et al (n 8) 7.
[42] G Hogben, *Botnets: Detection, Measurement, Disinfection and Defence* (Heraklion, ENISA, 2013).
[43] UNODC Report (n 9) 33.
[44] See legal dimensions in L Edwards, 'Dawn of the Death of Distributed Denial of Service: How to Kill Zombies' (2006) 24(1) *Cardozo Arts and Entertainment Law Journal* 23–59.
[45] Symantec Report (n 14).
[46] Symantec Report (n 14). Legal control of spam in DP law is discussed in Chapter 5.
[47] Symantec Report (n 14) 73.
[48] Symantec Report (n 14).
[49] ENISA Report (n 17) 46.

C. Security in the Internet of Things (IoT) and Cyberwarfare

The IoT involves networking physical devices with a range of sensors, from thermostats to security cameras. The goal is often to enable new value-added services for users. This could mean automating mundane activities, like heating management, or increasing home security by enabling remote monitoring of who enters or leaves via a mobile application. In the industrial setting, companies embed sensors into different stages of product or service supply chains to identify efficiencies. This can lead to a number of risks, in cyber-physical systems leading to physical harms in the real world.[50] The diversity of IoT application domains introduces a vast range of stakeholders from traditional IT hardware and software firms to energy firms, car manufacturers and city councils. From a security perspective, there are many challenges, including: (i) the pervasive heterogeneity in the technical nature of IoT devices with different networking protocols, interfaces, sensing and processing capabilities; (ii) different contexts of use, from transport to security to energy; and (iii) the nascent nature of the industry, in which security practices are either non-existent or are yet to be harmonised. With domestic IoT ecosystems, for example, devices from different manufacturers layered with services from different organisations may all be interacting, each with varying levels of security safeguards.[51] Indeed, poor security practices in IoT are prevalent, where devices may lack even basic security measures, for example passwords. Compromised security vulnerabilities of smart domestic technologies like cars, insulin pumps and children's toys have all been shown.[52]

These IoT vulnerabilities pose new routes for exploits.[53] We already see IoT devices being compromised and used in hacks. For example, the Shodan search engine has been used to find unsecured IP connected devices, for example baby cameras, whose live video feed can be observed openly from anywhere in the world.[54] The scale is significant, and as the UK NCA note, 'the Shodan search engine reveals, for example, over 41,000 units of one insecure model of DVR are connected to the Internet as of January 2017'.[55] Recent DDoS attacks on a domain name service (DNS) company were mounted, in part, by the Mirai IoT botnet, made up of compromised IP connected security cameras and digital video recorders (DVRs).[56] Since Mirai, other IoT botnets

---

[50] L Urquhart and D McAuley, 'Avoiding the Internet of Insecure Industrial Things' (2018) *Computer Law and Security Review*.

[51] D Barnard-Wills, L Marinos and S Portesi, *Threat Landscape and Good Practice Guide for Smart Home and Converged Media* (Heraklion, 2014).

[52] A Greenberg, 'Hackers Remotely Kill a Jeep on the Highway – With Me in It' (*Wired*, 21 July 2015), available at www.wired.com/2015/07/hackers-remotely-kill-jeep-highway; J Finkle, 'J&J Warns Diabetic Patients: Insulin Pump Vulnerable to Hacking' (*Reuters*, 4 October 2016), available at http://uk.reuters.com/article/us-johnson-johnson-cyber-insulin-pumps-e-idUKKCN12411L; D Goodin, 'Creepy IoT Teddy Bear Leaks >2 Million Parents' and Kids' Voice Messages' (*Ars Technica*, 28 February 2017), available at https://arstechnica.com/security/2017/02/creepy-iot-teddy-bear-leaks-2-million-parents-and-kids-voice-messages.

[53] ENISA Report (n 17).

[54] JM Porup, 'How to Search the Internet of Things for Photos of Sleeping Babies' (*Ars Technica*, 19 January 2016), available at https://arstechnica.co.uk/security/2016/01/how-to-search-the-internet-of-things-for-photos-of-sleeping-babies.

[55] NCA Report '17 (n 25) 6.

[56] NCA Report '17 (n 25) 6.

have emerged, such as Persirai which targets IP Cameras specifically,[57] and the Reaper botnet, created by actively hacking software instead of just hunting for default passwords.[58] As the recent Internet Society report frames it, IoT devices have both inward and outward security implications, where the former impacts users, and the latter sees IoT becoming infrastructure for further attacks.[59]

Addressing these issues, we see efforts towards standardisation in the IoT market, as well as initiatives like Hypercat and the development of new standards, bringing safety concerns into security too.[60] However, there is a long, political process between competing companies, governments, professional bodies and civil stakeholder groups, all of whom must work together to agree on optimal security standards that provide protection without stifling innovation.[61] In seeking to establish responsibility within IoT supply chains, the recent UK Government *Secure by Design Report* maps IoT security obligations onto a variety of stakeholders. So, device manufacturers need to ensure no use of default passwords and provide software integrity whilst IoT service providers should monitor usage data for unusual activity or build in outage resilience.[62] Similarly, the ACM *Statement on IoT Privacy and Security* asserts a need for full life cycle management against threats, for example as devices change maintenance ownership.[63] As has been seen with the WannaCry ransomware attacks being based on exploits in legacy software, the scope for harm with IoT devices that are not effectively managed over time could be huge. These could involve significant physical and information security harms in a variety of domestic and workplace contexts.

D. Cyberwarfare

Cyberwar is a contested term, but[64] most commentators often agree that the use of the 'world's first digital weapon', Stuxnet, was an act of cyberwarfare.[65] The state sponsored 2010 Stuxnet worm attack (allegedly from the US and Israel)[66] on the Iranian Natanz nuclear enrichment plant targeted specific Siemens industrial control

---

[57] J Leyden, 'Another IoT Botnet Has Been Found Feasting on Vulnerable IP Cameras' (*The Register*, 10 May 2017), available at www.theregister.co.uk/2017/05/10/persirai_iot_botnet/.

[58] A Greenberg, 'The Reaper IoT Botnet Has Already Infected a Million Networks' (*Wired*, 20 October 2017) available at www.wired.com/story/reaper-iot-botnet-infected-million-networks/.

[59] Internet Society, *IoT Security for Policy Makers* (Geneva, 2018).

[60] E Leverett, R Clayton and R Anderson, 'Standardisation and Certification of the "Internet of Things"' (2017) *Proceedings of WEIS*.

[61] A Bouverot, *GSMA: The Impact of the Internet of Things, The Connected Home* (2015); IoT-UK, *Establishing the Norm: Introduction to IoT Standards* (London, 2017).

[62] Department for Digital, Culture, Media and Sport, *Secure by Design Report* (London, 2018).

[63] USACM/ACM, *ACM Statement on Internet of Things Privacy and Security* (2017) available at www. acm.org/binaries/content/assets/public-policy/2017_joint_statement_iotprivacysecurity.pdf.

[64] L Urquhart, 'Cyberwar: Hype or Reality?' (*Naked Security*, 20 March 2012), available at https://nakedsecurity.sophos.com/2012/03/20/cyber-war-hype-or-reality; L Urquhart, "Do We Need Another Word for Cyber War?' (*Naked Security*, 21 August 2012), available at https://nakedsecurity.sophos.com/2012/08/21/do-we-need-another-word-for-cyber-war.

[65] K Zetter, 'An Unprecedented Look at Stuxnet, the World's First Digital Weapon' (*Wired*, November 2014), available at www.wired.com/2014/11/countdown-to-zero-day-stuxnet.

[66] E Nakashima and J Warrick, 'Stuxnet Was Work of U.S. and Israeli Experts, Officials Say' *The Washington Post* (2 June 2012), available at www.washingtonpost.com/world/national-security/stuxnet-was-work-of-us-and-israeli-experts-officials-say/2012/06/01/gJQAlnEy6U_story.html?utm_term=.9ee2a60c2170.

systems, using a combination of fake authentication certificates and zero day exploits.[67] Ultimately it aimed to delay production of purportedly nuclear weapons using enriched uranium as part of the Iranian nuclear programme.[68]

The legality of cyberwarfare has been considered within international law, in respect of both *jus ad bellum* and *jus in bello*.[69] The targeting of critical civilian infrastructure as the 'battlefield' for playing out international tensions is one particular problem in reconciling cyberwar with the law. Difficulties attributing the source of cyber-attacks also lead to blurring of the lines between cybercrime, terrorism, espionage and warfare. For example, online activity during the conventional armed conflict of the 2008 South Ossetia War saw Georgian websites targeted by state sponsored hacker group Russian Business Network.[70] Similarly, sustained DDoS attacks against government departments, political parties, universities and financial services perpetrated by 'patriotic Russian hackers' protesting the removal of the Bronze Soldier War Memorial from Tallinn Square in 2007 prompted NATO's sustained attention.[71] The NATO Cooperative Cyber Defence Centre of Excellence in Tallinn has created the Tallinn Manuals which interpret the application of public international law to cyber operations during armed conflict[72] and, more recently, during peacetime.[73]

To further complicate the picture, there is growth in cyber-espionage threats, known as Advanced Persistent Threats (APTs). High profile campaigns like Operation Shady RAT or Operation Aurora involve targeting of state and large-scale industrial infrastructure to steal foreign intellectual property and intelligence.[74] The actors involved in these campaigns again range from state sponsored hacking groups to nation states, making attribution difficult. The term is also increasingly being used as an umbrella term in relation to a range of Russian cyber activities. These range from alleged intervention in foreign elections through misinformation, spreading of fake news and 'troll farms';[75] increasing hacking of routers and connected

---

[67] ie unpatched vulnerabilities in IT systems that can be exploited. A market exists in buying these exploits before they are patched by vendors.

[68] K Zetter, 'How Digital Detectives Deciphered Stuxnet, the Most Menacing Malware in History' (*Wired*, 7 November 2011), available at www.wired.com/2011/07/how-digital-detectives-deciphered-stuxnet.

[69] HH Dinniss, *Cyber Warfare and the Laws of War, Cyber Warfare and the Laws of War* (Cambridge, Cambridge University Press, 2012).

[70] J Markoff, 'Before the Gunfire, Cyberattacks' *The New York Times* (12 August 2008), available at http://www.nytimes.com/2008/08/13/technology/13cyber.html.

[71] J Richards, 'Denial of Service: The Estonian Cyberwar and Its Implications for US National Security' (2009) 18(2) *International Affairs Review*; Establishment of NATO Cooperative Cyber Defence Centre of Excellence.

[72] Split into two parts – Part I International Cybersecurity Law (ie primarily *jus ad bellum*) with state attribution (Rules 6–9); Use of Force (10–12); Self Defence (13–17); then Part II on Law of Cyber Armed Conflict (ie primarily *jus in bello*) with detailed rules on cyber weapons, legitimate targets, cyber espionage and the nature of attacks (Rules 25–66).

[73] CCD COE NATO, *Tallinn Manual 2.0 on the International Law Applicable to Cyber Operations*, 2nd edn (Tallinn, Cambridge University Press, 2017); CCD COE NATO, *Tallinn Manual on the International Law Applicable to Cyber Warfare* (Tallinn, Cambridge University Press, 2013).

[74] D Alperovitch, 'Revealed: Operation Shady RAT' (*McAfee*, 2011), available at www.mcafee.com/us/resources/white-papers/wp-operation-shady-rat.pdf; J Finkle, 'Hacker Group in China Linked to Big Cyber Attacks: Symantec' (*Reuters*, 17 September 2013), available at www.reuters.com/article/us-cyberattacks-china-idUSBRE98G0M720130917.

[75] Minority Staff Report, *Putin's Asymmetric Assault On Democracy In Russia And Europe: Implications For U.S. National Security* (Washington, 2018) at www.foreign.senate.gov/imo/media/doc/FinalRR.pdf.

devices;[76] and cyber-attacks masking as ransomware, such as attacks on critical infrastructure from NotPetya.[77]

Whilst zero-day vulnerabilities are often exploited to carry out cyber-attacks on critical infrastructure, such as energy, transportation or industrial control systems,[78] traditional phishing campaigns are also often used. A good example is the blackouts and power outages from attacks on Ukrainian electricity distribution companies Prykarpattya Oblenergo and Kyiv Oblenergo which affected over 220,000 customers and which utilised malware distributed through phishing emails and malicious Microsoft Word files.[79]

III. Legal and Technical Responses

We look here at the UK, EU and international legal frameworks. In the UK, we focus on the Computer Misuse Act 1990 (hereinafter 'CMA 1990') and its case law. At a European level, we look briefly at data breach notification provisions in the forthcoming General Data Protection Regulation (GDPR),[80] and also briefly summarise the Network and Information Security (NISD) Directive 2016.[81] Lastly, we reflect on the Council of Europe Convention on Cybercrime, and the challenges of cyberwarfare.

A. UK Law

In policing cybercrime, UK police have powers under the Investigatory Powers Act 2016 (for powers of equipment interference see Chapter 6), and within the Fraud Act 2006 in relation to online attacks that create financial loss.[82] However, in this chapter we focus on the CMA 1990, and look at case law to unpack the challenges therein.

---

[76] N Kobie, 'Nobody is Safe from Russia's Colossal Hacking Operation' (*Wired*, 21 April 2018), available at www.wired.co.uk/article/russia-hacking-russian-hackers-routers-ncsc-uk-us-2018-syria.

[77] NCSC, ' Russian Military Almost Certainly Responsible for Destructive 2017 Cyber Attack' (*NCSC News*, 15 Feb 2018), available at www.ncsc.gov.uk/news/russian-military-almost-certainly-responsible-destructive-2017-cyber-attack; for background on the attack, see I Thomson, 'Everything You Need to Know About the Petya, er, NotPetya Nasty Trashing PCs Worldwide' (*The Register*, 28 June 2017).

[78] For a discussion of the disruption of SCADA control systems used in power stations, see VM Igure, SA Laughter and RD Williams, 'Security Issues in SCADA Networks' (2006) 7(25) *Computers and Security* 498–506; See Urquhart and McAuley (n 50) on cyber-attacks and industrial infrastructure.

[79] HM Government (n 33) 21.

[80] Regulation (EU) 2016/679 of the European Parliament and of the Council of 27 April 2016 on the protection of natural persons with regard to the processing of personal data and on the free movement of such data, and repealing Directive 95/46/EC (General Data Protection Regulation or GDPR) [2016] OJ L119/1.

[81] Directive EU 2016/1148 of the European Parliament and of the Council of 6 July 2016 concerning measures for a high common level of security of network and information systems across the Union [2016] OJ L194/1.

[82] See J Zoest, 'Computer Misuse Offences' (2014) *Westlaw UK Latest Update*, 4; Crown Prosecution Service, *Legal Guidance on Fraud Act 2006*, available at www.cps.gov.uk/legal/d_to_g/fraud_act. In the 2006 Act see s 2 ('Fraud by false representation'); s 6 ('Possession of articles for use in frauds'); and s 7 ('Making or supplying articles for use in frauds').

i. Section 1 CMA 1990: Unauthorised Access to Computer Material

A section 1 CMA 1990 offence occurs when a person causes a computer to:

1. perform any function with intent to secure access to any program or data held in any computer,[83] (or to enable any such access to be secured);
2. where 'the access he intends to secure [or to enable to be secured] is unauthorised'; and
3. 'he knows at the time when he causes the computer to perform the function that that is the case'.[84]

The term computer, frustratingly, is not defined in the CMA, but in subsequent case law it has been held to mean a 'device for storing, processing and retrieving information'.[85]

The *intent* to commit an offence does not have to be directed at any particular:

1. programme or data, for example Microsoft Word;
2. a programme or data of any particular kind, for example a word processing program; or
3. a program or data held in any particular computer, for example on Alice's computer.[86]

With the CMA 1990, interpretation is provided in section 17, with sections 17(2) and 17(5) being particularly important for defining 'securing access' and 'unauthorised access', respectively. Section 17(2) states:

A person secures access to any program or data held in a computer if by causing a computer to perform any function he:

a) alters or erases the program or data;
b) copies or moves it to any storage medium other than that in which it is held or to a different location in the storage medium in which it is held;
c) uses it; [i.e. if the function he causes the computer to perform (a) causes the program to be executed; or (b) is itself a function of the program][87]
d) has it *output* from the computer in which it is held (whether by having it *displayed* or in any other manner);
e) and references to access to a program or data (and to an intent to secure such access [or to enable such access to be secured][88]) shall be read accordingly.[89]

---

[83] Section 17(6) includes 'references to any program or data held in any removable storage medium which is for the time being in the computer; and a computer is to be regarded as containing any program or data held in any such medium'.

[84] CMA 1990, s 1(1)(a)-(c) as Amended by Police and Justice Act 2006, s 35.

[85] *DPP v Jones* [1997] 2 CR App R 155, *per* Lord Hoffman at 163.

[86] CMA 1990, s 1(2)(a)-(c).

[87] CMA 1990, s 17(3).

[88] Added by Police and Justice Act 2006, Sch 14, para 29.

[89] CMA 1990, s 17(4) clarifies s 17(2)(d), stating '(a) a program is output if the instructions of which it consists are output; and (b) the form in which any such instructions or any other data is output (and in particular whether or not it represents a form in which, in the case of instructions, they are capable of being executed or, in the case of data, it is capable of being processed by a computer) is immaterial.'

Section 17(5) defines unauthorised access as:

'Access of any kind by any person to any program or data held in a computer is unauthorised if:

a)   he is not himself entitled to control access of the kind in question to the program or data; and

b)   he does not have consent to access by him of the kind in question to the program or data from any person who is so entitled.[90]

A number of cases have clarified points. The case of *Attorney General's Reference (No 1 of 1991)*[91] clarified that section 1 CMA 1990 does not require the hacker to use a different computer from that hacked to complete the offence of unauthorised access; s 1 can be breached by 'using another person's identifier (ID) and /or password without proper authority in order to access data or a program; displaying data from a computer to a screen or printer; or even simply switching on a computer without proper authority'.[92]

In *Cuthbert*,[93] a system penetration tester donated £30 to a Tsunami appeal website run by the Disasters Emergency Committee. After donating, he became suspicious of the website because of the image banner and lack of confirmation message given. He tested the site[94] to ensure it was not a phishing scam, which triggered an intrusion response system. Despite his lack of intention to cause harm, he was convicted of breaching section 1 CMA 1990 because 'unauthorised access, however praiseworthy the motives, is an offence'.[95] This raised concern among the pen tester community around the consequences of their techniques.[96]

In *DPP v Bignall*[97] two married police officers with authorised access to the Police National Computer used the system to obtain information for private purposes. The Department of Public Prosecutions (DPP) claimed this was 'unauthorised access', as their access was meant to be only for police purposes. The DPP argued action taken for other purposes was no longer authorised, and thus a breach of section 1 CMA 1990. However, the Court held this action was not 'unauthorised', as defined in sections 17(2) or 17(5), stating instead that the role of the CMA 1990 is to protect against unauthorised access to computer material (ie hacking),[98] and not to

---

[90] Amended by Criminal Justice and Public Order Act 1994, s 162(2).

[91] *Attorney General's Reference (No 1 of 1991)* [1993] QB 94.

[92] Zoest (n 82) 1.

[93] 'Regrettable Conviction Under Computer Misuse Act' (*Out-Law*, 7 Oct 2005), available at www.out-law.com/page-6207.

[94] P Sommer, 'Computer Misuse Prosecutions' (*Society of Computers and Law*, 2005), available at www.scl.org/site.aspx?i=ed832. Sommer states that 'using a directory traversal test – in effect he re-formed the URL he could see in the command bar of his Internet browser to see whether the security settings on the remote Web site would allow him access beyond the web root. His attempt was rejected, he felt relieved and thought no more of the matter.'

[95] Stated by District Judge Mr Quentin Purdy.

[96] Although, according to Sommer, some in the community disagreed as to the appropriateness of using directory traversal as a test.

[97] *DPP v Bignell* [1998] 1 Cr App R 1.

[98] *Ibid* at 12, *per* Astil J.

protect integrity of information stored on the computer.[99] Under *Bignell*, 'a person does not commit an offence under the 1990 Act, s1 if he accesses a computer at an authorised level for an unauthorised purpose'.[100]

However in *R v Bow Street Magistrates Court ex Parte Allison No 2*,[101] the Court took a different stance towards authorised access.[102] Allison allegedly obtained customer account information from an American Express employee as part of a fraud scheme that cost the company $1m.[103] The employee had the *ability* to access all customer accounts, but was only *authorised* to access accounts related to her work. The information she accessed to commit fraud was taken from accounts she was not authorised to access.[104] The House of Lords therefore clarified the scope of section 1, stating that it

> refers to the intent to secure unauthorised access to any programme or data. These plain words leave no room for any suggestion that the relevant person may say: 'Yes, I know that I was not authorised to access that data but I was authorised to access other data of the same kind.'[105]

Interestingly, Lord Hobhouse still held that *Bignell* was still 'probably right', because the police officers had asked a computer operator, who was operating within the authority of his job, to obtain information for police officers in response to their requests.[106] MacEwan suggests that this reasoning is not persuasive, because the computer operator was 'blissfully unaware of the real reason behind the Bignells' requests'.[107] Instead, the operator was an 'innocent agent' and

> the fact that the computer operators lacked *mens rea* means that the true participants in the alleged offences were the police couple. In such circumstances, 'the principal is the participant in the crime whose act is the most immediate cause of the innocent agent's act'. The Bignells fitted this description.[108]

---

[99] This is the remit of data protection laws, specifically the Data Protection Act (1984) at that time – this would now be s 55 of the Data Protection Act 1998.

[100] *Halisbury's Laws of England*, Supplement to 11(1) (5th edn Reissue, 2008), para 604A.

[101] *R v Bow Street Magistrates Court ex Parte Allison No 2* (AP) [2000] 2 AC 216.

[102] *R v Bow Street Magistrates Court ex Parte Allison No 2* [1999] 3 WLR 620.

[103] *R v Bow Street* (n 101) at 220: '... she accessed various other accounts and files which had not been assigned to her and which she had not been given authority to work on. Having accessed those accounts and files without authority, she gave confidential information obtained from those accounts and files to, among others, Mr. Allison. The information she gave to him and to others was then used to encode other credit cards and supply P.I.N. numbers which could then be fraudulently used to obtain large sums of money from automatic teller machines'. This case also involved deliberations on extradition of Allison, which are not discussed further. Due to the nature of the attacks, many of these hacking cases involve extradition aspects, for example *R (on the application of McKinnon) v DPP* [2009] EWHC 2021 (Admin); *Ahzaz v United States* [2013] EWHC 216 (Admin); and *Maxwell-King v United States* [2006] EWHC 3033 (Admin).

[104] See K Stein, 'Unauthorised Access and the UK Computer Misuse Act 1990: House of Lords "Leaves No Room" for Ambiguity' (2000) 6(3) *Computer and Telecommunications Law Review* 63–66.

[105] *R v Bow Street* (n 101) at 224.

[106] *R v Bow Street* (n 101) at 225.

[107] N MacEwan, 'The Computer Misuse Act 1990: Lessons From its Past and Predictions for its Future' (2008) 12 *Criminal Law Review* 955–67, 958.

[108] *Ibid*, 958; internal quote from I Walden, *Computer Crimes and Digital Investigations* (Oxford, Oxford University Press, 2007) 166.

ii. CMA 1990 Section 1 – Sentencing

We now look at sentencing to see how the courts punish CMA 1990 offences, and due to lack of formal sentencing guidance in the Act, we again turn to case law. With indictment, conviction for a section 1 offence is up to two years, a fine or both, whilst on summary conviction, an offender in England and Wales can be imprisoned for 12 months, fined up to statutory maximum, or both (in Scotland the limits are identical, except the imprisonment cannot exceed six months).[109] *R v Mangham*[110] outlined several factors to be considered as aggravating factors when sentencing occurs, namely:

- whether the offence is planned and persistent;
- the nature of damage caused to the system and to the wider public interest – considering national security, individual privacy, public confidence and commercial confidentiality;
- the damage caused, including cost of remediation;
- motive and benefit, including revenge;
- whether the hacker tried to sell the compromised information;
- whether the information been passed to others;
- the value of the intellectual property impacted; and
- the psychological profile of the offender.[111]

R v Martin (Lewys Stephen)[112] is an example of the stricter view the courts are now taking in relation to CMA 1990 offences. This case involved offences under sections 1, 2, 3, and 3A,[113] and Leveson LJ stated that it highlighted a particularly high level of culpability due to the level of detail in planning the attacks and the nature of the targets. Martin perpetrated denial of service attacks against police forces and universities, as well as changing the Internet banking passwords of his victims. Given the wider implications of these crimes for society, Leveson LJ held that the sentences for the offences needed to 'involve a real element of deterrence … those who commit them must expect to be punished accordingly'.[114]

This approach can be seen in subsequent sentencing of perpetrators of high profile hacks, as in the 2013 case of *R v Cleary, Davis, Al-Bassam and Ackroyd*[115] from hacktivism collective Lulzsec and in the *Crosskey* case. With the former, they were tried for offences under section 3 of the CMA 1990, arising from Lulzsec DDoS attacks on high profile targets like the US Central Intelligence Agency, British Serious Organised Crime Agency and News International. They also modified websites of the

---

[109] Section 35(3)(a)–(c) as amended by Police and Justice Act 2006, s 35.
[110] *R v Mangham* [2012] EWCA Crim 973.
[111] *Ibid, per* Cranston J at 19.
[112] *R v Martin (Lewys Stephen)* [2013] EWCA Crim 1420.
[113] See Blackstone's Criminal Practice 2014, Section B17 Offences involving Computers – B17.14; in addition to two years' imprisonment, he also received a deprivation order from using various IT equipment under the Powers of Criminal Courts (Sentencing) Act 2000, s 143.
[114] *R v Martin* (n 112) [39].
[115] Southwark Crown Court, May 2013, reported in Zoest (n 82) 5.

UK National Health Service, Twentieth Century Fox, and Sony Pictures Entertainment. These actions resulted in fairly severe custodial sentences from 24 months to 36 months, and five-year Serious Crime Prevention Orders for computer/internet use for all the offenders involved.

This can be contrasted to an extent with *R v Crosskey (Gareth)*.[116] Crosskey misrepresented his identity to deceive Facebook into providing him with a password which he then used to access the Facebook account of actress Selena Gomez for a period of three days. He offered to sell stories to the celebrity press based on what he learned from this access, and posted a video on YouTube about the hack. Crosskey pled guilty, and mitigating factors like his act being a result of 'bravado', his regret for his actions, his previous good character, and the activity taking place over a short time meant his sentences for section 1 and 3 offences were reduced from 18 months of imprisonment to 12 months' detention in a young offender institution.[117]

iii. CMA 1990 Section 2 – Unauthorised Access with Intent to Commit or Facilitate Commission of Further Offences

Section 2 of the CMA 1990 covers 'unauthorised access with intent to commit or facilitate commission of further offences' where, after already committing a section 1 offence, the perpetrator intends to commit or facilitate the commission (by himself or a different person) of another offence.[118] The further offence will be one which carries either a sentence fixed by law, or one that would carry a five-year sentence (if the offender is over 21 and does not have previous convictions).[119] This further offence does not need to be committed at the same time as the section 1 offence – it can be 'on any future occasion'[120] – and it does not actually have to be possible for the subsequent offence to be committed.[121] Examples of section 2 offences include 'accessing without authority another person's personal data (such as name and bank account number) from a computer with the intention of using those details to transfer money from an on-line bank account'.[122] For a summary conviction the sentence is 12 months' imprisonment, a fine not exceeding statutory minimum, or both, in England and Wales (the maximum imprisonment in Scotland is six months). On indictment, the maximum imprisonment is five years, as well as a fine, or both.

iv. CMA 1990 Section 3 – Viruses and Malware

Section 3 covers 'unauthorised acts with intent to impair, or with recklessness as to impairing, operation of computer, etc'. An offence under this section is committed

---

[116] *R v Crosskey (Gareth)* [2012] EWCA Crim 1645.

[117] *Ibid*; Zoest (n 82) 6.

[118] CMA 1990, s 2(1)(a) and (b).

[119] *Ibid* part (b) also includes this: '(or, in England and Wales, might be so sentenced but for the restrictions imposed by section 33 of the Magistrates' Court Act 1980)'.

[120] *Ibid*, s 2(3).

[121] *Ibid*, s 2(4).

[122] Zoest (n 82) 1.

if an unauthorised act in relation to a computer is committed, where the perpetrator knows it is unauthorised.[123] By doing the act they intend to:[124]

- 'impair the operation of any computer';
- 'prevent or hinder access to any program or data held in any computer';
- 'impair operation of any such program or the reliability of any such data'; or
- enable any of the above to be done.[125]

The conditions of not requiring intent or recklessness to be directed at specific computers, programmes, or data are the same as in section 1, discussed above. Section 3(5) states that doing an act includes 'causing an act to be done', and includes a series of acts. Furthermore, the impairing, preventing, or hindering can be temporary. On indictment conviction carries the penalty of up to 10 years, a fine or both; for summary procedure in England and Wales the maximum penalty is 12 months' imprisonment, a fine not exceeding statutory maximum, or both (in Scotland the maximum imprisonment is six months).[126] Typical section 3 offences include sending viruses, embedding malware in email, and DDoS attacks.[127] DDoS case law is an interesting area to consider in more depth.

v. CMA 1990 Section 3 and DDoS

DPP v Lennon was a pre-Police and Justice Act 2006 reform case in which section 3(1) still required an unauthorised 'modification' to a system (whereas now it is unauthorised 'act').[128] In this case, Lennon used a mail bombing campaign[129] against his former employers, sending 500,000 emails to the company servers.[130] The Court accepted that sending emails was a modification to the system; hence the question was the authority of Lennon to do so, especially when sending emails is ordinarily an authorised activity. It was held that the implied consent of a user to receive emails is not without limits,[131] and such consent does not stretch to cover situations where the purpose of emails is to overwhelm the system. As Keene LJ stated, the recipient 'does not consent to receiving emails sent in a quantity and at a speed which are likely to overwhelm the server. Such consent is not to be implied from the fact that the server has an open as opposed to a restricted configuration.'[132] As discussed above, the Police

---

[123] See also s 17(8), 'An act done in relation to a computer is unauthorised if the person doing the act (or causing it to be done)–(a) is not himself a person who has responsibility for the computer and is entitled to determine whether the act may be done; and (b) does not have consent to the act from any such person. In this subsection 'act' includes a series of acts.' Amended by Police and Justice Act 2006, Sch 14, para 29.

[124] CMA 1990, s 3(1)(a)-(c).

[125] *Ibid*, s 3(2)(a)-(c). If the person is reckless as to whether the act will have these consequences, then that is an offence under s 3(3).

[126] *Ibid*, s 3(6).

[127] Zoest (n 82) 2.

[128] CMA 1990, s 3, amended by Police and Justice Act 2006, s 36.

[129] Using the Avalanche v3.6 program.

[130] The emails were made to appear to come from a manager within the company.

[131] See CMA 1990, s 17(8)(b) on definition of an 'unauthorised act'.

[132] *DPP v Lennon* [2006] EWHC 1201 (Admin) at 14; see also Jack J at 9: 'the owner of a computer which is able to receive emails is ordinarily to be taken as consenting to the sending of emails to the computer.

and Justice Act 2006 amended the CMA 1990[133] to deal with unauthorised acts, where this act can be a series of acts, and any 'impairment, prevention or hindering of something can be temporary'. As DDoS attacks do not ordinarily cause permanent damage to the server, merely knocking it offline temporarily, this brings them within the scope of section 3.

In *R v Caffrey*,[134] Caffrey was charged under section 3 for remotely modifying computer systems at the US Port of Houston, and impairing management of logistics at the port. He managed successfully to claim that he lacked the *mens rea* for the offence by alleging the act was carried out by a self-deleting Trojan horse. Despite no evidence of this Trojan ever being present on the machine, he was acquitted. Edwards has argued this result is 'somewhat analogous to a murder case where the accused claims that he performed the act but only while possessed by aliens, or perhaps more likely, while sleepwalking' and due to the subject matter being computer science, unlike medicine, juries' lack of expertise might cause them to err on the side of caution and to acquit.[135] In another unusual basis for acquittal, one of the first CMA 1990 cases, *R v Bedworth*,[136] saw the hacker acquitted based on lack of *mens rea* due to expert witness testimony that he suffered from 'computer tendency syndrome' and thus had an addiction to computers.

vi. CMA 1990 Section 3ZA – Unauthorised Acts Causing or Creating Risk of Serious Damage

Section 3ZA was added by section 41 of the Serious Crime Act 2015 and applies when the accused does any unauthorised act in relation to a computer: (i) knowing at that time it is unauthorised; (ii) causing, or creating a significant risk of serious damage of a material kind; and (iii) intends by doing the act to cause such damage or being reckless as to whether it is caused.[137] Material damage could include damage to the environment or human welfare in any place or to the economy or national security of any country.[138] Material damage to human welfare is a broad concept, including loss of human life, illness, or injury, disruption to supply of money, food, water, energy or fuel, and disruption of communications systems, transport facilities or health services.[139] When causing material damage, it matters not if the act causes the damage

His consent is to be implied from his conduct in relation to the computer. Some analogy can be drawn with consent by a householder to members of the public to walk up the path to his door when they have a legitimate reason for doing so, and also with the use of a private letter box. But that implied consent given by a computer owner is not without limit. The point can be illustrated by the same analogies. The householder does not consent to a burglar coming up his path. Nor does he consent to having his letter box choked with rubbish.'

[133] See s 3(5).
[134] *R v Caffrey* Southwark Crown Court, 17 October 2003.
[135] Edwards (n 44) 42.
[136] *R v Bedworth* 1993 (unreported), but see some brief discussion in S Fafinski, 'Access Denied: Computer Misuse in an Era of Technological Change' (2006) 70(5) *Journal of Criminal Law* 435.
[137] CMA 1990, s 3ZA(1).
[138] *Ibid*, s 3ZA(2).
[139] *Ibid*, s 3ZA(3).

directly, or is the only or main cause of the damage.[140] Doing an act includes causing an act to be done, including if it is a series of acts. A country includes reference
to a territory, and any place in, or part or region, of a country or territory.[141] When
convicted on indictment, the sanctions for this offence are up to 14 years, a fine, or
both.[142] When the act caused or created significant risk to human life, or human illness
or injury, or serious damage to national security, the penalty can be life imprisonment,
a fine, or both.

vii. CMA 1990 Section 3A – Making, Supplying or Obtaining Articles for Use in Section 1, 3, and 3ZA Offences

Section 3A, as amended by section 41 of the Serious Crime Act 2015, seeks to control
trade in tools used for computer misuse offences. An individual is guilty if they:

- make, adapt, supply or offer to supply any article for use to commit, or assist
  commission of, a section 1, 3, or 3ZA offence;
- if they supply an article believing it is likely to be used in commission of these
  offences;
- if they obtain an article intending to, or with a view to, using it to commit
  (or to assist with commission of) these offences.[143]

Interestingly, an article means any program or data held in 'electronic form'.[144]
Conviction on indictment carries up to two years' imprisonment, a fine, or both, and
on summary procedure the standard 12 months' imprisonment in England and Wales
(six months for Scotland), a fine not exceeding statutory maximum, or both.[145]
    A risk is with dual-use articles, for example those that may have a lawful purpose
in penetration testing or for managing security of computer systems, but also could
be used for unlawful purposes. The Crown Prosecution Service[146] clarifies that mere
possession of articles is not an offence; intent is a key element to establish this offence.
In determining the likelihood of the article being used for such purposes, CPS guidance
states that prosecutors should consider whether the article is developed mainly for
committing such offences, if it is commercially available through legitimate distribution routes, what its user base is, and what its normal use cases are. As they argue,
'prosecutors should look at the functionality of the article and at what, if any, thought
the suspect gave to who would use it; whether for example the article was circulated to
a closed and vetted list of IT security professionals or was posted openly'.
    The Low Orbit Ion Canon (LOIC) is an interesting example to consider.
Following political fallout from WikiLeaks sharing confidential US diplomatic

---

[140] s 3ZA(4) CMA.
[141] s 3ZA(5) CMA.
[142] s 3ZA(6) CMA.
[143] Ibid, s 3A(1)–(3).
[144] Ibid, s 3A(4).
[145] Ibid, s 3A(5).
[146] Crown Prosecution Service, Legal Guidance on Computer Misuse Act 1990, available at www.cps.gov.uk/
legal/a_to_c/computer_misuse_act_1990/.

cables online, a number of high profile organisations cut hosting or donation payment services to the website.[147] Hacktivist collective[148] Anonymous responded in support of WikiLeaks' agenda with a campaign of targeted DDoS attacks during 'Operation Payback'.[149] Interestingly, these DDoS attacks relied not on zombie botnets, but on individuals participating in the protest by volunteering their computers to be part of the network by downloading a piece of software called the Low Orbit Ion Canon.[150] This software has legitimate purposes in stress testing networks, so if an individual downloads the software but does not then participate in the attack there is scope for arguing that they did not breach section 3A(3).[151]

B. European Law: The General Data Protection Regulation and the Network and Information Security Directive 2016

The EU General Data Protection Regulation (hereinafter 'GDPR') includes provisions on security of personal data.[152] Here we focus on the new notification rules around personal data breach, ie 'a breach of security leading to the accidental or unlawful destruction, loss, alteration, unauthorised disclosure of, or access to, personal data transmitted, stored or otherwise processed'.[153] Any data controllers who suffer a personal data breach need to notify the UK data protection regulator, the Information Commissioner Office, within 72 hours of discovery of the attack.[154] They need to provide quite detailed information in a very short period of time, including:

1. the nature of the personal data breach including where possible, the categories and approximate number of data subjects concerned and the categories and approximate number of personal data records concerned.
2. communicate the name and contact details of the data protection officer or other contact point where more information can be obtained;
3. describe the likely consequences of the personal data breach;
4. describe the measures taken or proposed to be taken by the controller to address the personal data breach, including, where appropriate, measures to mitigate its possible adverse effect.[155]

In addition, they need to notify the data subject about the breach, in a clear and plain manner, without undue delay (but not within 72 hours) if it is likely to pose high risks

---

[147] MasterCard, Visa, Amazon Web Services.

[148] Hacktivism ordinarily involves targets chosen through political or social motives with the emphasis on protest.

[149] L Edwards, 'WikiLeaks, DDoS and UK Criminal Law: The Key Issues' (*Practical Law Company*, 22 December 2010), available at https://uk.practicallaw.thomsonreuters.com/1-504-3391.

[150] The LOIC leaves IP addresses of participants, making them easily identifiable, and as Edwards notes, *ibid*, the police can easily use powers under s 22 of the Regulation of Investigatory Powers Act 2000 to obtain subscriber information from ISPs to cross reference with IP addresses of alleged attackers.

[151] See Edwards (n 149) at section 'Is Merely Downloading the LOIC Tool a Crime?'.

[152] GDPR, Art 32. See fuller discussion of the GDPR in its whole in Chapter 4.

[153] *Ibid*, Art 4(12).

[154] *Ibid*, Art 33.

[155] *Ibid*, Art 33(3).

to their rights and freedoms.[156] This is unnecessary, however, if the following three conditions are met:

1.   the controller has implemented *appropriate technical and organisational protection meas-ures*, and those *measures were applied to the personal data affected* by the personal data breach, in particular those that render the personal data unintelligible to any person who is not authorised to access it, such as *encryption*;

2.   the controller has taken subsequent measures which ensure that the *high risk* to the rights and freedoms of data subjects referred to in paragraph 1 is *no longer likely to materialise*;

3.   it would involve *disproportionate effort*. In such a case, there shall instead be a *public communication* or similar measure whereby the data subjects are informed in an equally effective manner (my emphasis).[157]

Given the notification provisions here, end users are still often likely to be finding out about data breaches through news stories or public messages from companies, particularly given the rise in the number of breaches (the number in 2016 was 45 per cent higher than in 2014).[158] The knock-on effects from a breach are significant; compromised usernames and passwords can be used in further attacks, and a large market in compromised credentials has thus arisen). Websites like *haveibeenpwned.com* let users check if their credentials have been compromised, for example in the famous LinkedIn or Adobe hacks.[159] However, smaller attacks are not publicised, or might not even be known about, and thus it is harder for users to know whether or not their data is at risk.

There is a risk that by shifting the responsibility of responding to security breaches onto users, the emphasis is shifted away from organisations' obligation to put in place good security practices, for example encryption by default. We should not be blaming end-users for bad passwords or poor security practices when so many factors make it hard for them to do otherwise.[160] Nevertheless, supporting users with education about risks, and creating more usable security tools is an important step. The field of usable privacy and security does much here to help, from making encryption tools easier to use, to improving password and authentication technologies.[161]

A recent EU Eurobarometer survey of over 28,000 EU citizens has shown that 87 per cent of respondents see cybercrime as a significant challenge, with 75 per cent concerned about security of their online personal information with websites. There are fears around being a victim to cybercrime, particularly with finding malware on devices and identity theft (69 per cent for both) and banking fraud (66 per cent).[162] Early initiatives like the UK's *Get Safe Online* service have long sought to raise awareness of users and businesses on fraud, identity theft and other online risks.[163] The National

---

[156] *Ibid*, Art 34.
[157] *Ibid*, Art 34(3).
[158] ENISA Report (n 17).
[159] M Burgess, 'How to Check If Your LinkedIn Account Was Hacked' (*Wired*, 24 May 2016), available at www.wired.co.uk/article/linkedin-data-breach-find-out-included.
[160] A Adams and MA Sasse, 'Users Are Not the Enemy' (1999) 42(12) *Communications of the ACM* 40–46.
[161] See Cylab for example research: http://cups.cs.cmu.edu/#password.
[162] Eurobarometer, *Special Eurobarometer 464a: European Attitudes towards Cyber-Security* (European Union, Brussels, 2017) 5–6.
[163] Website at www.getsafeonline.org/about-us.

Crime Agency has continued this work, for example by creating guidance on how to download and update security software, or how to report cybercrimes to the Action Fraud service,[164] as part of the 2014 UK Government campaign *Cyber Streetwise* which advised citizens on avoiding online scams, monitoring online privacy, and using strong passwords.[165] Small and Medium Enterprise (SME) interests are also targeted with this programme,[166] largely due to their vulnerabilities to cyber-attacks. As a 2013 former UK Department of Business, Innovation and Skills report showed, '87 per cent of small firms surveyed suffered an online security breach in the previous 12 months, including data corruption and loss as well as hacking and fraud'.[167]

Beyond SMEs, larger organisations have an increasing role to play in addressing cybersecurity risks, especially those companies providing critical infrastructure. The 2016 EU Network and Information Security Directive (hereafter 'NISD'), was transposed into domestic law in May 2018.[168] It establishes minimum harmonised standards for network and information security across the EU for critical infrastructure, requiring Member States to adopt national measures and implementation strategies. It includes many provisions on cross-border cooperation, like the creation of a network of computer security incident response teams (CERTS) and a strategic cooperation group to bring states together to share information about attacks.

Under NISD, Member States need to identify the operators of 'essential services' in their territory from across the energy, transport, banking, financial markets and health sectors.[169] This includes bodies like energy operators involved in supply, distribution and storage of natural resources (for example oil pipelines, refineries and rigs), transportation providers (for example air carriers, intelligent transport systems, or traffic management), banking (for example credit institutions), financial trading (for example stock markets), and healthcare providers (for example hospitals and clinics). Curiously, it also extends to three specific digital services, namely online marketplaces, online search engines and cloud computing services.[170] Online marketplaces are places where sales or services contracts are concluded with companies like eBay, or mobile application stores like Google Play or the Apple App Store. It does not include platforms that are intermediaries for third parties to conclude contracts later. An interesting question arises as to how 'gig economy' services such as Uber or Amazon's Mechanical Turk would be treated in this respect. With regard to search engines, NISD relates to services that enable search for all content online as services like Google/Bing or Yahoo provide, as opposed to price comparison sites or content search bars within

---

[164] Website at www.actionfraud.police.uk/report_fraud.

[165] *Cyber Streetwise* campaign website at www.cyberstreetwise.com/partners (this website has since been superseded by the Government's *Cyber Aware* campaign at www.cyberaware.gov.uk.

[166] HM Government, *Cyber Streetwise – Open for Business*, available at www.gov.uk/government/uploads/system/uploads/attachment_data/file/273330/cyber_streetwise_open_for_business.pdf.

[167] *Ibid*, and Department for Business, Innovation and Skills, *2013 Information Security Breaches Survey* (London, BIS 2013), available at www.gov.uk/government/uploads/system/uploads/attachment_data/file/191671/bis-13-p184es-2013-information-security-breaches-survey-executive-summary.pdf.

[168] Network and Information Systems Regulations 2018 (SI 2018/No 506).

[169] Directive (EU) 2016/1148 of the European Parliament and of the Council of 6 July 2016 concerning measures for a high common level of security of network and information systems across the Union [2016] OJ L194/1, Annex II.

[170] *Ibid*, Annex III.

an individual website.[171] It does not cover internet service providers (ISPs) or trust providers,[172] as these are covered by separate legislation, for example the e-Privacy Directive 2002 for ISPs.[173]

C. International Dimensions: Cybercrime and Cyberwarfare

As cybercrime and warfare exists across jurisdictions, international legal frameworks are important to reflect on. The new EU 'Police and Justice' Data Protection Directive 2016[174] provides a framework for law enforcement agencies to cooperate and share data across borders. However, the main substantive cross border instrument in this area is the Council of Europe's Convention on Cybercrime.

The Convention, which came into force in 2011,[175] seeks to create 'a common criminal policy aimed at the protection of society against cybercrime, inter alia by adopting appropriate legislation and fostering international co-operation'.[176] It contains both substantive and procedural provisions, and seeks harmonisation by defining five offences signatories need to incorporate in their domestic law, including hacking, computer based fraud and the distribution of illegal content.[177] The UK covers many of these in the CMA 1990. In keeping the Convention up to date, the Cybercrime Convention Committee (T-CY) has issued guidance notes[178] on applying the Convention to topics including critical infrastructure attacks, DDoS attacks, botnets, new forms of malware and identity theft, and phishing in relation to fraud.[179] As of April 2018, the Convention has 57 overall ratifications, with the UK signing in 2001 and ratifying in 2011.[180] It also contains more controversial procedural provisions for international cooperation which are intended to address the cross-border nature of cybercrimes and whereby states provide mutual assistance for investigations and evidence gathering.[181]

Similarly, international laws need to be applied to understand how the frameworks accommodate the challenges of cyberwarfare.[182] The law on the use of force

---

[171] *Ibid*, Recitals 14 and 15.

[172] *Ibid*, Recital 7.

[173] Directive 2002/58/EC of the European Parliament and of the Council of 12 July 2002 concerning the processing of personal data and the protection of privacy in the electronic communications sector (Directive on privacy and electronic communications) [2002] OJ L201/37.

[174] Directive (EU) 2016/680 of the European Parliament and of the Council of 27 April 2016 on the protection of natural persons with regard to the processing of personal data by competent authorities for the purposes of the prevention, investigation, detection or prosecution of criminal offences or the execution of criminal penalties, and on the free movement of such data, and repealing Council Framework Decision 2008/977/JHA [2016] OJ L119/89.

[175] Council of Europe, Chart of signatures and ratifications of Treaty 185, ETS No 185, available at www.coe.int/en/web/conventions/full-list/-/conventions/treaty/185/signatures.

[176] See the Preamble of the Convention on Cybercrime (Budapest, 23 November 2001).

[177] *Ibid*, Ch II, s 1.

[178] Adopted by the 9th Plenary of the T-CY (4–5 June 2013).

[179] Guidance Notes numbers 2–7.

[180] See Council of Europe (n 175).

[181] Convention on Cybercrime, Arts 23–25.

[182] For more detail see (2012) 17(2) *Journal of Conflict and Security Law* (special edition on cyberwarfare).

and self-defence in Articles 2(4) and 51 of the UN Charter are being applied in a new and difficult context of cyberwarfare, beyond the originally-intended scope of armed attacks causing kinetic damage. Overcoming challenges in attributing an attack to a nation state requires cooperation from technical and legal communities. Traffic can be masked and routed via several countries to hide the identity of perpetrators, making establishment of state responsibility for cyber-attacks difficult.[183] Furthermore, given the messy crossover between cyber-war, -crime, -espionage, and -terrorism, to name a few, the holding of nation states responsible for acts of groups that may be acting autonomously, without knowledge or authority of the armed forces, poses further issues. Determining proportionate responses to interstate cyber-attacks raises political and ethical questions too, for example whether the use of kinetic attacks in response to cyber-attacks can be deemed legal,[184] and whether it is or can be morally correct to do so. With states designing and building cyber weapons like Stuxnet, debates open up around appropriate controls over the cyber arms trade, through perhaps a treaty to control use of these weapons, or even to ban some, as with nuclear or chemical weapons.[185] Nevertheless, despite all these difficult questions, in order to balance against the fear, uncertainty and doubt surrounding cyberwarfare[186] some experts recommend focusing on more mundane, but very real, threats to power grids: outages from unfortunate electrocuted squirrels and birds who get caught up in grid infrastructure.[187]

IV. Conclusions

Throughout this chapter, we have explored the dynamic and adversarial nature of cybersecurity threats, actors, and the legal responses to them. As we increasingly augment our homes, cities and bodies with sensors and computational devices, we need better strategies to secure attack vectors and patch vulnerabilities. The embedding of systems capable of physical actuation in our daily lives means the implications of exploits and hacks go beyond the desktop or smartphone screen, and begin to pose physical harms.[188] Guarding against these risks requires more than just recourse to *ex ante* legal measures. Instead, we need more holistic approaches to building security into devices and networks. This can only occur from closer alliance between legal,

---

[183] J Carr, 'Responsible Attribution: A Prerequisite for Accountability', *The Tallinn Papers: A NATO CCD COE Publication on Strategic Cyber Security* (2014).

[184] D Alexander, 'U.S. Reserves Right to Meet Cyber Attack with Force' (*Reuters*, 15 November 2011), available at www.reuters.com/article/us-usa-defense-cybersecurity-idUSTRE7AF02Y20111116.

[185] L Arimatsu, 'A Treaty for Governing Cyber-Weapons' (2012) *Cyber Conflict (CYCON), 2012 4th International Conference on Cyber Conflict*.

[186] RA Clarke and RK Knake, *Cyber War: The Next Threat to National Security and What to Do about It* (Ecco, 2010).

[187] C Wootson Jr, 'Most Cybersecurity Experts Are Worried about Russian Hackers. One Says: Look, a Squirrel!' (*The Washington Post*, 18 January 2016), available at www.washingtonpost.com/news/the-switch/wp/2017/01/18/most-cybersecurity-experts-are-worried-about-russian-hackers-one-says-look-a-squirrel/.

[188] Urquhart and McAuley (n 50).

policy, and technical communities, working together in more agile ways to understand both the threats and what appropriate responses might be. Regulation in this domain, like many areas of technology law, is challenged by the pace of technological change. Nevertheless, to enable greater resilience to cybersecurity vulnerabilities we need to address risks of harm to users in a more prospective manner. This means finding ways to create technically secure, resilient systems that are supported by appropriate and effective cybersecurity regulation strategies.

Index